LOGISTICAL
MANAGEMENT

A Systems Integration of Physical Distribution, Manufacturing Support, and Materials Procurement

Third Edition

Donald J. Bowersox
Michigan State University

David J. Closs
Michigan State University

Omar K. Helferich
Dialog Systems Incorporated

Macmillan Publishing Company
New York
Collier Macmillan Publishers
London

Earlier edition copyright © 1974 and 1978 by Macmillan Publishing Company. A portion of this material has been reprinted from *Physical Distribution Management*, First Edition, by Edward W. Smykay, Donald J. Bowersox, and Frank H. Mossman, © 1961 by Macmillan Publishing Company; Second Edition, by Donald J. Bowersox, Edward W. Smykay, and Bernard J. La Londe, copyright © 1968 by Macmillan Publishing Company.

Macmillan Publishing Company
866 Third Avenue, New York, New York 10022

Collier Macmillan Canada, Inc.

Library of Congress Cataloging-in-Publication Data

Bowersox, Donald J.
  Logistical management.

  Bibliography: p.
  Includes index.
  1. Physical distribution of goods—Management.
2. Materials management.   I. Closs, David J.
II. Helferich, Omar Keith.   III. Title.
HF5415.7.B66 1986   658.7   85-16822
ISBN 0-02-313090-3

Printing: 1 2 3 4 5 6 7 8   Year: 6 7 8 9 0 1 2 3 4 5

The Logistician

Logisticians are a sad and embittered race of men who are very much in demand in war, and who sink resentfully into obscurity in peace. They deal only in facts, but must work for men who merchant in theories. They emerge during war because war is very much a fact. They disappear in peace because peace is mostly theory. The people who merchant in theories, and who employ logisticians in war and ignore them in peace, are generals.

Generals are a happily blessed race who radiate confidence and power. They feed only on ambrosia and drink only nectar. In peace, they stride confidently and can invade a world simply by sweeping their hands grandly over a map, pointing their fingers decisively up terrain corridors, and blocking defiles and obstacles with the sides of their hands. In war, they must stride more slowly because each general has a logistician riding on his back and he knows that, at any moment, the logistician may lean forward and whisper: "No, you can't do that." Generals fear logisticians in war and, in peace, generals try to forget logisticians.

Romping along beside generals are strategists and tacticians. Logisticians despise strategists and tacticians. Strategists and tacticians do not know about logisticians until they grow up to be generals—which they usually do.

Sometimes a logistician becomes a general. If he does, he must associate with generals whom he hates; he has a retinue of strategists and tacticians whom he despises; and, on his back, is a logistician whom he fears. This is why logisticians who become generals always have ulcers and cannot eat their ambrosia.

—Author unknown
Made available by Major William K. Bawden, RCAF.

PREFACE

For nearly three decades, I have had the good fortune to participate actively in the development of business logistics. I have come to have a deep respect for the importance of logistics in a free-enterprise system. Because of the growing complexity of logistical management, I have asked two former students to join as authors in the third edition. Omar Keith Helferich and David J. Closs have joined with me to describe the current content and future direction of logistical management.

The history of the *Logistical Management* manuscript started in 1958. As some readers are aware, portions of the first edition of *Logistical Management* were initially published in two editions of *Physical Distribution Management*. The first, published in 1961, was a collaboration with two other authors and was the initial attempt to integrate physical distribution activities in a single book. In 1968, the second edition of *Physical Distribution Management*, again a collaboration, was substantially rewritten as a new book because of the vast changes that had occurred in the field during the intervening seven years. The first edition of *Logistical Management*, published in 1974, contained a great deal of the material from the earlier two works. However, by 1974, the horizons of subject content once again expanded so as to make a new and broader approach to logistics essential. The viewpoint of total logistics was further developed and refined in the second edition of *Logistical Management*, published in 1978. Thus, this third edition of *Logistical Management* represents the fifth refinement of selected materials. However, like all the previous versions, it represents a significant expansion of subject matter.

Logistical Management is presented as a systems integration of physical distribution, manufacturing support, and procurement. Business logistics is viewed as involving all aspects of physical movement to, from, and between the business locations that constitute the physical facilities of an enterprise. We hope that the text achieves two fundamental objectives—first, to present a comprehensive description of existing logistical practice within the private and public sectors of society, and second, to provide a conceptual approach for integration that illustrates how the discipline is likely to change in the future.

It would be impossible to list all of the individuals who have made significant contributions to the contents of this book. Special thanks are due to Professor Donald A. Taylor of Michigan State University, who has actively helped all of the authors throughout our careers. In addition, for their specific aid with the manuscript, appreciation is due Professors Bixby Cooper, Frank Mossman, John Hazard, Robert Monczka, and George Wagenheim of Michigan State University and Bernard J. LaLonde of The Ohio State University. We also wish to acknowledge the contribution of Pat J. Calabro, The University of Texas at Arlington, John J. Coyle, Pennsylvania State University, Grant M. Davis, University of Arkansas, and David L. Shrock, Arizona State University, all of whom provided detailed reviews of the initial manuscript and who offered numerous suggestions to improve the quality of presentation. It is an honor to acknowledge the guidance over the years of close friends who counsel freely: Walter L. Jeffrey, retired Vice Chairman of the E. F. MacDonald Company, Robert J. Franco, Executive Vice President ARA Transportation Sector, and

Mark Egan, former Executive Director of The National Council of Physical Distribution Management, Rick Price, Vice President, Nabisco Brands, Inc., Bill Partipello, Vice President, Coca-Cola Foods, Inc., and C. Richard Polzello, Senior Vice President, J. E. Seagram, Inc., and the influence of two former mentors who are deceased: Edward A. Brand and George A. Ramlose.

The authors in combination have been active members of The Council of Logistics Management, formerly the National Council of Physical Distribution Management since its inception. It would be impossible to elaborate the contributions of the many Council members who have been of assistance in the preparation of this manuscript. In particular, we wish to acknowledge the continued contribution of George Gecowets and his staff who are always willing to help the academic community. Over the past sixteen years, business executives who have attended the annual Michigan State University Logistics Management Executive Development Seminar have been exposed to the basic concepts developed in the text and have given freely of their time and experience.

The roster of those who teach various aspects of logistics around the world has expanded so as to make acknowledgment of key individuals impossible. To this group in general, and in particular to our colleagues at Michigan State University whose advice and assistance made it possible to complete this manuscript, we express our sincere appreciation.

It is difficult to pinpoint the continuous contribution that teachers receive from students over the years. In many ways, the final day of judgment of a professional career comes in the seminar room. We have been fortunate to have the counsel of a great many outstanding young scholars who currently are making their marks upon the academic and business worlds. In particular, we wish to acknowledge the assistance of all of the doctoral students who participated in simulation research dealing with LREPS and SPSF over the past decade. Bonnie Clift assisted in the preparation of examples and tables for the 3rd edition.

We wish to single out the contribution of Felicia Kramer, who served as coordinator of manuscript preparation in several earlier editions. Pamela Cook, who assisted in preparation of the current edition, continued the outstanding support of the 3rd edition. Without Pam and her word processor this extensive revision would not be reality.

Finally, authors must have an understanding family, or the preparation of a manuscript would be impossible during the demanding years of life. This book is dedicated to our families.

With so much able assistance, it is difficult to offer any excuse for any shortcomings that might appear. However, the faults are solely our responsibility.

> Donald J. Bowersox
> David J. Closs
> Omar Keith Helferich

BRIEF CONTENTS

APPENDICES

DETAILED CONTENTS

PART FIVE **Future Environments**

CHAPTER **15**   Dimensions of Change—A Seminar Focus   **473**

INTEGRATED LOGISTICAL MANAGEMENT

Logistical Management

The subject of this book is logistical management. Logistical management is unique and, to some degree, represents a paradox because it is concerned with one of the oldest and also newest activities of business and government. Logistical system components—facility location, forecasting and order management, transportation, inventory, warehousing and packaging—have been performed since the start of commercial and industrial activity. It is difficult to visualize any marketing or manufacturing that could be completed without logistical support. Likewise, logistical support is vital to government, military, and nonprofit organizations. There is no doubt that logistical performance is and always has been a vital economic activity.

The newness of logistics stems from the emergence of a radically different and widespread approach to the integrated management of the logistical process. For a variety of reasons detailed later in this chapter, management practices regarding logistics began to abruptly change during the 1950s. The concept of integrated logistics has continued to expand to the point where modern logistics is defined as:

> a single logic to guide the process of planning, allocating and controlling financial and human resources committed to physical distribution, manufacturing support and purchasing operations.[1]

---

[1] The term *logistics* is not qualified specifically as business or military. The basic concepts of logistical management are applicable throughout private and public enterprise activities. Over the

The objective of logistics is to arrange delivery of finished inventory, work in process inventory, and material assortments, when required, in usable condition, to the location where needed, and at the lowest total cost. It is through the logistical process that materials flow into the vast manufacturing capacity of an industrial nation and products are distributed through marketing channels for consumption. The complexity of logistical systems is awesome. In the United States alone, channels of marketing contain over 2.2 million retailers and more than 350 thousand wholesalers.[2]

In the overall arrangement of both profit and nonprofit ventures, logistical performance provides time and place utility for inventory. Such utility is equally important to business and government operations. When materials, work in process, and finished goods inventory are positioned at the desired location, in a timely manner, value is added by virtue of logistical performance. Such added value is costly to achieve. Although difficult to measure precisely, most experts agree the annual logistical expenditure of the United States exceeds 12 per cent of the total gross national product.[3] Expenditures for transportation services represent approximately 7 per cent of GNP. In other words, for every trillion dollar of GNP, the national logistical bill is estimated to be $120 billion annually, of which transportation represents approximately 70 billion.[4]

The above estimates provides an order of magnitude feel for where logistical costs fit at a gross national level. For individual companies, total cost expenditures range from 10 to 35 per cent of gross sales depending on the business, the geographical area of operations, and the weight/value ratio of the

---

years, common titles used to describe all or parts of the material discussed in this text have been *business logistics, physical distribution, materials logistics management, materials management, physical supply, logistics of distribution, marketing logistics, rhochrematics,* and *total distribution.* In 1976 the Council of Logistics Management modified its 1962 definition of *physical distribution management* as follows: "Physical distribution management is the term describing the integration of two or more activities for the purpose of planning, implementing and controlling the efficient flow of raw materials, inprocess inventory and finished goods from point of origin to point of consumption. These activities may include, but are not limited to, customer service, demand forecasting, distribution communications, inventory control, material handling, order processing, parts and service support, plant and warehouse site selection, procurement, packaging, return goods handling, salvage and scrap disposal, traffic and transportation, and warehousing and storage." Although this definition does not incorporate the specific managerial titles used in this text, it does reflect the need for total movement management from point of materials procurement to location of finished-product distribution.

[2] U.S. Bureau of the Census of Retail and Wholesale Trade, Summary Statistics, 1982.

[3] The estimate of 12 per cent of gross national product is the authors' projection. Other estimates of aggregate United States' logistics costs for 1982 range from $418 billion to $650 billion. The $418-billion estimate was provided by Robert V. Delaney of Leaseway Transportation Corporation. An estimate of $419 billion has been provided by Booz, Allan and Hamilton. A. T. Kearney, Inc., provided an estimate of $650 billion. The estimate of 12 per cent of the gross national product used by the authors reflects a conservative estimate based on activities included in logistics management which is defined to encompass physical distribution, manufacturing support, and purchasing. Based on a 1984 GNP of $3.66 trillion, the total cost of logistics is estimated to represent approximately $440 billion. The 12 per cent estimate reflects a decline in percentage expenditure over the last decade as logistics productivity has improved.

[4] Based on a 1984 expenditure of $250 billion, Transportation Association of America, *Transportation Facts and Trends.* Washington, D.C. 1985.

finished products and raw materials involved. In terms of cost, logistics often represents the highest single operating expenditure, second in dollars spent to materials or cost of goods sold. It is clear that the logistical contribution of time and place utility is vital to business and government operations and is costly to realize.

This book is concerned with the process of integrated logistical management. Such integration involves the coordination of physical distribution, manufacturing support, and purchasing. In a broad sense logistical coordination involves all aspects of inventory movement and storage. To achieve logistical objectives, managerial attention must be directed to the design of a logistical system and to its operation. From an accountability perspective, logistical management responsibility is defined as:

> the managerial responsibility to design and administer a system to control the flow of materials, work in process and finished inventory to meet the strategic objectives of the enterprise.

The goal of logistical performance is to achieve a predetermined level of manufacturing-marketing support at the lowest possible total cost expenditure. The logistical manager has the fundamental responsibility for planning and administering an operating system capable of realizing this goal. Within this broad responsibility of system planning and administration, a multitude of detail and complex tasks exists. The hallmark of logistics is integration of the varied dimensions and demands for strategic movement and storage.

This initial chapter introduces and defines the basic concepts involved in logistical management. Attention is first directed to a brief review of forces contributing to the development of contemporary logistics. Next, an overall perspective of logistics is presented by discussing physical distribution, manufacturing support, and procurement in terms of both unique and common features. The third part provides an overview of system components involved in logistical performance. The fourth part explains the systems approach to logistical system design and identifies critical trade-offs that must be reconciled to achieve integrated performance. Next, the logistical mission of an enterprise is detailed. The chapter concludes with an overview and synthesis of subjects developed in subsequent chapters.

THE EVOLUTION OF LOGISTICAL MANAGEMENT

Prior to 1950, the typical enterprise treated the process of logistical management on a fragmentary basis. Although a great many authors acknowledged the fundamental importance of logistics to marketing and manufacturing, no formal or integrated concept prevailed.[5]

Since the Industrial Revolution, the United States' capacity to mass produce and mass market far outstripped the capacity to mass distribute. The advent of

---

[5] Numerous early references to logistics can be located in business literature. Arch W. Shaw, *An Approach to Business Problems* (Cambridge, Mass.: Harvard University Press, 1916), pp. 101–10, discussed the strategic aspects of physical distribution. Other early references are found in Fred E. Clark, *Principles of Marketing* (New York: Macmillan Publishing Co., Inc., 1922); Theodore N.

the marketing concept intensified the chaotic and segmented nature of logistical operations. The priority that modern marketing placed upon (1) line-item proliferation, (2) selling identical products through a wide variety of marketing channels and different types of retailers, and (3) the widespread offering of product-contained services combined to create a *need* for a new and less expensive approach to physical support. The following quote from a 1954 speech of the late Paul D. Converse provides a general appraisal of the situation prevailing during the early 1950s.[6]

> in the study of marketing and the operation of marketing departments and business a great deal more attention is paid to buying and selling than to physical handling. In fact, the physical handling of goods seems to be pretty much overlooked by sales executives, advertising men, and market researchers. ... problems of physical distribution are too often brushed aside as matters of little importance. I have for years been reading business and economics magazines. Such publications over the years have devoted relatively little space to physical distribution.

The neglect and subsequent late development of logistics can be logically attributed to at least two factors. First, prior to the time that computers were commonplace and before quantitative techniques were widely used, there was no reason to believe that integration of logistical activities would improve performance. The late 1950s were destined to witness the start of a major change in logistical management practices. Neither computers nor quantitative techniques were to be denied the fertile area of logistical application. From a historical perspective there is little doubt that early developments in computers and quantitative technologies were as effectively utilized in logistics as in any other management area.

A second major factor contributing to a change in traditional management practices during the 1950s was the volatile economic climate. The profit squeeze which started in the early 1950s and continues today created a managerial attitude conducive to cost containment and reduction. Logistics provided a fertile area for realizing such cost control.

Thus technology and economic necessity changed abruptly during the 1950s. The subsequent development of integrated logistics is reviewed in four time periods during which revised attitudes and practices emerged regarding movement and storage management.

Beckman, *Wholesaling* (New York: The Ronald Press Company, 1926); Percival White, Scientific Marketing Management (New York: Harper and Low, Publishers, 1927), Ralph Borsodi, *The Distribution Age* (New York: Appleton-Century-Crofts, 1929); and Richard Webster, "Careless Physical Distribution: A Monkey-Wrench in Sales Management Machinery, " *Sales Management*, Vol. 19 (July 6, 1929), p. 21. For a comprehensive review of early literature, see Bernard J. La Londe and Leslie M. Dawson, "Early Development of Physical Distribution Thought," in *Readings in Physical Distribution Management* (New York: Macmillan Publishing Co., Inc., 1969), pp. 9–18. The historical review presented in this introduction is updated from an article originally published in 1969; see Donald J. Bowersox, "Physical Distribution Development, Current Status, and Potential," *Journal of Marketing*, Vol. 33 (January 1969), pp. 63–70.

[6] Paul D. Converse, "The Other Half of Marketing," *Twenty-Sixth Boston Conference on Distribution*, Boston, 1954, p. 22.

1956 to 1965—A Decade of Conceptualization

The period from 1956 to 1965 was a decade during which the integrated logistical concept began to crystallize. Four major developments solidified this conceptualization: (1) development of total cost analysis, (2) application of the systems approach, (3) increased concern for customer service, and (4) revised attention to marketing channels. A brief discussion of each follows.

Development of Total Cost Analysis

In 1956 a specialized study of air freight economics provided a significant integrative concept.[7] The study, in an effort to explain the economic justification for high-cost air transport, introduced the concept of total cost analysis. Total cost was presented as *all* expenditures required to accomplish a specified logistical mission. The authors illustrated selected situations wherein the high freight rates characteristic of air transport could be more than offset by reductions in inventory holding and warehouse operation costs. They concluded the least total-cost method of logistical operations might utilize high-cost transportation.

The concept of total cost, although basic, had not previously been applied to logistical economies.[8] Probably because of the economic climate of the times, the impact of the study focused attention to the total cost of logistical systems. Subsequent refinements provided a more comprehensive identification of logistical cost components and further elaborated the critical need for functional cost analysis.[9]

Application of the Systems Approach

The first prominent applications of systems technology occurred during World War II.[10] The concept of total integrated effort toward the achievement of

---

[7] Howard T. Lewis, James W. Culliton, and Jack D. Steel, *The Role of Air Freight in Physical Distribution* (Boston: Division of Research, Graduate School of Business Administration, Harvard Univesity, 1956).

[8] The total cost concept, developed in greater detail in Chapter 9, is a specialized form of break-even analysis. For some early applications, see J. Brooks Heckert and Robert B. Miner, *Distribution Costs* (New York: The Ronald Press Company, 1940), Chap. 15; and Donald R. Longman and Michael Schiff, *Practical Distribution Cost Analysis* (Homewood, Ill.: Richard D. Irwin, Inc., 1955), pp. 35–37.

[9] In particular, see Marvin Flaks, "Total Cost Approach to Physical Distribution." *Business Management*, Vol. 24 (August 1963), pp. 55–61; Raymond LeKashman and John F. Stolle, "The Total Cost Approach to Distribution," *Business Horizons*, Vol. 8 (Winter 1965), pp. 33–46; and Douglas M. Lambert and Bernard J. La Londe, "Inventory Carrying Costs," *Management Accounting* (August 1976), pp. 31–35.

[10] For an early discussion of the systems approach to problem solving, see Geoffrey Gordon, *System Simulation* (Englewood Cliffs, N.J.: Prentice-Hall, Inc., 1969), Chaps. 1 and 2; Jay W. Forrester *Principles of Systems* (Cambridge, Mass.: Wright-Allen Press, 1969); Stanford L. Optner, *Systems Analysis* (Englewood Cliffs, N. J.: Prentice-Hall, Inc., 1960); Stanely F. Stasch, *Systems Analysis for Marketing Planning and Control* (Glenview, Ill.: Scott, Foresman and Company, 1972); Van Court Hare, Jr., *Systems Analysis: A Diagnostic Approach* (New York: Harcourt Brace Jovanovich, 1967); and/or Robert H. Kupperman and Harvey A. Smith, *Mathematical Foundations of Systems Analysis* (Reading, Mass.: Addison-Wesley Publishing Company, Inc., 1969).

specified military goals was tailor-made for logistical analysis. Whereas total-cost analysis offered a method for measuring logistical activities, the systems concept provided an framework for analysis of complex relationships.

The first general articles describing the potential of integrated logistics relied heavily upon systems analysis.[11] The systems approach highlighted the deficiency of treating logistical activity centers as isolated performance areas.

When evaluated from a systems viewpoint, integrated logistics identifies a need for compromise between and among traditional practices. For example, manufacturing traditionally has desired stable production runs and low procurement costs. In contrast, logistics raises questions concerning the total cost and strategic impact of these practices. The traditional financial position favors low inventories. While inventory commitments should be minimized, arbitrary reductions that force inventory below necessary levels can increase total cost of operations. Marketing's traditional preference for forward finished goods inventory commitment to local markets and broad product assortments in anticipation of sales is a risky practice. Such anticipatory logistics may be in direct conflict with the most economical total system arrangement. The significant point is that logistical trade-offs must be included in strategic planning. The basic belief that integrated system performance produces superior end result became the primary focal point of logistical planning.

Increased Concern for Customer Service

By the early 1960s, the horizons of integrated logistics began to expand. During this period, management emphasis began to include customer service performance.[12] The result was a realistic evaluation of logistical service with respect to manufacturing and marketing. Several different logistical arrangements can be utilized to support marketing and or manufacturing. Each is capable of providing different levels of operational support and involves significantly different operating costs and resource commitments. To develop an effective and efficient logistical systems, the relationships of cost and service must be simultaneously evaluated. The strategic objective is to develop and implement a logistical operation capable of obtaining specified customer service performance at the lowest possible total cost.

Revised Attention to Marketing Channels

Most logistical systems were initially studied from the vantage point of a single or vertically integrated enterprise. During this early decade, breakthrough firms came to recognize that logistical activities and responsibilities seldom stopped at the point of initial ownership transfer.[13]

---

[11] For example, see Harvey N. Shycon and Richard B. Maffei, "Simulation—Tool for Better Distribution," *Harvard Business Review*, Vol. 38 (November–December 1960), pp. 65–75; Donald D. Parker, "Improved Efficiency and Reduced Cost in Marketing," *Journal of Marketing*, Vol. 26 (April 1962), pp. 15–21; J. L. Heskett, "Ferment in Marketing's Oldest Area," *Journal of Marketing*, Vol. 26 (October 1962), pp. 40–45; and John F. Magee, "The Logistics of Distribution," *Harvard Business Review*, Vol. 40 (July–August 1962), pp. 89–101.

[12] For examples, see Peter Drucker, "The Economy's Dark Continent," *Fortune*, Vol. 72 (April 1962), pp. 103–104; William Lazer, "Distribution and the Marketing Mix," *Transportation and Distribution Management*, Vol. 2 (December 1962), pp. 12–17; and Wendell M. Stewart, "Key to Improved Volume and Profits," *Journal of Marketing*, Vol. 29 (January 1965), pp. 65–70.

A channelwide perspective of logistics illustrates that significant costs may occur as a result of the practices of individual enterprises engaged in a channel arrangement. The interface of two or more individual logistical systems may result in excessive cost generation and customer service impairment for the overall channel. Even if individual logistical systems are fully compatible, the total cost for the channel may escalate as a result of functional duplication. A great deal of the attention to channel relationships resulted from the 1957 classic work of Wroe Alderson.[14] The functional approach to channel analysis he provided served to revive, expand, and update the contributions of early marketing scholars concerning the relationship of risk and the understanding of commitment in channelwide logistical operations.

Further insight into channelwide logistical arrangements resulted from the study of information lags and product commitments. In 1958 Forrester introduced dynamic analysis of channel arrangements.[15] In terms of physical flow, Forrester illustrated the channelwide impact of information upon inventory fluctuation and accumulation. Until Forrester's contribution, the impact of time had been generally neglected in logistics in favor of facility location. The integration of time and location offered a new understanding of the logistical process. Over subsequent years the integration of temporal and spatial analysis served to establish the theoretical foundations of integrated logistics.[16]

In summary, the study of integrated logistics in comparison to the history of business and economics is relatively new. The development of tools of analysis and high-speed computers provided the opportunity to improve logistical operations. In addition, the economic climate of the period encouraged cost reduction. The result was a decade during which the concept of integrated logistics materialized. Although many factors contributed to logistical development, the four discussed in this part had particular significance. During 1962 and 1963 the National Council of Physical Distribution Management was established. NCPDM represents the initial professional organization founded for the sole purpose of advancing the state of the art and practice of integrated performance in a significant area of overall logistics. Originally founded by thirteen individuals, membership in the organization exceeded 5,000 by the mid-1980s. In 1985 NCPDM officially changed its name to The Council of Logistics Management to formally acknowledge the expanding scope of logistical management.

1966 to 1970—A Time to Test for Relevancy

By the mid-1960s, those concerned with logistical management had developed a rather segmented, but theoretically sound, approach to guide integrated

---

[13] The issue of legal ownership is critical to transaction analysis. Logistical responsibility may extend long after the time of actual ownership transfer. For an expanded treatment, see Chapter 3, pp. 89–92.

[14] Wroe Alderson, *Marketing Behavior and Executive Action* (Homewood, Ill.: Richard D. Irwin, Inc., 1957).

[15] Jay W. Forrester, "Industrial Dynamics," *Harvard Business Review*, Vol. 36 (July–August 1958), pp. 37–66; or Jay W. Forrester, *Industrial Dynamics* (Cambridge, Mass.: The MIT Press, 1961).

[16] This concept of temporal/spatial integration is critical to the development of integrated logistics. The concept is developed in detail in Chapter 9.

planning. The flurry of attention that Professor Converse perceived as a critical need in 1954 had become a reality by 1966.

The period from 1966 to 1970 represented a time during which the basic concepts of logistics were tested. The general result was that the predicted cost and service benefits became reality. For the most part, logistical concepts passed the test of time. Managerial emphasis focused on improved operating performance as countless firms implemented integrated logistics.

Within a single enterprise initial attention typically focused on either physical distribution or purchasing. A general observation concerning the pattern of adoption was that few firms simultaneously undertook change in both physical distribution and purchasing practices. The typical situation was for initial development to begin in one or the other area.

Firms that had a primary orientation to the marketing of relatively low-price consumer products, such as grocery and pharmaceutical manufacturers, as well as retailers, tended to place a great deal of attention on finished-goods inventory management and support of customer orders. The overall field of physical distribution developed to the point where it became common practice for firms to seek the management of order processing, warehousing, transportation, and inventory control on an integrated basis.

In contrast, materials management began to develop as an attempt to integrate the planning and logistical dimensions of purchasing and manufacturing. Those firms that were early leaders in materials management typically produced consumer durables such as automobiles and appliances. Emphasis in materials management, as contrasted to physical distribution, focused around the orderly flow of raw materials and component parts to support manufacturing operations.

The establishment of physical distribution and materials management organizations faced significant opposition in many firms. Managers who had traditionally been responsible for specific areas, such as transportation or purchasing, often were suspicious of the organizational integration required to implement either physical distribution or material management concepts. The basic idea that overall total cost might be reduced by spending more on a specific activity was difficult to establish, given traditional methods of performance measurement. For example, traffic managers had typically been measured by dollars expended for transportation as a percentage of gross sales. Given traditional performance measurement, it became clear that increased transportation expenditures to realize superior physical distribution performance could appear on the record as a deterioration of transport purchasing. It is understandable why all managers did not embrace the integrated concepts with equal enthusiasm.

A second deterrent to widespread adoption of either physical distribution or materials management was the difficulty in presenting a case to support the hard-core return on investment that would materialize from implementation. In part, measurement problems resulted from the widespread practice of not evaluating the true cost of maintaining inventory. Given the accounting practice of the times, it was also difficult to place a monetary return or value on superior customer service performance.

The impact of the above noted factors combined with a multitude of other reasons for resisting change meant that not all efforts to implement logistical principles were accepted. Several notable attempts to implement new concepts failed. However, because of some outstanding success stories, the fundamental concept of integrated logistics passed the relevancy test.

1971 to 1979—A Period of Changing Priorities

The years from 1971 to 1979 represented a period of prolonged uncertainty in almost every dimension of enterprise activity. For the first time since World War II the availability of low-cost energy became a critical concern. Energy shortages, coupled with rising prices for fuel and petroleum-based materials, culminated in widespread shortages of many basic materials and manufactured products. During the early part of the decade, concerns of near crisis proportion struck the logistics community with the advent of the OPEC oil embargo. Logistics faced a need to improve energy productivity since transportation and storage are among the largest and most visible energy consumers.

The crises of the decade extended beyond energy to include ecological concerns. Across the board, logistics activities ranked high among the sources of environmental impact and potential pollution.

Finally, the economy failed to withstand the many strains that were characteristic of the decade, ranging from Watergate to the demise of the Eastern railroads. During the early 1970s the United States' economy fell into a deep recession during which unemployment reached heights surpassed only during the Great Depression. The recessions of the 1970s created a situation which has been labeled "stagflation."[17] In terms of growth, the economy became stagnant. However, at the same time inflation continued at rates unprecedented within the United States. Toward the later part of the decade interest rates reached unpredicted double-digit heights.

The impact of the 1971–1979 period upon the development and implementation of logistical concepts was significant. Overnight, enterprise priorities and related programs to cope with the ever-changing situation shifted from *servicing demand* to *maintaining supply*. Top-management attention focused on procurement because of the sheer consequence of supply failure. The result was the rapid adoption of materials management concepts. Whereas the physical distribution profession originally developed to support the marketing concept, materials management matured from the hazards of potential supply discontinuity. In response to an immediate need, traditional methods of material procurement changed overnight. In replacement, a new systems orientation based on adoption of just-in-time movement and long-term contractual commitments emerged. Emphasis began to focus on proactive rather than reactive procurement. In other words, rather than planning operations to react to marketing needs, management began to formulate plans around the maintenance of continuous manufacturing and processing, given a high probability of material shortages.

From a technological perspective, the early 1970s was a prolific period of research and development in mainframe computer models for logistical system

---

[17] *Stagflation* is defined as simultaneous stagnation in gross national product growth coupled with inflation.

design and control.[18] Logistical models to assist in the evaluation of alternative logistical strategies became a reality.

The events of the period also confirmed a growing realization that significant logistical problems often have an organizational and institutional rather than a technical base. During the decade, attention began to be directed to the potential of third-party logistical arrangements as an alternative solution to the growing complexity of logistical support.[19]

In retrospect, the most significant overall impact of the 1971–1979 period was the institutionalization of logistics within the organizational structures of countless private and public enterprises. The concepts were proven as viable contributors to the attainment of enterprise objectives. The inception of integrated physical distribution and materials management provided a means to deal positively with uncertainty.

1980 to 1985—A Period of Significant Political and Technological Change

The early years of the 1980s experienced more abrupt change in logistical operations than was the case in any previous time period.[20] The most significant changes were (1) transportation deregulation, (2) the introduction of micro-computer technology, and (3) the communication revolution. A brief discussion of each as it impacted integrated logistics follows.

Transportation Deregulation

Within a few months in the summer and autumn of 1980, the economic and political infrastructure of transportation was radically reformed by the passage of the Motor Carrier Regulatory Reform and Modernization Act and the Staggers Rail Act.[21] While the basic intent underlying each act was significantly different, they combined to create a permissive environment for transportation innovation. The years following legislative enactment were characterized by a host of administrative and judicial actions which further relaxed restraints on what services, prices, and commitments for-hire transportation could provide the shipping public. In a similar vein, the range of permissible actions that private transportation could perform for internal as well as customer distribution and purchasing was radically altered. From 1980 forward, the transportation structure of the United States has increasingly become a free-market

---

[18] For an early review of system models, see Robert G. House and George C. Jackson, *Trends in Computer Application in Transportation and Management* (Columbus, Ohio: Ohio State University, 1976). Chapter 13 provides an up-to-date review.

[19] James L. Heskett, "Sweeping Changes in Distribution," *Harvard Business Review*, March–April 1973, pp. 123–32; or see Donald J. Bowersox, "Showdown in the Magic Pipeline: Call for New Priorities," Presidential Issue, *Handling and Shipping* (Fall 1973), pp. 12–14.

[20] For materials that elaborate the strategic potential of logistical management see Roy D. Shapiro, "Get Leverage from Logistics," *Harvard Business Review* (May–June 1984), pp. 119–126, and Graham Sharman, "The Rediscovery of Logistics," *Harvard Business Review* (September–October, 1984), pp. 71–79. Also see Ronald H. Ballou, *Business Logistics Management Planning and Control*, 2nd ed. (Englewood Cliffs, N. J.: Prentice-Hall, Inc. 1985), and Roy W. Shapiro and James L. Heshelt, *Logistics Strategy: Cases and concepts* (St. Paul: West Publishing Company, 1985).

[21] Public Laws 96–296 and 96–488, respectively. See Chapter 5, pp. 142–46.

system. Some experts feel that the Interstate Commerce Commission will, in the foreseeable future, be dismantled with remaining regulation of transportation being conducted under traditional antitrust agencies.

Chapter 5 provides a comprehensive treatment of significant changes in transportation that have resulted since 1980 and their impact on logistical performance. While the economic impact on shipper and carrier operations has been significant, one collateral benefit of deregulation is often neglected. As a result of the widespread publicity that surrounded deregulation, senior-management attention was attracted to the potential of taking advantage of the significant change. Emphasis was once again attracted to the logistical system as a source for productivity improvement. To fully exploit the newfound opportunity to capture transportation economies, it became opportune to reexamine the coordination of physical distribution, manufacturing support, and procurement. One key to increasing transportation productivity is improved utilization of equipment. Significant changes took place in the traditional methods and practices of physical distribution, manufacturing support, and procurement to improve transportation productivity. The fact of the matter is that freight transportation expenditures typically account for 5 to 10 per cent of a firm's gross sales. Any reduction in transportation expenditure offers instant profit improvement.

Microprocessor Technology

Some experts predict that the commercialization of microprocessor technology during the early 1980s will ultimately eliminate centralized data processing. The impact of the micro era is predicted to be particularly significant to the logistical system which has rapidly become the biggest user of computers.

The fact of the matter is that numerous desk-top computing resources are larger and more powerful than many mainframes being developed as recently as the late 1970s. These microcomputers are now abundant throughout logistical organizations. This hardware is cheap and, when combined with fourth- and fifth-generation development languages, it provides the processing power at the end-user level to resolve and conduct most transaction, assessment, and decision support processing. Software to permit microprocessors to participate interactively in distributed processing with data-base management systems resident on larger machines began to be marketed in 1985.

The impact of the microprocessor on integrated logistics stands to be far reaching. The computing resources are here today to coordinate complete information exchange between physical distribution, manufacturing support, and procurement. The capability to engage in logistical resource planning of these interrelated areas from a single integrated data base is the key to achieving unprecedented levels of logistical productivity.[22]

Communication Revolution

The impact of new communication technology upon logistical capability may nearly equal that of the microprocessor. During the very early 1980s managers began to unfold the operational problems related to implementation of Universal Product Coding (UPC) and Electronic Data Interchange (EDI). The

---

[22] This concept is developed in greater detail in Chapters 2 and 11.

technological impact of point-of-sale scanning was to increase the amount of raw data concerning various aspects of logistical performance. Computer-to-computer ordering became common to exploit the growing availability of data and the need to convert and transmit information to key decision points.

By the mid-1980s many experts began to predict that even more powerful communication technologies were on the verge of commercialization. The capability to transmit sight, sound, and written messages was predicted to become increasingly available and economical. In late 1984, Federal Express introduced ZAP mail that promised pickup, transmission, and delivery of documents through the United States in a total elapsed time of four hours or less. The technology of video text, with its many significant applications to logistics, began to be commercialized. The potential impact of communication change is highlighted by the following prediction of Robert V. Delaney.[23]

> Terrestrial radio has improved to the point where it is now possible to maintain voice communication with vehicles over most of the interstate highway system. By 1987, perhaps sooner, the Geostar Satellite System will permit distribution managers to locate and communicate with vehicles throughout North America, instantly and digitally. Mobilstar, Navstar and other technologies may follow. The application of satellite technology to just-in-time and other inventories velocity programs will be exciting.

Beyond doubt the communication technology impact will be exciting. What is in the offing is an unprecedented opportunity to utilize communication to further coordinate and integrate logistical operations. For over a decade the one significant component of logistical systems that has been becoming less expensive is information.[24] In contrast, all other components of logistical cost have increased equal to or greater than the prevailing inflation rate. This emerging technology that permits the integration of information into logistical system operations and control represents an unprecedented trade-off opportunity.

1986 and Beyond—Toward Integrated Logistics

For breakthrough enterprises the decades ahead offer the prospect for even greater payoffs from the full implementation of logistical management. The challenge for the future is to fully integrate the inherent complexities of physical distribution, manufacturing support, and purchasing operations. As traditionally constituted, each represented a partial solution to an important operating problem. The only long-term relevancy is to focus attention on attainment of enterprise strategic goals as contrasted to solving operating problems. The attainment of strategic goals rests with the development and

---

[23] Robert V. Delaney, "Key Physical Distribution Changes Impacting on Today's and Tomorrow's Opportunities," paper presented at Grocery Manufactures of America, Inc. Distribution Committee Conference, Hilton Head, South Carolina, April 26, 1984, p. 11.

[24] Bernard J. La Londe, "Transportation in the 21st Century," *Handling and Shipping Management: Presidential Issue,* 1984–85, p. 78, and *Some-Thoughts on Logistics Policy and Strategies: Management Challenges for the 1980s* (Columbus: College of Administrative Science, The Ohio State University, Working Paper Series, December 1984).

implementation of a *single* overall logic. Integrated logistical management provides such a logic and is becoming increasingly relevant for at least five reasons.

First, there is a great deal of interdependence between all logistical areas which can be exploited to the advantage of the enterprise. The perspective of a *total* movement/storage system provides a higher order of trade-offs and greater synergistic potential. Throughout the logistical system management is faced with ever-increasing labor cost. Logistical managers must develop methods to substitute capital for labor-intensive processes. Logistical operations are among the most labor intensive performed in an enterprise. Complete integration increases the economic justification for substitution of capital for labor.

A *second* reason for supporting integrated logistics is that a narrower or restricted approach creates the potential for a dysfunctional interface. To a significant degree, concepts related solely to physical distribution, manufacturing support, or purchasing place operational priorities on diametrically opposite goals. The failure to develop a dominant philosophy of logistical management creates the potential for classical suboptimization.

A *third* reason to integrate is that the control requirements for each operation are similar. The objective of logistical control is to reconcile the different operational demands confronted by physical distribution, manufacturing, and procurement.

A *fourth* reason for the integration of logistical operations is an increasing awareness that many trade-offs exist between manufacturing economies and marketing requirements that can be reconciled by a well-designed logistical system. The dominant pattern of manufacturing is to produce products in various sizes, colors, and quantities in *anticipation* of future sale. The *postponement* of final assembling to some later time in the order-processing cycle can greatly reduce risk and increase overall enterprise flexibility. Innovative new systems are emerging to make use of logistical facilities to reduce the traditional anticipatory nature of business.

A *final*, and perhaps most significant, reason for integrated logistics is that the complexity of contemporary logistics require innovative solutions. The challenge for the coming decades is to develop *new ways* of satisfying logistical requirements, not simply using technology to perform *old ways more efficiently.* The broad perspective of integrated logistical management is a prerequisite to attainment of this breakthrough.

As a result of these five reasons, the field of logistics has and will continue to be managed on an integrated basis. This text is written on the assumption that full integration of all logistically related operating systems into one highly coordinated effort will materialize, as a strategic commitment. The next section provides a brief overview of such an integrated process.

THE LOGISTICAL SYSTEM

The concept of integrated logistics is illustrated in Figure 1–1.[25] The logistical process is viewed as a system that links an enterprise with its customers and

---

[25] The flow concepts developed in this section are based on Donald J. Bowersox, Phillip L. Carter and Robert M. Monczka, "Computer Aided Purchasing, Manufacturing and Physical Distribution," *Proceedings NCPDM Annual Meeting* (Oak Brook, Ill: September 16–19, 1984), pp. 142–146.

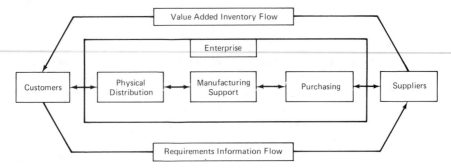

Figure 1–1 Logistics System

suppliers. Information flows from and about customers in the form of forecasts and orders and is refined through planning into specific manufacturing and purchasing objectives. As materials and products are purchased, a value-added inventory flow is initiated which ultimately results in ownership transfer of finished products to customers. Thus, the logistical process is viewed in terms of two interrelated efforts: (1) value-added inventory flow, and (2) requirements information flow.

Prior to reviewing each flow in greater detail, two considerations are important. First, the basic concept illustrated in Figure 1–1 is not restricted to business nor is it unique to manufacturing firms. The need to coordinate requirements and operations is found in all types of institutions which function in a specialized society. A retailing or wholesaling firm may directly link physical distribution and purchasing and not require manufacturing support. All political-economic societies have logistical requirements regardless of their reliance upon either free or controlled market systems. Logistics is universal to the process of growth and survival.

It is also important to point out that the normal value-added inventory flow toward customers must at select times be reversed. Product recalls are a common occurrence owing to rigid standards of quality control, expiration dating, and clear-cut responsibility for hazardous product consequences. A further need for reverse or return logistical performance is the increasing number of laws prohibiting the use of disposable beverage and food containers. Reverse logistics does not necessarily serve to improve logistical productivity. However, reverse movement is justified on a social basis and must be accommodated in logistical system design. The point of significance in reverse logistical operations is the need for maximum control when a potential health liability exists. In this sense, a recall program is similar to a strategy of maximum customer service which must be executed regardless of cost. In contrast, reverse logistics of reusable or recyclable containers requires movement utilizing the lowest-total-cost solution. The important point is that logistical strategy cannot be formulated without careful consideration of reverse logistical requirements.

Value-Added Inventory Flow

The operational aspect of logistics is concerned with management of the movement and storage of materials and finished products. As such, logistical operations are viewed as commencing with the initial transportation of a material or component part from a supplier and terminating with the final delivery of a manufactured or processed product to a customer.

From the initial purchase of a material or component, the logistical process adds value by placing inventory at the time and place required. At each step in the manufacturing effort, a material gains greater potential value as it is transformed into finished inventory. Throughout the manufacturing operation work-in-process inventory is transported to support final assembly. The cost associated with each of these movements is part of the value-added material flow. The ultimate value added is achieved by the final ownership transfer of finished-goods inventory to a customer at specified time and place.

For a large manufacturer, logistical operations may consist of thousands of movements, which ultimately culminate in the delivery of products to an industrial user, retailer, wholesaler, dealer, or other marketing intermediary. For a large retailer, logistical operations may commence with the purchase of products for resale and terminate either with consumer pickup or with delivery to the consumer's home. For a hospital, logistics starts with procurement and ends with full support of surgical and recovery operations. The significant point is that regardless of the size and type of enterprise, logistics requires a great deal of management attention. For discussion, logistical operations of an enterprise are divided into three categories: (1) physical distribution, (2) manufacturing support, and (3) purchasing. These are illustrated in the center of Figure 1–1 and combine as the logistical operational units of an enterprise.

The process of *physical distribution management* is concerned with movement of product to customers. In a physical distribution sense, the customer is viewed as the final stop in the marketing channel. The availability of product is a vital part of each channel member's marketing effort. Even a manufacturer's agent, who does not typically own inventory, must depend on product availability to perform expected marketing responsibilities. Unless a proper assortment of products is delivered when needed and in an economical manner, a great deal of overall marketing effort may be in jeopardy. It is through the physical distribution process that the time and space of customer service become an integral part of marketing. Thus, physical distribution links an enterprise with its customers. To support the wide variety of marketing systems that exist in a highly commercialized nation, many different physical distribution systems are utilized by individual enterprises. In total, such systems link together manufacturers, wholesalers, and retailers into marketing channels which provide product availability as an integral aspect of the overall marketing process.

The process of *manufacturing support* concerns control over work-in-process inventory as it flows between stages of manufacturing. The primary concerns of manufacturing support are to participate in development of a production plan and to provide materials and work-in-process inventory in a timely manner to support manufacturing operations. Thus, the overall concern of manufacturing support is not the *how* of production but rather the *what*, *when*, and *where* products will be manufactured.

Manufacturing support has one significant distinction when contrasted to physical distribution or purchasing. Whereas both physical distribution and purchasing deal with the uncertainty of market forces, manufacturing support is limited to movement within and ostensibly under the complete control of the enterprise. The uncertainties introduced by random customer ordering, erratic vendor performance, or critical material shortages are removed from manufacturing support. From the viewpoint of operational planning, the separation of manufacturing support from inbound and outbound movement provides an opportunity for optimal coordination.

Purchasing is concerned with the procurement and movement of materials, parts, and/or finished inventory from supplier location to manufacturing or assembly plants, warehouses, or retail stores.[26] Depending upon the situation, the process of acquisition is commonly identified by different titles. For the manufacturer, the process of material acquisition is typically called *purchasing*. In government circles, acquisition is traditionally referred to as *procurement*. At the retail and wholesale levels of overall marketing, *buying* represents the most widely used term. Acknowledging that operational differences do exist concerning each specific situation, in this text the term *purchasing* is used to refer to all types of procurement. The term *material* is used to identify and differentiate inventory moving inbound to an enterprise, regardless of its degree of readiness for immediate resale. The term *product* is used to identify finished inventory. Thus, *material* relates to inventory with respect to inbound flow and *product* is used to identify inventory for outbound customer shipment. The fundamental difference is that a product results from whatever value is added to material as a consequence of the enterprise's manufacturing, sorting, or assembly.

Similar to physical distribution, purchasing is concerned with availability of the desired material assortment where and when needed. Whereas physical distribution is concerned with outbound customer shipments, purchasing is concerned with the inbound support of manufacturing, sorting, or assembly. Under select situations, such as a grocery manufacturer shipping to an integrated retail chain, one firm's physical distribution is another firm's purchasing. Although similar or even identical transportation movements are involved, the degree of managerial control and associated risk related to the shipment varies substantially between physical distribution and purchasing.

From the perspective of the total enterprise, the three areas of logistical operations have substantial overlap. However, viewing each as a distinct dimension of value-added material flow provides the opportunity to capitalize upon the particular circumstances surrounding each, while maintaining a coordinated effort. The prime concern of integrated logistical management is the coordination of overall value-added inventory movement. The three types of movements combine to provide operational management of materials, semi-finished components, and products moving between locations, supply sources, and customers of the total enterprise. In this sense logistics is concerned with the strategic management of total movement and storage. Table 1–1 provides a summary statement of the specific operational concerns of physical distribution, manufacturing support, and procurement.

Requirements Information Flow

Requirements information flow is concerned with the identification of what specific inventory is needed at which locations within the logistical system. The

---

[26] For a comprehensive discussion of purchasing see Michael R. Leenders, Harold E. Fearon, and Wilbur B. England, *Purchasing and Materials Management*, 8th ed. (Homewood, Ill: Richard D. Irwin Inc. 1985).

TABLE 1–1 Summary Statements of Specific Operating Concerns of Physical Distribution, Manufacturing Support, and Purchasing in Overall Logistics

Physical Distribution

The process of providing customer service. Requires the performance of order receipt and processing, deployment of inventories, storage and handling, and outbound transportation within a channel of distribution. Includes the responsibility to coordinate with marketing planning in such areas as pricing, promotional support, customer service levels, delivery standards, handling return merchandise and life-cycle support. The primary physical distribution objective is to assist in revenue generation by providing strategically desired customer service at the lowest total cost.

Manufacturing Support

The process of planning, scheduling, and supporting manufacturing operations. Requires master schedule planning and the performance of work-in-process storage, handling, transportation, and time phasing of components. Includes the responsibility for storage of inventory at manufacturing sites and maximum flexibility in the coordination of geographic and final assemblies postponement between manufacturing and physical distribution operations.

Purchasing

The process of obtaining products and materials from outside suppliers. Requires the performance of requirement planning, supply sourcing, negotiation, order placement, inbound transportation, receiving and inspection, storage and handling, and quality assurance. Includes the responsibility to coordinate with suppliers in such areas as scheduling, supply continuity, hedging and speculation, and research leading to new sources or programs. The primary procurement objective is to support manufacturing or resale organizations by providing timely purchasing at the lowest total cost.

---

primary objective of developing requirements information is to establish a plan to integrate logistical operations. Such coordination is required to establish and maintain operational continuity. Within the three areas of logistical operations, different movement circumstances exist with respect to size of order, availability of inventory, and urgency of movement. The primary objective of requirements information flow is to reconcile these differentials.

Requirements information flow involves planning and coordination of logistical operations. This involves four areas of managerial concern: (1) product-market forecasting, (2) order processing, (3) master production scheduling, and (4) requirements planning.

The establishment of objectives to guide logistical operations requires that estimates be compiled concerning future sales expectations and inventory requirements. The formulation of a statistical estimate of future sales is *product-market forecasting*. The planning horizon of a product-market forecast is relatively short with three months to one year being most typical. Forecasting purchases by specific customers or in specific markets is the initial step in logistical planning. Almost all procurement, manufacturing, and distribution undertaken by an enterprise is in *anticipation* of future sale. For example, materials are purchased in *anticipation* of undertaking specific manufacturing and assembly, in *anticipation* of an order, which itself is in *anticipation* of future customer demand. Product-market forecasting constitutes a firm's initial effort to reconcile, program, and, to the extent possible, postpone the anticipatory logistical process inherent in a free-market system.

In contrast to forecasting, *order processing* constitutes a "here and now" activity. In a sense, order processing represents the realization of sales that were anticipated by the forecast. The arrival of a customer order initiates the physical distribution process which, when completed, provides the logistical effort necessary to support marketing. Order processing, including up-to-date information regarding the nature of demand, is an essential aspect of logistical coordination. First, it renders the logistical system dynamic. Second, the order provides a factual source of information to assist in adapting production and material plans. Seldom, if ever, is a product-market forecast directly on target. The more typical case is a degree of over- or underestimate of anticipated sales. Order processing provides an ongoing source of reconciliation between what was anticipated and what is in fact occurring.

The combination of product-market forecasting and order processing with inventory status and planned inventory requirements becomes the *Statement of Distribution Requirements* for a given planning period. To coordinate logistical activity, the statement of distribution requirements must be synthesized with manufacturing capability and capacity. This synthesis is referred to as the *Master Production Schedule* (MPS). The MPS integrates what the enterprise is capable of doing within the parameters of the strategic plan. The MPS specifies how the enterprise will deploy manufacturing capacity over a specified time period. The time period covered by the MPS varies depending upon the type of enterprise. For example, the buying and merchandising plan for retailers, which is the counterpart of the industrial MPS, is normally for 30 to 90 days and is based on seasonal and holiday periods. In contrast, master production schedules for manufacturing firms often develop preliminary schedules months in advance. The main point is that the MPS provides direction to the overall enterprise and specifies logistical support requirements.

The fourth aspect of information flow is requirements planning. If a finished product is being purchased for resale, the typical situation is to establish an open-to-buy to be used at the discretion of each buyer. The coordination of manufacturing and material procurement is, in contrast, typically a multiple-state process which entails more complex time phasing than either retail or wholesale buying. The term *Materials Requirement Planning* (MRP) is used to discuss coordination of this aspect of logistics. In manufacturing firms it is also necessary to evaluate and plan capacity to assure the master production schedule can be achieved. This form of requirements planning is referred to as *Capacity Requirements Planning*. In Chapter 2 the concept of *Logistical Resource Planning* (LRP) is introduced as the device utilized to coordinate requirements information flow. It is essential that the overall direction of logistical operations be coordinated with the strategic planning of the enterprise.

LOGISTICAL SYSTEM COMPONENTS

The performance of value-added inventory and requirements information flows is formulated into a integrated logistical process by the coordination of (1) facility structure, (2) forecasting and order management, (3) transportation, (4) inventory, and (5) warehousing and packaging. These system components provide the capacity to achieve the operating objectives of physical distribution, manufacturing support, and purchasing. In this section attention is directed to an overview of how these components interact in a typical business enterprise. Two qualifications are important to remember when viewing logistical components from the vantage of a single enterprise.

First, all enterprises require cooperation from others in the distribution and purchasing channels. Such alliances amount to limited agreements on common interorganizational policies and programs. Risk for performance of logistical functions will be accepted only to the extent that it corresponds with reward or results from counterbalance of power. Decisions as to who will perform which functions are matters for negotiation. Once these negotiations are stabilized, they become logistical operating parameters. Each individual enterprise involved in a marketing or purchasing situation, given negotiation of transaction conditions, must make its own arrangements in implementing its share of the channel's overall logistical responsibility. The outcome of such negotiations forms the base for planning the logistical system. It also follows that an individual enterprise may engage various functions of logistics and therefore will be more or less involved in each of the five system components.

Second, service firms such as transportation carriers or public warehouses often play an important role in the logistical system of an enterprise. In essence, such specialists are substitute choices for the internal performance of specific logistical functions. For-hire specialists only assume specified risk for performance. When included in a logistical system they are assumed willing to accept a degree of managerial direction and control from their customers. Attention is now directed to the basic components common to all logistical systems.

Facility Structure

Classical economic analysis has neglected the importance of facility location to operating performance. When economists studied supply-and-demand relationships within a variety of market structures, location advantages and transportation cost differentials were often assumed to be either nonexistent or equal among competitive firms. Business, in contrast, cannot neglect the impact of location. The network of facilities selected by an enterprise's management is fundamental to logistical efficiency. The number, size, and geographical arrangements of facilities have a direct relationship to customer service capability and cost.

The fact that a great deal of disparity exists between geographical market areas can not be disputed. The 10 largest metropolitan markets in areas in terms of population in the United States account for over 45 per cent of potential product sales or services. It follows that any enterprise marketing on a national basis must give serious attention to the location of logistical facilities to service these prime markets. A similar geographic disparity exists in raw-material and component-parts markets or source locations.

All business transactions must be developed within and between a framework of facility locations. The facility network of an enterprise represents a series of locations to which and through which materials and products flow. For planning purposes, such facilities include manufacturing plants, warehouses, and retail stores. If the service of for-hire transportation or public warehousing is used, the facilities of these specialists are also part of the network.

The importance of selecting the best possible network of facilities cannot be overemphasized. Although relocation of all enterprise facilities at one time is inconceivable, considerable latitude exists in location selection and facility design over time. The selection of a superior locational network can result in a substantial competitive advantage. Logistical efficiency is directly related to and limited by the facility network structure.

CHAPTER 4

Forecasting and Order Management

Communication is an often-neglected activity in the logistical system. Historically, neglect was the result of a lack of data-processing capability to handle the necessary information flow. There has also been a lack of managerial understanding regarding the impact that fast and accurate communication can have on logistical performance.

Deficiencies in the quality of information can result in countless problems. Such deficiencies fall into two broad categories. First, information received may be incorrect with respect to trends and events. Because a great deal of logistical flow takes place in anticipation of future transactions, an inaccurate appraisal can result in inventory shortage or overcommitment. Second, information may be inaccurate with respect to a specific customer's needs. An enterprise that processes an incorrect order confronts all the costs of logistics without the resultant sale. Indeed, the costs are often compounded by the cost of inventory return and, if the sales opportunity still exists, another attempt to provide the proper products.

The speed of information flow is directly related to the integration of facilities, transportation, and inventory. It makes little sense for a firm to accumulate orders at a local sales office for a week, mail them to regional office, send them to the data-processing department, assign them to a distribution warehouse, and then ship them via air for fast delivery. Perhaps on line order entry from the customer's office with surface transportation would have achieved the desired fast delivery at a lower total cost. The key objective is balance among all components of the logistical system.

Forecasting and order management are the two managerial tasks directly associated with logistical communication. Each of these activities was discussed earlier. While the forecast represents an estimate of future events, a customer order is the critical information flow that initiates logistical performance.

The more efficient the design of a firm's logistical system, the more sensitive it is to disturbances in information flow. Finely tuned systems have no extra inventory. In such situations, safety stocks are maintained at the minimum possible level. Incorrect information can cause a serious disturbance in system performance. Delays in communication flow can amplify information errors, causing a series of oscillations in system corrective performance. Communication renders a logistical system dynamic. The quality and timeliness of information are the prime determinants of system stability.

Transportation

Given a facility network and communication capability, transportation provides place utility. Transportation and traffic management have received considerable attention over the years. Almost every enterprise of any size has a traffic manager responsible for administration of its transportation program.

Generally, an enterprise has three alternative ways to obtain transportation capacity. First, a private fleet of equipment may be purchased or leased. Second, specific contracts may be arranged with transport specialists to provide movement service. Third, an enterprise may engage the services of any legally authorized transport company that offers point-to-point transfer at specified charges. These three forms of transport are known as *private*, *contract*, and *common carriage*. From the logistical system viewpoint, three factors are of primary importance in establishment of the transport service capability: (1) cost, (2) speed, and (3) consistency.

The *cost* of transport accrues from the actual payment for movement between two points, plus the expenses related to owning in-transit inventory. Logistical systems should be designed to minimize the transport cost in relation to the total system cost. However, this does not mean that the most inexpensive method of transportation is always desirable.

Speed of transportation service is the time required to complete a movement between two locations. Speed and cost are related in two ways. First, transport specialists capable of providing faster service will charge higher rates. Second, the faster the service, the shorter the time interval during which materials and products are captured in transit.

Consistency of transportation service refers to the variance in time for a number of movements between the same locations. In essence, how dependable is a given method of transportation with respect to time? In many ways, consistency of service is the most important characteristic of transportation. If a given movement takes two days one time and six the next, serious bottlenecks can develop in the flow of goods which impair inventory control. If transport capability lacks consistency, inventory safety stocks must be provided to protect against service breakdowns. Transport consistency influences both the seller's and buyer's overall inventory commitment and related risk.

In the design of a logistical system, a delicate balance must be established between transportation cost and quality of service. In some circumstances low-cost slow transfers will be preferred. Other conditions may require faster methods. Finding the proper transportation balance is one of the primary objectives of logistical system analysis.

Three aspects of transportation should be kept in mind as they relate to the logistical system. First, facility selection established a structure or network that limits the range of transport alternatives and determines the nature of the transfer effort that must be accomplished. Second, the total cost of transportation involves more than a carrier's freight bill for movement between two locations. Third, the entire effort to integrate transport capability into a logistical system may be defeated if the service is sporadic and inconsistent.

Inventory

The requirement for transport between facilities is based on the inventory policy followed by an enterprise. Theoretically, an enterprise could stock each and every item carried in inventory in the same quantity at every facility. Few enterprises, however, would follow such a luxurious inventory program, since the total cost would be prohibitive. The objective is to maintain the lowest possible inventory consistent with customer service and manufacturing goals.

Excessive inventories can compensate for errors in the design of the basic system and may even help overcome poor administration of logistical activities. However, inventory used as a crutch will result in higher than necessary total cost.

Logistical programs should be initiated with the objective of committing as few assets to inventory as possible. The answer to a sound inventory program is found in selective deployment based on five factors: (1) customer qualities, (2) product qualities, (3) transport integration, (4) manufacturing concerns, and (5) competitor performance. Each of these factors is discussed briefly.

Every enterprise selling to a variety of customers is confronted with a range of relative profitability. Some customers are very profitable and others are not. Such profitability stems from range of product-line purchases, volume of purchases, price, marketing services required, and the support activities necessary to maintain an ongoing relationship. Highly profitable customers constitute the core market of an enterprise. Inventory policies should be designed to protect core customers by providing rapid and consistent logistical service.

Most enterprises experience a substantial variance in the volume and profitability of individual products within a product line. The typical enterprise with a wide product assortment finds that 20 per cent of the products marketed account for 80 per cent of the profit. A realistic appraisal should be made of the reason low-profit items are carried. On the surface, it would seem obvious that an enterprise would want to provide a high degree of consistent delivery service on highly profitable products. Less profitable items, however, may be necessary to provide full-line service to core customers. Therefore, all factors must be considered when developing a selective inventory policy. Many enterprises find it desirable to hold product inventories on slow-moving or low-profit items at a centralized distribution warehouse, utilizing rapid transportation methods when these items are ordered by a customer.

Selection of a product assortment to be stocked at a specific facility will have a direct impact on transportation cost. Most transportation rates are based on shipment size. Thus, it may be sound policy to stock more items at a specific facility to generate larger-volume shipments. The corresponding savings in unit transportation cost may more than offset the increase in unit inventory holding cost.

Concern with reduction of work in process inventories has a direct relationship to overall logistical strategy. The Just-In-Time (JIT) concept of managing inventory is based on the philosophy that well-run manufacturing plants do not require stockpiling of parts and components. The alternative to stockpiling is to receive inventory necessary to support manufacturing in the exact quantity and at a specified time. While JIT programs will reduce work-in-process inventory to absolute minimums, the savings must be balanced between the impact on other inventories and transportation costs incurred in the logistical process.

Finally, inventory stocking programs are not created in a competitive vacuum. An enterprise is more desirable to do business with if it provides rapid and consistent delivery. Therefore, inventory may be placed in a specific warehouse to improve logistical strategic impact even when such commitments increase cost. Such inventory policies may result from an effort to gain a differential advantage over a competitor or to neutralize one that a competitor currently enjoys.

Material inventory exists in the logistical system for different reasons than finished-product inventory. An understanding that an integral relationship exists among facilities, transportation, and inventory is fundamental. With inventory, it is desirable to be as selective as possible in policy development.

Warehousing and Packaging

Four of the components of a basic logistical system—facility location, forecasting and order management, transportation capacity, and inventory allocation—are subject to a variety of alternative design arrangements, each of which has a degree of potential effectiveness and a limit in attainable efficiency. In essence, these four activity centers provide a system structure for integrated product flow. The final area of design—warehousing and packaging—also represents an integral part of the logistical system but does not fit the neat structural scheme of the other components. Warehousing and packaging directly involve all other system components.

When warehouses are justified in a logistical system, a firm can select between obtaining the services of a specialist or operating its own facility. The concern is more extensive than a place to store inventory since many functions essential to the overall logistical process are performed at warehouses. Examples are such functions as customer order selection, transportation consolidation, and in some cases final product assembly.

Within the warehouse material handling represents an important activity. Handling accounts for a great deal of logistical cost in terms of operation and capital expense. It stands to reason that the fewer times a product is handled, the lower the damage potential and the greater the potential efficiency of the total physical flow. A great many mechanized and automated devices exist to assist in the performance of material handling. In essence, each warehouse and its material-handling capability represent a minisystem within the overall logistical process. To facilitate handling efficiency, cans, bottles, boxes, or whatever are combined into larger cartons. This *master carton* performs two functions. First, it serves to protect the product throughout the logistical process. Second, the master carton services as a primary load, allowing handling of one larger package rather than a multitude of individual units. For efficient handling, master cartons are grouped into large lots. These large lots may be further grouped into unit loads or containers for handling.

When effectively integrated into an enterprise's logistical operations, warehouse and packaging can substantially reduce problems related to speed and ease of movement through the system. In fact, several enterprises have been able to design unit loads to move large assortments of products from manufacturing directly to customers.

Conclusion—Logistical Components

The main strength of logistics results from treating system components on an integrated basis. Systems technology provides the framework for evaluating alternative logistical designs on a total cost basis. A systems orientation stands in direct contrast to the traditional approach of treating the activities of logistical management on a separate or diffused basis.

In a strategic context, the central focus of logistics is inventory commitment. Products and materials are viewed as a combination of form, time, place, and possession utilities. Inventory has little value until form is placed at the right time at a location which provides the opportunity to transact possession. If a firm does not consistently meet the requirements of time and place closure, it has nothing to sell. Unless such time and place closure is efficiently achieved, profits and return on investment may be jeopardized. Until the utilities of time and place are achieved, little, if any, value has been added by the logistical process. Attention is now directed to systems technology which provides the basis for integrating logistical components.

SYSTEMS ANALYSIS

The exact origin of the systems analysis is difficult to trace since the concept of a system is closely related to all forms of organized activity. Faced with the challenges of global war, scientists during World War II developed an organized methodology to guide the research and development of complex physical and organizational problems. This approach is now commonly referred to as *systems analysis*. A basic understanding of the systems concept is desirable for a full appreciation of integrated logistics.

The systems concept stresses total integrated effort toward the accomplishment of a predetermined objective. Objectives for a logistical system can be varied. For example, one objective might be the lowest cost operation. Another objective could be consistent customer service. Given objectives, a system capable of obtaining the desired results can be designed.

Utilizing the systems approach, attention is directed to the interaction of all parts of the system. These parts are referred to as system *components*. Each *component* has a specific function to perform toward attainment of system objectives. To illustrate, consider a high-fidelity stereo system. Many components are integrated for the single purpose of sound reproduction. The speakers, transistors, amplifier, and other components only exist to assist in producing the desired sound quality.

Some principles can be stated concerning general systems architecture. *First,* the performance of the total system is of singular importance. Components exist and are justified only to the extent that they enhance total system performance. *Second,* components do not individually require optimum design. Emphasis is based upon the integrated relationship of components in the system. *Third*, a functional relationship, called *trade-off*, exists between components that may stimulate or hinder combined performance. *Finally,* components linked together as a system can, on a combined basis, produce end results greater than possible through individual performance. In fact, the desired result may be unattainable without such synergistic performance.

These principles are basic and logically consistent. Without question, a logistical system with balanced integration of component parts will attain greater results than one deficient in coordinated performance. Although logical and indisputable in concept, effective application of the systems approach is operationally difficult.

Until recently, the activities of logistics were most often performed within enterprises on an independent basis. For example, transportation and inventory were managed by separate organizational units with little or no attention given to integration. To the extent that isolated performance is common practice, a serious barrier to the attainment of logistical objectives may exist. In the final analysis, it matters little how much a firm spends on any individual component, for example, transportation, as long as overall logistical objectives are achieved at the lowest total cost expenditure.

THE LOGISTICAL MISSION

The logistical mission of an enterprise is to develop a system that meets objectives at the lowest possible dollar expenditure. The logistical system is primarily concerned with support of manufacturing and marketing operations. At the policy level, the critical question is to determine the desired level of performance and determine the associated cost of logistical operations. Thus, the planning of logistics involves two policy considerations: (1) service performance, and (2) total cost expenditure. The challenge is to establish a balance between performance and cost that will result in attainment of the logistical objectives of the enterprise. This logistical policy provides the managerial mandate for system design.

Logistical Service

With respect to total performance, almost any level of logistical service can be obtained if an enterprise is willing to pay the price. For example, a full-line inventory could be situated in close geographical proximity to all major customers. A fleet of trucks could be held in a constant state of delivery readiness. To facilitate order entry, a dedicated communication line could be installed between the customer's facility and the supplier's distribution warehouse. Under this hypothetical situation, a customer's order could be entered into the system within a matter of seconds. The availability of inventory could be set even higher by consigning merchandise to each customer. Although this hypothetical service situation might constitute a sales manager's dream, such extreme performance is neither practical nor necessary to support most marketing and manufacturing systems.

Logistical performance is, in the final analysis, a question of priority and cost. If a specific material is not available when required by the manufacturing system, it may necessitate a plant shutdown, with resultant cost and possible loss of sale. The penalty of such a failure is great. Therefore, the priority placed upon performance in such situations is typically high. In contrast, the impact of a two-day delay in delivery of products to a grocery chain store warehouse may be limited to the rescheduling of a supermarket delivery. The priority placed on performance should be directly related to impact of failure.

Logistical performance is measured with respect to availability, capability, and quality. *Availability* concerns the system's capacity to consistently satisfy material or product requirements. As such, availability deals with inventory level. As a general rule, the lower the frequency of planned stockouts, the greater the investment in average inventory.

Capability of logistical performance refers to the elapsed time from receipt of an order to inventory delivery. Performance capability consists of the speed of delivery and consistency. Naturally, all firms desire to provide customers fast delivery. However, rapid delivery is of little value unless it is consistently achieved. It may hinder a firm to promise second-day delivery if in actual performance the standard is achieved only a small percentage of the time. An enterprise on the receiving end of a logistical system typically values consistency over speed of service.

Performance *quality* relates to how well the overall logistical task is completed with respect to damage, correct line items, and resolution of unexpected problems. There is no point in speedy delivery of a damaged product. Quality relates to the maintenance of low error rates and a respected track record for resolving problems.

Performance standards should be established on a selective basis. Some products are more critical than others because of their importance to the purchaser and their profitability. The stated level of delivery performance should be realistic. In general, firms tend to be overly optimistic when stating performance standards. Inferior or substandard performance in adherence to an unrealistic service policy might well cause greater operating and customer problems than the statement of less ambitious goals.

Logistical Cost

For a considerable period of time, it has been in vogue to talk about profit centers within an enterprise. The logistical system should be viewed as a cost center. As with all other expenses, every effort must be made to hold expenditures to a minimum. In the case of the logistical system the cost to be minimized is total cost across the overall process. The establishment of artificial profit centers may create a temptation to shift functional cost responsibility rather than minimize total cost.

The level of total cost has a direct relationship to the customer service policy. The simultaneous attainment of high availability, capability, and quality is expensive. The higher each of these aspects of total performance, the greater the cost of logistical operations.

A significant planning problem stems from the fact that logistical cost and increased performance have a nonproportional relationship. A firm that supports a service standard of overnight product delivery at 95 per cent consistency may confront nearly double the logistical cost of one that develops a program of second-morning delivery at 90 per cent consistency. The same firm committed to a delivery policy of overnight service at greater than 95 per cent consistency could easily dissipate profits by attempting to provide performance which is possibly not needed, expected, or even wanted by customers.

Logistical Objectives

From the viewpoint of logistical system design and administration, a firm must establish objectives and control several different operational areas. The following five objectives are required to realize effective and efficient logistical performance: (1) minimum variance, (2) minimum inventory commitment, (3) maximum consolidation, (4) quality control, and (5) life-cycle support. Each objective is briefly discussed.

Variance is any uncertainty or unexpected event that disrupts system performance. Whether the variance results from order cycle uncertainty, an unexpected disruption in manufacturing, goods arriving damaged, or delivery to an incorrect location, the result is unexpected variance that must be accommodated. Variance reduction involves both internal and external relationships. Each interface point within a logistical system represents a potential source of variance. To the extent that variances can be minimized, logistical productivity will be improved. Thus, one basic objective of overall logistical performance is to *minimize variance*.

The objective of *minimum inventory* involves level of commitment and velocity. Level of commitment is concerned with where inventory is positioned throughout the logistical system. Velocity is concerned with how much inventory is held for any authorized cause. Concepts like *Zero Inventory* have become increasingly popular to reflect a desire to eliminate as much inventory as possible.[27] The basic notion is that system defects do not appear until inventories are leaned to the lowest possible level. While the notion of eliminating inventory is attractive, it is important to remember that inventory performs some essential functions in a logistical system. Inventories may offer a sound return on investment when they result in economies of scale in manufacturing or procurement. The key objective is to reduce and control inventory to the maximum extent possible while simultaneously achieving operating objectives. To achieve the objective of *minimum inventory* the logistical system design must control location, level and velocity for the entire firm as contrasted to individual profit centers.

One of the most significant logistical costs is transportation. Transportation costs are directly related to size of shipment and the distance the shipment is transported. A great many concepts of integrated logistics result in a desire for small shipments to support just-in-time manufacturing. A basic goal of logistical system design is to provide the agreed-to customer service. This service commitment must be realized while maintaining *maximum transportation consolidation*. This means that innovative programs to assist grouping small shipments into consolidated movements must be incorporated in logistical system design.

A fourth logistical objective is to consistently achieve a specified level of *quality control*. A major change in logistical operations over the past decade has been a commitment to help achieve and maintain high levels of product quality. In today's world, product quality has become critical because of the high cost of failure. If a product is defective after the entire logistical process is complete, no value is added, but all costs are experienced. In fact, the total logistical process often must be recalled and repeated. The cost of satisfying a customer order that must be reworked as a result of incorrect shipment or damaged arrival is far more costly than a correct customer shipment. Emphasis on zero defect purchasing includes logistical quality control.

The final logistical design objective is *life-cycle support*. Few items are sold without some guarantee that the product will perform as advertised over a specified period. In fact, some products, such as copying equipment, enjoy their primary profit opportunity by selling supplies and providing aftermarket service. The importance of life-cycle support varies directly with the product and buyer. For firms marketing consumer durables or industrial equipment, the commitment to life-cycle support constitutes one of the most versatile operation situations and largest costs of logistical operations. The life-cycle support aspects of a logistical system must be carefully designed.

---

[27] Robert W. Hall, *Zero Inventories* (Homewood, Ill.: Dow Jones-Irwin, 1983).

Conclusion—Logistical Mission

The typical enterprise will find that the best overall relationship between logistical performance and cost is one that balances reasonable performance levels and realistic cost expenditures. Very seldom will either lowest total cost or highest service performance constitute the best logistical policy.

A well-designed logistical effort must have the capability to control operational variance and to minimize inventory commitments across the entire system. Total cost expenditure is directly impacted by achieving maximum possible transportation consolidation. In addition to cost containment, the objectives of quality control and life-cycle support are integral to the logistical mission.

Significant advances have been made in the development of tools to aid management in the measurement of cost-performance trade-offs. A sound policy can be formulated only if it is possible to estimate expenditures for alternative levels of system performance. Likewise, alternative levels of system performance are meaningless unless viewed in terms of marketing and manufacturing requirements. Determination of the logistical mission requires cost/revenue policy formulation.

Progressive firms have begun to realize that a well-designed and operated logistical system can create a strategic differential among competitors. The human and physical assets that combine to create a cost-effective logistical system are not easily duplicated. The design and implementation of such a system cannot be purchased or put into place without considerable commitment over an extended time horizon. *As a general rule, firms that obtain a strategic advantage from logistical operations establish the nature of industry competition.*

DEVELOPMENT PROFILE

The concept of integrated logistics is relatively new to enterprise management. The growth of logistics has resulted from an acute need to improve movement and storage efficiency. This growth has been stimulated by a vast array of technological developments. The decades ahead offer the prospect of even greater payoffs from full exploitation of integrated logistics.

Overall logistical management is concerned with operations and coordination. Operations deal with strategic movement and storage. To complete the total operations mission, attention must be directed to the integration of physical distribution, manufacturing support, and purchasing. These three areas combine to provide operational management of materials, semifinished components, and products moving between locations, supply sources, and customers of the enterprise.

The mission of the logistical system is measured in terms of total cost and performance. Performance measurement concerns the availability of inventory, capability in terms of delivery time and consistency, and quality of effort. Logistical costs have a direct relationship to performance policy. The higher planned performance, the higher total logistics cost. The key to effective logistical performance is to develop a balanced effort between service performance cost expenditure.

This first chapter has introduced and traced the development of basic concepts and ingredients of integrated logistical management. The overall text is divided into five parts. The objective of Part One is to introduce and scope integrated logistics. Following this overview chapter, the remaining chapters of Part One describe a strategic orientation to logistical operations and control. Chapter 2 provides a detailed treatment of interfaces and decision processes that provide the infrastructure for logistical process. In Chapter 3 the nature of customer service and the relationship to marketing strategy and channel structure is discussed.

The subject matter of Part Two concerns components of a logistical system. Chapter 4 develops concepts of forecasting and order management. Chapters 5 and 6 are concerned with transportation. In Chapter 7 the elements of inventory are treated. In Chapter 8 warehousing and packaging are covered.

Part Three is concerned with logistical policy and control. The foundations of logistical policy are developed in Chapter 9. Chapter 10 presents organizational considerations. Chapter 11 treats administration.

In Part Four, the emphasis shifts to techniques and methodologies. Chapter 12 is devoted to planning procedure and design methodologies. In Chapter 13 attention is directed to techniques available to assist management in the design of a logistical system. Chapter 14 reviews and illustrates techniques available to assist in operational planning and management.

Part Five deals with future environments that are expected to impact logistical operations. Chapter 15 presents a series of changes that appear to be on the logistical horizon. The format of the chapter is to present a dimension of change in a seminar format to serve as a nucleus for discussion.

Thus, the subject matter development begins with a comprehensive discussion of logistical management (Part One), followed by a detailed treatment of the fundamental components that combine to form the logistical system of the enterprise (Part Two). At the conclusion of the first two parts, the stage will have been set for in-depth treatment of the two fundamental responsibilities of a logistical manager: logistical management (Part Three) and planning (Part Four).

The decision to focus this text on the individual enterprise made it necessary to select subjects of concern to overall logistical management and omit others from explicit coverage. Three such omissions are noteworthy.

First, all logistical managers have a specific stake in the maintenance of a viable national transportation system. The determination of national policy and the encouragement of sound public investment in the transportation infrastructure require the active involvement of logistical professionals in all levels of government. Issues of macro-transportation are not specifically discussed at any point in the text material. Chapter 5 presents a background discussion of regulation, and Chapter 6 reviews the transportation infrastructure within which logistical systems must be designed. This material introduces the reader to major issues of national concern.

Second, many logistical managers have an active responsibility for multinational materials management and physical distribution. All indications suggest the years ahead will require greater involvement in the international logistical arena. At the present time it is difficult to make generalized statements concerning multinational logistical patterns. With the exception of transportation and containerization, most import-export arrangements are location specific. Therefore, at the possible sacrifice of total subject coverage, attention concentrates on domestic logistical operations. Multinational logistics is treated as a seminar focus in Chapter 15.

Third, the text does not extensively discuss the important subject of logistical ecology. Various aspects of logistical systems, particularly transportation and packaging, are potential causes of environmental pollution. On the positive side, the logistical delivery system is one of the nation's most available resources to be applied toward solving ecological problems. For example, solid-waste disposal and package-material recycling depend upon effective reverse logistical movement for successsful transfer of society's waste to processing points. The prime reason for not including logistical ecology, once again, is an inability to generalize regarding developments and responsibilities.

A final note concerning subject matter development is the format used to integrate locational analysis and theory. The network of facilities used in a logistical system provides and limits the potential for operating effectiveness and efficiency. To a large degree, facility location influences all components of the logistical system. To stress these interrelationships when most relevant, locational considerations are discussed at several points throughout the text. In Chapter 2 the network concept of fixed facilities and order cycles is introduced in a discussion of the logistical system concept. Location is also an integral part of transportation coverage in Chapters 5 and 6. The locational considerations of warehousing are contained in Chapter 8. The integration of spatial and temporal considerations in the formulation of logistical policy is developed in depth in Chapter 9. Techniques to assist managers in selecting specific locations are covered in Chapter 13. The basic issues involved in manufacturing plant location and associated checklists are treated in appendixes. Although this format spreads the treatment of location throughout the next, it has the advantage of developing the salient aspects of location as an integral part of each impacted subject matter.

QUESTIONS

1. Develop a statement regarding why no formal or integrated concept of logistics prevailed prior to 1950.
2. What is the basic logic that supports total-cost analysis?
3. Describe the concept of value-added inventory flow. How are the costs of logistics related to the value-added flow?
4. Describe the key operational differences between physical distribution, manufacturing support, and purchasing.
5. What is anticipatory physical distribution? How do modern concepts of logistics help reduce the risks associated with anticipation?
6. What reasons can you give for the traditional lack of attention to the cost of transferring inventory within an enterprise? Where do you think such internal transfer costs are typically included in accounting records?
7. Discuss and elaborate the following statement: "The selection of a superior locational network can result in a substantial competitive advantage."
8. Do you agree that all organized behavior is to some degree systems-oriented? Describe the concept of trade-off, and illustrate why it is an integral part of systems analysis.

9. Illustrate from your experience an example of failure to solve a problem on a total-systems basis.

10. A logistics system was described as having five objectives: (1) minimum variance, (2) minimum inventory commitment, (3) maximum consolidation, (4) quality control, and (5) life-cycle support. Provide an example of how each of the objectives can hinder efficiency and effectiveness if they are not realized.

CHAPTER 2

Logistical Strategy and Decision Processes

Introductory comments stressed that the primary objective of logistical management is to achieve integrated operations. Management of individual logistical activities is often under the direction and control of various departments within an enterprise. Such diffusion increases the possibilities for duplication and waste. Similarly, information flow between organizational units may be fragmented enough to jeopardize logistical coordination. The fundamental belief that integrated system performance will produce an end result greater than is possible from individual effort is the focal point of logistics. Systems technology provides a disciplined method for achieving integration.

The objective of this chapter is to describe the environment within which logistical performance must be planned and executed. The initial section provides an overview of the enterprise as a competitive entity. For planning it is important to develop a clear perspective of how logistics relates to other constituencies of an enterprise and its interface to the external environment.

The second section introduces the concept of the performance cycles as the process that links suppliers, enterprise facilities, and customers into a logistical system. The proposition presented is that, regardless of size and complexity, logistical systems can be understood and evaluated in terms of performance cycle structure. Section three is devoted to a brief overview of logistical resource planning which provides a control logic for integrated logistics. The final three sections of the chapter review strategic alternatives for physical distribution, manufacturing support, and purchasing.

Before proceeding, some comments are in order regarding organization. Managers are acutely interested in organizational structure because it directly reflects responsibility, title, compensation, and power. Implicit in the logistical management concept is the notion that grouping all responsibility for logistics into a single organizational unit will automatically improve integrated control. This notion has the fallacy of emphasizing structure in contrast to performance. Formal organization alone is not sufficient to guarantee performance. Some of the most effective logistical operations function without being formally organized under a single manager. Other enterprises with formal logistical groups also achieve superior results. Any generalization regarding organization is premature at this stage of subject development. Logistical organizations vary depending upon the specific mission, available personnel, and resource capabilities. Some basic patterns of organizational structure are available and are presented in Chapter 10 as managerial guides. Initially the objective is to foster a philosophy of operation that stimulates all levels of management within an enterprise to think and act in terms of integrated logistical capabilities and economies.

LOGISTICAL ENVIRONMENTS

A major responsibility of logistical executives is the development of strategic and operational plans. A logistical strategy consists of a long-range plan for commitment of financial and human resources to physical distribution, manufacturing support, and purchasing operations. The specific objective of the strategic plan is to provide policies, facilities, equipment, and operating systems capable of obtaining performance goals at the lowest total-cost expenditure. It is the strategic logistics plan that delineates policies concerning what type of warehouses will be used, where they will be located, where and what inventory assortments will be stocked in each, the philosophy of purchasing, how transportation requirements will be satisfied, which methods of material handling will be utilized, and the basic methods of order processing. The most important feature of the strategic plan is that it provides the system design by which the varied aspects of logistical operations are coordinated.

A useful perspective is to gain an understanding of internal and external forces that influence logistical strategy. *The only constant in today's dynamic business environment is change.* A significant input to logistical planning is to assess, monitor, and evaluate environmental changes. Table 2–1 provides a summary of selected environmental factors over time. The purpose of Table 2–1 is to illustrate the dynamic nature of key environmental factors. The purpose of environmental monitoring is to evaluate the varied direction and rate of change as they relate to logistical operations.

TABLE 2–1 Dynamics of Environmental Change

Selected Environmental Factor	Dominant View				
	1975	1980	1985	1990	1995
Inflation	Medium-High	High	Medium-Low	Medium	Medium
Interest	Medium	High	Medium	Medium	Medium
Energy	Short supply Medium cost	Available High cost	Available Medium cost	Varied projections	Varied projections
Population U.S. millions	215.5	—	238.8	—	260.5
Household U.S. millions	71.5	—	88.5	—	104.5
Transportation regulation	Full regulatory	Reregulation Legislative	Administrative Judicial	Sunset Administrative	Antitrust base
Productivity	Decreasing	Stabilized	Increasing	Varied projections	Varied projections

External to the enterprise are environmental forces that limit flexibility. One classification includes (1) industry competitive assessment, (2) geo-market differentials, (3) technology assessment, (4) material-energy assessment, (5) channel structure, (6) economic-social projections, (7) service industry trends, and (8) regulatory posture. Together these forces form the ecological planning environment. From the viewpoint of decision and planning, logistical executives should remain informed concerning each category by supporting a formal effort to collect, evaluate, and project data concerning the most probable direction and magnitude of change. Each category is briefly discussed to illustrate the potential impact on logistical operations.

Industry-Competitive Assessment

This assessment involves a systematic review of the limits and potential of a firm's industry based on such factors as market size and growth rate, profitability potential, critical success factors, import/export trends, and labor issues. Analysis of competitive forces involves such factors as leading firm influence and control, international competition, intensity of rivalry and confrontation, power of customers and suppliers, and the distinctive competencies of competing firms. A careful assessment of key competitor's logistical competency is important to understanding the minimum level of customer service performance that will be acceptable within the industry.

Geo-Market Differentials

The logistics facility structure of an enterprise is directly related to location of consumer and supplier markets. Population density of certain areas, traffic patterns, and population shifts over time all impact location decisions. The Census Bureau predicts that six out of every ten Americans will live in the

South or West Sun Belt by the year 2000.[1] The Bureau also predicts a transfer of employment and income from the industrialized North to the South and West. However, even within the Sun Belts, growth is erratic by areas and split within specific states.

Companies such as McDonald's and Southland (7–11 stores) study these factors in order to determine where favorable marketing opportunities lie. Demographic information such as age, income, and educational level characteristics of different locations can be beneficial for pinpointing markets. Mapping of industry demographics is essential when planning logistical requirements.

Technology Assessment

Among the technology areas that impact logistical systems, the most prominent are computers, communications, material handling, and transportation. In the area of communications, computers, satellites, scanning, bar coding, and integrated data bases have widespread influence. The flow of transaction information is critical to an enterprise. Integrated data bases capable of tracking the movement of raw materials, work in process, and finished-goods inventory are being used for improved managerial control and decision support.

Robots, computer vision, mechanized storage, and increased usage of automatic guided vehicle systems are tools with which technology is impacting material handling. Soft-sided trucks, development of intermodal concepts, and new packaging options are examples of changing transportation technologies. The need for technology assessment is highlighted by the fact that most of the technology discussed above was not commercially available a decade ago.

Material Energy Assessment

The continued dependence of logistical operations on fossil-based fuels is predicted for at least the remainder of the twentieth century. This dependency has increased managerial attention to an examination of potential substitutes for material and energy sources. Firms must continuously assess the resources upon which they are dependent and evaluate available alternatives. As key resources become scarce and their prices rise, or their usage is limited owing to environmental impact, transition to substitutes will be necessary. Trucking fleets are currently experimenting with conversions to natural gas and battery-powered vehicles.[2] An awareness of the range of alternatives supplemented by an assessment of the worst, best, and most likely scenarios provides the basis for planning. Advance planning will enable the enterprise to implement a strategic transition rather then a panic reaction when a conversion is required.

Channel Structure

Logistical capabilities need to be planned in terms of channel structure. All enterprises, regardless of size, must conduct physical distribution and purchasing operations within a set of business relationships. A marketing channel is

---

[1] Bureau of Census estimates as published in the *Wall Street Journal*, September 8, 1983, and October 18, 1983.

[2] For a discussion of energy conservation in logistics see Kenneth B Ackerman, *Practical Handbook of Warehousing* (Washington, D.C.: The Traffic Service Corporation, 1983), pp. 70–72.

defined as a system of relationships that exists among institutions involved in the process of buying and selling.[3] An enterprise must accommodate changes in channel structure and in selected situations should be proactive toward stimulating change if logistical performance can be improved. For example, throughout industry a reduction in the number of supplying vendors is being evaluated in an effort to improve the consistency of materials and delivery service. General Motors' Buick City in Flint, Michigan, represents a redesign of supply channels wherein vendors are being asked to position inventories to reduce manufacturing lead times.

Enterprises should regularly evaluate the relative advantage of buying or selling direct with company sales force or brokers as contrasted to using wholesalers. In some industries the trend is away from wholesalers, while in other industries wholesalers are gaining in popularity. Pharmaceuticals, for example, are increasingly being delivered through wholesalers which permits faster delivery and lower inventories to be maintained by pharmacists. The upward trend in mail order and telemarketing is having a major impact on traditional marketing channel structure for some industries. Changes in the composition of demand, structure of supply, number of channel participants, and traditional channel relationships need to be regularly monitored with respect to logistical system design.

Economic-Social Projections

The level of economic activity and change in dominant social perceptions are difficult to predict. They can have a major impact on logistical requirements. The aggregate demand for transportation services is directly related to gross national product. When domestic labor costs rise, or the dollar becomes strong in relation to foreign currencies, imports increase. Interest rates have been extremely volatile during the last decade. As interest rates increase, pressure to reduce inventory throughout the marketing channel also increases. High cost of inventory justifies utilization of high-cost transportation modes to decrease delivery time and increase inventory velocity throughout the logistical system.

Social mores, lifestyles, expectations, and attitudes all impact an enterprise and its logistical requirements. The potential spill of hazardous materials becomes a major social issue when it impacts public safety or jeopardizes quality of life. Monitoring public sentiment and leading economic indicators can help an enterprise avoid potentially disabling circumstances and regularly assess the risk involved in existing practices.

Service Industry Trends

Over the past several decades the service sector of the American economy has increasingly represented a greater portion of gross national product. The particular services of concern to logistical operations are for-hire transportation, warehousing, and computer resources. The portion of the logistical dollar allocated to the acquisition of service support has increased over the past

---

[3] Donald J. Bowersox, M. Bixby Cooper, Douglas M. Lambert, and Donald A. Taylor, *Management in Marketing Channels* (New York: McGraw-Hill Book Company, 1980), p. 1.

decade.[4] From the viewpoint of logistical system design, such services provide flexibility which is variable cost based. To be an astute buyer of logistical services it is essential that an enterprise keep abreast of prevailing practices and the rate of technology deployment throughout the service sector. The range of services provided by for-hire logistics suppliers has dramatically increased since 1980.[5] While a degree of consolidation is now taking place among firms that provide logistical service, the industry has traditionally consisted of a large number of small suppliers. Such a diverse supply structure places an extra burden on buyers to assure they receive competitive services and prices.

Regulatory Posture

Perhaps the most visible environmental change during the past decade has been in the regulatory structure of transportation and communication. Logistical managers must evaluate and predict the most likely national, state, and local government regulatory changes that will impact their enterprise. In review of the significant regulatory changes that occurred in transportation since 1980, it is clear that selected firms were far better positioned to take advantage of change then others. This failure of some firms to prepare a proactive program to accommodate change was apparent in both the demand and supply sides of for-hire transportation. To illustrate, over 100 class-I and II common motor carriers were forced to declare bankruptcy following passage of the Motor Carrier Regulatory Reform and Modernization Act of 1980. During the same time period other carriers reported record earnings.

Conclusion—Logistical Environments

In competition, the enterprise is viewed as a goal-seeking organization functioning within and adjusting to environmental constraints. Over a single planning horizon, environmental factors may be relatively constant. The enterprise and its competitors modify corporate strategies in an effort to increase market share. The enterprise that gains buyer favor enjoys a competitive differential advantage. This advantage may be rapidly eliminated by competitors, or it may be retained over a substantial period of time. To the degree that a differential advantage prevails, the recipient firm gains lasting distinctiveness and long-run goal achievement.

If an enterprise is to survive, all parts—marketing, manufacturing, financial, logistics, human resources, and senior management—must function as a totality. This overall integration is illustrated in Figure 2–1. Only to the extent that any given part contributes to the total effort does that part have economic justification.

Viewing an enterprise as a total system of goal-directed action is essential to maximize competitive impact. Within the enterprise the logistical system is essential. Those enterprises that develop a strategic logistical posture gain a competitive advantage in cost and service that is difficult to duplicate. Because of the potential permanency in competitive advantage, a great deal more attention to logistics is being incorporated in strategy planning. In the long run, quicksands of economic and institutional change may render a well-established

[4] Ackerman, op. cit., Part I.
[5] Ibid., pp. 17–24.

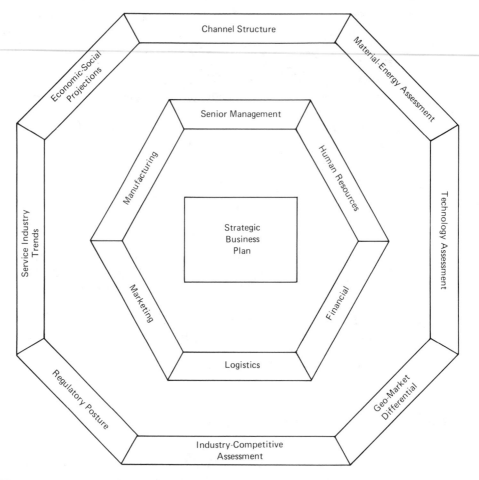

Figure 2–1 The Enterprise—A Competitive Environmental Setting

logistical system inadequate. Unless an enterprise regularly upgrades logistical performance, the results could be an increase in cost and a potential loss of competitive leadership to rival enterprises.

LOGISTICAL PERFORMANCE CYCLES

Viewing logistical operations in terms of performance cycles provides a basic perspective of interfaces and decision processes that can be used for design analysis and operational administration. At the most basic level, each member of the supply base, all enterprise facilities, and customers who participate in the logistical process must be connected by communications and transportation. The physical facility locations within performance cycles are identified as *nodes*. The communication and transportation connections are referred to as *links*.

In addition to nodes and links, a logistical performance cycle must be supported by a *level* of inventory which is an integral part of the operating system. Inventory committed to the system consists of average stock to cover reorder time and safety stock.

Finally, a performance cycle confronts an *input/output* requirement as it functions in a dynamic manner. The *input* to a performance cycle is the volume of product or material requirements the system must handle. If the average level of requirements is great, a substantial volume of throughput will be experienced. A high-volume system will typically require a variety of performance cycles to satisfy overall requirements. If input is not large, the complexity of the performance network is reduced. The design options are also reduced when requirements volume is low since little opportunity will exist to aggregate volume movement between any two nodal points.

System *output* relates to the capability of the overall performance-cycle structure to satisfy operational requirements. To the extent that operational requirements are satisfied, the performance-cycle structure is *effective* in accomplishing its stated mission. *Efficiency* is related to the amount of resource expenditure necessary to render the overall logistical system effective.

Depending upon the purpose of a particular performance cycle, all activities may or may not be under the complete control of the enterprise. For example, manufacturing support cycles are typically under complete control. In contrast, performance cycles related to physical distribution and purchasing normally include participants outside the enterprise.

It is important to realize that the frequency of logistical activity varies between performance cycles. Some performance cycles exist to support a one-time purchase or sales activity. In such a case the cycle is designed, implemented, and then abolished. In contrast, other performance cycles function continuously. An additional complicating fact is that any single node in a logistical system may be a participant in several different performance cycles. For example, the warehouse facility of a hardware wholesaler might receive merchandise from several hundred manufacturers on a more-or-less regular basis.

When one considers an enterprise of national or multinational scope, marketing a broad product line to many customers, engaged in basic manufacturing and assembly, and procuring raw materials and components from a variety of sources, the notion of a performance cycle linking every pair of locations may be difficult to comprehend. It is almost impossible to guess how many performance cycles exist in the logistical systems of General Motors or Sears.

Regardless of the number of performance cycles an enterprise uses to satisfy its logistical requirements, the important point is that *each* cycle needs to be individually designed and operated. A performance-cycle orientation is an important first step toward understanding logistical requirements. In essence, the performance-cycle structure provides a framework for implementation of the system approach.

Figure 2–2 illustrates the performance-cycle concept in terms of basic applications in each of the logistical operating systems. Figure 2–3 illustrates the more complex network of performance cycles one would expect to find in a multiecheloned structure.

Three points are significant in the performance-cycle approach to the anatomy of logistics. First, the performance cycle is the fundamental concept for achieving the integration of logistical functions. Second, the performance-cycle structure in terms of links and nodes is basically the same whether one is concerned with physical distribution, manufacturing support, or purchasing.

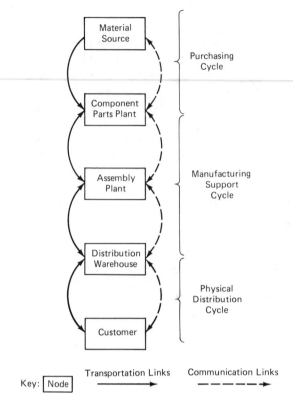

Figure 2–2 Logistical Performance Cycles

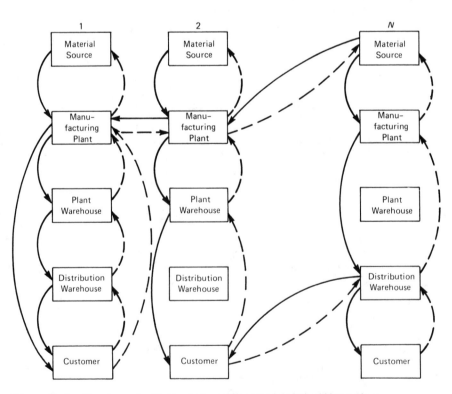

Figure 2–3 Structure of a Multiecheloned Flexible Logistical Network

However, considerable differences exist in terms of control that a single enterprise enjoys over a specific type of performance cycle. Third, regardless of how vast and complex the total logistical system structure, the essential interfaces and decision process can be identified and illustrated in terms of individual performance cycles.

Attention is now directed to the specific nature of operations associated with physical distribution, materials management, and inventory transfer.

Physical Distribution Performance Cycle

Physical distribution management is the aspect of overall logistics concerned with the processing and delivery of customer orders. Physical distribution is essential to marketing because timely and economical product delivery is critical for profitable transactions. The process of marketing can be broadly divided into transaction-creating and physical-fulfillment activities. Physical distribution is primarily concerned with the physical-fulfillment activities.

The development of physical distribution systems to support modern marketing is a dynamic aspect of management. An enterprise constantly changes parts of its marketing mix in an effort to gain and hold a competitive advantage in the marketplace. This relationship is developed in depth in Chapter 3.

The typical physical distribution cycle consists of five related activities. They are: (1) order transmission, (2) order processing, (3) order selection, (4) order transportation, and (5) customer delivery. The basic physical distribution performance cycle is illustrated in Figure 2–4.

From the viewpoint of logistical operations, physical distribution is the critical interface between customers and munufacturing. This interface is inherently conflictive. On the one hand, marketing is reluctant to deny customers. This reluctance is illustrated by the difficulty in eliminating gross sales volume as a measure of marketing success and the failure of marketing managers to implement principles of selectivity in terms of servicing customers. On the other side, manufacturing traditionally desires long production runs with as little change as possible. Continuous manufacturing processes result in lowest unit production cost. The traditional method of solving these natural marketing-manufacturing conflicts has been to build up inventory. The typical process is to move stockpiled inventory forward into the physical distribution system in anticipation of future sale. Products are transported with the risk of

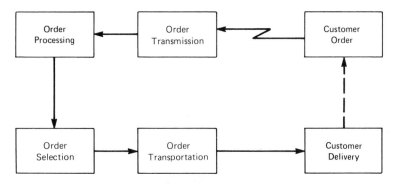

Figure 2–4   Basic Physical Distribution Performance-Cycle Activities

being shipped to the wrong market at the wrong time. They often end up completely out of logistical position to support customer service.

In the next section of this chapter attention is directed to the logistical resource planning as a way to gain integrated control over finished inventory allocation. The physical distribution performance cycle operates downstream from manufacturing and purchasing. Inventories committed to physical distribution include the maximum potential value that can be added by manufacturing and the logistical process. It is essential they be positioned to enjoy the maximum benefit of time and place utility.

The very fact that physical distribution deals with customer orders means that operations will be more erratic than is characteristic of manufacturing and procurement support. Attention to *how* customers order products is essential to reduce variance and simplify transactions. First, every effort should be made to improve forecast accuracy. Second, a program of advanced order substitutions should be initiated whenever possible. When customers commit to a specific item they often will accept substitutions if they are informed in advance and not surprised.

The key to understanding physical distribution performance-cycle dynamics is to keep in mind that the customer initiates activity by order placement. The logistical response capability of the selling enterprise represents one of the most significant competitive factors in overall marketing strategy.

Manufacturing Support Performance Cycle

The manufacturing support performance cycle is concerned with movement required to integrate physical distribution and purchasing operations within an enterprise and support production schedules. Manufacturing support has the primary objective of establishing and maintaining an orderly and economic flow of materials and work-in-process inventory into production. Specialization involved in physical distribution and purchasing can create a gray area concerning responsibility and control over the flow of materials required in manufacturing. The movement of product, materials, and semifinished parts and components between enterprise facilities is the responsibility of logistical manufacturing support.

The identification of manufacturing support as a distinct operating area is a relatively new concept in logistical management. The justification is that performance cycles related to all aspects of manufacturing should be designed within a particular set of objectives and constraints. Therefore, to realize maximum benefits, the allocation of logistical effort and control within each performance area should vary to accommodate specific requirements.

Manufacturing support has one significant difference in comparison with either physical distribution or purchasing operations. Manufacturing support movement is typically captive to the enterprise, whereas the other two areas must deal with the uncertainty of external suppliers and customers. Greater overall control is thus possible. *Maximum exploitation of this control is the prime justification for treatment of manufacturing support as a separate logistical operating area.*

The manufacturing support system controls components, semifinished products, and finished products after they are purchased or released from initial production. The purpose is to control the movement and storage of components and semifinished goods between stages of manufacturing and finished inventory to and between warehouses utilized by the enterprise. Products must be consistently available from manufacturing sources to provide high levels of customer service. The level of product availability in turn depends upon production scheduling and the capability to transfer components between manufacturing facilities. As such, manufacturing support serves as a safety valve between all production plants and field inventories.

In sequence, in a manufacturing organization, purchasing provides raw materials and externally purchased semifinished components when and where needed. Once the manufacturing operation is initiated, subsequent interplant movement of materials or semifinished products is classified as manufacturing support. Transfer operations are restricted to dock-to-dock movement and any intermediate storage required. When production is completed, transfer is arranged for initial allocation of finished inventory to the warehouses that service customer orders. At this point physical distribution operations are initiated.

In a multiplant firm, the manufacturing support system may constitute a vast network. To the extent that a number of different manufacturing plants participate in various stages of production and fabrication leading to final production, numerous handlings and transfers will be required prior to final product availability. With finished inventory allocation, products may flow directly from manufacturing plants to field warehouses or they may be funneled through a series of intermediate warehouses for purposes of accumulating product assortments. In select situations, the complexity of manufacturing support may exceed either physical distribution or purchasing operations.

As noted earlier, the manufacturing support system has one major difference in contrast to either physical distribution or purchasing. Support operations are limited to movements within and under internal management control. Therefore, in conducting manufacturing support, the variance introduced by random-order entry and erratic vendor performance is controlled, permitting more optimal time phased movement.

Procurement Performance Cycle

Several activities are required to maintain an orderly flow of materials and parts into manufacturing. They are (1) sourcing, (2) order placement and expediting, (3) transportation, and (4) receiving and inspection. These activities are required to complete the purchasing process. Once materials, parts, or resale products procured are in the possession of the enterprise, storage, inventory control, and materials handling are required to complete their flow into the manufacturing or retail complex.

In many ways, the procurement cycle is similar to the customer-order-processing cycle involved in physical distribution. However, three important differences exist.

First, delivery time, size of shipment, method of transport, and value of the products involved changes substantially in the material cycle. Generally, purchase requirements result in very large shipments, which may be transported by barge, deep-water vessels, multiple-car trains, and truckloads. While exceptions do exist, transport emphasis in purchasing is placed on realizing movement at the lowest cost. The lower value of materials and parts in contrast to finished products means that a greater potential trade-off exists between cost of maintaining inventory in transit and low-cost modes of transport. Since the cost of maintaining materials and most parts in the supply pipeline is relatively lower per day than the cost of maintaining finished products, there is normally no benefit in paying premium rates for faster transport. Therefore, performance cycles in purchasing are often longer than those in customer-order-processing cycles.

A second major difference is the involvement of fewer intermediaries in procurement as contrasted to the finished-product marketing channel. In physical distribution, any particular firm is only one participant in an overall channel which must achieve several specified functions through the combined efforts of all members.[6] In contrast, the procurement performance cycle is more direct. Materials and parts are most often purchased directly from a supply source. The procuring firm typically has little interest in the channel arrangements necessary for the supplier to realize source availability. The utilization of more direct channels is an important factor in purchasing system design.

Finally, since the customer-order-processing cycle handles orders at the convenience of customers, random ordering must be accommodated in the design of the physical distribution system. In contrast, the procurement system *places* orders. The degree of control is therefore far greater in purchasing as a result of a substantial reduction in this form of operational variance.

The three major differences in purchasing, as contrasted to the customer-order cycle, enhance more orderly programming of logistical activities. The major uncertainty in purchasing is the probability of future price changes or supply discontinuity.

Operational Uncertainty

One of the major objectives of logistical management is to reduce variance in day-to-day operations. The performance cycle is one of the major logistical environments that introduces variance.

Figure 2–5 provides an illustration of variance that can occur as performance-cycle activities are repeated. Using the total performance-cycle, statistical analysis is possible concerning each activity and for total elapsed performance time. In Figure 2–5 any given order could require as few as 5 days and as many as 40 days to complete the performance cycle.

From an operating perspective, variance over and under expected time must be controlled. Time variances can result from workloads exceeding capacity of order processing and warehouse facilities, lack of inventory, transportation delays, and unexpected changes in desired delivery schedule and times. Each performance-cycle activity has an expected or standard time. A key to achieving logistical operational goals and to reducing disruptive manufacturing and marketing interfaces is to control overall elapsed performance-cycle time within accepted tolerances. The next section directs attention to logistics resource planning as a logic to achieve integrated control.

LOGISTICAL RESOURCE PLANNING (LRP)

The primary goal of integrated logistical operations is to transport all inventory as directly as possible from procurement, through manufacturing, and to final

---

[6] For elaboration of the channel functions of exchange see Chapter 3, pages 83–86.

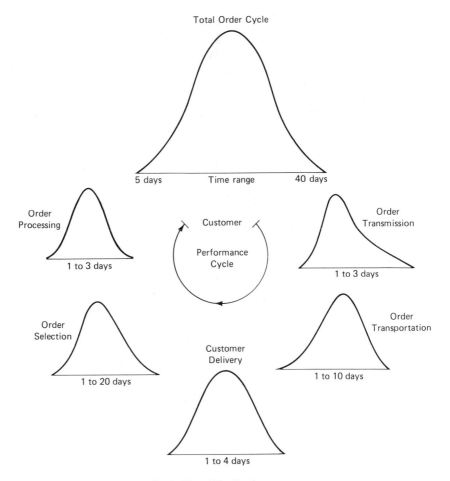

Figure 2–5   Performance Cycle Time Distribution

destination so that all physical handling and transportation contributes to the value-added process. This requires control across the entire materials logistics process as described in Figure 1–1. The objectives of logistical resource planning (LRP) have only become feasible as a result of rapid advancements in computer-based information systems.

The appeal of LRP is the emphasis placed on integrating the overall objectives of the enterprise with logistical requirements. The LRP process is initiated by interpreting the strategic business plan in terms of environmental monitoring and internal assessments. Environmental monitoring was discussed in the initial section of this chapter. Internal assessment concerns performance appraisal of past operating periods. The base goal of LRP is to implement the strategic business plan by the development of action plans related to physical distribution, manufacturing support, and purchasing. The concept of LRP represents an extension of manufacturing resource planning (MRP-II) to include the integration of functional planning and distribution requirements.[7]

---

[7] For presentation of the basic concept of MRP-II see Oliver W. Wight, *Manufacturing Resource Planning: MRPII Unlocking America's Productivity Potential*, rev. ed. (Essex Junction, Vt.: The Oliver Wight Companies, 1984).

Figure 2–6 illustrates the LRP process. LRP is a closed-loop process linking planning and execution of logistical commitments. This reconciliation is achieved by building a formal adjustment mechanism into the LRP process. The overall success of the logistical mission in an enterprise is dependent on plans being feasible and consistent with the strategic business plan. The adjustment feedback mechanisms are illustrated by return arrows in Figure 2–6. Using LRP logic, manufacturing resources and capacity are coordinated with the financial implications of distribution and procurement strategies. The potential of LRP relies on the computerized capability to collect, manipulate, and communicate manufacturing status and market-based trends. The key to LRP is an integrated data base which includes customer orders, finished-goods inventory, master production schedule, work-in-process inventory, raw-material inventory, and supply requirement information to be used for planning, control, and to simulate alternative plans. In essence, the command over information provided by LRP permits flexibility and rapid response capability to adjust to what is happening in customer and supply markets.

The LRP process contains four critical planning activities: (1) statement of distribution requirements, (2) master production scheduling, (3) materials requirement planning, and (4) capacity requirements planning. These planning activities are essential to manufacturing and logistics coordination.

Statement of Distribution Requirements (SDR)

The purpose of the statement of distribution requirements (SDR) is to provide a time-phased assessment of what finished-goods inventory is needed and where it is needed in the physical-distribution system. The four main inputs to the SDR are the forecast, customer orders, inventory status, and planned requirements. These inputs must be determined for each inventory stocking facility and then aggregated for the entire enterprise.

The *forecast* of customer demand is the fundamental input to determining distribution requirements. Customer demand is independent in that customers are free to choose what, when, and where they desire product delivery. Forecasting consists of a group of statistical and mathematical techniques that can be applied to reduce the impact of uncertainty on logistical operations. The term *forecast* is used exclusively to identify formal methodologies for estimating future demand. Forecasting methodology is discussed in Chapter 4.

Customer orders represent the trigger mechanism of the overall logistical system. Significant advances have been made in the application of computer technology to increase the speed and accuracy of order entry. Once orders are received, they represent customer commitments that the logistics system must satisfy. It is common throughout industry for customer orders representing different delivery times to be active at any one time in an order-processing system. Back-orders as the name implies, represent orders from past time periods that could not be filled because of inventory deficiencies. Advance orders represent customer commitments that will require inventory at a future point in time. To evaluate the full impact of customer orders on distribution requirements, current, back, and advance orders must be considered. The basic customer service platform of an enterprise is deeply routed in the order entry and processing capability of the LRP sytem. Customer service is treated in greater detail in Chapter 3 and order processing is a subject of Chapter 4.

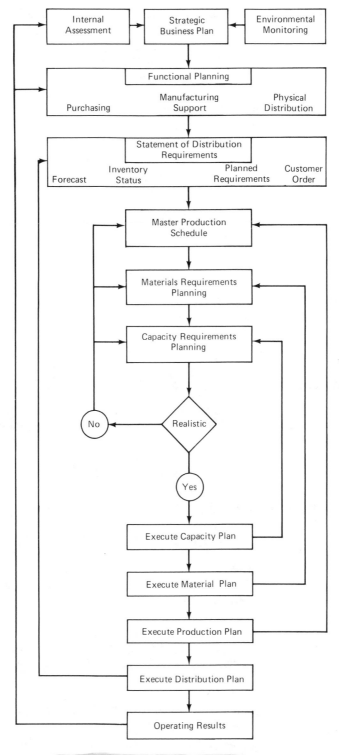

Figure 2–6 Logistical Resource Planning Process (LRP)

Critical to the determination of distribution requirements is the available inventory status. To the extent that inventory planning involves make-to-stock or safety-stock strategies, an assessment of available inventory is essential to identifying what should be produced to satisfy future requirements. Most sophisticated order-processing systems provide the capability to reserve or mortgage inventory to specific customer orders. The degree to which inventory is committed must be assessed in a review of inventory status. Inventory strategies are discussed in Chapter 7.

A final aspect of formulating a SDR is to include requirements for events that are known to managers involved in the planning process. An example might be a planned change in manufacturing capacity that will idle a given plant for a specified time. This event is known to management in advance and must be accommodated. To avoid a customer service discontinuity, inventory must be built and stockpiled in advance to service customers during the idle period. Other examples of planned requirements are seasonal sales or manufacturing contraints that must be accommodated by building inventories is advance of selling periods.

The SDR reflects an assessment of inventory requirements based upon the forecast, customer orders, inventory status, and planned requirements. The SDR provides the time-phased *pull* that guides manufacturing commitments. As such, market-paced manufacturing is initiated by the SDR.

Master Production Schedule (MPS)

Master scheduling is the process by which the manufacturing capability of an organization is reconciled with the statement of distribution requirements as determined from forecasts, customer orders, back-orders, and planned requirements. The MPS is used to resolve conflicts between manufacturing and marketing. The end result is viewed as a contract which states what purchasing intends to procure, what manufacturing intends to produce, and what marketing agrees to sell or place into inventory. The MPS must be well managed to result in attainment of service, quality, and profit goals. The MPS specifies what quantity of products is scheduled to be produced during future time periods. This is contrasted with an order point system which schedules production when a minimum inventory quantity is reached. The greatest advantage to an MPS is the capability to plan manufacturing activities over an extended horizon. A good MPS has several characteristics. *First*, it is complete in that all distribution requirements are considered, including customer orders, forecasts, service requirements, and interplant orders. The complete status is achieved by use of the statement of distribution requirements.

Second, the MPS should be as stable as possible. A schedule that manufacturing can meet may conflict with one that is fully responsive to the marketplace. This inherent conflict must be acknowledged and resolved from an overall perspective. Through the recognition of firm, planned orders, schedule adjustments, and the usage of time fences to establish periods within which different degrees of change are possible and cost effective, stability can be attained.[8]

---

[8] A time fence is a planning device used to set different priorities on when changes can be made in the master production schedule.

A *third* characteristic of a good MPS is feasibility with respect to the overall capability and business plan. If the MPS is totaled for all products in dollar terms, the total should be compatible in an upward sense with the financial plans of the organization. MPS should also be feasible in a downward sense with respect to the timing and utilization of manufacturing capacity and key human and material resources.

A *fourth* and final characteristic is that the MPS should represent the manufacturing game plan used to drive the materials requirement planning system and the capacity planning system.

Materials Requirement Planning (MRP)

The focus of MRP is the procurement of components and materials to support manufacturing. MRP logic originated in the United States during the 1960s.[9] The original MRP concept utilized computer capabilities to time phase procurement. The emphasis was to minimize inventory by arranging for delivery of exact requirements from vendors as required in manufacturing. To achieve time-phased procurement, MRP developed logic to manage long lead times characteristic of a geographically dispersed supply base. The essential concept necessary for MRP is the recognition that manufacturing demand can be classified as *dependent*. As originally defined, dependent demand is directly related to, or derived from, the demand for other items or end products.[10] Dependent demand is based on the master production schedule interpretation of distribution requirements and need not be forecasted. Once the components and materials necessary to support a specific manufacturing schedule are identified, MRP provides a time-phased logic to manage their timely arrival.

The material plan provides an assessment of what items will be required to support the MPS. A bill of materials (BOM) is used to determine the combination of assemblies, subassemblies, parts, and materials needed to support planned production. The materials plan specifies what work must be completed on lower level units to support the planned production as well as the materials that must be obtained from the supply base network.

An alternative use of MRP logic is to allocate finished-goods inventory from manufacturing to forward stock locations. This application is often called FORWARD MRP or DRP which stands for distribution resource planning.[11] The typical business situation that supports DRP is a make-to-stock manufacturing operation. From a physical distribution perspective the objective of DRP is to forward allocate as little inventory as practical while satisfying customer service goals. The DRP logic positions the forward warehouse as the dependent

---

[9] For early development of the MRP concept see George W. Plossal and Oliver W. Wight, *Materials Requirement Planning by Computer* (Washington, D.C.: American Production and Inventory Control Society, Inc., 1971); Joseph Orlicky, *Material Requirement Planning* (New York: McGraw-Hill Book Company, 1975); Jeffery G. Miller and Linda G. Sprague, "Behind the Growth in Materials Requirement Planning," *Harvard Business Review*, Vol. 53 (September–October 1975), pp. 83–91.

[10] For a comprehensive discussion of the concept of dependent demand in materials requirement planning see Thomas E. Vollmann, William L. Berry, and D. Clay Whybark, *Manufacturing Planning and Control Systems*, (Homewood, Ill.: Richard D. Irwin, Inc., 1984), pp. 34–35.

[11] Andre J. Martin, *DRP: Distribution Resources Planning* (Essex Junction, Vt.: The Oliver Wight Companies, 1983).

demand point for planning and executing inventory allocations. Gross requirements from forward warehouses are accumulated to help establish the master production schedule. This form of proactive allocation logic is treated in greater detail in Chapter 7.

This brief introduction of MRP and DRP points out that each concept has a focus that is functionally based. MRP is a procurement tool. DRP is a distribution tool. They are an integral part of overall logistical resource planning that seeks to control manufacturing and logistics on a fully integrated basis.

Capacity Resource Planninng (CRP)

The purpose of capacity resource planning (CRP) is to determine if the desired production can be accomplished when scheduled within the capacity limitations of manufacturing facilities. A master production schedule that appears feasible may turn out to be a mission impossible in terms of a firm's capability to produce component subassemblies.

To determine if the MPS can be supported, a capacity load projection is completed. A load projection is calculated for each work station by back scheduling from due date for each item contained in the MPS. The calculated load requirement is compared to available capacity. The extent of over- or underutilization is thus determined for each work center. Management involvement is required at this point to eliminate overutilization. Such overutilization can be resolved by subcontracting, scheduling overtime, revising human resource allocations, or revising the MPS. Likewise, if a work center is projected to be underutilized, management may decide to reduce work hours, lay off employees, bring subcontracted work in-house, reallocate human resources, or revise the MPS. The degree of capital intensiveness of a particular manufacturing operation dictates how level the MPS needs to be in order to efficiently utilize manufacturing capacity. A trade-off is required between equipment costs, human resource costs, inventory costs, and other less tangible factors such as resultant customer service levels and employees' quality of work life.

When an acceptable MPS is identified, it can be *frozen* as realistic. From this point forward the various functional plans can be implemented.

Conclusion—Logistical Resource Planning

Each enterprise must pick, choose, and blend alternative control logics in the implementation of integrated logistics. A broad-based concept like LRP is applicable to direct purchasing situations such as retailing and hospital materials management. In such situations the SDR and MRP processes can be directly linked to eliminate concern with MPS and CRP. It is important to stress that the basic concepts embedded in alternative planning logics are not mutually exclusive. The key to integrated logistics is to develop a customized control capability that utilizes available concepts and technology to the maximum strategic advantage of each unique enterprise. A few observations are noteworthy regarding the full impact of market-paced resource commitment upon business operations.

First, the premium placed in the capability to turn resource allocations on a dime to exploit market opportunity could result in a serious case of master schedule nervousness. The key is to accommodate change without introducing excessive expediting, uneconomic production, and high-cost transportation. While minimization of inventory is a prime logistical objective, equally important are the objectives of minimum variance, maximum transportation consolidation, quality control, and life-cycle support.[12]

Second, a variety of economic and market forces may justify building speculative finished-goods, work-in-process and component/material inventories. Finished-goods inventory may be required to provide customer service availability that is not possible using the most-responsive manufacturing operations. Seasonal consumption and/or production constraints may be the reason for finished-inventory accumulations. Economies of scale in manufacturing and transportation may offer economic benefits that trade-off in favor of accumulating work-in-process inventories. The objective is the achievement of the lowest total cost, not the optimization of a specific cost. In the procurement arena, obtaining continuous and sufficient supplies of critical materials may justify stockpiling inventories. These qualifications are presented as a reminder to avoid the dangers of a myopic fixation on achieving stockless production.

Third, the overall focus of logistics resource planning surpasses the operational areas of logistics and involves to a significant degree the how of manufacturing and marketing. It is essential that logistics operations be finely tuned with these areas of corporate effort. This coordination is made possible through involvement in the strategic business planning process and is realized on a day-to-day basis through logistical resource planning.

Each operational area of logistics embodies specialized operating strategies. The final three sections of this chapter review strategic alternatives as they relate to physical distribution, manufacturing support, and procurement.

PHYSICAL DISTRIBUTION STRATEGIES

In this section basic physical distribution strategies available to support integrated logistics are reviewed. The initial part reviews the operational nature of echeloned, direct, and flexible physical distribution systems. The second part discusses the strategy of postponement. The final part deals with consolidation strategies.

Physical Distribution Operational Patterns

The many facets of physical distribution make the design of an operating system a complex assignment. In designing a system with an acceptable balance of performance and cost, management must always keep in mind that any system will require constant adjustment. Thus, flexibility becomes an important part of system design. When one considers the variety of physical distribution systems around the world that service widely diverse markets, it is astonishing that any design similarity exists from one situation to the next. However, all systems have two characteristics in common. *First*, they are designed to encourage maximum inventory flow. *Second*, the systems must be designed within the existing technological state of logistical system components. Technological limits for the performance of major logistical activities result in common patterns among

---

[12] See Chapter 1, pages 28–29.

systems. Three basic patterns stand out as the most widely utilized for logistical operations: (1) echelon systems, (2) direct systems, and (3) flexible systems.

Echelon Systems

The term *echelon* implies that the flow of products proceeds through a series of consecutive locations as it moves from origin to final destination. Such steps involve positioning inventory in warehouses. The essential characteristic of an echelon system is that finished-goods inventory is stocked at one or more points prior to final destination shipment.

Two common echelon patterns involve the use of break-bulk and consolidation warehouses in physical distribution systems. The break-bulk warehouse typically receives large-volume shipments from a variety of suppliers for assortment into combinations desired by individual customers or retailers. Food distribution centers operated by major grocery chains are prime examples of break-bulk warehouses. The consolidation distribution warehouse is normally operated by a manufacturing enterprise that produces products at different plants. Consolidation of products at a central point makes it possible to combine all products manufactured into a single shipment. Major food-processing firms are prime examples of enterprises using consolidation facilities.

Echelon systems employ warehouses to provide inventory assortments and achieve low transportation rates. Additionally, inventories held in warehouses are available for rapid customer delivery. Rapid delivery can be accomplished without a warehouse network by using premium transportation. However, when volume is sufficient, a network of strategically located field inventories often provides the best balance of cost-service performance.

Direct Systems

Contrasting with the echelon pattern are physical distribution systems operating *direct* to final destination from one or a limited number of central stocking locations.

Direct-distribution enterprises find their particular marketing efforts are best supported by a central inventory from which customer orders are filled. Direct-distribution systems often utilize high-speed transport and electronic order processing to overcome geographical separation from customers. Examples of direct shipments are carload-to-customer movement, direct store delivery, and consumer mail-order deliveries. Direct-shipment systems are commonly used in purchasing materials because of the large average size shipment from vendor to purchasing source.

The overall potential to increase the number of direct-distribution shipments has basic appeal because it eliminates inventory commitment and multiple handlings. The limiting element to direct distribution is the high cost of transportation and potential loss of control. Advances in electronic communication capabilities are rapidly changing the situation. Today, technology exists to maintain control as well as reduce the labor-intensive nature of processing many small orders for direct delivery. The economic forces are shifting to the point where direct delivery is predicted to become the least-cost physical distribution solution in an increasing variety of situations.

Flexible Systems

The most common physical-distribution practice is to combine echelon and direct movement into a *flexible* operating system. As a general rule, inventory selectivity is encouraged in the design of a logistical system. A system can be designed to hold some products or materials in field warehouses, while others are distributed directly. In many cases, the size and composition of an order may determine the most economical location from which to service a specific customer.

For example, one automotive manufacturer supplies aftermarket replacement parts utilizing a flexible system strategy. The system is designed to warehouse inventories at various distances from dealer locations based on demand. The slower the part turnover, the more centralized the inventory. The slowest moving parts are held at a central location, which directly supplies the entire world.

A second enterprise, which supplies industrial components, follows a completely opposite flexible distribution strategy. In order to satisfy unexpected demand, this enterprise inventories sufficient quantities of slow movers at field distribution warehouses. In contrast to the automotive firm, fast turnover products are shipped directly to customers from manufacturing plants.

The difference in strategies is explained when one examines the market segment that each enterprise serves and the degree of product differentiation each enjoys. The automotive enterprise faces extensive competition on replacement parts for new models. As a model ages, competition decreases, making the original manufacturer the sole supplier. The industrial component supplier, on the other hand, sells a product with a high degree of competitive substitutability. Fast product demand can be forecasted. In contrast, slow-selling product demand is erratic and difficult to forecast. In this enterprise's market, a supplier is measured by purchasing agents in terms of how fast unexpected production breakdowns can be remedied.

Each enterprise faces a different marketing situation, and each utilizes a different flexible logistics strategy with respect to warehousing finishing-product inventories. An enterprise must determine the distribution strategy that will satisfy customer service requirements at the lowest total cost.

Flexible operations may also incorporate into the physical-distribution system design the capability to service a given customer from alternate warehouse. This form of flexible operation can be employed in two ways: (1) contingency and (2) routine.

Contingency Flexible Operations. Contingency flexible operation represents backup support for the preferred pattern of logistical performance. A typical situation is when a primary shipping point is unable to provide normal service. For example, a warehouse may be stocked out of a specific item with no inventory replenishment planned for the immediate future. To prohibit a prolonged customer back-order or to avoid order cancellation, a contingency policy may exist to fill all or at least short-supply items from a secondary shipping point.

A secondary source location in a contingency plan will typically result in higher logistical cost. The customer will be serviced but at an increased cost. This added variable cost must be justified by product contribution margin or because the product is critical to the customer. Conceptually, a firm can afford to spend up to the last penny of gross margin contribution on contingency logistical operations and still make a profit contribution.

Routine Flexible Operations. A form of flexible operational capacity which is gaining in popularity is to incorporate into system design a routine procedure for shipping to specific customers from more than one logistical facility. This practice of routine flexible operations may be justified in at least three different situations.

First, the customer may be located at or near a point of equal transportation cost between two warehouses. Customers who are located at points of nearly equal delivery cost from more than one warehouse offer an opportunity to fully utilize physical distribution capacity by alternating shipment origin according to inventory availability, workload, and/or equipment utilization. This form of flexible balancing offers a way of fully utilize capacity and balance system workloads based on demand variability.

A second situation wherein an enterprise may deliberately incorporate routine flexible distribution operations is when specific-size customer shipments have different logistical costs when serviced from different facilities. For example, the lowest-total-cost method to provide delivery of a small shipment may be through a warehouse. In contrast, shipments having total weight greater than 15,000 pounds may have the lowest total logistical cost when shipped direct from manufacturing plants. Provided that each alternative method of shipment can meet customer service requirements, total cost will be reduced by using a routine flexible operation.

A third type of routine flexible operation is when an enterprise selects to follow different warehouse stocking policies. The cost of supporting inventory requires that careful analysis be completed to determine which items to place in a particular warehouse. As illustrated above in the automotive example, a common practice is to stock selected items in specific warehouses with the total line being supported from a central facility. A retail store in a small community may stock a limited version of the overall line. When customers desire nonstocked items, the store will accept the order. However, customer shipments will be made from a larger store or a warehouse facility. The term *mother store* is often used to describe inventory policies that vary by market area with designated responsibility for backup support.

The variation of stocking policy by echelon level is a common strategy used to limit inventory exposure. Systems that utilize multiecheloned stocking strategies normally cannot justify full-line stocking in all warehouses. The reasons for echelon stocking range from low profit contribution to high per-unit cost of inventory maintenance. One way to operationalize a fine-line inventory classification strategy is to differentiate stocking policy by system echelons.[13]

Flexible operations can be contingency or routine based. A prerequisite to flexible operations is the capability to accurately interrogate inventory status and quickly switch orders between facilities. The use of flexible operations for contingency planning has a well-established track record. The incorporation of routine flexible arrangements as a basic part of system design is new and

---

[13] For example, one location might stock fast movers only, while another location could be stocked with a full line. This concept is further developed in Chapter 7, pages 225–30.

rapidly growing. To a significant degree, a programmed capability of flexible operations can offset the use of safety stock to provide customer service in a multiple facility physical distribution system.

Postponement

The concept of postponement has long standing in business literature. However, practical examples in logistics have not materialized until recently.[14] Postponement offers a way to reduce the anticipatory nature of physical distribution. Almost all movement and storage in a physical distribution system takes place in anticipation of future transactions. To the degree that final manufacturing or distribution of a product can be postponed until a customer order is obtained, the risk associated with inventory accumlation is automatically reduced or eliminated. Two types of postponement should be carefully reviewed when formulating operating procedures: (1) assembly postponement and (2) geographical postponement.

Assembly Postponement

The basic concept behind assembly postponement is to retain the product in a neutral status as long as possible in the manufacturing process. Several outstanding examples of assembly postponement are currently in practice. Mixing colors upon customer request has reduced dramatically the number of stockkeeping units required at retail paint stores. A similar postponement situation is Sunoco's system to mix gasoline octane grades at the retail pump. In other industries it has become common practice to process and store product in bulk to postpone final product packaging. In other situations products are packed, but private brand labeling is postponed until orders are received. Other examples of assembly postponement are the rapidly increasing practice of installing accessories at automobile and appliance dealerships, thereby customizing products to customer request and commitment. Another example of assembly postponement is the assembly and final accessory configuration of motorcycles at dealers.

These examples all have one thing in common. They introduce the capability to reduce the number of stockkeeping units required to support a broad-line marketing effort. Until the product is customized, it has the potential to serve many different end-customer requirements.

The impact of assembly postponement is twofold. First, the quantity of different products moved in anticipation of sale is reduced, therefore the risk of mislocation is lower. The second, and perhaps more important, impact is the increased use of distribution warehouses and dealers to perform light-manufacturing and final-assembly operations. To the extent that a degree of specialized talent or economies of scale does not exist in manufacturing, the

---

[14] For example, see Wroe Alderson, "Marketing Efficiency and the Principle of Postponement," *Cost and Profit Outlook*, Vol. 3 (September 1950); Wroe Alderson, *Marketing Behavior and Executive Action* (Homewood, Ill.: Richard D Irwin, 1950), p. 424; Louis P. Bucklin, "Postponement, Speculation, and the Structure of Distribution Channels," *Journal of Marketing Research*, Vol. 2 (February 1965), pp. 26–32; Thomas A. Staudt, Donald A. Taylor, and Donald J. Bowersox, *A Managerial Introduction to Marketing*, 3rd ed. (Englewood Cliffs, N.J.: Prentice-Hall, Inc., 1976), pp. 281–82.

process of customization may be best delegated and performed near the final destination market. The traditional mission of the warehouse in some industries is changing rapidly to accommodate assembly postponement.

Geographic Postponement

In many ways geographic postponement is the exact opposite of assembly postponement. The basic notion of *geographic postponement* is to maintain a full inventory assortment at a few centralized locations with no forward movement until a customer order is received. Once the logistical process is initiated, delivery is as direct as possible to the customer. Under the concept of geographic postponement the anticipatory nature of physical distribution is eliminated.

An example of geographic postponement is the Sears Store Direct logistical system. Utilizing rapid-order communications, the physical distribution of an appliance is not initiated until a customer order is received. An appliance purchased on Monday will be ready for in-home installation on Thursday. Beginning on Monday the actual order coordination will flow from Sears to Whirlpool Manufacturing. The physical distribution flow consists of overnight truck movement on Tuesday for store delivery on Wednesday and local delivery on Thursday. The distinct possibility exists that the appliance sold on Monday was not manufactured until that night or early Tuesday.

The potential of geographic postponement has resulted from the capability to process and transmit orders with a high degree of accuracy and speed. Geographic postponement substitutes rapid processing time for the anticipatory need to move products to forward stocking points to satisfy future sales. Unlike assembly postponement, systems utilizing geographic postponement can retain full manufacturing control and economies characteristic of centralized operations while still meeting customer service requirements.

The two types of postponement offer ways to refrain from final product-market commitment until a customer order is received. They both serve to reduce the anticipatory nature of overall physical distribution. The two types of postponement reduced anticipation in different ways. Assembly postponement moves *nondifferentiated* product toward the market with a plan to modify the product to customer requirements at some future time. Geographic postponement holds *differentiated* products at a central location until a customer order is received. The factors favoring one or the other form of postponement hinge on volume, value, competitive practices, economies of scale, and required customer service in terms of delivery speed and consistency. Both forms of postponement represent powerful alternatives to traditional anticipatory physical distribution.

Shipment Consolidation

A significant opportunity exists in all logistical operations to reduce transportation expenditures through shipment consolidation. Quantity discounts are provided for larger volume shipments in for-hire rate structures. Generally speaking, the larger the shipment, the lower the freight rate per hundredweight. To control physical distribution cost it is desirable to consolidate small shipments. The economy of scale of transportation cost has not changed as a result of deregulation or the increased demand for scheduled or just-in-time delivery. To reduce transportation cost a great deal of attention has been directed to the development of ingenious consolidation programs. To properly consolidate it is necessary to know both current and planned inventory status. It is desirable to be able to mortgage or commit planned production. To the extent practical, consolidations should be planned prior to order processing. All aspects of consolidation require timely and relevant information concerning order-cycle variances.

From an operational viewpoint, three opportunities exist to realize freight consolidation: (1) market area grouping, (2) schedule delivery, and (3) pool consolidation. The extent to which each can be realized in day-to-day operations must be considered in formulating physical distribution strategy.

Market Area Grouping

The most fundamental type of consolidation is when small shipments to a specific market area are combined for transportation. This type of consolidation does not interrupt the natural flow of the freight by trying to influence when shipments are tendered to common carriers. Rather, the quantity being shipped to or purchased by customers in the overall market provide the consolidation basis. Many firms participate in purchasing cooperatives that arrange multiple-shipper consolidations.

The difficulty of both inbound and outbound market area groupings is identification of sufficient daily volume to realize effective consolidation. To offset the volume deficiency three arrangements are commonly used. First, firms may consolidate shipments to an intermediate point for purposes of line-haul transportation savings. At the intermediate point the shipments are separated and forwarded to destinations on an individual basis. Second, firms may select to delay shipments to realize sufficient volume for consolidation on specific days to specific destination markets. Third, a given enterprise may join with other firms to form a pool of small shipments. The last two arrangements are discussed below.

Scheduled Distribution

Scheduled distribution consists of limiting shipments to specific markets to selected days each week. The scheduled distribution plan is normally communicated to customers in a way that sells the virtue of planned delivery. The performance cycle is stabilized by a commitment on the part of the shipping firm that orders received prior to an established deadline will be guaranteed to be delivered on the day of scheduled distribution.

Scheduled distribution may conflict with the trend toward specified customer delivery appointments. Specified delivery means an order is required to be delivered within a narrow time window. In today's world, a requirement to provide plus or minus one-hour delivery of a component or part may be specified in the purchase contract. Carried to its ultimate, the appointment or specified delivery time could require a physical distribution capability to arrange for any authorized size shipment to arrive at a specified time at any authorized customer facility. The challenge is to satisfy such demanding customer service standards while maintaining the benefits of consolidation.

Pooled Distribution

Participation in a pooled distribution plan typically means that a third-party organization arranges the consolidation. The term *third-party* refers to a freight forwarder or a public warehouse who consolidates shipments from many different organization. Available pooling services are further discussed in Chapters 5 and 8.

Conclusion—Physical Distribution Strategies

From the preceding discussion it should be clear that a wide variety of different strategies are available and should be evaluated in the design of a physical distribution system. Several of the available strategies are directly related to the manufacturing and procurement logics of an enterprise. Attention is now directed to selected manufacturing strategies.

MANUFACTURING STRATEGIES

The worldwide competitive climate of the mid-1980s has forced manufacturing to introduce techniques to lower unit costs while simultaneously improving quality. The change occurring in manufacturing logic is as far reaching as was Frederick Taylor's original concept of "scientific management" in the early 1900s.[15] The purpose of this section is to provide a logistical manager with an introduction to new manufacturing strategies that impact logistics.

The responsibility split between logistics and manufacturing must be clearly understood. Manufacturing is concerned with *how* to produce. As such, manufacturing involves all intraplant activities including materials handling. The manufacturing *support* aspects of overall logistics are concerned with providing inventory to support production. The common ground between manufacturing and logistics is the control logic used to determine the *what*, *when*, and *where* of production.

The first part of the section discusses market-paced manufacturing. Next, attention is directed to a variety of manufacturing strategies and and technologies being deployed to increase flexibility. These final concepts are discussed under the broad banner of just-in-time strategies.

Market-Paced Manufacturing

The new logic of manufacturing places primary emphasis on responding as rapidly as possible to market requirements. The ideal vision is that a product would never be manufactured or a component purchased until a customer order was received. Under this idealistic *pull* concept manufacturing and purchasing remain totally *flexible* to accommodate market requirements. To the degree that market-paced manufacturing strategies are realized, the *anticipatory* nature of purchasing, manufacturing support, and physical distribution would be eliminated.

Manufacturing under a pull system implies that a product will not be assembled or fabricated until specifically demanded. Pull logic is contrasted to a

[15] Frederick W. Taylor, *The Principles of Scientific Management* (New York: Harper, 1911).

push system wherein any authorized product may be produced to stock providing the necessary components and materials are available. Typical classification of manufacturing with respect of forecast and orders is (1) make-to-stock, (2) assemble-to-order, (3) fabricate-to-order, and (4) engineer-to-order. Within this classification the primary impact of pull logic is on the make-to-stock and assemble-to-order classes. In both situations manufacturing lead times would be extended if work-in-process and component inventories are not available as needed. The objective is to maintain acceptable inventories and response time while maintaining the maximum flexibility.

The ideal result of a pull manufacturing philosophy is improved efficiency owing to elimination of waste and production stock. Under a pull manufacturing logic components or materials necessary to support production or assembly are purchased to arrive at the specified production plant as needed and in the exact quantity required. Emphasis in procurement is placed on exact material/component lot sizes to accommodate specified production runs. The concept of market-paced manufacturing is based on a capability to rapidly switch what is being produced while maintaining product control.

Adoption of a flexible pull manufacturing philosophy permeates every logistical process and activity. The demands placed upon manufacturing support are exacting with little or no tolerance for error. Thus, logistical variance must be eliminated to adequately support market-paced manufacturing. The ultimate appeal of a pull logic is its focus on inventory minimization throughout the logistics system.

Just-in-Time Strategies

A great deal of the flexibility necessary to support market-paced manufacturing has resulted from adoption and expansion of just-in-time strategies (JIT).

The initial attention to applying pull concepts to manufacturing was established by the Japanese in the 1950s when the Toyota Motor Company introduced a system known as *Kanban*.[16] The popular appeal of JIT was the potential elimination of work-in-process inventories by limiting production and assembly to only what is required to support planned manufacturing or customer orders. This revolutionary approach to manufacturing management questioned the low cost benefits of economy of scale manufacturing in favor of minimizing inventory investment. The basic underlying logic was to produce an item only when needed and as efficiently as possible by eliminating wasted or duplicated activity. The basic philosophy of JIT is that inventory only exists to cover problems. By reducing inventories, problems in the manufacturing process are exposed. These problems must be solved before inventories can be further reduced.

Prime attention was directed to quality control to assure that products would be produced with zero defects the first time, thereby eliminating reruns.[17] The initial JIT concepts focused on moving materials into the manufacturing

[16] See Richard J. Shonberger, *Japanese Manufacturing Techniques* (New York: Macmillian Free Press, 1982); George C. Jackson "Just in Time Production: Implications for Logistics Managers," *Journal of Business Logistics*, Vol. 4, No. 2 (1983); and Richard J. Ackonberger, *Japanese Manufacturing Techniques, Nine Hidden Lessons in Simplicity* (New York: The Free Press, 1982).

[17] For an integration of JIT concepts into an overall framework of operations management see Richard J. Schonberger, *Operations Management, Productivity and Quality*, 2nd ed. (Plano, Tex.: Business Publications Inc., 1984).

environment so as to have only the exact quantity of material at the necessary time and place to support a production schedule. To achieve this goal a combination of requisition and production cards (sign boards) were utilized to control material flow and authorize component manufacturing. From a logical viewpoint, JIT was very similar to a two-bin inventory control logic for production inventory without any restriction regarding minimum lot size.[18] The implicit assumption was that everything manufactured was in direct and timely response to market need.

The natural expansion of the original JIT concept was to incorporate advanced production technology. Advanced JIT is a focused manufacturing logic that seeks to implement *zero inventory or stock less production*.[19] Emphasis has begun to be placed on changing manufacturing culture and technology to accommodate maximum flexibility. As such, JIT now embraces a variety of basic manufacturing concepts which are applicable to both made-to-stock and the variety of assemble and made-to-order manufacturing processes.

JIT logic places a great deal of emphasis on purchasing strategies. To the extent practical, the JIT goal is to position materials obtained from external suppliers directly into the manufacturing process in an effort to avoid performing any logistical activity that is not essential to the value-added process.[20]

This part concludes with the discussion of some strategies that are involved in JIT. They are (1) reduced lot sizes and set-up time, (2) load leveling, (3) group technology, (4) statistical process control, (5) preventive maintenance, and (6) team approach. These specific strategies are direct operation responsibilities or concerns of manufacturing. They do have a direct impact on the logistical support requirements for a JIT manufacturing system.

Reduced Lot Sizes and Set-Up Time

One way to reduce work-in-process inventory is to cut lot sizes. To reduce lot sizes economically, set-up costs and times must be reduced. Dramatic reductions have been accomplished by deploying new manufacturing procedures. The range of techniques varies from low-technology solutions such as having everything required to perform the changeover at the job site to high-technology solutions using robotics and numerically controlled machines. Reduced lot sizes and the usage of automatic equipment for loading and unloading have brought new factors into switch-over support. Technologies and procedures have been implemented that reduce set-up times to minutes, as contrasted to hours or even days. The logistical support system must be highly responsive to permit manufacturing complete flexibility in lot-size variance and set-up time.

Load Leveling

Load leveling is another part of the JIT strategy. Balancing the work schedule to the maximum extent possible permits fine tuning of manufacturing opera-

---

[18] Robert W. Hall, *Zero Inventories* (Homewood, Ill.: Dow Jones-Irwin, 1983), pp. 3–4.

[19] Yasukiro Monden, "Adaptable Kanban Systems Help Toyota Maintain Just-in-Time Productions," *Industrial Engineering* (May, 1981), pp. 29–45; and Kazuo Higashi, "A Zero-Inventory Manufacturing Approach," *Unpublished Paper*, Michigan State University, 1980.

[20] Hall op. cit., and Jinichiro Nakane and Robert W. Hall, "Management Specs for Stockless Production," *Harvard Business Review*, Vol. 61 (May–June, 1983).

tions at all levels. The master production schedule is the key to balancing workloads. The schedule for every day and every hour should reflect a balance of material, labor, and plant capacity. The schedule should also be balanced in regard to product mix required by the customer. Final scheduling is typically a repetitive process which takes place over time. The initial schedules are approximate and become progressively more refined as the planned production date approaches. Each change incorporated into the master production schedule to realize load leveling requires a corresponding change in logistical manufacturing-support plans.

Group Technology

To achieve manufacturing quality control and to help realize efficiency in material handling, attention to manufacturing equipment layout and material storage location is critical. The key is to minimize the distances traveled, the number of trips required, unnecessary movements, and to pinpoint responsibility to perform selected processes.

The popularity of the group-technology concept is based on material handling efficiency. Implementation of group technology requires that the material flow through a manufacturing plant be analyzed to identify products with common routings. These products should ideally be grouped and the manufacturing equipment required for their processing be physically located in a work cell to promote material handling efficiency. This requires conversion from a plant layout which has typically clustered manufacturing equipment by common type. For example, lathes have typically all been located together. Under group technology they may be spread throughout a manufacturing plant. The potential efficiencies of group technology are easy to illustrate. Assume two machines are utilized in a specific process and they are each located in common groups. To start the sequence, a part is placed in machine A for processing. When processing is completed, the part is removed and placed in a container for material handling to another department. When a sufficient quantity is accumulated to fill the container, it is moved to machine type B. The part is then loaded into machine B for processing. When the process on machine B is complete, the part is unloaded. Using conventional layout, five separate material handling moves are required, and work-in-process inventory is accumulated between process steps.

In comparison, a group-technology work cell would locate machines A and B adjacent to each other. To initiate the process, the part is loaded into machine A for processing. Upon completion the part is removed and placed into machine B. When the machine cycle is completed on machine B, the part is removed. Three material handling moves were required under group technology, and no work-in-process inventory was accumulated.

The way that group technology promotes quality control is that responsibility is pinpointed. Using the start-to-finish sequence, the specific machine responsible for each process is identified by group.

Statistical Process Control (SPC)

The quality of products produced is a critical element of the JIT strategy. Poor quality utilizes extra capacity to realize a level of output, requires greater amounts of inventory in the system, introduces schedule variance, requires rework or produces scrap, and negatively impacts employee morale and customer satisfaction. Statistical process control (SPC) is a technique used to resolve quality problems based on manufacturing variance.

Manufacturing is properly viewed as a series of repetitive events. One, two, or a large number of operations may be involved. Process variable refers to a defined condition which represents an indication of quality. Specific tests are used over time to measure the process variable. Variability is detected by fluctuations in measurement.

The reason for variations can be explained by a variety of causes. Variability measurements plotted over time are expected to produce a random pattern around the average expected value. This natural variability can be caused by such factors as tooling or material consistency. The reasons for this natural variability are referred to as *common causes*. A cause that results in a measurement outside of the normal range of variability is identified as a *special cause*. Conditions such as a new operator or tooling out of adjustment can be special causes.

Statistical process control monitors when the special causes in any process occur and are eliminated. A process regularly measured and determined to be within control assures that variations are within the specified tolerances of acceptable quality. When statistical process is implemented, full inspection of output is not required. If the system is measured as being in control, labor savings are realized by elimination of inspections. The advantages of statistical process control are that costs and quality performance are predictable, and special causes can be identified and eliminated with speed and reliability.

Preventive Maintenance

The introduction of preventive maintenance is an important JIT concept. Simply stated, preventive maintenance seeks to repair and adjust a machine *before* breakdown or out of calibration occurs. This procedure is contrasted to allowing a machine to run until repair is required because of breakdown.

In a traditional manufacturing situation work-in-process inventories serve to buffer processes when a breakdown occurs. Once this inventory is eliminated, an unexpected breakdown can cause serious variance in the overall manufacturing process. The concept of preventing maintenance is founded in the belief that regular inspection and adjustment will result in the lowest total-cost manufacturing.

Team Approach

Successful implementation of a JIT strategy relies upon employee involvement and mutual trust in decision-making and problem-solving. The team approach goes beyond the bounds of manufacturing and includes purchasing, the external supply network, physical distribution, and the customer. Management needs to recognize the contribution of each individual and place increased responsibility on employees to perform in a manner that benefits the entire system. This requires awareness of who the team members are, improved communications, long-term commitment, training, and continual reinforcement and encouragement to improve.

Conclusion—Manufacturing Strategies

With the basic commitment to market-paced manufacturing dawns a production era. The concepts of JIT are idealistic. Anything approaching ~~~ implementation of this manufacturing philosophy requires a maximum commitment to flexibility. In turn, the emphasis on manufacturing flexibility requires maximum responsiveness in manufacturing support. To a significant degree the attainment of JIT goals is totally dependent upon logistical support capability.

PURCHASING STRATEGIES

Purchasing is a boundary-spanning activity that links manufacturing and an external supply network. The focal point is to provide continuity and stability in procurement. The fundamental objective is to provide the correct assortment of materials, parts, or resale merchandise at the desired location, when needed, and in an economical manner. From 40 to 60 per cent of the cost of goods sold is accounted for by external payments to suppliers. Purchasing provides a key opportunity to realize competitive advantage. Utilizing supply management techniques and implementing scheduled delivery requirements are two strategies for improving procurement performance.

Supply Management

Supply management requires that buying firms identify and implement opportunities for long-term competitive advantage through purchasing. Management of this process involves (1) definition of vendor performance requirements, (2) obtaining comprehensive information, and (3) supply base selection and relations. Each activity is discussed.

Vendor Performance Requirements

Supply management is based on the careful specification of current and future manufacturing requirements as the foundation for designing a vendor network. Purchasing managers need to obtain realistic expectations regarding specific needs and the degree of variance acceptable. Information is required regarding product quality, logistical requirements, lead time, volumes, and engineering support. Understanding needs and priorities is necessary to evaluate potential vendors. The selection criteria established which vendors are candidates for long-term agreements.

Comprehensive Information

Purchasing is responsible for obtaining comprehensive and accurate data on supplier availability, procurement lead times, and historical performance. In the case of quality management it is not sufficient to determine that a producer is able to meet quality expectations. There should also be evidence that the specified quality level can be met consistently. The emphasis on quality control has increased substantially in recent years as a direct result of broader interest in consumer protection. Manufacturers are increasingly faced with assuring customers that their products meet performance and safety standards. Maintaining this commitment starts with procurement of quality materials and parts. This is clearly evident in the history of automotive recalls. To date, most recalls are the result of subassembly failure.

Engineering support from suppliers is becoming more critical. Increased foreign competition has required American producers to increase productivity in order to remain competitive. Vendors, in turn, are being pressed to improve their productivity and share gains in the form of lower prices. Engineering support to complement changes in methods or technology is required to meet this objective. Participation of vendors in initial product design or subsequent design changes, through value engineering efforts, is the way in which supplier engineering support is being utilized to improve productivity.

A great deal of effort on the part of purchasing personnel involves price negotiation and cost reduction. To determine a fair price and quantity discount schedule, it may be necessary to study supplier operations to develop a detailed understanding of supplier costs. Such an understanding of cost is integral to evaluate make-buy decisions.

Lowest unit price is not always the least-total-cost procurement option. Price must be viewed in terms of quality and consistency of supply. Poor quality is costly because of the value added to the part in form, time, and place utility. There are additional costs in having to return a part. Another factor to be considered in price evaluation is the possible disruption of production waiting for usable parts. Perhaps most important are the costs incurred if poor-quality parts were not discovered until they are incorporated into a final product.

Another element that influences cost is logistics. The objective is to design and operate an efficient system for acquiring procured items. To accomplish this objective, transportation, inventory, ordering communication, and storage and handling must be integrated into a balanced support system. In this respect the logistical cost required to gain possession must be carefully evaluated in source selection. Although a particular vendor may offer the lowest purchase price for a quality part, the logistical cost may prohibit doing business with that vendor.

With raw materials, the best price may well change as a function of supply and demand. The timing of purchases must be based on an appraisal of most likely future prices as well as the cost associated with maintaining stockpiles. A substantial element of risk is involved in procurement, which can make hedging economically justifiable at times.

Supply Base Selection and Relations

In determining the appropriate number of suppliers to ensure continuous supply, information is required concerning vendor business risks, capacity, and committed volume. To avoid erratic availability and to promote supplier relations it may be necessary to establish long-term commitments. The serious nature of maintaining continuity is easily understood when one considers the high cost of manufacturing disruption. If the shortage of mateials or parts causes work stoppage, the burden of manufacturing cost continues because of labor and capital commitments. In addition, an unplanned work stoppage will have a direct impact upon customer service performance. At the very least, the orderly processes of physical distribution will be disrupted as high-cost emergency measures are required to service customers.

Many firms are trying to reduce the number of suppliers with whom they do business. Although this may increase the supply risk, potential gains such as reduced variability in product, simplified communications, greater willingness on the part of suppliers to improve products may enhance relations.

Another benefit of good will with vendors concerns the inevitable emergencies that develop regardless of how well the operations plan is established. The ability to compensate for sudden failure of a supply source or to increase production rapidly may depend upon the willingness of suppliers to substantially modify operations. At times it may be necessary to cancel outstanding commitments or return materials or parts when actual sales lag behind forecast or when a product is discontinued. The ability to get full vendor cooperation in such situations is in part a question of economic leverage. However, if a positive relationship exists between purchasing and the supplier, such situations can be handled with a minimum of friction.

Scheduled Delivery Requirements

The time-sensitive requirements characteristic of MRP-II and JIT logics demand frequent delivery. Scheduled transportation requirements may require that components be delivered to the exact place in a manufacturing plant where they will be used. The performance of scheduled delivery requires that vendors be given exact information concerning quantity, delivery time, and location. Both buyers and sellers place a great deal of attention on quality information. Suppliers need to provide exact lead-time information. Purchasers must provide accurate requirements information to suppliers as far in advance as possible.

The key concept that must dominate buyer-seller relationships is *responsiveness*. If enterprises aspire to implement market-paced manufacturing, it follows that master production schedules will be held open longer and that they will be subjected to more frequent changes. The delay in freezing the MPS will reduce the response time available to the supplier network. Each change in the MPS will require purchase order adjustments that could whiplash throughout the supplier network.

To realize stable supply, an increased openness in business relationships is required between buyers and sellers. This openness is facilitated by computer-based two-way information exchange.

Conclusion—Purchasing Strategies

Traditional purchasing concepts have been dramatically changed by the emphasis on integrated logistics. Primary emphasis on price negotiation is being replaced by a partnership relationship between buyers and sellers. To receive the vendor support and responsiveness required to implement market-paced manufacturing, buyers are reducing their number of suppliers and providing longer-term contract commitments. The dominant view of purchase price is one that reflects the true value received from a vendor. Unlike typical past practice, the low-price vendor will not automatically receive a contract. Vendors who offer the lowest total cost for the full range of services provided will be the preferred suppliers.

SUMMARY

Many logistical costs are hidden between specific operations and are extremely difficult to identify and control. In addition, the actions of a specific unit of an enterprise can cause expensive duplication or the need to perform, logistical activities that might not otherwise be required. The attention directed to logistical interfaces and decision processes seeks to improve the productivity of overall logistical operations.

Logistical performance must be planned and executed in an uncertain environment. To assure the development of feasible strategic business plans, attention must be directed to a careful evaluation of environmental trends and past performance. Such planning requires coordination within the logistical system and between other critical processes within the enterprise.

The performance-cycle structure provides a logic for combining the nodes, links, and levels that are essential to physical distribution, manufacturing support, and purchasing operations. A great many similarities exist between performance cycles dedicated to these three vital areas of logistics. It is also important to understand that a number of critical differences exist between the nature and degree of control between physical distribution, manufacturing support, and purchasing operations. These similarities and differences are critical to planning and controlling the logistical process.

Considerable attention in this chapter has been directed to logistical resource planning (LRP) as an overall control process. While at times the various labels appear like alphabet soup, it is significant for each management to work out a scheme to realize effective information management. The various tools available should be adopted, modified, or rejected in an effort to realize effective control. The key to today's environment is to utilize state-of-the-art communication assistance and integrated data-base management to realize control objectives. LRP provides one scheme to achieve this control.

The final sections of the chapter dealt with strategies that are available to guide operations within the specific areas of physical distribution, manufacturing support, and purchasing. While several of these strategies involve the how of marketing and manufacturing, they have a profound impact on the what, when, and where of logistics requirements.

Attention in Chapter 3 is directed to marketing and customer service requirements that drive logistical requirements.

QUESTIONS

1. Discuss and illustrate the following statement: "The only constant in today's dynamic business environment is change."
2. Provide examples of specific industries that failed to properly monitor the business environment.
3. Can a logistical system be effective and not efficient? Can it be efficient and not effective?
4. Describe the fundamental differences between the purchasing, manufacturing support, and physical distribution cycles as they relate to logistical control.

5. Discuss uncertainty as it relates to a multicheloned logistical network.
6. What role does the statement of distribution requirements (SDR) play in the overall process of logistical resource planning (LRP)?
7. Discuss the relationship between MPS, MRP, BOM, and CRP. Be specific regarding feedback and establishment of the final logistics plan.
8. Provide examples of assembly and geographic postponement from your experience.
9. Discuss the concepts of market-paced and anticipatory manufacturing.
10. What is the impact of the just-in-time logic on purchasing strategy? What new vendor criteria does JIT create?

CHAPTER 3

Customer Service and Marketing Strategy

The fundamental objective of logistical management is to effectively meet customer needs by providing timely and accurate product delivery. As a prerequisite to logistical system design, it is imperative to determine the customer service deliverables contained within the overall marketing strategy. This chapter focuses attention on the formulation of a customer service policy.

Logistical management's ability to impact revenue generation is determined by customer service. This chapter discusses customer service as an interface between marketing and logistical management. The first section discusses the role of logistics in strategic marketing. Customer service strategies for various market environments are reviewed. The second section reviews distribution channel strategies and their impact on marketing and logistics. Next, customer service performance measures are identified and discussed. The fourth section discusses the role of customer service administration by providing a conceptual approach for formulating and implementing a customer service program. The final section identifies a procedure for designing a customer service strategy.

LOGISTICS IN STRATEGIC MARKETING

The objective of this section is to position logistics within the overall marketing mix. The first part discusses logistics as a marketing mix element. The second part positions the importance of logistics within marketing. The final part describes logistical requirements for supporting marketing.

Logistics as a Marketing Mix Element

In contemporary business the predominant philosophy of enterprise planning is a marketing orientation. Such an orientation is designed to underscore the need for successful penetration of markets and the importance of profitable transactions for the survival of an enterprise. This posture, referred to as the marketing concept, emerged during the shift from a seller's market to a buyer's market following World War II.[1]

The marketing concept is a market-based planning philosophy based on identifying customer needs and mobilizing resources to serve specific needs.[2] The marketing concept begins with the goal of satisfying consumer needs at a profit. All enterprises systems must be integrated toward this fundamental goal. If an enterprise is to survive, all systems—marketing, manufacturing, finance, and logistics—must function as a totality aimed at generation of profitable transactions.[3] The marketing concept provides the integrative force for corporate strategic planning.

Three basic pillars support the marketing concept: (1) customer needs are more basic than products, (2) products must be viewed in an end-use concept, and (3) volume is secondary to profit. Each of these is discussed.

The notion that customer needs are more basic than products places a priority upon studying market opportunities to determine which products are needed and will be purchased. Products that can be manufactured economically may or may not be sold profitably, depending upon customer needs. All products will die over time as new and better methods of satisfying consumer needs are discovered through research and development. Thus, the marketing concept begins with an in-depth study of markets in order to identify potential product opportunities. Once a marketing opportunity is isolated, a product may or may not materialize, depending upon the feasibility of successful production, adequate financial resources, logistical capability, and marketing skill. The opportunity for profitable transactions initiates in the marketplace—customer needs are more basic than products.

For successful marketing, products must be viewed in an end-use context. This second pillar of the marketing concept stresses that products be placed in a context where customers can readily make the transition from concept to use. Once again, the integration of total available resources is required. Four

---

[1] J. B. McKitterick, "Profitable Growth—The Challenge to Marketing Management," speech before the 45th National Conference of the American Marketing Association, June 20, 1962.

[2] For a full development of this concept, see Thomas A. Staudt, Donald A. Taylor, and Donald J. Bowersox, *A Managerial Introduction to Marketing*, 3rd ed. (Englewood Cliffs, N.J.: Prentice-Hall, Inc., 1976), Chapter 2.

[3] Ibid.

economic utilities add value to a product in a use context: (1) form, (2) possession, (3) time, and (4) place utility. The product's *form* utility is generated during the manufacturing process. Marketing creates the *possession* utility in the product by informing the potential customer of the product's availability and facilitating the exchange transaction of the overall process. Logistics creates *time* and *place* utility. Thus, marketing can specify the color, shape, and style of the product and create a convenient and economical transaction between buyer and seller. Manufacturing can build a high-quality product at the lowest possible unit cost. It remains for logistics to ensure that the right product is at the right place at the right time. Profitable transactions will materialize only if all four utilities are integrated in an end-use context.

The final pillar of the marketing concept highlights the importance of stressing profitability rather than volume in selecting priorities.[4] The important success measure is not the number of units sold but rather the degree of profitability resulting from accumulated transactions. Therefore, variations in all forms of the utility offered—form, possession, time, and place—can be economically justified if a particular market segment is willing to pay for the adjustment in offering. Markets typically consist of many different segments, each of which has a particular product preference. The refinement of market segmentation and product differentiation acknowledges that all aspects of an offering are subject to modification when justified on the basis of profitability.[5] The integrated marketing concept provides the foundation for planning overall operations for all facets of an enterprise.

Many attempts have been made to describe the managerial marketing activities. For purposes of illustration, the functional approach developed by Staudt, Taylor, and Bowersox is adopted. These authors describe integrated managerial marketing in terms of nine functions required to support profitable marketing transactions. The functions are: (1) market delineation, (2) purchase behavior motivation, (3) product-service adjustment, (4) channel selection, (5) physical distribution, (6) communications, (7) pricing, (8) organization, and (9) administration. Table 3–1 provides a brief definition of the managerial emphasis for each function.

This brief review of the functions of managerial marketing stresses the role of marketing as one part of the enterprise engaged in implementing the marketing concept. Two points are of particular importance. First, a clear distinction should be maintained between a market-oriented philosophy of planning as contrasted to those functions associated with the execution of the marketing task. Second, it is important to realize the integral nature of logistical operations to marketing performance. Although logistics has been introduced as a major system of the enterprise, considerable overlap exists between the logistical tasks and the marketing tasks. Prior to discussing the logistical requirements for marketing support, the importance of logistics within marketing is established.

---

[4] J. B. McKitterick, op. cit.

[5] The classic article on this point is Wendell R. Smith, "Product Differentiation and Market Segmentation as Alternative Marketing Strategies," *Journal of Marketing*, Vol. 20 (July 1956), pp. 3–8. Also see Theodore Levitt, "Marketing Myopia," *Harvard Business Review*, Vol. 38 (July–August 1960), pp. 45–56. More recent treatments are found in R. C. Blattberg and S. K. Sen, "Market Segmentation Using Models of Multidimensional Purchasing Behavior," *Journal of Marketing*, Vol. 38 (October 1974), pp. 17–28; and J. T. Plummer, "The Concept and Application of Life Cycle Segmentation," *Journal of Marketing*, Vol. 38 (January 1974), pp. 33–37.

TABLE 3–1 Managerial Functions of Marketing Defined

1. The *market delineation function*—the determination and measurement of potential purchasers and their identifying characteristics.
2. The *purchase behavior motivation function*—the assessment of those direct and indirect factors that underline, impinge upon, and influence purchase behavior.
3. The *product-service adjustment function*—those activities required to match the product-service offering with the market in which it is to be purchased and consumed.
4. The *channel selection function*—the selection and organization of institutions through which the product-service offering is made available to the marketplace.
5. The *physical distribution function*—the actual movement of goods from points of production to points of consumption.
6. The *communications function*—the design and transmitting of information and messages between the buyer and seller to the end that the most favorable climate for the seller is created in the marketplace.
7. The *pricing function*—the determination and administration of prices that meet the objectives of the enterprise.
8. The *organization function*—the structuring and incentive of human resources.
9. The *administration function*—the formulation of operating procedures and standards to control pretransaction and transaction performance and the measurement of posttransaction feedback to generate satisfactory marketing performance on a continuing basis.

Source: Adapted from Thomas A. Staudt, Donald A. Taylor, and Donald J. Bowersox, *A Managerial Introduction to Marketing*, 3rd ed. (Englewood Cliffs, N.J.: Prentice-Hall, Inc., 1976), p. 53.

Logistical Importance in Marketing

Marketing managers have traditionally dealt with the 4 Ps of product, price, promotion, and place. The product encompasses the physical attributes and characteristics of the product itself. Price encompasses the resources that must be expended to acquire title to the product. In addition to the exchange price, this component must include the costs associated with transportation, time, and financing. Promotion includes the resources allocated to advertising and promotion. Place, which includes physical distribution and marketing channels, is the concern of logistical management. The integrated combination of resources allocated to product, price, promotion, and place is termed the *marketing mix*. When developing the overall enterprise marketing strategy, management is concerned with resource allocation to individual mix components.

To determine the marketing mix, management must identify the relative emphasis to place on logistics. This evaluation requires that management determine the importance customers place on product availability in comparison to other marketing mix elements. A 1976 National Council of Physical Distribution Management Study by La Londe and Zinszer evaluated the relative importance of marketing mix elements for a number of different industries.[6] For each industry, managers were requested to allocate 100 points

[6] Adapted from Bernard J. La Londe and Paul H. Zinszer, *Customer Service: Meaning and Measurement* (Chicago: National Council of Physical Distribution Management., 1976), pp. 17–79.

TABLE 3–2   Logistics Importance Within Marketing Mix

Industry	All Manufac- turing	Chemicals/ Plastics	Food Manufac- turing	Pharma- ceuticals	Elec- tronics	Merchan- dise	Con- sumer Goods	Indus- trial Goods
Marketing Mix Element								
Product	38	38	36	47	48	30	31	28
Price	24	26	27	20	14	23	23	17
Customer service	20	18	15	12	22	25	23	39
Advertising, sales promotion	18	18	22	21	16	22	23	16
Total	100	100	100	100	100	100	100	100

Source: Adapted from Bernard J. La Londe and Paul H. Zinszer, *Customer Service: Meaning and Measurement* (Chicago: National Council of Physical Distribution Management, 1976), pp. 17–79.

among marketing mix elements to determine those perceived as most important. The research utilized the term *customer service* to represent the entire *place* marketing mix element. Table 3–2 lists the average relative importance placed on the various marketing mix elements by categories of industry. Note that the table presents the average perceived importance for an industry so the perceptions of an individual enterprise may vary. The table illustrates that customer service generally ranked behind product and price and is generally ranked more important than promotion. However, it is interesting to note that the importance of customer service increases significantly when dealing with industrial goods. Using the results of published surveys and marketing research, management must establish the relative importance of logistics for their specific situation.[7]

The second consideration in establishing logistical importance within marketing is to identify the potential impact of inadequate customer service performance. Table 3–3 lists potential problems associated with inadequate logistical support of marketing. The table lists the percentage of customers responding by type of reaction to inadequate customer service.[8] As Table 3–3 indicates, typical reactions range from a call to a salesperson or manager to stoppage of all purchases. Since many of these reactions may have significant impact on the long-term viability and profitability of an enterprise, manage-

[7] Other articles discussing the importance of customer service include Harvey N. Shycon and Christopher R. Sprague, "Put a Price Tag on Your Customer Service Levels, *Harvard Business Review*, Vol. 53 (July–August 1975), pp. 71–78, see also Ray T. Sanford and Jack W. Farrell, "A Study of Customer Service Perceptions, Requirements, and Effects on American Industry," *Proceedings of the 1982 Annual Conference* (Chicago: National Council of Physical Distribution Management), pp. 233–46.

[8] Steven G. Baritz and Lorin Zissman. "Research Customer Service the Right Way," *Proceedings of the 1983 Annual Conference.* (Chicago: National Council of Physical Distribution Management), pp. 608–19.

TABLE 3–3 Reactions to Inadequate Distribution Support of Marketing

	Per Cent Customers
Reduced volume	29
Call salesperson or manager	26
Stopped all purchases	18
Discontinued specific item	16
Refused to purchase new items	9
Refused to support promotion	2

Source: Steven G. Baritz and Lorin Zissman, "Research Customer Service the Right Way," *Proceedings of the 1983 Annual Conference* (Chicago: National Council of Physical Distribution Management, 1983), p. 611.

ment must consider the likely outcome when determining customer service policy. Another study investigated the relative impact of the quality and level of customer service for American industry as a whole.[9] The results indicate that, within a limited range, a 1 per cent customer service improvement yields a 1 per cent increase in market share. Conversely, noncompetitive customer service levels lead to faster declines in market share than if competitive service was being provided.

The brief review of available research provides an indication of the importance of logistics to overall marketing and the potential impact of poor customer service. The results demonstrate that customer service performance significantly impacts marketing effectiveness. To be effective, the logistical strategy must be integrated into overall marketing strategy. Conversely, a marketing strategy without the inclusion of logistics is incomplete.

Logistical Requirements for Marketing Support

This part identifies two major logistical requirements for effective marketing support: (1) market requirements and (2) strategic requirements. Market requirements are imposed by customer needs and are dependent upon the product and type of customer. Strategic requirements result from enterprise policy.

Market Requirements

The type of customer determines the basic customer service requirements that must be satisfied. As a general rule, consumer markets are less concerned with the customer service performance than industrial markets. One classification of market requirements is based on three time dimensions of the marketing transaction: (1) pretransaction, (2) transaction, and (3) posttransaction.[10] The pretransaction aspect of marketing includes activities necessary to create a meeting of minds among parties favorable to ownership transfer. Within

[9] Sanford and Farrell, op. cit., pp. 243–44.

[10] Adapted from Staudt, Taylor, and Bowersox, op. cit., p. 48.

TABLE 3–4 Market Requirements for Marketing Support

	Consumer Markets	Industrial Markets
Pretransaction Elements		
1. Written statement of policy		———————→
2. Customer receives policy statement		———————→
3. Organizational structure		———————→
4. System flexibility		———————→
5. Management services		———————→
Transaction Elements		
1. Stock-out level	←———————	
2. Order information		———————→
3. Elements of order cycle		———————→
4. Expedite shipments		———————→
5. Transship		———————→
6. System accuracy		———————→
7. Order convenience	←———————	
8. Product substitution	←———————	
Posttransaction Elements		
1. Installation, warranty, alterations, repairs, parts		———————→
2. Products tracing		———————→
3. Customer claims, complaints, returns	←———————	
4. Temporary product replacement		———————→
5. Implies increasing importance from one market type relative to another		———————→

Source: Listing of elements adapted from Bernard J. La Londe and Paul H. Zinszer, *Customer Service: Meaning and Measurement* (Chicago: National Council of Physical Distribution Management, 1976).

logistics, these pretransaction elements include product availability and quoted order cycle time. The transaction aspect of marketing administration concerns all activities that must be performed between the time a meeting of the minds occurs among parties and the actual transfer of ownership. Within the logistics framework, the transaction elements include the capability to expedite orders, to back order products, to substitute products, to provide order and delivery status, and to correct errors and damage on a timely basis. The posttransaction aspect of administration is concerned with the state of affairs that exists between buyer and seller after the ownership transfer is completed. This includes the ability to provide the actual delivery date and to provide life cycle support such as warranty and postwarranty service such as parts and repair.

Table 3–4 characterizes consumer and industrial markets in terms of their specific requirements for transaction elements. While the table provides a general indication of requirements for each broad market category, there are many situations where the characteristics of a specific customer will differ from those presented. The important point is to identify the characteristics of a specific target market. Once the customer's critical customer service dimensions are identified, the firm can develop a strategy to satisfy target market requirements. In addition to identifying and designing market needs, it is also necessary to appraise strategic requirements.

Strategic Requirements

From the discussion thus far, it is clear that logistics provides far more than passive support for marketing. In addition to economical delivery, customer service represents a strategic source of competitive superiority.

The marketing mix must be dynamic with respect to changes in the marketplace and competition. Thus, the level and response aspects of customer service will differ depending upon the specific situation confronted. Logistical strategic performance is examined in terms of tactical adjustments, new product support, service/cost trade-offs, and distribution channel support.

Tactical Adjustment Across Product Life Cycle. Perhaps the best illustration of the need for dynamic logistical performance is the product life cycle. The product-life-cycle concept has been developed by marketing planners to illustrate the varying competitive conditions which are expected during the market life of a product.[11] Figure 3–1 illustrates a four-stage product life cycle: (1) introductory, (2) growth, (3) saturation-maturity, and (4) obsolescence-decline. Detailed discussion of all marketing ramifications associated with each stage of the life cycle is beyond the scope of this book. The illustrations, however, emphasize that the firm's marketing mix should be different in each stage and that expectations concerning logistical performance should also vary.

[11] For an interesting discussion of overall marketing strategy during the product life cycle, see Theodore Levitt, "Exploit the Product Life Cycle," *Harvard Business Review*, Vol. 43 (November–December 1965), pp. 81–94, or John E. Smallwood, "The Product Life Cycle: A Key to Strategic Marketing Planning," *Business Topics*, Vol. 12 (Winter 1973), p. 30. For a discussion of the changing customer service requirements across the product life cycle, see John C. Chambers, Satinder K. Mullick, and Donald D. Smith, "How to Choose the Right Forecasting Technique," *Harvard Business Review*, Vol. 49 (July–August 1971), pp. 47–76.

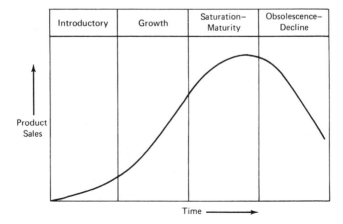

Figure 3–1   Product-Life-Cycle Concept

During the introductory stage of a new product, a high level and responsive logistical performance are desirable. Since the primary objective is to gain a market foothold, a high premium is placed on having available stock for customers to draw upon and providing rapid and consistent service on replacement orders. For example, a retail chain may add a new product but invest in only a slim stock. If the product gains customer acceptance, rapid reorder is required. There must also be a high degree of marketing communication during the introductory stage as potential customers are informed of product availability and persuaded to purchase. Product shortages during this critical time could dilute the impact of the introductory marketing strategy. Thus, during the introductory stage, logistics plays a prominent role in the integrated marketing offering. Since the market position is not secure, shipment sizes tend to be small and the frequency of orders erratic as customers do not want to be left holding unsalable merchandise. As a result of these characteristics of introductory markets, logistical costs associated with providing the necessary service level are high.

During the growth stage of the product life cycle, the product has gained market acceptance, and sales become more predictable. Logistical emphasis during the growth stage shifts from high customer service levels to a more balanced service/cost performance. Thus, customer service standards may be reduced in an effort to realize a reduction in delivered unit cost. Expanded market coverage and a high level of profitability in transactions is characteristic of the growth stage of the product life cycle. Terms and conditions of sale are adjusted to reflect economies associated with physical flow and efforts made to encourage maximum efficiency. During the growth stage, an enterprise experiences maximum latitude in controlling logistical performance to realize low total cost.

The saturation-maturity stage is characterized by intense competition. A product confronts extensive competition from a variety of substitutes, with price manipulation a typical competitive tactic. Logistical performance during the saturation stage is expected to become highly selective. Competitors adjust their service performance to provide high levels of availability and response to major customers. Higher expenditures are allocated to logistical performance to assure service to those customers who represent the core of the enterprise's market.

The product's volume declines during the obsolesence-decline stage of the product life cycle. During this period, management is faced with a decision on whether to close out the product or to continue distribution on a restricted basis. During this stage, the logistical system must support existing business while avoiding excessive risk in the event that the product is discontinued. Minimum risk thus becomes more important than achieving the lowest per-unit cost of performance.

The product life cycle illustrates the variety of logistical strategies that a firm may implement at different times. No "must do" rules exist. Logistical performance, like all other elements of the marketing mix, must be altered to strategically meet the market and competitive situation. The level and response of performance change over time, and the enterprise's willingness and ability to absorb logistical cost also vary across the life cycle. In general, this means that new product situations command higher emphasis on level of service and availability. The emphasis will shift toward service/cost trade-offs during later stages in the cycle.

As the foregoing life cycle discussion indicates, the degree of customer service and associated logistical cost must be adjusted to fit the marketing situation. In addition to change across time, the physical distribution system must maintain flexibility and adjust to complexity at any specific point in time. The requirements to support a single product throughout one life cycle may be clear. The more prevalent situation, however, involves support of multiple products serviced to different customers through multiple channels. In such a complex situation, a system must be flexible and capable of coping with change. The remainder of this part provides examples of these dynamics.

New Product Support. Logistical support of new product introductions was briefly discussed in the introductory stage of the product life cycle. It was pointed out that the typical system is expected to provide a high level of product availability and rapid order response during the introductory period.

The extent of new product activity anticipated for the future is worth discussion. In the past, growth was easily generated from existing products or acquisition of other enterprises. The pattern for future growth is expected to depend upon new product development. This changing emphasis is important to logistics for at least three reasons.

First, greater emphasis on new product development means that the logistical system must be able to accommodate a wider variation in product line. Special handling, transportation, and packaging requirements will increase as the product line expands, forcing greater system flexibility. Should the expanded product line require special equipment, such as refrigerated trucks or rail tankcars, the task of logistics becomes more complex.

A *second* consideration is the requirement to service many different markets through multiple channels. With an expanding market offering, products typically will become more specialized and will be sold to smaller and highly service-oriented market segments. To reach these markets, it may be necessary to use several different marketing channels. The result will be smaller product volume flowing through any specific channel and less opportunity to aggregate volume for cost reductions.

A *final* implication of increased new product introduction stems from the knowledge that marketing is far from an exact science when it comes to the development of new products. As noted earlier, the development of new products requires an interpretation of customer needs. In addition, the potential product must be communicated into a use context to inform and persuade potential buyers. In more than half the cases of new product development, the product offered does not experience sufficient longevity in the marketplace to recover development cost. From a logistical viewpoint, it is difficult to project which products will win or lose. Extreme care must be taken not to influence product failure by being unable to support the product during critical introductory stages. On the other hand, inventory stockpiling and anticipatory logistics to support sales that never materialize can be extremely expensive. The impact of logistics on the firm's balance sheet and income statement is becoming a concern to top management.

Customer Service Myopia. Just how much customer service should be provided to support the integrated marketing strategy is a complex strategic question. The system capacity to provide both high levels of product availability and rapid and consistent response to customer orders is costly. The next section provides a concrete illustration that the *cost* of improving the level of customer service increases at a far faster rate than the corresponding performance increases. Therefore, enterprises offering extremely high degrees of customer service will confront high total costs of logistics.

Failure on the part of managers to appreciate the relationship of incremental customer service and associated cost can result in commitments to high degrees of performance. The ideal result is the selection of a service level and response that will support sales without setting standards so high as to endanger performance. This proper degree of service can be determined only by experimentation and a willingness to formulate a policy regarding customer service to be offered.

With modern logistics technology, almost any degree of service can be provided if an enterprise is willing to pay the cost. In fact, most firms provide service in excess of that necessary for successful marketing. One of the major tasks in logistics planning is to replace the tendency to overservice with a sound approach to the determination of necessary customer service. The desire to locate a warehouse in every customer's backyard or to consign inventories must be replaced with a systematic approach to logistics. Such design should be based upon cost-revenue benefit analysis. Overcoming customer service myopia is one of the most difficult tasks of logistical planning.

Scrambled Merchandising. In today's economy, retailers sell wholesale, wholesalers sell retail, hardware stores sell soft goods, department stores sell food, food stores sell applicances, they all sell toys, and discount stores sell everything. This new structure of retailing is often referred to as scrambled merchandising or channel jumping.

Scrambled merchandising is not restricted to retailing. Finished goods often move to the same retailer from wholesalers, distributors, jobbers, assemblers, and direct from producers. In some cases, goods bypass retailers altogether and move directly to consumers. These changing patterns of shipments have forced substantial alterations in logistical support systems.

To accommodate multiple-channel physical distribution, many manufacturers and retailers have been forced into operating distribution warehouses. To a significant degree, manufacturer warehouses have replaced many of the specialized wholesalers, such as food and hardware, who were once the dominant distribution channel members. Such specialized intermediaries were unable to service adequately the distribution patterns of multiple channels.

Thus today's complex business arena demands that an enterprise provide physical distribution service within many different channels. The simple task of delivering almost all manufacturing output to a few wholesalers has been replaced by a variety of physical fulfillment systems delivering to numerous customer warehouses and, in many cases, direct to retail stores. Under multichannel distribution, less volume is delivered to any one location, which often results in higher per-unit costs. On the other hand, customer demands for high degree of service exist, since no intermediary exists between manufacturer and retailers in many channels. The practice of channel jumping has simultaneously increased the complexity of physical distribution and reinforced the need for operational flexibility.

Cost/Benefit Analysis. The importance of not being customer service myopic with regard to establishing service levels that are unnecessarily high was discussed

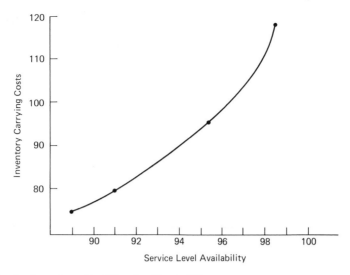

Figure 3–2   Inventory Cost/Service Trade-Off

earlier. The important point is that the customer service level must be justified in terms of relative costs and benefits.

The evaluation should take the form of an analysis of the costs of providing a specified service level with the potential gains that all expected. The following example illustrates an approach for this analysis.

In an effort to identify the most appropriate customer service level, it is necessary to identify the relationship between the benefits of stock availability and the inventory costs associated with holding that stock. Figure 3–2 illustrates the basic relationship. the horizontal axis is customer service level in terms of a quantity fill rate. The vertical axis is the cost of holding inventory. The figure illustrates that the inventory holding costs increase at an increasing rate as the customer service requirements increase. The service level or availability is expressed in terms of the percentage of quantity that could be shipped when ordered. The inventory holding costs are the costs incurred due to investment, risk, taxes, and insurance. Chapter 7 discusses inventory costing in detail.

Assuming the current policy is to offer customers a 91 per cent availability rate, the inventory cost and service curve can be used to evaluate the costs and benefits of alternatives. Table 3–5 summarizes the cost impact of service changes from the current 91 per cent based on the relationship in Figure 3–2. As shown in the table, reducing the service level to 89 per cent reduces the inventory holding cost by $48,000, while increasing the service level to 98 per cent increases the cost by $391,000. While it is not difficult to identify the

TABLE 3–5   Total Cost Impact for Service Change from 91 Per Cent Level

Cost savings for service reduction to 89 per cent	$ 48,000
Cost increase for service increase to 95 per cent	$166,000
Cost increase for service increase to 98 per cent	$391,000

TABLE 3–6   Incremental Sales for Break-even Profits (000s of Dollars)

Net Profit as A Per Cent of Sales	89% Alternative	91% Existing	95% Alternative	98% Alternative
At 2% net of sales	(2,400)	0	8,300	19,550
At 4% net of sales	(1,200)	0	4,150	9,775
At 6% net of sales	(800)	0	2,766	6,517
At 8% net of sales	(600)	0	2,075	4,888
At 10% net of sales	(480)	0	1,660	3,910

cost impact, the resulting benefits are more difficult to determine. Table 3–6 illustrates one approach to identify the benefits necessary to break even with increased service levels. If net profits are 2 per cent of sales and service level is decreased from the current 91 to 89 per cent, the break-even point is $2.4 million in sales. In other words, a loss of up to $2.4 million in sales owing to the reduced service level, could be experienced while still being better off because of the reduction in inventory cost. Conversely, if the service level is increased from the current 91 per cent to 98 per cent, the increased sales required, assuming that the net profit is 2 per cent of sales, is $19.55 million to break even. If management does not believe that the sales increase is possible, then the increased service level is not justified. The table summarizes the break-even points for other service levels and net profit levels.

The above approach illustrates cost/benefit analysis that is part of the customer service decision. It is a primary role of logistics to position customer service within the other components of the marketing mix and evaluate the alternative costs and benefits.[12]

CHANNEL STRATEGIES TO SUPPORT MARKETING AND LOGISTICS

As a part of establishing a customer service strategy, it is important to identify distribution channel requirements and create a structure to support the desired logistical operations. This section discusses logistics in a channel context, identifies some of the functions that the channel must perform, and presents alternative channel strategies. One of the basic realizations about specialization in trade is the fact that no single enterprise can be self-sufficient. Regardless of the size of an enterprise and the vastness of its operation, it must rely upon other organizations to provide selected services and materials. Thus, attention is directed to selected aspects of the distribution channel environment.

Among the least-understood areas of business are the institutional and activity groupings referred to as distribution or marketing channels. Distribu-

---

[12] Another example of the application of a trade-off analysis in setting customer service is demonstrated in W. D. Perreault and F. A. Russ, "Improving Physical Distribution Decisions with Trade-off Analysis," *International Journal of Physical Distribution and Materials Management*, Vol. 7, No. 93. (1977), pp. 117–27.

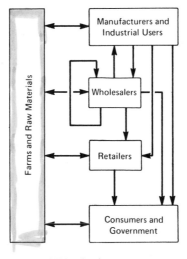

Figure 3–3 Typical Channels of Distribution

tion structure is of fundamental importance because the channel is the arena within which marketing and logistics culminate in customer transactions. The American Marketing Association defined the distribution channel as the structure of intracompany organizational units and extracompany agents and dealers, wholesale and retail, through which a commodity, product, or service is marketed. The distribution channel is a grouping of intermediaries who take title to a product during the marketing process, from first owner to last owner.

Figure 3–3 provides a graphic illustration of the typical institutional arrangement alternatives found at all levels of the marketing process. Of particular interest in Figure 3–3 are the many institutions that products or materials may pass through and the alternative paths they can follow between original owner and final buyer. For example, retail stores may purchase from all levels of supply, from farm to wholesaler.

One advantage of a channel flow diagram is that it places the multiplicity of institutions used in modern marketing into a logical sequence. However, the simplicity of the flow diagram understates the complexities involved in selecting a channel structure for an individual enterprise. Appendix I provides a more comprehensive review of the various ways channels of distribution are treated in the marketing literature. To fully understand the importance of channel considerations in operational system design, it is important to view the logistical process in a multienterprise structure.

The Channelwide Logistical Process

The logistical channel consists of a number of independent enterprises which combine to deliver product and material assortments to the right location at the proper time. A number of functions must be performed jointly by all channel members in the logistical process. From the total channel viewpoint, these functions should be performed with a minimum of duplication in order to minimize overall channel costs. The following discussion expands the basic components of the single-enterprise logistical system to include multiple enterprises functioning in a channel context.

Logistical flow in a channel is analogous to the mechanics of a ratchet wrench. Physical movement is best designed for economies of one-way movement toward the final customer location. Although products often have to be returned from retailer to manufacturer, such as for repair work or product recall, reverse movement is an expensive exception rather than the rule. In today's environment of consumer protection and product liability, it is imperative that the system design considerations for reverse logistics be incorporated into the channel structure.

The distribution channel must be designed to perform five basic functions. These functions are: (1) Adjustment, (2) transfer, (3) storage, (4) handling, and (5) communications. Each is described.

Adjustment

The adjustment function has received considerable attention in marketing literature. Adjustment is concerned with the creation of an assortment of goods. At some geographical point or points in the distribution channel, goods must be concentrated, selected, and dispersed to the next location level.

Concentration refers to the collection of large quantities of a single good or large groupings of several goods specified for final sale in an assortment. A manufacturer's distribution warehouse is a prime example of a logistical concentration point. Large shipments of products produced at various factories are transferred to the distribution warehouse. The distribution warehouse, in turn, holds concentrations until an order is received for a particular assortment. The concept of concentration reduces the number of channel relationships required since the manufacturers and retailers must only deal with a single distributor instead of requiring each manufacturer to deal with each retailer.

The process of gathering individual products into an assortment is referred to as *selection*. The selection process results in custom grouping of products to satisfy one customer's specifications. Manufacturers commonly offer customers mixed carloads or truckloads of products. Such mixed shipments allow customers to carry the minimum necessary inventory of all items in the product line while retaining the benefits of the lower freight rates per unit that result from volume shipments.

Dispersement consists of placing selected assortments in the right place at the proper time. Dispersement represents the final level of performance and results in customer service.

The particular enterprise performing the overall adjustment function may be company-operated or a specialized channel intermediary. Wholesalers find economic justification in performing the adjustment function and thereby reduce the risk on the part of other channel members. Over the past several years, merchant wholesalers have increased at the very time when vertical integration by large retailers and manufacturers was to have eliminated their economic justification. It would appear that the economies of vertical integration may not offset the corresponding loss of innovative specialization and risk spreading. The strategically placed merchant wholesaler is able to perform the adjustment function for a number of different retailers and manufacturers, thereby reducing the risk as well as the number of transactions required in the total logistical process.

Transfer

The transfer function consists of the mechanics of concentration and dispersement. A single good or an assortment of goods must be physically transported to support transactions. In the collection phase of the adjustment function, the typical transfer consists of large, limited commodity shipments. In the dispersement phase, the typical transfer is a product assortment. As a general rule, transfers related to dispersement are more costly than concentration. Concentration is typically a maximum-volume movement between manufacturers and wholesalers. Chapter 5 and 6 discuss transportation strategies.

Storage

The storage function occurs in the logistical channel owing to the great deal of concentration, selection, and dispersement that are performed in anticipation of future transactions. Since there are typically conditions of uncertainty for both demand and supply, the logistical process typically incorporates safety inventory to accommodate transaction requirements. Chapter 7, Inventory, discusses inventory strategies.

Handling

The handling function is one of the most costly aspects of channel performance. Once a concentrated quantity or an assortment of goods reaches a transfer point, shuffling begins. Cartons are moved in, placed, moved about, moved about more, and finally moved out. The objective is to reduce handling in the logistical channel to an absolute minimum. Each handling operation has a separate and unique cost in addition to increasing the potential for product damage. Consequently, the fewer the total handlings in the channel, the lower the total cost. Channel structures requiring the movement of product or material through several different facilities represent one of the most excessive areas of logistical duplication. Chapter 8, Warehousing and Packaging, identifies and discusses the strategies to accommodate handling.

Communication

Communication is a two-way function in the logistical channel. In one direction, messages relay customer orders. In the other direction, communication assures desired end results such as shipment expediting. Channel communication is continuous as products are transferred, adjusted, and stored. Communications also exist with respect to assortment, quantity, location, and time of exchange. Chapter 4, Forecasting and Order Management, discusses communication requirements.

From initial stimulant to feedback, direct communication costs are overshadowed by the cost of a faulty message. Since a great deal of logistical action is initiated in anticipation of future transactions, communications containing overly optimistic predictions or projections may stimulate a fever of ultimately useless work. Analysis of communications between channel members suggests that anticipation has a tendency to amplify as it proceeds between participants

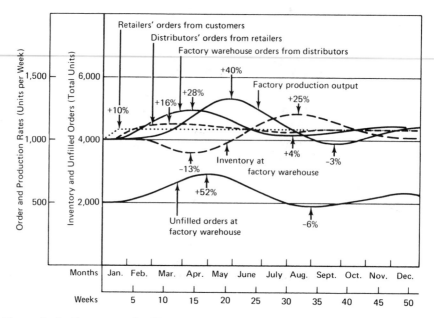

Figure 3–4 Response of a Simulated Production-Distribution System to a Sudden 10 Per Cent Increase in Sales at the Retail Level

in a logistical network. Each error in the interpretation of transaction requirements creates a disturbance for the total logistical channel. In a classical work, Forrester simulated channel interrelationships to demonstrate how the total channel may enter into an oscillating corrective pattern, resulting in a series of over- and underadjustments to real market requirements.[13] Figure 3–4 illustrates the channel inventory oscillations that were simulated when the retailer increases demand by 10 per cent.

By the very nature of its mission, a distribution channel must be sensitive to transaction requirements. The system stands ready to initiate the logistical process upon receipt of a message. Extreme care must be taken to structure the communication function with a high degree of reliability while retaining the flexibility required for change and adaptation.

Interorganizational Considerations

Since a sequence of functions must be performed in the logistical process, it is not surprising that a number of individual enterprises combine to create a channel. Only through coordination can transaction requirements be fully satisfied. Each organization exists for a reason and performs services in anticipation of a return on investment and effort. Unnecessary duplication of functions in the channel impairs the total efficiency of the combined effort. Over the long run, each channel member enjoys rewards or suffers losses based upon the success of the overall logistical channel.

---

[13] Jay W. Forrester, *Industrial Dynamics*, (Cambridge, Mass.: The MIT Press, 1961), and "Industrial Dynamics," *Harvard Business Review*, Vol. 36 (July–August 1958), p. 43.

Enterprises that make up the logistical channel are specialists in performing one or more functions. Specialization by function increases overall efficiency. The greater the degree of specialization the intermediary has in the performance of logistical functions, the less risk that specialist will assume in overall performance.

A motor carrier performing a single-transfer function in a channel incurs relatively little risk. Carriers attempt to hedge risk involvement in any single logistical channel by performing similar functions for a variety of channels. A retailer or a merchant wholesaler incurs risk in the sale of a single manufacturer's products. Each attempts to hedge risk by offering a total assortment much broader than any single manufacturer's product mix.

In contrast, a processor or manufacturer of a single product line may risk survival on the capabilities of a single distribution channel. This disproportionate risk among channel members is of central importance for logistical planning. Some channel members have a deeper vested interest in the ultimate accomplishment of successful exchange than others. Therefore, members with a greater vested interest are forced to play a more active role and assume greater responsibility for channel performance.

Without guidance, significant logistical costs may be rapidly accumulated by functional duplication. In addition, costs may be unfavorably influenced by enterprises with very little at stake in the channel. Such costs must be controlled if the channel is to realize maximum efficiency. Control in the logistical channel is difficult to realize because the only alternatives to ownership are persuasion or coercion.

Ownership control consists of vertical integration, by a single enterprise, of two or more consecutive links in the logistical channel. The ultimate in vertical integration is the manufacturer shipping via private transportation to vertically integrated warehouses and retail outlets. Such complete vertical integration is rare. The exact extent to which vertical integration has materialized during recent decades is difficult to appraise. As noted earlier, merchant wholesalers have tended to increase in number rather than decrease. Ample evidence exists that the selling intermediaries have undergone more dramatic vertical integration than the logistical specialists.

Even when a firm is vertically extended with respect to integrated wholesaling, the services of specialized transportation companies rarely can be eliminated. Sears and Wards use extensive common carrier transportation in addition to their own vast fleet of private and contract transportation. It is doubtful that a firm could ever be fully integrated in a complex society.

Tactics of persuasion and coercion are the most practical methods other than ownership for directing and controlling logistical activities. This need for common action under leadership guidance is referred to as *superorganization management*. The prerogative of spearheading coordinated activity often goes to the channel member with the greatest economic power. Domination by virtue of economic leverage comprises what are termed vertically controlled in contrast to vertically owned operations. In many situations, an enterprise coordinates the activities of specialized intermediaries through market strength. The name *channel captain* has been suggested for the enterprise able to stimulate interfirm coordination.

Although all enterprises in a logistical channel desire to cooperate, individual profit orientation and legal barriers tend to create conflict. In addition, a degree of conflict exists over those in the channel willing to assume responsibility for performance of the more risky logistical activities. The enterprise with the greatest economic power often is the one least directly concerned with the welfare of the specific channel. Under such conditions, economic power is often used to shift risk rather than stimulate coordination.

Conflict resolution in distribution channels receives substantial attention in the marketing literature. Detailed treatment is beyond the scope of this text. The essential point is that the ultimate survival of a channel may depend upon constructive leadership. This total channel perspective is particularly important to logistical operations. The interdependence is developed in greater detail in the next part.

Nature of Logistical Channels

Completion of the logistical process requires the utilization of a broad range of enterprise facilities and intermediary specialists. A facility is defined as an organizational unit engaged in the performance of all or some part of the logistical process. Thus, a distribution warehouse or a company-managed truck are logistical facilities. However, either one also may be an intermediary specialist. The warehouse may be public, and the truck may be owned and operated by a common carrier. The intermediary specialist is an independent business operated for profit. In the design of a logistical system, the services of an intermediary specialist can be substituted for those provided by the enterprise. The objective is to select the proper combination of facilities and specialists to meet objectives at the lowest total cost.

Two factors are of critical importance in planning logistical channels. First, planning must encompass the total channel rather than a single enterprise. Second, care must be exercised to select intermediary specialists for reasons of logistical competence rather than marketing capability only. Each of these considerations is discussed below.

Range of Channel Planning

The traditional approach to channel planning seldom extended beyond the legal boundaries of the enterprise because normal control and profit measurement end when a product is transferred to a new owner. Depending upon conditions and terms of sale, exchange of legal ownership is usually accomplished immediately before or after the final physical transfer of the product. However, in special cases, such as consignment selling or forward buys, a product's physical exchange may be completed long before the legal ownership exchange.

The logistical process does not end once ownership transfer occurs. It does not end when the product is turned over to the next level in the distribution channel or even when it is delivered to a buyer, unless all conditions of the transaction are satisfied. Ultimate responsibility for logistics does not end until the product in question is finally accepted by the person, family, or enterprise that will utilize it. Therefore, to properly direct logistical activities, planning horizons must transcend the total distribution channel.

Many significant costs of logistics occur between enterprises engaged in a distribution channel. As noted earlier, the control of such costs may rest with an intermediary specialist who has very little risk or vested interest in the overall success of the marketing or logistical process. For example, an infrequently used common carrier who takes 20 days to transfer a shipment scheduled for three-day delivery and delivers in split quantities of the original shipment may substantially increase total channel costs.

In addition, many costs—such as inventory holding expense—may accumulate from duplicated effort at various levels within a channel. Duplication increases the cost of total marketing resulting in channel adjustments justified on the basis of a single firm's cost-control program. Such modifications, however, may increase the costs of all other enterprises in the channel and hinder the ability of the total channel to survive. Consequently, logistical planning should be channelwide in perspective.

Intermediary Selection

A second factor of prime importance in channel planning involves selection of specialized intermediaries for reasons of logistical competence. Traditionally, when an enterprise decided to locate a branch or district sales office, it was almost axiomatic that a field inventory be located at the facility. If an enterprise selected a market plan to utilize a specific wholesaler, it was assumed that the same wholesaler would inventory a full line product assortment.

This single-structure system ignores the possibility that a very effective marketing intermediary may not be either an effective or an efficient logistics intermediary. Successful marketing of an enterprise's product may require a wide range of channels to effectively reach various market segments. Using the same structure for logistical flows may force small uneconomical shipments. Substantial economies of scale and related advantages might otherwise be realized in physical flow. The most suitable structure for marketing channels may not, and often is not, satisfactory for logistical operations.

The Concept of Channel Separation

The term *structure* is widely used to describe a number of interrelationships which are part of, but subordinate to, the whole. Thus, the arrangement and interrelationship of a logistical system are properly viewed as the system's structure. In logistical channels, structure relates to the framework for processing basic flows that pass through the channel. Careful analysis and classification of such flows provide the basis for specialization of effort.

Several authors have developed the idea of flow separation within the overall structure of the distribution channel.[14] The present approach singles out two

[14] A number of authors have developed the flow concept; contributions of noteworthy mention in the authors' opinion were presented by Roland Vaile, E. T. Grether, and Reavis Cox, *Marketing in the American Economy* (New York: Ronald Press, 1952); Ralph F. Breyer, "Some Observations on Structural Formation and Growth of Marketing Channels," in Reavis Cox, Wroe Alderson and Stanley J. Shapiro, eds., *Theory in Marketing* (Homewood, Ill.: Richard D. Irwin, Inc., 1964), pp. 163–75; George Fisk, *Marketing Systems* (New York: Harper & Row, Publishers, 1967), pp. 214–79; Louis P. Bucklin, "Postponement, Speculation, and the Structure of Distribution Channels," *Journal of Marketing Research*, Vol. 2 (February 1965), pp. 26–31; and Louis W. Stern and Adel I. El-Ansary, *Marketing Channels* (Englewood Cliffs, N.J.: Prentice-Hall, Inc., 1977), pp. 391–430.

flows. To achieve a satisfactory marketing process, a flow of transaction-creating efforts and a flow of logistical efforts must exist and be coordinated. There is no reason why these two flows must transpire sequentially through the same network of intermediaries. These two flows, logistical and transaction creating, are considered primary. All other flows in the total distribution channel are viewed as supportive.

The logic for separation of logistical fulfillment and transaction creation is based on the notion that no legal or economic laws require simultaneous treatment or performance.[15] Factors that tend to increase or decrease the total cost of physical flow have no relationship to ownership boundaries. Conversely, advertising, credit, personal selling, and other transaction-creating efforts of marketing have a significant influence upon the economics of physical flow. The responsiveness of each primary flow to specialization is unique to the circumstances surrounding that flow. In any given marketing situation, primary flows may best be accomplished by intermediary specialists. The most effective network for achieving profitable transactions may not be the most efficient arrangement of exchange intermediaries. Based upon specialization in primary flow, the overall distribution channel can be viewed as containing transaction and logistical channels.

The transaction channel consists of a group of intermediaries engaged in the process of trading. The goal of the transaction channel is to negotiate, to contract, and administer trading on a continuing basis. The full force of creative marketing action exists within the transaction channel. Participants in transaction-channel activities are marketing specialists, such as manufacturing agents, salesmen, jobbers, wholesalers, and retailers.

The logistical channel contains a network of intermediaries engaged in the functions of adjustment, transfer, storage, handling, and communication. Participants in this channel are logistical specialists. They are concerned with solving problems of time and space.

Examples of Separation

Figure 3–5 illustrates the concept of separation for the distribution of color television sets. In this situation, the transaction channel consists of five links: (1) general sales office, (2) district sales office, (3) distributor, (4) retailer, and (5) consumer. The logistical channel design consists of seven links: (1) factory warehouse, (2) company truck, (3) regional warehouse, (4) motor common carrier, (5) public warehouse, (6) local delivery, and (7) customer. Only at the point of transaction completion, the customer, do the two primary channels merge.

Figure 3–5 illustrates additional significant points. In the logistical channels, three specialized intermediaries are involved in distribution of the product. These three specialists are, at level 4, a common-carrier motor firm; at level 5, a public warehouse, and at level 6, a specialized local delivery firm. Three levels of physical distribution operation take place in the logistical channel using organization facilities of the producing enterprise. The television sets are warehoused at the factory, transported in company trucks, and stored in a

---

[15] The notion of transaction versus exchange is based on John R. Commons, *The Economics of Collective Action* (New York: Macmillan Publishing Co., Inc., 1950).

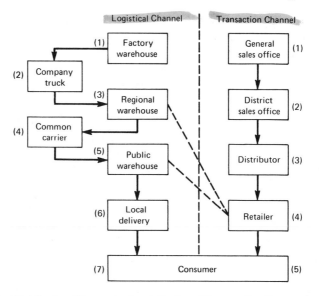

Figure 3–5 Distribution Channel—Logistical and Transaction Separation

regional warehouse before any specialized intermediary ever participates in the logistical channel.

The distributor, level 3 in the transaction channel, plays a unique role. The distributor, while never physically handling the television sets, has legal title from the time the sets leave the company warehouse (level 3, the logistical channel) until they are delivered to the consumer. Of course, the distributor could elect to warehouse in a private facility but in this example has selected to use a public warehouse specialist.

The retailer illustrated is only one of many who sell the line of television sets. The retailer displays limited sets and offers next-day delivery to consumers who enter into a transaction. Delivery is then made from the distributor's stock in the public warehouse, using the services of a specialized local delivery intermediary. When sets are required for display in the retailer's store, they may be obtained by the distributor from the factory's regional warehouse (level 3, logistical channel) or from stock in storage at the public warehouse (level 5, logistical channel). These two possibilites are illustrated as connections between the two channels utilizing common-carrier transportation.

Retailers commonly limit stocks to display models. Sales are negotiated with a commitment to deliver a specified model and color at a particular time and place. Although the transaction is initiated at a retail store, physical exchange may be completed by direct customer shipment from a warehouse strategically located many miles from the point of transaction.

An additional example of separation is the factory branch office that carries no inventory. The office exists for the sole purpose of transaction creation. The physical exchange between seller and buyer may move in a variety of combinations of transport and storage, depending upon value, size, bulk, weight, and perishability of the shipment. Generally, no economic justification exists for locating warehouses and inventories with each branch office. The network of branch offices is best selected to facilitate maximum transaction impact. The selection of logistical intermediaries is designed to achieve the desired physical performance and economies.

A final example of separation comes from the rapidly growing home delivery industry. An order placed at a local catalog desk or by phone may be drop-shipped from a distant factory directly to the buyer's home. Although the flow pattern described is only one of many observable arrangements in direct marketing, all such systems are designed to create separation and thereby the opportunity for specialization.

Interdependence of Transaction and Logistical Activities

The concept of separation of transaction and logistical flows should not be interpreted to mean that either can stand alone. The activities of both must be completed as the basis for a satisfactory sale. Both types of activities are essential to the marketing process. The major argument in favor of separation of transaction and logistics is that it increases the structural opportunities for specialization.

Separation does not necessarily require different enterprises to enjoy the benefits of specialization. The same intermediary may be very capable of performing both transaction and logistical activities. The degree of individual enterprise separation depends upon the necessity for specialization, economies of scale, available resources, and managerial capabilities. Transactions are never complete until the logistical process is fully administered. Depending upon the category of goods—convenience, shopping, or specialty—the logistical process may start in anticipation of, be simultaneous with, or follow negotiation. The final logistical act occurs in accord with specifications established during the negotiation phase of the transaction. Such specifications relate to time, location, or terms of transfer. Given specifications, minimization of logistical expense is essential to achieve a mutually satisfactory transaction.

Benefits of efficient logistics are not limited to cost reduction. By achieving time and place utility, logistics can enhance transaction capabilities. The ability to promise and provide dependable delivery of a proper assortment serves as a stimulant to purchase agreement and routinization.

CUSTOMER SERVICE PERFORMANCE

Once the overall marketing strategy has positioned customer service within the marketing mix, the next task is to operationalize the customer service program. The first part of this section provides a specific definition of customer service. The following part discusses customer service measures.

Customer Service Definition

Although most managers agree that customer service is important, the typical manager has difficulty in defining the exact meaning of the term. Two interpretations commonly used are *easy to-do-business with* and *sensitive to customer needs.*[16] While these perceptions are important from a qualitative perspective, it

---

[16] See Bernard J. La Londe and Paul H. Zinszer, op. cit., pp. 203–207, for an extensive list of corporate definitions of customer service. For the most part, the answers to the "define customer service" question were qualitative.

is difficult to interpret what *easy to-do-business with* means for a customer service representative who has to deal with the public on a daily basis. To develop a customer service strategy it is necessary to develop a working definition of customer service.

La Londe and Zinszer suggested a framework for defining customer service.[17] Customer service is illustrated through three models: (1) customer service as an activity, (2) customer service as performance levels, and (3) customer service as a management philosophy. The activity model suggests that customer service is a process to be managed, and the resulting goal is to complete the prescribed actions. The potential problem with the activity model is that actions may be completed but not achieve the desired benefits.

The second model defines customer service in terms of a series of performance levels. Examples of such an approach might be having a 95 per cent stock availability level or a 10-day order cycle time. While these performance measures facilitate the definition and measurement of customer service, the specific measures often become an end rather than the means. The measures that are identified as being important to customers must be tracked accurately. It is possible that the relative importance of the different measures may change over time. For effective customer service an enterprise must identify changes and respond accordingly. For example, when there is no product shortage, the most important measure might be consistent delivery times. On the other hand, when there is a product shortage, the customers may place more weight on product availability rather than shipment consistency.

Within the management philosophy model, the customer-oriented philosophy integrates and manages all of the elements of the customer interface within a predetermined optimum cost-service mix. Although this approach exemplifies the marketing concept, it does not provide adequate direction for managers.

The broad definition of customer service must balance elements from all three models. First, the enterprise must adopt an overall customer-oriented philosophy. This means that the management must direct resources to identify and meet customers needs. This philosophy must be instilled throughout the enterprise. Since it is difficult to measure performance against a management philosophy, the second task is to define specific measures for evaluating performance. Specific measures are usually quantitative in nature. The following discussion identifies some specific measures and their relative importance. However, the definition of service measures does not automatically satisfy customer requirements. The final task is to establish a process to perform and measure customer service activities. This task requires that the customer service managers be provided the human resources and information necessary to effectively process customer orders and provide necessary information. A complete customer service program integrates all three models to effectively meet customer requirements.

Customer Service Measurement

Chapter 2 introduced the primary customer service measures of availability, capability, and quality. This part discusses measures and measurement requirements.

---

[17] Ibid., pp. 157–59.

TABLE 3–7   Relative Importance of Customer Service Elements

Element	Importance — Manufacturing		Importance — Merchandising	
		Manufacturing		Merchandising
1. Product availability		42.7		43.1
2. Order cycle time		19.4		25.5
a. Entry	4.2		6.1	
b. Processing	5.1		4.7	
c. Pick and ship	4.9		7.9	
d. Transit time	5.2		6.8	
3. Distribution system flexibility		11.6		10.1
a. Expedite order	4.1		3.5	
b. Back order	2.6		2.0	
c. Substitute	1.6		2.2	
d. Faster transportation	2.7		2.4	
e. Other	0.6		0.0	
4. Malfunction handling		8.0		7.2
a. Administrative errors (credit)	2.1		1.1	
b. Picking errors	1.5		1.5	
c. Shipping errors	1.2		2.3	
d. Warehouse damage	1.2		0.8	
e. Company shipping damage	0.8		0.7	
f. Carrier shipping damage	0.9		0.8	
g. Other	0.3		0.0	
5. Information support		12.4		11.8
a. Inventory status	4.5		4.5	
b. Order status	3.6		3.2	
c. Data base	3.8		3.9	
d. Other	0.5		0.2	
6. Product support		5.1		2.3
a. Repair parts	1.1		0.4	
b. Repair service	1.1		0.2	
c. Technical advice	2.0		1.5	
d. Other	0.9		0.2	
7. Other		0.8		0.0
Total points		100.0		100.0

Source: Bernard J. La Londe and Paul H. Zinszer, *Customer Service: Meaning and Measurement* (Chicago: National Council of Physical Distribution Management, 1975), p. 118.

Measures

Table 3–7 summarizes attributes of the primary customer service measures and relative importance.[18] A summary is provided for both manufacturing and merchandising firms. As the table indicates, the only significant difference between the relative importance for the categories is the emphasis placed on

[18] Ibid., p. 118.

posttransaction product support by manufacturing firms. Since industrial firms typically purchase complex and critical products to support manufacturing, it is logical that they would be more concerned with the posttransaction support. Specific measures for evaluating performance are expanded below.

Availability Measures. Product availability measures ability to provide product when it is desired by the customer. This may be measured in terms of the per cent of orders, units, or lines that can be filled from existing stock. For example, a 95 per cent unit availability measure implies that the enterprise desires to fill 95 per cent of the units demanded when the order is placed. Other measures may be lines shipped complete or orders shipped complete. The shipped complete measures record the percentage of instances that orders or lines can be completely filled from existing stock.

Capability Measures. Customer service capability measures are order cycle time, distribution system flexibility, and malfunction handling capability. These measure an enterprises capability to make adjustments. The order cycle time is the customer perception of the elapsed time from when the order is placed until the shipment is received. The cycle time measures include average time and time variances associated with order communication, order processing, order consolidation, back-order delay, and delivery time. As an example, this measure may be defined by specifying that a percentage of orders be shipped or received within a ten-day cycle time.

The flexibility measure evaluates capability to provide special services for orders such as processing back-orders, providing substitute products, expediting orders, and providing faster transportation. The flexibility measure must record the relative effort involved in the changes and the enterprise's ability to respond.

The malfunction correction capability measures ability to respond to problems such as errors or damage. The errors may involve order entry, processing, picking, or shipping errors when an incorrect product or incorrect amount is sent to the customer. The damage may be incurred in the manufacturing process, warehouse handling, or transportation. Regardless of the source, the customer has received damaged goods and requires an adjustment. The measures that are appropriate to the malfunction include the number and percentage of orders that incur a malfunction, the corrective responses taken, and the cost of correcting such malfunctions.

Quality Measures. The three customer service measures that are quality related are: information, product support, and other. These measures evaluate ability to provide pre- and posttransaction support for the customer in terms of both information and service. As the date in Table 3–7 indicates, the ability of an enterprise to provide accurate information is the third most significant measure of customer service next to the product-availability and order-cycle-time measures. The information measure records an enterprise's ability to respond to customer inquiry for order and inventory status. More and more customers are indicating that complete knowledge concerning the contents and timing of an order are more important than the complete order fill. Customers can adjust to most of problems caused by stockouts or substitutions if they receive timely information.

The second quality measure concerns product support at all points in the transaction. An enterprise demonstrates product support ability by providing technical advice as well as maintenance and repair services. As Table 3–7 indicates, support is particularly critical for items sold to industrial firms since technical or maintenance problems could impair or shut down manufacturing. This measure could be reported in terms of the availability, accuracy, and completeness of technical product information. For repair and maintenance, the measure should report the average and consistency of response time along with the average number of problems encountered.

The final quality measure contains the remaining customer service elements not included in the other categories. As the table indicates, this category is not significant for either industrial or general merchandise.

The above discussion has identified and reviewed specific customer service measures. The relative importance of the individual measures has been positioned within the overall customer service concept. The following part discusses criteria that can be used to evaluate customer service.

Measurement

Although the previous part discussed the critical elements in the eyes of the customers, it did not present measurement specifics. When measuring service performance, three points must be considered: (1) the specific events to be measured, (2) the actual measures, and (3) the measurement base.

The specific events identify the variables to be measured. Table 3–8 presents a list of the variables that could be used to measure service performance. The table also notes whether the variable should be measured at a point in time or over time. Variables that are measured at a point in time are termed status or state variables and are useful for evaluating the logistics system's current situation. For example, a review of the current number of back orders or the current volume of in-transit inventory would provide management with an early warning of customer service problems. The variables that are measured over time, termed flow variables, record the system activities across a period of time such as a month or a quarter. Regardless of the specific variable measured

TABLE 3–8   Service Measurement Variables

Specific Variables	Measurement Period
Sales	Over time
Orders	Over time
Returns	Over time
Back orders	Over time/Point in time
Stockouts	Over time/Point in time
Cancelled orders	Over time
Cancelled lines	Over time
Back order recovery	Over time
Back order age	Over time/Point in time
Short shipments	Over time
Damage claims	Over time
Number of expedites	Over time

TABLE 3–9 Customer Service Physical Measures

1. Cases	5. Dollars
2. Units	6. Dozens
3. Lines	7. Broken cases
4. Weight	8. Gallons

TABLE 3–10 Customer Service Reporting Aggregation

1. Overall system level	5. Order level
2. Sales area level	6. Customer level
3. Product group level	7. Facility level
4. Brand level	8. Product level

to evaluate customer service performance, the event must be monitored appropriately. For example, it does not make sense to measure cancelled orders at a point in time.

The second consideration is the actual categories measured. Table 3–9 lists physical measures that may be reported. For example, it is possible to report stockouts in terms of both units and dollars. Although both measures are derived from the same source, they do not always provide the same managerial information. When stockouts are measured in terms of units, the performance measures for both high- and low-value product are weighted equally. On the other hand, the reporting of stockout performance in terms of dollars places more weight on the stockouts for higher value, and presumably higher margin, items. Management is usually more concerned when the stockouts are for high-volume items than for lower-value items.

The final consideration is the measurement base. The measurement base describes the reporting aggregation. Table 3–10 lists different levels of reporting aggregation in descending order. The overall system aggregation summarizes all activities to system totals. This level is easy to measure since it requires the maintenance of very little data. However, it tends to camouflage potential problems by averaging activities. On the other hand, when there is little aggregation such as when the performance is measured by product or customer, it is more difficult to analyze volumes of data and identify the overall status of potential problems. Although it is more difficult to capture and maintain the data at the customer or product detail level, it is much easier to identify problems.

Management must evaluate the trade-offs when selecting the most appropriate customer service measure and measurements. While a greater degree of detail facilitates the timely identification of potential problems, the resources required to collect, maintain, and analyze the information are substantial. However, with the significant advances being made in information technology with regard to collection, maintenance, and analysis, the costs associated with detailed customer service performance evaluation are declining. The use of improved information technology to provide more detailed customer service reporting will lead to more refined customer service offerings designed to meet the specific needs of customers. In order to provide competition and cost-effective offerings, management must continuously evaluate the information benefit trade-offs caused by dynamic change in today's environment.

Once the philosophy and measures have been defined and put into place, the final task in establishing a complete customer service program is the creation of a mechanism for administration. The final section discusses customer service administration.

CUSTOMER SERVICE ADMINISTRATION

Customer service administration ideally performs two roles. The first, and traditional, role is customer service operation. The second, and more recent role, involves customer service analysis. The following part discuss each role.

Operating Role

The customer service operating role involves order processing and handling of customer inquiries. The specific activities that must be performed include order entry, order processing, customer inquiry handling, order modifications, and coordination of special customer needs such as build to order manufacturing. These activities are relatively specialized and routinized. In addition, it is often necessary to complete a significant number of transactions within a given time period. As a result, the emphasis in operations is placed on efficiency. The system must be designed to perform the operations role with speed, accuracy, and at the lowest cost per transaction.

Analytical Role

The analytical role of customer service is used to obtain information to improve customer service performance or reduce cost. The specific analysis activities include customer tracking and evaluation, customer and competitive intelligence gathering, and demand management.

The customer tracking and evaluation activity reviews customer performance and requirements. The objective is to identify where the firm is not providing adequate customer service or where improved offerings could increase sales and profitability.

The customer and competitive intelligence gathering activity collects and synthesizes market intelligence to identify potential opportunities or problems. For example, through casual conversations with a customer, it may be determined that a competitor is changing its customer service policy. The intelligence activity should be designed to gather and synthesize such information and develop response strategies.

Demand management attempts to influence customer action through coordination and information transfer. For example, if a customer plans to offer a large promotion for a product, the demand management efforts should identify this requirement and ensure that this need is consistent with the enterprise's ability to support the promotion. If the requirements are not consistent with available support, demand management efforts should attempt to develop a mutually agreeable solution. For example, the customer may be persuaded to change the promotional timing or products for pricing incentives.

When compared with the operating role, the analytical role of customer service is not structured. As opposed to the efficiency stressed in the operating role, the analytical role must be designed for effectiveness. The systems and procedures must be flexible and facilitate communications between the customers and logistical decision-makers.

DESIGNING A CUSTOMER SERVICE STRATEGY

The preceding sections have discussed the role of customer service within marketing, customer service performance, and customer service administration. Once the general customer service characteristics have been identified, the next task is to develop an overall customer service strategy. This section presents a procedure for developing such a strategy.

Recent developments have demonstrated that customer service is becoming more significant in overall strategic planning. A review of the literature provides numerous articles that discuss the concept of customer service and describe procedures for development of customer service strategies.[19]

This section presents a four-step procedure for developing a customer service strategy. Since the market and the competition are both dynamic entities, a customer service strategy is not something that can be completed once and then set aside for a number of years. Although the complete process does not have to be performed on a continuing basis, the procedures must be in place to identify environmental change and suggest appropriate adjustments.

The four steps for designing customer service strategy are (1) audit customer service, (2) set performance objectives and standards, (3) institute management systems, and (4) institute control and review procedures. Figure 3–6 illustrates the process through a flow diagram. The following describes the activities for each of the above tasks.[20]

Audit Customer Service

The first task is the completion of a customer service audit to identify the market requirements and the competitive situation. This task is usually accomplished through a survey which is completed by customers and potential customers. The survey's objective is to identify the key elements of customer service and their relative importance as perceived by the customer. The survey must identify the customer's requirements in terms of availability, order cycle time, information, flexibility, problem-handling, and product support. In addition to identifying customer requirements, the ideal audit should also identify the competitive offerings. The competitive knowledge can be used to

---

[19] Articles discussing the customer service concept include Martin Christopher, "Creating Effective Policies for Customer Service," *International Journal of Physical Distribution and Materials Management*, Vol. 13, No. 2, pp. 3–23; and Michael Levy, "Toward an Optimal Customer Service Package," *Journal of Business Logistics*, Vol. 2, No. 2 (1981), pp. 87–109.

[20] See Martin Christopher, op. cit., p. 6, for a detailed discussion of a similar approach.

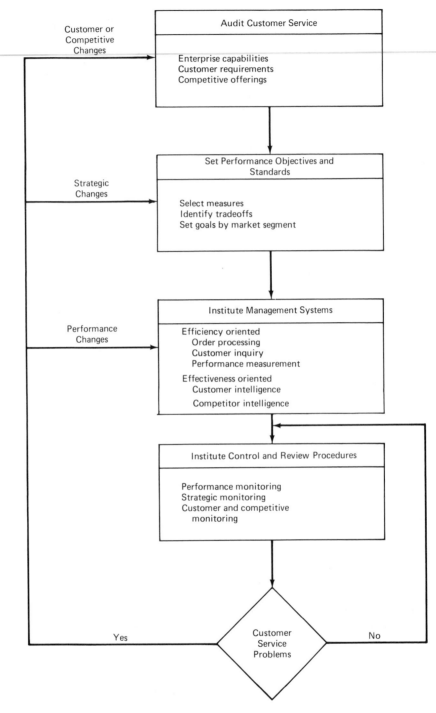

Figure 3–6 Customer Service Strategy Flowchart

develop strategies that can compete effectively with other firms. The audit must also attempt to identify the tradeoffs that customers are willing to make.

Although it is only necessary to complete an audit on a periodic basis, the overall environmental monitoring must be ongoing. The monitoring must identify and evaluate changes and trends to determine whether a change is significant enough to warrant a change in the customer service strategy.

Set Performance Objectives and Standards

Setting the performance objectives and standards requires the establishment of specific goals and measures for directing customer service. This requires the selection of specific measures from those discussed earlier and then establishment of quantitative goals for meeting those measures. For example, the objectives set may be to provide 95 per cent product case availability within 10 days. With this objective, 95 per cent of the cases demanded must be shipped within 10 days.

The identification of performance objectives requires that management consider the trade-offs between the benefits of a specific customer service level and its associated cost. There are two considerations in making this trade-off. First, the enterprise must establish its service position relative to customer requirements and the competition. Even though the customers may desire a 95 per cent product availability rate, if all the competitors provided less than an 85 per cent availability rate, it may not be necessary to set objectives at the 95 per cent level. Although the 95 per cent level may be what the customers think they want, the cost of providing such a level may be unprofitable. The first trade-off consideration is thus the customer's desires balanced against what an enterprise can provide while remaining competitive.

The second trade-off concerns the cost and benefit of specific performance objectives. Management must determine the expected benefits that can be obtained from a specific service level. The benefits would typically come in the form of increased revenue, profitability, or competitive position. The costs that must be evaluated include the cost of increased inventory, premium transportation, or faster communication.

The evaluation of both considerations should be completed by market segment since it may be desirable to define specific segmental strategies. There may be one segment that requires high product availability, while another segment may place more emphasis on low cost. The final outcomes of this task are specific objectives and strategies for each segment, along with the supporting material to defend them in light of other possible resource allocations.

Institute Management Systems

The third task is to design and institute management systems to accomplish and measure the desired customer service activities. The systems, procedures, and human resources must be employed to process orders, answer customer inquiries, measure performance, and gather and analyze customer and competitor intelligence. For the first three activities, the system design must emphasize efficiency while the systems effectiveness must be the primary design consideration for the last activity.

Institute Control and Review Procedures

The final task institutes the procedures to monitor and review the system's performance and initiate desired adjustments. The control procedures must identify when performance either significantly exceeds or drops below the prescribed service levels. When significant variances are identified, the system should suggest and initiate appropriate adjustments. The review procedures must embody enough authority to effect the desired changes. The review must also identify when the environment has changed enough to warrant the redesign of the customer service strategy.

SUMMARY

Chapter 3 has reviewed customer service concepts and positioned them within strategic marketing. It is necessary to consider the importance of logistics within marketing and then identify the logistical requirements to be allocated in support of marketing. The chapter introduced distribution channels and channel strategies available to support overall marketing. Customer service was defined, and measures for evaluating customer service performance were reviewed. The role of customer service administration was reviewed. The chapter concluded with a recommended procedure for the development and design of an integrated customer service strategy. The key fact to remember is that corporate survival occurs in the marketplace, not in the board rooms, warehouses, or the factories. A market orientation is essential. Logistics can be a proactive part of an overall marketing strategy if the customer service program is carefully orchestrated.

QUESTIONS

1. What measurements typically are used to evaluate customer service performance?
2. Discuss the differences between the market and strategic requirements for logistical support of marketing.
3. Discuss the tactical adjustments that the logistical function must make throughout the product life cycle.
4. Why does customer service not increase proportionally to increases in total cost when a logistical system is being designed?
5. Identify the elements and discuss the differences between the operating role and analytical role of customer service administration.
6. What procedure should an enterprise use to design a customer service strategy?
7. What considerations should be employed to identify the appropriate customer service measures and then define quantitative measures for ongoing evaluation?
8. Discuss the differences between improving customer service through faster and more consistent transportation, higher inventory levels, and/or expanded numbers of warehouses.
9. Discuss the different customer service requirements for industrial markets versus consumer markets.
10. In what ways can customer service performance be improved by incorporating flexible distribution operations into a logistical system design?

LOGISTICAL SYSTEM COMPONENTS

Forecasting and Order Management

Forecasting and order management are concerned with the establishment and communication of requirements and specifications that integrate logistical operations. Purchasing has the primary objective of maintaining an orderly flow of externally procured items into the enterprise. Physical distribution operations are concerned with outbound delivery of products to customers. Manufacturing support serves to balance operations by managing the movement of semifinished goods between stages of production and finished inventory to and between warehouses. To provide coordination, logistical information systems provide communication between customers and logistical operations.

When an enterprise performs substantial operations in both physical distribution and purchasing a high degree of coordination is necessary. The coordination provided by forecasting and order management can increase effectiveness by enabling managers to exchange information rather than move products. The technological advances in information processing introduce many opportunities for improving communications flow with customers and within the enterprise. This chapter develops the importance of forecasting and order management and discusses related trade-off opportunities.

The chapter initially discusses the nature and requirements for strategic communication. Next, demand forecasting is developed. The final section discusses order management and requirements for order management systems.

105

COMMUNICATIONS

Increasing importance is being placed on logistical communications. As stated above, information communication is an effective alternative to speculative physical distribution. For example, the advent of Federal Express and other premium transportation carriers and associated high-speed communication have allowed the centralization of parts inventories with a reduction in overall inventory requirements.

The application of communications processes and technology to improve logistical effectiveness places two requirements on an enterprise. First, the firm must understand the role of effective communications. Second, the systems to support the desired communications must be installed and applied. The following parts discuss the elements of logistical communications.

Elements of Logistical Communication

Logistical communications consists of two basic categories which each contain two elements. The logistical communications categories are operational communications, which include the elements of forecasting and order processing, and strategic communications, which include customer intelligence and demand management. Figure 4–1 illustrates the information flows for each category. The following sections define each communication category and discuss its importance to logistical management.

Forecasting

The fundamental input to planning and coordinating logistical operations is a forecast of customer demand. Such demand is independent of the enterprise in that customers are free to choose what and when they purchase. Forecasting is the way an enterprise seeks to anticipate future uncertainty on operations. The demand forecast provides the linkage between the firm and its market

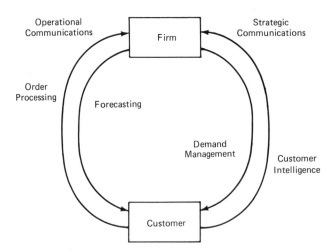

Figure 4–1 Logistical Communications Elements

environment. The desired result of forecasting is a common set of expectations among all managers concerning the expected level of future activity and anticipated performance of individual products.

Demand forecasting for logistical coordination must be detailed to the individual geographical location and product level. This forecasting level is referred to as product-market sales forecasting.[1] The planning horizon of a product-market forecast is relatively short, with a maximum time duration of one year. The typical forecast horizon is three months. Forecasting what products will be purchased by specific customers and in specific markets is the initial step in operational planning. Almost all purchasing, manufacturing, and distribution undertaken by an enterprise is in anticipation of future sales. For example, materials are procured in anticipation of undertaking specific manufacturing and assembly in anticipation of an order, which itself is in anticipation of future consumer demand. Product-market forecasting constitutes a firm's initial effort to reconcile, program, and, if possible, postpone the anticipatory process inherent in a free-market system.

Order Processing

In contrast to forecasting, order processing constitutes a "here and now" measure of marketing activity. In a sense, order processing represents the realization of sales that were anticipated by the forecast. The arrival of a customer order initiates the physical distribution process which, when completed, provides the logistical effort necessary to support marketing.

Order processing, including up-to-date information regarding the nature of demand, is an essential aspect of logistical communications. First, it creates a command status that renders the logistical system dynamic. Second, the order provides a factual source of information to assist forecasting. Seldom, if ever, is a product-market forecast directly on target. The more typical case is a degree of over- or underestimate of anticipated sales. The integration of order processing information into logistical communication provides an ongoing source of reconciliation between what was anticipated and what is in fact occurring. The communication process is improved if the order processing element includes significant bidirectional information flow between the customer and the enterprise.

Customer Intelligence

The third communication element flows from the customer to the firm. This communication concerns customer requirements such as special requests regarding shipment quantities, packaging, or delivery requirements. It is not uncommon for customers to develop and implement an aggressive promotional plan without informing a critical supplier's physical distribution operation. Communication channels must be designed to gather and promote the flow of customer intelligence information.

[1] For a detailed discussion of this level of forecasting, see Donald J. Bowersox et al., "Short Range Product Sales Forecasting," Proceedings, 14th Annual Conference of the National Council of Physical Distribution Management, Chicago, 1976.

Demand Management

The fourth communication element is directed toward the customer and controlled by the enterprise. The typical situation is for an enterprise to react to customer demands as presented. This requires a readiness to supply customer needs within the time frame specified. Since customer needs may vary significantly, this approach requires a firm to maintain significant inventories to safeguard against unpredictable needs. Demand management, which is a logical extension of requirements planning, involves communication between the enterprise and customers to coordinate product quantities and delivery dates. Demand management may take the form of advance notice of extra large quantities required for special promotions or an agreement to substitute alternate products when availability problems occur. Demand management takes place when orders are discussed in advance of processing with customers with the objective of making mutually beneficial adjustments. The effective execution of demand management requires an intimate knowledge of the current inventory situation and operational capabilities, along with a sensitivity to customer needs.

Conclusion—Communications

Effective communication is critical in the operation of a logistics system. In the past, communication has been accomplished by positioning the product near the market in anticipation of customer requirements. This procedure potentially leads to excessive speculative product distribution and unnecessary inventory. Effective operational communication aids the timely and accurate development of forecasts. Effective strategic communication provides the ability to identify opportunities and make adjustments to match market requirements and logistical capability.

DEMAND FORECASTING

The demand forecast drives all aspects of the plan. This includes everything from financial projections to distribution requirements. Figure 4–2 illustrates the various levels of forecast typically required. The logistical and sales forecasts both make projections of specific customer requirements. Although the sales forecast may be filtered through various levels of district and regional sales offices, it is ultimately included directly into the financial plan. On the other hand, the logistical forecast is used to operationalize a number of other activities including the statement of distribution requirements the master production schedule, and the materials requirements plan.

At an aggregate level, the financial forecast projects monetary position throughout the year. The forecast includes expected impacts on the balance sheet, the income statement and cash flow requirements. This forecast must include aggregate sales level, in quantities and dollars, and projected costs. Since the objective of the financial forecast is to project aggregate results, the level of detail is not particularly significant. For example, at this level it is not important whether the product is sold in one city as opposed to another. Similarly, the exact product color or model sold is not particularly important.

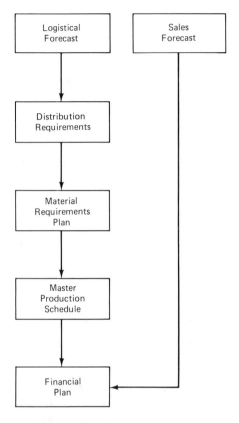

Figure 4–2   Company Forecast Requirements

On the other hand, when one is developing forecasts for logistical management, the specific product model, demand location, and time is important for planning customer service. The forecaster must develop projections for specific distribution facilities. Even if the aggregate forecast is correct, if a specific customer's product, location, and time requirements cannot be met, the logistical system is operating ineffectively since sales will be lost or additional costs will be incurred.

The remainder of this section focuses on forecasting for logistical management. The following parts first discuss the general nature of logistical forecasting. Second, a forecasting procedure is presented and discussed. The final part discusses specific forecast techniques and approaches.

General Considerations of Logistical Forecasting

Logistical forecasting is the projection of customer demands by location, product, and time period. Typical logistical forecasts are prepared at a detailed level. This part discusses five characteristics of the logistical forecast.

Forecasting Versus Prediction

Although the terms *forecast* and *predict* are often used interchangeably, there is a slight difference from a logistical perspective. Webster defines forecast as: "to anticipate or calculate usually as a result of rational study and analysis of available pertinent data."[2] On the other hand, predict is defined as: "to declare in advance such as a prophecy." While it would be desirable for each enterprise to employ individuals who are capable of accurately predicting detailed customer requirements, there are few such human beings.

Logistical management requires the use of forecasting to anticipate sales. The data include historical demand patterns, customer intelligence, and scheduled promotions and programs. These data must be gathered, analyzed, and integrated to develop the detailed logistical forecast. The historical demand patterns include actual sales by product and distribution facilities. The general assumption is that past demand patterns will repeat, subject to changes brought about by trends and business patterns. Customer intelligence data include information concerning special customer or competitor knowledge such as promotions. The promotions and programs data include the marketing promotional schedule to identify major factors changing the demand pattern.

Forecast Components

A second consideration is the relative weight to place on each forecast component. Each logistical forecast consists of four components: (1) seasonal, (2) trend, (3) cyclic, and (4) irregular. While some forecasts may not place emphasis on each component, the forecaster must consider each and incorporate them as is appropriate. Each component is briefly discussed.

The *seasonal* component is a generally recurring upward and downward movement in the demand pattern, usually on an annual basis. An example is the annual demand for toys which has a high demand just prior to Christmas and then drops off during the first three quarters of the year. It can be said that the demand pattern of toys exhibits low seasonality during the first three quarters with the peak seasonality being found in the last quarter. It should be noted that the seasonality discussed above refers to consumer retail seasonality. Seasonality at the wholesale level precedes consumer demand by approximately one quarter.

The *trend* component is defined as the long-range general movement in periodic sales over an extended period of time. This trend may be positive, negative, or neutral in direction. A positive trend means that sales are increasing across time. For example, the trend for personal computer sales during the decade of the 1980s is increasing. Over the product life cycle, the trend direction may change a number of times. For example, due to a change in people's drinking habits, beer consumption and the resulting demand for beer changed from an increasing trend to a neutral trend during the early 1980s. Increases or decreases in trend can be dependent on changes in overall population or consumption patterns. A knowledge of which factor impacts sales is significant when making projections. For example, a reduction in birth rates implies a reduction in the demand for disposable diapers will follow. However, a trend to use disposable as contrasted to cloth diapers by more individuals may cause an increase in demand even when the size of the overall market is decreasing. The above are obvious examples of forecast trend. While

---

[2] *Webster's Third New International Dictionary*, 1978 (Springfied, Mass.: G. & C. Merriam Company).

the impact of trend on short-range logistical forecasts is subtle, it must still be considered when developing the forecast.

The *cyclic* component is characterized by wide swings in the demand pattern lasting typically a year or more. These cycles may be either upward or downward. An example is the business cycle in which the economy typically swings from recessionary to expansionary cycles every three to five years. The demand for housing is typically tied to the business cycle as well as the resulting demand for major appliances.

The *irregular* component consists of the events that are completely unpredictable or random. Due to its random nature, this component is impossible to predict.

It is beyond the scope of this text to provide a detailed discussion of how to formulate each forecast component. There are a number of texts which provide such detailed calculations.[3] The important point is that the forecaster must recognize the potential impact of different components and treat them appropriately. For example, the treatment of a seasonal component as a trend component could result in an inaccurate forecast. The components significant to a particular forecast must be identified, analyzed, and incorporated with the appropriate techniques.

Forecast Approaches

Broadly speaking, there are two approaches for developing forecasts. The *first* approach, the top down or decomposition approach, develops a high-level forecast and then spreads it across markets or products based on historical sales patterns. The *second* approach is a bottom-up or aggregation method which develops detailed forecasts for each market or product and then builds up an aggregate forecast.

Although the two approaches are presented as opposite extremes, they are actually the end points on a continuum. The forecast may be generated using a combination of top-down and bottom-up approaches. The precise combination depends on the forecaster's needs and capabilities.

Figure 4–3 illustrates the two alternatives. The left side of the figure illustrates the top-down approach, while the right side demonstrates the bottom-up approach. In both cases, the forecast is being computed for a manufacturing plant with two warehouses. In the first case, the manufacturing forecast is estimated to be 100 per month. This monthly forecast is then spread to the warehouses using the historical percentages of 40 and 60, respectively.

The bottom-up approach generates an individual forecast for each warehouse based on historical demand patterns coupled with other available information. These individual forecasts are then summed to develop the manufacturing forecast.

---

[3] Many of the texts used for business statistics provide detailed discussions of the methodology. A particularly good treatment is provided by Lawrence L. Lapin, *Statistics for Modern Business Decisions*, 3rd ed. (New York: Harcourt Brace Jovanovich, Inc.), 1982, pp. 339–436. A more thorough treatment of decomposition, particularly for management applications, is found in Steven C. Wheelwright and Spyros Makridakis, *Forecasting Methods for Management*, 3rd ed. (New York: Wiley-Interscience, 1980), pp. 123–45.

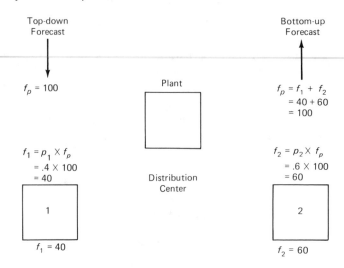

Figure 4–3   Forecast Approaches

The forecaster must decide which approach is applicable in a particular situation. The top-down approach is centralized and is appropriate for stable demand situations or when the demand levels are changing uniformly throughout the market. For example, when demand levels are increasing 10 per cent uniformly across all markets, the use of the top-down approach facilitates the development of new detailed forecasts since the relative percentage changes are constant.

On the other hand, the bottom-up approach is decentralized since each warehouse forecast is developed independently. As a result, each forecast can more accurately track and consider demand fluctuations within specific markets. However, the bottom-up approach requires more detailed record-keeping and makes it more difficult to factor in systematic demand factors such as the general impact of a major promotion.

While the forecaster does not have to accept one alternative at the expense of the other, an acceptable combination must be selected. The correct combination must trade-off detail tracking of the bottom-up approach with the data manipulation ease of the top-down approach. Muir and Newberry provide a detailed discussion of this pyramid forecasting approach.[4]

Forecast Reconciliation

The fourth consideration in establishing a logistical forecast system is a means for reconciling differences between sales, marketing, manufacturing, and logistics. In many firms independent forecasts are generated by each organizational unit. Since sales bonuses are typically based on the attainment of a quota, the sales forecast is often used to motivate salespeople. While sales forecasts are sometimes high due to quota requirements, they are usually understated to provide attainable goals. Since manufacturing is criticized

[4] James W. Muir and Thomas L. Newberry, "Management's Role in Designing Forecasting System." *Production and Inventory Management Review and APICS News* (October 1980), pp. 20–28.

when the finished-goods inventory becomes depleted, production forecasts are typically biased toward the high side. To compound the situation, manufacturing management may feel sales forecasts are overly optimistic and therefore may reduce what is already a low forecast. In this case, manufacturing will produce even less than forecasted, resulting in significant lost sales. Since logistical management must operate as the buffer between the sales and manufacturing, the logistical forecast is typically somewhere between the two extremes.

While specific operating areas of an enterprise have different objectives and requirements, there is no reason for significant differences in the forecast. The key is to coordinate forecasts across operating areas to provide one unified objective. The use of a single forecast for all areas allows each area to reach its respective goal without being dysfunctional to the overall enterprise. An effective forecasting system must incorporate a means of reconciling the individual requirements into a unified forecast.

Forecast Error

The fifth consideration when establishing a forecasting system is a mechanism for treating forecast error. Forecast error is defined as the difference between the actual and the forecasted demand. When considering forecast error, the forecaster must evaluate two factors. First, there must be a means of measuring the forecast error. Second, the forecaster must identify the potential impact of forecast error. Each of these factors are discussed.

Measurement. The forecast error is the difference between demand and the forecast. Stated mathematically, this is written as:

$$e_i = d_i - f_i$$

where:

$$e_i = \text{error}$$
$$d_i = \text{demand}$$
$$f_i = \text{forecast}$$

Table 4–1 provides the monthly demand and forecast in units for a personal computer store. This summary is used to illustrate the impact of alternative forecast error measures.

One approach for error measurement is to sum up the errors over time such as illustrated in column 4. With this approach, errors are summed over the year, and a simple average is calculated. As illustrated, the average error is very near zero, even though there are some months with significant error. The problem with this approach is that the positive errors cancel the negative errors, masking a significant forecasting problem. In order to avoid this problem, an alternative approach is to ignore if the error is over or under forecast and evaluate the absolute error.

Column 5 illustrates the computation of the absolute error and the resulting mean absolute deviation (MAD). While the MAD is often used to measure forecast error, an alternative is to square the error and then use the mean

TABLE 4–1   **Monthly Personal Computer Sales**

(1)	(2)	(3)	(4)	(5)	(6)
				Absolute	Squared
Month	Demand	Forecast	Error	Error	Error
January	10	11	−1	1	1
February	11	9	2	2	4
March	9	9	0	0	0
April	13	12	1	1	1
May	7	9	−2	2	4
June	11	12	−1	1	1
July	12	12	0	0	0
August	9	11	−2	2	4
September	12	7	5	5	25
October	9	13	−4	4	16
November	8	9	−1	1	1
December	9	10	−1	1	1
Sum			−4	20	58
Mean			−.33	1.67[a]	4.83[b]

[a] Mean absolute deviation (MAD).
[b] Mean squared error.

squared error for comparing forecast alternatives. Column 6 illustrates the squared error approach. The advantage of the squared error approach is that it penalizes larger errors more than smaller ones. For example, the MAD approach penalizes a forecast deviation of 2 only twice as much as a deviation of 1. The squared error approach penalizes a forecast measurement deviation of 2 four times more than a forecast deviation of 1. The use of the squared error approach penalizes a system more for a few large errors than for a large number of small errors.

Impact. When evaluating forecast error, it is important to identify the impact of potential error. In some cases, a relatively small error may result in significant increase in inventory-carrying cost. The forecast error magnitude impacts the amount of inventory that is required to provide specified customer service levels since more error or uncertainty implies that higher inventories will be required. When selecting the acceptable level of forecast error, the trade-off between error and inventory impact must be evaluated.

To illustrate, Figure 4–4 presents the inventory/customer service relationships for two forecast error levels. The curves were generated using a dynamic simulation testing environment.[5] Assume the desired service level, in terms of case fill availability is 94 per cent. Based on the simulated inventory/service curve, a distribution center would require an average inventory of approximately 2,225 units at an error rate of 20 per cent. At the 40 per cent error level, the required inventory level is approximately 2,500 units or a 12 per cent increase. If each inventory unit had a value of $4, the cost of carrying the additional inventory would be $275 based on a 25 per cent cost of carrying

[5] See Chapter 13, pages 415–19, for a more detailed discussion of dynamic simulation tools.

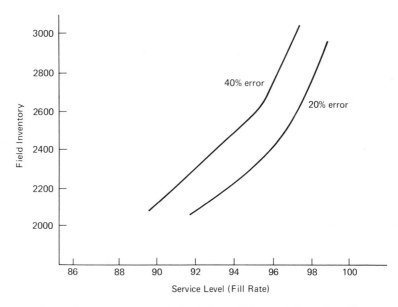

Figure 4–4   Performance Curve Under Different Forecast Error Conditions

inventory. Since the magnitude of the impact is not significant, there should be no major effort to reduce the forecast error from 40 to 20 per cent. On the other hand, if each unit was valued at $4,000, the annual savings in inventory-carrying cost would be $275,000. At this impact level, the forecaster would realize a significant return-on-investment if forecast error could be reduced.

The impact of the forecast error should be identified prior to expended significant resources to reduce the error. In some situations, the increased inventory cost justifies significant expenditures to improve forecast capability. On the other hand, in some situations the magnitude of additional inventory is minimal regardless of forecast error. The required accuracy of a forecasting system is directly related to the impact of error on cost or performance.

Conclusion—Demand Forecasting

The above five considerations should be addressed when selecting a forecasting system. There are trade-offs related to each consideration. Logistical management must identify trade-offs and define the approach that minimizes cost and achieves the best overall results.

FORECAST PROCEDURE

Logistical coordination requires the best possible estimate of individual product-market demand. Although forecasting is far from an exact science, more and more enterprises are relying on mathematical and statistical forecasting techniques. Forecast procedures vary depending on time horizon, time interval, and level of detail.

The purpose of the process and techniques discussed in this section is to generate forecasts concerning future demand that will be placed upon combined physical distribution, manufacturing support, and purchasing operations.

The time horizon for logistical operational forecasts is normally one year or less. Depending upon the plan's intended use, forecasts may be required on a daily, weekly, monthly, quarterly, semiannual, or annual basis. A survey of 161 companies revealed that the most popular forecast period is one month.[6] The important requirement is that the basic planning horizon be selected to accommondate logistical operations.

While the calendar interval is the most popular time period for forecasting, it is sometimes necessary to develop forecasts of demand during inventory replenishment cycle time to compute safety stock requirements. The forecasted demand during the cycle time, which incorporates demand and cycle time uncertainty, is a primary determinant of the safety stock requirements. While an estimate of demand during cycle time is a basic forecast, it is difficult to record and maintain since replenishment cycles occur on an irregular basis. Improved information technology has made it more feasible to forecast demand during cycle time.

Finally, with respect to level of detail, the purpose of the forecast is to develop an estimate of product requirements in individual markets. In the formulation of purchasing plans, production schedules, and distribution plans, the combined forecast for several markets provides on overall estimate of operational requirements. Since the market and product uncertainties tend to cancel each other, less detailed forecasts tend to be more accurate. For accurate logistical planning detailed forecasts are required.

Forecast Procedure Evaluation

Logistical forecasting requires the selection of an appropriate mathematical or statistical technique to generate periodic forecasts. There are many evaluations of the capabilities of alternative forecasting techniques.[7] Although there are many different forecasting techniques, they are not interchangeable. The effective use of a forecasting technique requires matching the characteristics of the market situation with the technique. Makridakis and Wheelwright suggest the following criteria for evaluating the applicability of a technique: (1) accuracy, (2) the forecast time horizon, (3) the value of forecasting, (4) the availability of data, (5) the type of data pattern, and (6) the experience of the practitioner at forecasting.[8] Each alternative forecast technique must be evaluated both qualitatively and quantitatively with respect to these six criteria.

---

[6] "Sales Forecasting Practices: An Appraisal," *Experiences in Marketing Management 25* (New York: National Industrial Conference Board, 1970), p. 23.

[7] Three of the most extensive evaluations are John C. Chambers, Satinder K. Mulick, and Donald D. Smith. "How to Choose the Right Forecasting Technique," *Harvard Business Review* (July/August 1971), pp. 47–76. Robin M. Hogarth and Spyros Makridakis. "Forecasting and Planning: An Evaluation." *Management Science*, Vol. 49, Vol. 47, No. 2 (February 1981), pp. 115–31. Spyros Makridakis and Steven C. Wheelwright, "Forecasting: Issues and Challenges for Marketing Management." *Journal of Marketing*, Vol. 55 (October 1977), pp. 24–37.

[8] Makridakis and Wheelwright, op. cit., p. 25.

There are literally hundreds of articles describing approaches and effectiveness of forecasting alternatives.[9] During the last two decades, forecasting techniques have become increasingly complex by the addition of advanced statistical and analytical capabilities. The general development hypothesis was that greater complexity and sophistication would result in improved forecast accuracy. While this is often true, recent research has indicated that simpler is often better. The more sophisticated techniques do not always provide significantly better results than the simpler techniques, particularly when one considers the resource requirements, both information and expertise, that the more complex techniques require.[10]

While it would be advantageous to be able to identify a specific forecast technique, simple or complex, that is appropriate for each application, the development and evaluation of forecast methodoliogies are not that exact. The selection of the appropriate forecast technique is an art much more than a science. Simply stated, logistical management should choose the technique or techniques that provide the best results. The concept of focus forecasting illustrates one approach to a combined methodology.[11]

Forecast Techniques

There are three general categories of forecast techniques: (1) qualitative methods, (2) time series methods, and (3) causal methods. The qualitative methods use qualitative data such as expert opinion and special information to forecast the future.[12] A qualitative method may or may not consider the past. The time series and projective methods focus entirely on historical patterns and pattern changes to generate forecasts. The causal methods, such as regression, use refined and specific information regarding variables to develop a relationship between a lead event and the event being forecasted. Qualitative methods rely heavily on expertise and are quite costly and time consuming. They are generally not appropriate for logistical forecasting. As a result, the next parts provide detailed discussion of time series and causal methods.

Time Series Methods

Time series methods are statistical techniques used when historical product sales data are available with relatively clear and stable relationships and trends. Using the historical sales data, time series analysis is used to identify: (1)

---

[9] Hogarth and Makridakis, op. cit.

[10] For a detailed analysis of the results, see J. Scott Armstrong, "Forecasting by Extrapolation: Conclusions from 25 Years of Research." *Interfaces*. Vol. 14, No. 6, (November–December 1984), pp. 52–66. A simulation analysis that draws a similar conclusion for alternative time series models is presented in Jeffrey R. Sims, *Simulated Product Sales Forecasting: Analysis of Forecasting Discrepancies in the Physical Distribution System*, Unpublished Ph.D. Dissertation (East Lansing, Mich.: Michigan State University, 1978).

[11] Bernard T. Smith and Oliver W. Wight, *Focus Forecasting: Computer Techniques for Inventory Control* (New York: Van Nos Reinhold, 1978).

[12] The discussion of forecast technique categories is generally based on the Chambers, Mulick, and Smith, op. cit.

systematic variations in the data due to seasonality, (2) cyclical patterns, (3) trends, and (4) growth rates of these trends. Once the individual forecast components have been identified, the time series methods assume the future will be similar to the past. This implies that existing demand patterns will continue into the future. This assumption is reasonably correct in the short term. Thus, these techniques are most appropriate for short-range forecasting. However, unless the demand patterns are reasonably stable, these techniques do not produce accurate forecasts.

When the rate of growth or trend changes significantly, the demand pattern experiences a turning point. Since the time series methods use historical demand patterns and weighted averages of data points, they are typically not sensitive to turning points. As a result, other approaches must be integrated with time series methods to predict when a turning point will occur.

Time series analysis includes a variety of forecasting techniques that analyze the pattern and movement of historical data to establish recurring characteristics. Based upon specific characteristics, techniques of varying sophistication can be used to develop time series forecasts. Four time series techniques are discussed in order of increasing complexity. They are: (1) moving averages, (2) exponential smoothing, (3) extended smoothing, and (4) adaptive smoothing.[13]

Moving Averages. Moving average forecasting is a two-step procedure. First, the average value of a series of data covering specific time periods, such as average weekly sales, is calculated. Second, the average value is used in conjunction with the trend of the data to forecast future sales. Each time a new period of actual data becomes available, it replaces the oldest time period's data. Thus, the number of time periods is held constant.

Mathematically, a moving average is expressed as

$$F_i = \frac{\displaystyle\sum_{j=i-(n-1)}^{i} S_j}{n}$$

where

F_i = moving average forecast
S_j = sales per time period; time periods are identified by the appropriate subscript
n = total number of time periods

For example, an April moving average forecast based on sales of 120, 150, and 90 for the previous three months is calculated as follows

$$F_{\text{April}} = \frac{120 + 150 + 90}{3}$$

$$= 120.$$

---

[13] This section draws heavily on Steven C. Wheelwright and Spyros Makridakis, *Forecasting Methods for Management,* 3rd ed. (New York: John Wiley & Sons, Inc., 1980), and Robert G. Brown, *Smoothing, Forecasting, and Prediction of Discrete Time Series* (Englewood Cliffs, N.J.: Prentice-Hall, Inc., 1963).

Although a moving average is easy to calculate, it has several limitations. The most significant are that it relies upon an average to change the forecast, it is unresponsive or sluggish to change, and a great amount of historical data must be maintained and updated to calculate forecasts. If the historical sales variations are large, average or mean values cannot be relied upon to render useful forecasts.

To partially overcome these deficiencies, weighted moving averages have been introduced as refinements. Exponential smoothing represents a form of weighted moving average.

 Exponential Smoothing. Exponential smoothing bases the estimate of future sales on the weighted average of the previous demand and forecast levels. The new forecast is a function of the old forecast incremented by some fraction of the differential between the old forecast and actual sales realized. The increment of adjustment is called the *alpha factor* (α). The basic format of the model is

$$F_t = \alpha D_{t-1} + (1 - \alpha) F_{t-1}$$

where

$$F_t = \text{forecasted sales for a time period } t$$
$$t = \text{forecast time period of constant duration}$$
$$D_t = \text{actual demand for time period } t$$
$$\alpha = \text{alpha factor or smoothing constant}$$

To illustrate, assume that the forecasted sales for the most recent time period were 100 units, and actual sales experience was 110 units. Further assume that the alpha factor being employed is 0.2. Then, substituting,

$$F_t = \alpha D_{t-1} + (1 - \alpha) F_{t-1}$$
$$= (0.2)(110) + (1 - 0.2)(100)$$
$$= 22 + 80$$
$$= 102$$

Thus, the new forecast is for product sales of 102 units.

The prime advantage of exponential smoothing is that it permits a rapid calculation of a new forecast without substantial historical records and updating. Thus, exponential smoothing is highly adaptable to computerized forecasting. Depending on the value of the smoothing constant, the sensitivity can be controlled.

A major issue in exponential smoothing is to determine the value assigned to the alpha factor. If a factor of 1 is employed, the net effect is to assume the most recent demand as the forecast of expected demand. A very low value, such as .01, would have the net effect of reducing the forecast to almost a simple moving average. Large alpha factors make the forecast very sensitive to change and therefore highly reactive. Low alpha factors tend to react slowly to change and therefore provide sluggish or delayed reaction. Thus, exponential smoothing does not eliminate the need for judgment decisions. In selecting the value of the alpha factor, the forecaster is faced with a trade-off between eliminating random fluctuations or having the forecast fully respond to demand changes.

Extended Smoothing. The basic exponential smoothing technique can be extended to include the impact of sales trend and seasonality in developing the sales forecast. The extended smoothing methods are termed exponential smoothing with trend and seasonality, respectively.[14]

The fundamental objective of extended exponential smoothing is to integrate the impact of trend and seasonality when specific values for these components can be identified. The method of calculation for extended smoothing is similar to that of the basic smoothing model, except that there are three components and three smoothing constants to represent level, trend, and seasonal components.

Similiar to basic exponential smoothing, extended smoothing allows rapid calculation of new forecasts with minimal record-keeping. The model's ability to respond depends on the smoothing constant values. Higher smoothing constant values provide rapid responses but may lead to overreaction. The major advantage of extended models is that they directly consider trend and seasonal components. While this is definitely an advantage, it is also their major weakness. The extended models are often characterized as being overly sensitive because of the inability to correctly segment individual forecast components. This oversensitivity may lead to forecast accuracy problems.

Adaptive Smoothing. Adaptive smoothing provides a regular review of the validity of the alpha factor. The value of the smoothing constant is reviewed after the forecast to determine the exact alpha value that would have resulted in a perfect forecast. Once determined, the alpha value used to generate the forecast is adjusted to a value that would have produced a more accurate forecast. Thus, managerial judgment is partially replaced by a systematic and consistent method of updating in determining an alpha factor.

More sophisticated forms of adaptive smoothing include an automatic tracking signal to monitor error in the smoothing constant. When the signal is tripped, the constant is automatically modified in an effort to reduce the error. As the forecast error is eliminated, the tracking signal automatically returns the smoothing constant to its original value.[15]

The adaptive smoothing models attempt to change their sensitivity based on the current situation. When the model detects a significant change, it changes the smoothing constant to place more weight on the most recent data.

Regression Methods

Forecasting by regression consists of estimating sales for a product based upon information regarding one or more other independent factors. If the product forecast is based upon a single factor, it is referred to as simple regression analysis. The use of more than one forecast factor is referred to as multiple regression.

The use of regression simply means that the forecast of future sales is based upon a correlation of one event to another. No cause-effect relationship need exist between the product's sale and the independent event if a high degree of

[14] P. R. Winters, "Forecasting Sales by Exponentially Weighted Moving Averages," *Management Science*, Vol. 6 (April 1960), pp. 324–42.

[15] D. W. Trigg and A. G. Leach, "Exponential Smoothing with an Adaptive Response Rate," *Operational Research Quarterly* (March 1967), pp. 53–59.

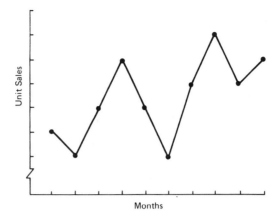

Figure 4–5 Example of Monthly Unit Sales

correlation is consistently present. A correlation assumes that the forecasted sales is proceeded by some leading independent factor such as the sales of a related product. However, the most reliable use of regression forecasting of sales is based on a cause-effect relationship.

Since simple and multiple regression is covered in depth in all business statistics textbooks, the present treatment is limited to the logic of regression forecasting.[16] The reader not familiar with regression is advised to review the technique in a basic source.

The initial step in a regression-based forecast is to accumulate past sales history for the product to be forecasted. Given a reasonable sales history, the average monthly sales and standard deviation of sales around the average should be calculated to determine the general distribution of historical sales. A typical pattern of monthly sales is illustrated in Figure 4–5. Regression forecasting assumes that monthly sales can be correlated to another factor, which will result in a forecast with a smaller uncertainty than the prediction obtained using basic time series analysis.

The second step is to collect data concerning an independent factor which may provide a better forecast. Assume for purposes of illustration that the objective is to forecast aviation propeller replacement sales. There is reason to believe that a positive correlation exists between total hours flown by private aviation in previous months and future months' propeller replacement sales. To test this assumption, historical data are collected on private aviation hours flown. An attempt is then made to establish a correlation relationship. The independent data must be lagged to accommodate the time interval between cause and effect. Assume that an appropriate time lag is three months.

The third step, once the data on private aviation are collected, is to plot the results in the form of a scatter diagram. Although it is not necessary to develop a scatter diagram, such a display makes it easier to observe a positive correlation. Figure 4–6 provides an example where monthly total hours flown by private aviation lagged three months is the independent variable, and monthly propeller sales is the dependent variable.

[16] For example, see Lapin, op. cit., Chapter 14.

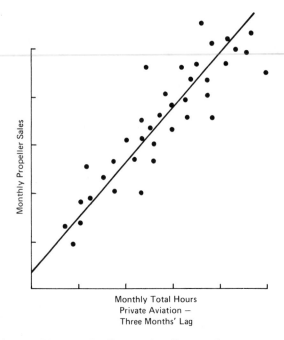

Monthly Propeller Sales

Monthly Total Hours
Private Aviation —
Three Months' Lag

Figure 4–6 Scatter Diagram for Regression Forecasting

The fourth and final step is to fit the solid line displayed on Figure 4–6 to the data plotted in the scatter diagram. The assumption is made that a linear relationship exists. The regression line is established by the formula

$$S = a + bx$$

where

S = predicted value of propeller sales associated with total monthly hours flown
x = monthly hours flown (3-month lag)
a,b = coefficients of the regression equation

Fitting the regression line resolves to finding the values for a and b that will minimize the sum of the squared deviations. The solution for these values is best found using a computerized statistical package. Manual procedures may be found in most statistical textbooks. Once the relationship of monthly sales and flying hours is determined, the regression line can be fitted and a three-month forecast of the expected sales is obtained.

The strength of the relationship between the dependent variable (sales) and the independent variable (flying hours) can be estimated by measuring the coefficient of correlation. The coefficient of correlation between two variables is determined by the formula

$$r = \frac{n \sum_i x_i y_i - \sum_i x_i \sum_i y_i}{\sqrt{\left[n \sum_i x_i^2 - \left(\sum_i x_i\right)^2\right]\left[n \sum_i y_i^2 - \left(\sum_i y_i\right)^2\right]}}$$

where

r = coefficient of correlation
x_i = independent variable for time period i
y_i = dependent variable (formerly noted as s; changed to y to conform to standard notation)

Correlation measures the regression-line fit between the independent variable and the dependent variable. The closer the value of the coefficient of correlation to plus or minus 1, the higher the correlation. A coefficient of 0 implies no relationship. Several assumptions underlie the application of regression forecasting. First, the development of a regression model requires a significant amount of data for the forecast variable and the causal variables. As a result, a significant amount of information must be stored and analyzed. The regression model can consider factors such as competitive actions, environmental changes, and promotions. The inclusion of such factors has the potential to predict reasonably good forecast turning points. The most serious limitation of regression is that it may not be possible to isolate a cause-effect relationship that has an acceptable coefficient of correlation. In addition, using multiple regression for a broad number of product forecasts in numerous markets is a cumbersome task.

Conclusion—Forecast Procedure

Through the forecast, the enterprise establishes the common goal to drive the entire logistics system. This goal identifies the what, where, and when of product sales. The objective is to assimilate as much information as possible, analyze it, and develop a forecast with the desired accuracy in a timely manner. With the advent of high-speed communication and information processing at relatively low cost, it becomes imperative that management assess their forecasting ability. There are some situations where improved forecasts will not achieve significant operational benefits. In other situations improved forecasts will result in significant inventory reductions.

To develop an effective forecast system, management must evaluate trade-offs either qualitatively or quantitatively. The evaluation of the accuracy trade-offs of individual forecast techniques aids in establishing the forecast system. While scientific evaluation can be completed to help identify the appropriate forecast procedures, much of the final determination remains an art. Attention is now directed to order management.

ORDER MANAGEMENT

Order management has the objective of managing communication between an enterprise and its customers. This communication includes all the activities required to process, ship and follow-up customer orders. This section discusses the potential of integrated order management, order types and their relative characteristics, and the order management functions. The final part defines order management stages.

Order Management Potential

The communications message is the trigger mechanism for the entire logistical system. The quality and speed of information flow facilitate integration of basic logistical system components. Conversely, a poor communication network, which allows order bottlenecks or information errors to go undetected, can create havoc within the logistical system. Such errors amplify and distort stock-out problems, production schedules, and inventory accumulation patterns.

Further, it is axiomatic that the more sophisticated the logistical system design, the more vulnerable it is to any internal or external communication malfunction. Take, for example, a zero-based inventory system, in which an order is placed following an item sale for replacement delivery. In such a system there is no safety stock at the retail level. The shoe retailer, for example, stocks one pair of a particular style of shoes. When this pair of shoes is sold, a replacement order is placed. The retailer is out of stock of this particular size and style until the replenishment order is received from the warehouse. In such a system the lag between sale (impulse) and order replenishment (response) must be dependable, or a prolonged out-of-stock situation might develop at the retail level. In a zero-based inventory system, the only way to ensure rapid response is through an efficient communications network. Enterprises using a zero-response inventory replenishment system rely on high-speed store-to-warehouse communication. The effect of a communication delay, either through mechanical failure or transmission error, can be serious. Delay increases the probability of an out-of-stock condition at the retail store and possible amplification of these problems throughout the supplier channel.

With the advent of the high-speed computer, new opportunities for effective use of communication in logistical operations have emerged. Management concern is with the speed and accuracy of messages. Time in the logistical system is both limited and inelastic.[17] If time is not fully utilized, it cannot be retained for the future. The more rapidly a specific task can be performed in the logistical system, the more time is made available for performance of other activities.

Two aspects of time influence the performance of all logistical components. The first is the time expected to elapse while performing a specified activity such as order transmittal. The second concerns message delay, experienced as a result of a variety of causes.

With modern information technology, a message can be transmitted with almost no elapsed time. Time saved in information transmission can be used in the performance of other logistical activities. The cost associated with obtaining rapid receipt of a customer order may be more than offset by savings realized in other logistical areas.

For example, assume that the total time elapsed in servicing a customer consists of three days for order transmittal, two days for warehouse processing,

---

[17] D. W. Boodman and R. C. Norris. "Progress in Distribution: Computer-to-Computer Ordering," *Handling & Shipping Management* (September 1981), p. 34.

TABLE 4–2   Direct Benefit Potential Estimates in the Food Industry from a Uniform Communication System

Savings	$Million/Year
Reduced clerical costs	
Orders and adjustments	$38.
Invoices	22.
Payment advices	12.
Announcements	4.
	$76.
Fewer clerical errors	
Clerical adjustments	$ 3.8
Freight	2.2
Labor	1.5
	7.5
	83.5
Minus operating costs	16.0
Net savings	$67.5

(At 50% transaction penetration.)

and one day for transport. Air freight is used to keep the total delivery time down to six days. An investment in data communications transmitting equipment integrated into warehouse operations could easily reduce transmittal and processing time to one day, which would allow five days for delivery. Given five days for possible outbound shipment, a number of transportation options less expensive than air freight might be available to achieve delivery within a total elapsed time of six days. The resultant transportation rate savings in such a situation could be more than adequate to offset the added cost of data communications.

The second impact of time upon communication concerns delay. Delay simply means that the message does not arrive when expected. Such delays can have a substantial impact upon logistical system performance. In particular, customer service can suffer as a result of stockouts, and production scheduling can be disrupted because of material or parts shortages.

Today's information technology has advanced to the point where more and more companies are considering or using direct electronic data interchange (EDI) of customer and supplier communications. EDI directly transfers information between customers and an enterprise. The adoption of uniform communication systems (UCS) requires a thorough analysis of the costs and benefits. Table 4–2 summarizes an estimate of the direct benefits of such a system in the food industry assuming that 50 per cent of the wholesale grocery transactions utilize a uniform communication system.[18] UCS is projected to have net savings potential of $68 million in the food industry. When one considers the indirect benefits, additional savings of $128 to 255 million, as shown in Table 4–3, are projected. While the projected benefits are substantial,

[18] Ibid.

TABLE 4–3   **Indirect Benefit Potential Estimates in the Food Industry from a Uniform Communication System**

Benefits	$Million/Year
Indirect savings	
Reduced inventory/stocking	$ 70 to 105
Reduced invoice adjustments	$ 33 to 55
More internal automation	$ 15 to 64
Fewer sales calls	10 to 32
Potential	$128 to 256

(At 50% transaction penetration.)

the application of such systems has realized mixed results. Even though the jury is still out concerning the benefits and costs of uniform communication systems, many firms will install, fine tune, and evaluate such systems through the 1980s. With improving information technology, more effective order management provides a fertile ground for reducing logistical costs and improving customer and supplier communications.

Order Types

The logistical system must deal with two order types: (1) customer orders and (2) purchase orders. Customer orders are the requests and resulting communication that takes place between the enterprise and its customers. Typically, the enterprise must process a large number of customer orders which range from very large to very small quantities. The firm usually maintains a limited amount of history base for each customer. The customer generally desires a rapid response, in terms of both product and information, and requires flexibility. These characteristics suggest that the customer order processing systems must be designed for efficient operations. The efficiency should maximize the application of new information technologies and reduce manual processing. Customer orders are demands upon the enterprise which must be integrated with sales forecast to develop logistical requirements. Since the forecast and orders often overlap, it is necessary to make judgments concerning whether the current customer orders reflect demands that are part of or are above and beyond the forecast. When the quantities of future orders are extensive, the procedure must make systematic or manual adjustments in the forecast. Throughout the order management system, efficiency is the key word for designing procedures.

Purchase orders are demands placed upon suppliers. The typical enterprise processes fewer purchase orders than customer orders. Purchase orders are usually larger in dollar size and provide for a longer order cycle time than customer orders. In order to enjoy purchasing efficiency, orders and suppliers must be constantly evaluated to identify potential problems and opportunities. This requires that detailed information be maintained for each supplier. The communication system must be designed to coordinate and track activity from purchase order generation to material receipt.

Order Management Components

All order management components must be integrated to achieve desired customer service at least total cost. Order management components have four links. The first link consists of inbound communication of the customer order. The second link in the system coordinates information with other enterprise units that are influenced by the order. The third link is the command function, which initiates activity. The fourth link is the control phase, where management establishes and monitors feedback to ensure desired logistical system performance. Each component of the order management system is discussed in detail.

Order Transmittal

A variety of methods exist to accomplish the task of order transmittal. Some common methods utilized are personal delivery, mail, teletype, and various forms of telephone transmittal. Telephone order transmittal ranges from personal calls to computer transmission. Each method of order communication can be classified according to speed, cost, dependability, and accuracy of message delivery. Table 4–4 presents a comparative ranking of methods.

As a general rule, the more rapid a form of order transmittal, the more costly it is per message unit. High-speed order communication may be desirable when rapid replenishment of inventory is necessary or when fast order transmittal can result in more economical performance in other areas of the logistical system.

Any increase in order processing speed should result in reduced inventories throughout the system. A decrease in overall cycle time improves reaction time to a customer order and consequently permits lower safety stocks. In this respect, there is a direct cost trade-off between increased communication cost and inventory level. However, as safety stocks are reduced and the system is brought into delicate balance, it becomes more vulnerable to any communication or information malfunction.

Alternative methods of order transmittal can be evaluated for dependability based on message consistency. In a sense, dependability is a mechanical measure of performance. As a general rule, the longer the elapsed time for message delivery, the greater the inconsistency of performance.

Inaccuracy in order transmittal results from human involvement. Written methods of order transmission using a standard format will be more accurate than verbal methods. The degree of accuracy will increase when data are coded and verified for mechanical transmission.

TABLE 4–4   Relative Characteristics of Alternative Order Transmittal Methods

Type	Speed	Cost	Dependability	Accuracy
Personal delivery	Moderate	High	High	Moderate
Mail	Slow	Low	Low	High
Teletype	Fast	Moderate	Moderate	High
Telephone				
Personal	Fast	High	High	Moderate
Data	Fast	High	High	High

A number of methods can be used to detect errors in order transmission and improve accuracy of data. Mechanical detection devices are available to perform consistency checks in the transmission of data. A computer can be programmed to select on an exception basis for managerial review any orders exceeding certain established ranges in quantity or cost. Computers can also be programmed to edit and cost extend product codes and other order details. In general, the more often a piece of information is handled, the greater the chance of error in communication. This is particularly true for manual transmission of information.

In summary, logistical operations are initiated with the transmittal of an order. Available methods of order communication can be evaluated with respect to speed, cost, dependability, and accuracy. Regardless of the method selected to transmit orders, it is desirable to limit the options and derive benefits of simplicity and routinization. There are three principles of order transmittal. First, the time span for order transmittal should be as consistent as possible, considering the risks of system malfunction and consequent stockout problems. Second, order transmission should be as direct as possible, with a minimum of change in order form and intermediate relay. Third, whenever possible, customer orders should be transmitted by mechanical rather than manual means to minimize human error.

Internal Coordination

The second component of an order management system is to ensure a timely and accurate flow of information to management areas outside logistics. Useful information derived from customer orders is often needed by other units of the organization. For example, sales reports and market evaluation data can be generated in a more timely and accurate manner as orders first arrive than at any other time in communication flow. Finance and accounting are concerned, for purposes of cash-flow management, with anticipated accounts receivable, credits granted, and purchases.

In a sophisticated logistical communication system, a great deal of the coordination surrounding order processing is accomplished automatically. For example, production scheduling may be linked directly to order processing and warehouse inventory control in order to level out production and realize an orderly overall manufacturing process.

In summary, logistical communication has an impact on many functions within the organization. A network must be designed that will ensure adequate two-way communication between logistics and other functional areas of the enterprise.

Logistical Command

After an order has been processed, the communication system must prepare logistical work directives. Inventory must be assigned, customer credit cleared, assignment to a warehouse completed, and shipping instructions and documentation formulated. This activity is called the *command function.*

The command function is extremely important in logistical operations because it activates system components. Unless the command function is accurate and timely, a great deal of inefficiency can result in logistical operations. The command function can be performed automatically through an integrated data-processing system in which inventories are automatically updated and shipping instructions prepared and released, or it can be done manually through verbal or written instructions. Modern logistical systems rely heavily upon automated communication command functions.

Command activities generally are limited to the internal logistical system. When common carriers, public warehouses and other third party service organizations are included in the logistical system, commands must extend outside the enterprise to ensure proper performance.

In summary, communication command initiates logistical performance. The efficiency of the logistical performance system depends upon the timeliness and accuracy of command.

Monitor and Control

If the order management system is used as a monitoring device, management must establish specific systems which ensure feedback. Feedback is the return of information for management review for all logistical activities requiring monitoring. These activities always relate to some aspect of customer service or to cost. It is one thing to promise a two-day delivery for 95 per cent of the orders and another to make certain that this target level is achieved. A multiplant or multiproduct enterprise generally will not review each individual shipment delivery to each customer but rather will review operations on an exception basis. Standards might be established to allow plus or minus one-day delivery deviation from programmed customer service levels. The only items selected for exception review would be shipment exceeding this range.

A similar review procedure can be designed to evaluate vendors, transportation suppliers, back orders, and damaged merchandise on a continuous basis. Exception reports from logistical monitoring also can be transmitted to other functional areas of the firm. For example, a listing of warehouse shipments expressed as turnover rates over time might be of interest to purchasing or marketing in evaluating suppliers or customers.

Another advantage of monitoring is the identification of developing trends. Shifts in color preferences and sizes, regional demand, and competitive actions can be identified by closely observing movement within the physical distribution system. Properly reviewing and evaluating this information and relaying it to decision points within the firm can result in a more accurate reaction to unanticipated or uncontrollable factors in the marketplace. The net effect of monitoring and control is a reduction of amplification and distortion in the logistical system. Additional aspects of performance measurement are discussed in Chapter 11.

Integrated Performance

The four components of the logistical order management are essential to overall performance. The fundamental purpose of an automated order-processing system is to integrate the four linkages into a coordinated order management system. Figure 4–7 illustrates the basic concept of the order management system.

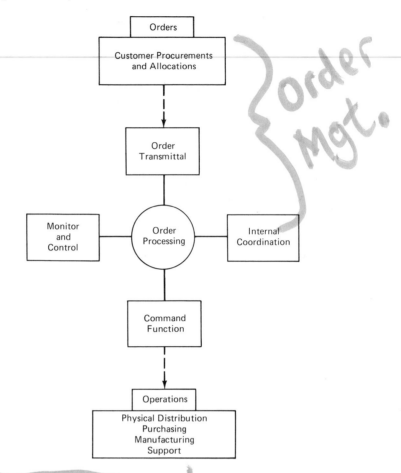

Figure 4–7 Logistical Order Management

Logistics Information Systems

Order management, as well as most of the other aspects of logistical communications, is operationalized through the logistics information system. A majority of the logistics information base of most enterprises are maintained in computerized form.[19] The logistical information system consists of a number of subsystems and files.

Figure 4–8 presents a schematic of the distribution segment of a logistical information system. The schematic contains five element types: (1) subsystems, (2) files, (3) management and data entry, (4) reports, and (5) communication links. The distribution segment interfaces with the remainder of the logistical information system through the distribution requirements plan. The remaining components of the logistical information system include the master production schedule, the manufacturing resource plan, the capacity requirements plan, and

[19] For a detailed summary of the applications, see Craig M. Gustin, "Trends in Computer Application in Transportation and Distribution Management," *International Journal of Physical Distribution and Materials Management*, Vol. 14 (November 1, 1984), pp. 52–60.

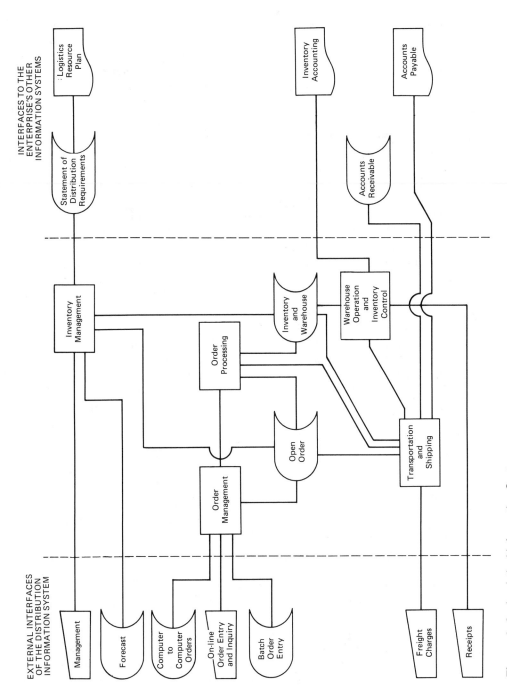

Logistics
Resource
Plan

Statement of
Distribution
Requirements

Inventory
Accounting

Accounts
Payable

Accounts
Receivable

Inventory
Management

Inventory
and
Warehouse

Warehouse
Operation
and
Inventory
Control

Order
Processing

Open
Order

Transportation
and
Shipping

Order
Management

Management

Forecast

Computer
to
Computer
Orders

On-line
Order Entry
and Inquiry

Batch
Order
Entry

Freight
Charges

Receipts

Figure 4–8 Logistical Information System

the purchasing subsystem. The subsystems consist of the transactions and processes that actually accomplish the logistical information processing.

The distribution information system should contain the following five subsystems: (1) order entry (2) order processing, (3) transportation and shipping, (4) warehouse operations and inventory control, and (5) inventory management. The files contain the data and information base to support the communications activities. The major data-base structures that are required for supporting distribution communications are: (1) order file, (2) inventory and warehouse files, (3) accounts receivable file, and (4) distribution requirements file.

The management and data entry activities occur when data must be entered into the system or when management must enter a decision. The general instances for this intervention include: order entry, order inquiry, forecast development and reconciliation, freight rating, and warehouse receipts and adjustments. The reports consist of numerous summary, detail, and exception listings to provide hard-copy information documenting system activities and performance. The links identify the information flow between the subsystems, files, entry activities, and reports.

The following segments discuss the activities typically accommodated within each subsystem.

Order Entry

The order entry subsystem supports the overall communications effort between the enterprise and its customers. In today's environment, this subsystem must accommodate both batch and on-line order entry as well as computer-to-computer processes. In addition to basic order entry, the subsystem must track the order from the time of entry to the receipt of customer payment. This tracking is necessary to be able to provide feedback for the customer at any time during the order cycle. Customer order changes and deletions must also be supported by the order entry subsystem.

Order Processing

The order processing subsystem performs the activities associated with the assignment and commitment of inventories to orders. These activities include the scheduling of order processing when the customer has submitted the order early. In addition, back orders must also be scheduled for fulfillment.

A major order processing decision involves inventory allocation when demands exceed supply. The subsystem must deal with product allocation among customer accounts. Many traditional order processing subsystems perform this allocation at a fixed time during the order cycle. This fixed time may be as a part of the order entry process or just prior to order shipment. To support segmented customer service, the subsystem should be flexible enough to provide inventory allocation at any time throughout the order cycle. For example, some customers may require specific quantities and cycle times and would thus like the inventory allocated early in the cycle. On the other hand, there may be another group of customers who may be willing to trade-off inventory guarantees for price discounts. Once the order processing subsystem has provided the inventory, the order is turned over to the transportation and shipping subsystem.

Transportation and Shipping

The transportation and shipping subsystem supports the activities that are required to schedule the transportation equipment, cause the orders to be picked in the warehouse, load the orders, generate transportation documentation, and trace the order. When the order sizes are relatively small, the subsystem must also support order consolidation procedures to minimize transportation costs. These procedures must evaluate, on a real-time basis, the trade-offs between the reduced transportation costs and the incurred order cycle time caused by holding customer orders for consolidation.

Warehouse Operations and Inventory Control

The warehouse operations and inventory control subsystem provides the information support for the inventory storage, inventory retrieval, physical inventory counts, and picking documentation generation. These include the activities to record warehouse receipts, inventory adjustments, and allocation of warehouse storage locations.

This subsystem coordinates the physical movement of goods in and through the warehouse with the information base that supports the movements. For example, the subsystem tracks the location of goods within the warehouse and initiates product movement from the storage locations to the shipping area. Since this subsystem requires such a high degree of coordination with the physical structure, the primary consideration in designing the subsystem is to provide adequate control without overburdening the system with a significant amount of data entry and reporting. While it might be advantageous to track warehouse movement, this would require that operating personnel record each movement. The application of new technologies such as scanning and bar coding facilitate this tracking process and make such coordination a reality.

Inventory Management

The inventory management subsystem supports the activities to develop and communicate the inventory requirements throughout the logistical system. On a timely basis, the subsystem should be capable of generating a schedule of distribution requirements based on the advanced and open orders, forecasted orders, scheduled production, and available inventory. In addition to scheduling distribution and production inventories, the subsystem must also coordinate the inventories at the various distribution facilities throughout the logistical network.

Conclusion—Order Management

The order management section has identified the functions, activities, and information to support order communications throughout the firm. The chapter emphasized the importance of effective communication to promote the attainment of a unified goal and efficient communications to minimize the cost per transaction. The introduction of new information technologies makes possible innovative approaches to facilitate the order management process. The ultimate objective of overall order management is to replace, as much as possible, the physical product movement with information movement.

SUMMARY

The forecasting and order management chapter has placed a significant emphasis on the enterprise's need to communicate. This logistical system must be designed to support both internal and external communication for the firm. The chapter's first section discusses the type of communications that are necessary to effectively support logistical operation. Two-way communication systems must be implemented between the enterprise and customers. This system must be both operational and strategic to provide for the processing of both customer orders as well as customer intelligence.

The second section presented the considerations for demand forecasting followed by a discussion of selected forecast techniques. The section identifies the trade-offs that must be considered when designing the forecasting system. In addition to suggesting the consideration of the impact of forecast error, the section presents the limitation of the general approaches to forecasting. The general conclusion is that no single approach to forecasting is perfect. Management should evaluate alternatives and select the one that appears capable of providing the best performance.

The final section discussed order management functions, activities, and systems. The chapter stresses the feasibility and potential of utilizing order and information management as a trade-off for physical product movement and manual processes. Significant advances in information technology makes the order management function a fertile field for reaping significant returns. Attention is now directed to transportation.

QUESTIONS

1. Discuss the elements of logistical communication and identify the characteristics of each.
2. What is the objective of forecast reconciliation and how should it be performed?
3. Discuss the impact of forecast error and identify the trade-offs that must be considered when considering the allocation of firm resources to forecasting.
4. What is the fundamental difference between time series and regression methods of forecasting?
5. Discuss the sensitivity of alpha factors in an exponentially smoothed forecast. How do extended and adaptive smoothing methods improve forecasting ability?

6. Discuss the potential benefits that can be gained through improved order management and identify the techniques that can be used to bring these benefits.
7. Discuss the relative capabilities of various techniques available for order transmittal.
8. Identify and discuss the subsystems that comprise a logistics information system.
9. What is the logistical command function and how does it relate to the logistics information system?
10. Discuss the differences between customer orders and replenishment orders. How do these differences impact the procedures that must be used in controlling and processing these orders?

CHAPTER 5

Transportation—Regulation and Administration

Transportation provides logistical system geographical closure by linking facilities and markets. In most firms more dollars are spent on transportation than on any other single element of logistical operations. Total expenditures on intercity freight in the United States in 1984 were 250 billion. This expenditure represented 7 per cent of the 1984 gross national product. Naturally, the ratio of transportation cost to total logistical cost varies among industries. Industries that produce high-value products such as cameras, jewelry, computers and electronic components have low transport cost as a percentage of sales. In contrast, coal, iron ore, basic chemicals, and fertilizers have high relative transport cost.

The requirement for transportation services varies greatly from industry to industry. For some basic commodities, transportation requirements command dedicated unit trains. In automobile logistics, the most common method of transport is the trilevel railcar. Several hundred trilevel railcars are required to transport a single week's automotive assembly. In iron ore transport, ships and barges moving on the Great Lakes and inland waterways may satisfy requirements most economically. To the meatpacker, transportation means refrigerated railcars or motor trailers. For the crude oil processor, transportation involves pipelines. For the retailer, United Parcel Service may constitute the primary method of customer delivery. In contrast, a producer of electronic components may use air freight or Federal Air Express for product delivery.

The treatment of transportation is divided into two chapters. In this chapter attention is directed to the regulation and administration of transportation. In Chapter 6 alternative transportation strategies are reviewed in terms of supply infrastructure and carrier services.

136

The first section of this chapter provides an overview of transportation regulation. In order to gain a clear perspective of transportation supply and demand in the 1980s it is necessary to trace significant regulatory actions from 1887 to the present day. From within the legal and market structure of transportation supply and demand each firm must formulate a transportation strategy. The final section of this chapter covers selected aspects of traffic management and administration.

TRANSPORTATION REGULATION

From 1887 until today all forms of transportation have been subject to some degree of regulation. With the passage of the Act to Regulate Interstate Commerce on February 4, 1887, the federal government began to undertake an active role in protecting the public interest with respect to the performance and provision of transportation services. In a broad sense the regulation of transportation can be classified as (1) regulation of business practice or economic regulation and (2) regulation of safety or social regulation. Both types of regulation are important in logistical management.

Regulation of business practice is the oldest type of regulation. In order to provide a dependable transportation service and to foster economic development, the federal and state governments took an active role in economic regulation. Governmental regulatory involvement spanned almost a century and sought to make transportation equally available to all users without discrimination. The basic regulatory policy was to foster competition among privately owned transportation companies. To encourage an economically sound transportation supply, government invested in public infrastructure such as highways, airports, waterways, and deep-water ports. To actually provide transportation service, government supported and regulated a system of privately owned for-hire carriers. The prime focus of business practice regulation was to control prices, degree of competition, and level of service provided by for-hire carriers. This resulted in a traditional regulatory practice of treating each carrier mode of operation on a stand-alone basis. By 1970 the degree of federal economic regulation had reached the point where it affected 100 per cent of rail and air ton-miles, 80 per cent of pipeline, 43.1 per cent of trucking, and 6.7 per cent of domestic water carriers.[1] This degree of direct government economic regulation began to change during the 1970s and took a dramatic turn in 1980 with the passage of major deregulatory legislation. Today's regulatory environment continues to be dominated by a trend toward free-market competition.

In direct contrast, to the trend toward more relaxed business practice regulation, the direction of the 1970s and 1980s has been toward more demanding safety and social regulation. Since its inception in 1967, the Department of Transportation (DOT) has taken an active role in the federal goverment's control over transport and handling of hazardous material, rules related to maximum work hours, and vehicle safety. The scope of this activity was further institutionalized by the passage of the Transportation Safety Act of

---

[1] Derived from the *1972 National Transportation Report* (Washington, D.C.: Department of Transportation, U.S. Government Printing Office, November, 1972), pp. 2–44.

1974. Since the early inception of DOT, the trend in safety and social regulation has intensified to include such far-reaching areas as consumerism, occupational safety and health, environmental impact, and equal opportunity employment.

The parts of this section seek to provide an overview of the transition from regulated to strategic transportation. The first part provides a brief regulatory synopsis from 1887 to 1975. This historical review provides the basis in the next part for viewing the economic deregulatory acts of the 1980s. The next part reviews regulatory activities since 1980 with emphasis on subsequent legislative administration and judicial actions. The final part reviews current federal transportation policy and reviews the future administrative outlook.[2] To the student unfamiliar with transportation subject matter, it is suggested that this section be initially scanned and then studied in detail after reading the balance of the chapter. No comprehensive review of transportation is possible without an understanding of the massive regulatory change that has occurred during the 1980s.

Brief History of Interstate Regulation

The purpose of interstate regulation is to scrutinize the activities of for-hire carriers in the public interest. Since railroads dominated early overland transportation, they initially enjoyed the position of a near monopoly. Individual states maintained the legal right to regulate discriminatory practices within their borders, but no federal regulation existed until the "Act to Regulate Commerce" was passed.[3] This initial act was the forerunner of the regulatory structure. It created the Interstate Commerce Commission (ICC).

The gradual definition of the federal government's regulatory power over carrier pricing resulted from a series of enactments and judicial decisions from 1900 through 1920.[4] At the turn of the century, destructive competitive practices resulted from independent rate-making among carriers. Although the ICC had the authority to review groups of rates with respect to their just and reasonable nature once rates were placed into effect by individual carriers, no regulation existed over *proposed* rate-making. Attempts at joint rate-making by railroads had been declared illegal. In 1903 the railroads supported the passage of the Elkins Act. This act reduced under-the-table rebates and special concessions, and increased the penalty for departing from published rates. It did not, however, eliminate the cause of discriminatory practices—independent and nonregulated rate-making.

The passage of the Hepburn Act in 1906 began to establish federal regulatory power over rate-making. The just-and-reasonable-review authorization of the 1887 act was expanded to include examination of maximum rates. However, the

---

[2] The discussion that follows is limited to an overview of business practice and economic regulation as they impact logistical management. For added depth in the specifics of regulation see John T. Coyle, Edward J. Bardi, and Joseph L. Cavinato, *Transportation* (St. Paul: West Publishing Company, 1982), and Temple, Barker and Sloane, Inc., *Transportation Strategies for the Eighties* (Oak Brook, Ill.: The National Council of Physical Distribution Management, 1982).

[3] For an early history of legislative attempts prior to 1887, see L. H. Hanley, *A Congressional History of Railroads in the United States, 1850–1887*, Bulletin 342 (Madison, Wis: University of Wisconsin, 1910).

[4] The following material is based upon a format established in D. Phillip Locklin, *Economics of Transportation*, 6th ed. (Homewood, Ill.: Richard D. Irwin, 1972).

regulatory posture remained after the fact until passage of the Mann-Elkins Act in 1910. This act permitted the ICC to rule on the reasonableness of proposed rates in advance of publication and to suspend such rates when they appeared discriminatory.

The posture for modern rate regulation was completed with the passage of the Transportation Act of 1920. The review power of the ICC was expanded to prescribe minimum as well as maximum reasonableness of rates. The ICC was instructed to assume a more aggressive nature concerning proposed rates. The original Act To Regulate Commerce was modified to instruct the Commission to initiate, modify, and adjust rates as necessary in the public interest. The 1920 act also changed the name of the 1887 Act to the Interstate Commerce Act.

Several additional transportation laws were enacted. With some exceptions their primary objective was to clarify issues related to the basic acts of 1887 and 1920. In 1935 the Emergency Transportation Act further instructed the ICC to set standards with respect to reasonable rate levels. By the 1930s motor carriers had become a prime transportation factor. In 1935 the Motor Carrier Act placed the regulation of common-carrier highway transportation under the jurisdiction of the ICC. This Act, which became Part II of the Interstate Commerce Act, defined the basic nature of the legal forms of common, contract, and exempt motor carriers.

In 1938 the Civil Aeronautics Act established the Civil Aeronautics Authority (CAA) as the ICC's counterpart for regulating air transport. The powers and charges of the CAA were somewhat different from those of the ICC, in that the Act specified that the CAA would promote and actively develop the growth and safety of the airline industry. In 1940 the functions of the original CAA were reorganized into the Civil Aeronautics Board (CAB) and the Civil Aeronautics Administration, now known as the Federal Aeronautics Administration (FAA). In addition, the National Advisory Committee on Aeronautics was formed in the mid-1930s and in 1951 became known as the National Aeronautics and Space Administration (NASA). Through the 1960s NASA concentrated attention on aerospace. However, NASA is specifically charged with the responsibility for increasing aviation safety, utility, and basic knowledge through the use of science and technology. Thus, in the structure that resulted, the CAB regulated rate-making, the FAA administered the airway system, and NASA was concerned with scientific development of aerospace, commercial, and civil (private) aviation.

The regulation of pipelines had not been as clear-cut as that of railroads, motor carriers, and aviation. In 1906 the Hepburn Act declared that selected pipelines, primarily oil, were in fact common carriers. The need for regulation developed from the early market dominance that Standard Oil Company gained by developing crude oil pipelines to compete with rail transport. In 1912 the ICC took action, which was upheld by the Supreme Court, to convert private pipelines into common carriers. While there are substantial differences between pipeline and other forms of regulation, for all effective purposes, the ICC was made responsible for pipeline regulation. Interestingly, a significant difference in pipeline regulation is that this type of common carrier was allowed to transport goods owned by the carrier.

Regulation of water transport prior to 1940 was extremely fragmented. Some regulation existed under both the ICC and the United States Maritime Commission. In addition, a series of specific acts placed regulation of various parts of the domestic water transport network under specific agencies. The Transportation Act of 1940 placed domestic water transportation under ICC jurisdiction and gave the Federal Maritime Commission authority over water transport in foreign commerce and between Alaska, Hawaii and other United States ports.

It is important to understand that the ICC did not set or establish rates for carriers under its regulatory jurisdiction. Rather, the ICC reviewed and either approved or disapproved rates. Carriers under federal regulation were exempt from the antitrust provisions of the Sherman, Clayton, and Robinson-Patman acts with respect to collaboration in rate-making. Such exemption was provided by the Reed-Bulwinkle Act of 1948, which permitted carriers to participate in rate-making bureaus. Cooperative rate-making was a common feature among for-hire carriers. In particular, for-hire transportation carriers in motor and rail organized freight bureaus that standardized cooperative pricing and published price tariffs for specific geographical areas. Motor carriers, for example, utilize eight rate-making bureaus to coordinate the establishment and publication of new or modified rates. The action of the bureaus was subject to ICC sanction.

Over the years a maze of federal agencies was created to assist in various phases of overall transport regulation. The Department of Transportation (DOT) was established to draw the majority of transport-related agencies together under a single administrative head at presidential cabinet level.

From 1970 until 1973 several acts were passed to aid the rapidly deteriorating rail situation in the United States. In 1970 the Rail Passenger Service Act established the National Railroad Passenger Corporation (Amtrak). The Regional Rail Reorganization Act of 1973 (3-R) was passed to aid seven major northeastern railroads that were facing bankruptcy. As a result of the 3-R Act provisions the Consolidated Rail Corporation (Conrail) began to operate portions of the seven railroads on April 1, 1976.

The establishment of Amtrack and Conrail represented the first modern attempt by the federal government to own and operate transportation services. While the subsequent passage of the Rail Revitalization and Regulatory Reform Act of 1976 (4-R) and the Rail Improvement Act of 1976 provided financial support for Amtrak and Conrail, these acts also began to reverse the trend of regulatory expansion that prevailed for nine decades.

Beyond 1975—A New Regulatory Era

In the early 1970s a concentrated attempt was underway to review and modify existing economic regulation to accommodate demands and requirements of contemporary society. As early as 1955 a Presidential Advisory Committee recommended increased competition in transportation. Their recommendations were published in a 1960 report issued by the Commerce Department.[5] A Senate Committee in 1961 drafted a recommended "National Transportation Policy." Among other recommendations the 1961 report advocated formation of the Department of Transportation (DOT).[6] After its formation it was the

[5] Department of Commerce, *Federal Transportation Policy and Program* (Washington, D.C.: U.S. Government Printing Office, 1960).

[6] Senate Committee on Commerce, *National Transportation Policy*, 87th Congress (Washington, D.C.: U.S. Government Printing Office, 1961). The Department of Transportation was established by Public Law 86–670 in 1966 and initiated operation on April 1, 1967.

Department of Transportation that became the dominant force seeking regulatory modification. From 1972 to 1980 DOT introduced or significantly influenced legislation at two-year intervals to modify the regulatory scope of for-hire carriers.[7]

The initial direct effort at regulatory reform was administrative in nature. From 1975 to 1978 Chairman Alfred Kahn forced *de facto* deregulation of the Civil Aeronautics Board by virtue of administrative rulings that encouraged air carriers to actively compete in free-market discounting and by easing new carrier entry. In 1977 the Federal Aviation Act was amended to deregulate domestic air cargo carriers, freight forwarders, and shipper associations with respect to pricing and entry. The standard for entry into the air cargo industry was modified to require that a new competitor be judged *fit*, *willing*, and *able* to carry out the proposed service. This modification in entry qualification dropped the traditional regulatory criteria of judging entry applications on the basis of *public convenience* and *necessity*. On October 24, 1978, the Airline Deregulation Act was passed which extended free-market competition to all forms of passenger air transport. A significant provision of the Airline Deregulation Act was the mandate to the Executive Branch to *sunset* the Civil Aeronautics Board on or before January 1, 1985.[8]

A significant step toward deregulation was taken with the passage of the Railroad Revitalization and Regulatory Reform Act of 1976 (4-R). The 4-R Act introduced a wide range of guidelines for the regulation of railroad marketing. A significant provision was the introduction of a *zone of reasonableness* or *zone of rate flexibility* (ZORF) in pricing. This concept, which permitted carriers significant latitude in pricing, was to become a common feature of subsequent legislation. ZORF permitted rail carriers to increase or decrease prices by 7 per cent from the level of rates in effect at the beginning of a year. While many advocates of deregulation were critical of the 4-R Act because it "didn't go far enough," the Act did introduce some significant new standards and practices in rate-making. The concepts of just and reasonable rates, market dominance, protective rate-making, and peak demand considerations were embodied in the Act.

The basic drive toward a careful review of existing regulatory policy and practice intensified as Congress established in 1976 a 19-member National Transportation Policy Study Commission (NTPSC). The Commission's charter was mandated by Public Law 94–280 (May 5, 1976). The broad base

---

[7] For varied opinions regarding the desire for and preferred nature of regulatory revamping, see *Analysis and Criticism of the Department of Transportation Motor Carrier Reform Act* (Washington, D.C.: American Trucking Association, 1976); Rupert L. Murphy, "Private or For-Hire?" *Distribution Worldwide* (September 1975), pp. 39–41; Stephen Tinghitella, "The Day the ICC Died." *Traffic Management* (December 1975), p. 14; Jim Dixon, "The Spectre of Distribution," *Distribution Worldwide* (September 1975), pp. 29–30. Harry J. Newman, "The Key to Reform Is Gradualism"; W. Doyle Beatenbough, "There Is Room for Improvement"; Lee Cisneros, "Regulation Is Simply the Balance Wheel"; J. B. Speed, "There Has to Be a Cross-Subsidization of Freight Rates"; B. A. Franzblau, "There Must Be a More Rational Approach"; Tom Cornelius, "Deregulation Would Cause a Chaotic Situation"; W. Stanhaus, "Our System Can Be Improved"; and E. Grosvenor Plowman, "The Need Is for Rational Regulatory Improvement," all in "Deregulation, Reregulation, or Status Quo?" *Distribution Worldwide* (September 1975), pp. 31–38. W. K. Smith, "Shipper/Common Carrier Relationship" and Wayne M. Hoffman, "Regulation of Transportation: How Much Is Enough?" both in *Transportation at a Turning Point* (Syracuse, N.Y.: Syracuse University Printing Service, 1981).

[8] The CAB was officially closed December 31, 1984.

mission of this Commission reflected the regulatory climate of the times. The law required:[9]

> ... a full and complete investigation and study of the transportation needs and of the resources, requirements, and policies of the United States to meet such expected needs.
>
> [Further the NTPSC was to] ... take into consideration all reports on National Transportation Policy which have been submitted to Congress.... It should evaluate the relative merits of all modes of transportation in meeting our transportation needs...[and]...recommend those policies which are most likely to insure that adequate transportation systems are in place which will meet the needs for safe and efficient movements of goods and people.

The Commission's final report was issued in June, 1979. The 527-page report contained 16 chapters, 5 appendices, 74 figures, and 211 tables. As will be highlighted later in this section, a study of the scope and magnitude of the NTPSC report was needed to help congeal fragmented National Transportation Policy. However, the 37-month study and reporting time was too long to contain the momentum for regulatory change.

Upon assuming office as Chairman of the Interstate Commerce Commission in 1977, A. Daniel O'Neil appointed a special task force to recommend ways by which the ICC could internally improve the regulation of motor carriers. The report, commissioned on June 2, 1977, was completed in 34 days and proposed 39 reform proposals. In many ways Chairman O'Neil's approach was similar to that previously followed by Alfred Kahn at the CAB. The task force report was significant because it represented the first major effort on the part of the ICC to internally respond to pressure for regulatory reform.

The struggle for regulatory change in railroads and trucking resulted in 1980 in the passage of the Motor Carrier Regulatory Reform Act and the Staggers Rail Act. Significant aspects of each are highlighted. *why enacted*

obj?

Motor Carrier Regulatory Reform and Modernization Act of 1980 (MCA–80)

The landmark motor carrier legislation since enactment of the Motor Carrier Act of 1935 was the passage of Public Law 96–296 which was signed into law by President Carter on July 1, 1980. The swift resolution of differences in House and Senate provisions of existing bills then under committee consideration, followed by rapid passage by the House and Senate, and presidential approval illustrate how fast the democratic process can work when it is politically advantageous. Even the most dedicated proponents for change were shocked by the rapid compromise and approval. After over 18 months of study and review the controversial bill was resolved into an acceptable form within days and signed into law within hours.

---

[9] National Transportation Policy Study Commission: *National Transportation Policy Through the Year 2000* (Washington, D.C.: U.S. Government Printing Office, 1979). For a discussion of specific policy issues see Gayton E. Germane, *Transportation Policy Issues for the 1980s* (Reading, Mass: Addison-Wesley Publishing Company, 1983).

The significant point concerning this rapid approval is that most observers agree that MCA–80 fell far short of providing a sound motor carrier deregulatory platform. In a later part of this section a review of the significant legislative, administrative, and judicial changes that have followed in the wake of the passage of MCA–80 will testify to the lack of comprehensiveness of the initial law. For those who were proponents of deregulation the law was a long-awaited first step. To opponents, MCA–80 represented the end of stability and the start of turbulent, if not chaotic, competition. The following paragraphs review the underlying philosophy of MCA–80 and highlight its basic features.

MCA–80 was designed to encourage competition and efficiency within the for-hire motor carrier industry. The basic philosophy of the Act was that authorization for carriers to enter the industry had been too restrictive over the years, resulting in too few carriers for effective competition. The traditional practice had been for the ICC to authorize operating rights in the form of a *Certificate of Convenience and Necessity*. As the name implies, the approval of a new certificate was only granted when it could be proved that the proposed service was necessary and in the public interest. Until passage of MCA–80 it was the responsibility of the carrier seeking new or expanded rights to prove necessity under potential protest by interested parties. MCA–80 reversed the burden of proof by requiring that those opposed must prove that the granting of the requested operating rights would be inconsistent with the public convenience and necessity. The new basis for review was that applicants be fit, willing, and able to perform the proposed service similar to that introduced earlier in air regulation.

In addition to relaxed entry, MCA–80 expanded the effective number of industry competitors by changing regulations regarding existing carriers. A highly controversial provision of the law authorized private carrier–compensated intercorporate hauling. The so-called back-haul provision of the law authorized pickup allowances to encourage effective utilization of private trucks in the food industry wherein products had traditionally been sold on a uniform zone-delivered basis. Regulations concerning contract carriers and independent owner-operators were relaxed to permit a broader range of participation in for-hire transportation. Finally, exemption status was expanded with respect to agricultural carriers and small shipments incidental to air transport. Agricultural cooperatives were authorized to haul up to 25 per cent of their total interstate tonnage in the form of nonfarm, nonmember goods.

Several provisions of MCA–80 relaxed industry pricing practices. The zone of rate flexibility (ZORF), originally tested in the 4-R Act, was introduced to the motor carrier industry. A zone of 10 per cent increase or decrease was established within which the ICC could not investigate, suspend, revise, or revoke any rate on the basis of reasonableness. Further the ICC was authorized to expand the ZORF by 5 per cent if justified by competitive conditions. This expansion was authorized by the ICC in 1984. Under provisions of MCA–80 the ZORF is adjusted to reflect changes in the Producer Price Index. The introduction of ZORF did not eliminate ICC involvement in motor carrier pricing. The ICC retained the authority to protect against discriminatory practices and predatory pricing. Carriers were also given more freedom regarding the nature of released value rates without ICC approval. Finally the Act made a serious challenge concerning the collective rate-making practices of the industry. As noted earlier, carriers were permitted to collectively set rates through the use of rate bureaus. MCA–80 limited the scope of collective rate-making by prohibiting discussion of single-line rate proposals after January 1, 1984. In general, MCA–80 challenged the status and practice of rate bureaus by requiring review by a Motor Carrier Rate-Making Commission. Subsequent developments in this area are further discussed in Chapter 6 dealing with common carrier pricing.

Other significant provisions of MCA–80 dealt with rule changes designed to increase industry efficiency. While carriers were given a more liberal hand in expanding services, they also were authorized to modify existing service if they could increase efficiency. As a result of the traditional process of granting operating rights, many carriers were restricted to specific routes or were required to pass through specified gateways during line haul movements. MCA–80 encouraged carriers to eliminate gateways and circuitous routes in an effort to increase direct routing. Carriers were also permitted to apply for relaxation of commodity requirements and the need to service specified cities if operating efficiency could be improved.

It is still too early to fully calabrate the structural impact of MCA–80 on the for-hire motor carrier industry. It is clear that the number of authorized motor carriers has increased significantly. Approximately 3,500 new operating authorities were granted in 1981.[10] Estimates of total new entrants between 1980 and 1984 have been as high as 18,000 and as low as 8,000.[11] Without question, numerous new firms only participated in small contract or irregular route authorities. Prior to passage of MCA–80 no single general commodity common carrier was authorized to service all locations within the continental United States. In 1985, the number of new and expanded all-location rights exceeded 50 authorizations. A significant concern is the high degree of failure among carriers who were in operation prior to the passage of MCA–80. Since 1980 over 35 major carriers have filed for bankruptcy. Even as late as 1984 long-standing industry names such as Interstate, ICX, Mason-Dixon, IML, and Branch initiated bankruptcy proceedings.

A great deal of industry turmoil has resulted from the pricing latitude provided by MCA–80. While some carriers have carefully tied the quality of transportation service offered to rates, others have engaged in massive discounting without cost justification based on modified operating practices.[12] The common carrier for-hire trucking market has dramatically shifted to less-than-truckload (LTL) concentration. Within the LTL sector of the industry many traditional carriers have become significantly stronger in terms of financial performance and industry tonnage share. In 1983 after-tax income for the nation's top 100 trucking fleets was higher than at any time since 1977. In 1984 motor carrier tonnage, net income, and revenue were all up over 1983. The carriers, new or old, that have prospered since MCA–80 are those who improved efficiency by eliminating undesirable activities, increased equipment

---

[10] *Investor News* (November, 1982).

[11] Robert V. Delaney, "Fixing What Was Broken," unpublished version of paper presented at NCPDM Annual meeting, Dallas, Texas, September 17, 1984, p. 14.

[12] Some pricing practices followed by motor carriers offered such dramatic price reductions that they were commonly referred to as kamikaze rates. Discounts as high as 40 per cent off published rates were offered without changes in operational practices following passage of MCA–80.

utilization, and decreased operational variance. This form of quality performance became possible and was rewarded within the provisions of MCA–80.[13]

What was original olig.?

The Staggers Rail Act

On October 14, 1980, President Carter took the next step toward overall deregulation by signing Public Law 96–488 known as the Staggers Rail Act. For the railroad industry the Staggers Rail Act was a continuation of a trend initiated in the 3-R and 4-R acts as supplemented by passage of the Rail Transportation Improvement Act in 1976. The prevailing regulatory policy was to be proactive toward rebuilding a strong rail system. The Staggers Rail Act continued this trend.

The dominant philosophy of the Staggers Act was to provide railroad management the freedom necessary to revitalize the industry. As such, the most significant provisions of the Staggers Act expanded the freedom in rate-making initiated by the 4-R Act.

The concept of ZORF pricing expanded to permit adjustment of any rate based on the percentage increase in the railroad cost recovery index. The significant feature of this provision is that railroads were authorized to lower rates to meet competition and also to raise rates to cover operating cost increases. Carriers were also given increased flexibility with respect to surcharges and cancellations, rules regarding burden of proof in judgments of market dominance, minimum rates, and general rate increases. Contract rate agreements between individual shippers and carriers were specifically legalized.

In addition to price flexibility, railroad management was given liberalized authority to proceed with abandonment of existing service supported by a streamlined approval process. The Act also provided the framework for a liberalized attitude toward mergers and increased railroad involvement in motor carrier service.

Similar to MCA–80, the Staggers Act raised serious questions concerning the future role of rate bureaus. The act prohibited the discussion of, or voting on, single-line rates and significantly altered existing practice on joint-line rates.

The impact of the Staggers Rail Act has resulted in significant changes in the structure and vitality of the rail industry. Prior to deregulation, one leading railroad executive referred to the industry as offering plain vanilla service with plain vanilla equipment.[14] Prior to deregulation, little differentiation existed between railroads. Rates were set by consensus, followed specific industry structures, such as grain or steel, and were insensitive to marketplace requirements. Deregulation has created the opportunity to quickly adjust prices and equipment allocations to specific markets, to tailor rates and services, to develop contract and incentive rates, to eliminate unprofitable routes, and to manage a railroad on an innovative basis.

[13] For a discussion of the importance of quality performance, see D. Daryl Wyckoff, "Transportation Quality: User Friendly," Third Annual William A. Patterson Distinguished Chair in Transportation Lecture, Northwestern University, May 9, 1984.

[14] Based on unpublished remarks by James A. Hagen, "Sales and Services in a Deregulated Environment," presented at Northwestern University Transportation Center, Evanston, Ill., January 25, 1984.

Similar to the reactions of motor carriers to MCA–80, not all railroads reacted in a positive manner regarding the Staggers Rail Act. Typical behavior ranged from excessive and ruinous rate-cutting to far-ranging innovation based on satisfying market needs. By 1985 selected shippers formed a group called Consumers United for Rail Equity (CURE) to protest against the way that the provisions of the Staggers Act were implemented by the ICC. Nevertheless after the initial five years of operation under the Staggers Act, the industry began to show increased stability and financial revitalization. The railroad industry is finding prosperity by responding to customer needs and has clearly overcome the famous Levitt criticism of being *market myopic*.[15] Current railroad growth reflects a strong trend toward intermodal operations as advances are made into merging, starting, or acquiring motor carrier operations. On July 24, 1984, the ICC voted unanimously to approve merger of the CSX Corporation and American Commercial Lines, Inc. This merger of the nation's then second largest railroad holding company and one of the largest barge operations represents an unprecedented step toward intermodal ownership. The most startling indication of the renewed railroad spirit is evidenced by the fact that when bidding for the purchase of Conrail from the government was officially closed at midnight on June 18, 1984, DOT had received 14 purchase offers.[16]

Regulatory Activity Since 1980

The nature of the United States government process is that prevailing law can result from legislation, administrative actions, and judicial rules. The passage of the MCA–80 and Staggers Rail Acts were legislative. However, they set off a series of administrative actions and judicial rulings that have had far-reaching implications. In addition, several new legislative actions have been passed or proposed since 1980. Some of the key activities in each category are reviewed in this part.

Legislative Action

Significant legislation has been proposed or enacted in both business practice and social regulation since 1980. Both types are discussed.

In terms of economic or business practice regulation, the Motor Bus Regulatory Modernization Act of 1982, the Ocean Shipping Act of 1983, the Surface Freight Forwarder Deregulation Act of 1984 and 1985, and the Custom Brokers Act of 1984 completed the first round of mode-by-mode deregulation.

The original provisions of the MCA–80 Act left a great many issues open to interpretation.[17] To some degree, questions were answered by passage of the

---

[15] Theodore Levitt, "Marketing Myopia," *Harvard Business Review* vol. 38 (July–August 1960), pp. 45–56.

[16] The return of Conrail into the private sector represents full circle of the conditions that prompted passage of the 3-R Act. Congress may accept one of existing bids, seek submission of new bids, or may follow a public stock offering. No deadline is mandated for the completion.

[17] Donald V. Harper, "The Federal Motor Carrier Act of 1980: Review and Analysis," *Transportation Journal* (Winter 1981), pp. 30–33, and statements on oversight hearings on the Motor Carrier Act of 1980 held before the House Committee on Public Works and Transportation, October 25. 1983, or before the Senate Commerce Committee, September 21, 1983. Annual oversight hearings are required by the Motor Carrier Act of 1980.

Surface Transportation Assistance Act of 1982. However, by 1983, DOT began to float a new regulatory act for public reaction. The initial DOT effort, entitled the Surface Transportation Deregulation Act of 1983, was a comprehensive law dealing with motor carriers, water carriers, freight forwarders, brokers, and pipelines. A revised draft, limited to further reform of motor carrier regulation, was titled The Truck Deregulation Act of 1983. DOT Secretary Elizabeth Dole predicted the proposed 1983 act would, if it had been enacted, eliminate most of the remaining ICC regulatory authority over the motor carrier industry. An expanded version of this act, entitled the National Motor Carrier Productivity and Safety Act of 1985, was introduced in the fall of 1985. If enacted into law, the 1985 act would for all effective measures fully eliminate motor carrier regulation. It is clear that the legislative posture is to further reduce or eliminate all ICC Regulatory control of motor carriers.

Other laws passed since 1980 do not strictly fit either the category of economic or social regulatory legislation. The Highway Revenue Act of 1982 and the Tax Reform Act of 1984 directly influenced motor carrier operations by increasing public highway use tax. The Tandem Truck Safety Act of 1984, in conjunction with the Surface Transportation Assistance Act (STAA) of 1982, sought to clarify standard rules concerning semitruck weight, overall length, and trailer width. The STAA mandated that the full interstate system be available for the operation of maximum authorized size commercial vehicles. The standard semitrailer as a result of these acts has become 48 foot, 102 inch wide with tandems authorized to 28 1/2 feet for each trailer. In addition to interstate availability, federal law has mandated that Federal-Aid primary highways, as designated by DOT, be available for maximum authorized size commercial vehicles. This has resulted in a national highway network of approximately 180,000 miles available to maximum-size vehicles. The Tandem Truck Safety Act prohibits authorities from restricting the use of maximum vehicles on local or state highways when moving to or from loading or unloading locations.

It is clear that the final chapter on deregulatory legislation is far from complete. Numerous legislative acts have been proposed since 1980, and a few key acts have become law.

Administrative-Judicial Rulings

Following the enactment of major regulatory legislation it is typical for agencies to make interpretative rulings to clarify the administration of the law. In the case of the ICC, proposed rulings are typically floated in the form of *ex parte* statements in an effort to seek reaction from interested parties. As one might expect, *ex parte* activity following the passage of MCA–80 and the Staggers Act was extensive.

In the initial four years following passage of the acts, the most significant rules and procedures established by the ICC were authorization and expansion of corporate back haul, deregulation of piggyback and boxcar freight, restricted antitrust immunity on single-line rates, expanded contract carrier industrywide authority, implementation of single-source leasing of equipment and drives, expansion of rail carriers' authority to engage in nonregulated for-hire trucking, authorization of owner-operators to participate in contract and private truck-ing, and authorization of computerized bills of lading. Rulings were also proposed and at least temporarily withdrawn to change the overall freight classification scheme and to fully deregulate all motor common carrier shipments 1,000 pounds or less. It is clear that the administrative process of the ICC has significantly expanded the deregulatory impact of MCA–80 and the Staggers Act.

The rules and procedures of the ICC are subject to legal review when and if interested parties feel the original intent of the law is violated and they have not received satisfaction from ICC administrative law reviews. Since passage of MCA–80 and the Staggers Act, the federal courts have been busy. The typical procedure is for the specific rule or procedure to be first tested in the United States District Court with typical review by the Court of Appeals. If the District or Appeals Court agrees to review, a decision is issued regarding the legality of the rule or procedure in terms of the enabling law. The final legal recourse is appeal to the United States Supreme Court. For the most part, the Supreme Court has supported deregulation by refusing to hear cases wherein the Appeals Court has ruled in favor of ICC rulings. Significant court rulings or refusal to review ICC actions concerned such far-reaching items as antitrust immunity, deregulation of boxcar traffic, numerous merger approvals, and single-source leasing.

As a general rule, both the administrative and judicial processes of government have enforced the trend toward deregulation of for-hire transportation. The combined efforts of the legislative, administrative, and judiciary from 1980 to 1985 have resulted in a rapid transition from a highly regulated to a free market for buying and selling transportation services.

National Transportation Policy and Administration

The federal government commitment to development and maintenance of a sound national transportation system was one of the basic reasons that regulation was initially proposed in 1887. The Transportation Act of 1940 contained a broad policy statement that guided government action until the passage of the Motor Carrier Act of 1980. During the 40-year period numerous study commissions reviewed and reported on policy matters and several Presidents made transportation policy statements. In 1976 Congress mandated a comprehensive study commission to review the nation's transportation needs through the year 2000.[18] The report of the commission issued in June, 1979, based its recommendations on six major policy themes: (1) national transportation policy should be uniform; (2) there should be an overall reduction in federal involvement; (3) economic analysis of intended federal actions should be used; (4) when the transportation system is used to pursue social goals, it should be done in a cost-effective manner; (5) federal involvement in transportation safety and research is required; and (6) users and those who benefit from federal actions should pay. Based on these themes the commission offered Congress policy recommendations on (1) regulation, (2) ownership and operations, (3) finance, pricing and taxation, (4) planning and information, and (5) government organization.[19]

---

[18] National Transportation Policy Study Commission, op. cit., pp. 247–49.

[19] Ibid., pp. 249–67. A review of Chapter 13 of the NTPSC report is essential for a logistical manager to understand where transportation policy stood in 1979 and where it was headed.

The Motor Carrier Act of 1980 contained a section titled National Transportation Policy. The following eight national transportation goals were articulated: (1) meet the needs of shippers, receivers, and consumers; (2) allow a variety of price and service options; (3) allow the most productive use of equipment and energy resources; (4) enable adequate profits and fair wages; (5) provide and maintain service to small communities and small shippers; (6) maintain a privately owned motor carrier system; (7) promote minority participation; and (8) promote intermodal transportation. While these specific goals are legally restricted to motor carrier operations, they do reflect the spirit and direction of federal regulatory posture for the 1980s.

Federal Administration

A serious question remains for private sector managers concerning what branch and organization of the federal government will administer transportation law and policy. The 1979 NTPSC report found 64 federal agencies administering over 1,000 policies and programs that involved transportation. In addition, 30 congressional committees were found to have legislative and oversight responsibilities directly affecting transportation.[20]

The theme and content of legislation proposed in the mid-1980s call for the complete abolishment of the Interstate Commerce Commission in all matters relating to trucking. Other proposals advocate a complete "sunset" of the ICC with the formation of a new National Transportation Commission to coordinate the residual regulatory activities for all modes of transportation. Two forces within federal government appear to be positioned to take an active role in the future direction of national transportation administration: (1) The Department of Transportation and (2) federal regulatory agencies such as the Justice Department and the Federal Trade Commission. Each is briefly discussed.

As noted earlier, the Department of Transportation was established April 1, 1967, and initiated operation in 1968. Since its establishment, DOT has been a proactive proponent of reduced economic regulation of transportation. Given current deregulatory trends, it appears that DOT is ideally positioned to coordinate most federal enforcement. Figure 5-1 provides an overview of the comprehensive organizational structure of DOT.

The future role of the Justice Department and the Federal Trade Commission in transportation regulation is just emerging. Prior to the passage of the Motor Carrier Act of 1980 and the Staggers Rail Act, the right for transportation agencies to engage in collective rate-making was mandated by law. Both of the 1980 acts established the basis for elimination of antitrust immunity in single-line rates. The Staggers Act made such collective rate-making immediately illegal. MCA-80 established a study commission to make a full and comprehensive investigation of collective rate-making processes for all rates of motor common carriers and the need for continued antitrust immunity. The study commission presented its report as directed. Based on this report it has been ruled by the ICC and upheld by judicial review that as of January 1, 1984, motor carriers could not collectively discuss and set new released value rates or rates that limit carrier liability, and as of July 1, 1984, they could no longer

---

[20] Ibid., p. 265.

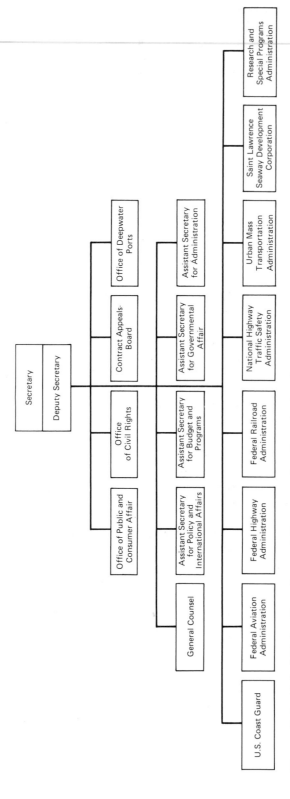

Figure 5–1 United States Department of Transportation Organization Chart

discuss and set single-line rates. To implement this ruling, the ICC defined a single-line rate as follows:

> If the proposed rate would apply to another carrier's single line operations, or would apply for both single line and joint line service, it is a single line rate on which collective activity is barred.

This definition limited legal collective rate-making for all effective purposes to LTL general commodity movements.

With the elimination of antitrust immunity, it appears that the door is open for the Justice Department to take an active role in transportation pricing matters. Likewise, the Federal Trade Commission has taken an increasingly active role. In September, 1984, the Justice Department filed an antitrust suit against the Rocky Mountain Motor Tariff Bureau claiming price-fixing and maintaining excessive rates. During the same month the Federal Trade Commission filed separate complaints against three motor carrier rate bureaus charging their *members* illegally conspired to establish and maintain collective rates on interstate traffic. In July, 1984, the Missouri Pacific Railroad Company and For-Mar-Company each paid fines of $50,000 for violation of the Elkins Act by agreeing to a payment of less than published rates.

The question of potential discrimination in price and service in transportation is becoming a major issue of the 1980s.[21] The potential issue of unreasonable discrimination caused by specific shipper tariffs issued by carriers has become a new concern of both the regulatory agencies and courts. A great deal of controversy exists concerning the relationship of traditional antitrust enforcement and the newfound carrier pricing freedom. Given all current signals, it is safe to conclude that both the Justice Department and the Federal Trade Commission will be actively involved in pricing, mergers, and evaluation of potentially discriminatory practices.

Conclusion—Transportation Regulation

This section has reviewed the dramatic regulatory change of the past decade. As a general statement, the purchase and performance of transportation services are now guided by the market forces of supply and demand. However, the posture of business practice and social regulation of the transportation industry is in a transition period characterized by uncertainty and inconsistency. It is also important to keep in mind that all states except Arizona, New Jersey, Florida and Wisconsin currently have some form of transportation regulation. It is more essential than ever before that logistical managers develop a basic transportation strategy. As logistical managers proceed to negotiate service and price with carrier management, they must be fully aware of the potential consequences of their actions in terms of antitrust implications as well as safety and social regulation. In addition to understanding the direction of change, it is essential that logistical managers seek to influence change in an effort to improve national transportation capability and the operational efficiency of their own organizations. Given this background, attention in the next section is directed to a review of transportation administration.

[21] Sam E. Somers Jr., "The Future Regulation of Discrimination in the Motor Carrier Industry," a paper presented at the Western Transportation Law Seminar, Dallas, Texas, March 6–9, 1983.

TRANSPORTATION ADMINISTRATION

read don't memorize

With, the significant degree of deregulation that has occurred, responsibilities for exacting traffic management have increased substantially. In the past it was not unusual for the traffic manager responsibilities in purchasing transportation to be limited to offers as published in tariffs. However, in the new context, traffic management duties frequently involve negotiation of all types of rates and services with carriers. This section reviews the role of traffic management in a logistical organization. Because many books are devoted to this subject, the content here does not constitute a detailed professional development of the field of traffic management. The objective is to sensitize the reader to the importance of transportation purchasing in logistical operations.

The administration of transportation consists of (1) freight classification, (2) negotiating the lowest rate for a movement consistent with service requirements, (3) equipment scheduling, (4) documenting, (5) tracing and expediting, (6) auditing, (7) claim administration, and (8) research.

Freight Classification

All products normally transported are grouped together into uniform classifications. The *classification* takes into consideration the characteristics of a product or commodity that will influence cost of handling or transport. Similar products are grouped into a class, thereby reducing the wide range of possible ratings to a manageable size. The particular class that a given product or commodity receives is its *rating*. A product rating is not the price that must be paid to have the product transported. The rating is the product's classification placement. The actual price to be paid is called the *freight rate*. As will be explained, the rate is printed in a pricing sheet called a *tariff*. Thus, a product's rating is used to determine the freight rate.

Motor carriers and rail carriers each have independent classification systems. The motor carrier system is the "National Motor Freight Classification," and rail classification are published in the "Uniform Freight Classification." The motor classification has 23 classes of freight, and the rail system has 31. In local or regional areas, individual groups of carriers may publish additional classification listings. Since deregulation, considerable attention has been directed to overall simplification of the classification scheme. Such change is highly probable in the future.

Classification of individual products is based on a relative percentage index of 100. Class 100 is considered the normal class, with other classes running as high as 500 and as low as 35 in the motor system. Each product is assigned an item number for listing purposes and then a classification rating. As a general rule, the higher a class rating, the higher the transportation cost of a product. Thus, a product classified as 400 would be approximately four times more expensive to transport than a product rated class 100. Products are also assigned classifications based upon the quantity shipped. Less-than-truckload (LTL) shipments of identical products will have higher ratings than carload (CL) or truckload (TL) shipments. This in reality is a form of exception rate.

To illustrate, assume item 70660 from the National Motor Freight Classification is described as "carpet or rug cushions, cushioning or lining, sponge rubber, in wrapped rolls." Item 70660 falls under the general product grouping

70500, "floor coverings or related articles." For LTL shipments, item 70660 has a 77 1/2 rating, whereas in TL shipments it is assigned class 45, provided that a minimum of 30.2 hundredweight is shipped. Many products are assigned different ratings based upon packaging. Sponge-rubber cushions may have a different rating when shipped loose, in bails, or in boxes than when shipped in wrapped rolls. Thus, a number of different classifications may apply to the same product, depending upon where it is being shipped, the size of the shipment, the transport mode being used, and packaging.

One of the major responsibilities of the traffic department is to obtain the best possible rating for all products shipped by the enterprise. Although there are differences in rail and motor classifications, each is guided by classification rules. These rule are similar. However, the rail rules are more comprehensive and detailed than those for motor freight classification. It is essential that members of a traffic department have a comprehensive understanding of classification rules.

It is possible to have a product reclassified by written application to the appropriate classification board. The board reviews proposals for change or additions with respect to minimum weights, commodity descriptions, packaging requirements, and general rules and regulations. All changes other than corrections in classification require public hearings prior to publication. All interested parties are provided an opportunity to be heard prior to acceptance or rejection of the proposal. After the proposal is accepted or rejected, methods of appeal are provided.

An alert traffic department will take an active role in classification. Many dollars can be saved by finding the correct classification for a product or by recommending a change in packaging or quantity shipped that will reduce the rating of an enterprise's product.

Negotiation of Freight Rates

Earlier in the chapter, an overview of rate regulation was presented. For any given shipment it is the responsibility of the traffic department to obtain the lowest possible rate consistent with service requirements. The prevailing transport price for each method of movement—rail, air, motor, pipeline, parcel post, United Parcel, freight forwarders, and so on—is found by reference of tariffs.

Under conditions that have existed since 1980 the prevailing tariff represents the point at which transportation negotiation is initiated. The key to effective negotiation is to seek WIN-WIN agreements wherein both carriers and shippers share productivity gains. As indicated several times throughout this text, the lowest possible cost for transportation may not be the lowest total cost of logistics. The traffic department must seek the lowest rate consistent with service standards. For example, if two-day delivery is required, the traffic department seeks the method of transport that will meet this standard at the lowest possible cost.

Equipment Scheduling

One major responsibility of the traffic department is scheduling, either for common carriers or private transportation. A serious operational bottleneck can result from carrier equipment waiting to be loaded or unloaded at a shipper's dock. Scheduling requires careful load planning.

In equipment scheduling, special charges for demurrage and detention should be held to a minimum. However, in special cases, it may be desirable to pay penalties to reduce other expenses. For example, demurrage charges may represent a favorable trade-off if labor overtime can be reduced. Each situation must be evaluated on the merits of the alternatives. Demurrage and detention as well as other services that carriers typically provide shippers are discussed in Chapter 6.

Documentation

Several documents are involved in transportation management. Two of the most important are the bill of lading and the freight bill.

Bill of Lading

The bill of lading is the basic document in the purchase of transport services. It serves as a transaction receipt by documenting commodities and quantities shipped. For this reason, accurate description and count are essential. In case of loss, damage, or delay, the bill of lading is the basis for freight claims.

The bill of lading specifies the terms and conditions of carrier liability and includes all possible causes of loss or damage except those defined as acts of God. It is important that terms and conditions be clearly understood so that appropriate actions may be taken in the event of inferior performance. Recent ICC rulings permit uniform bills of lading to be computerized and electronically transmitted between shippers and carriers.

There are variations in bills of lading. In addition to the *uniform* bill of lading, others commonly used are order notify, export, and government. It is important to select the correct bill of lading for a specific shipment.

An *order-notified* or *negotiable* bill of lading is a credit instrument. It provides that delivery not be made unless the original bill of lading is surrendered to the carrier. The usual procedure is for the seller to send the order-notified bill of lading to a third party, usually a bank or credit institution. Upon customer payment for the product, the credit institution releases the bill of lading. The buyer then presents it to the common carrier, who, in turn, releases the goods.

An *export* bill of lading permits the domestic use of export rates, which are sometimes lower than domestic rates. When a shipment is being exported, the use of export rates for the domestic origin or destination line-haul transport might reduce total cost. An export bill of lading also permits extended time at the port for transfer of freight from a railcar to a ship. In many cases the export bill also eliminates the need for special broker services at port facilities.

Government bills of lading may be used when the product is owned by the US government. A government bill of lading allows the use of *Section 22 rates*, which are normally lower than regular rates.

The named individual or buyer on a bill of lading is the only bona fide recipient of goods. A carrier is responsible for proper delivery according to instructions contained in the document. In effect, title is transferred with accomplishment of delivery.

Freight Bill ✳

The *freight bill* represents a carrier's method of charging for transportation services performed. The freight bill is derived from information contained on the bill of lading. It may be either prepaid or collect. A *prepaid* bill means that transport cost must be paid for prior to the transportation performance, whereas a *collect* shipment shifts payment responsibility to the buyer.

A great deal of transportation administration is involved in preparation of bills of lading and freight bills. Several shippers and carriers are working with the Transportation Data Coordinating Committee to reduce this administrative burden. Some firms elect to pay at the time of creating the bill of lading, thereby combining the two documents into one. Such arrangements are based upon financial analysis of the relative benefits of advanced payment to reduce paperwork costs. Many attempts are also underway to produce all documents in the required number of copies simultaneously. This has become more practical with the advent of computer facilities of aid in document preparation.

Tracing and Expediting

Another important responsibility of transportation management is tracing and expediting. Shipment committed to the vast transportation network of the United States are bound to go astray or be delayed en route from time to time. Most large carriers maintain a tracing department and a computerized service to aid shippers in locating a shipment. The tracing action must be initiated by the shipper's traffic department, but, once initiated, it is the carrier's responsibility to provide the desired information.

Under conditions of exacting product movement control such as just-in-time procurement, the shipper may desire to expedite a given shipment to overcome some unexpected change of events. Under these conditions the shipper is provided a "pro" number, which corresponds to the carrier's waybill and vehicle number. Identification of the shipment's pro number assists in the determination of its location at transfer and point-of-destination terminals.

Auditing

Auditing of freight bills is another important function of the traffic department. Owing to the complexities involved in finding the correct rate, the probability of an error in rate determination is higher in purchasing transportation than in most other purchasing decisions. Given that transportation represents nearly 50 per cent of total logistical cost, a small error in rate calculation could result in a significant loss to either carriers or shippers. The purpose of auditing is to assure billing accuracy.

There are two types of freight audits. A *preaudit* determines the proper rate and charges prior to payment of a freight bill. A *postaudit* makes the same determination after payment.

Auditing may be either external or internal. If external, freight auditing companies are utilized who have personnel specialized in reviewing specific commodity groupings. Payment for an external audit is usually based on a percentage of the revenues reclaimed through overcharges. It is crucial that a highly ethical firm be employed because valuable marketing and customer information is contained in the freight bill, and corporate activities may be adversely affected if it is not held confidential.

A combination of internal and external auditing is frequently employed. The division of this activity is typically based upon the freight bill. Thus, for a bill of $600, a 10 per cent error results in a $60 recovery, but for a $50 bill a 10 per cent error results in only a $5 recovery. Bills with the larger recovery potential are typically audited internally.

External versus internal auditing may also be affected by the size of the firm and the degree of rate computerization. Large traffic departments are in a position to have audit specialists. Firms on computerized systems of freight payment can build in rates on a majority of points and weights. In that case automatic checks on proper payment can be made by computer programs designed for that purpose.

Claim Administration

When transportation services or fees do not meet the predetermined standards, shippers can make claims for restoration. The majority of claims fall into two categories: (1) loss and damage and (2) overcharge-undercharge. Loss and damage claims represent a shipper's demand for carrier payment of partial or total financial loss resulting from improper fulfillment of the transport agreement. Charge claims result from a variation in charges from those published in tariffs.

A specialized body of rules applies to the proper procedure for claim filing and the responsibility of involved parties. Two factors regarding claim administration are of primary importance. First, detailed attention should be given claim administration because such recoveries are realized only by aggressive audit programs. Second, the emergence of a large volume of claims indicates that the involved carriers are not performing their service obligation. Regardless of the dollars recovered by claim administration, the breakdown in customer service performance from loss and damage claims impacts a shipper firm's reputation with customers.

Research

Beyond traffic administration, the traffic department carries a research responsibility. A distinction of professionalism in traffic management is the capability to do meaningful traffic research.

Traffic research is divided into two areas. The first involves activities to improve the cost of transportation services and/or the quality of service received. The second constitutes activities aimed at improving overall logistical operations.

Transport Services Research

Traffic managers should always be on the lookout for information to improve carrier service or obtain lower freight rates for the desired quality of service. This means that an aggressive program of performance measurement should be a continuing activity of transportation research.

Carrier performance measurement is one of the least developed areas of traffic research. Information is normally accumulated from individual carrier claims. Shippers should also attempt to measure how well carriers meet stated service obligations. Such obligations involve (1) equipment availability, (2) tracing efficiency, (3) expediting capability, and (4) transit consistency.

Among these four measures of performance, the one most difficult to obtain reliable information about is transit consistency. In Chapter 7, where the subject of inventory control is developed, it will be pointed out that a vital aspect of control is order cycle speed and consistency. Regardless of how fast a supplier is able to ship, if the transport carrier provides inconsistent delivery, problems in inventory control will result. Likewise, sales can be lost and production lines shut down if carriers fail to meet their service obligation. Generally speaking, the smaller a given shipment, the greater the service variance between consecutive shipments. Thus, while a truckload or carload shipment may regularly meet published schedules, the same efficiency may break down in LTL or package shipments. Some carriers are superior to others, and the task is to determine which carrier is most consistent.

One shipper purchasing from a number of suppliers for delivery to several different warehouse locations obtains transit information as follows. When suppliers ship, they are required to record the time, date, and other critical information on a postcard which is mailed to purchasing. At the warehouse the arrival time and date are recorded and transmitted to the central purchasing. Both dates are recorded and retained in a computer by the individual carrier along with a statement of expected performance. The variation between actual and expected performance is calculated and updated on a regular basis. At specified times the performance record of each carrier is tabulated for purchasing and traffic management review.

This consistency report, coupled with statistics on equipment availability, tracing, and expediting performances, provides valuable information for carrier evaluation. Unless this information is collected on a routine basis it is difficult to be specific or take corrective action about erratic carrier performance.

The effectiveness of transportation negotiation depends upon a shipper's ability to support proposals with accurate and complete information. Review of carrier performance and continuous examination of beneficial changes in existing classifications and tariffs are required for effective research. Such information can only be collected by a well-administered research and analysis program.

Logistical System Research

For any given operating period, traffic management is expected to provide the required transportation services within the stated expenditure budget. It is also traffic management's responsibility to seek ways that transportation can be used to reduce total logistical costs. For example, a slight change in packaging may open the door for negotiation of a lower classification rating for a product. Although packaging costs may increase, this added expense may be offset by a substantial reduction in transportation cost. Unless such proposals evolve from the traffic department, they may not be detected.

As indicated earlier, transportation is the highest single cost area in most logistical systems. Because of this cost and the dependence of the logistical system on an effective transport capability, the traffic department must play an active role in future planning.

SUMMARY

At the outset of this chapter considerable attention was directed to the regulation of transportation. Beginning in 1975 significant forces were at work trying to increase the competitive nature of the transportation industry. Since 1980 the forces of deregulation have become a reality.

Many benefits of integrated logistics are recognized and accomplished by aggressive and innovative traffic management. Transportation administration is a specialized area of management. The final section of this chapter provided a short review of the duties and responsibilities of traffic management. A distinction was made between administrative and research activities. It is in the area of transport research that the skills of the traffic management are vital. Chapter 6 focuses attention on transportation infrastructure and carrier services.

QUESTIONS

1. Why did the federal government originally engage in regulation of transportation?
2. What are the major features of the Staggers Rail Act?
3. What are the major features of the Motor Carrier Act of 1980 (MCA–80)?
4. What does *de facto* deregulation consist of, and how is it accomplished?
5. Describe and illustrate the concept of zone of rate flexibility. How does it apply to motor carrier and rail pricing?
6. What is an *ex parte* action, and what role has it played in transportation regulation since 1980?
7. What is the current status of transportation deregulation? What future role do you project for DOT?
8. What is the difference between a rate and a rating? Do you feel that classification will be important in a deregulated environment? Support your position.
9. Discuss computer applications in transportation administration. In what specific areas can the paperwork traditionally associated with transportation be reduced or eliminated?
10. Explain the difference between a preaudit and a postaudit.

6

Transportation—Infrastructure and Services

A wide range of transportation alternatives are available for product or raw-material movement in a logistical system. In addition to for-hire transportation, an enterprise may decide to operate private transportation or enter into a contract with a transport specialist. This chapter provides an overview of available transportation services and their customer service capabilities. The chapter development places emphasis on the range and cost of available transportation services.

The first section provides a review of transportation infrastructure in terms of modal choice and characteristics. The second section reviews common carrier rate structures and describes special or accessorial services that carriers offer to customers.

TRANSPORTATION INFRASTRUCTURE

In this section infrastructure is viewed in terms of the legal variety and relative characteristics of transportation modes and multimodal systems. The term *mode* is used to identify a basic method or form of transportation.

Basic Modes

The five basic transportation modes are rail, highway, water, pipeline, and air. The relative importance of each mode can be measured in terms of system mileage, traffic volume, traffic revenue, and the nature of traffic composition. Each mode is reviewed with respect to these relative measures.[1]

---

[1] For a more detailed discussion, see Charles A. Taff, *Management of Physical Distribution and Transportation*, 7th ed. (Homewood, Ill.: Richard D. Irwin, Inc., 1984); Roy J. Sampson, Martin T.

Rail

Historically, railroads have handled the largest number of ton-miles within the continental United States. As a result of the early establishment of a comprehensive rail network connecting almost all cities and towns, railroads dominated intercity freight tonnage until after World War II. This early superiority resulted from the capability to transport large shipments economically, frequent service, and a somewhat monopolistic position. However, with the advent of serious competition following World War II, the railroad's share of ton-miles and revenues has been declining.

In 1982 rail transport accounted for 34.3 per cent of total intercity tonnage. Projections to the year 2000 indicate that rails will experience a moderate decline in market share to 31.9 per cent of total intercity ton-miles. This market share trend represents a major accomplishment compared to the 1947 to 1970 period, during which railroads experienced a serious decline in market share. In terms of total share of intercity transportation ton-miles, railroads transported 54.0 per cent in 1947, 39.2 per cent in 1958, 38.8 per cent in 1965, and 35.9 per cent in 1970. The decline in share of revenue was even more significant, dropping from almost 40 per cent in 1950 to 20.9 per cent in 1982.

The miles of railroads in service once ranked number one among all modes. In 1982 the total miles of railroad was 165,000 miles which ranked last among all modes. This mileage has further declined during the mid-1980s due to the liberalized abandonment provisions of the Staggers Rail Act.

The capability of railroads to transport very large tonnages efficiently over long distances is the main reason they continue to command significant intercity tonnage and revenue. Railroad operations experience high fixed costs because of expensive equipment, right-of-way, switching yards, and terminals. This fixed capacity, coupled with the nature of rail power, results in a relatively low variable operating cost. The replacement of steam by diesel power reduced the railroad's variable cost per ton-mile, and electrification offers a potential for even greater reductions. A minimal of power, combined with limited labor, allows a large volume of traffic to be transported considerable distances at low variable cost per ton-mile.

In recent times the character of traffic transported by rails has shifted from a wide range of commodities to an emphasis on extracting industries, heavy manufacturing, and agricultural commodities. The greatest sources of railroad tonnage are the raw-material-extracting industries located a considerable distance from improved waterways.

Despite operational problems, the inherent fixed-variable cost structure of railroads still offers economic superiority for numerous long-haul movements. Since the 1950s, railroads have tended toward a policy of market segmentation by eliminating small-shipment (LCL) traffic and several accessorial services. This emphasis on marketing has increased since passage of the Staggers Rail Act. To provide improved service to major rail users, progressive railroads have

Farris and David L. Shrock, *Domestic Transportation: Practice, Theory, and Policy*, 5th ed. (Boston: Houghton Mifflin Company, 1985); John T. Coyle, Edward J. Bardi, and Joseph L. Cavinato, *Transportation* (St. Paul: West Publishing Company, 1982); and *National Transportation Statistics Annual Report*, 1983, (Washington, D.C.: U.S. Department of Transportation, U.S. Government Printing Office, August 1984).

concentrated on the development of specialized equipment, such as the enclosed trilevel automobile car, cushioned appliance cars, unit trains, and new pricing techniques. Operations have been expanded in terms of integrated motor carrier operations. In an overall sense, railroads in the 1980s have become the leaders in intermodalism.

These examples are by no means a comprehensive review of recent railroad innovations. They are characteristic of the attempts being made to retain and improve railroad's share of the overall transportation market. It is clear that significant changes are occurring in traditional concepts of railroading. The 1970 issues of survival and potential nationalization have given way in the 1980s to the revitalization of a rail network.

Highway

Highway transportation has expanded rapidly since the end of World War II. To a significant degree, the rapid growth of the motor carrier industry resulted from flexibility of door-to-door operation and speed of intercity movement.

In 1982, expenditures on intercity freight moved by for-hire truck exceeded $34 billion, which was equal to 88 per cent of the combined total for rail, air, water, and pipeline. In terms of relative increase, motor carriers transported 5.2 per cent of total ton-miles in 1947, 12.5 per cent in 1958, 14.6 per cent in 1965, 15.9 per cent in 1970, 19.7 per cent in 1975, and 23.8 per cent in 1982. The forecasted market share of intercity for-hire truck ton-mileage for the year 2000 is projected to remain around 22 per cent.

Motor carriers have flexibility in that they can operate on all types of highways. The 1975 improved highway mileage available to motor carriers exceeded 3.8 million miles, which was greater than the combined total of all other modes of transport. The total interstate system represents approximately 42,500 statute miles, while total federal-aided primary roads consist of nearly 300,000 miles of highway.

In comparison to railroads, motor carriers have relatively small investment in terminal facilities and operate on publicly maintained right-of-way. Although the cost of license fees, user fees, and tolls is considerable, these expenses are directly related to the number of over-the-road units operated. The variable cost per mile for motor carriers is high because a separate power unit is required for each trailer or combination of tandem trailers. Labor requirements are high because of driver safety restrictions and the need for substantial dock labor. The net result is a structure of low fixed cost and high variable cost. In comparison to railroads, motor carriers are economically adapted to handling small shipment moving short distances.

The character of motor carrier traffic favors manufacturing and distributive trades. In particular, motor carriers have made significant inroads into rail traffic associated with medium and light manufacturing. Because of delivery flexibility, motor carriers have captured almost all freight moving from wholesalers or warehouses to retail stores. The prospect for maintaining relative market share in highway transport remain bright. In 1984, with the exception of small package goods moving in premium service, almost all less than-15,000-pound intercity shipment (LTL) were transported by motor carriers.

The motor carrier industry is not without problems. The primary difficulties relate to the increasing cost of labor as reflected in equipment replacement, driver wages, maintenance, and, in particular, platform and dock wages. Although accelerating labor rates influence all modes of transport, the labor-intensive nature of motor carrier operations causes the impact to be felt severely. To counteract this trend, carriers have placed a great deal of attention on improved line-haul scheduling that bypasses terminals, computerized billing systems, mechanized terminals, tandem operations that pull two trailers by a single power unit, and utilization of coordinated transport systems, such as trailer on flat car (TOFC) to perform a portion of line-haul movement.

The greatest threat to the for-hire motor carrier industry is over-the-road transportation by shipper-owned trucks or by specialized carriers that perform transport services for shippers under contract. In 1980 over 50 per cent of all intercity truck tonnage was hauled in private fleet operations. The low fixed cost structure of motor carrier operations results in easy entry by new firms. Since 1980 deregulation has encouraged new firms to enter all forms of trucking.

It is apparent that highway transportation will continue to function as the backbone of logistical operations for the foreseeable future. The area of primary concern to logistical planning is service, rates, and special charges associated with shipments under 15,000 pounds.

Water

Water is the oldest mode of transport. The original sailing vessels were replaced by steamboats in the early 1800s and by diesel power in the 1920s. A distinction is generally made between deep-water and navigable inland water transport. Domestic water involves the Great Lakes, canals, and navigable rivers.

In 1982 domestic water transport accounted for 15.9 per cent of total intercity tonnage. Its relative share of intercity ton-miles was 31.3 per cent in 1947 and 31.7 per cent in 1958. Tonnage declined to 27.9 per cent in 1965 but increased in 1970 to 28.4 per cent. This short-term increase did not last. Market share dropped to 16.4 per cent in 1972 and was 15.9 per cent in 1982. Forecasted market share for the year 2000 is 23.1 per cent of total intercity tonnage.

The exact miles of improved inland waterways in operation do not include the Great Lakes or coastal shipping. In 1982 25,543 miles of improved inland waterways were operated. Fewer system miles exist in inland water than any other transportation mode.

The main advantage of water transport is the capacity to move extremely large shipments. Deep-water vessels are restricted in operation. In contrast, diesel-towed barges have considerable flexibility. Water transport ranks between rail and motor carrier with respect to fixed cost. The fixed cost of operation is greater than that of motor carriers but less than that of railroads. The main disadvantage of water is the limited degree of flexibility and the low speeds of transport. Unless the source and destination of the movement are adjacent to a waterway, supplemental haul by rail or truck is required. The capability of water to transport large tonnage at low variable cost places this mode of transport in demand when low freight rates are desired and speed of transit is a secondary consideration.

Freight transported by inland water is oriented to mining and basic bulk commodities, such as chemicals, cement, and selected agricultural products. In addition to the restrictions of navigable waterways, terminal facilities for bulk and dry-cargo storage and load-unload devices limit the flexibility of water transport. Labor restrictions on loading and unloading at dock level create operational problems and tend to reduce the potential range of available traffic. Finally, highly competitive situation has developed between railroads and inland water carriers in areas where parallel routings exist.

Inland and Great Lakes water transport will continue to be a viable transportation option in future logistical systems. The full potential of the St. Lawrence Seaway has not been realized with respect to domestic freight.[2] The slow passage of inland river transport can provide a form of warehousing in transit if fully integrated into overall system design. Improvements in ice-breaking equipment appear on the verge of eliminating the seasonal limitations of domestic water transport.

Pipeline

The initial pipelines were in operation in domestic commerce in 1865. Although growth was not dramatic, by 1947, 9.5 per cent of intercity tonnage moved by pipeline. A major increase in utilization occurred between 1947 and 1958 when the percentage of total intercity freight ton-miles jumped to 16.5 per cent. In 1956 pipeline transport constituted 18.7 per cent of total intercity tonnage, 19.6 per cent in 1970, 21.0 per cent in 1975, and 25.8 per cent in 1982. The forecasted market share for the year 2000 is 22.8 per cent. Pipelines for the past several decades have represented the fastest-growing transportation mode. A great deal of this growth is directly attributable to the energy crises which resulted in direct government subsidies for substantial increases in capacity such as the Trans-Alaska pipeline.

The most frequent commodity transported by pipelines is petroleum. In 1960, 190,944 miles of pipeline were operational in the United States. By 1970, that figure had jumped to 218,671 miles. The operational figure in 1982 declined to 213,699 miles. Pipelines have the highest fixed cost and the lowest variable cost among transport modes. The high fixed cost results from the right-of-way for pipeline, construction, and requirements for control stations and pumping capacity. Since pipelines are not labor-intensive once constructed, the variable cost of operation is extremely low.

The basic nature of a pipeline is unique in comparison to all other modes of transport. Pipelines operate on a 24-hour basis, seven days per week, and are limited only by commodity changeover and maintenance. An obvious disadvantage is that pipelines are not flexible and are limited with respect to commodities that can be transported. Experiments on the potential movement of solid products in the form of slurry or in hydraulic suspension continue to be conducted. For the immediate future petroleum products will remain the primary commodity transported by pipelines.

Air

The newest, most glamorous, and by far the least utilized mode of transport is air freight. The glamor of air freight lies in the speed with which a shipment can

---

[2] For a detailed discussion concerning the Seaway, see John L. Hazard, *Transportation: Management, Economics, Policy* (Cambridge, Mass.: Cornell Maritina Press, Inc., 1977), pp. 371–414. This work is currently being updated.

be transported. A coast-to-coast shipment via air requires a few hours, as contrasted to days via other modes of transport. The trade-off of speed for cost associated with other elements in the logistical system, such as field warehousing, has attracted considerable attention to the potential of air freight.

Air transport still remains more of a potential than a reality. Although the mileage is almost unlimited, for over two decades air freight has accounted for less than 0.2 of 1 per cent of all intercity ton-miles. Air transport capability is limited by lift capacity and availability of aircraft. Traditionally, most intercity air freight has been transported on scheduled passenger flights. While this practice was economically justified, it caused a subsequent reduction in both capacity and flexibility of freight operations. The high cost of jet air craft, coupled with the erratic nature of freight, has limited the assignment of dedicated aircraft to all-freight operations. Likewise, research and development on special-purpose cargo air craft, such as STOL-capable aircraft and cargo helicopters, had lagged because of the slow maturation of high-volume air freight.

The fixed cost of air transport is not high in comparison to those of rail, water, and pipeline. Airways and airports are generally developed and maintained with public funds. Likewise, terminals are normally maintained by local communities. The fixed costs of air freight are associated with aircraft purchase and the requirement for specialized handling systems and cargo containers. Air transport ranks second only to highway with respect to low fixed cost. On the other hand, air freight variable cost is extremely high as a result of fuel, maintenance, and the labor intensity of both inflight and ground crews.

No particular commodity dominates the traffic carried by air freight operations. Perhaps the best distinction is that most freight handled is on an emergency, rather than a routine, basis. Most firms utilize scheduled or nonscheduled air cargo movements when the situation justifies high cost. Products with the greatest potential for regular air movement are those having high value or extreme perishability. When the marketing period for a product is extremely limited, such as with Christmas, high fashion items, or fresh fish, air transport may be the only practical method for logistical operations.

The prospects for increased utilization of air cargo in logistical operations remain promising. Although movement by air requires prior and subsequent land movement, the speed of service between two points can reduce overall logistical costs sufficiently to offset the added cost of air transport.

Modal Classification

The basic modes of transportation were reviewed in terms of historical development and share of intercity ton-miles and freight revenue. The essential operating characteristics of each mode were noted, including the relationship of associated fixed and variable cost structures. Table 6–1 provides a comparison of modes in terms of system mileage, intercity ton-miles, traffic revenue, and forecasted market share. These data are presented for 1972 and 1982. Table 6–2 provides a summary of the fixed-variable cost structure of each mode. Table 6–3 summarizes the operating characteristics of each mode with respect to speed, availability, dependability, capability, and frequency.

Speed refers to the elapsed time for intericty movement. Air freight is the fastest of all modes. Availability refers to the ability of a mode to service any

TABLE 6–1   Modal Comparison Vital Statistics and Dominant Traffic Composition

1972 and 1978*; Forecasted to 2000[†]

Mode		System[a] Mileage	Traffic Volume (Intercity Ton-Miles)	Forecast Traffic Volume (Intercity Ton-Miles)	Traffic Revenue (Per/ Ton-Mile)	Nature of Traffic Composition
Rail	72	203,299	37.6%	31.9%	$ 1.62	Extracting industries
	82	165,000	34.3%		$ 3.21	Heavy manufacturing Agricultural commodities
Highway	72	270,259[b]	22.8%	22.0%	$ 7.97	Medium and light manufacturing Distribution between wholesalers and retailers
	82	298,219	23.8%		$14.09	
Water	72	25,543[c]	16.4%	23.1%	$ .47	Mining and basic bulk commodities Chemicals
	82	25,543	15.9%		$ 1.10	Cement Some agricultural products
Pipeline	72	221,127[d]	23.1%	22.8%	$ .29	Petroleum
	82	213,699	25.8%		$ 1.25	Coal slurry
Air	72	300,126	.016%	.2%	$22.75	No particular commodity Most freight handled on
	82	352,292	.2%		$46.78	emergency rather than regular basis

* National Transportation Statistics Annual Report, 1983, U.S. Department of Transportation, U.S. Government Printing Office, August
[†] National Transportation Policies through the Year 2000, National Transportation Policy Study Commission, U.S. Government Printing Office, June, 1984, Forecast Based on Medium Growth Scenario, Appendix Table 38.
[a] Statute miles
[b] Federal-aid primary
[c] Inland waterway
[d] Petroleum and other liquid products
[e] Class I and II intercity common carriers excluding household goods
[f] Index = 100 in 1967

TABLE 6–2   Nature of Cost Structure for Each Mode   *FC vs. VC*

Mode	Cost Structure
Rail	High fixed cost in equipment, terminals, track, etc. Low variable cost
Highway	Low fixed cost—highways in place and provided by public support Low variable cost—fuel, labor, maintenance, etc.
Water	Medium fixed cost—ships and equipment Low variable cost—capability to transport large amount of tonnage
Pipelines	Highest fixed cost—rights of way, construction, requirements for control stations and pumping capacity Lowest variable cost—no labor cost of any significance
Air	Low fixed cost—aircraft and handling and cargo systems High variable cost—fuel, maintenance, and labor

TABLE 6–3   Relative Operating Characteristics—Five Basic Transportation Modes

Operating Characteristic	Transportation Mode				
	Rail	Highway	Water	Pipeline	Air
Speed	3	2	4	5	1
Availability	2	1	4	5	3
Dependability	3	2	4	1	5
Capability	2	3	1	5	4
Frequency	4	2	5	1	3

given pair of locations. Highway carriers have the greatest availability. Dependability refers to potential variance from expected or published delivery schedules. Pipelines, because of their continuous service, rank highest in dependability. Capability is the ability of a mode to handle any transport requirement. Water transport is the most capable. The final classification is frequency, which relates to the quantity of scheduled movements. Pipelines, again because of their continuous service between two points, lead all modes in frequency.

As Table 6–3 shows, the appeal of highway transport is in part explained by its high ranking across all five characteristics. Operating on a world-class highway system, motor carriers rank first or second in all categories except capability. Although substantial improvements in motor capability resulted from relaxed size and weight limitations on interstate highways and approval to use tandem trailers, it is not realistic to assume motor transport will surpass rail or water capability.

Legal Forms of Transportation

In addition to classifying transportation alternatives on the basis of mode, another method of grouping is on the legality of carrier operating rights. Each carrier must comply with some form of legal authorization to transport goods and commodities. The four traditional types of legal carrier are common, contract, private, and exempt. In recent years the independent provider of transportation services has become a vital part of supply. Each type of carrier may exist within any basic transportation mode. The traditional structure of regulated transportation was for carrier ownership to be limited to a single legal type and mode. Since deregulation, many firms have been granted dual operating authorities in two or more legal forms of transport. For example, some private carriers have been granted common and contract carrier rights. In addition, there has been a trend on the part of government to encourage intermodalism wherein two different modes are joined by operating agreement and/or ownership.

Common Carrier

The most basic category of legal transportation consists of different types of common carriers. A common carrier is a company that offers to transport property for revenue at any time and any place within its operating authority without discrimination. A common carrier is authorized to conduct for-hire transportation after receiving a Certificate of Public Convenience and Necessity from the appropriate regulatory agency. Common carriers are required to publish rates charged for transport service. The operating authority received by a motor common carrier may include transport of all commodities or may limit transport to specialized commodities such as steel, household goods, or computers. In addition, the operating authority specifies the geographical area the carrier may service and indicates if such service is to be on a scheduled or nonscheduled basis.

Contract Carrier

Contract carriers perform transport services on a selected basis. Although contract carriers must receive authorization in the form of a permit, such permits normally are less restrictive than common carrier operating authority. The basis for contract cartage is an agreement between a carrier and a shipper calling for the provision of a specified transportation service at an agreed-to cost. The business agreement becomes the basis for the contract carrier to receive a permit. The permit authorizes the contract carrier to transport specified commodities. The contract carrier may transport for more than one shipper and is not required to charge the same rate for all shippers. Recent regulatory rulings are moving toward the authorization of contract carriers to service all firms within an industry. This move is reflective of the overall trend to liberalize services that a contract carrier can legally provide.

Exempt Carrier

Exempt carriers do not confront direct regulation with respect to operating rights or pricing policies. Exempt carriers, however, must comply with licensing and safety laws of the states in which they operate. If the exempt carrier is engaged in interstate movement, rates must be published. Exemptions for motor and water carriers originated from the need to transport seasonal and unprocessed agricultural products to manufacturing centers. Today, exempt carriers operate across a broad range of commercial activity. Exemptions are granted on the basis of service area and to support selected associations.

An example of service area exemption is local cartage within the commercial zones surrounding municipalities. In a controversial and contested ruling in early 1977, the ICC dramatically expanded commercial zones. In the case of municipalities with populations of 1 million or more, the commercial zone was expanded from 5 to 20 miles beyond municipal limits.

An association exemption refers to shipper alliances for the purpose of aggregating small shipments at a buying center for transport in consolidated shipment. The two primary modes engaged in exempt cartage are highway and water.

The general scope of exemption has expanded since 1980. Several provisions of the 1980 deregulatory acts increased exempt privileges. Administrative rulings since 1980 have fully exempted boxcar, trailer on flat car, and rail-associated trucking from the need to comply with freight classifications.

Private Carrier

Private carriage consists of a firm providing its own transportation service. The firm must provide managerial direction over the transport operation and must have an ownership basis in the goods or commodities transported. It is legal for a transportation subsidiary of a conglomerate to transport for divisions or corporations within the family group of businesses. Although private transport does not come under the regulatory laws of the federal or state governments, it is subject to license safety, and weight restrictions. Private trucking has increased significantly during the past decade, and all forecasts indicate continued expansion. The flexibility and economy of a private truck operation customized to the needs of a particular shipper are difficult for a common carrier to match. A recent change in transportation law that encourages private trucking was the 1984 Supreme Court approval of single-source leasing. Under the provisions of single-source leasing, a firm can obtain the services of a driver and the necessary equipment under a single lease. This provision reduces the number of transactions necessary to place a private fleet in operation.

Independent Carrier

A special type of legal transportation is the owner-operator or independent trucker. The owner-operator typically owns a tractor and may own a trailer. Using their own equipment owner-operators provide line-haul service on a regular or trip-by-trip basis for other legal forms of transportation. Recent rule changes authorize owner-operators to make business arrangements with common, contract, exempt, and private carriers. Prior to the 1980s owner-operators were limited to providing service to common and contract carriers.

Conclusion—Legal Forms

From the perspective of logistical system design, the distinctions between legal forms of transportation are slight. The main considerations are the degree of restriction, the extent of financial commitment, and the flexibility of operation.

Since deregulation, the restrictions surrounding what a given legal form of transportation can and cannot do have been greatly relaxed. However, restrictive laws and regulations still exist regarding each form of cartage. These restrictions must be understood in logistical system design.

The extent of commitment refers to the degree of financial involvement or obligation which the shipper has to offer the carrier. The least amount of commitment is experienced with common carriers, since an agreement reached for each shipment specifies the obligations of all parties. Contract operations have a greater degree of commitment in the sense that the typical contract between a carrier and shipper is for six months to one year. It is important to point out that the degree of involvement normally associated with both common and contract carriers is variable cost in nature and is directly associated with the tonnage transported. In private transport, the extent of commitment is longer and involves both fixed cost of equipment and variable cost of operation. This obligation can be reduced by equipment leasing or utilizing owner-operators. The commitment associated with exempt cartage is difficult to generalize since it can range from very little to extensive.

The greatest latitude in terms of flexibility is naturally associated with private transport. However, it should be noted that failure to schedule private transport in an economical and routine manner can lead to costly operations. Exempt and contract cartage rank second to private carriage for operational flexibility. Since the contract operator is captive to the shipper, a great deal of direction can be exercised in operational scheduling. The number of common carriers means that the availability of service is great. However, the shipper does not legally have a great deal of direct control concerning the common carriers' operation. While the common carrier must service all shippers on an equal basis and at a common price, the prudence of good management dictates that the common carrier will design service around the requirements of large and frequent shippers.

The vitality of a sound national transportation system rests with common carriers, the backbone of the transport network. Most enterprises utilizing private, exempt, and contract carriers also tender frequent shipments to common carriers. In fact, the largest users of private trucking are usually the largest users of common carrier transport. The general belief among professional traffic managers is that every effort should be made to support a sound common carrier network capacity.

Intermodal Transportation

Intermodal transportation refers to two carriers representing different modes providing joint service. Many efforts have been made over the years to combine the inherent advantages of different transport modes into single-shipment movement. Initial attempts at modal coordination trace back to the early 1920s. Such services became common during the 1950s.

Technically, coordinated transportation could be arranged among all basic modes. Descriptive jargon is popular—piggyback, fishyback, trainship, and airtruck have become standard transportation terms. The important distinction of coordinated arrangements is that the line-haul portion of the shipment is split between two different modes.

The best-known and most widely used coordinated system is the trailer-on-flatcar (TOFC), commonly known as *piggyback*. As the name implies, a motor carrier trailer is placed on a railroad flatcar for some portion of the intercity line haul.

A variety of piggyback service plans are available. However, not all railroads offer each. The most significant plans are summarized in Table 6-4. Among the piggyback arrangements the most popular is Plan II 1/2 wherein the shipper provides the terminal service at either origin or destination. This plan covers nearly 50 per cent of all TOFC movements.

Containers also move via TOFC service. Containerization is discussed in greater detail in Chapter 8. The basic concept is that goods are enclosed in a protective device to facilitate handling during transit from origin to destination. The containers are placed on flatcars similar to TOFC service, except that containers are generally smaller. A special label has been applied to container-on-flatcar service—COFC.

As noted earlier, TOFC is just one type of intermodal transport currently in operation. One of the oldest is fishyback, when over-the-road trailers or containers are loaded on ships or barges for long-distance transport. Such services are provided in coastal waters between Atlantic and Gulf ports, Great Lakes to coastal points, and along inland navigable waterways.

Because of the economic potential of linking two modes in a coordinated effort, the intermodal concept appeals to shippers and carriers. In fact, several

TABLE 6–4 Summary TOFC Plans

Plan I	Railroad movement of common motor carrier's trailers, with the shipment moving on one bill of lading with billing being done by the trucker. Traffic moves under rates in regular motor carrier tariffs. Motor carrier handles ramp-to-door terminal service at origin and destination.
Plan II	Railroad does line haul and performs terminal service, moving rail-owned trailers or containers on flatcars under one bill of lading.
Plan II 1/4	Railroad provides trailer, flatcar, and line haul and performs either origin or destination terminal service.
Plan II 1/2	Railroad furnishes the trailer, flatcar, and line haul, but the shipper performs the origin and destination terminal service.
Plan III	Railroad provides line haul, while shipper and/or consignee provide trailers and perform terminal service. Typical rates are based on a flat charge per trailer.
Plan IV	Shipper or forwarder furnishes a trailer-loaded flatcar, either owned or leased. The railroad makes a flat charge for loaded or empty-car movements, furnishing only line haul.
Plan V	Traffic moves generally under joint rate. Either mode may solicit and bill for traffic.

authorities have suggested that the only way to maintain a strong national transportation network is to encourage and foster increased intermodalism. Efforts to increase intermodalism are of prime interest to logistical planners because such development increases the options available in system design. The deregulatory trend of the 1980s substantially relaxed barriers to multimodal ownership. As a consequence, a large number of railroads have acquired common motor carriers, and joint ownership of barge and rail firms is now a reality. The next decade should witness expanded development of intermodal arrangements.

Package Services

Over the past several decades a serious problem has existed in small-shipment transportation. The typical common carrier has difficulty in providing a reasonably priced small-shipment service due to the overall cost associated with pickup and delivery, terminal and line-haul service. To solve this problem, motor carriers have followed the practice of requiring a minimum charge for any shipment handled. Most railroads do not offer small-shipment service. Because of the minimum charge practice, an opportunity existed for companies offering specialized service to enter the small-shipment or package-service market.

Package services represent an important part of transportation infrastructure. However, the variety of services offered does not fall neatly into the modal classification scheme. Package services can be classified as providing regular and premium transportation. Each is discussed.

Regular Package Service

Numerous carriers offer package delivery services within the commercial zones of metropolitan areas. As noted earlier, this type of service is classified as an exempt common carrier who specializes in parcel delivery. Other carriers offer package delivery service on an intrastate and interstate basis. The best known of these carriers are United Parcel Service and the United States post office.

The original service offered by UPS was contract delivery of local shipment for department stores. In this sense, the service was limited to delivery of merchandise to consumers. During the past two decades, UPS has made substantial inroads into overall intercity package movements. Since its inception, UPS has been constantly expanding the scope of its overall operating authority. The basic concept is that individual packages conforming to specified size and weight restrictions may be shipped intercity via UPS. By specializing in a specific size of package, UPS has been able to provide overnight cost-effective service between most cities within 150 miles. Provided that shippers are located at key commercial centers, UPS two-day service can cover approximately 55 per cent of the continental United States' population.

The United States post office parcel service provides nationwide service similar to that of UPS. Because of a unique operating characteristic regarding line haul, parcel service is discussed in the next section under auxiliary transportation. Other forms of routine package services are offered by various bus companies that provide intercity passenger transport.

The importance of regular parcel service cannot be overemphasized. One of the fastest-growing forms of marketing in the United States is nonstore retailing, in which orders are placed by telephone or mail from catalogs for subsequent home delivery. The bulk of nonstore retailing for home delivery which transcends a local municipal area is transported via United Parcel Service and parcel post.

Premium Package Service

Most organizations that provide routine package service also have a premium service. UPS, for example, offers a Blue Label Service and the post office provides Priority Service. Several specialized carriers who specialize in providing premium service have entered the package transportation market in the past decade.

The most widely recognized premium package service is provided by Federal Air Express (FAE). FAE provides nationwide overnight service utilizing a fleet of dedicated cargo aircraft. The original FAE service attracted attention because of the innovative line-haul plan wherein all packages were flown each night to a terminal hub located in Memphis, Tennessee, for sorting and redistribution. FAE's original service has been expanded to include a form of two-hour document transmission throughout the country marketed as ZAP-Mail and expansion of package size and weight allowances.

The potential for rapid growth in parcel service has attracted many competitors into the overnight premium package service. In addition to specialized firms like FAE, UPS, Airborne Freight, Emery Worldwide, and Purolator, major motor carriers and airliness have begun to offer competitive service. These services appeal to commercial businesses because they fill a need for rapid delivery to cover emergency requirements. They also appeal to infrequent business and personal shippers.

Auxiliary Transportation

Auxiliary transportation is provided by firms that operate in a manner somewhat analogous to wholesalers in marketing channels. They purchase a major share of their intercity or line-haul transport from legal forms of transport. In some situations they operate their own over-the-road equipment. It is common practice for auxiliary users to operate as exempt carriers within the commercial zone of municipalities for purposes of pickup and delivery.

The economic justification of auxiliary carriers is that they offer shippers lower rates for movement between two locations than would be possible by direct shipper utilization of common carriers. A more detailed explanation of the peculiarities in the common carrier rate structure that provide the opportunity for auxiliary transport are discussed later in this chapter. The enabling conditions for auxiliary transport are the existence of minimum charges, surcharges, and less-than-volume rates. A quantity of small shipments from various shippers is aggregated by the auxiliary user, who then purchases intercity transportation on a volume-rate basis. The auxiliary carrier typically offers shippers a rate lower than the corresponding common carrier rate for the shipment size. The profit margin of the auxiliary carrier is the per-pound difference between the rate charged the shipper and the cost of transport service purchased from the carrier. In some cases auxiliary carriers charge even higher rates than shippers could obtain directly from primary carriers. The justification for higher charges is faster delivery and more complete service. The three main auxiliary carriers are freight forwarders, shipper associations, and parcel post.

Freight forwarders accept the full responsibility for performance on all shipments tendered to them by shippers. Freight forwarders are common in surface and air cargo. In both cases, they consolidate small shipments and then tender a bulk shipment to common carriers for transport. At the destination, the freight forwarder splits the bulk shipment into the original shipments. Local delivery may or may not be included in the forwarder's service. The main advantage of the forwarder is a lower rate per hundredweight and, in most cases, speedier transport of small shipments than would be experienced by direct tender to a common carrier.

Shipper associations are similar in operation to the freight forwarder. As the name implies, shipper associations are voluntary nonprofit entities with membership centered around a specific industry in which small-shipment purchases are common. Department stores, for example, often participate in shipper associations since a large number of different products may be purchased at one location, such as the garment district in New York City. The basic idea is that a group of shippers establish an administrative office at a point of frequent merchandise purchase. The office arranges for all members' purchases to be delivered to a local facility. When sufficient volume is accumulated, the staff arranges for consolidated shipment to the association's membership base city. As indicated earlier, some associations operate their own intercity transportation, with the legal status of an exempt carrier. Each member is billed on a proportionate basis to traffic moved plus a prorated share of the association's fixed costs.

The United States post office operates surface and air parcel service. The charges for parcel post are based on weight and distance. Generally, parcels must be delivered to the post office at a point of shipment origination. However, in the case of large users and when it is to the convenience of the government, post office service may be established on the premise of the shipper. Intercity transport is accomplished using air, highway, rail, and even water, and the legal forms utilized in parcel post include common and contract cartage. Delivery is provided at the destination by the postal service.

The auxiliary forms of transportation utilize the services of one or more of the modes and legal forms of transport except pipelines. Auxiliary carriers represent a major source of small shipment distribution.

Conclusion—Transportation Infrastructure

The transportation infrastructure available to the logistics planner in the United States is superior to that of any other nation. Although problems do exist within and between the modes, the shipper has many choices with respect to how a particular shipment will be transported between two locations. Within the five basic modes, several legal forms exist. In addition, intermodal arrangements, specialized carriers, and auxiliary transportation exist to round out the alternatives. The task in logistical system design is to select the transport mix that satisfies overall transportation requirements.

Ultimately, the selection of a transportation mix must be fully integrated into the overall logistical effort. In evaluating the potential transportation mix, the value or service rendered by a specific combination of carriers must be measured in terms of corresponding cost. The next section disccusses the common carrier rate structure.

COMMON CARRIER RATE STRUCTURE

A comprehensive treatment of all aspects of common carrier rates is beyond the scope and intent of this overview. The primary purpose of this section is to introduce the basic logic and prevailing practice in common-carrier rates. First, the most popular types of rates are discussed. The final part reviews special services that carriers provide which are important to logistical planning. This discussion is limited to common carrier rates because they are required to be published by law. Rates related to contract and exempt carriers are negotiated and are difficult to generalize.

Common Carrier Line-Haul Rates

Common carriers have traditionally utilized three basic types of line-haul rates: (1) class, (2) exception, and (3) commodity. Each type of rate is reviewed.

Class Rates and Classification

The term *class rate* evolves from the fact that all products transported by common carriers are classified for purposes of transportation pricing. The classification scheme reduces the number of rates a common carrier would have to offer to transport all commodities. In standard transportation terminology a products classification is referred to as its *rating*. The classification does not provide the price charged for movement of a commodity. The price in dollars and cents per hundredweight to move a specific product classification between two locations is referred to as the *rate*. To avoid confusion in understanding common carrier rates, a clear distinction should be made between the rating and the rate. The specifics of freight classification were discussed in greater detail in Chapter 5.[3]

Once the classification rating for a product is obtained, the applicable rate per hundredweight between any two locations can be determined from a price list referred to as a tariff. All products legally transported in interstate commerce can be shipped via class rates. The actual price charged for a specific shipment is normally subjected to a minimum charge and may also be subject to a surcharge or an arbitrary assessment.

The *minimum charge* represents the minimum a shipper must pay to make a shipment regardless of weight. To illustrate, assume that the applicable class rate is $6/cwt (hundredweight) and the shipper wants to ship 100 pounds to a specific location. If no minimum charge existed, the transportation cost would be $6. However, if the minimum charge is $12 per shipment, the cost for completing the shipment would be the minimum. Under the assumed conditions, the minimum charge renders all shipments from 1 to 200 pounds at equal transportation cost.

An *arbitrary* is a special assessment added to a shipment charge. In some cases, arbitraries exist to provide carriers extra compensation for servicing selected destinations or areas. Arbitraries are particularly common in the South, where added charges have traditionally been placed upon shipments in selected weight categories. In other cases, the applicable rates to specific destinations are published in terms of hundredweight charge to a major city plus an arbitrary charge for delivery beyond.

An additional charge, often added for small shipments, is a *surcharge* to help cover specific carrier costs. The surcharge may be a flat charge or a sliding scale based on the size of the shipment.

Class rates, minimum charges, arbitrary charges, and surcharges form a pricing structure which, in various combinations, is applicable between all locations within the continental United States. Commodity classification provides a basis for grouping all products into a few ratings. The tariff specifies the class rate for any rating group between specified origins and destinations. With the advent of widespread computerization, class rates are now published between Zip-code areas and are provided to shippers in computer media. In combination, the classification scheme and class rate structure combine to form a generalized pricing structure for rail and motor common carriers. Because of the generalized nature of class rates, they represent the highest transport prices.

---

[3] See pages 152–53.

Exception Rates

Exception rates, or exceptions to the classification, are special rates published to provide shippers rates other than the prevailing class rate. The original purpose of the exception rate was to provide a special rate for a specific area, origin-destination, or commodity when either competitive or high-volume movements justified a downward rate adjustment. Rather than publish a new tariff, an exception to the classification or class rate was established.

Just as the name implies, when an exception rate is published, the classification that normally applies to the product is changed. Such changes may be the assignment of a new class or may be a percentage of the original class. Technically, exceptions may be higher or lower, but most exception rates are reductions from class rates. Unless otherwise noted in the tariff, all services associated with the movement remain the same as the class rate when a commodity moves under an exception rate.

Since deregulation, a number of new types of exception rates have gained in popularity. An *aggregate tender rate* is one wherein a shipper agrees to provide a carrier multiple shipments in exchange for a discount or exception to the prevailing class rate. The primary objective of an aggregate tender rate is to reduce carrier cost by permitting multiple shipment pickup during one stop at a shipper's facility. Since 1980 numerous pricing innovations have been introduced by common carriers based on variations of aggregation principles. A *limited service rate* is one wherein a shipper agrees to perform one or more services typically performed by the carrier, such as trailer loading, in exchange for a discount. In both aggregate tender and limited service, as well as other innovative exception rates, the basic economic justification is the lowering of carrier cost and sharing of benefits based on shipper-carrier cooperation. These new forms of exception rates are typically negotiated between shippers and carriers based on specific freight and operating characteristics.

Commodity Rates

When a large quantity of a product moves between two locations on a regular basis, it is common practice for carriers to publish a *commodity rate.* Commodity rates are special or specific rates published without regard to classification. The terms and conditions of a commodity rate are typically specified in a contract between the carrier and the shipper. The Staggers Rail Act specifically made contracts between carriers and specific shippers legal. Commodity rates are typically published on a point-to-point basis and apply only on specified products. Today, most rail freight moves under commodity rates. Commodity rates are less prevalent in motor carrier tariffs. Whenever a commodity rate exists, it supersedes the corresponding class or exception rate.

Conclusion—Line-Haul Rates

The three main line-haul rates form the nucleus of the motor and rail common carrier rate structures. Each mode has specific characteristics applicable to their tariffs. In water, specific tariff provisions are made for cargo location within the ship or on the deck. In addition, provisions are made to charter total vessels. Similar specialized provisions are found in air cargo and pipeline tariffs. Auxiliary users and package services publish tariffs specialized to their service.

Thus, although this part described the most frequently used common carrier line-haul rates, it did not provide comprehensive coverage.

Special Rates and Services

A number of special rates and services provided by for-hire carriers are available for logistical operations. This final part describes some important examples.

Freight-All-Kinds Rates

Rates for *freight-all-kinds* (FAK) are important to physical distribution operations. Under FAK rates, a mixture of different products are delivered to a single or limited number of destinations. Rather than determine the classification and applicable rate of each product, an average rate is applied for the total shipment. In essence, FAK rates are line-haul rates since they replace class, exception, or commodity rates. Their purpose is to simplify the paperwork associated with the movement of a mixture of commodities. As such, they are of particular importance in physical distribution.

Local, Joint, Proportional, and Combination Rates

Numerous *special rates* exist that may offer transportation savings on specific freight movements. When a commodity moves under the tariff of a single carrier, it is referred to as a *local rate* or *single-line rate*. If more than one carrier is involved in movement of the freight, a *joint rate* may be applicable wherein the freight moves on a through bill of lading even though multiple carriers are involved in the actual transport. Because many motor and rail carriers operate in restricted territory, it may be necessary to utilize the services of more than one carrier to complete a shipment. Utilization of a joint rate can offer substantial savings over the use of two or more local rates.

Proportional rates are in fact special price incentives to utilize an attractive tariff that applies only to part of the desired route. If a joint rate does not exist and proportional provisions do, the cost of moving a shipment under the proportional provisions of a tariff are applicable to origin or destination points outside the normal geographical area of a single-line tariff. Proportional rates provide a discount on the single-line part of the movement, thereby resulting in a lower overall freight charge.

Combination rates are similar to proportional rates in that two or more rates may be combined when no published single-line or joint rates exist between two locations. The rates may be any combination of class, exception, and commodity rates. The utilization of combination rates often involves several technicalities, such as intermediate rules and aggregation of intermediates, which are beyond the intent of this treatment. The use of a combination rates may substantially reduce the cost of an individual shipment. In most cases that involve regular movements, the need to utilize combination rates is eliminated by the publication of a through rate.

Transit Services

Transit services are, with some exceptions, limited to railroads. A transit privilege permits a shipment to be stopped at an intermediate point for a specified reason. When transit privileges exist, the shipment is charged a through rate from origin to destination plus a transit privilege charge. From the viewpoint of the shipper, the use of this specialized service is restricted to specific geographical areas once the product enters transit service. Therefore, a degree of postponement is lost when the product is placed in transit because the area of final destination can be altered only at significant added expense or, at the least, loss of the through rate and assessment of the transit charge. Finally, the utilization of transit privileges increases the paperwork of shippers, both in terms of meeting railroad record requirements and ultimate settlement of freight bills. The added cost of administration must be carefully weighed in evaluating the true benefits gained from utilizing a transit privilege. During the last decade railroads have generally discouraged the use of transit services.

Diversion and Reconsignment

For a variety of reasons, a shipper or, for that matter, the *consignee* (receiver of shipment) may desire to change routing, destination, or even consignee once a shipment is in transit. This flexibility can be extremely important. It is a normal practice among certain types of marketing intermediaries to purchase commodities with the full intention of selling while in transit with subsequent diversion or reconsignment.

Diversion consists of changing the destination of a shipment while it is en route and prior to arrival at the originally planned destination. *Reconsignment* is a change in consignee prior to delivery. Both services are provided by railroads and motor carriers for a specified charge.

Split Delivery

At destination, carriers will provide split delivery where delivery at more than one physical location is desired. Under specified tariff conditions, pickup and delivery will be extended to points beyond the initial destination. The typical practice is to pay the rate for the total shipment to the final destination plus a charge for each stop-off.

Demurrage and Detention

Demurrage and detention are carrier charges when freight cars or truck trailers are retained beyond the specified loading or unloading time. The term *demurrage* is used by the railroads for delay in excess of 48 hours in returning a car to service. Motor carriers use the term *detention* to cover similar delays. In the case of motor carriers, the permitted time is specified in the tariff and will normally be limited to a few hours. The assessment of a penalty charge is mandatory on the part of carriers and is subject to ICC policing and fine if not properly administered.

From the viewpoint of logistical operations, the degree of demurrage and detention experienced must be carefully administered. Situations exist wherein it is desirable to pay the charge to gain time in processing a particular shipment. In effect, the boxcar or trailer can be used as temporary warehouse space by payment of demurrage or detention.

Accessorial Services

Motor and rail carriers offer a wide variety of services that can be important in planning a logistical operation. Diversion, reconsignment, transit, demurrage, detention, and split delivery are examples of special services discussed above. The list of additional special services is almost unlimited. Of particular importance to logistics are environmental, special equipment, and delivery services.

Environmental services refer to special control of freight while in transit. Refrigeration, ventilation, and heating are examples of controlled-environment transport. *Special equipment charges* refer to per-trip assessment for the use of special equipment which the carrier has purchased for the economy and convenience of the shipper. The *delivery* services provided by carriers are particularly important to logistical operations. Although this brief coverage of special services is not all inclusive, it does provide examples of the range and type of services carriers provide. Thus, the role of a carrier in a logistical system is often far greater than line-haul transportation.

SUMMARY

The critical nature of transportation to logistical operations can be developed from a number of perspectives. Transportation provides spatial closure for the logistical system by linking geographically separated facilities and markets. Transportation is a total cost-reducing activity in the sense that expenditures for transport services permit specialization and economies in the process of manufacturing and marketing.

The transport infrastructure consists of five basic modes of transport. Rail, highway, water, pipeline, and air can be compared on the basis of speed, availability, dependability, capability, and frequency of service, as well as fixed and variable costs. Within these modes, legal forms of transport identify specific carriers as common, contract, private, exempt and independent operators. In addition, intermodal package and auxiliary transportation round out the infrastructure. The task in the design of a logistical system is to select from among all alternatives the combined transport mix that best fits the need of a particular enterprise.

The common carrier rate structure provides a basis for evaluating the benefits in overall logistical operations in terms of corresponding cost. Specific common carrier line-haul rates can be grouped as class, exemption, and commodity rates. A wide variety of special rates and services exist which are of particular importance to logistical operations.

In combination, Chapters 5 and 6 have provided an overview of transportation. Because of the large proportion of total logistics dollars spent on movement, it is essential that high-quality transportation management be established and maintained. Many benefits of integrated logistics are first identified and then accomplished as a result of aggressive and innovative traffic management. In Chapter 7 attention is directed to inventory.

QUESTIONS

1. Describe the five modes of transportation, identifying the most significant characteristics of each. What is the basic concept behind intermodal movement?

2. Why have the railroad miles declined during a period of national growth?

3. Railroads have the largest percentage of intercity freight ton-miles, but motor carriers have the largest revenue. How do you justify this relationship?

4. Why is motor carrier freight transportation the most overall preferred method of product shipment?

5. Given deregulation, is there any real difference between common, contract, and exempt carriers?

6. Are independent or owner-operators a legal form of transportation given current regulatory provisions? Support your answer.

7. Among the TOFC plans, which is most popular and why?

8. How can the recent rapid growth of premium package services such as Federal Air Express be justified on an economic basis?

9. Why are freight-all-kinds (FAK) rates important to an enterprise engaged in the delivery of a broad product line to customers?

10. Provide an example of how diversion and reconsignment can be used to increase logistical efficiency and effectiveness.

Inventory

Inventory is one of the riskiest decision areas in logistical management. Commitment to a particular inventory assortment and subsequent market allocation in anticipation of future sales represent the vortex of logistical operations. Without the proper assortment of inventories, serious marketing problems can develop in revenue generation and customer relations. Likewise, inventory planning is critical to manufacturing operations. Raw-material shortages can shut down assembly or require modification of the production schedule, which, in turn, introduces added expense and potential of finished inventory shortage. Just as shortages can disrupt planned marketing and manufacturing operations, overstocked inventories can also create problems. Overstocks increase cost and reduce profitability through added warehousing, capital tieup, deterioration, excessive insurance, added taxes, and obsolescence.

Inventory management seeks to achieve a balance between shortage and excess stock within a planning period characterized by risk and uncertainty. The principles of inventory management are developed in this chapter. The first section presents an overview of risk and functionality associated with inventory decisions from a strategic perspective. The second section reviews the elements of inventory policy. The third section introduces the concept of inventory lot sizing and discusses some alternative lot-sizing rules. The fourth section restates the goals of inventory management and provides a detailed discussion concerning the nature and treatment of uncertainty. Section four also outlines procedures for inventory control. The fifth section identifies inventory management alternatives and provides guidelines for application of options. The final section discusses the development of an integrated inventory management strategy.

STRATEGIC INVENTORY MANAGEMENT

Strategic inventory management is the development and execution of policies and procedures to decide where to place inventories, when to trigger replenishment inventory movement, and the size of replenishment or inventory allocations. Inventory control, on the other hand, is primarily concerned with ensuring that accounting records match physical inventory count and that inventory is protected from loss, damage, and pilferage. Given the recent high cost of capital, additional emphasis is being placed on management of resources committed to inventory. This emphasis is demonstrated through an increased desire for understanding strategies and tools for managing inventory. This section discusses the nature of inventory and examines its functionality.

Nature of Inventory in the Logistical System

Formulation of an inventory policy requires an understanding of the role of inventory in a manufacturing-marketing or service enterprise.[1] This segment provides background understanding by presenting financial characteristics of inventory investment, discussing inventory risk, and identifying some conflicts characteristic of inventory management.

Financial Considerations

In order to understand the importance of inventory, one must grasp the magnitude of assets committed in a typical enterprise. Table 7–1 presents selected financial and inventory investment information for eight consumer and industrial goods manufacturers. As the table indicates, a significant percentage of all assets of these firms is committed to inventory. As new products are added, this inventory investment increases, resulting in higher inventory asset deployment. The large size of typical assets committed and the relative percentage of total resources involved mean that inventory represents a significant cost center. The reduction of a firm's inventory commitment by a few percentage points through effective inventory management can provide dramatic profit improvement.

---

[1] For a variety of background discussions, see John F. Magee, *Production Planning and Inventory Control* (New York: McGraw-Hill Book Company, 1958); M. K. Starr and D. W. Miller, *Inventory Control: Theory and Pratice* (Englewood Cliffs, N. J.: Prentice-Hall, Inc., 1962); E. S. Buffa and J. G. Miller, *Production-Inventory Systems: Planning and Control*, 3rd ed. (Homewood, Ill.: Richard D. Irwin, Inc. 1979); G. Hadley and T. W. Whitin, Analysis of Inventory Systems (Englewood Cliffs, N. J.: Prentice-Hall, Inc., 1963); Rein Peterson and Edward A. Silver, *Decision Systems for Inventory Management and Production Planning* (New York: John Wiley & Sons, 1979).

TABLE 7-1 Selected 1984 Financial Data for Consumer and Industrial Goods Manufacturers ($ Millions)

Company	Sales	Net Income	Total Assets	Inventory Investment	Inventories as a Per Cent of Assets
American-Cyanamid	$ 3,536	$ 166	$ 3,056	$ 507	16.6%
Bristol-Myers	3,907	408	3,007	551	18.3%
General Foods	8,600	317	4,432	1,097	24.8%
General Mills	5,551	245	2,944	487	16.5%
General Motors	74,581	3,730	45,695	6,622	14.5%
Hewlett-Packard	4,710	432	4,161	748	18.0%
IBM	23,274	5,485	37,243	4,381	11.8%
Johnson & Johnson	5,973	489	4,462	992	22.2%

Inventory Types and Characteristics

The holding of inventory is risky. It is important to understand that the nature and extent of risk vary depending upon an enterprise's position in the distribution channel.

Retail Inventory Risk. For a retailer the management of inventory is fundamentally a buying and selling process. The retailer purchases a wide variety of products and assumes a substantial risk in the marketing process. The retailer's inventory risk can be viewed as wide but not deep. Because of the high cost of store location, the retailer places prime emphasis on turnover and direct product profitability of inventory items.

Although retailers will assume a risk position on a variety of products, their position on any one product is not deep. Risk is spread across more than 10,000 stockkeeping units in a typical supermarket. A discount store offering general merchandise and food often stocks over 25,000 stockkeeping units. A full-line department store may have as many as 50,000 stockkeeping units. Faced with this width in inventory, retailers attempt to reduce their risk by pressing manufacturers and wholesalers to assume greater and greater inventory responsibility. Pushing inventory "back up" the marketing channel has resulted in retailer demand for fast delivery of mixed-product shipments from wholesalers and manufacturers. Specialty retailers, in contrast to mass merchandisers, normally experience less width of inventory risk because the lines they handle are narrower. However, specialty retailers must assume greater risk with respect to depth and duration of inventory holding.

Wholesale Inventory Risk. The risk exposure of wholesalers is narrower but deeper and of longer duration than that of retailers. The merchant wholesaler purchases in large quantities from manufacturers and sells in small quantities to retailers. The economic justification of the merchant wholesaler is the capability to provide to retail customers a merchandise assortment produced by different manufacturers. When products are seasonal, the wholesaler is often forced to take an inventory position far in advance of the selling season, thereby increasing depth and duration of risk.

One of the greatest hazards of wholesaling is product-line expansion to the point where the width of inventory risk approaches that of the retailer, while depth and duration of risk remain characteristic of traditional wholesaling. For example, traditional full-line hardware and food wholesalers have faced a difficult situation during the past decade. Expansion of product lines has increased the width of inventory risk. In addition, their retail clientele have forced a substantial increase in depth and duration by shifting inventory risk. The pressure of product-line proliferation, more than any other single factor, has forced a decline in general wholesalers with replacement by specialized operations.

Manufacturing Inventory Risk. For the manufacturer, inventory risk has a long-term dimension. The manufacturer's inventory commitment starts with raw material and component parts, includes work-in-process, and ends with the finished goods. In addition, finished goods often must be transferred to warehouses in close proximity to wholesalers and retailers prior to sale. Although a manufacturer may have a narrower line of products than retailers or wholesalers, the manufacturer's inventory commitment is relatively deep and of long duration.

If an individual enterprise plans to operate at more than one level of the distribution channel, it must be prepared to assume additional inventory risk. For example, the food chain that operates a regional warehouse assumes risk typically related to the wholesaler operation which is over and above normal retail operations. To the extent that an enterprise becomes vertically integrated, inventory must be managed at all levels of the marketing channel.

Inventory Conflicts

Since all members of a marketing channel must accept some degree of risk, emphasis on inventory reduction results in conflict. More and more retailers are attempting to reduce risk by forcing suppliers to maintain inventories. As a result, suppliers must deliver smaller orders on a timely basis. In turn, suppliers have forced some risk back to manufacturers. The resulting conflict is that each customer wants to reduce inventory commitment and rely on suppliers to provide accurate and timely replenishment. Of course, the customer is not generally willing to give up any sales margin for increased level of inventory support.

Conflict is not restricted to the marketing channel. Conflict also exists between physical distribution, manufacturing, and purchasing within an enterprise. Each area has a natural desire to have others maintain inventories.

Emphasis on inventory reductions has intensified these conflicts. In order to resolve conflict management must understand the impact that revised inventory strategies will have within an enterprise and across the channel. This understanding must lead to integrated strategies which consider the economic and service implications for all involved. For example, it may be beneficial for the overall enterprise to have manufacturing maintain higher work-in-process inventories to support more flexible physical distribution operations.

In addition to the conflict between functions, there is also substantial potential conflict between inventory investments and other enterprise investments. Instead of tying up scarce resources in inventories, assets could be invested in new product development or in the financial markets. When all forms of conflict are considered, it is clear that the return-on-investment of assets committed to inventory must be evaluated against alternative investments.

Inventory Functionality

The basic function of inventory is to increase profitability through manufacturing and marketing support. The ideal concept of inventory would consist of manufacturing a product to a customer's specifications. Such a system would not require raw materials or finished goods in anticipation of future sales. While a zero-inventory manufacturing distribution system is not practical, it is important to remember that each dollar invested in inventory should be committed to achieve a specific objective.

Inventory is a major area of asset deployment which should be required to provide a minimum return on capital investment. A measurement problem exists, however, since the typical profit-and-loss statement does not adequately display the true cost or benefit gains of inventory investments.[2] Lack of measurement sophistication makes it difficult to specify the desired inventory level. Most enterprises carry an average inventory that exceeds their basic requirement. This generalization can be understood better through a careful examination of the four prime functions underlying inventory commitments.

Geographical Specialization

One function of inventory is to allow *geographical specialization* for individual operating units. Based on requirements for factors of production such as power, materials, water, and labor, the economical location for manufacturing is often a considerable distance from geographical areas of demand.[3] For example, tires, batteries, transmissions, springs, and so forth are significant components in automobile assembly. With geographical separation, each automobile component can be produced on an economical basis and then, through internal inventory transfer, fully integrated in assembly.

The function of geographical separation is also related to assortment collection in finished-goods physical distribution. Manufactured goods from various locations are collected at a single warehouse in order to offer customers a mixed-product shipment. Such warehouses are common examples of geographical separation and integrated distribution made possible by inventory.

Geographical separation permits economic specialization between the manufacturing and distribution units of an enterprise. To the degree that geographical specialization exists, inventory in the form of raw materials, semifinished goods or components, and finished goods is introduced to the logistical system. Each location requires a basic inventory. In addition, intransit inventories are necessary to link manufacturing and distribution. Although difficult to measure, the economies gained by geographical specialization are expected to more than offset the added cost of inventory and transportation.

[2] Douglas M. Lambert, *The Development of an Inventory Costing Methodology* (Chicago: National Council of Physical Distribution Management, 1976), p. 3, and *Inventory Carrying Cost, Memorandum 611* (Chicago: Drake Sheahan/Stewart Dougall, Inc., 1974).

[3] See Appendices II and III.

Decoupling

A second function of inventory is to provide maximum efficiency of operations within a single manufacturing facility. This function is referred to as *decoupling*.[4] Stockpiling work in process within the manufacturing complex permits maximum economies of production without work stoppage. Likewise, production-to-warehouse inventory allows economy of scale in manufacturing. Warehouse inventory produced in advance of need permits distribution to customers in large-quantity shipments at minimum freight rates per unit.

The decoupling function of inventory permits each product to be manufactured and distributed in economical lot sizes. In terms of marketing, decoupling permits products manufactured over time to be sold as an assortment. Thus, decoupling tends to buffer the operations of the enterprise. Decoupling differs from geographical specialization. Decoupling enables increased efficiency of operation at a single location, while geographical specialization includes multiple locations. To a significant degree modern concepts of manufacturing, discussed in Chapter 2, have reduced but not eliminated the economic benefits of decoupling.

Balancing Supply and Demand

A third function of inventory is *balancing*, which involves elapsed time between consumption and manufacturing. Balancing inventory exists to reconcile supply availability with demand. The most notable examples of balancing are seasonal production and year-round consumption. Orange juice is one such product. Another example of year-round production and seasonal consumption is antifreeze. Inventories in a balancing capacity link the economies of manufacturing with time variations of consumption.

The managerial reconciliation of time lags in manufacturing and demand involves a difficult planning problem. When seasonal demand is concentrated in a very short selling season, manufacturers, wholesalers, and retailers are forced to take an inventory position far in advance of the peak selling period. For example, in lawn-furniture manufacturing, production must be in high gear by early fall for units that will not be sold until the following spring or summer. In early January and February manufacturers' inventories peak and start to decline as orders for furniture begin to flow through the marketing channel on their way to wholesalers and retailers. Retail sales begin in early spring and hit a peak between Memorial Day and Labor Day. However, after July 4 the retail market shifts from a seller's market to a buyer's market. Price competition dominates as retailers attempt to reduce inventory and eliminate seasonal carry-over. Thus, from a retailer's viewpoint, an inventory position for the entire selling system must be planned six months prior to the peak selling season. Any attempt to supplement inventories after Memorial Day is risky.

Although lawn furniture is an extreme example of seasonal selling, almost all products have some seasonal variation. Inventory stockpiling allows mass consumption or mass manufacturing of products regardless of seasonality. The balancing function of inventory requires investment in seasonal stocks which are expected to be fully liquidated within the season.[5] The critical planning

---

[4] Buffa and Miller, op. cit., p. 21.

[5] This type of buying is often referred to as *promotional buying*.

problem is how much to stockpile to enjoy maximum sales without running the risk of carry-over into the next selling season.

Safety Stock

The *safety stock* or *buffer stock* function concerns short-range variation in either demand or replenishment. A great deal of inventory planning is devoted to determining the size of safety stocks. In fact, typical overstocks result from improper planning of safety stocks.

Safety stock requirement results from uncertainty concerning future sales and inventory replenishment. If uncertainty exists concerning how much of a given product will be sold, it is necessary to protect inventory position. In a sense, safety stock planning is similar to purchasing insurance.

Safety stock protects against two types of uncertainty. The first type of uncertainty is concerned with demand in excess of forecast during the replenishment period. The second type of uncertainty concerns delays in replenishment. An example of demand uncertainty is a customer request of more or less units than planned. Replenishment uncertainty results from a delay in order receipt, order processing, or transportation.

Statistical and mathematical techniques for aiding managers in planning safety stock policy are developed later in the chapter. At this point it is important to realize that the probability, magnitude, and impact of each type of uncertainty can be estimated. The safety stock function of inventory is to provide a specified degree of protection against both types of uncertainty.

Conclusion—Inventory Functions

The four functions of inventory are geographical specialization, decoupling, balancing supply and demand, and safety stock. These functions define the inventory investment necessary for a specific system to perform to management objectives. Given a specific manufacturing-marketing complex, inventories planned and committed to operations can be reduced only to a minimum level consistent with performing the four inventory functions. All inventories exceeding the minimum level represent excessive commitments.

At the minimum level, inventory invested to achieve geographical specialization and decoupling can be modified only by changes in the facility location and manufacturing procedures of the enterprise. The minimum level of inventory required to balance supply and demand relates to the difficult task of estimating seasonal requirements. With experience over a number of seasonal periods, the inventory required to achieve marginal sales during high periods of demand can be projected fairly well. A seasonal inventory plan can be formulated based upon this experience.

The inventories committed to safety stocks represent the greatest potential for improved performance. Commitments to safety stocks are operational in nature. They can be adjusted rapidly in the event of error or a desired change in policy. A variety of techniques is available to assist management in planning safety stock commitments. Therefore, this chapter focuses on a thorough analysis of safety stock relationships and policy formulation. To the extent that an enterprise becomes vertically integrated, inventory must be managed at multiple levels of distribution. The management of echeloned inventories characteristic of vertically integrated enterprises is complex because of a need for a multilevel policy formulation and control. Regardless of whether the inventory requirement is at the manufacturing, wholesaling, or retailing level, or whether it is single level or echeloned, the basic techniques and principles of inventory management apply.

ELEMENTS OF INVENTORY POLICY

This section reviews the definitions related to an inventory management policy. The section begins by defining specific terms and relationships that are fundamental to inventory dynamics. The second part discusses the relationship between the performance cycle and average inventory.

Inventory Definitions

Inventory policy consists of guidelines concerning what to purchase or manufacture, when to take action, and in what quantity. The development of sound policies is the most difficult area of inventory management. The focal point of policy formulation is the establishment of average inventory commitment.

Average inventory consists of the finished products, raw materials, components, and work-in-process typically stocked in logistical facilities. The average inventory is the level of stock maintained across time. From a policy viewpoint, the appropriate level of inventory must be determined for each facility. Average inventories consist of base and safety stock.

Base stock is the portion of average inventory that results from the replenishment process. The amount ordered at a single time during the replenishment process is termed the order quantity. The average inventory held as a result of the order process is referred to as base stock. Another commonly used term to identify this aspect of inventory is *lot size stock*.[6] *Given the order formulation and disregarding safety stock, average base stock equals one-half order quantity.*

The second part of average inventory is the stock held to protect against the impact of uncertainty on each facility. This portion of inventory, as noted earlier, is called *safety stock.* The basic premise of safety stock is that a portion of inventory should be devoted to cover short-range variation in demand and replenishment. *Given safety stock, average inventory equals one-half order quantity plus safety stock.*

A subject of special interest is the ownership of in-transit inventory. This portion of total inventory is referred to as *transit* or *pipeline inventory.* Transit inventory is necessary to achieve replenishment. A specific enterprise may or may not have legal ownership of transit inventory depending upon terms of purchase. If ownership is transferred at shipment destination, inventory in transit is owned by the shipper. The opposite is true when merchandise is purchased at origin. Under conditions of origin purchase, transit inventory should be treated as part of average inventory. The determination of *how much* inventory to hold and the delineation of *when* and in *what* quantities to order are the primary concerns of inventory policy.

---

[6] These terms are used interchangeably.

Inventory control is a mechanical procedure for implementing an inventory policy. The accountability aspect of control measures how many units are on hand at a specific location and keeps track of additions and deletions to the basic quantity. Accountability and tracking can be performed by manual or computerized techniques.[7] The primary differentials are speed, accuracy, and cost.

One major problem in applied inventory management is failure to separate the formulation of policy from control. The formulation of inventory policy is an executive responsibility. The determination of policy guidelines integrates inventory into the overall logistical process. In turn, all other functional areas of the enterprise are influenced by the implementation of inventory policy through logistical performance. While effective inventory control is essential for smooth operations, problems in control normally do not create the same disruption or failure to achieve goals as problems of improper policy. The remainder of this chapter focuses on various aspects of inventory policy formulation.

Relationship of Performance Cycle and Average Inventory

In policy formulation, it is necessary to determine how much inventory to order at a specified time. For purposes of illustration, assume the following conditions. First, the performance cycle duration is constant. Second, the daily rate of sales during replenishment is constant. For example, the performance cycle is always 20 days and the rate of sale is always 10 units per day. Third, the ordering enterprise takes ownership of the inventory upon delivery. Although such assumptions concerning certainty remove the complexity involved in the formulation of inventory policy, they serve to illustrate some basic principles.

Figure 7–1 illustrates these relationships. This type of chart is referred to as a *sawtooth diagram* because of the series of right triangles. Since complete certainty exists with respect to replenishment and usage, orders are scheduled to arrive just as the last unit is sold. Thus, no inventory beyond average base stock is held. Since the rate of sale in the example is 10 units per day and it takes 20 days to complete inventory replenishment, a sound reorder policy might be to order

[7] See Chapter 4, pages 127–28.

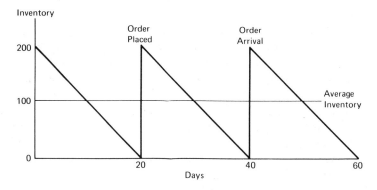

Figure 7–1   Inventory Relationship Constant Sales and Performance Cycle

200 units every 20 days. Given these conditions, terminology related to policy formulation can be identified.

First, the reorder point is specified as 200 units on hand. Order size based on demand would have no reason to exceed 200 units. Every time an order is received, an additional order for 200 units is placed.

Second, average base inventory is 100 units, since stock on hand exceeds 100 units one half of the time (10 days) and is less than 100 units one half of the time. In fact, average base inventory is equal to one half of the 200-order quantity.

Third, assuming a work year of 240 days, 12 purchases will be required during the year. Therefore, over a period of one year, 200 units will be purchased 12 times (2,400 total units). Sales are expected to equal 10 units 240 times (2,400 total units). An average base inventory of 100 units is planned. Thus average inventory turnover will be 24 times (2,400 total sales/100 average inventory). The turn rate assumes that the enterprise is not responsible for intransit inventory.

In time, the sheer boredom of such routine operations would lead management to ask some questions concerning the arrangement. What would happen if orders were placed more frequently than once every 20 days? Why not order 100 units every 10 days? Why order as frequently as every 20 days? Why not reorder 600 units once every 60 days? Assuming that the inventory performance cycle remains a constant 20 days, what would be the impact of each of these alternative ordering policies on reorder point, average base inventory, and inventory turnover?

The policy of ordering a smaller volume of 100 units every 10 days means that two orders will always be outstanding. Thus, the reorder point would remain 200 committed units on order to service average daily sales of 10 units over the 20-day inventory cycle. However, average base inventory on hand would drop to 50 units, and inventory turnover would increase to 48 times per year. The policy of ordering 600 units every 60 days would result in an average base inventory of 300 units and a turnover of approximately eight times per year. These alternative ordering policies are illustrated in Figure 7–2. Despite this analysis, a dilemma would still exist concerning the most desirable ordering policy.

An exact policy concerning order quantity can be calculated by balancing the cost of ordering and the cost of maintaining average base inventory. The economic order quantity (EOQ) model provides a specific answer to the balancing of these two critical cost categories. By determining the EOQ and dividing it into forecasted annual demand, the frequency and size of order that will minimize the total cost of inventory are identified. Prior to reviewing EOQ, it is necessary to identify costs typically associated with ordering and maintaining inventory.

Identification of Inventory Costs

Since inventory is related to all aspects of logistical operations, it is difficult to isolate the cost of inventory ordering and maintenance. In fact, accounting practice is to group inventory costs. The net result is that the functional cost of inventory is difficult to isolate for purposes of policy formulation.

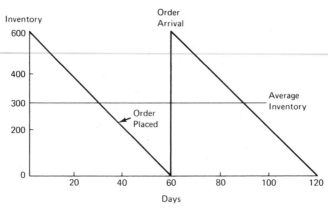

Example: Order 600

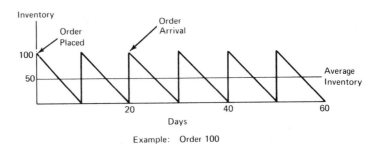

Example: Order 100

Figure 7–2   Illustration of Alternative Order Quantity and Average Inventory

Maintenance Costs

The accounts traditionally included in the cost of maintaining inventory are taxes, storage, capital, insurance, and obsolescence.[8] The costs associated with taxes and insurance are relatively easy to determine. Insurance cost is a direct payment based upon estimated risk or exposure over time. Tax cost is a direct levy normally based on inventory holding on a specific day of the year or average holding over a period of time, depending upon local laws.

Storage cost must be allocated to specific products since it is not related directly to inventory value. Depending upon the type of warehouse facility used, public or private, total storage charges may be direct, or it may be necessary to impute costs. With privately owned facilities, the total annual depreciated expense of the warehouse must be reduced to a standard measure such as cost per day per square or cubic foot. The cost of total annual occupancy for a given product can then be assigned by multiplication of daily occupied space times the standard cost factor accumulated for the year. This figure can then be divided by the total number of units of merchandise processed through the facility to determine the average storage cost per merchandise unit. In assignment of such costs, care must be taken to make appropriate allowances for idle space.

[8] Lambert, op. cit., p. 57, provides a detailed review of accounts.

Obsolescence cost is calculated on the basis of past experience. The type of obsolescence of concern in inventory planning is the deterioration of product while in storage which is not covered by insurance. Obsolescence also can be expanded to include marketing loss when a product becomes obsolete in terms of model design. Again, care must be exercised to avoid costs not directly related to inventory. The assignment of obsolescence cost should be approached with caution and should be limited to direct loss related to storage. Charges related to obsolescence should be expressed on a per unit basis similar to storage cost.

The most controversial aspect of maintenance cost is the appropriate charge to place on invested capital. Experience with a variety of enterprises indicates figures ranging from the prevailing prime interest rate to 25 per cent.[9] The logic for using the prime interest rate or a specified rate pegged to prime is that cash to replace capital invested in inventory can be purchased in the money markets at that rate. Managerially specified interest rates are based on a target return on investment expected from all dollars available to the enterprise. A dollar invested in inventory loses its earning power, restricts capital availability, and prohibits alternative investment.

Zinszer suggests another approach to arrive at the invested capital cost based on the type of inventory.[10] He suggests that the inventory valuation depends on whether the inventory represents cycle inventory, safety inventory, or speculative inventory. Cycle inventories are valued at relatively low rates since they are necessary for operating the business. Speculative inventories are valued at much higher rates since they are truly a risk investment.

Confusion may result from the fact that top management has not established a clear-cut capital cost policy to be applied uniformly in financial decision-making. For logistical planning, the cost of capital must be thought out clearly, since the final rate of assessment will have a profound impact on system design. Low investment cost tends to encourage multilocations and liberal inventory allocations. High costs have the opposite effect, almost to the point of restricting facility expansion.[11]

The cost of maintaining inventory involves management judgment, estimation, assignment, and a degree of direct measurement. The final figure should be expressed on an annual basis as a percentage value to be applied to average inventory. Determination of maintenance cost across a broad group of products or raw materials requires substantial analysis. While cost of capital can be applied to average inventory holdings, expenses associated with taxes, insurance, storage, and obsolescence vary, depending on the specific attributes of each product. Once agreement has been reached on the appropriate assessment for maintenance, the figure should be held constant during logistical system analysis.[12]

---

[9] For a list of 13 different approaches to arriving at this figure, see Lambert, op. cit., pp. 24–25.

[10] Paul H. Zinszer, "Inventory Costing: A Return on Inventory Approach to Differentiating Inventory Risk," *Journal of Business Logistics*, Vol. 26 (1983), pp. 20–39.

[11] In Chapter 9, pages 281–88, the impact of inventory cost on facility location is examined in detail.

[12] This is developed in greater detail as an aspect of management procedure in logistical strategic planning. See Chapter 12, pages 355–58.

Ordering Costs

The cost of placing an order consists of estimating the full expense of inventory control, order preparation, order communication, update activities, and managerial supervision. Similar to maintenance cost, ordering costs are built up for each element of expense until a total cost of order placement is obtained. The combined figure should include assignment of a share of fixed cost related to order preparation plus the direct variable cost associated with ordering. For example, if the total fixed cost associated with ordering activities is $550,000 per year and the historical pattern has been the placement of 220,000 orders per year, the fixed-cost factor per order would be $2.50. The variable cost of placing an order represents a calculated cost which, when combined with fixed cost, results in a total cost per order.

A great deal of difference exists among organizations and managers concerning what they feel the cost is to place an order. The important point is to include all costs in assignment of fixed and variable expenses. Once the total cost of placing an order is estimated, the typical assumption is to hold it constant regardless of how many orders are placed during a planning period. This assumption of linearity is not typically accurate. However, as long as order quantity remains fairly constant from one planning period to the next, only a limited error is introduced.

Nature of Demand

Demand forecasts, updated by timely information from order processing, as discussed in Chapter 2 provide major inputs to the formulation of the enterprise's statement of distribution requirements.[13] The nature of this linkage in commercial organizations varies between manufacturing businesses and enterprises purchasing merchandise for resale, such as wholesalers or retailers. The statement of distribution requirements provides a critical input in the overall process of Logistical Resource Planning (LRP). As such, LRP integrates growth objectives, forecasts, and all forms of information into a concise statement. Once stated, the statement of distribution requirements represents the transition from independent to dependent demand.[14]

Demand for a given item is *independent* when it is not dependent upon the demand for another item. For example, demand for a refrigerator is not dependent upon the demand for household furniture. Demand is dependent when the quantity of a specific component is directly based on the demand for an end product or subassembly, as in the relationship of axles to automotive assembly. The essential characteristics of dependent demand is that it can be calculated, given the operational plan.

---

[13] For a detailed discussion see Chapter 2, pages 48–50.

[14] For an expanded discussion, see Joseph Orlicky, *Material Requirement Planning* (New York: McGraw-Hill Book Company, 1975), pp. 22–29. For product procurement, the situation is independent. For materials and parts procurement, the situation is dependent. For varied MRP applications, see George W. Plossl and Oliver W. Wight, *Materials Requirement Planning by Computer* (Washington, D. C.: American Production and Inventory Control Society, Inc., 1971); Robert M. Monczka, Philip L. Carter, and Richard F. Gonzales, "Materials Requirements Planning Implementation Scenario for a Successful User," unpublished paper, Michigan State University, 1976; and Jeffery G. Miller and Linda G. Sprague, "Behind the Growth in Materials Requirement Planning," *Harvard Business Review*, Vol. 53 (September–October 1975), pp. 83–91.

Dependent demand illustrates the vertical sequence in purchasing or manufacture of specific items. Requirements are expressed in direct quantity such as cases of corn or tons of coal necessary to meet end-product requirements. In manufacturing situations, vertical dependence may extend through several organizational levels. Horizontal dependent demand is a special situation where an attachment, promotion item, or operator's manual is included with each item shipped. In this situation the item demanded is not required to complete the manufacturing process but may be necessary to complete the marketing process.

The important point to remember is that the estimated demand for the item to be purchased for resale or to be manufactured is initially determined by a combination of forecasting, order processing, inventory status and requirements planning. However, once the plan is formulated, component-parts requirements or insertions to the product can be directly calculated and do not need to be forecasted separately. If substantial changes develop in distribution requirements, it may be necessary to modify the logistics resource plan. However, the dependent demand status of procurement does not change.

INVENTORY LOT SIZING

The lot sizing concept balances the cost of maintaining inventories against the cost of ordering. The key to understanding the relationship is to remember that average base inventory is equal to one-half order quantity. Therefore, the larger the order quantity, the larger the average base inventory and consequently the greater the maintenance cost per year. However, the larger the order quantity, the fewer orders required per planning period and consequently the lower the total ordering cost. The lot quantity formulations identify the precise quantities at which the annual combined total cost of ordering and maintenance is at a lowest point for a given sales volume. Figure 7–3 illustrates the basic relationships. The point at which the sum of ordering cost and maintenance cost is minimized represents the lowest total cost. The above discussion presents the basic lot sizing concept and identifies the fundamental objectives. Simply stated, the objectives are to identify the ordering quantity or period that minimizes the total cost of inventory maintenance and ordering.

Economic Order Quantity (EOQ)

The economic order quantity is the replenishment order quantity that minimizes the combined cost of inventory maintenance and ordering. The identification of such a quantity assumes that demand and costs are relatively stable throughout the year. Since the EOQ is calculated for each individual product, the basic formulation does not consider the impact of joint-ordering of products. The next part discusses some EOQ extensions.

The most efficient method for calculating economic order quantity is mathematical. Earlier in this presentation a policy dilemma was faced regarding whether to order 100, 200, or 600 units. The answer can be found by calculating the applicable EOQ for the situation. Table 7–2 contains the necessary information.

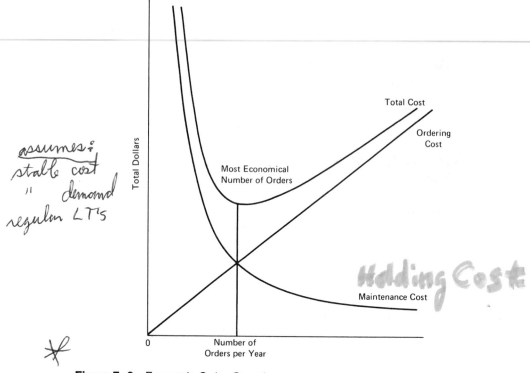

assumes:
stable cost
" demand
regular LT's

Figure 7–3 Economic Order Quantity

To benefit from the most economical purchase arrangement, orders should be placed in the quantity of 300 units rather than 100, 200, or 600. Thus, over the year eight orders would be placed, and average base inventory would be 150 units.

TABLE 7–2 Factor-Input EOQ Sample Formulation

Annual sales volume	2,400 units
Unit value at cost	$5
Maintenance cost	20% per year
Ordering cost per order	$20

To calculate the above, the standard formulation for EOQ is

$$EOQ = \sqrt{\frac{2C_oS}{C_mU}}$$

where

$$C_o = \text{cost per order}$$
$$C_m = \text{cost of maintenance per year}$$
$$S = \text{annual sales volume, units}$$
$$U = \text{cost per unit}$$

Substituting from Table 7–2,

$$EOQ = \sqrt{\frac{2 \times 20 \times 2400}{0.20 \times 5.00}}$$

$$= \quad 96,000$$
$$= 310 \text{ (rounded to 300)}$$

Total ordering cost would amount to $160 and maintenance cost $150. Thus, after rounding to allow ordering in multiples of 100 units, annual reordering and maintenance costs have been equated.

Referring back to Figure 7–3, the impact of ordering in quantities of 300 rather than 200 can be observed. The EOQ of 300 means that additional inventory in the form of base stock has been introduced into the system. Average inventory has been increased from 100 to 150 units on hand.

Based upon examination of the relationship of the inventory performance cycle, inventory cost, and economic order formulations, several basic relationships useful for inventory planning have been introduced. First, the EOQ is found at the point where annualized order cost and maintenance cost are equal. Second, average base inventory equals one-half order quantity. Third, the value of the inventory unit, all other things being equal, will have a direct relationship on the duration of the performance cycle in that the higher the value, the more frequently orders will be placed.

EOQ Extensions

The straightforward simplicity of the EOQ formulation does confront some difficulty in application. The most persistent problems are those related to various adjustments necessary to take advantage of special purchase situations. Three typical adjustments are: (1) volume transportation rates, (2) quantity discounts, and (3) other adjustments. Each category is discussed briefly.

Volume Transportation Rates

In the EOQ formulation discussed, no consideration was given to the impact of transportation cost upon order quantity. When products are on a delivered basis and the seller pays transportation cost from origin to the inventory destination, such neglect may be justified. However, when the item is procured at origin, the impact of transportation rates upon total cost must be considered when determining order quantity.

As a general rule, the greater the weight of an order, the lower the cost per pound of transportation cost from any origin to destination.[15] A freight-rate discount for larger-size shipments is common to both truck and rail and is found in class, exception, and commodity rates. Thus, all other things being equal, an enterprise naturally wants to purchase in quantities that offer maximum economies in transportation expenditure. Such quantities may be larger than the purchase quantity that would otherwise constitute the EOQ.

Increasing order size has a twofold impact upon inventory cost. Assume for purposes of illustration that the most desirable transportation rate is obtained

---

[15] For an expanded discussion, see Chapter 9, pages 279–81.

when a quantity of 480 is ordered as compared to the EOQ-recommended order of 300 calculated earlier.[16] The first impact of the larger order is to increase the average base inventory from 150 to 240 units. Thus, ordering in larger quantities increases inventory maintenance cost.

The second impact is a decrease in the number of orders required to satisfy annual requirements. Given the modification, the frequency of orders required to realize the maximum economies of transportation in the example will be five.

To complete the analysis it is necessary to formulate the total cost with and without transportation savings. While this calculation can be directly made by modification of the EOQ formulation, direct comparison provides a direct answer.[17] The only additional data required are the applicable freight rates for ordering in quantities of 300 and 480. Table 7–3 provides the data necessary to complete the analysis.

Table 7–4 provides the analysis of total cost. Taking into consideration the potential transportation savings by purchasing in larger lot sizes, total annual cost by purchasing 480 units five times per year rather than the EOQ solution of 300 units eight times per year results in a $570 saving.

The impact of volume transportation rates upon total cost of procurement cannot be neglected. In the example above, the rate per unit equivalent dropped from $1 to $0.75, or by 25 per cent. In actual practice, freight-weight breaks may not drop that abruptly. However, it is common to have multiple weight breaks applicable between any given origin and destination. Under such situations, the cost-per-hundredweight range, from minimum shipment LTL to carload minimum weight, may far exceed 25 per cent. Thus, any EOQ must be

[16] To determine transportation rates, the unit quantity must be converted to weight.

[17] For an expanded discussion, see Peterson and Silver, op. cit., pp. 162–200.

TABLE 7–3 Modified Input EOQ to Accommodate Transportation Volume Rates

Annual sales volume	2,400 units
Unit value at cost	$5
Maintenance cost	20% per year
Ordering cost/order	$20
Small-shipment rate/unit	$1
Large-shipment rate/unit	$0.75

TABLE 7–4 EOQ Modified to Accommodate Volume Transportation Rates

	Alternative 1: EOQ = 300	Alternative 2: Modified Order = 480
Maintenance cost	$ 150	$,240
Ordering cost	160	100
Transportation cost	2,400	1,800
Total cost	$2,710	$2,140

tested for transportation cost sensitivity across a range of weight breaks if the merchandise is purchased at origin.

A second point illustrated in the data of Table 7–4 is the fact that rather substantial changes in the size of order and the orders placed per year resulted in only modest change in total cost of maintenance and ordering. The EOQ quantity of 300 had a total annual cost of $310, whereas the revised order quantity had a comparative cost of $340. EOQ formulations are only sensitive to significant changes in order cycle or frequency. Likewise, substantial changes in cost factors are necessary to result in a major impact on the economic order quantity.

Finally, three factors regarding inventory cost under conditions of origin purchase are noteworthy. First, purchase at origin means the buyer assumes full risk for inventory at time of shipment. Depending upon time of required payment, this could mean that transit inventory is part of the firm's average inventory and therefore subjected to an appropriate charge.[18] It follows that any change in weight break leading to a shipment method with a different in-transit time should be assessed the added cost or savings as appropriate in the total cost analysis.

A second factor regarding transit time and related inventory is that when purchasing on a delivered basis, no direct liability is associated with transit inventory. However, as is pointed out shortly, the length and consistency of transit time as well as the quantity of inventory in transit are major factors when planning inventory under conditions of uncertainty.

The final factor deals with the addition of transportation cost to the value of inventory for purposes of correct maintenance costing. Table 7–4 is not totally correct in that the transportation cost per unit is not added to the value of the inventory for costing purposes.[19] Thus, the savings possible from buying in larger quantities are understated.

Quantity Discounts

An analogous situation to transportation volume rates is when the item purchased is subject to quantity discounts. Table 7–5 illustrates a sample schedule of discounts. Quantity discounts can be handled directly with the basic EOQ formulation by calculating total cost at any given volume-related purchase price to determine associated EOQs. If the discount at any associated

---

[18] In such situations, the cost of money invested in inventory should be appropriately charged, provided that it is paid for at origin.

[19] Lambert, op. cit., pp. 57.

TABLE 7–5   Example of Quantity Discounts

Cost	Quantity Purchased
$5.00	1–99
4.50	100–200
4.00	201–300
3.50	301–400
3.00	401–500

quantity is sufficient to offset added cost of maintenance less reduced cost of ordering, then the quantity discount offers a viable alternative.[20] It should be noted that quantity discounts and transportation volume rates each affect larger quantity purchases. This does not mean that the lowest total cost purchase will always be larger than would otherwise be the case under basic EOQ.

Other EOQ Adjustments

A variety of special situations may occur that will require adjustments to the basic EOQ. Examples are: (1) production lot size, (2) multiple-item purchase, (3) limited capital, and (4) private trucking. In all adjustment situations the focal point of attention is total cost of the basic EOQ in comparison to the modified purchase condition.[21]

Discrete Lot Sizing

Not all inventory management situations require procurement to support uniform usage rates that are common to EOQ reorder situations. In manufacturing situations the demand for a specific component tends to occur at irregular intervals and for varied quantities. The irregular nature of usage requirements results from demand being dependent upon the production schedule. At the time of manufacturing, the necessary assembly parts must be available. Between requirement times, no need exists to maintain inventory of the component in stock if it can be obtained when needed.[22] Inventory servicing of *dependent demand* requires a modified approach to the determination of order quantities, which is referred to as *discrete lot sizing*. The identification of the technique as "discrete" means that the procurement objective is to obtain a quantity of a component that equals the net requirements at a specific time. Because component requirements fluctuate, purchase quantities using discrete lot sizing will vary between orders. A variety of lot sizing techniques are available. In this part: (1) lot-for-lot, (2) period order quantity, and (3) time-series lot sizing are briefly presented.

Lot-for-Lot

The most basic form of discrete ordering is to plan purchases to cover net requirements over a specified period. No consideration is given to the cost of ordering under the *lot-for-lot* methodology. In one sense, lot-for-lot sizing is pure dependent-demand-oriented, since no economies of discrete ordering are considered. Once manufacturing requirements are identified, no additional lot sizing is performed. The basic technique is often used when the item being purchased is inexpensive and the requirements are relatively small and irregular. Actual time to procure the item can be held to a minimum by the use of electronic order transfer and premium transportation.

---

[20] The exact calculation is a form of break-even analysis. See Chapter 13, pages 398–400.

[21] For an expanded discussion of EOQ adjustments, see Peterson and Silver, op. cit., pp. 162–200.

[22] Plossl and Wight, op. cit., pp. 6–8.

Period Order Quantity

The *period order quantity* (POQ) technique builds upon the logic of EOQ. The POQ technique performs three steps to accomplish component procurement. First, the standard EOQ is calculated. Second, the EOQ quantity is divided into the forecasted annual usage to determine the frequency of ordering. Third, the number of orders is divided into the relevant time period (52 for weeks or 12 for months) to express the order quantity in time periods covered.

To illustrate, carry forward the data from Table 7–2 which resulted in an EOQ of 310. To adjust to a 12-period year, the POQ technique would be as follows:

$$EOQ = 310$$
$$Forecast = 2,400$$
$$Orders\ per\ year = \frac{2,400}{310} = 7.74$$
$$Order\ interval = \frac{12}{7.74} = 1.5\ months$$

Under the POQ application, orders are planned approximately every six weeks. The typical order is 310 units unless planned usage has not materialized or order duration requires procurement for advance periods.

The main advantage of the POQ approach is that it takes into consideration the cost of maintenance and thereby reduces carry-over inventories to a minimum. The disadvantage is similar to that of basic EOQ, in that derived demand needs to be continuous to realize the full potential.

Time-Series Lot Sizing

The fundamental objective of time-series lot sizing is to combine requirements over several periods to arrive at a procurement logic. The time-series approach is dynamic because the order quantity is adjusted to meet best-estimate requirements. This dynamic approach is contrasted to basic EOQ, which is static in the sense that the order quantity, once computed, continues unchanged in the planned purchasing activity.[23]

The key to dynamic lot sizing is that requirements are expressed in varying quantities across time rather than in usage rates per day or week, as is typical of EOQ. Given substantial usage fluctuation, fixed-order quantities must give way to a lot sizing system that can calculate an economical order given changing and intermittent usage.[24] Three such techniques are widely discussed in the literature and are briefly reviewed: (1) least unit cost, (2) least total cost, and (3) part-period balancing.

The *least unit cost* seeks to identify a combination of requirements over a number of periods that results in the lowest cost per piece. Starting with the net

---

[23] Thomas Gorham, "Dynamic Order Quantities," *APICS Production and Inventory Management Journal* (First Quarter, 1968).

[24] Plossl and Wight, op. cit., p. 7.

requirements of the initial period, each future period is evaluated on a per-unit basis to arrive at the combined quantity for a given number of periods wherein the unit cost is minimized. Thus, order quantities and frequency vary substantially as a function of the least-unit-cost determination. The least-unit-cost approach does provide a way to overcome the static features of EOQ and POQ. The main shortcoming is that unit cost may experience wide variation between time periods that would not be evaluated using the least-unit-cost methodology.

The *least-total-cost* approach seeks the quantity that minimizes total cost for successive periods. In this sense, least total cost, which is the balancing of ordering and carrying, is similar to EOQ in objective. The fundamental difference is that order interval is varied to seek least total cost. The least-total-cost calculation is based on a ratio of ordering to maintenance cost (Co/Cm), called the *economic part-period*. The economic part-period defines the quantity of a specific component which, if carried in inventory for one period, would result in a maintenance cost equal to the cost of ordering. The least-total-cost technique selects order sizes and intervals that most nearly approximate the economic part-period calculation. Thus, order sizes remain fairly uniform; however, substantial differences do occur in elapsed time between order placement. The least-total-cost technique overcomes the failure of the least unit cost to consider trade-offs across the overall planning period.

Part-period balancing is a modified form of the least-total-cost technique that incorporates a special adjustment routine called *look ahead/look back*.[25] The main benefit of this feature is that it extends the planning horizon across more than one ordering point to accommodate usage peaks and valleys when calculating order quantities. Adjustments are made in order time or quantity when a forward or backward review of more than one order requirement indicates that modifications to the economic part-period may be beneficial. The typical procedure is to first test the *look-ahead* feature to determine if more time results in approximation of the economic part-period quantity. *Look back* is typically utilized if look ahead leaves the lot size unchanged. In this sense, look back means that a future order, which under the economic part-period rule would normally be scheduled for delivery during the fourth period, would be advanced if earlier delivery would reduce total cost. The net result of incorporation of the look-ahead/look-back feature is that it renders the application of the economic part-period concept to a simultaneous review of multiple periods.

Conclusion—Discrete Lot Sizing

The varied approaches to discrete lot sizing all seek to overcome assumptions regarding uniform usage that are required for EOQ calculations. Whereas EOQ results in a uniform order quantity that may be ordered in a fixed or variable time interval, discrete-lot-sizing techniques seek greater flexibility to accommodate irregular usage. The techniques reviewed have had varying degrees of success in meeting the basic objective of discrete lot sizing.[26]

---

[25] J. J. DeMalteis, "An Economic Lot Sizing Technique: The Part-Period Algorithms," *IBM System Journal*, Vol. 7 (1968), pp. 30–38.

[26] Orlicky, op. cit., pp. 120–37.

INVENTORY MANAGEMENT GOALS AND UNCERTAINTY

Prior to discussing the alternative strategies for inventory management, this section reviews the goals of the inventory management function and characterizes the nature of logistical uncertainty. It is important to consider these goals and characteristics so that the appropriate trade-offs can be identified, evaluated, and selected.

Inventory Management Goals

Inventory management must consider four goals when attempting to define an effective strategy. These goals are: (1) customer service, (2) profitable allocation, (3) predict and control, and (4) total cost integration. The following part discusses each and identifies critical considerations.

A primary inventory management goal is to provide the desired level of customer service. This customer service objective reflects the basic logistical output. Whether the desired customer service level is defined in terms of quantity or order fill rate, order cycle time, or back-order delay time, inventory management must incorporate procedures to meet the desired standards. While customers may request a service level that is above the stated policy, they may not be willing to pay the price to support such customer service. The customer service level must be selected to trade-off the benefits of additional revenue against the costs of higher inventories. The system should not be designed to handle higher-than-requested service levels due to associated higher costs.

The second goal is a profitable allocation of available inventories. While it is usually desirable to attempt to service all customer demands, situations are often confronted where it becomes unprofitable to service all customer requests. When there is a shortage in available inventory or when a customer requests orders in uneconomical lot sizes, inventory management must have a policy to guide allocation of available resources. The allocation decision also concerns the length of time inventory will be reserved for a customer. Factors to consider when making the allocation decision include current and projected inventory availability, customer demands, and segment profitability.

The third goal is to predict inventory requirements and control inventory movement through distribution facilities. While determining the controlling inventory requirements, management must minimize inventory resources committed. This goal is accomplished by tracking inventories and integrating information to project current and future requirements. In the process of tracking and projecting, inventory management must evaluate all inventory resources to determine if the logistical system could operate as effectively with lower inventory. This process is similar to maintaining the navigability of a waterway. There are two approaches that may be used. The first approach increases the water level until there are no vessels that run aground. Another approach is to keep reducing the water level in an attempt to identify the problem areas. When a problem area is identified, the waterway is dredged to allow the vessels to pass. For the inventory manager, the first approach is the equivalent of adding inventory until maximum assets available are deplored. The second approach attempts to isolate bottlenecks and then make changes in the system to bypass or eliminate the problem. A basic inventory management goal is to identify and take advantage of these opportunities.

The last goal is to integrate inventory with the other activities of the enterprise and the channel. The costs and benefits gained from maintaining inventories at various stages within the enterprise and within the channel must be considered in terms of other activities. Inventory management must be able to justify costs and benefits in perspective.

The Nature of Uncertainty

Although it is useful to review basic inventory relationships under conditions of certainty, formulation of inventory policy must take into consideration the realistic situation of uncertainty. One of the main functions of inventory management is to provide safety stock protection against uncertainty.

As noted earlier, two types of uncertainty have a direct impact on inventory policy. Demand uncertainty concerns the fluctuation in rate of orders during the inventory performance cycle. Replenishment uncertainty deals with variations in the length of the inventory performance cycle. In this part demand uncertainty is treated with respect to setting safety stocks when the duration of the inventory performance cycle is assumed constant. In the next part both types of uncertainty are handled on a simultaneous basis.

Nature of Demand Uncertainty

The purpose of unit sales forecasting is to project sales during the inventory performance cycle. Even with good forecasting, demand during the replenishment typically exceeds or falls short of anticipated demand. To provide protection against a stockout when demand exceeds forecast, safety stock is added to base inventory. Under conditions of demand uncertainty, average inventory is defined as one-half order quantity plus safety stock. Figure 7–4 illustrates the inventory performance cycle under conditions of demand uncertainty. The dashed line reflects the forecast. The solid line illustrates inventory on hand from one cycle to the next. The task of planning safety stock consists of three steps. First, the likelihood of stockout must be gauged. Second, demand potential during periods of stockout must be estimated. Finally, a policy decision is required concerning the degree of stockout protection to introduce into the system.

Assume for purposes of illustration that the inventory performance cycle is 10 days. Historical experience indicates that daily sales range from zero to 10 with average daily sales of 5 units. The economic order is assumed to be 50, the reorder point is 50, the planned average inventory is 25, and sales during the performance cycle are expected to be 50 units.

Table 7–6 provides a recap of actual sales history over three consecutive inventory performance cycles. During the first cycle, while daily demand experienced variation, the average of 5 units per day was maintained. Total demand during cycle 1 was 50 units, as expected. During cycle 2, demand totaled 50 units in the first 8 days, resulting in an out-of-stock. Thus, no sales were possible on days 9 and 10. During cycle 3, demand reached a total of 39 units. The third performance cycle ended with 11 units remaining in stock.

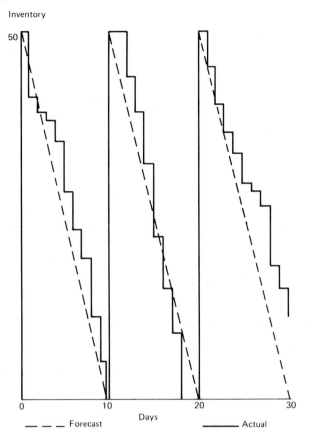

Figure 7–4   Inventory Relationship Demand Uncertainty and Constant Performance
Cycle

Over the 30-day period, total sales were 139 units, for an average daily sales of
4.6 units.

Based on the history recorded in Table 7–6, management can observe that
stockouts occurred on 2 of 30 total days. Since sales never exceed 10 units
per day, no possibility of stockout exists on the first 5 days of the performance
cycle. Stockouts could occur on days 6 through 10, on the remote possibility
that demand on the first 5 days of the cycle averaged 10 units per day and no
inventory is carried over from the previous period. Since over the three
performance cycles 10 units were sold only once, it is apparent that the real risk
of stockout occurs only during the last few days of the performance cycle, and
then only when sales have exceeded the average by a substantial margin.[27]

Some approximation is also possible concerning the amount of sales that
could have been enjoyed had stock been available on days 9 and 10 of cycle 2. A
maximum of 20 units could have been sold if inventory had been available. On

---

[27] In this example, daily statistics are used. An alternative, which is technically more correct from a
statistical viewpoint, is to utilize performance related to reorder cycles.

The major limitation of order cycles is the length of time and difficulty required to collect the
necessary data.

the other hand, it is possible that even if stock had been available, no demand would have occurred on days 9 and 10. Based on average demand of 4 to 5 units per day, a reasonable appraisal of lost sales is from 8 to 10 units.

It should be apparent that the degree of risk related to stockouts created by variations in sales is limited to a short time and includes a small percentage of total sales. However, management should take some protective action to realize available sales and to avoid the risk of possible deterioration in customer relations. Although the sales analysis presented in Table 7–6 helps toward an understanding of the problem, the appropriate course of action is still not clear. Statistical probability can be used to assist management in the development of a safety stock policy.

In order to provide a basis for understanding this statistical analysis, the following part discusses the application of statistical probability to the demand uncertainty problem.

The sales history over the 30-day period has been arranged in Table 7–7 in terms of a frequency distribution. The main purpose of the frequency distribution is to make an appraisal of variations around the average daily demand.

TABLE 7–6　Typical Demand Experience During Three Replenishment Cycles

	Forecast Cycle 1		Stockout Cycle 2		Overstock Cycle 3	
Day	Demand	Accumulated	Demand	Accumulated	Demand	Accumulated
1	9	9	0	0	5	5
2	2	11	6	6	5	10
3	1	12	5	11	4	14
4	3	15	7	18	3	17
5	7	22	10	28	4	21
6	5	27	7	35	1	22
7	4	31	6	41	2	24
8	8	39	9	50	8	32
9	6	45	Stockout	50	3	35
10	5	50	Stockout	50	4	39

TABLE 7–7　Frequency of Demand

Demand/Day	Frequency (Days)
Stockout	2
Zero	1
One unit	2
Two units	2
Three units	3
Four units	4
Five units	5
Six units	3
Seven units	3
Eight units	2
Nine units	2
Ten units	1

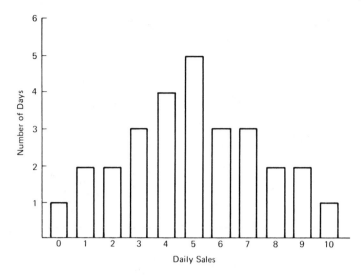

Figure 7–5 Historical Analysis of Demand History

Given an expected average of 5 units per day, demand exceeded average on 11 days and was less than average on 12 days. An alternative way of illustrating a frequency distribution is by a bar chart, as in Figure 7–5.

Given the historical frequency of demand, an exact calculation is possible of how much safety stock would be necessary to provide a specified degree of protection. Probability theory is based on the random chance of a given occurrence out of a large number of occurrences. In the situation illustrated, the frequency of occurrences is 28 days. Although in actual practice more than 28 events would be desirable, a limited sample illustrates the application of probability theory to setting safety stocks.

The probability of occurrences assumes a pattern around a measure of central tendency, which is the average value of all occurrences. While a number of frequency distributions are utilized in inventory control, the most basic is the *normal distribution*.[28]

A normal distribution is characterized by a symmetrical bell-shaped curve, illustrated in Figure 7–6. The essential characteristic of a normal distribution is that the three measures of central tendency are identical. The mean (average) value, the median (middle) observation, and the mode (most frequently observed) value all have the same numerical value. To the extent that these three measures are the same or nearly identical, a frequency distribution is classified as normal.

The basis for prediction using a normal distribution is the standard deviation of observations around the measures of central tendency. The *standard deviation* is a measure of dispersion of events within specified areas under the normal curve. Within ±1 standard deviation, 68.27 per cent of all events occur. Within ±2 standard deviations, 95.45 per cent of all events occur. At ±3 standard deviations, 99.73 per cent of all events are included. In terms of inventory

[28] For a useful discussion of the application of statistical concepts to logistical problems, see Harry J. Bruce, *How to Apply Statistics to Physical Distribution* (Philadelphia: Chilton Book Company, 1967).

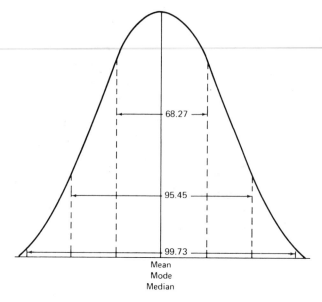

Mean
Mode
Median

Figure 7–6 Normal Distribution

policy, the standard deviation provides a means of estimating the safety stock required to provide a specified degree of protection above the average demand.

The first step in setting safety stocks is to calculate the standard deviation. The formula for standard deviation is

$$\sigma = \sqrt{\frac{\Sigma\, fd^2}{n}}$$

where

σ = standard deviation
f = frequency of event
d = deviation of event from mean
n = total observations available

The necessary data to determine the standard deviation are contained in Table 7–8. Substituting from Table 7–8,

$$\sigma = \sqrt{\frac{181}{28}}$$

$$= \sqrt{6.46}$$

$$= 2.54 \text{ (rounded to 3)}$$

Owing to the inability to add stock except in complete units, the standard deviation of the data in Table 7–8 is rounded to 3 units. In setting safety stocks, 2 standard deviations of protection, or 6 units, would protect against 95.45 per cent of all events included in the frequency distribution.

However, in setting safety stocks, the only situations of concern are the probabilities concerning events that exceed the mean value. No problem exists

TABLE 7–8   Calculation of Standard Deviation of Daily Demand

Units	Frequency (f)	Deviation from Mean (d)	Deviation Squared (d²)	fd²
0	1	−5	25	25
1	2	−4	16	32
2	2	−3	9	18
3	3	−2	4	12
4	4	−1	1	4
5	5	0	0	0
6	3	+1	1	3
7	3	+2	4	12
8	2	+3	9	18
9	2	+4	16	32
10	1	+5	25	25
$n = 28$	$\bar{s} = 5$			$\Sigma fd^2 = 181$

concerning inventory to satisfy demand equal to or below the average. Thus, on 50 per cent of the days when sales are less than average no safety stock is required. Safety stock protection at the 95 per cent level will, in fact, protect against 97.72 per cent of all possible events. This added benefit results from what is typically called a one tail statistical application.

In order to use statistical probability in setting safety stocks, it is important to test the compatibility of the historical data with the expected theoretical frequency distribution. Although the frequency distribution illustrated in Figure 7–5 or Table 7–7 is very similar to a normal distribution, this may not always be the case. In other situations where the actual data are exponential, binomial, Poisson, or nearly normal, a test of goodness of fit should be completed.[29] One such test is the chi-square (χ^2) test of fit, the formula for which is

$$\chi^2 = \sum_{i=1}^{k} \frac{(o_i - e_i)^2}{e_i}$$

where

$$\chi^2 = \text{measure of fitness}$$
$$o_i = \text{observed frequencies}$$
$$e_i = \text{expected frequencies}$$

If the value of χ^2 is zero, the fit between the historical data and the theoretical expectation would be perfect. As the computed value of χ^2 increases, the goodness of fit decreases.

Statistical tables are available to assist in the acceptance or rejection of the theoretical distribution as a valid statistical representation.[30] While the inventory planner does not need to understand the full process, the planner should be

[29] For example, see Lawrence Lapin, *Statistics for Modern Business Decisions*, 3rd ed. (New York: Harcourt Brace Jovanovich, Inc., 1982), pp. 597–610.

[30] Ibid.

assured of a valid *fit* prior to utilizing statistical probability in establishing safety stock.

The preceding example illustrates how statistical probability can assist with the quantification of demand uncertainty. However, demand is not the only source of uncertainty. Therefore, attention is now directed to the treatment of replenishment uncertainty.

Nature of Replenishment Uncertainty

Replenishment uncertainty simply means that inventory management cannot count on consistent delivery. The planner should expect that the replenishment duration time will have a high frequency around the average and be skewed in excess of the planned duration.

From a planning viewpoint, it would be possible to establish safety stock policy around the minimum possible days, the average expected days, or the maximum possible days of the inventory performance cycle.

Using the minimum or maximum limits, the resultant safety stock would be substantially different. Remember that safety stocks exist to protect against demand uncertainty during replenishment. Consequently, policies centered around minimum performance value would provide inadequate protection, and those formulated around maximum value would result in excessive safety stocks.

If the impact of replenishment uncertainty is not evaluated statistically, the most common practice is to formulate safety stock policy on the planned or average expected replenishment days. However, if substantial variation in replenishment duration is experienced, statistical treatment is necessary. In manufacturing planning situations dealing with derived demand, the major form of uncertainty is the performance cycle.

Table 7–9 presents a frequency distribution of performance cycles. Although 10 days is the most frequent experience, replenishment ranges from 6 to 14 days.

TABLE 7–9 Calculation of Standard Deviation of Replenishment Cycle Duration

Performance Cycle (days)	Frequency (f)	Deviation from Mean (d)	Deviation Squared (d)²	fd²
6	2	−4	16	32
7	4	−3	9	36
8	6	−2	4	24
9	8	−1	1	8
10	10	0	0	0
11	8	+1	1	8
12	6	+2	4	24
13	4	+3	9	36
14	2	+4	16	32
				$\sum fd^2 = 200$

$$N = 50 \qquad \bar{t} = 10$$

$$\sigma = \sqrt{\frac{fd^2}{N}} = \sqrt{\frac{200}{50}} = \sqrt{4} = 2 \text{ days}$$

If the performance cycle is assumed to follow a normal bell-shaped distribution, an individual performance cycle would be expected to fall between 8 and 12 days 68.27 per cent of the time.

From a practical viewpoint, when cycle days drop below 10, no immediate problem exists with safety stock. If the actual performance cycle was consistently below the planned over a period of time, then adjustment of expected duration would be in order. The situation that is of most immediate concern is when the time duration of the performance cycle exceeds the expected value of 10 days.

From the viewpoint of the probability of exceeding 10 days, the frequency of such occurrences from the data in Table 7–9 can be restated in terms of performance cycles greater than 10 days and equal to or less than 10 days. In the example data, the standard deviation would not change because the distribution is normal. However, if the actual experience had been skewed in excess of the expected cycle duration, the theoretical distribution most appropriate may have been a Poisson distribution.[31] In Poisson frequency distributions the standard deviation is equal to the square root of the mean. As a general rule, the smaller the mean, the greater the degree of skewness in the Poisson distribution.

Treatment of Combined Demand and Performance Cycle Uncertainty

The inventory performance cycle has been identified as the combination of order communication, processing, transportation, and update. These elements create an information and physical product flow between two locations. The integrated performance cycle forms the central context for planning inventory policy. Up to this point, all discussions related to safety stock have assumed a constant time value for the duration of the performance cycle. For example, in the illustration concerning the establishment of safety stocks to cover sales uncertainty, the duration of the cycle was assumed as a 10-day constant. The more typical situation confronting the inventory planner is illustrated in Figure 7–7, where both demand and inventory performance cycle uncertainties exist. In this part the nature of uncertainty concerning the performance cycle is reviewed, and methods are introduced for estimating combined probabilities of both types of uncertainty.

Treating demand uncertainty and performance cycle uncertainty consists of combining two independent variables. The duration of the cycle is, at least in the short run, independent of the daily demand. However, in setting safety stocks, the joint impact of the probability of individual variation in each must be related.

Table 7–10 presents a summary of sales and replenishment cycle performance. The key to understanding the potential relationships of the data in Table 7–10 is illustrated by reviewing a six-day replenishment cycle. Total demand during the six days could range from 0 to 60 units. On each day of the cycle, the demand probability is independent of the previous day, and so forth for the six-day duration. Assuming the full range of potential situations illustrated on Table 7–10, total sales during replenishment could range from 0 to 140 units. With this basic relationship between the two types of uncertainty in mind, safety stock requirements can be determined by either numerical or simulated procedures.

[31] Ibid., pp. 577–85.

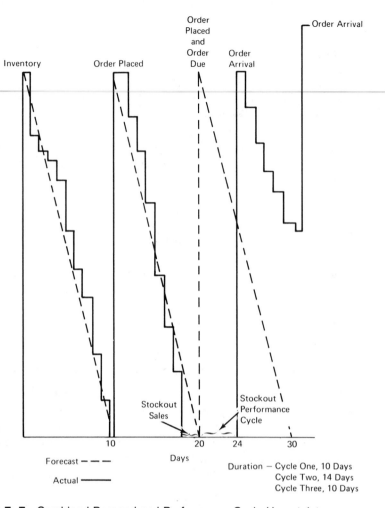

Figure 7-7 Combined Demand and Performance Cycle Uncertainty

TABLE 7-10 Frequency Distribution—Demand and Replenishment Uncertainty

Demand Distribution		Replenishment Cycle Distribution	
Daily Sales	Frequency	Days	Frequency
0	1	6	2
1	2	7	4
2	2	8	6
3	3	9	8
4	4	10	10
5	5	11	8
6	3	12	6
7	3	13	4
8	2	14	2
9	2		
10	1		

$$n = 28 \qquad n = 50$$
$$\bar{s} = 5 \qquad \bar{t} = 10$$
$$\sigma_s = 2.54 \qquad \sigma_t = 2$$

Numerical Compounding: Demand and Replenishment Uncertainty

The exact compounding of two independent variables involves multinomial expansion. While this type of procedure requires extensive calculations when the data approximate the scope of those illustrated in Table 7–10, the solution provides a direct measure of encountering various levels of usage during the replenishment cycle.

A direct method to convolute the standard deviations of the two frequency distributions in order to approximate the combined standard deviation of the two sets of data is by the formula:

$$\sigma_c = \sqrt{\bar{t}\,\sigma_s^2 + \bar{s}^2\,\sigma_t^2}$$

where

σ_c = standard deviation of combined probabilities
$\bar{t}$ = average performance cycle time
σ_t = standard deviation of the performance cycle
$\bar{s}$ = average daily sales
σ_s = standard deviation of daily sales

Substituting from Tables 7–8 and 7–9,

$$\sigma_c = \sqrt{10.00\ (2.54)^2 + (5.00)^2(2)^2}$$
$$= \sqrt{64.52 + 100}$$
$$= \sqrt{164.52}$$
$$= 12.83\ (\text{rounded to } 13)$$

This formulation provides the convoluted or combined standard deviation of $\bar{t}$ days with an average demand of $\bar{s}$ per day when the individual standard deviations are σ_t and σ_s, respectively. The average for the combined distribution is simply the product of t and s or 50.00 (10.00 × 5.00).

Thus, given a frequency distribution of daily sales of from 0 to 10 units per day and a range in replenishment cycle duration of 6 to 14 days, 13 units of safety stock are required to protect for 68.27 per cent of all order cycles. To protect at the 97.72-per cent level, it is necessary to plan a 26-unit safety stock.

It is important to note that the event that is being protected against is a stockout during the replenishment order cycle. The 68.27- and 97.72-per-cent levels are *not* product availability levels. These percentages reflect the probability of a stockout during a given order cycle. For example, with a 13-unit safety stock, stockouts would be expected to occur on 31.73 (100 − 68.27) per cent of the replenishment order cycles. This implies that over time, if the distribution facility had released 100 replenishment orders while maintaining a 13-unit safety stock, the stock location could expect to deplete the stock prior to receiving on approximately 32 per cent of the replenishment orders.

While this percentage provides the probability of a stockout, it does not indicate the relative magnitude of the stockout. The relative magnitude of a stockout indicates the percentage of units stockout relative to the total amount demanded. In addition to being impacted by the probability of a stockout, the

TABLE 7–11 Summary of Alternative Assumptions Concerning Uncertainty and Impact on Average Inventory

	Order Quantity	Safety Stock	Average Inventory
Assume constant $\bar{s}$ sales and constant $\bar{t}$ performance cycle	50	0	25
Assumes demand protection $+2\sigma$ and constant $\bar{t}$ performance cycle	50	6	31
Assume constant $\bar{s}$ demand and $+2\sigma$ performance cycle protection	50	20	45
Assume joint $+2\sigma$ for demand and performance cycle	50	26	51

relative magnitude is influenced by the replenishment order size. This concept is further detailed in the next part.

In terms of average inventory, no safety stock requires 25 units, whereas protection for both types of uncertainty requires 51 units. An average inventory of 51 units is sufficient to provide a combined 97.72-per cent protection against the independent possibility of daily demand or performance cycle variation. Table 7–11 summarizes the alternatives confronting the planner in terms of assumptions and corresponding impact on average inventory.

Estimating Fill Rate

The fill rate represents the magnitude of a stockout rather than the probability. Fill rate is the desired availability goal in setting customer service objectives. Figure 7–8 illustrates the difference between stockout probability and stockout magnitude. Both illustrations in Figure 7–8 have a safety stock of one standard deviation or 13 units. For both situations, given any replenishment cycle, the probability of a stockout is 31.73 per cent. However, during a 20-day period, the top example in Figure 7–8 illustrates two instances where the stock may be depleted. These instances are at the ends of the cycle as noted. In the lower example where the order quantity has been doubled, the system only has the possibility of stocking out once during the 20-day cycle. So, while both situations face the same demand patterns, the first one has more opportunities for stockout. To generalize the above observation, for a given safety stock level, increasing the order quantity decreases the relative magnitude of potential stockouts and, conversely, increases customer service availability.

The precise mathematical formulation of the relationship is:

$$SL = 1 - \frac{f(k)\sigma_c}{EOQ}$$

where:

SL = the stockout magnitude (the product availability level);

$f(k)$ = a function of the normal loss curve which provides the area in a right tail of a normal distribution;

σ_c = the combined standard deviation considering both demand and replenishment cycle uncertainty; and

EOQ = the replenishment order quantity.

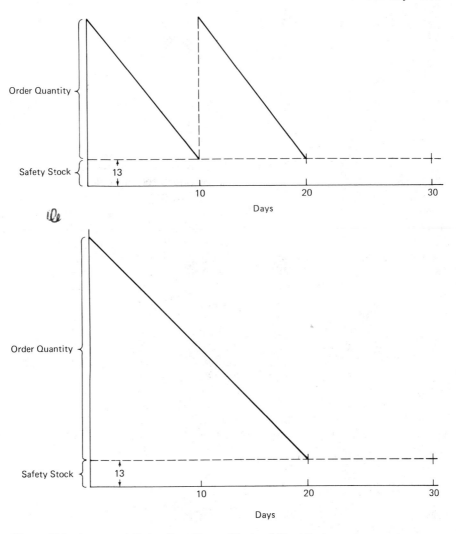

Figure 7-8   Impact of Order Quantity on Stockout Magnitude

To complete the example, suppose a firm desired 99 per cent product availability. Assume the EOQ was calculated to be 300 units. Table 7–12 summarizes the required information.

Since $f(k)$ is the item to calculate safety stock requirements, the above equation must be solved for $f(k)$ using algebraic manipulation. The result is:

$$f(k) = (1 - SL) \times (EOQ \times /\sigma_c).$$

Substituting from Table 7–12,

$$f(k) = (1 - .99) \times (300/13)$$
$$= .01 \times 23.08$$
$$= .2308$$

The calculated value of $f(k)$ is then compared against the values in Table 7–13 to find the value that most closely approximates the calculated value. For this

TABLE 7–12 Information for
              Determining Required
              Safety Stock

Desired service level	99 per cent
σ_c	13
EOQ	300

TABLE 7–13 Table of Loss Integral for
              Standardized Normal
              Distribution

k	f(k)	k	f(k)
0	.3989	1.5	.0293
.1	.3509	1.6	.0232
.2	.3068	1.7	.0142
.3	.2667	1.8	.0110
.4	.2304	1.9	.0084
.5	.1977	2.1	.0064
.6	.1686	2.2	.0048
.7	.1428	2.3	.0036
.8	.1202	2.4	.0027
.9	.1004	2.5	.0020
1.0	.0833	2.6	.0014
1.1	.0686	2.7	.0010
1.2	.0561	2.8	.0007
1.3	.0455	2.9	.0005
1.4	.0366	3.0	.0003

example, the value of k that most closely meets this condition is 0.4. The required safety stock level is:

$$ss = K \times \sigma_c$$

where

> ss = safety stock in units;
> k = the k factor that corresponds with $f(k)$; and
> σ_c = the combined standard deviation.

So, substituting in for the example

$$ss = k \times \sigma_c$$
$$= 0.4 \times 13$$
$$= 5.2 \text{ units}$$

The safety stock level required to provide a 99-per cent product fill rate when the order quantity is 300 units is approximately 5 units. Table 7–14 illustrates the calculated safety stock levels for other order quantities.

TABLE 7-14   Impact of Order Quantity on Safety Stockz

Order Quantity	k	Safety Stock
300	0.4	5.2
200	0.65	8.4
100	1.05	13.6

Table 7–14 illustrates that there is a trade-off between the order quantity and the safety stock. An increased order size can be used to compensate for decreasing the safety stock levels or vice versa. The existence of such a trade-off implies that there is an optimum combination of order size and safety stock that will result in the desired customer service level at the minimum cost. The analysis to identify this optimum is beyond the scope of this text.[32]

Simulating Demand and Performance Cycle Uncertainty

As an alternative to numerically compounding uncertainty, the joint relationship of demand and performance cycle variation can be approximated by using *Monte Carlo simulation*.[33] The Monte Carlo simulation approach consists of selecting representative performance cycles and sales levels on a random basis. Although Monte Carlo requires a large number of observations to establish safety stock policy, the procedure can be extremely useful when frequency distributions related to either sales or performance cycle history are not known or do not have a good fit to either a normal or Poisson distribution.

To illustrate the Monte Carlo procedure, Table 7–15 provides historical statistics similar to those presented on Table 7–10, with the addition of

[32] For a good discussion of the concepts and calculations required, see Harvey M. Wagner, *Principles of Operations Research* 2nd ed. (Englewood Cliffs N. J.: Prentice-Hall, Inc., 1925), pp. 821–38.

[33] Robert B. Fetter and Winston C. Dalleck, *Decision Models for Inventory Management* (Homewood, Ill.: Richard D. Irwin, Inc., 1961), pp. 52–54.

TABLE 7-15   Summary of Demand and Performance Cycle Probabilities for Monte Carlo Simulation

Daily Unit Demand	Frequency Probability	Probability ≤ Demand	Random Number	Performance Cycle Duration	Frequency Probability	Probability ≤ Duration	Random Number
0	0.04	0.04	001–040	6	0.04	0.04	001–040
1	0.07	0.11	041–110	7	0.08	0.12	041–120
2	0.07	0.18	111–180	8	0.10	0.22	121–220
3	0.11	0.29	181–290	9	0.17	0.39	221–390
4	0.14	0.43	291–430	10	0.20	0.59	391–590
5	0.17	0.60	431–600	11	0.17	0.76	591–760
6	0.11	0.71	601–710	12	0.12	0.88	761–880
7	0.11	0.82	711–820	13	0.08	0.96	881–960
8	0.07	0.89	821–890	14	0.04	1.00	961–1,000
9	0.07	0.96	891–960				
10	0.04	1.00	961–1,000				
	$N = 28$ $\bar{s} = 5$				$N = 50$ $\bar{t} = 10$		

probabilities and random numbers. The probability related to each indicates the frequency with which that value would be expected to occur provided a large sampling. For example, with respect to daily demand, demand of 5 units is expected to occur 17 out of 100 times. The accumulated probability is also displayed and indicates the number of times the value of the occurrence is equal to or less than a particular value. For example, 60 out of 100 times the daily demand value is expected to be equal to or less than 5 units. In addition, random numbers proportional to the frequency of each event are displayed in Table 7–15.

The Monte Carlo process consists of selecting a random number for an inventory performance cycle. A random number is typically selected from a pregenerated table of numbers or is produced by a computer. To illustrate, assume that the random number 386 is selected for the inventory performance cycle duration. The corresponding value is 9 days. Next, random numbers for 9 individual days of sales are selected. Table 7–16 illustrates two rounds of Monte Carlo simulation where the random value of the performance cycle was selected as 9 and 11 days, respectively. In order to simulate a complete approximation of the joint relationships of both demand and performance cycle uncertainty, a sample of several hundred cycles and related sales would be required for reliability.

If the purpose of the simulation is formulating a safety stock policy, then only selections where demand during the performance cycle are greater than expected need be considered. For example, if expected average demand is 5 units per day and the expected performance cycle is 9 days, all simulations with total demand of less than 45 units can be dropped from the analysis. All situations in which simulated average demand exceeded the value of expected average sales during replenishment would be tabulated for purposes of formulating a safety stock policy.

TABLE 7–16 Example Results of Monte Carlo Simulation: Two Observations

Performance Cycle Duration: R386 = 9 days		Performance Cycle Duration: R721 = 11 days	
Random Number	Unit Sales	Random Number	Unit Sales
097	1	796	7
542	5	520	5
422	4	805	7
019	0	452	5
807	7	685	6
065	1	594	5
060	1	481	5
269	3	124	2
573	5	350	4
		916	9
		085	1
$\sum s = 27$		$\sum s = 56$	
$\bar{s} = 3$		$\bar{s} = 5.09$	

The Dependent Demand Situation

Prior to reviewing the strategy of the customer service availability level, clarification is needed regarding safety stocks in dependent situations.[34] The essential aspect of dependent demand is that inventory requirements can be calculated. Dependent demand, therefore, does not require forecasting, since uncertainty is eliminated. It follows that no specific safety stock is necessary to support a time-phased procurement program such as MRP.[35] The basic notion of time phasing is that parts and subassemblies need not be carried in inventory as long as they are available when needed.

The case for no safety stocks under conditions of dependent demand rests on two assumptions: (1) that procurement replenishment is predictable and constant, and (2) that vendors and suppliers maintain adequate inventories to always satisfy 100 per cent of purchase requirements. The second assumption may be operationally attainable by virtue of volume-oriented purchase contracts which assure vendors and suppliers of eventual purchase.[36] In such cases the safety stock requirement still exists for the overall channel with the responsibility shifted to the supplier.

The assumption of replenishment certainty is more difficult to achieve. Even in situations where private transportation is used, an element of uncertainty is always present. The practical result is that safety stocks do exist in most dependent demand situations.

Three basic approaches have been used to introduce safety stocks into a system coping with dependent demand.[37] First, a common practice is to put *safety time* into the requirements plan. Thus, a component is ordered one week earlier than needed to assure timely arrival. A second approach is to increase the requisition by a quantity based on an estimate of expected forecast error. For example, it is assumed that forecast error will not exceed 5 per cent. This procedure is referred to as overforecasting top-level demand. The net result is to increase procurement of all components in a ratio to their expected usage plus a cushion for forecast error. Components common to different end products or subassemblies under the overforecasting technique will naturally experience greater quantity buildups than single-purpose components and parts. To accommodate for the unlikely event that all common assemblies will simultaneously require safety stock protection, a widely used procedure is to set a total safety stock for the item at a level less than the sum of 5-per cent protection for each potential use.[38] The third method is to utilize the previously discussed statistical techniques for setting safety stocks directly to the component rather than the item of top-level demand. The essential point is to recognize that safety stocks *are* normally required under conditions of derived demand.

---

[34] Orlicky, op. cit., pp. 22–25.

[35] This lack of need for safety stock is conceptually correct. However, in practice, safety stocks are used in MRP systems. See Orlicky, op. cit., pp. 7–9, and Plossl and Wight, op. cit., pp. 9–10.

[36] The practice became more common as a result of emphasis being placed on just in time procurement strategies.

[37] Plossl and Wight, op. cit., pp. 31–33. See also D. Clay Whybark and J. Greg Williams, "Material Requirements Planning Under Uncertainty," *Decision Sciences*, Vol. 7 (1976), pp. 595–606, for an analysis of the effectiveness of these alternatives.

[38] Ibid.

Inventory Control

In order to implement the desired inventory management logic, control procedures must be implemented. This part reviews control alternatives and discusses the implications of each.

A variety of inventory reorder systems exist. Most are based on either perpetual or periodic review. The following part reviews each method and presents some concepts regarding modification.

Perpetual Review

An inventory control approach based on perpetual review is basically a reorder-point system. To utilize this type of control system, an accurate accountability is necessary for all stockkeeping units. If the line is broad, computer assistance is necessary to implement the perpetual concept effectively. The perpetual approach is described as follows:

$$ROP = ss + \bar{s} \times \bar{t}$$

where

ROP = reorder point
ss = safety stock
$\bar{s}$ = average expected daily demand
$\bar{t}$ = duration of expected inventory replenishment cycle

Thus, with an expected replenishment cycle of 10 days, expected average demand of 5 units per day, and a safety stock of 32 units, to cover uncertainty, the ROP would be as follows:

$$ROP + ss + s \times t$$
$$= 32 + 5(10)$$
$$= 82 \text{ units}$$

and average inventory would be

$$\bar{I} = ss + \frac{q}{2}$$

where

$\bar{I}$ = average inventory
ss = safety stock
q = order quantity

Implementing an order quantity of 50 units, average inventory would be as follows:

$$\bar{I} = ss + \frac{q}{2}$$

$$= 32 + \frac{50}{2}$$

$$= 57 \text{ units}$$

Most illustrations throughout this text are based on a perpetual review system utilizing a fixed reorder point. The reorder formulation is based on two assumptions: (1) purchase orders for the item under control will be placed when the reorder point is reached, and (2) the method of control provides a continuous monitoring of inventory status. If these two assumptions are not satisfied, the method of perpetual review must be modified.

Periodic Review

An inventory control system based upon periodic review assumes that item status is reviewed at a specified time. For example, the status of a particular item may be reviewed every 20 days. Therefore, modification in the basic reorder point must be implemented to take into consideration the fixed time interval of each review.

The periodic approach is described as follows:

$$ROP = ss + \bar{s}\left(\bar{t} + \frac{p}{2}\right)$$

where

ROP = reorder point
ss = safety stock
$\bar{s}$ = average expected daily demand
$\bar{t}$ = duration of expected inventory replenishment cycle
p = review period in days

Since inventory status counts are only completed at a specificed time, any item could fall below the desired reorder point prior to the review time. Therefore, the assumption is made that the inventory will fall below ideal reorder status prior to the periodic count time on approximately one half of the review times. Assuming a review period of 20 days and using conditions similar to those of the perpetual example, the ROP then would be as follows:

$$ROP = ss + \bar{s}\left(\bar{t} + \frac{p}{2}\right)$$
$$= 32 + 5\left(10 + \frac{20}{2}\right)$$
$$= 132 \text{ units}$$

Implementing an order quantity of 50 units, average inventory could remain 57 units. However, because the review period is of greater duration than the replenishment cycle, the order quantity would have to be increased to accommodate the 10 days' difference. Average inventory thus would become 82 units. Because of the time interval introduced by periodic review, periodic control systems generally require larger average inventories than perpetual systems.

Modified Control Systems

To accommodate specific situations variations and combinations of the basic periodic and perpetual control systems have been developed. Most common are the replenishment level system and the optional replenishment system. Each is briefly noted to illustrate the range of modified systems available for control purposes.

The *replenishment level system* is a fixed-order-interval system that provides for short interval periodic review. With complete status on inventory similar to the perpetual concept, an upper limit or replenishment level for reordering is established. The review period is added to the lead time and the replenishment level is defined as

$$L = ss + \bar{s}\,(\bar{t} + p)$$

where

L = replenishment level
ss = safety stock
$\bar{s}$ = average daily sales
$\bar{t}$ = duration of expected inventory replenishment cycle
p = review period in days

The general reordering rules become

$$q = L - I - q_0$$

where

q = order quantity
L = replenishment level
I = inventory status at review time
q_0 = quantity on order

Assuming a review period of 5 days, average expected sales of 5 units, safety stock of 32 units, and a replenishment cycle of 10 days:

$$
\begin{aligned}
L &= ss + \bar{s}\,(\bar{t} + p) \\
&= 32 + 5(10 + 5) \\
&= 107 \text{ units}
\end{aligned}
$$

Since the replenishment cycle is greater than the review period, it is necessary to take into consideration outstanding orders. Assume that one order is outstanding for 25 units and the inventory status at time of review is 25 units. Then

$$
\begin{aligned}
q &= L - I - q_0 \\
&= 107 - 25 - 25 \\
&= 57 \text{ units}
\end{aligned}
$$

Under the replenishment system concept, the size of order is determined without reference to lot sizing. Emphasis is placed upon maintaining inventory levels below a maximum, which is the replenishment or order-up-to level. The maximum is protected as an upper level since inventory will never exceed the replenishment level and can only reach the replenishment level if no unit sales are experienced between the order communication and update. Under these conditions the average inventory becomes

$$\bar{I} = ss + \frac{\bar{s}p}{2}$$

The *optional replenishment system* is sometimes referred to as *SS* or the *min-max system*. Similar to the replenishment system, the optional system substitutes a variable order quantity for a specific lot size. However, a modification is introduced to limit the lower size of the variable order quantity. As a result, inventory is controlled on a perpetual basis between an upper and lower range. The upper range exists to limit maximum accumulation of inventory, and the lower limit serves to protect against small orders. The basic ordering rule becomes

$$q = S - I - q_0 \text{ whenever } I + q_0 \text{ is } < \text{ROP.}$$

INVENTORY STRATEGY ALTERNATIVES

Broadly speaking, three approaches are available to manage inventory distribution. The reactive or pull inventory approach uses customer demand and availability to pull product through the distribution channel. The proactive planning or push inventory approach pushes product through the channel based on forecasted demand and availability. A hybrid approach, the alternating logic, utilizes a combination of the two basic approaches to create an inventory management strategy which is uniquely fitted to the product situation. Each approach is reviewed and application guidelines are presented below.[39]

Reactive Systems

A reactive inventory system, as the name implies, reacts to inventory needs by drawing the product through the distribution channel. Replenishment shipments are initiated when available stock level at a warehouse falls below a predetermined minimum or reorder point. The amount ordered is usually based on some lot sizing formulation, although it may be some variable quantity which is a function of current stock levels and a predetermined maximum level. The reordering levels and quantities are usually based on a forecasted demand, but inventory is not shipped until a replenishment order has been actioned by customer demand on existing inventories. In summary, a reactive system waits for customer demand to pull inventory through the system. Inventory commitment is postponed until customer demand depletes warehouse stock.

A reactive inventory system is based on the assumption that all customers, market areas, and products contribute equally to profits. ABC or fine-line classification techniques can be used to strategically establish inventory levels.

[39] This discussion is adopted from David J. Closs, "An Adaptive Inventory System as a Tool for Strategic Inventory Management," *Proceedings of the 1981 Annual Conference of the National Council of Physical Distribution Management* (Chicago: National Council of Physical Distribution Management), pp. 659–78.

However, a pure reactive inventory system does not position inventory prior to the establishment of a need, which is determined by the current inventory position relative to the minimum prescribed level. Thus, using a reactive system, there is no logic to force the positioning of fast-moving stock in proximity to consistent or profitable markets.

The reactive inventory logic is also based on the assumption that infinite inventory is available at the supply location. This assumption is necessary to guarantee that replenishment shipments will arrive at the ordering warehouse and not fall victim to unplanned stockouts. The reactive inventory logic plans no back-orders or stockouts when placing replenishment orders.

The assumption concerning infinite availability implies no significant manufacturing or storage capacity limitations in the logistical system. This assumption implies products can be produced as desired and stored at the producing facility until required by the distribution system. This is probably one of the most significant limitations of the reactive inventory system.

When replenishment orders are initiated, the reactive decision rules assume performance cycle time can be predicted and that cycle length is independent from one replenishment to another. The basic assumption is that management cannot alter cycle times through expediting or delaying tactics. Although reactive logics assume no control over cycle times, many managers do in fact impact cycle performance.

For best performance of a reactive inventory logic, customer demand should be relatively stable and consistent. Most of the reactive inventory system decision rules are based on standard normal, gamma, or Poisson distributed demand functions. If the actual demand patterns do not closely resemble any of the above functions, available inventory decision rules will be of questionable value. For example, if the typical sales pattern were lumpy due to the existence of several large accounts, a higher level of safety stock would be required than might be predicted using a standard normal distribution. In addition, the demand function should be stable over the relevant planning cycle. Since the demand patterns for most products are constantly changing due to trends and competitive actions, it can be very difficult to determine what the appropriate stable demand pattern should be.

Since a reactive inventory system is pulling the product based on local demand it does not require information concerning the stock position at warehouses other than the one being replenished. Thus, there is little potential for effectively coordinating the inventory stocking policies of multiple warehouses. With the current capability for communication and information processing, this feature does not take advantage of valuable information.

Another assumption of the traditional reactive inventory management system is that the replenishment quantities must be greater than the expected demand over the cycle time. This implies that there should only be one replenishment order in the pipeline at a time and that replenishment orders should not pass in transit. Although this makes sense for most situations, there are some cases where a smaller order quantity might be advantageous to decrease average inventory.

A final assumption necessary for the mathematical derivation of the optimal reactive inventory system is that the cycle time length must not be correlated with demand. This is required to obtain an accurate approximation to the variance of the demand over the cycle time. In many cases, however, larger demand levels mean longer lead times, since times with higher-than-average demand levels are also the times that typically put the most stress on distribution channel operations.

The above discussion has outlined many of the assumptions and the resulting problems in the classical reactive inventory logic. The problems include overly simplified demand patterns, "infinite" availability and capacity, no segmented profitability consideration, and failure to utilize the coordination capability of multiple facilities. Operationally, most inventory managers overcome these limitations through the skillful use of manual overrides. However, these overrides often lead to suboptimal inventory decision-making, since the resulting combination of decisions uses neither consistent decision rules nor consistent inventory management criteria.

Inventory Planning Logic

In contrast to the reactive systems, planning systems attempt to plan future inventory levels. Using a detailed plan of customer needs, inventory requirements are time-phased from manufacturing through the distribution channel. The concept of distribution requirements planning (DRP) exhibits this approach to inventory management.[40] This part first illustrates the planning approach and then discusses some of the assumptions that are necessary to make the inventory planning approach operate effectively.

The Mechanics of DRP

The fundamental tool for distribution requirements planning is the DRP display which time-phases the requirements across the planning horizon. The horizon is typically divided into weeks. The display reports the current on-hand balance, the safety stock, replenishment cycle time, and order quantity for the item. In addition, for each planning period, the display provides gross requirements, scheduled receipts, projected on-hand, and planned orders. The gross requirements reflect the demands from customers and other distribution warehouses. The scheduled receipts are the replenishment shipments that are scheduled to be received at the warehouse. The projected-on-hand is the weekly inventory level, and the planned orders are the planned replenishment orders that should be initiated. Figure 7–9 illustrates a sample DRP display for a simulated warehouse located in Detroit. The weekly on-hand projections are equal to the prior week's on-hand less the current week's gross requirements plus any scheduled receipts. The example indicates the projected on-hand level for a specific week would drop below the safety stock level because a planned order is not scheduled for arrival until 2 weeks later. The procedure has identified that replenishment orders must be released during weeks 1, 4, and 8 for arrival during weeks 3, 6, and 10, respectively. The added benefit of an integrated planning approach is that the system also knows the time-phased requirements that will be placed on the replenishment source for Detroit. In this case, the replenishment source, whether it is a manufacturing plant or a central

---

[40] For a complete discussion of the concepts and procedures for DRP, see Andre Martin, *Distribution Resource Planning: Distribution Management's Most Powerful Tool* (Englewood Cliffs, N. J.: Prentice-Hall, Inc., 1983).

On hand balance: 200
Safety stock: 50
Lead time: 2 weeks
Order quantity: 300

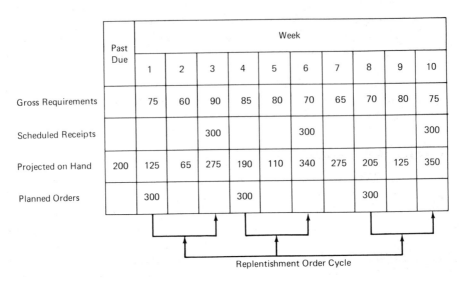

	Past Due	Week									
		1	2	3	4	5	6	7	8	9	10
Gross Requirements		75	60	90	85	80	70	65	70	80	75
Scheduled Receipts				300			300				300
Projected on Hand	200	125	65	275	190	110	340	275	205	125	350
Planned Orders		300			300				300		

Replentishment Order Cycle

Figure 7–9   Detroit DRP Display

distribution warehouse, would know that it must schedule shipment to Detroit during weeks 1, 4, and 8. Now that the DRP process has been presented, the following part discusses the required assumptions.

Basic Assumptions

A planning system does not use either a fixed reorder point or a fixed order point of time. Instead, using requirements at the customer level and the time required to move the product through the distribution channel, a master plan schedules inventory through the system for arrival on time. The inventory planning or DRP approach theoretically does not need safety stock, since the time-phasing should make the product available when and where it is required. However, when demand or cycle time uncertainty exists, planning systems may utilize safety stock or safely lead time to compensate for the uncertainty.

For inventory planning systems to be effective, a detailed and accurate forecast is required on a time-phased basis at each warehouse. This is necessary to direct the flow of goods through the distribution channel. The system, in general, does not have excess inventory at any location so there is not room for error in the theoretically operated planning system. To the extent that this level of forecasting accuracy is possible, the inventory planning system operates well. However, many organizations cannot forecast accurately at the required level of detail. The forecasts must be timely and accurate at the warehouse and product detail level. This means forecasts must be made for each warehouse and product with adequate lead time to allow transport. With such requirements, there are three sources for potential error. The forecast may be wrong. The forecast may have predicted demand at the wrong location. Finally, the forecast may have predicted demand at the wrong time. In any case, the forecast error could force an incorrect allocation of inventory.

To facilitate movement of inventory through the logistical system, it is imperative that allocations be controlled to coordinate stock at multiple warehouse locations. The information base must maintain stock requirements for facility, stock availability, and transportation time between facilities. This information must be current and up-to-date. If such a sophisticated information base is not available, a planning system would not operate effectively.

An inventory planning system also assumes relatively consistent replenishment cycle times. Since orders must be time-phased, rules used to allocate inventory must rely on cycle time estimates. Operationally, variable leadtimes can be partially overcome through the use of safety lead times.

Just as in the case of the reactive inventory system, much research has been done concerning the optimal operation of a planned inventory system. The typical practice is to use one of the discrete lot sizing algorithms discussed earlier in this chapter.

Even with the recent advancement in information-processing capabilities, there are still problems associated with implementation of an integrated inventory planning system for finished-goods distribution. The major problems are associated with the forecast accuracy required. Although modern inventory planning algorithms allow some uncertainty, distribution systems, unlike production schedules, must satisfy independent customer demands. The distribution system cannot usually establish and follow a detailed delivery schedule. Thus, a major problem area for inventory planning systems revolves around the fact that accurate forecasts are not possible at such a detailed level.

Another problem, which technology is beginning to overcome, is the level of communication and coordination that is required between facilities to allow for effective planning. A master control system must be implemented that maintains stock availability and forecasts needs for all facilities within the logistical system.

A third problem related to inventory planning is the consistency required for the replenishment cycles. Since inventory needs are time-phased through the system, potential delays between warehouses must be considered.

Adaptive Logic

A combined inventory management system may be used to overcome some of the problems inherent in using either a reactive or an inventory planning system. The factors that might make a reactive system better in one situation may change over the course of time to favor a inventory planning system. Thus, the ideal approach is an adaptive inventory management system.

Description

An adaptive inventory management system is one that combines reactive and inventory planning logics. Ideally it adapts the logic used to accomodate changing environments. The fundamental concept is that customer demand must usually be treated as independent demand, but there are some locations within the channel where demand can be treated as dependent. Thus, at some locations and times within the distribution channel, there must be an interface between independent and dependent demand. The uniqueness of an adaptive inventory management logic is that it changes as environmental conditions change. During some parts of the year, it may be possible to push products to field warehouses, while at other times the most efficient alternative may be to hold the stock at the manufacturing location and wait for customers to pull it through the distribution channel. An adaptive inventory system must adjust by location and time, thus, the information base for such a system must be totally integrated. With existing data-management techniques, it is possible to maintain the required level of information. The primary difficulties in implementing such a system are the decision rules that should be used for making adjustments and adaptations. Using these factors, the following part presents heuristic decision rules.

Adaptive Decision Rules

Adaptive inventory management decision rules can incorporate the relative contribution or profitability of various market segments. For segments or products which are highly profitable and consistent movers, the appropriate decision rule is to push inventory to the market since there is little likelihood of poor allocation. This rule overcomes two limitations of the reactive system while not taking the risk of a pure inventory planning system. First, inventories can be moved from upper echelon facilities which may be over capacity, at volume levels that provide transport economies of scale. Second, an adaptive and selective approach does not push slow or inconsistent movers. The markets and products that are selected to utilize the inventory planning logic must be reviewed periodically.

The difference between independent and dependent demand is the second factor that influences the selection of an appropriate inventory management logic. Since the adaptive system recognizes that the two are different, it attempts to utilize the logic that best fits the situation. Basically, the decision rule is to utilize the planning policies whenever possible to minimize costs, but don't overcommit stock where there is a high degree of uncertainty. The key decision is whether demand can best be treated as independent or dependent.

The third factor concerns the nature of the distribution channel interfaces, which include economies of scale, uncertainty, and capacity. The nature of each of these interfaces affects the type of system that would be appropriate for the location and time.

If the interface displays substantial economies of scale, the inventory management logic utilized should be oriented to a planning logic since lower costs will result from volume transportation. The planning system is designed to make shipments that take advantage of volume movement rates. An evaluation must be made for the channel institutions involved at the particular point in time. If the interface between the institutions exhibit scale economies, inventory should be pushed between the institutions.

Many forms of uncertainty exist at each interface in the channel. The three broad uncertainty categories include supply uncertainty, replenishment cycle uncertainty, and demand uncertainty. The inventory management logic must be designed to treat all three uncertainty types at different points in time. Reactive inventory systems consider cycle time and demand uncertainty but fail to allow for supply or availability uncertainty. Inventory planning systems allow for supply uncertainty but have limited consideration for cycle and demand uncertainty. The ideal inventory logic should be able to treat all three uncertainty sources.

Just as in the case of economies of scale, the uncertainty factor must be addressed for each interface in the distribution channel. However, as a general rule, once the decision is made to utilize a planning system at one echelon in the channel, a proactive system must be used at all echelons above the one where the initial decision was applied. To determine which type of system is appropriate, the combination of the three uncertainties must be investigated for each echelon or location. The following heuristic decision rules should be used in selecting the appropriate type of system for each stage.

For situations where there are supply uncertainties or allocation restrictions, a planning-based system is the most appropriate to efficiently allocate the existing resources. An inventory planning system facilitates the supply of the product to markets where it can be sold more profitably or with a greater degree of certainty. The planning approach can also be used to manage shipments to markets or customers who can most easily survive without them. Replenishment cycle time uncertainty should be treated with a reactive inventory system between the locations involved. The use of a planning system in this situation could cause a large shipment to be delayed or arrive early. The reactive logic leads to smaller shipment quantities and less risk of overcommitment. The third type of uncertainty is the demand level at each location. For situations where demand is relatively stable or predictable, the planning logic is the most efficient since it can take advantage of the movement economies. For situations where demand is not consistent or predictable, the reactive logic is the most appropriate since it postpones stock commitment to lower echelons until there is some evidence of need.

The final factor for deciding the most appropriate inventory management system is the capacity of the channel interface. The interface capacity refers to either the production capacity of manufacturing facilities or the storage capacity of the various distribution centers and warehouses. The reactive logic assumes that there are no capacity limitations on any distribution facilities, so such logic may cause problems when there are restrictions. Thus, when there are capacity restrictions either at the plant or storage facilities, the inventory planning logic moves product out from an overcapacity location more efficiently.

The above heuristic decision rules indicate the general logic requirements for various channel situations. Table 7–17 summarizes the management logic most appropriate for the various environmental conditions. Each channel situation may consist of a combination of factors.

TABLE 7–17   Suggested Inventory Management Logic

Use proactive logic under conditions of:	Use reactive logic under conditions of:
Highly profitable segments	Cycle time uncertainty
Dependent demand	Demand uncertainty
Economies of scale	Destination capacity limitations
Supply uncertainty	
Source capacity limitations	
Seasonal supply build-up	

So far the discussion has described an adaptive inventory system and has identified the factors to which it should be able to adapt. The following section discusses the adjustments that an adaptive inventory logic should be able to manage.

There are three situations when an adaptive inventory system should consider change. The three general categories are temporal adjustment, spatial adjustment, and product adjustment.

First, the system must have the ability to adapt over time. The factors discussed above certainly change characteristics through time. For example, agricultural products are widely available in the late summer and early autumn so processing for the entire year must be done then. For many firms, this means that the manufacturing locations may have an overcapacity so that a planning approach is appropriate. However, in the spring and summer, as supplies are decreasing, it may be wise to switch to a reactive system to avoid product overcommitment.

Second, the system should have the ability to adapt by location and echelon. This can be termed spatial adjustment. For each channel segment, the factors discussed must be investigated to determine which inventory logic would be the most appropriate. In general, the echelons closer to the product source would tend to use a planning logic, while those closest to the final customer would tend toward a reactive logic. However, the stage at which the logic shifts from inventory planning to reactive may change over time. In the above agricultural situation, during the packing season, it would probably be appropriate to push the product all the way through the channel to the final customer. On the other hand, during the spring and summer when supplies are low, a reactive system is the most appropriate for most stages within the channel.

The final adjustment that an adaptive system must make is by product. As product availability or demand changes, the system should be able to switch from one system to the other to provide the most efficient means for distributing the available product. In some situations this capability may call for the operation of dual distribution systems, one for proactive products and one for reactive products.

SYSTEM INVENTORY MANAGEMENT

The previous discussions focused on the development of inventory management procedures for an individual product. While this was necessary from the point of view of understanding the concepts, it is important to emphasize that all inventories must be managed to allow the enterprise to meet the desired objectives. Assuming all things are equal, the management approach utilized for each product line should be that which matches the marginal inventory cost with the marginal revenue gained by the last unit sold.

If the specific inventory situation includes a policy of back-ordering customer orders, the associated costs should be considered when establishing the inventory policy. For example, a back-order requires duplicate order processing, added administrative cost, wasted marketing effort, and loss of profit contribution on available cash flow when unable to fill an order. These cost factors can be eliminated by maintaining high inventory availability. Once again, the solution is found at the point of equating appropriate marginal costs and revenue. For practical planning, a high degree of selectivity must be exercised in establishing inventory policy across a broad product line. Not all items have the same degree of importance. The task in establishing sound inventory policy is to classify the inventory line on the basis of enterprise objectives.

The fine-line classification of a product line can be based on a variety of measures. The most commonly used are sales, profit, unit value, usage rate, and critical nature of the item. By classifying the overall product line, different inventory policies can be established for each product grouping. Those groups of extreme importance can be assigned high protection. In contrast, those with limited importance can be given little or no protection.

Classification by sales volume is one of the oldest methods employed to establish selective policy for an inventory line. In most marketing situations a small percentage of products account for a large percentage of sales. This generalization is often called the 20/80 rule. It is based on the rule that 20 per cent of the products typically account for 80 per cent of the sales. The most common sales classification is to rank-array and then group products into categories labeled, for example, ABC. Table 7–18 presents a rank array of 20 products with three classification groupings. With fine-line classification, inventory policies can be set for each group to assure that the fast-moving products are afforded the lion's share of protection.

In special situations the classification system used to develop safety stock policy may be based upon multiple factors. For example, sales, profitability,

TABLE 7–18   Fine-Line Classification on Basis of Sales

Product Identification	Annual Sales (in thousands)	Per Cent Total Sales	Accumulated Sales (%)	Accumulated Products (%)	Classification Category
1	$ 45,000	30.0	30.0	5	A
2	35,000	23.3	53.3	10	A
3	25,000	16.7	70.0	15	A
4	15,000	10.0	80.0	20	A
5	8,000	5.3	85.3	25	B
6	5,000	3.3	88.6	30	B
7	4,000	2.7	91.3	35	B
8	3,000	2.0	93.3	40	B
9	2,000	1.3	94.6	45	B
10	1,000	0.7	95.3	50	B
11	1,000	0.7	96.0	55	C
12	1,000	0.7	96.7	60	C
13	1,000	0.7	97.4	65	C
14	750	0.5	97.9	70	C
15	750	0.5	98.4	75	C
16	750	0.5	98.9	80	C
17	500	0.3	99.2	85	C
18	500	0.3	99.5	90	C
19	500	0.3	99.8	95	C
20	250	0.2	100.0	100	C
	$150,000				

TABLE 7–19   Sample Inventory Strategy Guide

Product Class	Forecast Procedure	Management Logic	Desired Service Level	Review Period
A	Top-down	Inventory planning	98 per cent	Weekly
B	Bottom-up	Reactive	95 per cent	Biweekly
C	Bottom-up	Reactive	85 per cent	Monthly

and critical nature could be weighted together in a combined index. The level of safety stock protection is then assigned according to the weighted rank-array.

For classification on the basis of unit usage, it is important to realize that a differential will exist in a product line between total dollar sales and unit movement. Often items with a high frequency of unit sales during an inventory performance cycle account for only a small percentage of total dollar sales. Grouping of such items into broad categories can reduce the task of setting management strategies.

With respect to unit value, it is important to keep in mind that high-value items are more expensive to protect than items with lower value. The reader should recall that the higher the unit value and the greater the sales rate, the more frequently orders would be placed under the rules of economic order quantity. The ideal inventory performance cycle would be short for items having high value and high usage. Therefore, the need to provide safety stocks for sales uncertainty during replenishment is reduced.

The key to selective establishment of management strategies is to realize from the outset that different products have various degrees of importance. Variations in the desired inventory performance cycle and in the degree of stockout protection during the cycle should be programmed in the best interest of meeting planned objectives.

The classification scheme can then be used to develop specific inventory management strategies for each product group. The segmentation could focus on forecast procedure, inventory management logic, and desired service level. Table 7–19 illustrates such an inventory strategy guide. The guide can then be used to systematically direct the inventory management resources to the products that provide the most benefit. In actual practice, it may be necessary to refine the product classifications to provide more specific strategies.

SUMMARY

In summary, the chapter reviewed the importance of inventory for logistical operations. The risks associated with holding inventory at each level of the distribution channel were reviewed, along with potential conflicts, both internal and external, to the enterprise. The basic inventory functions of geographical specialization, decoupling, balancing supply and demand, and safety stock protection against uncertainty were identified.

The second section reviewed the basic elements of inventory policy. The section provided basic inventory definitions and relationships. The relationship between the performance cycle, order quantity, and average inventory was discussed and illustrated. The inventory carrying cost elements of maintenance and ordering costs were defined and trade-offs discussed. The difference between independent and dependent demand were presented.

The concept of economic order quantity was developed as the traditional approach to determining how much to order. Several special adjustments to the basic EOQ were noted, with emphasis placed on volume transportation rates and quantity discounts. In addition, a discussion was devoted to discrete-lot-sizing techniques commonly used in manufacturing procurement situations.

A critical aspect in formulating inventory policy is the identification of the inventory management goals of customer service, profitable inventory alloca-tion, prediction and control of inventory requirements, and total cost integra-tion. A thorough review of demand and replenishment uncertainty was presented, followed by a discussion of methods for determining safety stock requirements based on desired service and uncertainty level. The perpetual and periodic inventory review procedures were described and illustrated.

The fifth section reviewed the inventory management alternatives of reactive, inventory planning, and adaptive. For each logic, the text presented a description of the logic, basic assumptions and guidelines.

The final segment discussed considerations for an overall system inventory management strategy. The basic consideration is that cost of inventory must be evaluated in terms of potential revenue. Various concepts of selectivity offer ways to reduce inventory risk. Attention is now directed to warehousing and packaging.

QUESTIONS

1. What impact does the cost of carrying inventory show on the traditional profit-and-loss statement of the enterprise?
2. Describe the differences between the demand and replenishment cycle uncertainty and identify the activities that can be performed to reduce the uncertainty.
3. Discuss the relationship between service level, uncertainty, safety stock, and order quantity. How can trade-offs between these elements be made?
4. Discuss the disproportionate risk in the holding of inventory by retailers, wholesalers, and manufacturers. Why has there been a trend to push inventory back up the channel of distribution?
5. Discuss the differences between reactive inventory logics and inventory planning logics. What are the advantages of each?
6. In developing an inventory management logic, what factors should be considered in identifying the appropriate procedures for each product?
7. What is the difference between the probability of a stockout and the magnitude of a stockout?
8. Discuss the major inventory management goals. Why should manage-ment consider profitable allocation as a goal?
9. What procedure and strategies can be used to reduce safety stock requirements for a fixed distribution system design? What are the trade-offs?
10. Discuss the difference between discrete and EOQ lot sizing.

Warehousing and Packaging

Warehousing and material handling do not fit the neat classification possible when discussing order processing, transportation, or inventory because they involve all logistical components. For example, material handling engages inventory as it flows through warehouses and as it is being transported. Such material handling is initiated in response to a customer order within the physical distribution, manufacturing support, or purchasing system. The main concern of this chapter is the development of a unified treatment of strategic warehousing and product packaging throughout the logistical system.

A major problem in logistical operations during the past several decades has been the level of labor productivity. The basic nature of raw materials, parts, and finished goods flowing through and among a vast network of facilities makes logistics a labor-intensive process. Productivity is the ratio of physical input to physical output. To increase productivity, it is necessary either to obtain greater output with the same input or to maintain existing output with a reduction in effort.

Labor productivity growth is influenced by the boom and recession pattern of business which has been characteristic of American industry since the early 1950s. When business is extremely good and the economy approaches full employment, output per worker-hour falls as marginal quality workers are employed. Warehousing operation gets more than its fair share of such new employees because few, if any skills are required to perform many of the required manual tasks. When business activity plummets, labor contract provisions typically prohibit a rapid reduction in payrolls. Separate productivity figures for warehouse workers are not available. However, it is safe to assume that warehouse labor productivity has lagged behind most other areas in the private sector. Four factors contribute to this conclusion.

First, the sheer number of labor hours involved in warehouse operations creates a vulnerability to any drop in output rate per labor hour. Second, the nature of warehouse operations has restricted the direct benefits gained by the introduction of computers. Third, until recently warehousing has not been managed on an integrated basis, nor has it received a great deal of top management attention. Finally, automation technology capable of reducing warehouse labor is only now, in the mid-1980s, beginning to reach its full potential.

Within the warehouse system, material handling is the prime consumer of labor. The application of labor to product selection and handling represents one of logistics' overall highest costs. The opportunity to reduce labor intensity and improve productivity lies with the emerging technology of handling. In a logistical warehouse primary emphasis is placed on material and product inbound and outbound handling in contrast to inventory storage. The warehouse represents the primary arena for material handling operations. Therefore, warehouse design is an integral aspect of overall handling efficiency and is vital for obtaining increased labor productivity.

In this chapter the activities of packaging, containerization, material handling and inventory storage are treated as a single managerial area. The objective of attaining maximum productivity throughout the logistical system provides the primary logic for this grouping. The first section provides an overview of the strategic nature of warehousing. The role of warehousing in a logistical system is reviewed, followed by a discussion of the cost and service justification for warehouses. The section concludes with a review of warehouse ownership options. The second section is concerned with the impact of products on the warehouse system. The first part of section two treats packaging. Emphasis is placed on protective packaging rather than marketing or motivation considerations. Attention is then directed to containerization. Containerization is defined to include all aspects of unitization. In the third section, warehouse operation is the focus of attention. The final section of the chapter provides an overview of material handling alternatives. For readers interested in planning and establishing a mechanized warehouse, a general guide is provided in Appendix II. The overall objectives of the chapter are the establishment of the strategic warehousing concept and development of a unified approach to the treatment of material handling throughout the logistical system.

STRATEGIC WAREHOUSING

This section develops the role of warehousing in a logistical system. The initial part reviews the strategic importance of warehousing. The second part discusses the cost and service benefits provided by warehousing. The final part reviews warehouse ownership options.

The Concept of Strategic Storage

Storage has always been an important aspect of economic development. In the early stages of economic expansion the Untied States consisted of individual households which functioned as self-sufficient economic units. Consumers performed storage and accepted the attendant risks. Meats were stored in smokehouses, and perishable products were protected in underground food cellars.

As transportation capability developed, it became possible to engage in economic specialization. Product storage was shifted from households to retailers, wholesalers, and manufacturers. Early literature indicates that the warehouse was initially viewed as a storage facility that was necessary to accomplish basic marketing processes. Storage was necessary to match products in a timing sense with consumers. Warehousing provided product storage until market demand required distribution. This view of storage resulted in a tendency to consider warehouses a necessary evil that added cost to the distribution process. This resulted in criticism of operating cost with little appreciation of the broader logistical spectrum in which warehousing played a vital role. The warehouse served as a static unit in the material and product pipeline. The warehouse's capability to group products into an assortment desired by customers was given little emphasis. Internal control and maximum inventory turnover received little managerial attention.

Literature of the early era correctly described the situation. Firms seeking to operate effectively between points of procurement, manufacturing, and consumption gave little attention to internal warehouse operations. The establishment of warehouses was essential for survival, but little emphasis was placed on qualitative storage and handling. Engineering efforts were centered on manufacturing problems.

Operation of early warehouses illustrated the lack of concern with material handling principles. The typical warehouse received merchandise by railcar or truck. The merchandise was moved manually to a storage area within the warehouse and handpiled in stacks on the floor. When different products were stored in the same warehouse, merchandise was continually lost. Stock rotation was handled poorly. When customer orders were received, merchandise was handpicked for placement on wagons. The wagons were then pushed to the shipping area where the merchandise was reassembled and handloaded on delivery trucks.

Because of inexpensive labor, human resources were used freely. Little consideration was given to efficiency in space utilization, work methods, or material handling. Despite their shortcomings, these early warehouses provided the necessary bridge between marketing and production.

Following World War II, managerial attention shifted toward increasing warehouse efficiency. Management began to question the need for so many warehouses. In the distributive industries it was not unusual for every sales territory to have a dedicated warehouse and inventory. Forecasting and production scheduling techniques improved, reducing the need for extensive inventory buildup. Production became more coordinated as time delays during the manufacturing process were reduced. Seasonal production still required warehousing, but the overall need for storage to support manufacturing was reduced.

The changing requirements of retail logistics more than offset any reductions in warehousing requirements gained in the manufacturing area. The retail store, faced with the necessity of stocking an increasing variety of products, could not order products in sufficient quantity from a single supplier to enjoy consolidated shipment. Cost of transporting small shipments made direct ordering prohibitive. This resulted in a need to utilize warehouses to provide timely and economical inventory assortments to retailers. At the wholesale level of the channel of distribution the warehouse became a support unit for retailing. Progressive wholesalers and integrated retailers developed state-of-the-art warehouse systems capable of providing the necessary retail logistical support.

Improvements in warehousing efficiency related to retailing soon were adopted in manufacturing. For enterprises producing products at multiple locations, efficient warehousing offered a method of reducing raw material and part storage and handling costs, while maximizing production operations. When fully integrated into the manufacturing process the warehouse is a vital part of logistical systems.

On the outbound side of manufacturing, warehouses opened the door for direct shipment of mixed products to the customer. The capability to provide factory-direct mixed-product shipments was appealing to marketing because it enhanced service capability. For the customer, direct, mixed shipments have two distinct advantages. First, logistical cost is reduced as a result of consolidated transportation of a full product assortment. Second, inventory of slow-turnover products can be reduced as a result of their availability as part of a consolidated shipment. As competition increased, the manufacturer capable of rapidly providing direct, mixed shipments gained a competitive advantage.

During the 1960s and 1970s emphasis in warehousing focused on the application of new technology. Technology-based improvements impacted almost every area of warehouse operations, creating new and better ways to perform storage and handling. During these decades significant advancements were made in handling techniques and procedures throughout all types of warehousing work. The central focus of the 1980s is on improved configuration of warehousing systems and advanced handling technology.

Warehouse Benefits

Benefits realized from strategic warehousing are classified on the basis of economics and service. At a conceptual level no warehouse should be included in a logistical system unless fully justified on a cost/benefit basis. In this part, basic warehouse benefits are reviewed. Without question, the benefits overlap.

Economic Benefits

Economic benefits of warehousing result when overall logistical costs are directly reduced by utilizing one or more facilities. It *is not* difficult to quantify the return-on-investment of an economic benefit because it is reflected in a direct cost-to-cost trade-off. For example, if adding a warehouse to a logistical system will reduce overall transportation cost by an amount greater than the cost of the warehouse, then total cost will be reduced. Whenever total cost reductions are attainable, the warehouse will be economically justified. Four basic economic benefits are attainable from warehouses: (1) consolidation, (2) break-bulk; (3) processing/postponement, and (4) stockpiling. Each is discussed.

Consolidation. A basic service offered by warehousing is the multimanufacturing plant consolidated shipment. Under this arrangement, the warehouse receives and consolidates merchandise from a number of manufacturing plants destined to a specific customer in a single transportation shipment. Consolidation results in the lowest possible transportation cost and reduced congestion at a customer's receiving dock.

In order to effectively consolidate, each manufacturing plant must use the warehouse as a forward stock location or as a sorting and assembly facility. The primary benefit of consolidation is that it combines the logistical flow of several small shipments to a specific market area or customer. Consolidation warehousing may be accomplished by a single firm, or a variety of firms may join in a third party for-hire consolidation service. Through the use of a warehouse consolidation program, each individual plant or shipper can enjoy lower total distribution cost than could be realized on a direct-ship basis.

Break-Bulk. Break-bulk warehouse service does not involve inventory storage. A manufacturer can combine orders from different customers within a market area into one consolidated shipment to a break-bulk warehouse. The warehouse sorts or splits out individual orders and arranges for local delivery. Using a break-bulk warehouse results in volume freight rates and reduces the difficulty of controlling small shipments to a given market area.

Processing/Postponement. Recently, a great deal of attention has been directed to the prospect of using warehouses to perform light manufacturing and processing. Using warehouses, assembly can be postponed until demand materializes.[1] For example, vegetables can be cooked, frozen, packed in large containers, and shipped to field warehouses. Actual packaging into consumer and institutional packs can be postponed until customers orders are received.

This example of postponement has two advantages. First, final packaging is reduced to the time of lowest possible risk. Second, inventories are reduced by using the basic product to support a variety of different package configurations.

Stockpiling. The basic benefit of stockpiling is to provide storage to accommodate seasonal production or demand. The direct economic benefit of this type of warehousing service is secondary to the fact that such storage is essential to the conduct of selected types of businesses. For example, lawn furniture and toys are produced year-round and are sold during a very short marketing period. In contrast, agricultural products are harvested at specific times with consumption being year-round. Both situations require warehouse storage to support marketing. The basic trade-off in stockpiling is between type and location of warehouse.

Service Benefits

Service benefits gained from warehouses in a logistical system may or may not reduce costs. When a warehouse is primarily justified on service, the supporting rational is that the time and place capabilities of the overall logistical system are improved. It is often difficult to quantify the return-on-investment of such a rationale because it involves cost-to-service trade-offs. For example, placing a

---

[1] For more detailed discussion, see Chapter 2, pages 57–58.

warehouse in the logistical system to service a specific market area may increase cost, but it might also increase market share, revenue, and gross margin. At a conceptual level, a service-justified warehouse would be added if the net effect was profit-justified. The problem is measurement of the direct revenue impact. Four basic service benefits are attainable from warehouses: (1) spot stock, (2) assortment, (3) mixing, and (4) production support. Each is discussed.

Spot Stock. Spot stocking is most often used in the physical distribution system. In addition, manufacturers with limited or highly seasonal product lines are partial to this service. Rather than placing inventories year-round in warehouse facilities or shipping direct from manufacturing plants, delivery time can be substantially reduced by advanced inventory commitment to strategic markets. Under this concept a selected inventory of a firm's product line is spot stocked in a warehouse to fill customer orders during a critical marketing period. Utilizing warehouse facilities for spot stocking allows inventories to be placed in a variety of markets adjacent to key customers just prior to a maximum period of seasonal sales. Following the sales season the remaining inventory is withdrawn to a central warehouse.

Assortment. A complete line-assorting warehouse may be employed by a manufacturer, wholesaler, or retailer. In an assortment warehouse products are stocked in anticipation of customer orders. Customized assortments are grouped as specified by customers.

The differential between stock spotting and complete line assortment is the degree and duration of warehouse utilization. A firm following a stock spotting strategy would typically warehouse a narrow product assortment and place stocks in a large number of small warehouses dedicated to specific markets for a limited time period. The distribution assortment warehouse is typically full line, limited to a few strategic locations, and is functional year-round.

Mixing. Warehouse mixing is somewhat similar to the break-bulk process, except that several different factory-consolidated shipments may be involved. When manufacturing plants are geographically separated, overall transportation charges and warehouse requirements can be reduced by in-transit mixing. In a typical mixing situation carloads or truckloads of products are shipped from manufacturing plants to warehouses. Each large shipment enjoys the lowest possible transportation rate. Upon arrival of two or more volume shipments, products are mixed and sorted as required by specific customers using the warehouse facility. Upon arrival at the warehouse, factory shipments are unloaded and the desired combination of each product for each customer order or market is selected.

The economies of in-transit mixing have been traditionally supported by special transportation tariffs.[2] These special mixing tariffs are variations of storage in-transit privileges. Under the mixing warehouse concept inbound products may also be combined with products regularly stored in the warehouse. Warehouses that provide in-transit mixing have the net effect of reducing overall product storage in a logistical system. Mixing is classified as a service benefit because inventory is sorted to exact customer order specifications.

---

[2] See Chapter 6, page 117.

Production Support. The use of product support warehousing is to provide a steady supply of components and materials to assembly plants. The economics of manufacturing may justify relatively long production runs of specific components. Safety stocks on items purchased from outside vendors may be justified because of long lead times or significant variations in usage. In these, as well as a variety of other situations, the most economical total cost solution may be the operation of a production support warehouse to feed manufacturing requirements.

In a pure sense, the just-in-time (JIT) philosophy discussed in Chapter 2 would eliminate the need for production warehousing.[3] In reality, safety stocks exist in manufacturing for a wide variety of reasons. The role of the production support warehouse is to feed processed materials, components, and subassemblies into assembly in an economic and timely manner.[4]

Conclusion—Warehouse Benefits

In conclusion, many services are possible from the use of warehouses that involve a great deal more than inventory storage. In fact, many of the services reduce the need for storage. This adaptation of traditional warehouse capabilities to contemporary service requirements and cost reduction is an excellent example of modern logistical management. Figure 8–1 provides flow diagrams of five benefits available from warehousing. The benefits not illustrated, processing/postponement, stockpiling, and spot stock, are primarily time-related as contrasted to flow-related.

Ownership Options

Three warehouse ownership alternatives are available: (1) private, (2) public, and (3) combinations of the two. A private warehouse facility is one operated and managed by the enterprise that owns the merchandise handled and stored at the facility. A public warehouse, in contrast, is operated as an independent business offering a range of services on a contract or fee basis.

Private Warehouse

A private warehouse may be owned or leased. The decision as to which best fits an individual enterprise's requirements is essentially financial. Often it is not possible to find a warehouse facility for lease which satisfies exact requirements. If a considerable amount of material handling is planned for a warehouse, an available building may not be conducive to efficient handling. As a general rule, an efficient warehouse should be designed around a material handling system in order to encourage maximum efficiency of product flow.

Real estate developers are increasingly willing to build and lease customized distribution warehouses. Such custom construction is available in many markets on a lease as short as five years.

---

[3] See pages 61–65.

[4] R. Scott Whiting, "Public Warehousing and the 'Just-in-Time' Production System," *Warehousing Review*, 1983, and "Challenge, Opportunity in Kanban Concepts Seen for Warehousing," *Traffic World* (June 18, 1984).

CONSOLIDATION

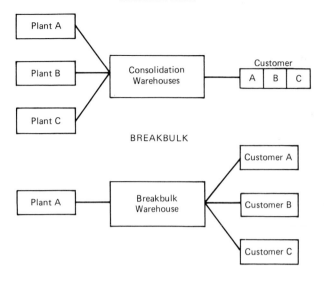

BREAKBULK

DISTRIBUTION ASSORTMENT

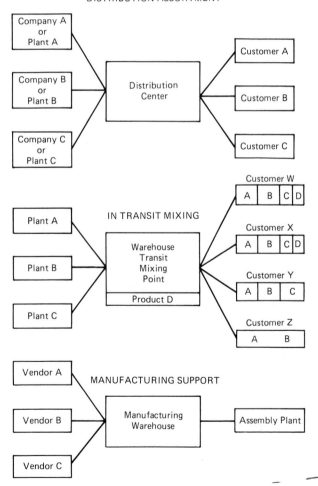

IN TRANSIT MIXING

MANUFACTURING SUPPORT

Figure 8–1   Warehouse Benefits

Public Warehouse

Public warehouses are used extensively in logistical systems. Almost any combination of services can be arranged with the operator of a public warehouse. These services can be arranged for a short term or may be contracted over a long time duration. A classification of public warehouses has been developed based upon the range of specialized operations performed. Public warehouses are classified as: (1) general merchandise, (2) refrigerated, (3) special commodity, (4) bonded, (5) household goods and furniture, and (6) field warehouse. Of course, many public warehouses offer combinations of these operations.

In physical distribution, a great many firms utilize public warehouses because of the range of services available and the flexibility. In procurement, attention is more often focused on storage. In both situations public warehouse facilities and services can be obtained to meet the exact requirements of the operations.[5]

A public warehouse charges in a variety of ways for services. Basic charges are for hundredweight stored or handled. Such charges normally exceed the cost of private warehousing, providing adequate product volume is available. However, when economy of scale is not possible, the public warehouse may be the low-cost alternative.

Combination Systems

As would be expected, many enterprises utilize a combination of public and private distribution warehouses. A private facility may be used to cover basic year-round requirements, and public facilities to handle peak requiremets. In other situations central warehouses may be private, with market area warehouses being public.

Full utilization of a warehouse throughout a year is remote. As a planning rule, a warehouse designed for full-capacity utilization will, in fact, be fully utilized between 75 and 85 per cent of the time. Thus, from 15 to 25 per cent of the time, space required to meet peak requirements is not utilized. In such situations it may be most efficient to build private facilities to cover the 75-per-cent requirement and use public facilities to accomodate peak demand. Figure 8–2 illustrates this concept.

The second form of combined public/private warehousing may result from market requirements. A firm may find that private warehousing is justified at specific locations based upon sales volume. In other markets public facilities may cost least. In logistical system design the objective is to determine whatever combination most economically satisfies customer service objectives.

Comparative Benefits of Public and Private Alternatives

In recent years, the traditional role of public warehouses as supplemental storage facilities has changed dramatically. The nature of modern business places a great deal of emphasis on inventory turnover and the ability to satisfy customer orders rapidly. To achieve these two benefits, flexibility must be

[5] Kenneth B. Ackerman, *Practical Handbook of Warehousing* (Washington, D.C.: The Traffic Service Corporation, 1983), pp. 29–36.

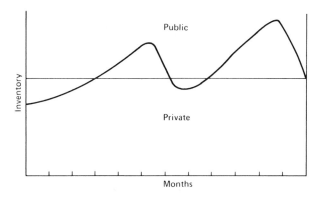

Figure 8-2   Combined Private and Public Warehouse Facilities

maintained within the logistical structure. Public warehouse management has been very progressive in designing warehouse systems that can be placed at the immediate disposal of logistics managers with little fixed or long-term commitment.

Many public warehouses have formed associations that allow a firm to obtain order processing and local delivery services in a number of cities across the United States. In addition to basic warehousing, these associations coordinate specialized services, such as inventory control and invoicing.

Some larger public warehouse firms are expanding operations to encompass a network of warehouses located in key markets. This trend has the ultimate potential to offer manufacturers a service which is effectively a logistical utility. Under the utility concept, all functions required to service customers are provided by the public warehouse logistics specialist. That is, transportation, order processing, inventory control, warehousing, and selected administrative matters are provided as an integrated service. Although still in the formulation stages, indications are that these multifacility public warehouse networks under one management coordination will increase in number and geographic coverage during the coming decade.[6]

Such innovative trends in public warehousing services are important in the appraisal of whether or not to use public or private warehouse facilities. Traditionally, the decision to use public warehouses was based on relative storage economics and flexibility. In the future, the choice will be based on the public warehouse organization's ability to perform necessary logistical tasks more effectively and efficiently than private systems.

From an analytical viewpoint, the private versus public warehouse decision is analogous to the purchasing decision to make or buy a component part. Private warehouse facilities require substantial investment, and such commitments should provide the same rate of return as other capital investments.

A final consideration regarding the use of public warehouse associations and single-ownership networks is the natural reluctance of an enterprise to turn over managerial responsibility to a third party for an operational area as vital as logistics. The risks—potential loss of control, problems in customer goodwill, and the inability to rapidly replace or supplement a system that fails to perform—are the prime reasons given by logistical managers for not adopting

[6] Ibid.

single-management public warehouse networks. Although many organizations use public warehouses exclusively, the typical arrangement is for each facility to be under individual ownership, with logistical network control resting with the manaufacturing, wholesaling, or retail enterprise. Whether or not future conditions will change the prevailing attitude and reluctance of public warehouse customers to accept the network concept remains to be seen.

PRODUCT IMPACT

The focal point in warehousing is the product that is stored and handled. Individual products or parts are normally grouped into cartons, bags, bins, or barrels for handling efficiency. These devices used to group individual products are referred to as *master cartons*. When master cartons are grouped into larger units for handling, the combination is referred to as *containerization* or *unitization*. In the material movement system, master cartons and containers perform two functions. First, the master carton and the unit load provide the basic handling unit. Second, each serves to protect individual products as they move through the logistical environment. This section discusses the role of master cartons and containers in the logistical system.

Packaging

The weight, cube, and fragility of the master cartons in an overall product line determine transportation and material handling requirements. If the package is not designed for efficient logistical processing, overall system performance will suffer. In this part packaging is reviewed in terms of protection and design.

The Benefits of Standardized Packaging

Final package design is most often based on manufacturing and marketing considerations at the neglect of logistical requirements. For example, shipping such products as motor cycles fully assembled results in a substantial reduction in density. A low-density package means higher transportation rates and greater cubic utilization of warehouse storage space. The proper package design should be based on a comprehensive assessment of logistical packaging requirements. This assessment requires an evaluation of how the package is influenced by all components of the logistical system.

The retail sale quantity should not be the prime determinant of master carton size. For example, beer typically sold in units of six and eight individual containers is normally packed in master cartons (cases) in quantities of 24 units. The prime objective is to determine a limited assortment of standard master cartons. Standardization of master cartons facilitates material handling and transportation.

The importance of standardization can be illustrated by an example adapted from a shoe retailer. The initial system used to ship shoes from the warehouse to retail stores consisted of reusing vendor cartons. Individual pairs of shoes were grouped as best as possible into available repack cartons. The result was a variety of carton sizes going to each retail store.

The method of order selection used to assemble a store's order was to work from a warehouse-sequenced picking list that grouped requirement by shoe style and quantity. Shoes were selected in the warehouse, packed into cartons, and the cartons were then manually stacked on a four-wheel wagon for transfer to the shipping dock. The cartons were then loaded into over-the-road trailers for transport to the retail store. While the order picking list provided a summary of all shoes in the total shipment, it was impossible for the retail stores to determine the contents of any given carton.

Viewing material handling as an intergrated system resulted in the economically justified decision to discontinue reusing vendor cartons. This new procedure required a standard shipping master carton which was cost-justified by changes in the method of order picking and material-handling. The revised system was designed around two concepts. First, standardized shipping cartons were adopted to permit continuous conveyor movement from point of warehouse order selection to the over-the-road trailer. Second, the integrated system used a computer process to assure that each standardized master carton was packed to maximum practical cube utilization.

Under the new system a picking list was generated for each carton. After the individual pairs of shoes were placed into the carton, the pick list was attached to the carton, providing a summary of contents for retail store personnel.

The advantages of a standarized carton extended even to the retail store's stock room. Because the contents of each master carton were easily determined, it was not necessary to search through many cartons for a particular style or size of shoe. Standardization allowed master cartons to be more efficiently stocked, resulting in less back-room congestion. Finally, complete identification of master carton contents facilitated completion of retail inventory and merchandise reordering.

As expected, the new integrated system required the purchase of master cartons, since each could be reused only about three times. However, this added cost was more than justified by improved order-picking productivity, continuous movement of cartons into over-the-road trailers, and more efficient utilization of transportation capacity. Since each master carton was cubed out to near capacity, dead space was reduced substantially. The standardized carton size was selected for maximum conformity with a high-cube over-the-road trailer, thereby eliminating dead space in stacking. The end result of standardized master carton usage was a substantial reduction in total cost combined with a far more effective material-handling system at both the warehouse and retail store.

This example illustrates both the systems approach to logistical planning and the principle of total cost. However, the most important point to be derived from the example is that master carton standardization facilitated system integration.

Naturally, few organizations can reduce their master carton requirements to a single size. When master cartons of more than one size are required, extreme care should be taken to arrive at an assortment of compatible units. Figure 8–3 illustrates one such concept utilizing four standard sizes. The sizes of the four master cartons result in modular compatibility.

Of course, logistical considerations cannot fully dominate packaging design. The ideal package for material handling and transportation would be a perfect cube having equal length, depth, and width with the potential to handle

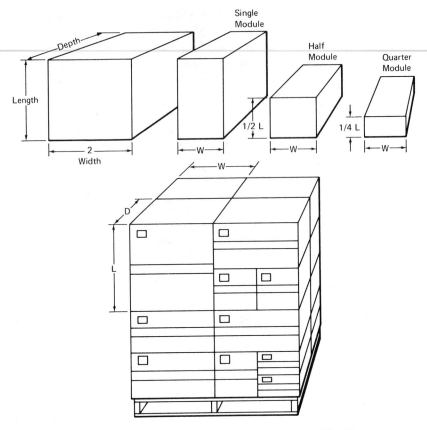

Figure 8–3 Example and Benefits of the Modular System of Packing

Adapted from the work of Walter Frederick Friedman and Company.

maximum possible density. Seldom will such a package exist. The important point is that logistical requirements should be evaluated along with manufacturing, marketing, and product design considerations when selecting master cartons.

Protective Packaging

A major function of the master carton is to protect products from damage while being moving and stored in the logistical system. The master cartons also serve as a deterrent to pilferage. Achieving the desired degree of protection involves tailoring the package to the product and selecting proper material for package construction. The crucial question is the desired degree of product protection.

For most products, the cost of absolute protection is prohibitive. The determining factors are the value and fragility of the product: the higher the value, the greater the economic justification for nearly absolute protection. If a product is fragile and has high value, then the cost of absolute protection can be significant.

The susceptibility to damage of a given package is directly related to the logistical environment. The fragility level of a product can be measured by product/package testing utilizing shock and vibration equipment. The result allows the predetermined level of product cushion to be built into the package to protect the product while in the logistical system. If packaging requirements and cost are prohibitive, alternative product designs can be evaluated utilizing the same testing equipment. The end result is the determination of the exact packaging required to protect the product.[7] The environment should be evaluated in terms of its physical and element characteristics. Each is briefly reviewed. A discussion then follows on package design.

Physical Environment. The physical environment of a product is the logistical system. The physical environment both influences and is influenced by the damage potential.

Package damage results from the transportation, storage, and handling systems utilized. If privately owned and operated transportation is used, the product will move to its destination in a relatively controlled environment. On the other hand, if common carriers are utilized, the product enters a noncontrolled environment. In the common carrier situation, the product may be handled by one or more break-bulk terminals and transported on a variety of vehicles. The less control a firm has over its physical environment, the greater the packaging precautions required to prevent damage. The logistical environment thus influences the packaging design decision.

During the logistical process, the product can experience a number of situations that can cause damage. The four most common causes of damage are vibration, impact, puncture, and compression. Within the logistical system, combinations of these forms of damage can be experienced whenever a package is in transit or being handled. In addition, stacking failure can result in damage while the product is in storage. The potential physical damage ranges from surface scuffing and marring to complete product crushing, buckling, and cracking.

Damage can be limited to a significant degree by securing packages while in transit. Typical methods of securing are strapping, tiedowns, and various dunnage materials which prevent product shift or limit virbration and shock. The best method of prevention is to load the over-the-road trailer or railcar in a tight pattern to reduce shifting.[8] Securing and proper loading reduce the damage prevention burden that the product package must provide.

As noted earlier, package requirements also influence logistical system design. The standard logistical practice for mainframe computers is an excellent example. Because the basic product is of high value and extreme fragility, a substantial investment in packaging would be required using normal common carrier services. Consequently, computers are often distributed using specialized household movers. The equipment and handling procedures employed by household-moving specialists are highly oriented to damage prevention. Therefore, while the cost of transportation is higher, product packaging capable of providing absolute product protection is not required.

---

[7] Discussion based on notes and suggestions presented by Kevin A. Howard, unpublished term paper (Michigan State University, 1983).

[8] James W. Goff, Joseph Gnebe, Diana Twede, and Todd Townsend, "You'll Never See It from the Road," (East Lansing, Mich.: School of Packaging, Michigan State University, Technical Report #26, 1984).

Element Environment. The element environment of a package refers to potential damage from temperature, humidity, and foreign matter. For the most part these environmental factors are beyond the control of logistical management. However, the protective package must be designed to cope with the range of possible adversity during transit.

To illustrate, it is not unusual for a package to be exposed to snow and below-freezing temperatures during loading, to be exposed to rain at an intermediate transfer point, and to arrive at a hot and humid destination. The crucial problem in evaluating the element environment is to determine in advance how the contents of the package will react with respect to these various elements in terms of instability and deterioration.

Temperature extremes naturally will affect package contents. At very high heat levels, some products will melt, spoil, blister, peel, fuse together, and discolor. Exposed to cold, the contents may experience cracking, brittleness, or complete spoilage. The package can offer only minimal protection from extreme temperatures. For example, frozen food temperature in prolonged transit cannot be maintained merely by package construction. The package design should be capable of protecting against natural environmental elements for a reasonable period of time.

Another potential product impact involves water and vapor. The humidity problem is in many ways far more severe than the impact of temperature upon package contents. The typical product has extremely limited tolerances for water exposure without causing dissolution, separation, corrosion, or pitting. For the most part, water exposure occurs during transfer between transport carriers and distribution organizations. Therefore, the package may constitute the product's sole source of protection. Even if the product is protected, the package could very well lose its exterior identification if exposed to excessive moisture.

The foreign-matter elements consist of any damage or loss of content stability caused by miscellaneous factors. For example, package contents can become contaminated or absorb tastes and odors if exposed for prolonged periods to chemical, noxious, or toxic elements. For certain kinds of products, extreme care must be taken to protect against insects and rodents. Sometimes the package must protect against deterioration caused by prolonged exposure to air or light.

Many products, such as film, chocolate, confectionery, livestock, and produce, are so perishable that logistical systems must be designed to provide controlled environmental movement. Surprisingly, products clearly identified as perishable often do not cause as severe of an element problem as their more durable counterparts. It is the unexpected short-term excessive temperatures, high humidity, or foreign matter that cause most product damage.

Package Design

Development of new packaging materials has been one of the most prolific areas of logistical research and development. A vast range of materials is employed in packaging. The most common are corrugated, solid fiberboard, wood, and expanded polystyrene. The question confronted in package design is to determine the degree of protection required to cope with the anticipated physical and element environments. The package design and material would combine to achieve the desired protection without incurring the expense of overprotection.

It is possible to design a package that has the correct material content but does not provide the necessary protection. Arriving at a satisfactory packaging solution involves defining allowable damage in terms of expected overall environment and then isolating a combination of design and material capable of meeting the specifications. The important points are: (1) in most cases the cost of absolute protection will be prohibitive, and (2) package construction is properly a blend of design and material.

The determination of final package design requires a great deal of testing to assure that specifications are satisfied at minimal cost. Such tests can be conducted in a laboratory or on an experimental shipment basis. During the past decade the process of package design and material selection has become far more scientific. Laboratory analysis has become the most reliable way to evaluate package designs because of advances in testing equipment and measurement techniqes. To a large degree, care in design has been encouraged owing to increased federal regulation of hazardous materials.

New instrumented recording equipment is available that measure severity and nature of shock while a package is in transit. Use of instrumented shipments on a selected sample of movements can reduce the bias inherent in trial-and-error test shipments. This form of testing is expensive and is difficult to conduct on a scientific basis. To obtain increased accuracy, computerized environment simulations can be used to replicate typical conditions that a package will experience in the logistical system. Laboratory test equipment is available to evaluate the impact of shock upon the interaction of product fragility and packaging materials and design.[9]

Containerization

An important part of overall storage and materials handling is containerization. The term *container*, which is used interchangeably with unitization, describes the physical grouping of master cartons into one restrained load for material handling or transport. The concept of containerization includes all forms of unitization, from taping two master cartons together to the use of specialized transportation equipment. All types of containerization have the basic objective of increasing material-handling efficiency. The present discussion is limited to methods of unitization that extend up to, but do not include, total vehicles. The first part discusses unit loads that do not utilize rigid enclosure. Next, the rigid-enclosure approach to unitization is discussed. Finally, the relative advantages and disadvantages of both are reviewed.

Nonrigid Containers

As the name implies, nonrigid containerization is not protected by complete enclosure. The most common variety consists of stacking master cartons on pallets or slipsheets. A hardwood pallet is illustrated in Figure 8–4. A slipsheet is similar to a pallet in size and purpose. The primary difference is that the

---

[9] For a discussion of cooperative industry research to improve carton design, see Pat Peterson, "The Industry Tackles the Problem with Cases," *Grocery Distribution* (September/October 1984), pp. 12–18.

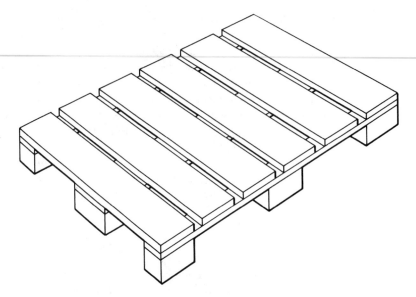

Figure 8–4 Example of Hardwood Pallet

slipsheet is a single layer of solid fiberboard, corrugated board, or plastic used to provide a unitization platform. Because the slipsheet lies flat on the floor, special fork trucks are required to handle slipsheet unit loads. The primary advantages of slipsheets are that their cost is sufficiently low to permit one-way utilization and the weight of the sheet is insignificant. Pallet and slipsheet types and sizes will be discussed first. Next, methods of stacking master cartons on pallets are briefly reviewed. Finally, alternative ways to secure unit loads during transport and material handling are discussed.

Unit Load Platforms. Most industry associations recommend a standardized pallet or slipsheet size to be used as a unit load platform. The Grocery Manufacturers of America have adoped the 40- by 48-inch pallet with four-way entry and similar-size slipsheets for food distribution. Throughout industry, the sizes most frequently used are the 40 by 48, 32 by 40, and 32 by 36 (all dimensions in inches). It is common practice to identify first the dimension of most frequent entry by handling equipment.

Generally, the larger a unit load platform, the more economical will be the resultant material handling. For instance, the 40- by 48-inch pallet provides 768 more square inches per stacking tier than the 32- by 36-inch size. Assuming that master cartons can be stacked as high as 10 tiers, the total added unitization space of the 40- by 48-inch pallet is 7,680 square inches. This is 60 per cent larger than the 32- by 36 inch size. The final determination of size should be based upon load, compatibility with the handling and transport equipment used throughout the logistical system, and standardized industry practice. With modern handling equipment, few restrictions are encountered in weight limitations.

Master Carton Stacking. While a variety of different approaches can be used to tier master cartons on slipsheets and pallets, four are most common: (1) block, (2) brick, (3) row, and (4) pinwheel. The block method is used with

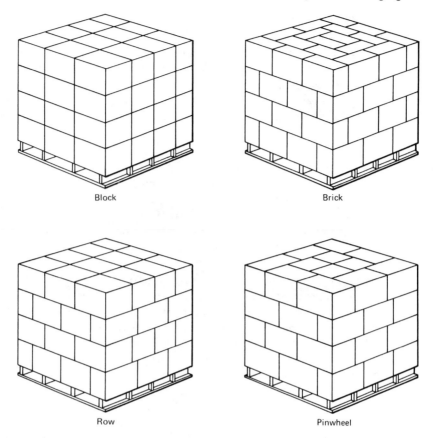

Block Brick

Row Pinwheel

Figure 8–5 Basic Pallet Master Carton Stacking Patterns

Adapted from palletization guides of the National Wooden Pallet Manufacturers Association.

cartons of equal width and length. With differential widths and lengths, the brick, row, or pinwheel pattern is employed. Figure 8–5 illustrates these four basic patterns. Except for the block method, cartons placed in the unit load are arranged in an interlocking pattern with adjoining tiers placed at 90-degree angles to each other. Load stability is increased by interlocking. The block pattern does not have this benefit.

Load Securing. A unit load can increase damage potential if it is not properly restrained during handling or transport. In most situations, the stability of stacking is not sufficient to secure the unit load while being handled or in transit. Standard methods of additional stability include rope tie, corner posts, steel strapping, taping, antiskid treatment, breakaway adhesives, and wrapping. Shrink wrap and stretch wrap securing has increased in popularity recently.

Shrink wrapping consists of placing a prestretched plastic sheet or bag over the platform and master cartons. The material is then heat-shrunk to secure the cartons to the platform. Stretch wrap consists of wrapping the unit load with a tightly drawn external plastic material. The unit load is rotated on a turntable to place the stack under tension. The platform is wrapped directly into the unit load. With shrink and stretch wrapping, the unit load assumes many of the characteristics of a rigid container. However, shrink and stretch wrap provide greater physical protection than a rigid container because of exact fit and weight support. Other benefits of wrapping are reduced exposure of master cartons to logistical environment, low cost, adaptability to various shipment size, insignificant added weight, and ability to identify contents and damage.[10] The major problem of wrapping is waste-material disposal.

Rigid Containers

A rigid container provides a device within which master cartons or loose products are placed during warehousing and transportation. The premise is that placing merchandise within a container will both protect it and make it easier to handle. The prospects for extensive domestic containerization have been the subject of a great deal of attention since the early 1950s.[11] The potential for increased productivity by containerization is obvious. Approximately one half of the total cost of transporting domestic goods is spent in shuffling between vehicles, transporting across docks and platforms, in packaging, for loss and damage claims, for pilferage, and for insurance. Table 8–1 summarizes the potential benefits of increased containerization.

Despite the potential benefits, domestic rigid containerized shipments are not common. In contrast, the expansion of container movements in international logistics proves the concept works and offers the potential for increased productivity. A challenge for the future is to make domestic containerization a reality.

Integrated Shipping Programs. Although discussed separately, packaging, containerization, and material handling represent integral parts of the logistical operating system. All three areas influence each other. For example, automated handling cannot be efficiently designed without a high degree of master carton standardization, which, in turn, provides the opportunity to containerize individual products. This section illustrates some aspects of the interaction of packaging, material handling, and containerization in the context of a total movement system.

[10] "Unitization: Getting It All Together," *Handling and Shipping Management* (May 1981), pp. 83–90.

[11] For a review of the development of customerization, see Vernon C. Seguin, *An Investigation of the Forces Inhibiting Growth of Containerization in Domestic Surface Freight Shipments* (Unpublished Ph.D. dissertation, Michigan State University, 1971).

TABLE 8–1   Potential Benefits of Rigid Containerization

1. Improves overall material movement efficiency
2. Reduces damage in handling and transit
3. Reduces pilferage
4. Reduces protective packaging requirements
5. Provides greater protection from element environment
6. Provides a shipment unit that can be reused a substantial number of times, thereby reducing waste and the need to dispose of the container

A number of integrated shipping programs between manufacturing concerns and customers have been successfully implemented. The impetus for such programs is to integrate material-handling capability, transportation, warehousing, inventory policy, and communications into the customer's logistical system. The objective is to minimize handling during the exchange of merchandise. To the degree that duplication can be reduced, cost savings are possible for both the manufacturer and the customer. This type of integrated exchange is most common in physical distribution.

Unit load shipment has many benefits. First, unloading time and congestion at destination are minimized. Second, products in unit load quantities facilitate material-handling. Inbound shipment checking is simplified, and inventory can be positioned rapidly for order selection. Unit loads utilize approximately one fifth the time required for manual unloading. Finally, damage in transit can be reduced by unit load shipping and specialized transportation equipment. All these factors reduce logistical cost.

Industry organizations such as the Grocery Manufacturers of America have been very active in encouraging unitized shipment programs. In many industries, pallet shipments are common in the manufacturing support phase of logistics, where shipments are often between company facilities. For interorganizational systems to function efficiently, a high degree of standardization and cooperation is required.

WAREHOUSE OPERATIONS

The warehouse contains materials, parts, and finished goods on the move. Warehouse operations consist of break-bulk and regrouping procedures. The objective is to efficiently move large quantities of inventory into and specific customer orders out of the warehouse. The ideal arrangement would be for products to arrive and depart the warehouse during a single working day. The functions performed in a warehouse are classified as movement and storage. Movement is emphasized. Storage is secondary. Within these two broad categories, movement is divided into three activities and storage into two activities.

Handling Requirements

As a result of the movement function, inbound quantity shipments are sorted into precise customer order assortments. The three handling activities are: (1) receiving, (2) instorage handling, and (3) shipping. Each is discussed.

Receiving

Merchandise and materials normally arrive at the warehouse in carload and truckload quantities. The first handling is unloading the transportation vehicle. In most warehouses, unloading is manual. Limited automated and mechanized handling methods have been developed which are capable of adapting to varying product characteristics at time of shipment arrival. Generally, one or two people unload the shipment. The product is hand-stacked on pallets or slipsheets to form a unit load for warehouse handling efficiency. In some cases, conveyors are employed to unload vehicles rapidly.

Larger merchandise may be unloaded directly from the car or truck by material handling equipment for movement into the warehouse. As discussed previously, shipments moving in containerized or unit loads dramatically reduces unloading time.

Instorage Handling

Instorage handling consists of all handling within a warehouse facility. Following receipt, it is necessary to transfer merchandise within the warehouse to position it for storage or order selection. Finally, when a customer order is received, it is necessary to accumulate the required products from around the warehouse and to move them to the shipping area. The two types of instorage handling are transfer and selection.

At least two, and sometimes three, *transfer* handlings are required within a typical warehouse. The merchandise is first moved into the warehouse and placed at a designated storage location. The inbound movement is handled by fork-lift trucks when pallets or slipsheets are used whereas other mechanical handling systems are used for larger unit loads. A second internal move may be required prior to order assembly, depending upon the operating procedures of the warehouse. When products are required for order selection, they are moved to a selection area. When the merchandise is large, such as a stove or washing machine, this second movement may be omitted. In the final handling, the assortment of products required for a customer shipment is moved from the warehouse to the shipping dock.

Selection is the primary function of the warehouse. The selection process groups materials, parts, and products into customer orders. It is typical for one section of the warehouse to be established as a selection area to minimize travel distance. The typical selection process is coordinated by a computerized control system. The primary focus for warehouse automation is the selection process. Various forms of automation are discussed later in this chapter.

Shipping

Shipping consists of checking and loading orders onto transportation vehicles. As in receiving, shipping is performed manually in most systems. Shipping unit loads is becoming increasingly popular because considerable time can be saved in vehicle loading. A checking operation is typically required to verify load contents when merchandise ownership changes. Checking is typically limited to carton counts, but in some situations a piece-by-piece check for proper brand, size, and so on is necessary to assure that all items the customer ordered are being shipped.

Storage Requirements

The warehouse performs two types of storage: planned and extended.

Planned Storage

As previously noted, primary emphasis is placed upon product flow in the warehouse. Regardless of velocity of inventory turnover, all goods received must be stored for at least a short time period. Storage for basic inventory replenishment is referred to as planned storage. Planned storage duration varies in different logistical systems based on replenishment cycles.[12] Planned storage must provide sufficient inventory to fulfill the reason why the warehouse was established within the logistical system.

Extended Storage

Extended storage, a somewhat misleading term, refers to inventory in excess of that planned for normal warehouse operation. In some special situations, storage may be required for several months prior to customer shipment. A warehouse may be used for extended storage for at least five reasons. In controlling and measuring warehouse performance, care should be taken to separate inventory turnover related to planned and extended storage.

The basic nature of some products requires they be stored to await demand or to spread supply across time. Extensive storage may be required to match supply and demand, resulting in very little turnover. As noted earlier in the chapter, a primary justification of warehousing is to accommodate *seasonality* in the logistical system.

When a product has *erratic demand* fluctuations, it may be necessary to carry additional supplies or safety stocks to satisfy customer service standards. An example is air conditioners. Because air conditioners are expensive items, dealers prefer to carry small inventories. When a period of high temperatures begins, manufacturers have limited time to distribute additional units.

Conditioning is required for some products and can be accomplished at the warehouse. These products may be stored for a limited period of time. The ripening of bananas is an example. Food distribution centers typically have ripening rooms to hold products until they reach peak quality.

The warehouse may contain goods purchased for *speculative* purposes. The degree to which this activity takes place will depend upon the specific materials and industries. For example, it is not unusual to store grain for speculative reasons.

The warehouse often is used to *realize special discounts*. Early purchase discounts may justify extended storage. The purchasing manager may be able to realize a substantial forward buy discount during a specific period of the year Under such conditions the warehouse holds inventories in excess of planned storage. Manufacturers of fertilizer, toys, and lawn furniture often attempt to shift the warehousing burden to customers by offering off-season storage allowances.

MATERIAL HANDLING FINAL

One extremely encouraging aspect of contemporary logistics is the productivity potential that can be realized from capital investment in material handling. Material handling cannot be avoided in the performance of logistics. It should, however, be minimized. The technical aspects of material handling are extensive and beyond the scope of this text. The following discussion places emphasis upon handling methods and efficiency. A final discussion treats recent developments in automated handling.

---

[12] See Chapter 7, pages 208–12.

Basic Handling Considerations

Material handling in the logistical system is concentrated in and around the warehouse facility. In particular, the three handling activities discussed earlier must be performed: (1) receiving, (2) instorage handling, and (3) shipping. These three types of handling are common to warehousing involved in purchasing, manufacturing support, or physical distribution operations.

A basic difference exists in the handling of bulk materials and master cartons. Bulk handling is a situation where protective packaging at the master carton level is unnecessary. Specialized handling equipment is required to unload solids, fluids, or gaseous materials. The following discussion focuses on master carton handling within the logistical system.

Over the years a variety of guidelines have been suggested to assist management in the design of material-handling systems. The following six guidelines are representative:

1. Equipment for handling and storage should be as standardized as possible.
2. When in motion, the system should be designed to provide maximum continuous product flow.
3. Investment should be in handling rather than stationary equipment.
4. Handling equipment should be utilized to the maximum extent possible.
5. In handling equipment selection, the ratio of dead weight to payload should be minimized.
6. Whenever practical, gravity flow should be incorporated in system design.

Handling systems are classified as mechanized, semiautomated, automated, and information-directed. A combination of labor and handling equipment is utilized in mechanized systems to facilitate receiving, processing, and/or shipping. Generally, labor constitutes a high percentage of the overall cost in mechanized handling. Automated systems, in contrast, attempt to minimize labor as much as possible by substituting capital investment in equipment. An automated handling system may be applied to any of the basic handling requirements, depending upon the situation. When selected handling requirements are performed using automated equipment while the remainder of the handling is completed on a mechanized basis, the system is referred to as semiautomated. An information-directed system uses computers to maximize control over mechanized handling equipment. Mechanized handling systems are most common. However, semiautomated and automated systems are rapidly increasing. As noted earlier, one factor contributing to low logistical productivity is that automated handling has yet to achieve its full potential. This situation is predicted to change dramatically during the late 1980s.

Mechanized Systems

Mechanized systems employ a wide range of handling equipment. The types of equipment most commonly used are fork-lift trucks, towlines, tractor-trailer devices, conveyors, and carousels.

Fork-lift Trucks

Fork-lift trucks can move loads of master cartons both horizontally and vertically. The pallet or slipsheet forms a platform upon which master cartons are stacked. A fork-lift truck normally transports a maximum of two unit loads at a time. Fork-lift trucks are not limited to unit load handling; skids or boxes may be transported, depending upon the nature of the product.

Many types of fork-lift trucks are available. High-stacking trucks capable of up to 40 feet of vertical movement, palletless side-clamp versions, and trucks capable of operating in aisles as narrow as 56 inches can be found in logistical warehouses.[13] The fork-lift truck is not economical for long-distance horizontal movement because of the high ratio of labor per unit of transfer. Therefore, fork-lifts are most effectively utilized in shipping and receiving, and to place merchandise in high cube storage. The two most common power sources for fork-lift trucks are propane gas and electricity.

Towline

Towlines consist of either in-floor or overhead-mounted drag devices. They are utilized in combination with four-wheel trailers on a continuous-power basis. The main advantage of a towline is continuous movement. However, such handling devices do not have the flexibility of fork-lift trucks. The most common application of towlines is for order selection within the warehouse. Order pickers manually place merchandise on a four-wheel trailer, which is then towed to the shipping dock. A number of automated decoupling devices have been perfected which route trailers from the main towline to selecting shipping docks.

A point of debate involves relative merits between in-floor or overhead towline installation. In-floor installation is costly to modify and difficult to maintain from a housekeeping viewpoint. Overhead installation is more flexible, but unless the warehouse floor is absolutely level, the line may jerk the front wheels of the trailers off the ground and risk product damage.

Tractor-Trailers

A tractor-trailer consists of a driver-guided power unit which tows a number of individual four-wheel trailers. The typical size of the trailers is 4 by 8 feet. The tractor-trailer, like the towline, is used to support order selection. The main advantage of tractor-trailers is flexibility. It is not as economical as the towline because it requires more direct labor and is often idle. Considerable advancements have been made in automated guided vehicle systems (AGVS). These are discussed under semiautomated material handling.

Conveyors

Conveyors are used widely in shipping and receiving operations and form the basic handling device for a number of order-selection systems. Conveyors are classified as power or gravity and roller or belt movement. Conveyors are flexible, permitting the basic installation to be modified with minimum difficulty. Portable gravity-style roller conveyors are often used for loading and unloading and in some cases are transported on over-the-road trailers to ease destination unloading. A great deal of conveyor flexibility is sacrificed in power-drive and belt configuration installations.

---

[13] Bernie Knill, "Lift Trucks: New Development Boosts a Sagging Market," *Material Handling Engineering* (April 1981), pp. 62–69.

Carousels

A carousel operates on a different concept than most other mechanized handling equipment. The carousel delivers the desired item to the order picker. A typical carousel consists of a series of bins mounted on an oval track. The entire carousel rotates, bringing the bin to the operator. A wide variety of different types of carousels are available. The typical carousel application involves selection of individual packages in such operations as repack areas, parts and service, and various types of supplies.

The types of mechanized material-handling equipment discussed are examples of the range available. Most systems combine handling devices. For example, fork-lift trucks may be used for vertical movement, while tractor-trailers are used for horizontal transfers.

Semiautomated

The semiautomated system supplements a mechanized handling system by automating specific handling requirements. Thus, the semiautomated warehouse is a mixture of mechanized and automated handling. Typical equipment utilized in semiautomated warehouses are automated guided vehicle system, computerized sortation, robotics, and various forms of line racks.

Automated Guided Vehicle System

The automated guided vehicle system (AGVS) performs the same type of handling function as a mechanized tractor-trailer. The essential difference is that an AGVS does not require an operator. The AGVS is automatically routed and positioned at destination without operator intervention.

Typical AGVS equipment relies on an optical or magnetic guidance system. In the optical application, tape is placed on the warehouse floor. The AGVS is guided by a light beam that focuses on the guidepath. Magnetic AGVS follows an energized wire installed in the floor. The primary advantage of AGVS is the elimination of a driver.

Sortation

Automated sortation devices are typically used in combination with conveyors.[14] As products are selected in the warehouse and conveyorized out, they must be sorted to specific shipment docks. For automated sortation the master carton must have a distinguishing code. These codes are read by a optical scanner or similar device, and products are automatically routed to the desired destination. Most controllers are programmable which permits sortation flexibility.

The automation of sortation provides two primary benefits. The first benefit is the obvious reduction in labor hours. The second benefit is significant increase in speed and accuracy. High-speed sortation systems can divert and align packages at rates exceeding one per second. In these system, packages are

---

[14] For an update in sortation concepts, see "Computerized, High-Speed Sortation System Handles Peak Volume Demand," *Material Handling Engineering* (September 1981), pp. 108–110; and "Sortation Enters the Electronic Age," *Material Handling Engineering* (February 1981), pp. 47–54.

diverted to the desired destination and can be positioned to accommodate unit loading.

Robotics

The robot is a humanlike machine that can be programmed as a result of microprocessors to perform one or a series of handling functions. The popularity of robotics resulted from their widespread adoption in the automotive industry during the early 1980s to replace selected manual tasks. The environment of a warehouse provides a different type of challenge to robotics than that found in a typical manufacturing plant. The nature of warehousing is to accommodate the exact merchandise requirements of a customer's order. Warehouse specification can vary extensively from one customer order to the next, resulting in far less routine than is typical in manufacturing.

The primary use of robotics in warehousing is to break down and build unit loads. In the breakdown of unit loads, the robot is programmed to recognize stocking patterns and to place products in the desired position on a conveyor belt. The use of robots to build unit loads is essentially the reverse of breakdown.

Another prime potential use of robotics in warehousing is in environments where it is difficult for human beings to function. Examples could be in high-noise areas or in extreme temperature environments such as freezers.

Significant potential exists to use robots in a mechanized warehouse to perform selected functions. The appeal is the ability to program the robot to function as an expert system capable of implementing decision logic in the handling process. For example, the robot can be programmed to recognize a specific situation or series of situations and to modify its performed tasks to accommodate the handling requirement. The capability to incorporate artificial intelligence, in addition to the speed, dependability, and accuracy, are the advantages of the robot in comparison to manual handling.

Live Racks

A device commonly used to reduce manual labor is to design storage racks so product automatically flows forward to the desired selection position. The typical live rack contains roller conveyors and is constructed for rear loading. To complete the installation, the rear of the rack is elevated higher than the front, causing gravity to flow products forward. When unit loads are removed from the front, all other loads in that specific rack automatically move forward.

Live racks are a prime example of incorporating gravity flow into material-handling system design. The use of the live rack replaces the need to use fork trucks to reposition unit loads. A significant advantage of this form of storage is the automatic rotation of product that results from rear loading of a live rack. Rear loading facilitates first-in, first-out inventory rotation.

Automated Handling

For several decades the concept of automated handling has been long on potential and short on accomplishment. Initial efforts toward automated handling concentrated upon order-selection systems for master cartons.

Recently, emphasis has switched to automated high-rise storage and retrieval system (ASRS). Each is discussed in turn after a brief review of automated handling concepts.

Potential of Automation

The appeal of automation is that it substitutes capital investment in equipment for labor. In addition to using less labor, an automated system typically operates faster and more accurately than a mechanized system. Its shortcomings are the high degree of capital investment and the complex nature of development and application.

To date, most automated systems have been custom designed and constructed for each application. The six guidelines previously noted for selection of mechanized handling systems are not applicable to automated systems. For example, storage equipment in an automated system is an integral part of the handling capability and can represent as much as 50 per cent of the total investment. The ratio of dead weight to payload has little relevance in an automated handling application.

Although computers play an important part in all handling systems, they are essential to automated systems. The computer provides programming of the automated selection equipment and is used to interface the warehouse to the remainder of the logistical system. The warehouse control system is vastly different in automated handling. One factor that prohibited rapid development of automated systems was the high cost of minicomputers. Breakthroughs in the cost of microprocessors have eliminated this barrier.

Order Selection Systems

Initially, automation was applied to master carton selection or order assembly in the warehouse. Because of high labor intensity in order selection, the basic objective was to integrate mechanized and automated handling into a total system.

The initial concept was as follows. An automated selection device was preloaded. The device itself consisted of a series of merchandise racks stacked vertically. Merchandise was loaded from the rear and permitted to flow forward in the "live" rack on gravity conveyors until stopped by a rack door. Between or down the middle of the racks, power conveyors created a merchandise flow line, with several flow lines positioned above each other, one at each level of rack doors.

Upon receipt of an order, punch cards were created for each product to be selected and sorted in rack sequence. The cards were then processed through a reader, which tripped the rack doors in sequence allowing the desired merchandise to flow forward onto the powered conveyors. The conveyors, in turn, transported merchandise to an order-packing area for shipment.

When compared to modern applications, these initial attempts at automated package handling were highly inefficient. A great deal of labor was required during the merchandise input and output phases, and the automated equipment was expensive. Applications were limited to merchandise of extremely high value or to situations where working conditions justified such investment. For example, systems were designed for frozen-food order selection.

Substantial advances have been made recently in automated selection of case goods. The handling of fast-moving products in master cartons can be fully automated from merchandise receipt to placement in over-the-road trailers. Such systems use an integrated network of power and gravity conveyors linking power-motivated live storage. The entire system is controlled by a computer coupled with the inventory and order-processing control systems for the warehouse facility.

Upon arrival, merchandise is automatically routed to the live storage position and inventory records are updated. Upon order receipt, merchandise is precubed to vehicle size and scheduled for selection. At the appropriate time, all merchandise is selected in loading sequence and automatically transported by conveyor to the loading dock. In most situations, the first manual handling of the merchandise within the warehouse is when it is stacked into the transport vehicle.

The solution of the input/output interface problem and the development of sophisticated control systems resulted in a highly effective and efficient package-handling system. Such systems are common today.

ASRS Systems

The concept of automated unit-load handling using high-rise storage has received considerable attention recently. The high-rise concept of handling is fully automated from receiving to shipping. Four main components constitute the basic system: (1) storage racks, (2) storage and retrieval equipment, (3) input/output systems, and (4) control systems.

The name *high-rise* derives from the physical appearance of the storage rack. The rack is a structured steel vertical storage as high as 120 feet. When one considers that the stacking height of palletized cartons in a mechanized handling system is normally 20 feet, the potential of high-rise storage is clear.

The typical high-rise facility consists of rows of storage racks. The rows are separated by aisles running from 120 to over 800 feet. It is within these aisles that the primary storage and retrieval equipment functions. The storage and retrieval machine travels back and forth in an aisle. Its primary purpose is to move products in and out of storage. A variety of storage and retrieval equipment is available. Most require guidance at the top and bottom to provide the vertical stability necessary for high-speed horizontal movement and vertical hoisting. Horizontal speeds range from 300 to 400 feet per minute (fpm) with hoisting speeds of up to 100 fpm or more.

The initial function of the storage and retrieval equipment is to reach the storage position rapidly. A second function is to deposit or retract a load of merchandise. For the most part, load deposit and retraction are achieved by shuttle tables, which can enter and exit from the rack at speeds up to 100 fpm. Since the shuttle table moves only a few feet, it must be able to accelerate and stop rapidly.

In some installations, the storage and retrieval machine can be moved between aisles by transfer cars. Numerous transfer arrangements and layouts have been developed. Such transfer units may be dedicated or nondedicated. The dedicated transfer car is always stationed at the end of the aisle in which the storage and retrieval equipment is working. The nondedicated transfer car works a number of aisles and retrieval machines on a scheduled basis to achieve maximum equipment utilization. The decision as to whether or not to include aisle-to-aisle transfer in a high-risk storage system rests with the economics of throughput rate and number of aisles included in the overall system.

The input/output system in high-rise storage is concerned with moving loads to and from the rack area. Two types of movement are involved. First, loads must be transported from receiving docks or production lines to the storage area. Second, within the immediate peripheral area of the racks, loads must be positioned for entry or exit. The greatest potential handling problem is in the peripheral area. A common practice is to have pickup and discharge stations assigned to each aisle capable of staging an adequate supply of loads to fully utilize the storage and retrieval equipment. For maximum input/output performance, it is normal to have different stations for transfer of inbound and outbound loads assigned to the same aisle. The pickup and discharge stations are linked to the handling systems that transfer merchandise to and from the high-rise storage area.

The control system in high-rise storage is similar to that described earlier when discussing automated order-selection systems. In the case of high-rise storage systems, a great deal of sophistication in programming and control measurement is required to achieve maximum equipment utilization and rapid command cycles. Recent advances in the speed and cost of microprocessors have resulted in computers being fully dedicated to the ASAR system.

Figure 8–6 illustrates the concept of a high-rise storage system. Merchandise flowing from production is automatically stacked on 48- by 40-inch slipsheet and shrink-wrapped to create a unit load. The unit load is then transported to the high-rise storage area by power conveyor. When the load arrives, it is assigned to a storage bin and transferred by power conveyor to the appropriate pickup station. At this point the storage and retrieval equipment takes over and moves the unit load to its planned storage location.

In addition to scheduling arrivals and location assignments, the control system handles inventory control and stock rotation. When orders are received,

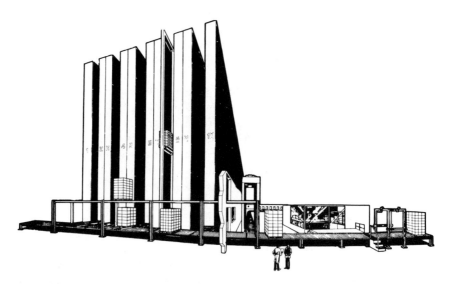

Figure 8–6   High-Rise Warehouse Facility

Reproduced by permission of Kenway Engineering

the command control system directs the retrieval of specified unit loads. From the outbound delivery stations, the unit load flows by power and gravity conveyor to the appropriate shipping dock. While retrieval and outbound delivery are being accomplished, all the paper work necessary to initiate product shipment is completed.

This example is typical of ASAR systems currently operating in a variety of industries. They are all designed to increase material-handling productivity by providing maximum storage density per square foot of floor space and to minimize the direct labor required in handling. The highly controlled nature of the system combines reliable pilferage-free and damage-free handling with extremely accurate control.

Information-Directed Systems

The concept of information-directed handling is relatively new and is still being evaluated. The concept is appealing because it combines the control of automated handling with the operational flexibility of mechanized systems.

The information-directed system uses mechanized handling equipment. The typical source of power is the fork-lift truck. In layout and design, the warehouse facility is essentially the same as any mechanized facility. The difference is that all fork-truck movements are directed and monitored by the command of a microprocessor.

In operation, all required handling movements are fed into the computer for analysis and equipment assignment. A computer program is utilized to analyze handling requirements and to assign equipment in such a way that direct movement is maximized and deadhead movement is minimized. Work assignments are provided to individual fork trucks by terminals located on the truck or from printouts picked up at selected terminal locations throughout the warehouse.

Information-directed handling has noteworthy potential in that selected benefits of automation can be achieved without substantial capital investment. The potential for gains in productivity results from substantial reduction in deadhead movements. The main drawback in the concept is the flexibility of work assignment. As a specific fork truck proceeds during a work period, it may be involved in loading or unloading several vehicles, selecting many orders, and completing several handling assignments. This wide variety of work assignments increases the complexity of work direction and could decrease the accountability for performance.

Special Handling Considerations

As expected, the primary focus of material movement is merchandise flowing in an orderly and efficient manner from manufacturer to point of sale. However, material-handling systems must also be capable of handling reverse flow within the logistical network.

For a variety of reasons, merchandise may be recalled by a manufacturer or returned to the manufacturer. Normally, such return flows are not of sufficient quantity or regularity to justify containerized movement. Therefore, the only convenient method for processing reverse flow is manual handling. To the degree practical, material-handling design should consider the cost and service impact of reverse logistics. Such flows often involve pallets, cartons, and packaging materials, in addition to damaged, dated, or excessive merchandise. In addition, ecological pressure to eliminate disposable containers will increase the quantity of returnable bottles moving in the logistical system. Handling and overall logistical systems in such industries will need to handle two-way movement efficiently.

Conclusion—Handling Alternatives

The managerial question is whether a specific handling system should be designed on a mechanized, semiautomated, automated, or information-directed basis. The initial cost of an automated system will be higher than a mechanized system. An automated system will require less building space, but the equipment investment will be greater. The return on investment from automation is in reduced cost of operation. An automated handling system, if properly designed and controlled, should outperform a mechanized system in terms of labor, damage, accuracy, product protection, and rotation. In the final analysis, the design to be used must be evaluated on the basis of return on investment.

SUMMARY

The primary concern of this chapter was to develop an integrated approach for the treatment of handling and storage. Material-handling occurs throughout the logistical system. The process of material handling is a prime consumer of labor. Because warehouse labor productivity has not been increasing at the same rate as that of other areas, considerable managerial attention is being concentrated on the improvement of material-handling efficiency.

The concept of strategic storage has caused a dramatic change in the range of available logistical systems. By utilizing the principles of warehousing, better service often can be rendered at lower cost. When product storage is required, it can be accomplished at strategic locations in the product-flow pipeline. A wide variety of public warehouse capacity and service are available for-hire in logistical operations.

The master carton is the nucleus of material handling. Care must be taken to prevent manufacturing and marketing from dominating package design. Logistical system factors must also be considered. From a logistical perspective, the greater the degree of package standardization, the more inherently efficient the material-handling function. To this end, a modular system of packaging is a noteworthy goal. The protective aspects of packaging consist of selecting a design and material capable of coping with physical and element environmental influences. Although absolute protection will in most cases not be necessary, the package should be scientifically designed to satisfy clear-cut protective specifications.

A great deal of attention is being directed to keeping freight on the move. A wide choice of handling equipment and systems is available to process master cartons and unit loads. All have one objective—to eliminate unnecessary handling. The choice among mechanized, semiautomated, automated, or information-directed handling systems depends upon the nature of the handling task and capital investment cost benefits.

While recent advancements in automated handling are encouraging, similar prospects are not materializing for containerization. The main advances in domestic containerization are centered upon nonrigid containers and coordinated transport arrangements.

With the completion of Chapter 8, each of the basic components of the logistical system has been covered. The essence of integrated logistics is that decisions related to order processing, transportation, inventory, packaging, and warehousing be treated on a combined basis. Unfortunately, not all markets can support a warehouse operation. Therefore, the number of facilities, their location, and the product mix stocked at each are primary concerns of logistical system design. Part III deals with the formulation and control of logistical policy.

QUESTIONS

1. Provide a definition and an example of strategic storage from a logistical system you are familiar with.
2. Under what conditions could it make sense to combine private and public warehouses in a logistical system?
3. What benefits can be gained by a modular system of packaging?
4. In terms of basic handling, describe the role of a unit load.
5. Discuss the differences between rigid and nonrigid containers. Discuss the role of load securing in unitization.
6. What is an integrated shipping program?
7. Why might it be economically justified to have multiple instorage handlings of a product in a warehouse?
8. Contrast planned and extended storage.
9. Explain the following statement: "A warehouse should merely consist of a set of walls enclosing an efficient handling system."
10. Until recently, why have automated handling system failed to meet their expected potential? What changed to encourage automation in the 1980s?

PART THREE

LOGISTICAL POLICY AND CONTROL

Foundations of Logistical Policy

The fundamental managerial objective is to achieve integration of all components in the logistical system. Integration must be achieved at three levels within the enterprise. First, within the individual areas of physical distribution, manufacturing support and purchasing, the components of facility location structure, forecasting and order management, transportation, inventory, and warehousing and packaging must be integrated on a total-cost basis. Next, physical distribution, manufacturing support, and purchasing must be coordinated into a single logistical effort. Finally, the total logistical policy must be consistent and supportive of marketing, manufacturing and financial efforts, and the overall goals of the enterprise. The objective of Chapter 9 is to present the framework for formulating logistical policy.

The initial section of the chapter introduces fundamental system design considerations. The total-cost approach to logistical policy is presented in detail as the analysis framework. The section initially deals with procedures and problems associated with implementing total-cost analysis. Attention is then directed to a review of customer service performance objectives. The initial section concludes with a discussion of the integration of logistical performance into overall enterprise operations by expanding the analysis to include cost-revenue trade-offs.

The second section discusses the relationships and basic principles of network location design. First, the relationship of transportation and facility location is developed. Second, the relationship of inventory and facility location is developed. The section concludes by the integration of the spatial aspects of transportation with the temporal aspects of inventory into the least-total-cost network design.

The final section provides the framework for integrating service and cost to arrive at a logistical policy. The concept of threshold service is introduced as the basis from which sensitivity analysis is launched to achieve a workable logistical program.

In total, this chapter provides a theoretical framework to guide the formation of logistical policy. The logistical system should be designed to provide a specified level of customer service performance at the lowest possible total cost. A well-designed logistical system offers a strategic capability that can contribute to competitive differential advantage.

SYSTEM DESIGN CONSIDERATIONS

The least-total-cost logistical policy requires the integration of all system components. The planning objective is to identify customer service performance goals and then to modify the least-total-cost system design as necessary to achieve the desired cost-revenue balance. This section presents basic system design considerations that are relevant to logistical policy formulation. The treatment proceeds from a basic discussion of total-cost analysis to the task of integrating performance goals for the determination of final system design.

Total-Cost Analysis

The basic integrative concept in logistical design is total-cost analysis. The original application of total-cost analysis was presented by Lewis, Culleton, and Steel in *The Role of Air Freight in Physical Distribution.*[1] Their study illustrated the total-cost justification for using air freight. If the speed and dependability of delivery permit other costs, such as warehousing and inventory, to be reduced or eliminated, then the high cost of air freight can be justified on a total-cost basis. The Lewis, Culleton, and Steel framework demonstrated cost-to-cost trade-off analysis and illustrated how total cost could be reduced by careful integration of all logistical components.

The basic concept of total cost is simple and complements the notion of designing logistical operations as an integrated performance system. The significant problem in operationalizing total cost is that traditional accounting practices for classifying and reporting costs do not adequately serve the needs of logistical measurement. The remainder of this part briefly reviews traditional accounting methods in terms of logistical analysis requirements and identifies costs relevant to logistical policy planning.

Public Accounting Interface

The two main financial reports in a business enterprise are the balance sheet and the profit-and-loss statement (P&L). The balance sheet reflects the financial position of a firm at a specific point in time. The balance sheet purpose is to summarize assets and liabilities of the firm and to reflect the net worth of

---

[1] Howard T. Lewis, James W. Culleton, and Jack D. Steel, *The Role of Air Freight in Physical Distribution* (Boston: Division of Research, Graduate School of Business Administration, Harvard University, 1965).

ownership. The P&L statement reflects the revenue and cost associated with operations over a period of time. As the name "profit and loss" implies, its purpose is to determine the financial success of operations for a specified time period. Logistical operations influence and are an integral part of both statements. For logistical policy planning, the primary concern is the method by which costs are identified, classified, and reported.

Accountants are concerned with the preparation of statements that follow accepted accounting practices. It is a legal requirement that organizations with public investors be audited regularly to assure that accounting practices are standardized and sound. What has resulted over the years is a reporting method designed to meet the requirements of investors and the internal revenue services of federal, state, and local governments. Unfortunately, conventional methods of accounting do not fully satisfy logistical planning requirements.

The first problem results from the fact that accepted accounting practice is to aggregate costs on a standard or natural account basis rather than on a functional basis. The practice of grouping expenses into natural accounts such as salaries, rent, utilities, depreciation, and so on does not identify operational responsibility. To help overcome the natural-account deficiency, it is common for statements to be subdivided by managerial or organizational areas of responsibility within an enterprise in an effort to measure each unit's performance. This process of classification helps but does not satisfy the requirements of logistical costing. Internal P&L statements generally group costs along budgetary lines. Thus, costs are provided in detail on an organizational basis. In reality, many of the costs associated with logistics cut across organizational units. The result is a data deficiency for integrated logistical planning.

The practice of classifying costs on a natural basis also creates a problem in functional analysis. In order to plan logistical operations, it is necessary to identify costs associated with performing specific tasks. This means that the logistical functions must be identified and assigned. The data are available in most accounting systems to classify costs by logistical function. The deficiency is the lack of accepted procedures for assignment of logistical costs. As far back as 1972 Schiff highlighted the problem and discussed prevailing practice.[2]

> What is of primary concern ... is the suitability of [logistics] cost reporting for internal use, and failure to identify these costs and classify them as operating expenses can only suggest that management and accountants do not think these costs are important enough to warrant the attention and concern of the receiver of the report or that they can be influenced by the manager to whom the report is addressed. It is difficult to find a logical basis for this position. The costs are identified and assembled in accounts and in all cases they are of significant dollar value to warrant identification. It would take a minimum of effort and re-education to alter the classification wherein freight and other distribution costs would be identified as operating expenses and thus more closely relate responsibility with reported results.

A great deal more logistical functional costing is taking place now than ever before. The Council of Logistics Management has sponsored a series of studies to

[2] Michael Schiff, *Accounting and Control in Physical Distribution Management* (Chicago: National Council of Physical Distribution Management, 1972), pp. 1–10.

help close the gap between traditional accounting and distribution cost accounting.[3] While progress is being made, much more managerial attention and research are needed before functional logistical cost accounting will become a universal practice.

A somewhat overlapping deficiency of traditional accounting concerns methods of reporting transportation expenditures. A standard practice in retailing is to deduct freight from gross sales to arrive at a net sales figure. This is similar to the way discounts and returns are handled and has evolved over the years as a firmly entrenched accounting practice. In part, the practice seems to be based on the belief that freight is a necessary evil about which management can do very little. The problem extends beyond *where* freight is reported. In many purchasing situations, freight is not reported as a specific cost. Many products are purchased at a delivered price which includes transportation costs. This practice of delivered pricing has changed radically since the passage of the transporation acts of 1980 and the increasing practice of customer pickup allowances.

A final deficiency in traditional accounting practice is the failure to specify inventory cost. This deficiency is twofold. First, costs associated with the maintenance of inventory, such as insurance and taxes, are not directly related to inventory decisions, thereby resulting in an understatement or obscurity in reporting inventory cost. Second, the cost impact of assets invested in inventory is not measured and separated from other forms of capital expense incurred by the enterprise. In fact, if a firm uses internal funds to support inventory investment, no capital cost will be reported in the profit-and-loss statement.

In summary, several modifications in traditional accounting are required to get a handle on costs for logistical policy planning. In particular, the two largest individual cost centers, transportation and inventory, have traditionally been reported in a manner that results in obscurity. Although the situation is improving, routine isolation and reporting of logistical functional costs are a long way from standard practice.

Logistical Costing Concepts

Which costs should be identified for purposes of logistical planning, and how should they be reported? The initial concern in logistical costing is to identify which specific accounts to include in a functional classification. A second concern is to identify the costing time frame. Finally, a decision must be reached concerning the manner in which cost data will be structured.

Each of the above areas is judgmental. It should be clear from numerous examples throughout this book that the judgment exercised in cost identification and grouping can substantially influence both logistical system design and operation. Therefore, the judgmental factor and supporting assumptions must be reviewed thoroughly at all levels of management in order to develop a realistic set of specifications.

Cost Identification. To have a comprehensive presentation, all costs associated with the performance of physical distribution, manufacturing support, and purchasing must be included in functional cost classification. The total costs associated with forecasting and order management, transportation, inventory,

---

[3] To date, studies have been completed in inventory, transportation, warehousing.

and warehousing, and packaging must be isolated and grouped functionally. Total logistical cost involves three types of specific expenditures: direct, indirect, and overhead.

Direct or *operational costs* are those expenses experienced during the performance of logistical activities. Such costs are not difficult to identify. The direct cost of transportation, warehousing, material handling, some aspects of order processing, and inventory can be extracted from natural cost accounts. Likewise, limited difficulty is experienced in isolating the direct administration cost of logistical operations.

Indirect costs are more difficult to identify. These costs are experienced on a more-or-less fixed basis as a result of allocation of resources to logistical operations. For example, the cost of capital invested in real estate, transportation equipment, and inventory—just a few of the areas within the capital structure of logistics—must be identified to arrive at a true cost. The manner by which indirect costs are imputed for inclusion into total logistical cost is based on managerial judgment.

All capital allocated to the logistical system represents a scarce commodity. Therefore, all expenses necessary to support capital investment in logistical operations must be included in total cost. If capital requirements are sourced from the asset base of an enterprise, a charge based on a hurdle rate for utilization should be imputed for inclusion into total cost.[4] The amount of such indirect cost may range from the prime interest rate to a figure which takes into consideration alternative uses of capital and expected rate of return. The judgment applied in arriving at cost of capital will greatly influence logistical system design. In turn, system design greatly influences operating costs. Thus, procedures and standards used in arriving at indirect logistical costs are critical.

The final costing allocation concerns *overhead*. An enterprise incurs a great deal of expense on behalf of all functional organizational units. A judgment is involved in how and to what extent this overhead should be allocated to specific operations. One method is to directly assign all corporate overhead on a uniform basis to all operational units. At the other extreme, some firms withhold all overhead allocations to avoid distorting the ability to measure direct and indirect logistical expenditures. Given these extremes, it is difficult to generalize regarding standard practice. From the viewpoint of formulating logistical policy, a sound guideline is not to allocate any overhead cost that cannot be directly influenced by logistical policy.

This discussion illustrates that gray areas exist in identifying logistical cost. Which costs are included in total cost is highly dependent on management judgment. A general rule to follow is that a specific cost should not be assigned when determining logistical policy unless it is under the managerial control of the logistical organization. Because of the judgmental factor involved, enterprises in the same industry will report vastly different total costs. It is important to realize that such cost differentials may have no direct relationship to the actual efficiency of logistical operations.

Cost Time Frame. A basic concern is to identify the period of time over which costs are accumulated for measurement. Generally accepted accounting principles call for accrual methods to relate revenues and expenditures to the actual

---

[4] For a complete discussion, see Douglas M. Lambert, *The Development of an Inventory Costing Methodology* (Chicago: National Council of Physical Distribution Management, 1975).

time period during which services are performed. Significant timing differentials are associated with logistical operations. From procurement through physical distribution, almost all logistical operating cost is incurred in anticipation of a future transaction.

To overcome the time problem, accountants attempt to break costs into those that can be assigned to a specific product and those that are associated with the passage of time. Using this classification, an attempt is made to match appropriate product and time period costs to specific revenue generation.

From a logistical perspective, a great many of the costs associated with procurement and manufacturing support are absorbed into direct product cost. Thus, because they can be assigned on a specific product basis, inventories can be valued on the basis of fully allocated cost. Such practices greatly influence logistical system design. In situations where a considerable period of time elapses between production and sales, such as in highly seasonal businesses, significant costs of logistical operations will be disassociated with revenue generation. Unless this potential mismatch is clearly understood and accommodated, logistical operations can be significantly mismeasured.

Cost Formatting. Logistical costs can be presented in a number of ways for managerial review. Three common ways are: (1) functional groupings, (2) allocated groupings, and (3) activity-level groupings. Each method is discussed.

To format costs by *functional grouping* means that for a specified operating period all expenditures for direct and indirect logistical services performed are listed by master and subaccount classifications. Thus, a total-cost statement is derived that can be compared from one operating period to the next. No standard format for functional cost grouping is available to fit the needs of all enterprises. Logistical functional cost statements should be designed to facilitate control within each unique environment. It is important to identify as many cost-account categories as practical and to develop a coding system that will facilitate grouping costs into these accounts.

Allocated cost formatting consists of assigning logistical expenditures to a significant measure of physical performance. For example, total logistical cost per ton, per hundredweight, per product, per order, per line item, or some other physical measure provides a basis for comparative analysis between consecutive operating periods.

Activity-level groupings are the most useful for evaluating alternative logistical policies. This method of formatting consists of grouping costs on the basis of fixed and variable as a function of volume. The purpose of classifying on the basis of fixed and variable cost is to approximate the magnitude of change in operating expenditure that will result from different volumes of logistical throughput. All cost elements that do not vary with volume are classified as fixed. In the short run, these costs would remain if volume was reduced to zero. Costs influenced by volume are classified as variable.

Total-Cost Groupings

For purposes of using total-cost analysis to determine logistical policy, it is recommended that emphasis be placed upon inventory and transportation which are the two cost groupings that directly influence logistical system design. Both inventory and transportation costs can be defined in a format sufficiently

TABLE 9-1 Total-Cost Grouping by Inventory and Transportation Components

Inventory-Related Costs	Transportation-Related Costs
Maintenance	Direct
Tax	Rates
Storage	Accessorial charges
Capital	Indirect
Insurance	Liability not protected by carrier
Obsolescence	Managerial
Ordering	
Communication	
Processing, including material handling and packaging	
Update activities, including receiving and data processing	
Inventory control	
Managerial	

broad to include the functional cost relationship to all other logistical components. For example, communication cost can be included in order processing. Likewise, warehouse and handling cost can be included in inventory cost.

In terms of inventory, total cost includes all costs related to maintenance and ordering. Maintenance cost includes taxes, storage in terms of fixed facility cost, capital, insurance, and obsolescence. The cost of ordering includes the full expense of inventory control, order preparation, communications, update activities, and managerial supervision.

The total cost of transportation includes published rates and accessorial charges plus expenses related to the hazards incurred in utilizing the various modes and legal forms of transport and the associated administrative costs. If private or contract carriers are used, accounts can be structured to identify the associated direct, indirect, and overhead costs.

A brief summary of the total cost of logistical activities is presented in Table 9–1. From the perspective of total-cost accounting, provision must be made to assign all costs related to logistical system design. The technique of grouping costs in association with the major accounts of inventory and transportation highlights the basic cost-to-cost trade-offs and maintains a clear perspective of the critical factors in logistical planning.[5]

Customer Service Performance

In Chapter 3 the nature of logistical performance was defined in detail to include availability, capability, and quality.[6] The point was made that almost any level of logistical service was attainable if an enterprise was willing to pay the associated cost. The objective of logistical policy formulation is to determine

---

[5] The basic logic to focus on transportation and inventory as the key accounts is based on the fact that they represent the trade-off base between costs associated with time and space in system design. All other costs of logistics are directly or indirectly related to transportation or inventory decreases.

[6] See pages 93–98 for a complete discussion of customer service.

the balance between performance and cost that will achieve the desired return on investment or other goals of the enterprise.

In customer service performance, *availability* is a system's ability to provide a product or material on a predictable basis. Availability in a system results from safety-stock policy. *Capability* is the ability to provide a stated speed and consistency of delivery. A system's capability results from the design and dependability of components that make up the performance cycle structure. *Quality* of performance relates to how effectively the logistical task is performed. The maintenance of quality performance is a responsibility of logistical operations measurement. To be effective, a logistical system must have some level of each attribute of customer service performance. It is also necessary to develop performance measures for each aspect of the overall logistical service mix.

The measurement and control of service can be approached from a number of vantage points. The suggested approach is based upon three sets of performance measurement data. The first centers on availability. The second is built around the total order cycle and provides a measure of capability. The final measure deals with quality.

Availability Measurement

The most visible measure of customer service is inventory availability. A typical measure of inventory availability is the percentage of items out of stock to total items carried in stock. The fallacy in this measure is that it does not take into consideration the velocity movement of various items in a product line. For example, 10 slow-moving items may be out of stock but not create serious customer service problems. On the other hand, one fast-moving item out of stock could cause havoc and result in a flood of customer complaints.

The desired measurement of inventory availability is an analysis over time of fill-rate performance. For example, specific reporting of orders with one or more items out of stock, average cases out of stock per order, average percentage availability of all items requested, back-order frequency, and back-order recovery rate provides comprehensive and factual measure of dynamic inventory availability.

Capability Measurement

The total performance cycle consists of the time measured in days from order placement to shipment receipt. In physical distribution, the cycle ideally should be measured from time of order receipt to customer delivery. In procurement the order cycle extends from time of purchase order release until receipt of supplier shipment. As noted earlier, order cycle performance confronts a number of uncertainties which complicate performance.[7] The task of capability measurement is to evaluate the impact of these uncertainties upon operational effectiveness.

At the single-echelon level, the typical total order cycle consists of four time elements. They are: (1) order transmission, (2) order processing, (3) order selection, and (4) order transportation. A fifth dimension of time is the delay

---

[7] See Chapter 2, pages 40–46.

experienced in the performance of any one or all of the order cycle activities. Using the total order cycle as a capability measurement framework, statistical analysis is possible concerning each element and the total cycle performance time. The task of capability service measurement is to determine the combined impact and cause of all delays over an operating period. Attention must also be directed to an enterprise's capability to introduce flexibility and exception handling into the normal order processing routine when unusual situations are encountered.

Quality Measurement

Delivery of incorrect or damaged merchandise in a timely manner does nothing to help an enterprise reach its operating goals. The measure of operational quality, similar to the other customer service performance measures, requires analysis over time. For example, occurrence of incorrect items on an order, shipments to improper locations, percentage of damage incidence by shipments or line items, and damage claims per quantity of shipments are representative of quality measurement indicators.

Cost-Revenue Analysis

The policy objective is to design a system capable of achieving logistical goals. For most commercial enterprises the overall goal is to maximize profits. To maximize profits, the theoretical solution to logistical design is simply stated: *continue to increase expenditures for improved logistical performance to the point where marginal cost equals marginal revenue.* At this point, short-run profits would be maximized. Although easily stated, marginal equality is difficult if not impossible to accomplish. Some of the major problems are: (1) measurement of incremental cost, (2) isolation of logistical performance from the remainder of enterprise performance, (3) inability to make incremental or minor changes in logistical system components, which in fact prohibits a truly marginal solution, (4) inability to modify commitments related to the logistical system quickly, such as leases, and, perhaps most significant, (5) inability to measure revenue elasticity as a function of logistical performance.

Various attempts have been made to approach the marginality solution by identifying the revenue loss when available sales are not realized. The cost of stockout represents logistical expenditure without benefit of marginal revenue analysis.[8] This approach provides assistance in arriving at a justified level of inventory availability. It does not answer the question of what might have been sold with superior logistical performance. Even though measurement and flexibility preclude exact solutions to the marginality problem, the objective of logistical policy formulation is to at least approximate the ideal solution. The approach recommended is to undertake sensitivity analysis initiating with the least-total-cost logistical system design. The final section of this chapter provides a generalized approach to evaluating marginal productivity of incremental customer service levels.

---

[8] For an example of research related to the problem of marginal service benefits, see Roy T. Sanford and Jack W. Farrell, "A Study of Customer Service Perceptions, Requirements and Effects on American Industry," Proceedings of the 1982 Annual Conference (Chicago: National Council of Physical Distribution Management), pp. 233–46.

FACILITY LOCATION STRUCTURE

Prior to the availability of low-cost overland transportation, most of the world's commerce was transported by water. During this early era, commercial activity centered around port cities, and overland transport of goods was costly and slow. For example, if a lady in a far-western state wanted to be married in a designer dress, the lead time for ordering could exceed 9 months. Although the need for fast and efficient transportation existed, it was not until the application of steam power to water and the invention of the steam locomotive in 1829 that the transportation technological revolution began in the United States. Today, the transportation system of the United States is a highly developed network of rail, water, air, highway, and pipeline services. Each transport alternative provides a different type of service available to be used within a logistical system.

The importance of location analysis has been recognized since at least the middle of the nineteenth century, when the German economist von Thünen developed *The Isolated State*.[9] To von Thünen, the primary determinant of economic development was the price of land and the cost of transport to market. The price of land resulted from the relative cost of transport and the ability of a product to command a price capable of absorbing transport cost. His basic thesis was that the value of specific produce at the growing location decreases with distance from the primary selling market.

Following von Thünen, Weber generalized location theory from an agrarian to an industrial society.[10] Weber's theoretical system consisted of numerous consuming locations spread over an area and linked together by linear weight-distance transportation costs. Weber developed a scheme to classify major materials as ubiquities and localized. Ubiquities were those materials available at all locations which could not in themselves serve to draw industrial facilities. Localized raw materials consisted of mineral deposits found only in selected locations. Based upon an analysis of the relative weight of localized raw materials and finished products, Weber developed a *material index*. The material index was a measure of the proportion of the weight of localized raw materials to the weight of the finished product. Each type of industry, based on the material index, could be assigned a *locational weight*. Utilizing these two measures, Weber generalized that specific industries would locate at the point of consumption if the manufacturing process was weight-gaining. They would locate facilities near the point of raw-material deposits if the manufacturing process was weight-losing. Finally, if the manufacturing process was neither weight-gaining nor weight-losing, firms would locate at an intermediate point or location of convenience.

Several location theorists followed von Thünen and Weber. The most notable contributions towards a general theory of location have been presented by Lösch, Hoover, Greenhut, Isard, and M. J. Webber.[11] All these authors have highlighted the importance of geographical specialization in industrial location,

---

[9] Joachim von Thünen, *The Isolated State* (Rostock, 1842–1863; reprinted Jena, 1921).

[10] Alfred Weber, *Theory of the Location of Industries*, Carl J. Friedrich (trans.) (Chicago: University of Chicago Press, 1928).

[11] August Lösch, *Die Räumliche Ordnung der Wirtschaft* (Jena: Gustav Fischer Verlag, 1940); Edgar M. Hoover, *The Location of Economic Activity* (New York: McGraw-Hill Book Company, 1938); Melvin L. Greenhut, *Plant Location in Theory and Practice* (Chapel Hill, N.C.: University of North Carolina Press,

including a thorough development of the fundamental importance of transportation.

In the most basic sense, transport capacity makes goods and commodities available that must be mined or manufactured elsewhere. Without transportation a community would have to be self-sufficient. The consequence would be limited variety of products, high prices, and inefficient utilization of natural resources.

From the vantage point of logistics planning, transportation links geographically dispersed manufacturing, warehousing, and market locations into an integrated system. As such, transportation provides *spatial* closure and permits specialization. Transportation should be viewed as cost-reducing in the sense that expenditures permit greater economies in the process of manufacturing and marketing.

The Spectrum of Location Decisions

In a broad sense, facilities included in the logistical system consist of all locations at which materials, work-in-process, or finished inventories are stored. Thus, all retail stores, finished-goods warehouses, manufacturing plants, and material storage warehouses constitute logistical locations. Among these many different types of facilities, the number and location of distribution and material warehouses are the most flexible in logistical system design.

A manufacturing plant location decision may require several years to capitalize. In contrast, some warehouse arrangements are so flexible that they are only used for spot stocking at specified times during an operating year. The selection of retail locations represents a specialized type of location analysis that is deeply influenced by marketing and competitive conditions. The discussion that follows concentrates on warehouse location analysis. Among all the location decisions, those related to warehouse policy will be reviewed most frequently. When, from time to time, manufacturing facility decisions are required, a great deal of attention should be directed to the impact of logistical operations on determining the best overall location. A refined body of knowledge concerning the location of manufacturing facilities has emerged over the years. Today, management can draw upon analytical sophistication tempered by sound theory to guide the selection of plant locations offering maximum economic and competitive benefits.[12] Appendix III provides material specific to manufacturing location analysis.

Warehouse Location Patterns

In logistical system design a warehouse will exist if it can render service or cost advantages. The number and geographic locations of warehouses are determined by manufaturing locations and markets. Warehouses represent one part

---

1956); W. Isard et al., *Methods of Regional Analysis: An Introduction to Regional Science* (New York: John Wiley & Sons, Inc., 1960); W. Isard, *Location and Space Economy* (Cambridge, Mass.: The MIT Press, 1968); and M. J. Webber, *Impact of Uncertainty on Location* (Cambridge, Mass.: The MIT Press, 1972).

[12] See Melvin L. Greenhut and H. Ohta, *Theory of Spatial Pricing and Market Areas* (Durham, N.C.: Duke University Press, 1975). Two additional sources published on an annual basis are *Plant Location* (New York: CIMMONS-Boardman Publishing Corp.), and *Site Selection Handbook* (Atlanta: Conway Publication Inc.).

of an overall effort to gain time and place utility. From a policy viewpoint, one or more warehouses will be utilized in a logistical system only if sales and marketing impact is increased or total cost is reduced.

Logically, three types of locational patterns evolve when warehouses are utilized. Using a classification developed by Hoover, these may be identified as market-positioned, production-positioned, or intermediately positioned.[13]

Market-Positioned

The market-positioned warehouse's function is to replenish customer inventory assortments. A warehouse geographically positioned near the market affords maximum inbound transport consolidation economies from inventory origin points with relatively short-haul local delivery. The geographic market area served from a market-positioned warehouse will depend on the desired speed of inventory replenishment, size of average order, and cost per unit of local delivery. Market-positioned warehouses may be operated by a retailer, manufacturer, or wholesaler. The mission of the warehouse will depend on the operating arrangement.

Market-positioned warehouses are designed to serve as break-bulk points for products purchased from various suppliers. The product line processed through a market-positioned warehouse is typically very wide. In contrast, the demand for any specific product is small in comparison to the warehouse's total volume. A retail store typically does not have sufficient demand to order inventory in consolidated quantities directly from manufacturers. The typical retail requirement is a variety of small lot size purchases from widely scattered manufacturers. In order to obtain rapid inventory replenishment of this broad product line and to lower logistical cost, a retailer may establish a warehouse.

Examples of market-positioned warehouses are found in the food industry. The modern food distribution warehouse usually is located near the point of highest retail sales concentration. From this location, local distribution to retail food stores can be accomplished rapidly while minimizing ton-miles. The maximum acceptable delivery time determines the proximity of the warehouse to the most distant retail outlet. Another example of a market-positioned distribution warehouse is Buick City near Flint, Michigan, where automotive assembly components are grouped to support just-in-time manufacturing strategies.[14]

This description of market-positioned warehouses represents one location pattern. Location of the warehouse close to the market served is based upon the need to replenish inventory rapidly and at the lowest cost.

Production-Positioned

A production-positioned warehouse is located close to manufacturing plants in order to act as a consolidation point for products. The fundamental reason for production-positioned warehouses is the manufacturer's desire for maximum

---

[13] Hoover, op. cit., p. 35.

[14] For a discussion of market-positioned warehouses to support manufacturing, see R. Scott Whiting, "Public Warehousing and the 'Just-in-Time' Production System," *Warehousing Review*, December 1983.

service to customers. Quantities of products from each plant are shipped to the warehouse from which full-line customer orders can be filled.

Strategic location of warehouses with respect to manufacturing plants allows mixed carloads or truckloads of customer shipments to move at consolidated transport rates. This mixed full-vehicle service stimulates purchase of products that would normally move under less-than-volume rates. A full-vehicle order may have shorter transit time than smaller orders. Therefore, the advantage of a production-positioned warehouse is the ability to furnish superior service for a total product assortment. If a manufacturer can offer all products at consolidated transportation rates, a competitive differrential advantage may be gained in customer service.

Several major manufacturing firms currently operate production-positioned warehouses. Leading examples are Pillsbury, Johnson & Johnson, General Foods, and Nabisco Brands. At Nabisco Brands, a shipping warehouse is located adjacent to each bakery. Quantities of all major products are maintained at each branch, thereby allowing full-service shipments.

Intermediately Positioned

Warehouses located between customers and manufacturing plants are classified as intermediately positioned. These warehouses, similar to production-positioned warehouses, find justification by providing increased customer service and reduced distribution cost.

Industrial location theory illustrates that focused manufacturing plants that produce a specific product line often must locate near sources of energy or required raw materials.[15] To realize competitive or cost-effective manufacturing, firms may be faced with a need to geographically decentralize manufacturing. When products from two or more plants are sold to a single customer, a collection warehouse may be justified at an intermediate location.

Transportation Economies

From the preceding discussion it is clear that warehouses enter a logistical system only when a differential advantage results from their inclusion between manufacturing and customers. Differential advantage gained by adding warehouses results from a distribution cost or service benefit to a given market. From the viewpoint of transportation economies, cost differential is realized as a result of using the warehouse as a consolidation point. In this part the consolidation potential of using a single warehouse is examined, followed by a discussion of transportation cost minimization across a network of facilities.

Warehouse Justification—Cost

A basic economic principle underlying the use of warehouses to serve a market area is consolidated transportation shipment. A manufacturer typically sells over a broad geographical market area. If customer orders tend to be small, then economic justification may exist for establishing a warehouse.

For example, assume that the average shipment size is 500 pounds and the rate between the manufacturing plant and a market for shipments of the

---

[15] Greenhut, op. cit., p. 117.

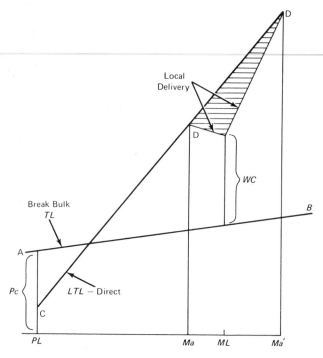

Figure 9–1 Economic Justification of a Single Warehouse Facility Cost per CWT

product is $7.28 per hundredweight. Each shipment made direct from the manufacturing location to the market would have a transportation cost of $36.40. Assume that the volume rate for shipments of 20,000 pounds between the manufacturing plant and the market is $2.40 per hundredweight and that the cost of local delivery within the market is $1.35 per hundredweight. Under these conditions, products shipped to the market via quantity rates and distributed locally would cost $3.75 per hundredweight or $18.75 per 500-pound shipment. Thus, if the warehouse facility and associated inventory level costs could be established for less than $17.65 per 500-pound shipment (36.40-18.75) or $3.53 per hundredweight, the overall cost of distributing to the market would be reduced. Under these conditions a warehouse would reduce total cost.

Figure 9–1 illustrates the basic principle of warehouse economic justification. *PL* is identified as the manufacturing location, and *ML* is the warehouse location within a linear market area. The vertical line at point *PL* labeled *Pc* reflects the handing and shipping cost associated with the preparation of a 500-pound *LTL* shipment (*C*) and a 20,000-pound truckload shipment (*A*). The slope of line *AB* reflects the truckload freight rate from the plant to *ML*, the warehouse which is assumed linear with distance.[16] The vertical line labeled *WC* at point *ML* represents the cost of warehousing and associated inventory maintenance. The lines labeled *D* reflect delivery cost from the warehouse to customers located within the area *Ma* to *Ma'*. The slope of line *CD* reflects the

---

[16] As explained in Chapter 6, pages 173–76, this assumption of linearity does not reflect typical transportation rates because of the tapering principle.

less-than-truckload rate from the plant to customers located between the plant and the boundary Ma'. The shaded area represents the locations to which the total cost of 500-pound customer shipment would be lower via the warehouse than direct from the manufacturing plant. From the perspective of total cost it would make no difference if customers located at points Ma and Ma' were serviced from the manufacturing plant or the warehouse.

Transportation Cost Minimization

As a general rule, warehouses would be added to the logistical system in situations where

$$\sum \frac{P_{\hat{v}} + T_{\hat{v}}}{N_{\hat{x}}} + W_{\hat{x}} + L_{\hat{x}} \leq \sum P_{\hat{x}} + T_{\hat{x}}$$

where

$P_{\hat{v}}$ = processing cost volume shipment
$T_{\hat{v}}$ = transportation cost volume shipment
$W_{\hat{x}}$ = warehousing cost average shipment
$L_{\hat{x}}$ = local delivery average shipment
$N_{\hat{x}}$ = number of average shipments per volume shipment
$P_{\hat{x}}$ = processing cost of average shipment
$T_{\hat{x}}$ = direct freight cost average shipment

The only limitation to this generalization is that sufficient volume of shipments be available to justify the fixed cost of the warehouse facility. As long as the total cost of warehousing, including local delivery, is equal to or less than the total cost of direct shipments to customers, the facility is economically justified.

The general relationship of transportation cost to location is illustrated in Figure 9–2. The total transportation cost will initially be reduced as warehouse locations are added to the logistical network. The reduction in transport cost results from consolidated volume shipments to warehouses coupled with short-haul small shipments from warehouse locations to customers. The cost of shipping small orders direct from manufacturing to customers is illustrated at the extreme left of Figure 9–2. At the low point on the transportation cost curve, the number of facilities required to enjoy the lowest total cost of transportation is identified.

If facilities are added beyond the optimum number of warehouses, total cost will increase. The main reason for the cost increase is that the quantity of consolidated volume shipments to each warehouse decreases, which results in a higher rate per hundredweight for inbound shipments. In other words, the frequency of small shipments inbound increases. Finally, as more and more warehouses are added to the network, the benefit of consolidated shipments is diminished, and total transportation cost begins to increase.

Inventory Economies

Inventory level and flow satisfy time requirements throughout a logistical system. The framework for planning inventory strategy is the performance

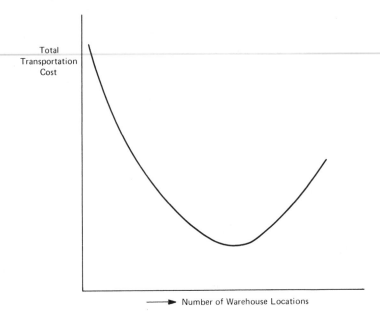

Figure 9–2 Transportation Cost as a Function of the Number of Warehouse Locations

cycle. Although one element of the performance cycle is transportation, which provides place utility, the key focus in inventory planning is time. The inclusion of forward inventory in a logistical system improves customer service capability. In this part, the impact of adding warehouses to a logistical system is examined, followed by a discussion of the impact of multiple warehouses on total system inventory requirements.

Warehouse Justification—Service

Warehouses can be vital to firms engaged in national distribution. To be competitive, firms are often required to market over broad geographical areas to realize maximum sales volumes. The general economies of manufacturing and marketing compel firms to locate manufacturing plants where low production costs can be enjoyed or large amounts of industry demand exist.

The dynamics of spatial competition enter the industry when products begin to gain acceptance in other than prime markets or near manufacturing locations. The enterprise may find it desirable to decentralize inventory to support marketing effort. In highly competitive industries the policy may be to locate a warehouse in a particular market area even if operation of the facility increases total cost. The availability of a local inventory permits high levels of customer service. For customers this means faster replenishment and an overall reduction of basic inventories. Thus, the enterprise who commits to the warehouse has used logistics to gain a differential advantage.

The inventory required to support a warehouse consists of transit, base, and safety stock. Transit stock is inventory captive in transportation vehicles. While in transit, this inventory cannot be physically utilized. It can be committeed to customers by use of a reservation or mortgaging capability in the order processing system. Base stock is a function of the replenishment logic used to determine order quantity. In a typical situation the transit stock and base stock combine to represent the minimum inventory committed to support a warehouse. As a general rule, the shorter the time required to replenish warehouse inventory, the lower the average inventory required to support the warehouse.

Safety stock is added to base and transit stock to protect against sales and lead time uncertainty. Both aspects of uncertainty are time related. Sales uncertainty is concerned with usage in excess of forecasted sales during replenishment. Lead time uncertainty is concerned with the total days required to replenish a warehouse.

For the total logistical system, average inventory commitment would be

$$\bar{I} = \sum_{i=1}^{n} \frac{Q_z}{2} + SS_i$$

where

$\bar{I}$ = average inventory in the total network

n = number of performance cycles in the network

Q_z = order quantity for a given performance cycle identified by the appropriate subscript

SS_i = safety stock for a given performance cycle identified by the appropriate subscript

Adding warehouses to a logistical structure increases the number of performance cycles. The impact on transit inventory and safety stock can be significant. In contrast, the impact on base stock by adding warehouses will not be significant. The base-stock level within a logistical system is determined by manufacturing and transportation lot sizes which do not change as a function of the number of warehouses. The combination of maintenance and ordering cost adjusted to take into consideration volume transportation rates and purchase discounts determines the replenishment EOQ and the resultant base stock. In just-in-time procurement situations, base stock is correlated to the discrete order quantity needed to support a specific manufacturing run or assembly situation. In either situation, the base-stock determination is independent of whether or not multiple warehouses are utilized to reduce logistical cost.

Transit. Transit inventory must be considered in the design solution because product inventory is committed. The inventory in-transit requires capital commitment. As performance cycles are added to the logistical network, the expected result is a reduction in transit inventory. This reduction occurs because the total transit days in the system are reduced. Assume that a single product is being sold in markets A and B and is currently being supplied from warehouse X, as illustrated in Figure 9–3. Assume also that the forecasted average daily sales is six for market A and seven for market B. The performance cycle duration is 6 days to market A and 10 days to market B.

With all other things held constant, what will happen to transit inventory, if a second warehouse is added, such as illustrated in Figure 9–4? Table 9–2 provides a summary of results. The main change is that the performance cycle to market B has been reduced from 10 to 4 days. Thus, the second warehouse reduced average transit inventory for the network from 53 to 32 units. It should

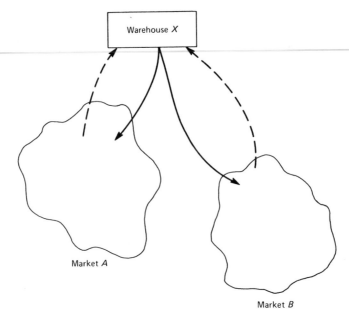

Figure 9-3 Logistical Network—Two Markets, One Warehouse

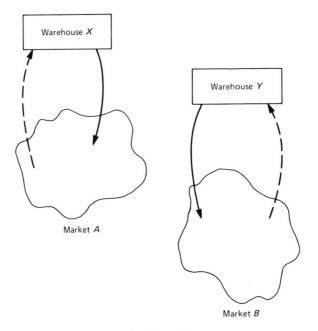

Figure 9-4 Logistical Network—Two Markets, Two Warehouses

be noted that the second warehouse did not create additional performance cycles on the physical distribution side of the logistical flow. However, on the inbound side each product stocked in the new warehouse requires a replenishment source. Assuming a full product line at each warehouse, the number of performance cycles will increase each time a new warehouse is added. However,

TABLE 9–2 Transit Inventory Under Different Logistical Networks

Forecasted Average Daily Sales	Market Area	Warehouse X Only	Two-Warehouse Facilities		
			Warehouse X	Warehouse Y	Combined
6	A	36	36	—	36
7	B	70	—	28	28
	$\sum A + B$	106			64
	$\bar{I}_a$	18			18
	$\bar{I}_b$	35			14
	$\sum \bar{I}$	53			32

TABLE 9–3 Logistical Structure: One Warehouse, Four Plants

	Warehouse X			
Manufacturing Plant	Performance Cycle Duration	Forecasted Average Sales	Transit Inventory	$\bar{I}$
A	10	35	350	175
B	15	200	3,000	1,500
C	12	60	720	360
D	20	80	1,600	800
	57	375	5,670	2,835

the average in-transit inventory for the total system is expected to drop as new warehouses are added because of a reduction in total system replenishment days. Assume that warehouse X is supplied by four manufacturing plants whose individual performance cycles and forecasted average usage are as illustrated in Table 9–3. For purposes of comparison, assume a unit value of $5 for all products handled at the warehouses. Utilizing only warehouse X, the average transit inventory would be 2,835 units at $5 each, or $14,175. Table 9–4 illustrates the addition of warehouse Y. Average transit inventory under the two-warehouse logistical structure dropped to 2,248 units at $5 each or $11,240. Thus, even though four new performance cycles were added to the logistical system, the average transit inventory was reduced because of the reduction in total replenishment days.[17]

In summary, the addition of facilities generally will have the net effect of reducing total in-transit days and thus inventory levels. This result, while typical, is not always the case. Each network of locations must be carefully analyzed to determine the exact impact upon average transit inventory. The key to understanding the impact of more warehouses on transit inventory is that total transit days are reduced even though performance cycles are added. To realize the benefits of reduced transit inventory, average shipment sizes must be sufficiently large to obtain volume rates. A qualification is that an increase in the number of performance cycles may reduce transit days, but it may also

[17] Experience with simulation indicates that the typical result of adding locations is an increase in the number of performance cycles and a decrease in performance cycle days.

TABLE 9–4 Logistical Structure: Two Warehouse, Four Plants

Manufacturing Plant	Performance Cycle Duration	Forecasted Average Sales	Transit Inventory	$\bar{I}$
		Warehouse X		
A	10	20	200	100
B	15	100	1,500	750
C	12	35	420	210
D	20	30	600	300
	57	185	2,720	1,360
		Warehouse Y		
A	5	15	75	38
B	8	100	800	400
C	6	25	150	75
D	15	50	750	375
	34	190	1,775	88
	$\sum xy = 91$	$\sum xy = 375$	$\sum xy = 4,495$	$\sum \bar{x}xy = 2,248$

increase lead time uncertainty. As performance cycles are increased in number, the potential need for safety stocks to protect against late delivery will also increase. This impact is treated under safety-stock.

Safety Stock. From the viewpoint of safety stock, the expected result of adding warehouses is an increase in average system inventory. In Chapter 7 the uncertainty related to sales and performance cycle uncertainty was evaluated using two independent frequency distributions. The purpose of safety stock is to protect against unplanned out-of-stocks during warehouse inventory replenishment. Thus, if safety stock increases as a function of adding warehouses, the overall system uncertainty must also be increasing.

The addition of warehouses to the logistical system impacts uncertainty in two ways. First, since performance cycle days are reduced, the variability in sales during replenishment and the variability in the cycle are both reduced. Therefore, reducing the length of the performance cycle relieves, to some degree, the need for safety stock requirement.

The second impact of adding locations has a direct and significant effect on average inventory. The addition of each new performance cycle creates the need for an additional safety stock. The introduction of additional warehouses to service a given level of demand in effect reduces the size of the statistical data base for determining safety-stock requirements with no corresponding reduction in uncertainty. For example, when the demand of several markets can be aggregated into a single warehouse with one statistical distribution, the variability of demand is averaged across markets. In essence, the use of probability allows the unused stock of one market to be used to meet safety-stock requirements of other markets.

To illustrate, Table 9–5 provides a summary of monthly sales in three markets on a combined and separate basis. Average sales for the three markets

TABLE 9–5   Summary of Sales in One Combined and Three Separate Markets

Month	Combined Sales All Markets	Unit Sales per Market		
		A	B	C
1	18	9	0	9
2	22	6	3	13
3	24	7	5	12
4	20	8	4	8
5	17	2	4	11
6	29	10	5	14
7	21	7	6	8
8	26	7	7	12
9	18	5	6	7
10	24	9	5	10
11	23	8	4	11
12	23	12	2	9
Total sales	265	90	51	124
Average monthly sales	22.0	7.5	4.2	10.3
Value greater than average	7	5	3	4

combined is 22 units per month, with the greatest variation above the average in month 6, when sales reached 29 units, 7 over average. Assuming, for ease of illustration, that it is desirable to provide 100-per-cent protection against stockouts and that total sales of 29 units had an equal probability of occurring in any month, a safety stock of 7 units would be required.

For individual markets, the average monthly sales for markets A, B, and C are 7, 4, and 10 units (rounded). The maximum demand in excess of forecast is for market A, 5 units in month 12; for market B, 3 units in month 8; and for market C, 4 units in month 6. The total of each of these three extreme months equals 12 units. If safety stocks were being planned for each market on a separate basis, 12 units of safety stock would be required for the total system, as contrasted to 7 units if all markets were serviced from a single warehouse. A total increase in overall system safety stock of 5 units is required to provide equal protection if each market is serviced from its own warehouse.

Although this is a simplified example, it illustrates the impact of additional locations on system safety stock. The important point to understand is that the increase in safety stock results from an inability to aggregate the sales across a large market area. As a consequence, separate safety stocks are required for each market to accommodate local demand variation.

Inventory Cost Minimization

The overall impact upon average inventory of adding warehouse locations in a logistical system is generalized in Figure 9–5. A reduction in average transit inventory is assumed as illustrated by the line. $\bar{I}_t$. The assumption is that a linear relationship exists between average transit inventory and the number of locations in the network.

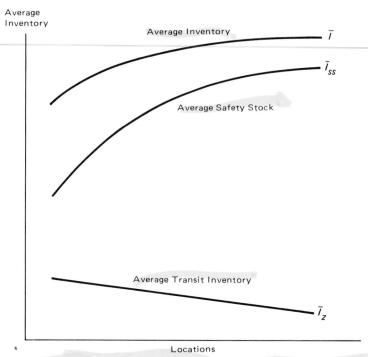

Figure 9–5   Average Inventory as a Function of Number of Warehouse Locations

The curve labeled $\bar{I}_{ss}$ (average safety stock) increases as warehouse locations are added. The actual increase is at a decreasing rate, since the net increase per location is the added safety stock required to accommodate demand uncertainty less the reduction in lead time uncertainty as a result of shorter replenishment cycle. The incremental inventory required to maintain customer service performance diminishes as warehouse locations are added to the system.[18] The average inventory curve, $\bar{I}$, represents the combined impact of safety stock and transit inventory. The significant point is that the safety stock dominates. In terms of the total system, the average inventory is the safety stock plus one half of the order quantity (base stock) and transit inventory. Thus, total inventory increases as the number of warehouse locations increases, given the same demand and customer service goals.

Least-Total-Cost Design

Over the past several years the identification of the least-total-cost system design has received considerable attention in the logistics literature.[19] The basic concept of total cost for the overall logistical system is illustrated in Figure 9–6. The low point on the total transportation cost curve is eight facilities. Total cost

[18] This reduction in the rate of safety-stock increase results from an increase in homogeneity of demand as the geographic size of the market area serviced by a facility is reduced.

[19] For complete early development of the total cost concept, see Raymond Lekashman and John F. Stolle, "The Total Cost approach to Distribution," *Business Horizon's*, Vol. 44 (Winter 1965), pp. 33–46; or Marvin Flaks, "Total Cost approach to Physical Distribution," *Business Management*, Vol. 24 (August 1963), pp. 55–61.

related to average inventory commitment increases with each additional warehouse. The lowest total cost for the overall example warehouse network is six locations.

Trade-off Relationships

The identification of the least-total-cost design in Figure 9–6 illustrates the trade-offs between cost-generating activities. *The minimal total-cost point for the system is not at the point of least cost for either transportation or inventory. This is the hallmark of integrated logistical analysis.*

In actual practice, a great many problems must be overcome for effective total-cost analysis. Foremost among implementational problems is that many assumptions must be made to operationalize the logistical system analysis. A second concern is the fact that a two-dimensional analysis, such as illustrated in Figure 9–6, does not encompass the complexity of total-cost integration. Each of the critical assumptions and associated implementational problems is discussed.

Critical Assumptions and Limitations

The two-dimensional display in Figure 9–6 represents a single level of sales volume across a single planning period. The assumption is that transportation consists of one representative average-size shipment. In actual operations neither of these conditions is true. First, the nature of logistical network design is not a short-term planning problem. Because of the basic nature of fixed-facility decisions, the planning horizon extends across several years of operations and a range of different annual sales volumes. Second, actual shipment

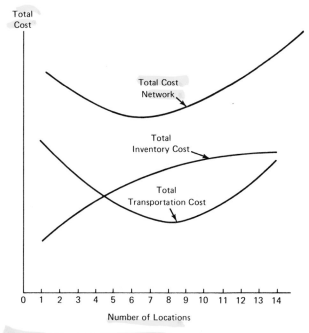

Figure 9–6 Total-Cost Logistical Network

size or order size will vary substantially around the average shipment size. In fact, the assumption that shipments must be serviced through a warehouse must be relaxed to include customer direct truckload and carload distribution. A realistic approach to planning must consider the range of shipment sizes accommodated by a variety of logistical methods within customer service constraints. In practical operation, alternative modes of transportation can be employed to upgrade the speed of delivery.[20]

The significant cost trade-offs occur between inventory and transportation. Inventory cost as a function of the number of warehouses is directly related to the desired level of inventory availability. If no safety stock were desired, the total inventory required would consist of base and transit stock. Under a no-safety-stock situation the total least cost for the system would be near the point of lowest transportation cost. Thus, the assumptions made regarding level of desired inventory availability and fill rate are essential to trade-off analysis and have a significant impact on the least-total-cost design solution.

The locational selection aspect of planning is far more complex than deciding how many facilities to utilize from a single array as illustrated in Figure 9–6. A firm engaged in nationwide logistics has a wide latitude of potential warehouse locations. Within the United States there are 50 states within which one or more distribution warehouses could be located. Assume that the total allowable warehouses for a logistical system cannot exceed 50 and locations are limited to a maximum of one in each state. Given this range of options, there are 1.1259×10^{15} combinations of warehouses that could be selected in seeking the total-least-cost network.

To overcome some simplifying assumptions, variations in shipment size and transportation alternatives can be introduced to the two-dimensional analysis presented in Figure 9–6. The refinement requires that a range of two-dimensional relationships be linked. The three variables under consideration are shipment size, transportation mode, and number of locations. The constants or givens are level of inventory protection, performance cycle duration, and the specific warehouse locations.

In constructing a more comprehensive analysis, shipment size can be grouped in terms of frequency of occurrence and the transportation mode economically justified to handle each size shipment within performance cycle time constraints. For each shipment size, a total-cost curve is identified. The result is a series of two-dimensional charts for each combination of shipment size and associated transportation mode. Next, the individual charts are linked by joining the points of least cost by a planning curve. In a technical sense, the planning curve is an envelope curve that joins the low total-cost points of individual shipment size–transport mode relationships. Figure 9–7 is a three-dimensional representation of shipment size, transportation mode, and location.

The planning curve joins points of total least cost for each shipment size. It does not join locational points. For example, the desirable number of locations to support least cost for one size of shipment may be more or less than for another. Further refinement is necessary to identify the specific locations that offer the least-cost alternative for each shipment size and transport combina-

---

[20] Lewis et al. op. cit.

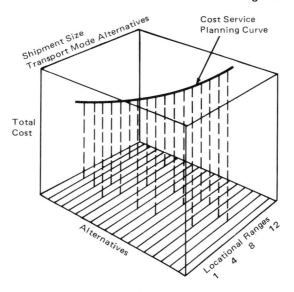

Figure 9–7 Three-Dimensional Total-Cost Curve

tion. Assume that the locational range consisted of from 1 to 12 warehouse alternatives. Within this range the planning curve will isolate a smaller range of acceptable locations. In Figure 9–7 the points of least-cost shipment size and transportation combinations fall within four to eight locations. A compromise is required to select the final warehouse network. Initially, the duration of the performance cycle and inventory available assumptions should not be varied. The levels of service and performance cycle serve as constants or parameters to determine the initial least-cost solution. At a later point in policy formulation the parameters can be subjected to sensitivity analysis. The fit of the least-cost planning curve requires marginal cost analysis for each shipment size–transportation mode combination for networks of four, five, six, seven, and eight warehouse locations. Providing customer service requirements are achieved within the four- to eight-warehouse range, the least-total-cost network of warehouses could be identified.

A final refinement to the planning problem concerns the selection of specific warehouses. In the case of Figure 9–7, the best-fit network of locations may not by cost superior to a different set of locations. Each warehouse network set will have a least-cost combination. The final policy may require that the analysis be completed with several different networks to identify the most practical locations for a given business situation. The final warehouse selections will never represent the mathematical optimal solution to minimize total logistical cost.

In order to take into consideration the wide range of variables in designing a logistical system, complex models have been developed. Several such models are be discussed in Chapter 13. The assumptions required to support integrated logistical system design are important from the viewpoint of their impact upon policy formulation. The integrated total-cost curve must take into consideration all relevant variables that are critical to system design.

FORMULATING A LOGISTICAL POLICY

To arrive at a final logistical policy, it is necessary to evaluate the relationships between alternative customer service levels and associated cost. While substantial difficulties exist in the measurement of marginal revenue, the comparative evaluation of marginal service performance and related marginal cost offers a way to approximate an ideal logistical system design. The general approach consists of: (1) determination of a least-total-cost system design, (2) measurement of service availability and capability associated with the least-total-cost system design, (3) conduct of sensitivity analysis concerning incremental service and associated cost in terms of revenue, and (4) finalizing a logistical policy. This section is devoted to a discussion of the logic that underlies the formulation of a service-oriented logistical policy.

The Least-Total-Cost Design

Just as a physical map of a geographical area illustrates the elevations, depressions, and contours of land surface, an economic cost map illustrates logistical cost differences. Generally, peak costs for labor and government services occur in large metropolitan areas. However, because of demand concentration, total logistics cost resulting from reduced transportation and inventory expenditures are often near minimum in metropolitan areas.

A policy of least total cost seeks a logistical system design with the lowest combined fixed and variable costs. The design of the least-total-cost system is determined purely by cost-to-cost trade-offs. In terms of basic relationships, the point of total least cost was illustrated in Figure 9–6. A level of customer service exists in a least-cost logistical design as a result of safety-stock assumptions and the proximity of warehouses to customers. The customer service associated with least-total-cost system design is referred to as the *threshold* service level.

Threshold Service

To identify a threshold service it is necessary to initiate the analysis with policies regarding minimum acceptable customer service *availability* and *capability* expected from the logistical system. A typical initial approximation is to permit the customer service capability to be a function of existing order transmission time, standard order-processing time at existing facilities, and transit time selected on the basis of lowest-cost transportation. Given these assumptions, existing cycle speed and consistency serve as the initial measure of customer service performance capability.

A typical initial approximation regarding customer service availability is to assume an acceptable minimum fill rate. Often the prevailing industry standard is used as a first approximation. For example, if safety-stock availability level is set at the 97.75-per-cent protection for the combined probability of demand and lead time uncertainty, it would be anticipated that approximately 98 out of 100 items ordered would be available.

Under initial conditions, each customer is assigned a shipment location on the basis of least total cost. In a multiproduct situation, selection of service territories for each facility will depend on the products stocked at each warehouse and the degree of product mixing required on customer orders.

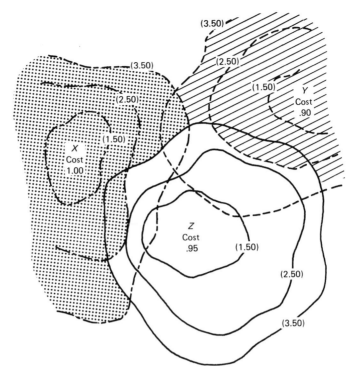

Figure 9–8 Determination of Service Territories—Three-Point, Least-Cost System

Because costs have significant geographical differentials, the service area of any given warehouse will vary in size and configuration. Figure 9–8 provides an illustration of the assignment of warehouse shipping areas based upon a line of equalized total delivered cost. The irregularity of service territories results from directional transportation cost differentials outbound from the three warehouses.

In Figure 9–8 the warehouses are identified by the letters X, Y, and Z. The hypothetical cost illustrated at each facility location represents the logistical cost for an average order with the exception of transportation. The differential of average order cost between facilities reflects geographical and individual system differentials.

Around each facility three total-cost lines are displayed, at intervals of $1.50, $2.50, and $3.50. The value on the line represents the total cost of logistics, including transportation to points located along the line. The area within a given line can be serviced at something less than the cost displayed on the line. The area serviced by each warehouse is based on lowest total cost. The territory boundary line represents the point of equal total cost between two warehouses. Along the line of equal costs, an enterprise would be indifferent on a cost basis as to which warehouse services a specific customer. From the customer's viewpoint, a substantial difference could result in terms of delivery time.

Two conditions are assumed in Figure 9–8. First, the illustration is based on an average order, thus distribution costs are equated on the average. To the degree that order size varies from the average, alternative territory boundaries based on shipment size are required. Second, an element of time is included based upon transportation miles. Transit inventory is calculated on standard time. Based on this limited analysis of threshold service, it cannot be concluded that delivery times will be constant within territories or that equal total logistics cost will be experienced within service areas.

The fact that a least-cost system is designed for maximum economy does not mean that threshold customer service will be necessarily low. The elapsed time from the customer's order placement to product delivery in a least-cost system will be longer on the average than for other types of systems. However, customers located in the heart of the market close to warehouses will enjoy rapid delivery. Because the least-cost array will tend to favor areas of highest demand concentration, a substantial number of customers will enjoy rapid service.

Given an estimate of expected order cycle time, management is in a position to make customer delivery commitments. Such a statement might be expressed as follows:

> Order performance for area A will be 5 days from receipt of orders at the warehouse facility. It is our policy to be able to fill 90 per cent of all orders within the 5 day period.

The actual performance of a logistical system is measured by the degree to which such service standards are met in practice. Given quantification of the variables involved, the threshold service related to the least-total-cost system can be identified. The next step in policy formulation is to test the desirability of the threshold service level.

Service Sensitivity Analysis

The *threshold* service resulting from the least-total-cost system design provides the base for sensitivity analysis. The basic service capabilities of a system can be increased or decreased by a variety of methods such as: (1) variation in number of warehouses in the system, (2) change in one or more performance cycle activities to modify speed or consistency of operations, and/or (3) change in safety-stock policy. Each form of modifying threshold service and the expected impact on total cost are briefly discussed.

Locational Modifications

The warehouse structure of the logistical system establishes the service that can be realized without changing the speed of the performance cycle or safety-stock policy. To understand the relationship between number of warehouses and service time, assume that the measure of logistical service is related to percentage of demand serviced within a specified time interval. The general impact of adding warehouses to the system is presented in Table 9–6. Several points of interest are illustrated.

First, incremental service is a diminishing function. For example, the first five locations provided 24-hour performance to 42 per cent of all customers. In order to double the percentage of 24-hour service, from 42 to 84 per cent, 9 additional or a total of 14 locations are required.

Second, high degrees of service are reached much faster for longer performance intervals than for the shorter intervals. For example, four locations can provide 85-per-cent performance within the 96-hour performance cycle. Increasing the total locations from 4 to 14 improved the 96-hour performance incrementally 9 per cent. In contrast, a total of 14 warehouses cannot achieve 85 per cent within the 24-hour performance cycle.

Finally, the total cost associated with each location added to the logistical network increases dramatically. Thus, while the incremental service resulting from additional locations is a diminishing function, the incremental cost associated with each new location is an increasing function.

Performance Cycle Modifications

Speed and consistency of service can be varied to a specific market or customer by a modification in one or more activities in the performance cycle. To improve service, computer-to-computer ordering and premium transportation can be utilized. Therefore, geographical proximity and number of warehouse do not equate directly with rapid or consistent delivery. The decision to increase service capability by faster performance cycle execution will increase variable cost. In contrast, service improvement by virtue of added warehouses involves a high degree of fixed cost and results in less overall system flexibility.

No generalizations can be offered regarding the cost/service improvement ratio attainable from performance cycle modification. The typical relationship of premium to lowest-cost transportation results in a significant incentive in favor of large shipments. Thus, if order volume is substantial, the economics of logistics can be expected to favor use of a warehouse or consolidation point to service a market area.

The impact of using premium transportation on the least-total-cost system is twofold: (1) the transportation cost curve will shift up to reflect higher per shipment expenditure; and (2) the inventory cost curve will shift down to reflect any reductions in average inventory resulting from lower transit stocks. In almost all cases, the net impact of these cost modifications will be an increase in total cost. Such adjustment from the least-total-cost system could be justified if higher service results in greater revenue.

Stocking Modifications

One direct way to vary service level is to increase or decrease the amount of safety stock held at one or more warehouses. The cost ramifications of providing high levels of inventory availability were discussed in detail in Chapter 7. At that point a substantial case was presented to support the logic of following a policy of selective safety stocks to protect availability of items most critical to attainment of operating goals.

The impact of increasing the safety stock across a total system will shift the average inventory cost curve up. The impact of increasing customer service availability will require larger safety stocks at each warehouse. As availability is increased, the safety stocks required to achieve each equal increment of availability increase.

Finalizing the Logistical Policy

Establishment of customer service performance standards constitutes a critical managerial policy. Customer service policy is integral to logistical system

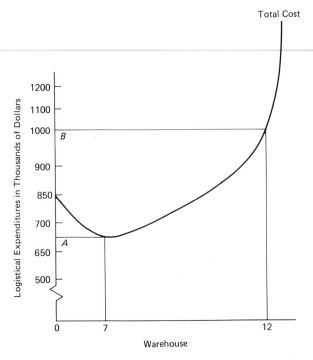

Figure 9–9 Comparative Total Cost for 7- and 20-Distribution Point Systems

design because service objectives must be obtained within acceptable cost. Management often falls into the trap of being overly optimistic in their service commitments. The result may be an excessively high commitment to customers followed by erratic performance. This dichotomy results from lack of understanding the total cost required to support high service commitments. The final step in isolating a policy is to relate the cost of incremental service to offsetting revenue requirements.

To illustrate, assume that the current system is geared to service at least 90 per cent of all customers at a 95-per-cent inventory availability within 60 hours of order receipt. Further, assume that the current logistical system is meeting these objectives at lowest total cost by utilizing five warehouses. Marketing, however, is not happy. Marketing management's opinion is that service capability should be increased to the point where 90 per cent of all customers would receive 97-per-cent inventory availability and 24-hour delivery. Top management is faced with a critical policy consideration.

Figure 9–9 provides helpful information for evaluating the customer service request. Marketing desires a 2-per-cent improvement in inventory availability coupled with a 36-hour improvement in delivery capability. Design analysis can isolate that 12 warehouse facilities would be the lowest-cost method for achieving the new service standards. The total cost of this expanded service capability is measured on the vertical axis of Figure 9–9 as the distance between points *A* and *B*. The total cost of meeting the marketing's desired service is $400,000 per year greater than current expenditures. If the firm had a before-tax profit margin equal to 10 per cent of sales, it would be necessary to generate $4 million in incremental sales to break even on the cost of providing the added service.[21]

Acceptance or rejection of the marketing proposal for increased service rests with senior management. Policy changes, once adopted, influence logistical design.

To finalize logistical policy, management must consider a full range of strategic alternatives. In addition to least total cost, logistical policy could be based on at least four other strategies: (1) maximum service, (2) profit maximization, (3) maximum competitive advantage, and (4) minimum asset deployment. Each basic strategy requires a different logistical system design.

Maximum Service

A maximum service strategy is rarely implemented. A system designed to provide maximum service usually would not attempt to deliver products faster than on a 24-hour basis.

Emphasis on maximum service shifts from cost to delivery time. For maximum service analysis a territory division can be developed similar to the least-cost service areas illustrated in Figure 9–8. However, the cost lines are replaced by time or service lines. The limits of each warehouse service area are determined by the capability to provide required delivery. As with cost-oriented service areas, time-oriented areas will be irregular because of transport-route configurations.

Total cost variation between least-cost and maximum-service models will be substantial. To service the total United States' market on an overnight basis requires 30 to 40 warehouses or the use of very high-speed, high-cost transportation.

Profit Maximization

Most business enterprises aspire to maximize profit in the design of logistical systems. Theoretically, the service area of each facility is determined by establishing a minimum allowable profit margin for customers located at varying distances from the facility. Because warehouses are normally located near high-volume markets, the greater the distance a customer is located from the service area center, the greater the costs of logistics. This occurs, not only because of distance, but also because of lower customer density at the periphery of the warehouse service area. At the point where the costs of serving peripheral customers results in minimum allowable profit margins, further extensions of the service territory become unprofitable on a total-cost-basis.

If the customer were offered better delivery service, more of the overall product assortment sold by an enterprise might be purchased. Conceptually, additional service should be introduced, to the point where marginal revenues equal marginal costs. At this point of equilibrium, no additional service is justified. Additional service may or may not result from increasing the number of warehouses. The service may be provided best by a supplemental system of

---

[21] This relationship is based on the assumption that no change, favorable or unfavorable, would take place in existing fixed or variable cost per unit as a result of an increase in volume.

TABLE 9–6 Service Capabilities Within Time Intervals as a Function of Number of Locations

Network Locations	Percentage Demand by Performance Cycle Duration (Hours)			
	24	48	72	96
1	15	31	53	70
2	23	44	61	76
3	32	49	64	81
4	37	55	70	85
5	42	60	75	87
6	48	65	79	89
7	54	70	83	90
8	60	76	84	90
9	65	80	85	91
10	70	82	86	92
11	74	84	87	92
12	78	84	88	93
13	82	85	88	93
14	84	86	89	94

direct delivery. The theoretical profit-maximization position is easier to state than to actually measure. However, equated marginal revenue and marginal cost represent a solution management should strive to approximate.

In the development of a policy based on profits, management is seeking a service and cost balance. Referring back to Figure 9–6, the balance normally will be found along the total-cost curve to the right of the least-cost point but considerably short of the point where total costs rise rapidly. For the situation illustrated in Figure 9–6, the profit-maximization system, as a first approximation, could be expected to fall between a network of 6 and 10 warehouses.

Table 9–6 presented a quantification of the service capabilities of 14 warehouses given a specific customer configuration. The actual service gains that result from adding warehouses will vary with each design situation. The dollar increase for adding each warehouse, Figure 9–6, reflects additional costs for providing higher delivery performance. These dollar estimates provide an assessment of the value of added service against added cost. Given a schedule of these cost-service relationships, management is armed with considerable information to help in the establishment of a customer service policy.

Maximum Competitive Advantage

Under special situations, the most desirable policy to guide logistical system design may be the accomplishment of maximum competitive advantage. Although there are many cases where systems may be modified to gain competitive advantage, two are developed here to illustrate the policy considerations.

Selective Cost Service Programs. The first case concerns modifications in system structure aimed at protecting major customers from competitive inroads. Management should be concerned with the welfare of major customers if

TABLE 9–7   Core-Customer Interrogative Results

Total Core Customers	Number of Core Customers Serviced by Hour Intervals			
	24	36	48	60
75	53	16	4	2

the existing service policy is only capable of providing 42 per cent of the customers with 24-hour delivery at 95-per-cent inventory availability.

To illustrate, assume that an enterprise is typical among those engaged in mass marketing and that 20 per cent of their customers purchased 80 per cent of their products. Further, assume that this group of critical customers are located at 75 different delivery destinations. The key is to determine if the 75 critical customer destinations are included in the 42 per cent of all customers receiving 24-hour delivery. Under conditions of equal customer geographical dispersion, the probability is about 0.5 that the array of 42 per cent of total customers would include all the significant 20 per cent. In other words, one would expect that on the average approximately 40 to 45 of the core customers would get 24-hour service.

Once core-customer locations are identified, it is a relatively easy process to isolate the customer service each receives. Core customers are identified as critical delivery points, and the frequency of service interval is obtained through an assessment process. Table 9–7 presents the type of results expected from such an assessment process.

The actual number of core customers receiving 24-hour delivery service in this example is 53. Thus, although 42 per cent of all customers receive 24-hour service, 76 per cent of the core customers receive prime consideration. In addition, the interrogative process points out that the remaining core customers receive varying degrees of service, with two of these critical customers receiving 60-hour delivery.

Provided that management is so inclined, this situation can be rectified by a restatement of objectives. The cost of a system providing 24-hour service to 90 per cent of all customers can be isolated, and management can equate the dollar-and-cents requirements of a core-customer policy. An alternative would be the use of premium transportation to service core customers currently receiving service greater than 24 hours.

Several additional systems modifications may be evaluated similar to the core-customer illustration shown. Management may wish to examine service provided to the most profitable customers. Evaluations can be made regarding customers or noncustomers with the greatest growth potential. In addition, an enterprise may wish to evaluate the incremental cost of providing prime service to the core customers of major competitors. Although all such modifications may increase total cost and decrease short-range profits, the long-range gain may be a substantial improvement in competitive position.

Justified High-Cost Location. An additional application of design modification to capitalize on competitive situations is the economically justified high-cost warehouse. This situation is pertinent especially to a small business.

Because of the rigidities inherent in large firms, pricing policies are likely to be inflexible. Antitrust legislation reinforces such rigidities. The result is that a large enterprise selling in a broad geographical market may tend to disregard unique cost-and-demand conditions in localized markets or find it nearly impossible to adjust marketing and logistical systems to accommodate these localized situations. This inflexibility creates opportunities for smaller enterprises. Such opportunities may encourage smaller enterprises to make significant investment in logistical capability to attract the localized market segment.

Location of a small-scale plant or warehouse facility in a minor market some distance from major competitors results in a localized service capability more or less insulated from competition. The logic of this special situation was developed under the general discussion of factors influencing facility location. At this time it is sufficient to highlight that large enterprises typically follow one or two policies concerning these special situations.

First, a large enterprise can elect to avoid such localized situations. This policy of concentrating on primary markets can be an opportunity for the higher-cost, smaller organization. Second, major producers may introduce smaller-scale facilities or institute direct logistical systems in an effort to service local-demand situations. Following the first policy will result in a system approaching a least-cost configuration. The second policy will require substantial system modification, with higher costs and lower short-range profits.

Minimal Asset Deployment. A final strategy that can guide logistical policy may be the desire to minimize assets committed to the logistical system. A firm that desires to maintain maximum flexibility may establish a policy of using variable-cost logistical components such as public warehouses and for-hire transportation. Such a policy might result in higher total logistical costs than could be realized by asset commitment to realize economies of scale.

Conclusion—Logistical Policy Formulation

In summary, integration of the logistical policy into overall corporate planning requires specified customer service performance. This customer service performance is viewed from product availability, performance time, and the probability that the desired delivery service will consistently materialize. The total-cost curve defines the point of least cost associated with each customer service level. From a design viewpoint, the point of total least cost with its associated threshold service capability offers ideal cost trade-offs. From the viewpoint of overall enterprise objectives, incremental service over and above the threshold level may be justified from the perspective of marketing or manufacturing operations. Service-cost trade-offs are required to identify the logistical policy that satisfies overall requirements.

SUMMARY

The objective of this chapter was to develop a basic framework for formulating logistical policy. Transportation and inventory were identified as the critical design considerations. Transportation deals with the spatial aspects of logistics and provides the primary justification for including warehouses in a system design. Inventory deals with the temporal aspects of logistics. Average inventory is expected to increase as the number of warehouses in a system increases. Total cost integration provides a methodology for simultaneous integration of these two basic logistical activities. Thus, total-cost analysis provides the methodology for integration within and between specific operational areas of logistics.

The formulation of a total-cost analysis is not without practical problems. Foremost is the fact that a great many important costs are not specifically measured or reported in standard accounting systems. A second problem involved in total-cost analysis is the need to consider a wide variety of design alternatives. To develop complete analysis of a planning situation, alternative shipment sizes, modes of shipment, and range of available warehouse locations must be considered.

These problems can be overcome if care is taken in the formulation of the design assignment. The cost format recommended for total-cost analysis is to group all functional costs associated with inventory and transportation. The significant contribution of total-cost integration is that it provides a simultaneous analysis of time- and space-related costs in logistical system design.

The formulation of a logistical policy requires that total-cost analysis be evaluated in terms of customer service performance. Logistical service is measured in terms of *availability, capability,* and *quality* of performance. The ultimate realization of each service attribute is directly related to logistical system design. To realize the final integration of logistical operations within overall enterprise planning, customer service should be provided to the point where marginal cost is equaled by marginal revenue. Such marginal balance is not practical to achieve. However, the relationship serves as a normative planning goal.

The formulation of a service policy starts from the identification and analysis of the least-total-cost system design. Given an assumed initial inventory availability level, the service capability associated with the least-cost design is referred to as the *threshold service level.* To evaluate potential modifications in the least-cost design, several forms of sensitivity analysis are possible. Three ways were identified to improve service levels: (1) variation in the number of facilities, (2) change in one or more activities of the performance cycle, and/or (3) change in safety-stock policy. The impact of each modification was explored in detail.

Next, attention was directed to finalizing a logistical policy. Beyond least cost, four additional strategies were identified: (1) maximum service, (2) profit maximization, (3) maximum competitive advantage, and (4) minimal asset deployment. Regardless of the final strategy selected, the desired level of customer service performance should be obtained at the associated lowest total cost.

QUESTIONS

1. Describe in your own words the meaning of spatial-temporal integration in logistical system integration.
2. What justification of logic can be presented to support the placement of a warehouse in a logistical system?

3. Why do transportation costs decrease as the number of warehouses in a system increase? Why do inventory costs increase as the number of warehouses in a system increase?

4. In your words, what is the locational impact of inventory? How does it differ for transit inventories and safety stocks?

5. What is meant by the level of threshold service of a least-cost system?

6. Why does customer service not increase proportionately to increases in total cost when a logistical system is being designed?

7. In Table 9–6 why does customer service speed of performance increase faster for customers located greater distances from a warehouse facility? What is the implication of this relationship for system design?

8. Discuss the differences between improving customer service through faster and more consistent transportation, higher inventory levels, and/or expanded numbers of warehouses.

9. What is the difference between minimum total cost and short-range profit maximization policies in system design?

10. In what ways can customer service performance be improved by incorporating flexible distribution operations into a logistical system design?

Organization

Management is the process of getting things done through others employed by the enterprise. An integral part of management is personnel motivation. The fundamental responsibility of top management is to create an environment within which each operating executive has maximum opportunity to achieve corporate objectives. To this end, organization structure is a vital part of management.

Traditional responsibility for logistical management has been fragmented throughout the organization. One basic premise underlying the integrated logistical concept is that organizational fragmentation of responsibility increases vulnerability to duplication, waste, and, at times, hinders mission accomplishment. With fragmented responsibility, communication flows are distorted, and lines of authority and responsibility become blurred.

Structuring of logistics as a separate organizational unit is a relatively new concept. The fact that logistical activities have always had to be performed has created a great deal of controversy on whether or not a unified organizational group is desirable or necessary. This chapter provides an overview of logistical organization practices.

The first section provides a brief review of logistical organization development. An evolutionary approach to logistical unification is described which reflects commonly observed patterns of organizational development. Section two reviews empirical research regarding evolving logistical organization. Section three focuses on the change process by which new logistical organizations evolve. In the final section typical issues confronted in achieving effective organization are discussed.

Two comments are in order concerning the manner in which organization structure is presented. First, recognizing that organization is a highly customized activity, no attempt is made to present charts of individual enterprises as representative models. No chart fits all structures. Rather, emphasis is placed on the logic of integrating functions as the logistical process matures within an enterprise. Accordingly, three model organizations are presented as types along a unification continuum. Applicability of this general treatment of organizational development will depend upon the individual enterprise.

A second point worth noting is that acknowledged principles of management are not reviewed. The established principles apply to all forms of management and provide valuable guidelines for designing an organizational structure. Since the principles of management are discussed in detail in basic management textbooks, they are not elaborated here.

ORGANIZATIONAL DEVELOPMENT

Logistical organizations change to meet the requirements of the business environment. In Chapter 1 development of the logistical concept was traced from 1950 to the present time. Throughout the 35-year period, logistical organizations evolved to satisfy the requirements confronted during each time period. In this section the evolution of logistical organization is classified into three types. In a longitudinal perspective, the types evolved along with the maturing of the overall logistical concept. The type I organization emerged during the 1950s and 1960s. Type II organizations became typical of the 1970s and early 1980s. The Type III organization emerged in the early 1980s and is expected to gain in popularity in the foreseeable future. However, at any point in time, specific firms and industries may reflect different levels of organizational maturity. As a result, Types I, II and III organizations can be readily observed in contemporary business.

If one accepts the premise that top management is generally not disposed to revolutionary change, it follows that a unified logistical organization would only evolve as necessary to meet specific requirements. As noted repeatedly, all functions of logistics have always been performed by successful enterprises. It is only natural that any attempt to reorganize management authority and responsibility will be resisted. Many logistical managers can testify that attempts at rapid reorganization are often met with rivalry and mistrust—not to mention accusations of empire building. The nature of organization is that budgets follow operational responsibility. Likewise, power and visibility result from large budgets. Logistical reorganization, therefore, has and will continue to be evolutionary in all but a few exceptional situations and needs to be preceded by substantial overall management education.

Unified organization is not a prerequisite to improved logistical efficiency. Likewise, it is not a guarantee that performance will automatically become more efficient and/or effective. The first condition that must exist within an enterprise is awareness that logistical performance can be improved through integrated effort. To unequivocally state that integrated organization is essential to total logistical cooperation erroneously places emphasis on structure rather than results.

Type I Organization

An organization with any degree of formal unification will emerge only after the basic concept and potential of logistics are accepted by management. The

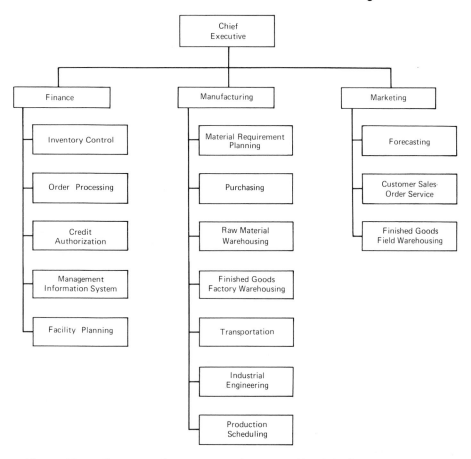

Figure 10–1   Traditional Organizational Structure of Logistically Related Functions

typical evolutionary pattern is for two or more logistics functions to be grouped organizationally without significant change in positioning within the hierarchy. This grouping may occur initially at the staff or line level of organization. Seldom will units engaged in purchasing and physical distribution be joined during this initial organizational development state. Finally, the initial logistical structure will seldom make organizational provisions to include direct management of manufacturing support.

Figure 10–1 illustrates a traditional organizational structure with dispersed logistical functions. *Only those functions typically involved in logistical operations are highlighted by the hypothetical organization chart.* In proceeding with the discussion of organization, it will be interesting to note that several activities that will be introduced as the comprehensive logistical organization evolves do not exist in the traditional organization structure displayed in Figure 10–1.

Figure 10–2 illustrates the form of unified organization likely to emerge initially. Although completely separated, physical distribution and materials management are identified as areas of functional control, and selected activities are grouped under these new control centers.

The critical point is that as recognition of integrated logistics develops within an enterprise, one or two clusters of unified operations can be expected to

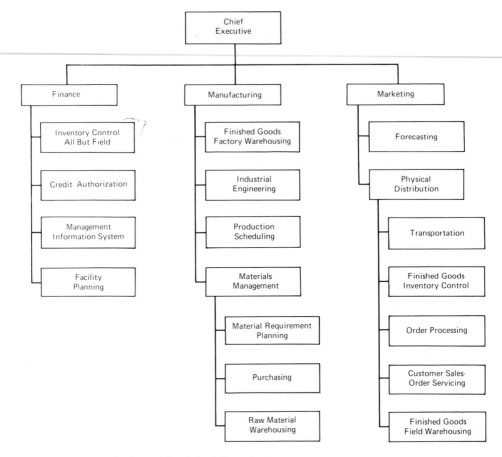

Figure 10–2 Type I Logistical Organization

emerge. In the marketing area, the cluster will typically center around customer servicing. In the manufacturing area, concentration can be expected in the materials or parts procurement areas. However, with few exceptions, most traditional functional departments will not be repositioned, nor will the hierarchy level of the newly created organization be altered significantly. For the most part, Type I organizational change involves grouping functions within the traditional areas of marketing and manufacturing. The notable deficiency of a Type I organization is the lack of direct responsibility for inventory control. For example, initial physical distribution organizations typically control warehousing, transportation, and order processing. Few Type I organizations have the direct responsibility to manage trade-offs between transportation and inventory.

Type II Organization

As the overall enterprise gains operational experience with unified logistics and the cost benefit of the approach is proved, a second stage of organization evolution may occur. Figure 10–3 illustrates a Type II organization posture.

The significant feature of the second stage of development is that some portion of the logistical area is singled out and elevated to a position of higher

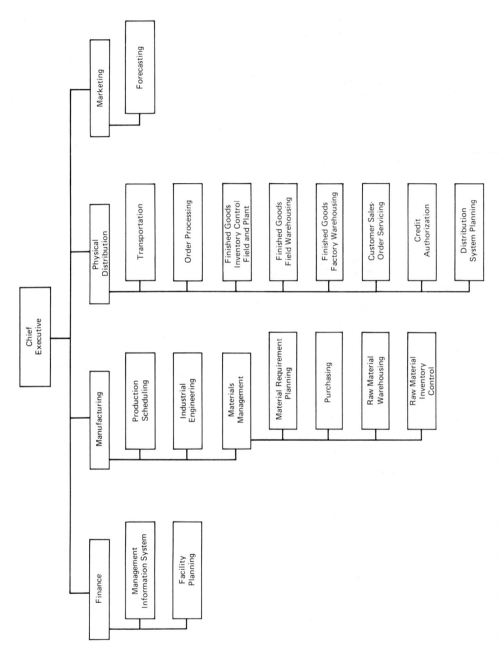

Figure 10-3 Type II Logistical Organization

organizational authority and responsibility. A likely candidate for initial independent status is physical distribution if improved customer service is conspicuous in overall enterprise performance. Typical of this enterprise type is the grocery manufacturing business. In industrial manufacturing and processing industries, materials management often increases in operational authority and responsibility as the integrated concept matures. Thus, the focal group elevated to a position of higher organizational prominence will depend, to a significant degree, upon the nature of the enterprise's primary business. The example in Figure 10–3 illustrates a situation wherein physical distribution has been restructured.

In order to structure a Type II organization, it is necessary to reallocate functions and to position the newly created organization at a higher level within the overall enterprise structure. In the Type II organization, note that the concept of fully integrated logistics is subordinated to the separate focus on physical distribution and materials management. This failure to synthesize logistical management into an integrated system is due in part to a preoccupation with specific tasks, such as order processing and purchasing, which are essential to continued operations. A second limiting factor to total unification is the lack of a fully operational logistical information system at this stage of development. A significant point about Type II organizations is that physical distribution and/or materials management begin to gain respectability among financial, manufacturing, and marketing counterparts. These other corporate offices begin to look to physical distribution and materials management as more than purely a reactive effort aimed at cost reduction or containment. In the Type II organization, it is common for physical distribution and purchasing operations to become proactive in business strategies as contrasted to reacting.

An equally important point is that Type II organizations create officer-level executives who have a voice in top management circles. These officers typically are vice presidents and are not exclusively concerned with cost reduction or containment. Their focus is on profit contribution, return-on-investment, asset deployment, and overall logistical efficiency.

Type III Organization

The third type of organization includes unification of all logistical functions and operations under a single management structure. Under Type III organization, the concept of logistical management as articulated throughout this book emerges as a fully integrated unit. Type III organizations with the comprehensive nature illustrated in Figure 10–4 remain rare. However, the trend in organization grouping is clearly toward the unification of as many logistical planning and operational functions as practical under single authority and responsibility. The goal of a Type III organization is the strategic management of all materials and finished-product movement and storage to the maximum benefit of the enterprise.

The rapid development of logistical information systems provided an impetus for Type III organizations. Information technology is currently available to plan and operate systems that fully integrate logistical operations. Several features of the Type III organization are noteworthy. The structure illustrated in Figure 10–4 is discussed by specific organizational units.

First, each aspect of overall logistical operation—purchasing, manufacturing support, and physical distribution—are structured as a separate line operation.

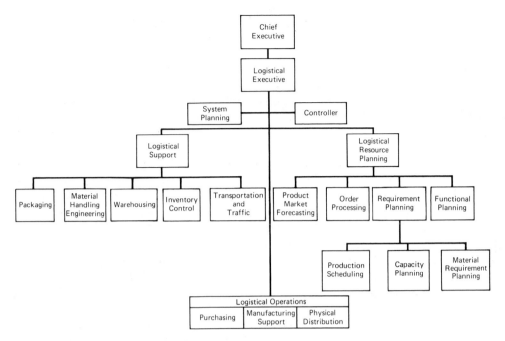

Figure 10–4 Type III Logistical Organization

The lines of authority and responsibility are direct for each major task to be performed within the logistical effort. Because of the well-defined areas of operational responsibility, it is possible to establish manufacturing support as an operational unit similar to purchasing and physical distribution. Each of the three units is operationally self-sufficient. Therefore, each is able to maintain the flexibility necessary to accommodate the peculiar nature of movement and storage within their respective operational areas. In addition, since all logistical activities are planned and coordinated on an integrated basis, joint opportunities between operational areas can be exploited.

Second, five functional areas are represented as logistical services. This operational unit facilitates integration of the logistical system. Care has been taken not to describe logistical services as a staff organization. Rather, the group is involved in day-to-day functional management with matrix accountability and direct liaison with physical distribution, manufacturing support, and purchasing.

Third, logistical resource planning embraces the full potential of management information systems to plan and coordinate operations. Order processing triggers the logistical system into operation and generates the integrated data base for controlling all phases of the operation. The logistical resource planning group is responsible for functional planning. The functional plans must be coordinated with forecasting, order processing, inventory status, and planned requirements to determine the statement of distribution requirements (SDR) applicable for any planning period. Based on the SDR, the requirements planning unit operationalizes manufacturing by performing master production scheduling, materials requirement planning, and capacity requirements planning. The organizational structure is based upon the data flow outlined in Chapter 1 and Chapter 2 (see Figure 2–6, Logistical Resource Planning Process).[1]

---

[1] Chapter 1 develops this concept of data and information; see pages 28–30. Chapter 2 discusses the planning process; see pages 46–53.

Finally, system planning and controllership exist at the highest level of the Type III organization. These two groups represent staff service for the integrated organization. The systems planning group is concerned with long-range strategic planning and is responsible for logistical system design studies and redesign recommendations.

The logistical controller measures performance of the logistical operation and provides data for managerial decision-making. The development of a program for logistical controllership is one of the most critical areas of integrated logistical administration. The task is extremely important because of the large operating and capital dollar expenditures involved in logistics. It is complicated by several barriers to effective costing which are inherent in accepted accounting principles and financial reporting. To develop effective logistical cost control, it is necessary to isolate functional accounts and to reconcile the impact of time upon operational expenditures. The key tool of logistical cost control is the combination of operating and capital budgets that regulate cash flow within the logistical sector. Of equal importance is the measurement of operational effectiveness in terms of customer service performance.[2]

It now appears that the Type III organization will be the dominant organization form of the future. It is important to realize that the concepts of physical distribution and materials management were useful during early stages of development. Both approaches offer a satisfactory organizational solution to specific operational problems. However, they are less than optimal because they offer partial solutions to total logistical control.

The logistics management concept offers a single logic to guide the efficient application of financial and human resources from material sourcing and purchasing into a multifacility manufacturing and assembly operations and then directing finished products through multiple channels of distribution to customers. Logistical management embraces a single system to manage trade-offs between purchasing, manufacturing support, and physical distribution.

It is clear that the future business environment will require more exacting performance. A Type III organization coordinates purchasing, manufacturing support, and physical distribution under single management guidance. This organizational logic permits maximum coordination of all trade-offs under a single top-level executive. Despite the ever-present uncertainties, significant productivity improvements appear obtainable if organizations are willing to seek new and innovative solutions to the problems and opportunities of tomorrow. Perhaps the single most distinguishing feature of the future is that top management has been conditioned to expect increasingly better performance from logistical management.

EMPIRICAL RESEARCH CONCERNING EVOLVING LOGISTICAL ORGANIZATIONS

The preceding discussion of organizational development was compiled based upon information reported in the literature and from review of individual company organization charts. Limited empirical research has been completed

---

[2] Chapter 9 reviews this in terms of policy; see pages 295–300. Chapter 11 presents a discussion of organizational effectiveness measures; see pages 328–32.

regarding overall patterns of logistical organization evolution. In this section, two major research studies are reported. Both confirm that the process of organization change is evolutionary and that the pattern is moving toward Type III structures.[3]

Ohio State University Research

In each of the past twelve years, Professor La Londe of The Ohio State University has conducted a survey of career patterns among United States logistics executives.[4] This research has sought to answer basic questions regarding background, training, work experience, and demographic characteristics of logistics executives. In addition, the research has quantified attitudes and opinions on critical issues related to organizational development.

Of particular interest are trends in responsibility, organization, and reportability from 1980 through 1984. Tables 10–1, 10–2, and 10–3 summarize results and describe trends over the five-year period.

A summary of results over the twelve-year study period identify several prominent changes which have occurred:[5] (1) a shift from staff to line or a combination of staff and line, (2) an upward repositioning of the chief logistical executive with more vice presidents and directors, (3) responsibility broadened to include more functional activities, (4) a shift in "outer directed" focus with a significantly larger share of time interacting with the marketing, production, finance, and data processing, (5) concerns shifting from activity-based areas to

---

[3] For a research study that indicates the integrated logistics system concept is not receiving greater acceptance, see Craig M. Gustin, "A Re-Examination of the Integrated Distribution Concept," *Journal of Business Logistics*, Vol. 5 (March 1984), pp. 1–15.

[4] Bernard J. La Londe, et al., "Distribution Careers," (Chicago, Ill.: Annual Proceedings of the National Council of Physical Distribution Management, 1972–1984).

[5] Adapted from Bernard J. La Londe and Larry W. Emmelhainz, "Distribution Careers: 1984" (Chicago, Ill.: Proceedings of the National Council of Physical Distribution Management, 1984), pp. 1–20.

TABLE 10–1 Organizational Responsibility

	1980	1981	1982	1983	1984
Line and staff	81%	77%	79.6%	76%	72.5%
Staff	8	8	5.6	7.6	7.0
Line	11	15	14.8	16.4	19.5

TABLE 10–2 Corporate Organization

	1980	1981	1982	1983	1984
Divisional	20%	20%	23.9%	20%	29.8
Centralized	26	17	22.5	20.6	19.0
Combined divisional and centralized	38	45	34.5	40	30.7
Distribution division	14	16	14.8	17.6	20.4
Other	2	2	4.2	1.8	5.1

TABLE 10–3 Reporting Relationships of Logistics Executives

Title	1980	1981	1982	1983	1984
Vice president reporting to					
Functional	28%	30%	41%	20.6%	14.7%
Senior (groups)	36	27	22	26.5	46.3
President	36	43	37	52.9	39.0
Directors reporting to					
Other directors	8	6	10	11.0	14.0
Vice presidents	80	71	76	75.6	65.1
Senior (group)					
vice presidents	7	11	7	6.1	2.3
President	5	12	7	7.3	18.6
Managers reporting to					
Other managers	13	4	10	7.3	7.1
Directors	27	33	50	58.2	25.0
Vice presidents	58	63	37	27.2	60.7
Presidents	2	0	3	7.3	10.0

broader economic and technological issues, and (6) steadily increasing recognition of a more "scientific" approach to logistics. The importance of basic analytical tools to solve problems has been recognized.

The Ohio State University research supports the hypothesis that the process of organization change is evoluntary. The decade of the 1970s witnessed some significant changes among United States corporations. A clear trend toward the Type III organization can be identified over the research period. The pace of organizational change has accelerated in the past few years and is predicted to continue to accelerate in the future.[6].

Kearney and Traffic Management Research

A research study conducted by Kearney Management Consultants and Traffic Management support the hypothesis that a massive realignment of management responsibilities is taking place among United State business firms.[7] This study, reported in 1981, concluded that companies are discovering that integrating management of the logistics process can produce favorable financial results. This conclusion is drawn from research into the manner in which companies have organized logistics from 1973 to 1980.
The key conclusions of the research were:[8]

1. An increasing number of companies are bringing an expanding group of logistics activities under centralized line planning and control.

[6] Bernard J. La Londe et al., op. cit.

[7] A. T. Kearney, "Organizing Physical Distribution to Improve Bottom Line Results" (Chicago, Ill.: Proceedings of the National Council of Physical Distribution Management, 1981), pp. 1–14; and A. T. Kearney, "Measuring and Improving Productivity in Physical Distribution" (Chicago, Ill.: National Council of Physical Distribution Management, 1984), Sections I and II.

[8] A. T. Kearney, 1981, op. cit., p. 2.

TABLE 10–4   Evolution of Logistics Organization

Trans.

Stage I

Management views its mission as controlling finished goods, transportation, and warehousing.
Primary orientation is operational.

*Phys.
structure*

Stage II

Management's mission is to integrate finished-goods distribution and control inbound transportation. Managers seek out opportunities to increase productivity by balancing trade-offs between all functions of physical distribution.

planning

Stage III

Management's mission is to integrate the total logistics process—combining physical distribution and materials management.
Orientation is strategic as well as operational.

---

2. The senior distribution/logistics executive is being elevated to corporate officer status, on a par with senior executives in marketing, sales, manufacturing, and finance.

3. There is a common pattern of organizational change involving three distinct stages of management development and reorientation.

4. Successful companies produce superior financial results by managing the process of change.

The research concluded that many companies by 1980 had not organized logistics as an integrated process. However, an increasing number of progressive companies were evolving such organizations. The study identified three evolutionary stages similar to the types described earlier in this chapter.[9] Table 10–4 summarizes the definition used in the research.

The research concluded that companies that have integrated logistical management to the level of Type I realized an additional contribution to pretax profits of 2.6 points in comparison to firms who had not responded organizationally to changing logistical pressures. Those firms that have extended integration to include the entire logistics process (Type III) show a total additional contribution to profits of 3.4 points over the less-integrated firms. The Type III firms also reported: (1) increased sales through improved customer service, (2) improved productivity of the resources devoted to logistics, (3) improved operating results from manufacturing and marketing, and (4) improved balance sheet strength as a result of reduced inventories, reduced accounts receivable, and increased cash flow.

The research supports the hypothesis that organization change is evolutionary and is accelerating. The research reported some significant trends from 1973 to 1980. During the period 92 per cent of respondent companies increased functions included in the distribution/logistical organization. The number of companies having at least Stage I responsibilities doubled over the period. Approximately 16 per cent of the companies with a line physical distribution organization in 1973 developed integrated Stage III logistics organizations by 1980. As organizations moved through the three stages, executive stature

---

[9] One notable difference between the authors' types and the A. T. Kearney stages is that the authors include manufacturing support in the statement of the mission.

increased. In 1980 a full 44 per cent of the senior logistics executives running Stage III organizations had the title vice president. Perhaps the most important conclusion was that over the eight-year period organization changes occurred at an accelerating rate. The 1980 study was updated in 1985. Preliminary results indicated that all trends reported in the earlier study had continued to materialize between 1980 and 1985.

EVOLUTIONARY CHANGE PROCESS

Throughout this chapter the point has been repeatedly made that organizational development is an evolutionary process. There are numerous concepts and theories regarding the actual change process.[10] The adaptive change theory correlates the rate of evolution to a firm's interaction with its environment. If a firm is experiencing rapid technological, market, competitive, and/or regulatory change, then it is expected to make organizational adjustments to accommodate such change.[11]

Figure 10–5 illustrates the process of change as concluded by the Kearney—Traffic Management research.[12] The study found that companies in the early stage of integration utilize information systems to focus on short-term operational needs to run the day-to-day business. Systems typical of Type I organizations were determined to be narrow in scope, seldom covering more than individual functions. Associated measurement and control systems usually were also narrow in focus, concentrating on basic measures such as warehouse costs and labor.

As logistical organization evolves to the Type II organization, planning horizons are extended beyond one year and across multiple functions. The information systems scope also expands to integrate functions such as order entry, order processing, inventory, and warehousing. Logistics managers begin to develop financial goals with budgets and a broader scope of productivity-related goals.

The broadening scope of responsibilities as organizations move toward Type III requires an information system with the total logistics system perspective. The information system must provide the appropriate interface and integration to link manufacturing and marketing with the appropriate logistics activities. The information systems must also support the strategic planning viewpoint as well as the broadened operational scope. The important point made is that

---

[10] See Rensis Likert, *New Patterns in Management* (New York: McGraw-Hill, 1961); Rensis Likert, *The Human Organization: Its Management and Value* (New York: McGraw-Hill, 1967); Bernard J. La Londe, "Strategies for Organizing Physical Distribution," *Transportation and Distribution Management* (January–February 1979), pp. 21–29; T. Burns and G. H. Stalker, *The Management of Innovation* (London: Travistock Publications, 1961); Jay W. Lorsch and Steven Trooboff, "Two Universal Models," in J. W. Lorsch and Paul R. Lawrence, *Organization Planning* (Homewood, Ill., Richard D. Irwin, 1972), pp. 7–16; Joan Coondward, *Industrial Organization: Theory and Practice* (London: Oxford University Press, 1965), Thomas J. Peters and Robert H. Waterman, Jr., *In Search of Excellence* (New York: Harper & Row, 1982); Lynn E. Gill, "Organizing for Effective Physical Distribution Management" (Chicago, Ill.: National Council of Physical Distribution Management Proceedings, 1977), pp. 103–120.

[11] Chapter 2 reviews the factors creating changes that require organizational adjustment; see pages 35–39.

[12] A. T. Kearney, 1981, op. cit., p. 14.

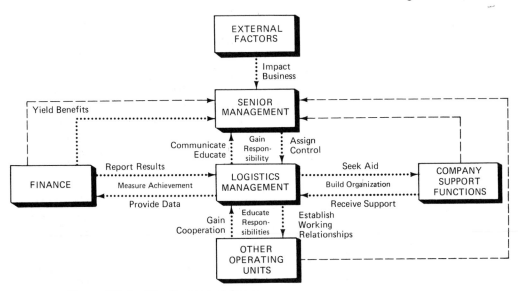

Figure 10–5   The Process of Change

Reprinted with permission from "Organizing Physical Distribution to Improve Bottom Line Results," National Council of Physical Distribution Management Proceedings, 1981, page 14, prepared by A. T. Kearney.

information systems are important in aiding a company in achieving maximum effectiveness at each stage of the organizational evolution.[13]

PERSISTENT ISSUES IN ORGANIZATION

The subject of organization always raises a number of issues. These issues are classified as persistent because they are easy to identify, commonly found, and are difficult to resolve. In this section six such organizational issues are discussed: (1) centralization-decentralization, (2) line and staff, (3) matrix structure, (4) conglomerate structure, (5) organizational positioning, and (6) interorganizational control.

Centralization–Decentralization

The distinction between centralization and decentralization in organization structure is based upon the degree of authority and profit responsibility delegated to specific operating units. Within an enterprise, units or divisions are considered highly decentralized if each is able to function on an autonomous basis. In a fully decentralized organization structure, each division would be responsible for providing its own logistical resource planning and execution.

Until recently, trends in logistical management supported centralized organization. The recent development of distributed processing for logistical

---

[13] Chapter 4 discusses the changes in information emphasis as the logistics organization evolves; see pages 130–33.

information systems no longer requires centralization to provide efficient data processing. The most recent Ohio State University research indicates a market shift toward decentralized logistical organizations.[14] A strong force for centralization is the high cost of logistical facilities and equipment that may be duplicated between divisions. A direct relationship exists between the degree of centralization and the nature of business operations. The conglomerate structure is a special situation that will be discussed later. Within a single business enterprise, a popular form of centralization is the distribution division that operates as a service support group for all individual business units or profit centers. Table 10–2 indicates that the distribution division concept increased during the five-year period from 1980 to 1984. All evidence suggests that integrated logistics can be successfully managed on either a centralized or decentralized basis in today's business environment. This latitude in organizational philosophy is possible as a result of the current state-of-the art capability in management information systems.

The Type III organization arrangement (Figure 10–4) offers a combination centralized and decentralized structure. The direct day-to-day logistical operations related to physical distribution, manufacturing support, and purchasing can be decentralized. The logistics support group could function equally well on a centralized or decentralized basis. The logistics resource planning group would typically be centralized.

Line and Staff

Managers have attempted to reconcile the difference between line and staff responsibilities since the advent of organization. The traditional distinction has been that line performs the operational tasks while staff is concerned with planning. This distinction is no longer valid. Today, all effective managers are involved to a significant extent in both operations and planning. What could be defined as a line function one day may very well be a staff function the next, depending upon the nature and urgency of the task. The impact of management information systems upon logistics has gone a long way to remove the traditional staff-line classification. The two groups are merging into a managerial resource base dedicated to maximum integration of the logistical operating system. For example, in the Type III organization structure the only traditional staff activities identified were system strategic planning and controllership. All other activities were integral to the conduct of routine logistical operations.

Matrix Structure

The dominant organizational structure in logistics is based on functional groupings. Under a functional structure logistical activities such as transportation and warehousing are grouped into clusters and related on direct lines of authority and responsibility. Such functional groupings typically utilize direct-line arrangements to allocate scarce resources to line operations.

As an enterprise begins to expand into multidivisional operations, it becomes difficult to maintain the clear lines of authority and responsibility of a functional organization structure. In a functional structure it is difficult to maintain the

---

[14] Bernard J. La Londe and Larry W. Emmelhainz, op. cit. See this chapter, page 311, Table 10–2.

flexibility required to satisfy unique requirements of each division. One solution to the multidivisional problem is to implement a matrix organization.[15]

In a matrix organization two types of senior managers are utilized. Business managers are responsible for the profitability of specific organizational units. Such units may be based on product line, geographical proximity, or class of business. Resource managers are established who are responsible for the human and physical resources to be assigned across business units.

This matrix form of structuring authority and responsibility is popular in service organizations such as consulting and public accounting. Business or project managers are given full accountability for the deliverables to a client. Such managers are assigned skilled personnel from resource pools for the duration of the assignment. These skilled personnel are directly responsible to a resource manager but are assigned to the business or project manager. The business or project manager has the direct authority for work design, assignment of functional staff, and project control. The business, or project manager usually participates with the resource manager in the recommendation of promotions, salary increases, and other benefits for the skilled personnel. Upon completion of the assignment, skilled personnel are returned to the functional pools for reassignment.

The value of matrix organization structures in logistical operating situations is a subject of considerable interest. The matrix approach typically requires a technical group which can be geographically assigned as necessary to satisfy line-unit requirements. The matrix approach offers a way to spread scarce technical resources on a flexible basis. As such, it reduces the potential duplication of highly skilled personnel across line units. An off-setting factor is that assigned resources may not feel the same commitment to missions that is characteristic of functional organizational arrangements.

The Type III organization structure can make effective use of matrix concepts. The logistics support group represents ideal functional skills to be related to physical distribution, manufacturing support, and purchasing through a matrix reporting structure.

Conglomerate Structure

Many enterprises have developed a conglomerate structure through ownership or control of other enterprises. Unlike typical mergers, the conglomerate approach preserves the organizational integrity of acquisitions. Once conglomerate control is achieved, the typical practice is to permit individual enterprises to continue to operate on an independent basis. Earlier discussion dealt with centralization versus decentralization within a single enterprise structure. The conglomerate issue involves management of several jointly owned enterprises.

A pressing question in strategic planning is whether selected services should be provided for individual enterprises on a consolidated basis. The concept of forming a separate service company to provide integrated logistics for all enterprises within the conglomerate as a profit-making logistics organization is

[15] Daniel W. DeHayes, Jr., and Robert L. Taylor, "Making Logistics Work in a Firm," *Business Horizons*, Vol. 15, No. 3 (June 1972), pp. 43–4; and James P. Falk, "Organizing for Effective Distribution" (Chicago, Ill.: Proceedings of the National Council of Physical Distribution Management, 1980), pp. 181–200.

one such consideration. The rationale is that the potential cost saving from consolidation would reduce each individual enterprise's existing logistical expense and provide sufficient economy of scale to achieve a substantial return on investment for the service company. Many experts feel this type of horizontal service capability may become the Type IV organization of the future.

When one considers that, on a combined basis, several major corporations have annual logistical operating costs in excess of $100 million, the service subsidiary offers productivity-improvement potential. A few initial steps have been taken toward service company development.[16] An interesting paradox is that the service company, focusing on either physical distribution or purchasing, could be of sufficient size to limit operations to either one or the other functions. For example, a maintenance, repair, and operating supply organization (MRO) or a distribution service company might be established to service all divisions of a large conglomerate. The size and operating scope of such organizations in a Fortune 100 corporation could parallel or even dwarf a Type III organization structure in a more typical-size enterprise. The full rationalization of the impact of conglomerate structures on logistical organization will be interesting to observe. The potential for productivity improvement is too large to deny the service subsidiary concept.

Organizational Positioning

Organizational unification has the net impact of improving the relative position of senior logistical executives in the overall enterprise structure. Twenty years ago executives with any form of a logistically related title were nearly impossible to locate. Today, vice presidents are common.

The overall logistical function, however, is just beginning to achieve the organization status that places it on an equal footing with marketing, manufacturing, and finance. Although the trend toward integration is undeniable, development of the integrated logistical management concept to the point where it is independent and functionally positioned in top management will be fully realized only over an extended period of time.

Interorganizational Control

In Chapter 2 the need for cooperation between enterprises that form a channel of distribution was discussed in terms of interorganizational dependency. Only through coordination of all functions required for effective logistics can transaction requirements be satisfied fully. Despite the need for cooperation, individual profit objectives and legal constraints create conflict between channel members. One issue of organizational concern is the extent to which one member of a channel of distribution can and should influence operational decisions and practices of other channel members. This extension of an enterprise's operational influence to the direction of other channel members results from an unbalanced power ratio.

[16] For an illustration, see "General Foods Logistics System" (Boston: Intercollegiate Case Clearing House, Harvard University, 1974); and A. D. Harvey, "Clark Distribution Services," *Distribution Management — Volume V of Computers in Manufacturing* (Pennsauken, N. J.: Auerbach Publishers, Inc.), 1985.

The acknowledgment that tactics of persuasion and coercion may be used effectively to further channel group objectives could eventually create a Type V organizational arrangement. Such arrangements could acknowledge the dependency relationship between channel members and lead to the interorganizational institutionalization of the process of functional transfer. Although such formalized interorganizational arrangements are not common today, some experts predict their inevitability in the future. A forerunner of this type of organization entity is the full-service distribution or purchasing organization owned and operated by a third party.[17]

SUMMARY

Logistical organization development is an evolutionary process. Traditionally, responsibility and authority for logistical performance have been fragmented. Definite trends are developing toward unification of logistical functions under a single management. This trend is evolving to the point where logistics is achieving equal stature with manufacturing, marketing, and finance. There is strong evidence to support the conclusion that Type III integration will continue to grow in the future. It is clear that the evolutionary process does not occur automatically. Achievement of integration requires continuous leadership and efforts by progressive managers and organizations. The evolution toward Type III organization can be expected to continue as long as the payoffs are substantial. Although organization is not a substitute for mature management, proper organization can increase the effectiveness of a sound managerial approach. Evidence exists to indicate that advanced Type IV and Type V organizations may develop in the future.

All organizational charts represent a customized approach to structuring the affairs of a specific enterprise. However, all enterprises face some persistent issues when reviewing organizational requirements. Issues related to: (1) centralization-decentralization, (2) line and staff, (3) matrix structure, (4) conglomerate structure, (5) organizational positioning, and (6) interorganizational control were reviewed in the chapter. The next chapter reviews logistics administration.

QUESTIONS

1. Is the organization of all logistical activities into a single management unit essential to the achievement of efficient operations?
2. Why is a Type I organization?

---

[17] For examples, see Donald J. Bowersox, "Showdown in the Magic Pipeline: Call for New Priorities," Presidential Issue, *Handling & Shipping* (Fall 1973), pp. 12–14; (March–April 1973), pp. 123–32; Walter F. Friedman, "Physical Distribution: The Concept of Shared Services," *Harvard Business Review*, Vol. 53 (March–April 1975), pp. 24–36; Richard C. Harris, "The Components of a Fully Integrated Physical Distribution Service," (Chicago, Ill.: Proceedings of the National Council of Physical Distribution Management, 1983), pp. 778–89; and Robert V. Delaney, "Fixing What Is Broken—A Strategy for Diversified Distribution Service Companies," (Chicago, Ill.: Proceedings of the National Council of Physical Distribution Management, 1984), pp. 269–308.

3. Why is it common for physical distribution and materials management to develop as separate entities in a firm? Is this bad?

4. Describe a Type II organization and distinguish it from a Type I organization.

5. What is the major distinguishing difference of a Type III compared with a Type II organization? Describe the role performed by the logistical controller.

6. The research sponsored by NCPDM indicates that many enterprises have not organized the logistics function as an integrated process. Explain whether this suggests that the Types I, II, and III were temporary phenomena?

7. Does the research conducted by The Ohio State University support the hypothesis of enterprises evolving through the three types? Explain by use of the study results.

8. Explain whether the NCPDM and Traffic Management Research Study conducted by A. T. Kearney supports the evolution hypothesis.

9. What are the concepts of Type IV and V organizations? Develop and illustrate each of these organizational types.

10. Among the persistent issues in an organization, why does centralization versus decentralization remain an issue? Explain why the ideas of conglomerate structure and interorganizational control are becoming more complex.

Administration

Organization is the structure by which human resources are aligned in a particular logistical operation. Logistical administration is concerned with allocation of resources and control. Integrated system administration is one of the least-understood areas of logistical management. The lack of clarity stems from the relative newness of integrated logistical systems and related performance measurement techniques.

This chapter is concerned with administration. Administration becomes effective through the establishment of clearly defined goals and continuous review of progress. The first section of this chapter presents management by objectives as a preferred logistics management style. In section two, operational planning is discussed. Section three is devoted to logistical controllership. The final section presents as overview of management information systems that are essential for the planning and control process.

MANAGEMENT BY OBJECTIVES

This section provides a brief overview of the basic concepts of management by objectives. The essential factor in management by objectives (MBO) is the establishment of goals and controls. In MBO the job description is not important. The important features are the individual job accomplishment objectives established for each administrative period. Job objectives are identified as goals. Given a goal or a series of goals, logistical administration then concerns itself with control in order to measure progress toward accomplishment.

The recommended approach to MBO is illustrated in Figure 11–1. The approach is summarized as follows:

1. At the beginning of the planning period, top management establishes overall goals or objectives for the entire organization. These overall objectives are then translated into action plans for every manager in the organization so that each has clear, unambiguous objectives for a particular area of responsibility—objectives in keeping with the overall organizational objectives.

2. Next, an organizational structure consistent with and capable of achieving these objectives must be established. Whereas objectives represent the "end," organization represents the "means" or the vehicle by which objectives will be achieved.

3. Position descriptions that clearly define the responsibilities of each individual in the organizational structure must then be developed.

4. The next phase involves establishing performance standards to guide and direct each individual's activities. These performance standards must be supportive and consistent with functional area and overall corporate objectives.

5. This step involves developing a reward structure that fairly and adequately compensates each individual who achieves the performance standards established for a position.

6. Finally, and perhaps most important, each individual's success or failure in achieving standards of performance *must* be appraised and corrective action taken where necessary. This represents the key to professional management.[1]

Management by objectives depends on the development of a sound operational plan. The approved plan becomes the basis for performance measurement during the operating period. The process of developing an operational plan is time-consuming and tedious. It is complicated by the need to view the total logistical system on an integrated basis. Such integration typically requires information not normally available from standard costing or accounting systems. The next section discusses operational planning.

OPERATIONAL PLANNING

Operational planning is crucial because managerial talent is always in short supply, and this shortage is expected to become even more acute in the future. Therefore, top and middle management cannot afford the luxury of becoming firefighters bogged down in operational problem-solving. One important technique for coordinating the efforts of an organization is the operational plan.

The operational plan for logistical administration is short range. Operations normally are not projected for more than a single fiscal year. The operational plan covers one segment of the overall business strategic plan. Given a strategic plan (long range), operational plans (short range) for physical distribution,

---

[1] Bernard J. La Londe and James F. Robeson, "Corporate Strategy and Organization for Distribution," *Journal of Business Policy* (Spring 1971), p. 55.

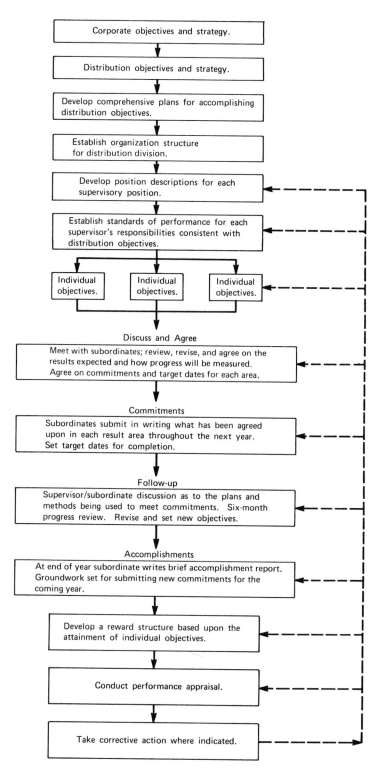

Figure 11–1   Process of Management by Objectives (MBO)

manufacturing support, and purchasing must be developed to direct day-to-day efforts. Long-range strategies represent a set of guideposts within which short-range operational plans detail goals to be accomplished during a specified time period. Such goals typically concern system modifications, performance, and budgeting. Each represents a set of short-term logistical management objectives.

Logistic System Modification Objectives

During any period, several adjustments in system structure may be planned for implementation. For example, an entreprise may have a long-range system strategy calling for consolidation of 25 warehouses into 10 regional distribution centers. The full implementational program may take a number of years and embrace several different operational plans. The initial operating plan may call for a commitment to open two regional facilities and to close a specified number of existing warehouses. Future operational plans may provide for initial occupancy of the two regional distribution warehouses, the commitment to establishing additional regional facilities, and the closing of other specified warehouses. The implementation of a logistical system redesign normally spans a number of years. Thus, consecutive operational plans will involve specific implementation of parts of an overall long-range strategic plan.

Two factors must be clearly understood when facility adjustments are included in operational plans. First, budget allocations must isolate the expense of the initial setup as well as once-and-for-all savings separate from day-to-day operational expenditures. Second, special efforts required to maintain customer service commitments during the period of system readjustment must be programmed adequately. Each of these expenditures is a result of a long-range plan for system redesign. As such, modification expenditures will not prevail between consecutive operational planning periods. Unless such one-time expenditures and interruptions are isolated, the capability for comparative analysis of operational results from one period to the next is substantially diluted.

The operational plan provides for scheduled modifications in logistical system facilities. It allocates resources and specifies managerial responsibility to achieve goals specified in the logistical strategic plan.

Performance Objectives

A significant portion of the operational plan concerns day-to-day operations. Operational performance objectives typically consist of specific goals as well as the schedule of planned activities to reach the goals. For example, during a specific operating period, assume the month of May, a grocery manufacturer may have a marketing objective to introduce two new products and to conduct three promotional activities in a specific marketing area. The physical distribution performance objectives for the operating period prior to May will require an inventory buildup and a degree of advance product movement to support inventory requirements during the promotional period. The goals may call for 100-per-cent availability of the new and promoted inventory items with two-day reorder capability during the first two weeks of the promotion, followed by somewhat less stringent performance during the final two weeks of the marketing effort. The detailed activities planned and the performance schedule to support the new product and promotional activity are typical of performance objectives found in an operational plan.

The development of performance objectives is based upon a combination of forecasts and managerial judgment regarding future marketing requirements. To develop appropriate goals and performance schedules, a great deal of coordination is required between managerial units. For logistical goals to be relevant, they must integrate marketing plans and manufacturing capabilities. Without effective coordination the basic benefits of integrated logistical performance will not materialize. In Chapter 2 the process of logistics resource planning was illustrated as a method of achieving such coordination.[2]

The activity schedules associated with a performance plan typically cover a short time period. While goals may remain the same from one performance period to the next, activity schedules are typically different. Many enterprises plan activities on the basis of calendar months. Others elect to operate on the basis of 13 four-week periods. The typical activity schedule will cover approximately 90 days, with the detail updated in 30-day intervals.

Thus, the performance schedule aspect of the operating plan provides the structure for achieving logistical objectives. It is the short-range "battle plan" which guides the allocation of authorized resources and priority ranks day-to-day activities. As such, the total logistical effort is synchronized through the statement of performance goals and scheduled activities.

Budget Objectives

Given system modification and performance objectives, the next step in the operations planning process is to budget expenditures. A typical procedure requests budgets from individual management units. Thus, line management, given a statement of objectives, is asked to formulate a request for operational funds. The budgets constitute each manager's estimate of resources required to achieve specific objectives. The budget is the key to formulating a logistical cost-control program. Four basic types of budgets are used in logistical controllership: (1) fixed, (2) flexible, (3) zero level, and (4) capital. The first three are used to control direct expenditures for logistical performance. The last is used when adjustment involving any component of the logistical system is scheduled during the operating period.

Fixed-Dollar Budgeting

As the name implies, the fixed budget is an estimate of functional costs by account associated with an anticipated volume of logistical activity. Given a volume projection, the budgeting process arrives at a realistic estimate of costs to be expended for the completion of logistical processing. The budget serves as a base for comparing desired performance in advance of the operational period with actual performance during and after the period. To a significant degree, budgeting is a management process in which top-level and operating executives attempt to arrive at joint estimates of funds required to realize desired

---

[2] See Chapter 2, pages 46–53, for a discussion of logistics resource planning as a method to integrate marketing plans and manufacturing capabilities.

performance. Naturally, top management desires lower budgets, whereas operating executives want to build in as much slack as possible. To overcome such bias in the budgeting process, many management groups structure budgets on a line-item basis. On the line-item basis, only a minimum transfer of expenditures between functional accounts is permitted unless the operating plan is modified.

Flexible Budgeting

The flexible budget is designed to accommodate unexpected variations in volume during the operating period. Normally, the flexible budget is based on standard costs for performing specific logistical functions. Expenditures are permitted to float automatically to the level of actual operations. Although this method is desirable, a high degree of cost sophistication is necessary for effective flexible budgeting.

Zero-Level Budgeting

Zero-level budgeting is used two ways in operational planning. At an operational-line management level a typical budgeting procedure starts with no authorized funds at the inception of the operational plan. Funding is then authorized from *zero up*, requiring justification of funds for each objective. A second type of zero-level budgeting is used in planning staff activities. This budgeting requires that all or a specified range of staff services be allocated back to line operations so that the final staff budget reflects *zero* unjustified expenditures. Both types of zero-level budgeting are attempts to tie operational expenditures to specific tasks, thus improving the base for subsequent managerial review and control.

Capital Budgeting

Capital budgeting controls the extent and timing of logistical investments. As noted earlier, during operational planning a number of logistical system changes may be initiated or completed. The capital budget, for example, commits cash or credit to construct a new warehouse, install a new order-processing system, purchase or lease transportation equipment, or institute any other planned expenditure.

When major system changes are planned, the capital budget formulation is straightforward. The difficulties arise when capital budgeting involves expenditures for research and development. At inception, such expenditures are nearly impossible to justify on a cost-benefit basis.

A creeping commitment can occur when day-to-day operations result in an unplanned capital expenditures. For example, logistical operations may experience unplanned buildups of inventory. If inventory is not rigorously controlled, a substantial unplanned capital commitment may result.

A final note concerns determination of those costs applicable to a particular capital investment decision. The accepted capital budgeting practice is to consider only investments that require new net capital. If system changes can be implemented that result in operational savings without new commitment, they are not subjected to the rigid control of capital budgeting.

Review of individual budget requests is a critical control process in logistical administration. Top management must be concerned with the total performance of the system and not the individual parts. Development of an integrated system provides top management with an estimate of the total dollars required to meet specified system objectives. The planning process becomes one of reconciling individual budget requests with total system resources.

Budget requests of middle managers will often exceed funds required for good performance. This is understandable because no single-unit manager is in a position to view the total system. A tendency also exists to view performance in any area on a unit-cost basis. This bias in unit-cost budgeting often forces uneconomic performance in one area without full evaluation of interrelationships to other areas. A traffic manager concerned with unit cost will tend toward low-cost transport alternatives.

Why are individual managers asked to formulate budget requests if such deficiencies are anticipated? The answer is twofold. First, it is essential that the individual manager participate in budget formation to gain a complete understanding of the integrated nature of total system programming. Budget formation is one of the most potent control and training tools available to top management. Second, individual unit managers are often aware of factors that must be considered in a specific operational plan which have not come to the attention of top management. The greatest danger in total system planning is top-management complacency concerning the continued validity of the long-range implementation strategy. Interaction between middle and top management is essential to the development of a realistic but demanding operational plan.

Final Operating Plan

The final operational plan is a blueprint for short-range performance. This written plan should contain a statement of objectives and detailed cost budgets for each logistical unit. The plan focuses on total system performance and objectives. It is designed to combine all relevant cost centers into a single unified effort. With the plan each operating manager is committed to budget performance on an overall basis, since cost increases or decreases in specific functions are no longer relevant. It is the total cost performance that counts. This concept of total accountability is one of the essential aspects of management by objectives. For the total system to achieve the highest possible performance, all managers must assume correlative responsibility for everyone else's job.

Operating Plan Modification

Once the final plan is developed, printed, and distributed, some aspects will typically require modification. Tactical adjustments to the operational plan will be required throughout the total operating period. Such modification results from planning errors and adjustments to accommodate unanticipated events.

Because individual managers have participated in development of the operational plan, each will be aware of the impact of decisions upon other functional areas. In day-to-day operations, managers may become aware of unanticipated changes that will adversely or favorably affect overall logistical activities. Significant modifications to operational plans are encouraged because superior results are achieved by exploiting timely opportunities. Two rules must be followed in implementing modifications. First, modifications must be formally requested prior to any deviation from plan. Second, all modifications must be evaluated in terms of total system performance. Once proposed modifications are adopted, formal written amendments to the operational plan should be distributed to all involved managers. Attention is now directed to controllership.

LOGISTICAL CONTROLLERSHIP

Increased competition and slower growth have forced industry to concentrate on improved productivity. A measurement/assessment system is essential to the control process. Logistics results compared to planned objectives are the outputs of the measurement system.

Need for Logistics Control

A study conducted for the NCPDM indicated that the most successful companies in achieving productivity improvements tend to have the most sophisticated measurement systems.[3] These successful companies have standards of performance for individual logistical functions and emphasize logistics planning. The report result was from a 14 to 22 per cent productivity gain in functional areas during the study period. The success profile indicated the characteristics listed in Table 11–1.[4]

Overall Measurement

There are at least seven distinct, although not necessarily mutually exclusive, measures of overall organizational performance. They are: (1) effectiveness, (2)

---

[3] For a detailed discussion, see A. T. Kearney, Inc., *Measuring and Improving Productivity in Physical Distribution*, (Oak Brook, Ill.: National Council of Physical Distribution Management, 1984), Sections I and II.

[4] Ibid.

TABLE 11–1   Characteristics of Firms Having Outstanding Logistical Control

1. Process of change is managed with same attention as day-to-day operations.

2. Employ project orientation for change with objectives and measurement of results.

3. Focus on real productivity gains from improved utilization and performance and from change of operational technology rather than simply cost reduction. This requires physical as well as financial measures.

4. Set goals to achieve success through basic programs rather than setting objectives that are too ambitious.

5. Provide good communications throughout organization of successes and persons/groups responsible.

6. Find a sponsor—the key expertise behind the program.

Adapted with permission from *Measuring and Improving Productivity in Physical Distribution*, A National Council of Physical Distribution Management study prepared by A. T. Kearney, 1984, page 9.

efficiency, (3) productivity, (4) quality, (5) quality of work life, (6) profitability, and (7) innovation.

The Productivity Measure

As noted above, productivity is only one measure of performance for an organization . It is not clear that it is the most important, or even necessarily a critical, measure of performance for all systems.

Productivity is a relationship (usually a ratio or an index) between output (goods and/or services) produced and quantities of inputs (resources) utilized by the system to produce that output. Productivity is thus a very simple concept. If a system has clearly measurable outputs and identifiable and measurable inputs that can be matched to outputs, productivity measurement is quite routine. However, if outputs are hard to measure, input resource utilization is hard to match up with outputs for a given period of time, input and output mix or type is constantly changing, data are difficult to obtain or not even available, then productivity measurement can be difficult and frustrating.

Conceptually there are three basic types of productivity measures: (1) static, (2) dynamic, and (3) surrogate. If all of the output and all of the input from a given system are included in the equation, it would be a total factor static productivity ratio. Ratio is considered static because it is based on one measurement.

The dynamic measure is completed across time. If outputs and inputs for a system compare static productivity ratios from one period to another, the result is a dynamic productivity index. An example of a dynamic productivity index is:

$$\frac{\text{Outputs 1984/Inputs 1984}}{\text{Outputs 1978/Inputs 1978}}$$

A third measure which does not adhere strictly to the common definition of the term is called a surrogate productivity measure. A surrogate productivity measure represents factors that are not typically included in the concept of productivity, but are highly correlated with productivity (customer satisfaction, profits, effectiveness, quality, efficiency, and so forth). Most managers operationalize productivity in this manner.

Performance Measurement Pitfalls

Substantial effort has been made to provide logistical managers with general decision-making information and techniques through computer-based systems. However, methods that help to measure, compare, and guide physical distribution performance have not received comparable attention. Old report formats need to be redesigned, and new, flexible, ad hoc reporting methods need to be added. In this part, five characteristics of an ideal control system are reviewed.[5]

[5] Ronald H. Ballou and Omar K. Helferich, "Measuring Physical Distribution Performance," Article No. 4.2.1 in *Distribution Management*—Vol. IV of *Computers in Manufacturing*, (Pennsauken, N. J.: Auerbach Publishers, Inc., 1983), pp. 1–2.

Dynamic Reporting

Variance reports are used widely to show change against previous period results, yet they do not give a dynamic picture of performance over an extended period of time. This lack of information limits the manager's ability to detect adverse trends before they are significantly out of control. In general, reports simply give the status of activity costs or asset levels, such as current period transport costs, warehouse costs, or current inventory stock levels. These type of reports are essentially static in nature.

Cost and Service Orientation

Because of the difficulty of obtaining the necessary data and accurately portraying the impact of customer service on revenue, a majority of reports show only logistical costs. They do not reflect cost-service trade-offs that are so important to include in revenue potential.

Productivity Orientation

Few reports adequately compare output performance with input requirements. Most show absolute levels of either output or input rather than a relationship between the two. Combination reporting would help to identify whether resources are being used in an efficient and effective manner and whether inputs are remaining at reasonable levels relative to outputs. One such input-output productivity measure is the inventory turnover ratio. More reports should be developed to measure logistical productivity relationships.

Cost-Trade-Off Reporting

The cost trade-off is a key concept on which integrated logistical management is built, yet few reports provide comparative information that encourages trade-off analysis among activities that are in cost conflict. For example, one report might combine both inventory and transportation costs, the two major costs in most logistical systems, without identifying the costs individually to permit trade-off analyses.

Management-Oriented Systems

Reporting systems should assist management in isolating areas of opportunity. Exception reporting and variance reporting provide this to a limited degree. Standard accounting practice frequently carries certain limitations on the reporting needed for decision-making purposes. For example, inventory carrying and inbound raw-material transportation costs are typically not reported. This can be a serious limitation to a logistics control system.

An important relationship exists between these shortcomings in logistics control and the inability to achieve needed productivity improvements. *First*, without a productivity measurement system, management lacks insight into the logistics process. *Second*, lack of ability (or desire) to communicate productivity measures undermines labor, supervision, and management motivation. The measurement system can be viewed as the control mechanism in the management of logistics. The logistics processes results compared against goals or standards are the outputs of the measurement system. Productivity improvements are achieved through making decisions and adjusting the process.

Performance Measurement

The operational plan provides the measurement base for overall control of logistical operations. The measurement system assures that resources are assigned and monitored to achieve managerial objectives.

Logistical performance should always be measured relative to the operational plan. Without an operational plan, measuring performance is difficult, if not impossible. In the retail field, Christmas toys might be purchased in early spring to realize special discounts and allowances. From a measurement perspective, such practices, although justified on a total-cost basis, may result in significant temporary increases in logistical costs far in advance of the normal season. These cost expenditures, when viewed in terms of the operational plan, cause little more than advanced planning for cash flow. Without the benefit of an operational plan, early expenditure for advanced distribution of Christmas merchandise could appear as an uncontrolled inventory buildup.

Logistical measurement is management by exception. The comprehensive and detailed nature of logistics requires that management review be limited to deviations from anticipated results. However, few managers are willing to sit back and wait for an exception to appear. The exception is proof that a problem exists. From a management perspective , a mechanism for system monitoring is essential. The assessment and control system exists to reassure management that the total system is tracking along the desired course.[6] A deficiency noted from system monitoring calls for a diagnostic evaluation of causal factors. The appearance of a significant exception means that a trend leading to a major deviation was overlooked during its formative stages.

The following example from inventory management illustrates the relationship between system monitoring and exceptions. Dollars allocated to an open-to-buy program at a given point in a planning period may be nearly depleted. At the same time a critical item may be approaching a reorder point. Placing the requirement order size as indicated by economic-order-quantity formulations could result in a commitment over and above authorized expenditures. One might assume that the individual merchandise controller would bring this situation to management's attention so that appropriate adjustments can be made.

However, if the original open-to-buy program was sufficient to cover needs, the current deficiency is a result of improperly allocated dollars for a past purchase decision by the same controller. Reports to management indicates that the controller needs help to rectify the error. Unfortunately, too few individuals feel free to expose themselves to open management scrutiny. This reticence may cause the controller to gamble that existing stock of the critical item will last until new funds are authorized. A rush order is then planned. In reality, the gamble involves customer service policy since it risks a stockout on a critical item. Given the opportunity for review, management might well choose to add dollars to the open-to-buy program to eliminate the risk of an out-of-stock

---

[6] See Chapter 3, pages 93–98, for a more detailed discussion.

situation. Unless the enterprise has a comprehensive monitoring system, management may never get the chance to express its choice until the out-of-stock situation turns up as an exception to stated policy.

In inventory management, the assessment and control system can signal that a critical item had passed the inventory level of normal reorder without the issue of a purchase order. The inventory control manager would be expected to take appropriate action and request aid from higher management if necessary. The combined procedure of management prevents the monitored trend from becoming a full-scale exception.

This discussion makes it clear that management would rather prevent than correct problems. The assessment and control system exists for this purpose. The performance reporting system exists to signal a breakdown within a segment of the organization that requires corrective action to prevent recurrence.

Levels of Measurement and Information Flow

The nature of measurement requires that several levels of information be developed within the enterprise. As a general rule, the higher the level of management review in the organization, the more selective information and reporting. The following four levels of information are appropriate to logistical measurement: (1) direction, (2) variation, (3) decision, and (4) policy. At each level the information may be related to trend monitoring or exception correction.

Direction

At the level of direction, information flow and measurement are concerned with execution of the operational plan. A stream of transaction documents signals a need, and the action document identifies appropriate steps necessary to meet objectives. For example, an order is received, credit is checked, the order is assigned to a warehouse, and it is picked, packed, and shipped. Upon shipment, the customer is billed in accord with the agreed-upon terms of sale. The order receipt is a transaction document; the remainder of the activities are generated by action documents.

At specified time intervals, all transaction and action documents are combined in a series of status reports. The status reports summarize individual activities in terms of existing capabilities to meet forecasted transaction requirements. For example, total inventory usage may be summarized by each item in the product line, and a comparison made to current inventories. Prompted by status reports, additional action documents may be issued to replenish stock on specific items.

Two important features should be kept in mind concerning information flow and measurement at the direction level. First, information at the direction level is concerned with day-to-day activities of the business on a transaction basis. Information at the direction level is selectively limited to status review in accord with predetermined decision rules. In total, information flow at the direction level is concerned with execution of predetermined programs.

The second feature of information flow at the direction level is accumulation of records to formulate a data bank for all other levels of control. The data base serves to generate all reports concerning effectiveness and efficiency, monitor all trends, and detect exceptions. Although managerial discretion at the direction level is limited, all that follows is based upon the accuracy of information processed and generated from transaction and action documents.

Variation

The variation level of measurement is concerned with accumulation of information regarding deviations from plan. As indicated earlier, variation measurement ideally results in interpretation of trends that could develop trouble. However, the variation may first appear as an exception to the desired level of performance at the direction level.

Managerial discretion concerning resource allocation initially occurs at the variation level. First, the manager must ascertain if the situation discovered is an isolated event or if it is symptomatic of a more serious problem. Second, the manager must determine if a solution to the problem is within the scope of delegated authority or if it will require additional resources. Depending on the manager's interpretation of these two questions, either corrective instructions will be issued to the direction level of operations, or assistance will be requested from the decision level.

It is important to realize that the scope of information reviewed at the variation level is considerably reduced in comparison to the direction level. Management at the variation level is concerned with the broader issues of effectiveness and efficiency related to a series of transactions.

Decision

Measurement at the decision level concerns operation plan modifications. Situations which have materialized at the direction and variation levels require a reappraisal of the original operational plan. As one would expect, the assortment of information presented at the decision level will be very selective. It is significant to note that the decision level is the initial measurement level at which a formal change in the operational plan is considered.

Modifications normally will require allocation of additional resources. The range of decisions will never involve a modification of system objectives. In other words, at the decision level customer service standards will not be changed if performance has been deficient. Rather additional expenditures will be authorized as required to meet system objectives. Managerial activities at the decision level must be evaluated in terms of total system consequences. As noted earlier, decisions that modify the plan must be relayed to all managers involved in total system performance.

Policy

Measurement at the policy level involves a basic change in objectives. Once again, the areas of system design and administration merge when questions of policy are confronted. The arena of concern becomes enterprise wide in scope and includes all members of management. The formulation of new policies requires an evaluation of planned system design as well as total cost of achievement. Requests for policy revisions may originate from any point within

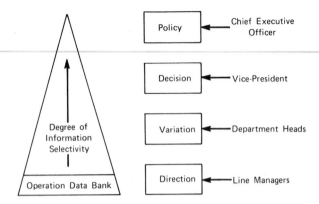

Figure 11-2 Information Flow and Levels of Measurement

the enterprise. Thus far, this discussion has centered around information generated from the logistical data base and from variations in either logistical performance or expenditure plans. However, policy changes may initiate from other areas of management. For instance, the marketing department may desire an overall upgrading of customer service standards.

Figure 11-2 will help clarify the four levels of measurement involved in logistical administration. Adjacent to each level, reference is made to the approximate corresponding organizational rank within an enterprise. On the left side of the chart a data pyramid is developed to reflect the selectivity of information considered at each measurement level. As noted earlier, each level is concerned with system monitoring as well as exception reporting. However, as information flows from the direction level to the policy level, the subject matter decreases in quantity and increases in importance to the welfare of the enterprise.

Performance Reporting

The essential feature of all measurement systems is the quality of reports generated from the management information system. Unless available information can be presented rapidly, accurately, and on relevant subjects, little in the way of positive control will transpire. In general, three types of reports are used in a logistical control system: (1) status, (2) trend, and (3) ad hoc reports. Each type of report is illustrated using inventory control. Similar types of reports are required for all functional areas of a logistical system to assure compliance to operational plan objectives.

Status Reports

As the name implies, a status report provides detailed information about some aspect of the logistical operation. One of the most common is the stock status report. The stock status report is used to keep track of multiple-item inventories at more than one stocking location. The amount of information contained in an individual report will depend upon the firm, its degree of inventory management sophistication, and the extent to which data processing is used.

In Table 11-2, inventory items are controlled from one central management location for distribution warehouses located in Detroit, Chicago, Atlanta,

TABLE 11-2 Example of a Stock Status Report

ABC Company Distribution
Warehouse Stock Status Report

Date 3-10-85
Controller A

| (1) | (2) | (3) | (4) Unit Inventory | (5) Unit Inventory | (6) Forecasted | (7) | (8) Suggested | (9) Dollars | (10) Inventory | (11) Open Purchase Order Detail | (12) | (13) |
			on Hand	on Order	Average Weekly Use	Back Order	Order Quantity	on Hand	on Order	Date Placed	Date Due	Quantity
10-326-01	Detroit	Normal	183		25			457.50				
	Chicago	Out of stock		365	40	45		0	912.50	2-15-85	2-26-85	365
	Atlanta	Expedite	29	145	15			72.50	462.50	3-1 -85	3-12-85	145
	Newark	Overstock	293		30			732.50				
	Los Angeles	Order	55		10		75	137.50				
	Dallas	Normal	103		23			257.50				
Total			663	510	143	45	75	1,657.50	1,375.00			530
10-327-05	Detroit	Normal										
	Chicago	Normal										
	Atlanta	Overstock										
	Newark	Order										
	Los Angeles	Order										
	Dallas	Order										
Total												
10-365-00	Detroit	Normal										
	Chicago	Expedite										
	Atlanta	Out of stock										
	Newark	Out of stock										
	Los Angeles	Expedite										
	Dallas	Expedite										
Total												

Newark, Los Angeles, and Dallas. The unit inventory is maintained on a central computer linked to the warehouses on a real-time basis. Individual items have been assigned to stock controllers, who are responsible for inventory status at all six distribution warehouses. This particular report is for a controller referred to as A.

The individual item or unit number is printed in column 1. These item numbers do not appear in numerical sequence since only items requiring attention are printed. However, if an item requires action at a specific distribution warehouse, status of that item in all other warehouses is printed on the report. Thus, when an inventory controller plans specific action concerning an item, the status at all stocking locations can be reviewed. The location is displayed in column 2, and status is reflected in column 3. Of particular interest is the required action printed in the status column 3. Based upon the rules of the inventory control system, the controller is informed of the reason the particular item appears on the stock status report. The remainder of the columns are self-explanatory. They provide the necessary information for the controller to direct the inventory procurement program.

Status reports can be developed for all logistical activity centers. Some relate to individual unit or transaction control; others are financial in nature. The purpose of the status report is to provide line managers with relevant information to fulfill their responsibility in the overall logistical system.

Trend Reports

Trend reports are used by administrators at levels of control higher than the line manager. In keeping with the flow of data outlined in Figure 11-2, trend reports are more selective in content than status reports. To illustrate, Tables 11-3 and 11-4 provide examples of trend reports that might be based upon the inventory stock status report.

Table 11-3 provides an inventory recap for all items, controllers, and stock locations. A report of this type is used by department heads to review the overall inventory situation. The data contained in the daily inventory summary are developed as a by-product of the stock status report printed for inventory controllers. Thus, management possesses a quick recap of the total system and can evaluate overall performance.

Table 11-3 provides a variety of information. General performance is available on all locations as well as individual controllers. For example, the Newark warehouse is 75 per cent in stock (column 1), 21 per cent of the items have been out of stock longer than five days (column 10), and 92 per cent of the orders scheduled for shipment were shipped as planned (column 12). The report also indicates that controller C is having problems. This person is in stock on only 82 per cent of the items (column 7), 15 per cent of the assigned items in stock currently require expedite efforts to prevent future stockouts (column 8), and the items out of stock fall heavily into the critical area of classified merchandise (column 9).

Armed with this information, the department head is in a position to review activities and take corrective action. If desired, ad hoc reports can be requested that will provide further detail to help analyze a possible trend. For example, the department head in this case would probably desire detailed information concerning the Newark facility and the activities of controller C. There is no end

TABLE 11-3 Daily Inventory Summary

	(1)	(2)	(3)	(4)	(5)
				Dollar Values Inventory	
Location	Total Items Stocked	Per Cent in stock	In Stock	On Order	Forecasted
Detroit	1,075	92	17,385	3,231	7,115
Chicago	1,093	91	20,265	3,695	5,940
Atlanta	1,041	88	15,197	3,780	8,201
Newark	1,073	75	18,243	9,361	11,116
Los Angeles	1,075	89	23,116	5,143	4,307
Dallas	1,026	90	19,450	2,184	1,993
Total system	6,383	87.5	$113,656	$27,394	$38,672

	(6)	(7)	(8)	(9)		
		Per Cent	Per Cent	Out of Stock by Class		
Controller	Total Items	in Stock	Expedite	A	B	C
A	1,250	91	10	30	40	50
B	1,300	89	9	36	71	38
C	1,100	82	15	65	47	91
D	1,275	85	9	15	81	95
E	1,458	95	8	20	70	40
Total	6,383	87.5	10	166	309	314

	(10)	(11)	(12)
			Per Cent
	Items	Items	Orders Shipped
Location	Out of Stock + 5 days	Overstocked	on Schedule
Detroit	12	31	96
Chicago	16	11	97
Atlanta	11	38	99
Newark	21	5	92
Los Angeles	14	17	87
Dallas	19	0	94
Total	93	120	96

to the selective information that can be generated from a date base of the type maintained to develop Tables 11–2 and 11–3.

Table 11–4 provides an executive summary of selected critical facts regarding inventory performance. Condensed information of this type would most often be used by executives at the vice-presidential or decision level of an operation (see Figure 11–2). As noted earlier, an executive who is content to wait for exceptions to appear is rare. Most executives would prefer to see the trend of performance in their areas of responsibility.

Table 11–4 covers a four-week period. The first three weeks are presented in aggregate, and the fourth week is developed on a daily basis. Reports of this nature provide the basis for trend evaluation and are useful in selecting areas for diagnostic analysis. For example, the data in Table 11–4 point out that although inventory performance over the past three weeks had deteriorated

TABLE 11–4   Logistical Performance Recap

Performance Area	Week C3	Week C2	Week C1	Current Week by Days				
				1	2	3	4	5
1. System in stock (%)	88.0	86.0	81.0	82.0	85.0	86.2	87.3	87.5
2. Weighted performance (%)	83.8	84.2	90.0	79.8	83.2	84.0	86.3	87.0
3. Dollars inventory	121,614	119,381	111,843	95,417	98,106	96,412	110,807	113,706
4. Shipments on schedule (%)	99	97	98	99	96	97	98	96
5. Back-orders	365	691	780	193	217	238	165	101
6. Selected data								
7. Other system								
8. Activity centers								

performance on the most recent days indicate that corrective action has been taken. Of particular interest in Table 11–4 is line 2, weighted performance. The weighted performance is a measure of stock availability in the quantities desired by customers. A system may enjoy a very high level of in-stock items but be out of stock on the items most wanted by customers. Measures of weighted performance generally run lower than measures of system in stock.

The data presented in Table 11–4 contain inventory trend information generated from the inventory stock status report (Table 11–2) and the daily inventory summary (Table 11–3). In all probability the executive receiving the performance recap would be responsible for additional logistical system activity centers. The report could be expanded to include data on transportation, warehouse performance, order processing, material movement, or any other desired areas. In addition, similar reports can be generated in materials management and inventory transfer operations. Because the information is selective and highly condensed, these reports can often be confined to a single page.

Ad Hoc Reports

Ad hoc reports may be created at any level of logistical administration and for a variety of reasons. Most often, ad hoc reports are developed to provide detail on specific areas of performance. Three types of ad hoc reports are common in administration.

The first type is a diagnostic report, which provides detail on a specific phase of operations. For example, a report might be requested to provide greater detail on current back-orders and subsequent corrective action. If the firm operates a real-time order-processing system, special diagnostic reports may be obtained in either hard or soft copy by direct interrogation.

The second type of ad hoc report is a position paper. Given a current or anticipated problem, a report outlining alternative courses of action and probable consequences is often desirable. In terms of control levels (see Figure 11–2), position papers are usually developed by line managers and department heads for use by executives at the decision level of the organization. These position papers will often request additional resources. If the request is approved, the operational plan will have to be modified. In accord with the levels of administrative control, position papers and related actions may involve a greater allocation of resources, but they will not involve changes in performance objectives.

The final ad hoc report is concerned with policy modification. Earlier in this chapter an example of a policy report was discussed when the marketing department requested that customer service objectives be substantially upgraded. Policy reports always are directed to or initiate from the chief executive officer of a firm. Their content almost always involves areas of activity beyond logistics.

The content of control reports is highly customized to the individual enterprise, its organization, and management information system sophistication. The content of reports should be geared to levels of administrative control: the higher the level of control, the more selective the nature of information contained in the report.

For the most part, status reports are used by line managers to direct logistical activities in accord with predetermined operational plans. Trend reports to monitor progress are highly condensed and are used by executives at the variation and decision levels. The higher the control level, the more condensed and selective the trend report. Trend reports prepared at the decision level should contain information related to all aspects of an integrated logistical system. Ad hoc reports contain selected information on certain units of the system. From the control center, interrogation of status and performance of individual units located at any geographic point may be initiated. Performance with respect to the operating plan can be evaluated to permit rapid and efficient management response to any externally or internally generated change.

MANAGEMENT INFORMATION SYSTEMS

The critical need for flexibility and productivity is responsible for the rapidly growing interest in logistical management information systems (MIS).[7] Figure 11–3 illustrates the traditional management information system pyramid. The success or failure of the logistics organization in the late 1980s and beyond will depend on how effectively information resources are utilized.

Perspectives on MIS

There are many approaches to the classification of management information systems. A Sloan School study classified MIS systems into four managerial categories: (1) routine systems that *monitor* daily transactions and provide

[7] Wendell M. Stewart, "Organization and Information—Keys to Effective Logistics Management in the 1980's," (San Francisco, Calif.: International Logistics Congress, 1981), pp. 25–8.

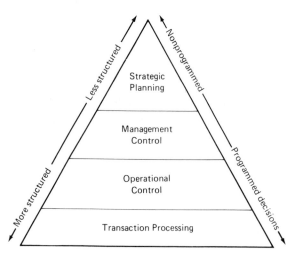

Figure 11–3 The MIS Pyramid

Types of Logistics Information Systems	TYPE of Logistics Organizational Integration		
	TYPE 1	TYPE 2	TYPE 3
Planning systems	Low to moderate	Moderate	High
Budgeting measurement, and control systems	Moderate	High	High
Operational management systems	High	High	High
Transaction processing systems	High	High	High

Figure 11–4   The Relative Importance of Logistics Information Systems to Logistics Organizational Integration

Adapted and reprinted with permission from Wendall Stewart, *Planning the Logistical Organization—An Evolutionary Approach* (Pennsauken, NJ: Auerbach Publishers, Inc., 1983).

reports on a schedule, (2) systems that produce reports about *exception* conditions, (3) systems that provide flexible "ad hoc" *inquiry* capability, and (4) systems that provide capability of data *analysis* to aid in decision support.[8]

Martin suggests that the mix of applications has radically changed over the past twenty years.[9] The majority of applications in the 1960s were routine batch processing such as order processing, payroll, and invoicing runs. In the 1970s on-line transaction systems became more common for order entry and processing. In the late 1980s and beyond the most important class of applications will be decision-support systems.

The development of MIS capability is typically evolutionary and may follow a pattern similar to that of the logistics organization development.[10] Figure 11–4 indicates the relative importance of MIS systems at each stage of organizational development.[11] The transaction systems form the MIS base. The next level is operational management systems. This is followed by budgeting, measurement and control. The final emphasis is on planning systems.

The Type I organization initially concentrates on the development of the transaction processing and management systems that are required for day-to-day logistics operations. Type I organization's information systems also include operational management systems for productivity measurement and control.

[8] R. B. Rosenberger, "The Information Center" (New York: SHARE 56, Proceedings, Session M372, Share, Inc., 1981).

[9] James Martin, *An Information Systems Manifesto* (Englewood Cliffs, N.J.: Prentice-Hall, Inc., 1984), p. 10.

[10] See Chapter 10, pages 304–10, for a discussion of the evaluation of the logistics organization from Type I through Type III.

[11] Wendell M. Stewart, "Planning the Logistics Organization: An Evolutionary Approach," Article No. 4.1.1 *Distribution Management*—Vol. V of *Computers in Manufacturing* (Pennsauken, N.J.: Auerbach Publishers, Inc., 1983), p. 5.

These systems are critical to provide management with the capability to track actual against planned performance levels and identify areas for improvement. These systems, typically driven by the transaction systems, support activities such as inventory stock location in a warehouse, vehicle routing, and scheduling.

The Type II logistics organization continues development of the transaction systems to cover the additional functions included in the expanded management scope. The Type II organization also begins to place emphasis on budgeting, measurement, and control systems. These systems must be interfaced with the accounting systems. The outputs of the systems might include variance reporting, exception reporting, budgets, and productivity measures for the key logistics resources. Capability for management inquiry and ad hoc reporting becomes important.

The Type III organization continues to expand systems to cover a broader logistics scope and places emphasis on integrated data base capabilities. The new emphasis is on development for systems to support planning at the strategic, tactical, and operational levels.

Classification of Logistics MIS

Logistics MIS applications can be classified as: (1) transaction systems, (2) decision-support systems, and (3) assessment and control systems.

Transaction systems are required to operate the logistics process on a day-to-day basis. Transaction systems cover routine logistical activities. Decision support systems provide computer-based logic to assist logistics managers in making operations and design decisions. Assessment and control systems provide a synthesizer of critical events and recommended decision points related to the operational plan. An assessment and control system provides information for comparison of progress to predefined objectives and policies.

Transaction Systems

Transaction systems are necessary to accomplish daily logistical operations. Typical transaction systems are order processing, inventory control, freight payment, and the accounting payable and receivables systems.

A complete materials and logistics transaction information system would include physical distribution, manufacturing support, and purchasing subsystems. Table 11–5 lists typical information included in each major subsystem.

Decision Support Systems

Recent advances in computer technology have stimulated interest in computer-aided tools to improve the effectiveness of management decisions. These tools, referred to as decision-support systems (DSSs), have become more practical as a result of the widespread use of microprocessors. DSSs are interactive computer-based systems that provide data and analytic models to help decision-makers.

A DSS is best used to solve problems that have specific characteristics. In *dynamic problem situations* issues continually change, either because the manager's perception of the problem changes or because the problem situation actually changes. *Limited solution times* develop where solution-response time is critical, and answers are needed quickly. *Dynamic data base* situations exist when the data necessary to perform the analysis continually change and are subject to uncertainty. In *High problem complexity* situations the variables are difficult or impossible to quantify, and their interactions for the problem being analyzed cannot be evaluated without the aid of a computer model. DSSs typically access transaction-processing systems and interact with the other parts of an overall information system to support the decision-making activities of managers.

The benefits generally attributed to use of DSS include: (1) insight into cost/service/profitability trade-offs, (2) identification of specific recommendations regarding logistics system improvements, (3) development of improved data bases, (4) identification of logistics' MIS improvement, and (5) quick responses to "what-if" questions.

The logistics DSS concept is illustrated in Figure 11–5. The DSS system requires a model, a data base, and a dialogue subsystem.

The purpose of the *model subsystem* is to provide a logic to guide analysis. The ideal model should be flexible to accommodate a variety of different decision situations. The range and characteristics of logistical models are discussed in greater detail in Chapter 13.

The *data-base subsystem* serves to manipulate information to support the decision process. Typical data-base information consists of unique logistics files

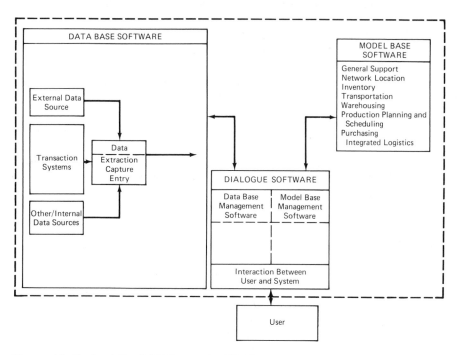

Figure 11–5   Logistics DSS Conceptual Design

Adapted with permission from O. K. Helferich, *Logistics Decision Support Systems*, Volume V of *Computers in Manufacturing* (Pennsauken, NJ: Auerbach Publishers, Inc., 1983), page 4.

and external data. The unique logistics data are typically generated by the transaction systems and consist of operational statistics. The external data sources include information that has relevancy to the logistical decision-support model. Such external data are typically accessed from the general data base. To provide an effective DSS, and ideal data-base subsystem and support program should include: (1) capability to combine a variety of data sources, (2) ability to rapidly add and delete data, (3) capability to present data in an easy-to-understand manner, (4) a full range of data-manipulation functions, and (5) flexibility to develop special data files for *what if* evaluations.

Dialogue software provides the interaction between the decision-support system and the user. Typical dialogue software provides conversational prompts that guide a user through a decision process. The key is to make the mechanics of preparing data and utilizing the model as easy as possible for the user. In addition, the dialogue software helps the user identify options and isolate problem solutions. Advanced dialogue software represents a form of *artificial intelligence* referred to as an *expert system*. The expert system contains the logic and experience necessary to guide a user to the best conclusion. While such expert systems are common in such fields as medicine, they are just evolving in logistics. Chapter 15 provides additional discussion on the long-range potential of artificial intelligence.

Assessment and Control Systems

Assessment and control systems are the key to ensuring that performance is consistent with management's operational plans. By improving operational efficiency and tracking progress, assessment and control systems help support an organization's efforts to obtain logistical objectives.

The logistics assessment and control activity serves several functions. *First*, it measures performance through reports, audits, and observations. *Second*, it makes comparison of actual to planned performance. *Third*, it identifies corrective action. A diagram of this process is presented in Figure 11–6. The assessment and control objective is to provide a prototype system for measuring the productivity, utilization, and performance of the overall logistics system, functional areas, and individual managers. Providing management with a system to automate and improve the review process is one of the key objectives to computer-based assessment and control systems.

SUMMARY

Logistical administration consists of operational planning and control. Administration in the logistical organization should be guided by a clear statement of objectives. The control process provides a measure of accomplishment.

Operational planning is concerned with the day-to-day activities of an enterprise within the framework of the business strategic plan. The formulation of an operating plan requires the coordination of objectives related to system modification, performance, and budgets into one integrated effort. As noted, consecutive operating plans often contain features of longer-term system implementational strategy. Therefore, logistical system design and administra-

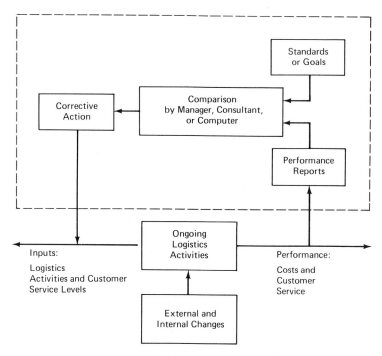

Figure 11-6   Logistics Assessment and Control Process

Adapted and reprinted with permission from Ronald H. Ballou and O. K. Helferich, *Measuring Physical Distribution Performance* (Pennsauken, NJ: Auerbach Publishers, Inc., 1983).

tion are unified through the relationships between operational plans and implemental strategies.

The control process is one of the most complex aspects of logistical management. The problem is not limited to information availability. In today's business enterprise data are abundant, and continued refinements in management information systems make data increasingly available. The challenge in logistical controllership is to format required data in a manner that results in consistent performance information and measurement.

Two types of data are required for logistical controllership. Cost-control data, although readily available, require a great deal of restructuring to be useful to logistical administration. Service performance data normally are not available within the corporate record base. However, the fact that all elements of the total performance cycle are under logistical management control in a unified organization structure renders the data for service measurement attainable. Logistical controllership must isolate cost and performance data to provide management with facts concerning the overall logistical operations. All levels of management control require timely and accurate data. From a logistical viewpoint, the ideal management information system should provide transaction, decision-support, and assessment and control information. In the final analysis, a logistical operation can be only as efficient and as effective as the management information system that guides its destiny.

QUESTIONS

1. Describe the concept of management by objectives (MBO). How is this applied to logistic management?
2. What types of factors or activities would be included in a typical operational plan?
3. Describe the role of the goals of operational planning: (1) system modification, (2) performance, and (3) budget.
4. Is it a good practice to modify operational plans once established?
5. Describe the concept of productivity. Include an example of each of the basic types of productivity measures.
6. Describe the different types of control commonly found in a logistical system.
7. Describe the classification of logistics management information systems. Give an example of each of the three types as applied to physical distribution.
8. What are the differences the emphasis of management information systems as a logistics organization evolves?
9. Describe the differences among fixed, flexible, and capital budgeting. Which method do you prefer and why?
10. What are the basic purposes of status, trend, and ad hoc reports?

LOGISTICAL TECHNIQUES AND METHODOLOGIES

Planning and Design Methodology

Just as there exists no ideal logistical system suitable for all enterprises, procedures followed in the conduct of logistical design vary extensively. As one would expect, developing a logistical management information system is considerably different than studying the potential modification of a warehouse network. However, several general steps are applicable to most logistical design situations. The purpose of this chapter is to present a general managerial guide for the planning and design process. Figure 12–1 illustrates the flow diagram of a generalized managerial guide for logistical design.

The generalized guide includes three phases: (1) system definition, (2) system development, and (3) system implementation. These phases are necessary in all logistical design projects.

Each phase is referenced to the prime areas of managerial concern on the right side of Figure 12–1. The left-hand side illustrates the process of (1) heuristic analysis and (2) continuous adjustment to change. From a managerial viewpoint, a final plan never really exists. Any system should be under constant review to take advantage of change. Thus, the total process of logistical system planning and design is a never-ending responsibility subject to modification with passing time. Each of the major phases illustrated in Figure 12–1 is discussed in this chapter. Because of the comprehensive nature of logistics, the discussion that illustrates the managerial guide is based upon general logistical system design.

The first three sections of this chapter present a review of Phase I, System Definition, followed by a brief overview of Phase II, Systems Development,

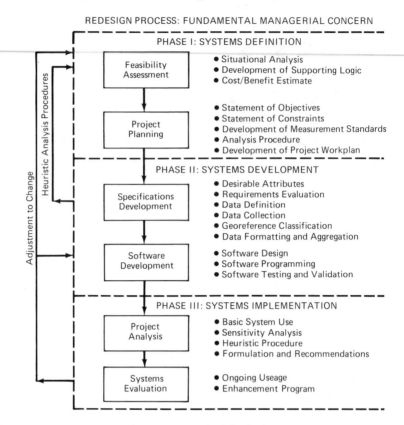

REDESIGN PROCESS: FUNDAMENTAL MANAGERIAL CONCERN

PHASE I: SYSTEMS DEFINITION

Feasibility Assessment
- Situational Analysis
- Development of Supporting Logic
- Cost/Benefit Estimate

Project Planning
- Statement of Objectives
- Statement of Constraints
- Development of Measurement Standards
- Analysis Procedure
- Development of Project Workplan

PHASE II: SYSTEMS DEVELOPMENT

Specifications Development
- Desirable Attributes
- Requirements Evaluation
- Data Definition
- Data Collection
- Georeference Classification
- Data Formatting and Aggregation

Software Development
- Software Design
- Software Programming
- Software Testing and Validation

PHASE III: SYSTEMS IMPLEMENTATION

Project Analysis
- Basic System Use
- Sensitivity Analysis
- Heuristic Procedure
- Formulation and Recommendations

Systems Evaluation
- Ongoing Useage
- Enhancement Program

Adjustment to Change · Heuristic Analysis Procedures

Figure 12–1 Managerial Guide to Logistical Redesign

and Phase III, System Implementation. These general phases apply to all logistics system redesign projects. In the discussion that follows Phases II and III are illustrated by a situation whereas a Decision Support System is being used as a design aid. The final section of the chapter presents comments on Phase II and III when applied to the development and implementation of a logistics management information system.

SYSTEM DEFINITION

Phase I of a logistics system redesign provides the basis for the entire project. A thorough and well-documented and -organized systems definition is a necessity for a successful systems redesign project. The major focus in phase I is on feasibility assessment and project planning. These two areas are discussed.

Feasibility Assessment

Logistics planning begins with a comprehensive analysis of overall requirements. The immediate managerial concern is to determine what, if any, modifications are needed to the existing logistical system. The process of evaluating the need and desirability of change is referred to as *feasibility assessment.* The recommended steps in completing the feasibility assessment are: (1) situational analysis, (2) development of supporting logic, and (3) cost-benefit estimate. Each is discussed.

Situational Analysis

Situational analysis involves the collection of facts concerning the logistical requirements confronted by an enterprise and the overall scope of current operations. The typical appraisal involves an internal review, a competitive appraisal, and a technology assessment to determine if a substantial area for cost or service improvement exists.

Internal Review. The purpose of the internal review is to develop a clear understanding of existing logistical activities. The internal review develops a profile that is a statement of historical performance, data, strategies, operations, and tactical policies and practices. The review usually covers the overall logistics organization as well as each logistics function.

A complete appraisal reviews all major resources such as personnel, equipment, and information. In particular, the review is directed at a comprehensive evaluation of the existing system's capabilities and deficiencies. Each aspect of the overall logistical system should be carefully examined with respect to how well its stated objectives are being realized. For example, is the physical distribution management information system consistently meeting the level and response of customer service performance desired by the marketing department? Likewise, is the materials management system meeting its goals with respect to support manufacturing requirements? Are the primary activities of logistical coordination being conducted in an orderly and integrated fashion? Finally, does an integrated concept of manufacturing support exist that takes maximum advantage of the captive nature of work-in-process inventory? These and many similar questions form the basis of the self-appraisal involved in the internal analysis. Through this comprehensive review, the opportunities that might justify potential system redesign are initially identified.

The specific content of the review is a function of the scope of the analysis. Table 12–1 presents some of the items frequently covered in an internal review. It would indeed be rare if all the data required in an internal review were available. Considerable research is typically required to assemble the necessary data. The purpose of the review is not detailed data collection. Rather, the review represents a diagnostic look at what is currently taking place in logistical operations as well as a probe to determine the availability of data. Most significantly, the internal review is aimed at the identification of areas where a substantial opportunity for improvement exists.

Competitive Appraisal. The focal point of the competitive appraisal is the external environment within which the logistical system functions. In particular, the competitive analysis is concerned with an appraisal of how well on a comparative basis, is the existing logistical system functioning in terms of customer requirements, vendor consistency, and competitor practices.

Although an internal review will indicate if the physical distribution operating system is satisfying the marketing organization's requirements, the competitive analysis is aimed at evaluating the fundamental need for existing customer

TABLE 12–1 Items Frequently Covered in a Situation Analysis

Item	Description
1. Facility network	Profile of geographical arrangements, capacity, and mission by facility
2. Performance cycles	Review of order-processing systems and procedures
3. Communication network	Delineation of network used to generate management information
4. Inventory management	Policies and control systems utilized to manage inventory
5. Traffic management	Review of practices—both common carrier and private fleet
6. Materials handling	Evaluation of materials handling techniques and practices
7. Forecasting	Appraisal of forecasting techniques and effectiveness
8. Production scheduling	Examination of methods and practices
9. Procurement	Delineation of techniques, accuracy of specifications, and vendor performance
10. Warehouse operations	Evaluation of receiving, inspection, put-away, and storage policies and practices
11. Finished products	Review from perspective of packaging, special handling, profitability, and costs by product
12. Performance measures	Practices, procedures standards/goals, "action triggers" to measure and control performance by logistics function based on costs, ROI, and service

service standards. For example, does the danger of developing a service myopia, as discussed in Chapter 3, in fact exist?[1]

The content of a competitive analysis is concerned with, but not limited to, such matters as: (1) examination of the logistical systems being used by major competitors in both the materials and finished-goods markets; (2) evaluation of existing marketing channel arrangements as well as major structural trends, including the presence or absence of separation in the transaction and logistical channels; (3) quantification of existing and potential customers and supply sources with respect to volume purchased, special logistical requirements, and structure of facilities that must be linked into the logistical system; and (4) measurement of delivery service consistently offered by major competitors.

As with the internal review, it would be rare to find all the data desired about the competitive and market environment readily available. Once again, the purpose of the competitive review is to appraise what is generally needed and to develop a comprehensive insight into the effectiveness of the existing logistical system.

Technology Assessment. As noted earlier, the period during which the concept of integrated logistics matured was dominated by a continuous stream of technological developments.[2] In particular, technologies related to computers

---

[1] See Chapter 3, pages 79–80.
[2] See Chapter 1, page 15.

and high-speed data transmission have been significant contributors to practical management of integrated logistics. The purpose of the technology assessment is to evaluate the findings of the internal review and competitive analysis in an effort to measure the extent to which available technology is being utilized.

To illustrate, if no major review has been completed recently regarding the technology of order processing, then substantial trade-off benefits related to real-time order entry may be available to the enterprise. Such an assessment should be completed with respect to each component of the logistical system as well as the status of overall integration.

Development of Supporting Logic

The second step in a feasibility assessment is to integrate the findings of the internal review, competitive analysis, and technology assessment into a logic to support logistical system modification. In many ways the development of a supporting logic constitutes the most difficult part of the strategic planning process. The purpose of the situational appraisal is to provide senior management with the best possible understanding of the strengths and weaknesses of the existing logistical system. From the comprehensive review, three specific end products are desired.

First, a determination must be made if sufficient areas for improved logistical performance exist to justify detailed research and analysis. In a sense, completion of the situational analysis provides a convenient go–no go point for additional study. The desirability, as well as the feasibility, of conducting detailed system review can be evaluated in terms of expected cost and benefit. While conducting the remaining steps in the managerial planning process does not commit a firm to implementation or even guarantee a viable new system design, the potential benefits of change should be fairly clear at the completion of the situational appraisal.

Second, the typical result of the appraisal is confirmation that a great many aspects of the existing logistical system are more right than wrong. This should not be a surprising conclusion. However, it is one that should be reached based on comprehensive factual analysis and not opinion. The delineation of areas where improvement potential exists, as well as those where operations are satisfactory, provides the foundation for determining the need for strategic system adjustment. For example, it may be apparent that a serious problem exists in inventory, which holds the potential for cost reduction and service improvement. Correspondingly, if there is no justification for questioning the existing structure of facilities with respect to location or size, then all subsequent analysis can focus on improvement of the inventory component without serious risk of suboptimization. The outputs of a logical review include a classification of issues-problems and opportunities faced by the logistics organization. The issue should be prioritized into primary "must" and secondary "nice to address" categories across short-term and long-range planning horizons.

The third output of the situational appraisal should be a clear statement of the logistical redesign alternatives available. The statement should include: (1) the current methods and systems, (2) the most likely options based on leading competitive and industry practices, and (3) innovative approaches based on new theory and technologies. The less frequently a redesign project is conducted to evaluate the selected issues, the more important it is to select a range of options for the evaluation. For example, a redesign project for a total logistics management information system and/or a manufacturing plant relocation project, either of which could probably be accomplished only once each 5 years, should consider a wide range of logical options with different technologies before a final decision is made.

At this point in the study process, it is well worth the effort to construct flow diagrams and/or outlines illustrating the basic concept associated with different alternatives. These diagrams will illustrate the opportunities for employing flexible operating patterns, clearly outline the transportation and communication requirements, and serve to provide a comprehensive overview of the study situation. Some variables available in identifying logistical options will be difficult to illustrate in a flow diagram. For example, regional variations, product-mix variations, and differential shipment policies are difficult to illustrate, although they do form the basis of design alternatives. Nevertheless, an attempt should be made to delineate the options. The techniques involved in this form of presentation are discussed in Chapter 13.

A recommended procedure is for the manager responsible for evaluating the desirability of a revamped logistical strategy to develop a logical statement and justification of potential benefits. Based upon the logic of customer service (Chapter 3) and foundations of logistical policy (Chapter 9), the projected logistical strategy alternatives should be committed to paper.

Cost-Benefit Estimate

The final deliverable of a feasibility assessment is a preplanning estimate of what benefits are expected to materialize if a logistical study is completed and the recommendations implemented. The benefits can be summarized in categories of service improvement, cost reduction, and cost prevention. Naturally the three categories are not mutually exclusive in that an ideal logistical strategy might realize some degree of all benefits simultaneously.

The category of service improvement simply means that the potential exists to generate more effective logistical performance as a result of the projected commitment of financial and human resources. For example, a reduction in the number of warehouses may increase inventory availability without a sacrifice in other attributes of customer service.

Potential cost reductions are of two types. First, a one-time commitment or reduction in financial or managerial resources required to operate the existing system may result from logistical redesign. The impact of reductions in capital deployment is significant in that the continuous cost associated with usage is eliminated, and the capital is freed for alternative deployment. The second type of cost reduction deals with the expenditure of out-of-pocket or variable costs to perform logistical tasks. The redesign of the system to employ new technologies often results in a particular function being accomplished more efficiently.

Cost prevention consists of instituting system changes in order to avoid continued involvement in programs and operations experiencing cost increases. For example, many recent entries into private transportation have been at least partially justified on a financial analysis that takes into account the estimated future level of for-hire rates. Naturally, any cost-prevention justification is based on an estimate of future conditions and is therefore vulnerable to error. While a logistical study would seldom be approved solely for cost prevention, consideration of such ramifications is recommended.

No rules exist to determine when a strategic planning situation offers adequate cost-benefits potential to justify an in-depth effort. Ideally, strategic review should be a continuous process undertaken at specific intervals to assure continued viability of the existing operational system. In the final analysis, the decision to undertake in-depth strategic planning must rest on how convincing the supporting logic is, to what degree the estimated benefits are believable, and an assessment of whether or not the estimated benefits offer sufficient return on investment to justify organizational and operational change. These potential benefits must be balanced against the out-of-pocket cost required to complete the strategic plan.

Identifying immediate improvement opportunities, although not always the goal of a planning project, is frequently the output of a feasibility assessment. Immediate improvements, whether in the form of suggestions to increase customer service and/or reduce costs, are often sufficient to justify the entire project. As the project team identifies potential improvement areas, a steering committee should evaluate each suggestion to determine the potential Return-on-Investment.

Project Planning

The second step in formulating a system definition is the establishment of the project plan. Five specific tasks must be accomplished at this stage of the managerial planning procedure: (1) statement of objectives, (2) statement of constraints, (3) development of measurement standards, (4) analysis procedure and (5) development of the project work plan.

Statement of Objectives

The strategic objectives deal with cost and service expectations for the revised system. It is essential that such objectives be stated specifically in terms of measurable factors. A typical procedure at this point in the study is to state specific service objectives, setting cost considerations aside until later in the study.

The following is a typical format of service objectives: (1) the system will be designed to provide 95 per cent inventory availability for category A products, 92 per cent for category B products, and 87 per cent for category C products; (2) desired delivery of all customer orders will be within 48 hours of order placement for 98 per cent of all orders; (3) customer service from secondary service points will be held to less than 10 per cent of orders; (4) mixed commodity orders will be filled without back-order on a minimum of 85 per cent of all orders; (5) back-orders will be restricted to five days' aging; and (6) the 50 most profitable customers will receive these minimum performance capabilities on 98 per cent of all orders.

Given these statements of customer service, a system can be planned that will deliver the specified performance. Total cost of the system can then be determined. To the extent that logistical cost does not meet managerial expectations, various levels of alternative customer service performance can then be evaluated using a process of sensitivity analysis.

An alternative approach to the statement of output objectives is to establish a maximum allowable total-cost logistical expenditure and then design a system that achieves the possible customer service with the acceptable logistical budget. Such cost-oriented objectives are practical because recommendations are guaranteed to function within acceptable budget ranges. The deficiency of a maximum-budget approach is a lack of sensitivity to service-oriented system design issues.

Statement of Constraints

An additional aspect of project planning deals with design constraints. From the situational analysis, it is expected that senior management will place restrictions on the scope of permissible system modifications. The nature of such restrictions will depend upon the specific circumstances of individual enterprises. However, two typical examples are provided to illustrate how constraints can impact the overall planning process.

One restriction common to distribution system design concerns the network of manufacturing facilities and the products produced at each. To simplify the study, management may elect to hold existing manufacturing facilities constant in logistical system planning. Such constraints are justified on the basis of financial considerations and capacity of the organization to absorb change.

A second example of constraints deals with marketing channels and physical distribution activities of separate divisions. In enterprises with a traditional pattern of decentralized profit responsibility, management may elect to omit certain divisions from study considerations. Thus, some divisions may be managerially determined to be candidates for consolidated physical distribution operations, whereas others are omitted from consideration.

All design constraints serve to limit the scope of the plan. However, as one executive stated: "Why study things we don't plan to do anything about?" Unless a reasonable chance exists that management is favorably inclined to accept recommendations, the subject or question should be structured as a study constraint.

The purpose of developing a statement of constraints is to have a well-defined starting point and overall perspective for the planning effort. If computerized analysis techniques are used to assist in the planning effort, major constraints can be evaluated later with minimum effort. If the planning is conducted on a manual basis, the degree of flexibility to vary constraints is significantly reduced. In contrast to study scope discussed above, the statement of constraints relates to specific buildings, systems, procedures, and/or practices to be retained from the existing logistical system.

Development of Measurement Standards

In most situations the feasibility assessment highlights the need for the managerial specification of measurement standards. Such standards will format cost structures and the cost of performance penalties. Management must provide guidelines for each category as a prerequisite to the formulation of the plan. Once formulated, standards should be held constant throughout system development. Although considerable managerial prerogative exists in the formulation of standards, care must be exercised not to dilute the validity of the analysis and subsequent results by setting impractical standards.

An important aspect of measurement is to quantify a list of assumptions which underlay or provide the logic supporting the standards. These assumptions should receive top managerial approval because they can significantly shape the results of the strategic plan. For example, a relatively small variation in the standard cost and procedure for evaluating inventory can result in major variations in the strategic plan.[3]

Analysis Procedure

Once the critical issues and alternatives are defined, the analysis procedure should be selected. There is a wide range of methodologies including: (1) manual analysis, (2) computerized decision-support models, and (3) information system development procedures.

For example, a decision-support model with linear programming and/or simulation algorithm(s) would likely be utilized to isolate a logistics warehouse strategy. A transaction-oriented management information system, whether for one function such as order entry and order processing or for the total logistics operations, would require software engineering to ensure successful methodology development. Many redesign projects require only manual analysis where the only computer assistance might be a spreadsheet software package on a microprocessor. An example of one such analysis would be to evaluate the price a shipper is willing to pay a carrier for freight movement in a given shipping lane.

The desired outputs and conclusions can be defined given the project issues and analysis methodologies to be used in the project. The input requirements include data required for the analysis tools plus all of the assumptions and parameters provided by senior management serve as constraints.

Development of Project Work Plan

The final step in project planning is development of a work plan. The project work plan specifies the resources and time required to complete the strategic design. The alternatives and opportunities specified during the feasibility assessment provide the basis for determination of study scope. In turn, the scope of the planning inquiry provides the basis for estimating the time required for completion.

A major overall management responsibility is to assure that expected results are realized within time and budget constraints. One of the most common errors in strategic planning is to underestimate the time required to complete the specified assignment. Extended time overruns will result in greater than planned expenditures and a deterioration of project creditability. Fortunately, several methodologies are available that can be adapted to the logistical planning project. Depending upon the nature of the planning project, structured methodologies are available to guide resource allocation and measure

---

[3] See Chapter 7, pages 201–15, and National Council of Physical Distribution Management, "Measuring and Improving Productivity in Physical Distribution" (Chicago, NCPDM, 1984).

progress. Such methodologies specify deliverables that must be presented for user walk-through and managerial overview at specified times during the planning process.

Scheduling is concerned with planning and accomplishment of nonrepetitive projects. In addition, scheduling techniques are concerned with the most efficient utilization of resources during the study. Two scheduling techniques, the *program evaluation review technique* (PERT) and the *critical path method* (CPM), are reviewed in Chapter 14. The illustration developed in Chapter 14 is specific to the time phasing and managerial guidance of strategic logistical planning.

Overview of System Development and Implementation

This initial section of the chapter has discussed feasibility assessment and project planning which combine to formulate a Phase I system definition. The activities involved in feasibility assessment and project planning are common to all types of logistical planning. The details of Phase II systems development and Phase III systems implementation depend upon the specific objective of the planning project.

The activities of each phase will be slightly different depending on the logistics redesign issues and project scope. For example, the strategic redesign of a logistics warehouse and production facility frequently utilizes a network computer model for analysis. A project where an existing DSS software package is utilized would not require all of the steps outlined in Phase II system development because the software is already developed and ready to utilize.

In contrast, a situation where a logistics management information system is under development would require a full Phase II system to develop the necessary software. All logistics system redesign projects require the implementation phase. The next section of the chapter focuses on managerial concerns in the development and implementation of system planning and redesign which involves the use of analysis techniques. The final section is concerned with Phases II and III when the major objective is the development of a logistics management information system redesign.

DECISION SUPPORT SYSTEM DEVELOPMENT

Significant advances in computer technology and increasing uncertainty regarding the economy, material resources, market competition, and governmental regulation are stimulating increased interest in computer-aided tools to improve the effectiveness of logistics management decisions.[4] These tools,

---

[4] For a review of the use of DSS applied to logistics management situations, see O. K. Helferich, "Logistics Decision Support Systems," *Computers in Manufacturing: Distribution Management* (Pennsauken, N. J.: Auerbach Publishers, Inc., 1984); Fred Glover et al., "An Integrated Production, Distribution, and Inventory Planning System," *Interfaces*, Vol. 9, No. 5 (November 1979), pp. 21–35; Paul S. Bender et al., "Practical Modeling for Resource Management," *Harvard Business Review*, Vol. 59 (March–April 1981), pp. 163–73; and Arthur M. Geoffrion and Richard F. Powers, "Management Support Systems," *The Wharton Magazine*, Vol. 5, No. 3 (Spring 1981), and M. K. Allen and M. A. Emmelhainz, "Decision Support Systems: An Innovative Aid to Managers", *Journal of Business Logistics* (Oak Brook, Ill.: National Council of Physical Distribution Management, Vol. 5, No.2, 1984), pp. 128–142.

referred to as decision support systems (DSSs), have become more practical as refinements to interactive computer terminals and personal computers have materialized. DSSs are basically interactive computer-based systems that provide data and analysis models to help decision-makers solve unstructured problems—problems with many difficult-to-define variables.

Until the 1980s, use of computer models required a major effort. The mainframe applications were slow, and models existed for only a limited number of decision support situations. The models were complicated and required significant effort to set up for each redesign situation. For example, it was not uncommon for data collection and preparation and the validation process to consume 75 to 90 per cent of the project time and budget. The rapid development of information technologies, however, is reducing the time and effort required to conduct logistics redesign through computer modeling. Technological development now offers much improved data-base management capabilities, faster computer capacity at lower costs, and through microprocessors complete control by the logistics end-user. In addition, a broad range of models are now available from sources such as software vendors, consulting organizations, and computer hardware manufacturers. Decision support model capability is often classified using a functional orientation. One such classification scheme is illustrated in Table 12–2.[5]

Decision Support System Specifications Development

Specifications development is critical to the determination of the type of DSS selected to address the logistics issues defined in Phase I. The analysis of specifications requires creative talent as well as analytical ability. This is normally the domain of the specialist. However, management still must plan as active role in order to maintain control, assume that the model will address the critical issues, and to develop appropriate data into a usable format. A technical treatment of modeling techniques is the subject matter of Chapter 13. At this point, emphasis is placed on the nontechnical aspects of logistical modeling.

The fundamental purpose of modeling is to attempt to make a valid prediction of how potential logistical configurations will perform in advance of implementation. A model constitutes a body of information and restrictions about a unique situation accumulated for the purpose of systems analysis.[6] The model is a substitute for testing actual logistical designs. By developing and testing a model, it is possible to evaluate the impact of alternative policies prior to resource commitment. Thus, modeling permits experimentation with different potential system modifications without resorting to trial and error or arbitrary changes in existing operations.

Models are of two general types: (1) physical and (2) abstract.[7] Physical models are replicas of the object under study. Common examples are the scaled

---

[5] Helferich op. cit., page 8.

[6] The classical classification of model types is found in J. W. Forrester, *Industrial Dynamics* (Cambridge, Mass.: The MIT Press, 1961), Chapter 4. Also see M. S. Scott Morton, *Management Decision Support Systems: Computer Based Support for Decision Making* (Cambridge Mass.: Harvard University, Division of Research, 1978). Also see R. H. Sprague, Jr. and E. D. Carlson, *Building Effective Decision Support Systems* (Englewood Cliffs, N. J.: Prentice-Hall, Inc., 1982).

[7] Forrester, op. cit., p. 49.

TABLE 12–2 Typical Analysis Capabilities of Logistics DSS Models

Integrated Logistics System	Production Planning and Scheduling
Total system optimization	Master production schedule
Total system costs/service trade-offs	"What if" production/inventory
"What-if" trade-offs between/among all	trade-offs
functions	Capacity planning
Network	Procurement/Purchasing
Type of facility	Price change/discount/
Number and location	time analysis
Size of warehouse	Inventory consolidation
Assignment of markets	analysis
Sourcing to plants	Material bid evaluation
	Quantity discount analysis
Inventory	Vendor analysis
Stocking policy	
Cost/investment	Warehouse
Stocking levels	Layout/design
Service levels	Storage allocation
Differential analysis by category (usage,	Space utilization
value, criticality, lead time)	
Transportation	
Freight consolidation	
Routing and scheduling	
Transportation budgeting	
Shipment planning	
Lane analysis/balancing	
Carrier analysis	

replications of aircraft within a wind-tunnel environment used to deduce performance of full-size aircraft. The process of physical modeling is frequently used in construction. Many logistical managers use physical models when planning a new warehouse layout. The disadvantage of using physical models in total system design studies is the complexity, time, and cost requirements of constructing the replication.

The abstract model uses symbols rather than physical devices to represent a system. A variety of abstract models exist, but the two most commonly used in logistical system design are block-flow diagrams and mathematical symbols. In a block-flow symbolic treatment, the system is illustrated by communication and product-flow diagrams. In a mathematical model or DSS, the components and interrelations of a system are expressed in terms of equations.

DSS development involves equations to handle operating relationships and, to the degree desired, feedback mechanisms. Programming consists of writing computer instructions to handle the required computations. The output or steps within the specifications development module are: (1) desirable attributes, (2) requirements evaluation, (3) data definition, (4) data collection, (5) georeference classification, and (6) data formatting and aggregation.

Desirable Attributes

A well-designed model will exhibit a number of desirable characteristics. The model developer and user select and weigh the most critical attributes for the situation as defined in Phase I. There are no exact rules to guide model builders in this critical effort. Experience, judgment, and a well-documented systems definition are the necessary ingredients to identify the appropriate attribute mix. The specific attributes of DSS models relate to construction of the analysis technique and application requirements. A comprehensive discussion of attributes is presented in Chapter 13.[8]

Requirements Evaluation

For logistical design the range of DSS models can be classified on the basis of the mathematical techniques they utilize in arriving at a design solution, their ability to represent the desired functional relationships, ability to represent temporal and spatial activities, and uncertainty. Each available solution technique, such as optimization or simulation, can be useful, depending on the specific logistics issues under consideration.[9]

Once the feasibility assessment is completed and the general attributes and requirements are weighted for priority, it is necessary to select an analysis technique. Given the availability of a broad range of models from vendors, a critical decision is whether to buy versus to develop a model in-house. The advantage of obtaining a model from an outside vendor is the experience of the previous users and developers in the evaluation of the model. External models are usually available with less delay than those developed internally. The primary advantage of developing a model in-house is that it probably will better reflect the uniqueness of and provide a more in-depth understanding of the problems for the internal staff.

Data Definition

The data preparation steps are frequently the most difficult and time-consuming in the modeling process. The data required to operationalize a computerized technique can be classified according to their utilization in the modeling process.[10] A well-defined body of knowledge exists concerning the relationship of data to model design. Four aspects of modeling that have data requirements are: (1) components, (2) variables, (3) parameters, and (4) functional relationships.

Components. The components of a model consist of the entities that are being described by a set of equations. They are the objects of primary interest in the system design. In terms of logistical system models, the entities or components are facility type and size, transportation, inventory, communication, and material handling. These factors constitute the resources of an enterprise that

[8] See Chapter 13.

[9] See Chapter 13, pp. 394–96.

[10] Helferich, op. cit., pages 4–6.

must be integrated to formulate a logistical system. Data must be collected for each system component.

Variables. The variables in a model serve the purpose of relating components. A number of variables exist within a complex model structure. The most common are exogenous, status, and endogenous variables.

Exogenous Variables. Exogenous variables are independent of the system being modeled. They constitute inputs to the model. As such, an exogenous variable's impact upon the system causes it to react or perform in a specified manner. Exogenous variables can be classified as instrumental or environmental on the basis of control exercised by the model builder or user.

Instrumental variables can be controlled or manipulated by the model user for experimental design. They are taken as given by the model but are controlled by the user. Thus, they can be changed at will for purposes of testing their impact upon the system design. In terms of logistical models, order-size policies, inventory dispositions, and customer service standards all represent instrumental variables.

Environmental variables cannot be controlled by the model user since no direct influence upon their nature or value exists. Thus, the impact of environmental variables is taken as given. A prime example of an environmental variable influencing logistical system design is the geographical distribution of product demand. The logistical system must service the product orders that evolve from basic demand determinants. No control exists over the geographical distribution of demand for purpose of improved logistical design. Environmental variables may have constant impact upon logistical system performance or may impact only at specific points in time. For example, while it is anticipated that demand impact will be continuous, the impact of a fire, flood, or other acts of nature will occur only rarely, if ever, it is hoped. Both types of environmental factors impact the model's performance and must be accommodated in design. While variables generated by the environment cannot be controlled with respect to actual impact, they can be manipulated by model users to evaluate system capability. In this form of evaluation, it is possible to determine how the logistical system would perform if unexpected environmentally based events occur. As a result, a logistical system design can be defined incorporating a high degree of capability to handle the most probable environmental changes with the least system disruption.

A critical aspect of model design is to define the system's boundary or dividing line between instrumental and environmental variables. The boundary influences the system's design range and will have a major impact upon the accuracy and relevancy of the resultant model.

Exogenous variables can also be viewed in terms of their purposes to the model. In this sense they are classified as set and flow variables. With respect to input, set and flow variables constitute the data necessary to establish and use the model.

Set data establish the prevailing system prior to the design process. To initiate the modeling procedure, it is necessary to define customers by location, size, and product demands. In addition, georeference coding is required for raw-material sources, suppliers, existing manufacturing plants, inventory accumulations, distribution warehouses, transport capacity, and all other factors involved in the existing logistical system. Set data also include values for various managerially determined constraints on system design. The degree of desired customer service and a statement of available resources are of critical importance.

Flow data represent the stream of operational demands to be placed upon the system during the study or planning period. At an operational level, flow data will be constructed as a series of customer orders or replenishment shipments. Such activity may be listed sequentially or randomly generated in order of occurrence for each time period under study. In seeking the best system design, flow data are held constant during analysis. The end result is a system status that will most effectively meet managerially determined service policies at the lowest total cost.

Status Variables. Status variables describe the system's state at any given time. In a logistical model, the system's state reflects the condition of all components with a particular design relationship or state. Each system state is based upon a set of relationships among components that will have a system service capacity and associated cost.

The starting system state is defined by the set data formulated under initial conditions. In logistical system modeling, initial state formulations must be sufficiently broad to allow inclusion of all potential system configurations. The fundamental purpose of the model is to modify state variables as a result of processing flow data, thereby isolating an improved system design.

Endogenous Variables. Endogenous variables are dependent upon system performance and constitute output. As a result of the interaction of exogenous and status variables, endogenous variables are generated.

The main managerial involvement with logistical design models is with the output screens and reports. Given an initial system state and both set and flow endogenous variables, the output expresses the degree of improvement projected from variations in system design. Depending upon the model under consideration, such output may take the form of operational status reports, profit-and-loss statements, or special analysis of problem situations.[11]

Parameters. In the design and operation of a model, parameters represent variables that do not change as a function of model operation. In other words, they constitute restrictions upon the model.

For purposes of this treatment, a parameter is defined as a design limitation on a model's structure and boundary. Parameters define the components that will be formulated by system state variables and the set limits of the endogenous variables that define the system boundary. The parameter is different than the managerial constraint identified during the project planning stage.

Constraints are limits placed upon the value of system state variables as well as both endogenous flow and set variables. These limits, both upper and lower, are enforced by the model design to exclude specific area of the study situation from system design modification. For example, manufacturing plant locations may be held constant in the design of a logistical system.

[11] See Chapter 11, pp. 334–40.

Both parameters and constraints may be varied by modification of the set data. The general procedure is to hold both constant in initial design of a logistical system. Once a system design is isolated that meets a specific operating requirement, parameters and constraints may be varied for sensitivity impact upon the design solution.

Functional Relationships. Functional relationships describe the interaction of all types of variables as the model functions. In modeling terminology, functional relationship, transformation, and algorithm are used interchangeably.

It is necessary to formulate the relationships among all variables included within the system structure. In essence, functional relationships are behavioral because they reflect the impact of change in system state. For example, the addition of a warehouse will result in substantial changes in transport, inventory, and communication demands placed upon the system. The functional relationship formulas provide a means for determining resultant changes in system state occasioned by the modeling process. As such, functional relationships are flow formulations, whereas system states are level equations.

An important part of the transformations of a model is the feedback mechanism. Feedback is essential to rendering the model dynamic. Given an initial system state flow, exogenous variables are processed to determine if an improved system state is possible. The degree of improvement is measured by change in the endogenous variables or output of the model. Such an improved system state results from analysis of operational relationships over a period of time. Feedback transformations are the manner by which time-related performance penalities and delays are formulated in a model.

The impact of feedback transformations influences the derived system state. Thus, stability is introduced into the modeling structure. A stable model will strive to maintain its original or initial state and make appropriate modification as disturbing events occur. An unstable model tends to amplify disturbances. Instability results because lags and unplanned interruptions are not dampened out by the ability of the system's functional relationships to take corrective system state action. The end result may be destruction of the system as it loses complete control.

Given a stable system, a disturbance, such as a two-week out-of-stock on a fast-moving product, would be expected to result in temporary adjustments in stock levels to protect the desired level of inventory availability. However, unless demand stabilized at a higher level, the model would seek to reinstate the original condition. In any event, a stable model would retain the desired performance level with a minimum of oscillation. In contrast, an unstable system would be more likely to experience prolonged oscillation between excessive and deficient inventories.

The typical manager may not view out-of-stock performance in terms of stability. However, the odds are high that instability has been experienced in actual operations. An unstable situation seldom improves until some external force intervenes. In consecutive periods, such external force may well be the controller when inventories peak and the sales manager at times of inventory drought. The development of stability in the logistical system can greatly reduce this conflict.

Data Collection

In actual design practice, the process of data collection began with the feasibility assessment. In addition, a fairly detailed specification of data is required in the formulation or adaptation of the system model. However, at this point in the planning procedure, detailed data must be accumulated and organized for use in analysis. One aspect of data collection is that the model can often be initially calibrated and validated using assumed or artificial data. Once operational, the model can be subjected to sensitivity analysis to determine the categories of data of particular importance to the design solution. Once identified, the data preparation area can concentrate on the critical information categories.

For purposes of discussion, the types of data required in a logistical design study are grouped as internal and external. Each is briefly discussed.

Internal Data. The majority of data required in a logistical study can be obtained from internal records. Although considerable digging may be required to come up with all the necessary pieces, most of the information is available.

The first category of required data concerns sales and customer orders. The annual sales forecast and percentage sales by month, as well as seasonality patterns, are necessary to structure the total volume to be modeled. A historical sample of customer order invoices is necessary to classify order characteristics. This sample, stratified by size and type of customer, can be used to generate orders to be processed by the system model.

Specific customer data are required, and ideally the data should be classified on a georeference basis. Location, type, size, order frequency, growth rate, and special logistical services required are perhaps the most significant groupings of data needed.

For procurement it is necessary to identify the sources of manufacturing and purchasing. In addition, a classification of raw materials and parts by demand and type is required. While manufacturing plant locations may not be a variable in a logistical design, it is necessary to specify the number and location of plants, the product mix produced, production schedules, and seasonality of production. With respect to inventory transfer, reorder priorities, shipment policy, warehouse processing times, and cost must be identified. In particular, inventory control rules and product allocation procedures are required. For each current and potential warehouse, it is necessary to establish operational costs, maximum-product-mix storage, and service capabilities. For the model structure it is necessary to identify the location and size of all existing warehouses, as well as locations that may be added during analysis.

In the area of transportation, the number and type of modes utilized, as well as the criteria for selecting each mode, must be established. Rates and transit times by modes, as well as shipping rules and policies, must be quantified. If private transportation is included in the analysis, then all relevant data are required.

In the area of inventory and communication, it is necessary to identify reorder policies, costs of inventory maintenance, order-processing time, and cost. Definition of the existing and potential reliability and capability of the order-communication system is required to provide the basis for alternative systems analysis.

Obviously, the collection of data for a detailed logistical system is a time-consuming and expensive task. The problem is complicated by the fact that synthetic costs and operating data are necessary to accommodate system modifications that require modeling of nonexistent logistical component arrangements.

While the various types of data here noted may be more or less than those required to evaluate a specific logistical system modification, the description provides an overall perspective. The prime justification of placing formal data collection following analysis technique selection is to limit the possibility of collecting unnecessary data. In final analysis, the design solution will be no better than the data it is based upon.

External Data. In most logistical planning situations, a selected amount of basic environmental data is required to model the system into future time. Management can normally provide an estimate of expected or desired sales for a planning horizon up to 10 years. The difficulty comes in obtaining a market-by-market distribution of such projections.

One solution to the problem is to use demographic factor projections that correlate highly with sales. For example, assume that a multiple correlation exists among sales, school enrollment, family size, and total population. Based on this correlation, future sales in any geographic area can be forecast by projection of these demographic factors.

The task of collecting demographic base data has become relatively simple. The United States Department of Commerce now makes available the Census of Population and Housing Fifth-Count Tallies Classified By ZIP Code Area.[12] These data are available as computer-coded input and provide all necessary information to develop correlations. A variety of projections concerning demographic factors are regularly published by various government agencies and universities. Thus, a reasonable data bank of environmental information is readily available.

Additional external data typically required is information concerning competitive logistical system designs and the marketing channel. An important interest will be competitive facility locations. In most cases this is readily available from published reports, annual reports, and the general knowledge possessed by company executives. The main purpose in collecting these data is that during the analysis phase of the study, it is desirable to compare the customer service capabilities of one or more major competitors to the system under consideration.

Georeference Classification

For modeling purposes, data concerning sales, customers, product, raw materials, and demographics need to be classified on a geographical basis. Distribution of such data by individual markets provides the geographical structure of demand or material source that must be serviced. The purpose of the model is to arrange the logistical system components in such a manner as to provide a level of service to individual markets at the lowest total cost. Thus,

---

[12] For a complete discussion of the usefulness of ZIP data, see *Rand McNally ZIP Code Atlas* (Chicago: Rand McNally & Company, 1975).

TABLE 12-3   Criteria in Georeference System Evaluation

Comparative georeference system attributes

Size of unit
Stability
Homogeneity
Flexibility
Mutual exclusiveness
Geographical continuity
Availability of periodically updated data

Model-oriented georeference system attributes

Availability of relevant data at the basic data unit
Appropriateness of data unit coverage to the markets serviced by the firm
Ability to determine distance from logistical facilities to data unit
Compatibility of data unit to the firm's management information system

---

selection of the georeference classification method is an extremely important aspect of the system design procedure.

A number of georeference classification structures have been developed. The six most useful to logistical modeling are: (1) customer point locations, (2) county, (3) standard metropolitan statistical area (SMSA), (4) economic trading area, (5) ZIP code, and (6) grid structure.

For purposes of selection in any given modeling situation, the alternative georeference structures can be evaluated on the basis of two criteria: (1) data attributes and (2) specific modeling requirements. Table 12-3 provides a summary of the major considerations in evaluating each criterion.

Customer Point Locations. The individual customer or material location is the most detailed georeference classification. One disadvantage of developing a model structured on individual customers is that sheer numbers can greatly slow processing. However, in some cases where a relatively few customers or supply sources are critical to logistical system design, specific customer detail may be justified.

When it is desirable to classify on the basis of specific customers, their geographic location can be identified by latitude and longitude or by use of a point reference system. A point reference system used in the past is PICADAD, which stands for *PI*, place identification; *CA*, characteristics of area; and *DAD*, procedure for computing distance and direction. Developed by the United States Department of Commerce, PICADAD provides a method to pinpoint almost every city in the United States. A special feature is that the reference system includes the computation procedure for calculation of distance. Determination of whether or not to use a point reference system rests with the level of detail desired. All other systems group geographical areas for purposes of data collection.

County. The county provides a reference system that for the most part is structured on historical political patterns. A great deal of data is available on a county basis. It is the basis for grouping of census data and can be readily identified to larger data sources such as SMSAs and states. Thus, the county structure is easily controlled from the viewpoint of data availability and processing.

In terms of model usage, it is sufficiently homogeneous for many products, is mutually exclusive, stable, and provides geographical continuity. Distance can be determined by use of key or central cities in the county without introducing significant error.

The primary disadvantage of the county is that it does not represent a trading area. The number of counties, approximately 3,000, is also a disadvantage in system model processing.

Standard Metropolitan Statistical Area. The SMSA is defined as a county or group of 300 continuous counties that contain at least one or twin cities with a population of 50,000 or more.

The primary advantage of using the SMSA as a georeference base is that 300 data units can be used to represent over 70 per cent of the consumer sales or other demographic information needed to project future demand. Data are easy to collect, and a great many are readily available in computer-processing format. As with the county, distance can be determined on a key-city basis.

The major limit is that the total set of SMSA units does not result in geographically continuous control structure. In addition, the SMSA structure is designed to change as a function of growth patterns.

Economic Trading Area. The concept of an economic trading area (ETA) is to design a georeference system to suit the requirements of a specific firm's demand and management information.

For example, an ETA classification system could be developed on the following basis: (1) all SMSAs and (2) each county where sales exceed a specific minimum that is not included in an SMSA. The main advantage of an ETA approach is custom design. Distance can be calculated on a key-city basis.

The primary disadvantage of ETAs is that they will be geographically large. The exact number would fall between the 300 SMSAs and the 3,000 counties, depending on the particular situation under analysis.

ZIP Code. A ZIP-based georeference system is formulated on the United States Postal Service ZIP Code Sectional Center System, which divides the country into 552 areas, including about 314 multicoded cities. The postal service describes an area as follows:[13]

1. It includes a hub city that is a national center for location and transportation.
2. It includes between 40 and 75 post offices.
3. The most remote post office is not more than 3 hours' normal driving time from the hub city.

It is possible to further subdivide the ZIP areas into 20,000 specific geographical units if the five-digit classification is employed and even greater with the full ZIP nine-digit classification.

---

[13] For a detailed study of geocoding systems, see Pamela A. Werner, *A Survey of National Geo-Coding Systems* (Washington, D. C.: U. S. Department of Transportation, 1972).

The primary advantage of the ZIP georeference system is flexibility. The classification is geographically continuous and relatively stable. It is common for firms to maintain ZIP codes in their data files, which greatly assist in obtaining internal data. Finally, distance can be determined on a hub-city basis.

The only significant limitation of the ZIP code reference system is that it is not as homogeneous as some other data-classification units. The geographic size of an area can vary greatly.

Grid Structure. Under a grid-structure classification base, the United States is divided into geographically standardized blocks. The original example of this form of classification was the REA grid. REA express developed the grid for purposes of pricing their transportation service. The concept divides the United States into 1°-square blocks based on latitude and longitude. Each block is further divided into 256 smaller squares, each containing approximately 41 square miles.

The grid system is relatively the smallest, most homogeneous, completely stable, highly flexible, mutually exclusive, and geographically continuous among the georeference systems available. In addition, it has been modified to accommodate distance by the elimination of curvature distortion.[14]

The primary limitation of a grid reference system is significant. In most cases it cannot be used without significant modification and adjustment of both internal and external data. The relevant data required in a logistical design are not grouped in a manner compatible to grids. Depending upon the situation, one or more georeference systems may be combined to formulate the data-classification structure for a system model.[15]

Among the six georeference systems reviewed, the ZIP code appears to be most widely used for logistical system models. The ZIP configuration meets all the desirable attributes specified in Table 12–3. The only serious limitation is that the areas are not uniform in size, which somewhat prohibits analysis based on density. However, the increasing availability of precoded and updated data is the main attribute of a ZIP-based reference system.

Data Formatting and Aggregation

Given the project period, data must be developed for use as flow input and as set constants for the study. The flow input represents historical records placed into a georeference code for analysis. Set constants represent a restatement of managerial parameters in terms of the system model. The technical aspects of each of these input formats are not a managerial responsibility.

In most situations it is necessary to aggregate data to reduce the amount of detail in a modeling situation. An example of aggregation would be the use of a limited number of products to reflect the activities of several different individual stockkeeping units. While aggregation is necessary, extreme care is required not to dilute data relevancy by excessive aggregation.

---

[14] Richard Lewis, *A Logistical Information System for Marketing Analysis* (Cincinnati, Ohio: South-Western Publishing Company, 1970), pp. 33–34.

[15] For a thorough discussion of georeference market classification, see Charles Smith, *Description and Technical Documentation of the LOKATE Geo-File* (Nabisco Brands, Inc., 1983).

To a significant degree, the exactness of data rests upon the model. In analytical formulations, where precise answers are anticipated, extreme care must be taken to maintain accuracy. Some latitude exists in simulations. However, the assumptions upon which aggregation procedures are based must be checked prior to use.

The logistics model should be developed to interface with a data-base management system (DBMS) to manipulate information from internal and external data bases. DBMS capabilities include: (1) ability to combine a variety of data sources through a data capture and extraction process, (2) ability to add and delete data sources quickly and easily, (3) ability to present data in terms readily understood by users, (4) a full range of data manipulation functions, and (5) flexibility to develop other data files to evaluate alternative "what ifs." The trend is toward data-base management systems that operate from real-time, regularly updated data, and promptly generate output to provide the necessary input for a wide variety of analysis techniques.

Although corporate data files/bases can supply the logistics DSS data files, more typically the DSS data base is separate from the operational data bases. Primary DSS input comes from internal operating systems. External data files serve as secondary sources.

Internal input to a complete logistics data base comes from routine transaction systems. Table 12–4 presents typical data input from these internal transactions.[16]

External data files also provide valuable input to a complete logistics data base. Table 12–5 details data elements of some typical files maintained in a logistics DSS data base.

Decision Support Systems Software Development

The steps for development depend on the decision to build or buy the decision support system software. A decision to build requires completion of the full software development steps of: (1) design, (2) programming, and (3) testing and validation. In this discussion the DSS is assumed to be purchased from a software vendor. Therefore, software development only requires testing and validation. In situations where original software is developed on a custom basis attention must be directed to design and programming. Detailed treatment of techniques and procedures to follow in these two steps is beyond the scope of this text.

Testing and Validation

A critical managerial responsibility is the testing and validation of the DSS. Because mathematical model building is a complex task, the risk is always present that the technical expert will not understand or have sufficient knowledge of the specific situation under study. Thus, before a model is used for logistics system design, its validity must be tested. If the model is not a

---

[16] Helferich op. cit.; D. S. Potter, "Managing the Computer Modeling Process," and D. G. deRoulet and D. G. Seguin, "The Application of Computer Models to Distribution Planning," all in *Computers in Manufacturing: Distribution Management*, (Pennsauken, N. J.: Auerbach Publishers, Inc., 1984); J. Elam, D. Klingman, and R. Schneider, "Experience with an Integrated Logistics Planning System," Conference Proceedings, National Council of Physical Distribution Management (San Francisco, 1982).

TABLE 12–4   Internal-Transaction Input to Logistics DSS Data Base

Administration
  Order entry/editing
  Order scheduling
  Order/shipping set preparation
  Invoicing
  Customer communication

  Credit and collection

Warehousing
  Receipts
  Put-away
  Storage
  Replenishment
  Order selection
  Checking
  Clerical/administrative
  Packing and marking
  Staging and order consolidation
  Shipping
  Overall warehouse

Transportation
  Loading
  Line-haul movement
  Overall fleet measure
  Trip log
  Overall costs/unit (ton, miles, stops, volume)
Overall service

Purchasing/Inventory/Production
  Sourcing/Procurement
  Overall purchasing
  Forecasting
  Planning and budgeting
  Execution and control
  Overall inventory management
  Production planning
  Production control
  Scheduling and dispatching
  Shop floor data collection
  Overall production management

Overall
  Service measure
  Cost measure
  Other performance measures

Reprinted with permission from O. K. Helferich, "Logistics Decision Support Systems," *Computers in Manufacturing: Distribution Management* (Pennsauken, NJ: Auerbach Publishers, Inc., 1983).

TABLE 12–5   Data Files Maintained for Logistics DSS Data Base

Basic Files
  Sales—product/market
    History
    Forecasts
  Transportation—mode/weight/class
    Shipment pattern
    Rates/costs
    Shipments
  Inventory—item/location
    Inventory levels
    Cost factors
    Service levels
  Production—item/plant/line
    Production levels
    Costs
    Capacity
  Warehousing—item/location
    Throughput
    Capacity
    Costs

Critical Factors
  Planning horizon
  Product mix
  Scope of analysis
  Other assumptions, guidelines, constraints
Policies/Parameters
  Inventory policy
  Production policy
  Shipment planning
  Service levels
  Inventory carrying costs
Solution Files
  Minimum costs
  Maximum service
  Optimistic sales
  Pessimistic sales
  Change in costs

Reprinted with permission from O. K. Helferich, "Logistics Decision Support Systems," *Computers in Manufacturing: Distribution Management* (Pennsauken, NJ: Auerbach Publishers, Inc., 1983).

reasonable approximation to the situation under study, little in terms of improvements can be anticipated.

In development of a validity test two conditions are desirable. First, the original model state should be structured to represent a known situation. As a start, the first system state is often structured as a replica of the existing system. Second, extreme care must be exercised to use all input flow data associated with the study period. Given these two conditions, it is possible to test validity by appraising the model's capability to represent results of a known situation.

A popular procedure is to operationalize the model on the basis of assumed data. Provided that the components and the functional relationships of the model can be defined, the model can be validated in part on a diagnostic basis to determine sensitivity range. A well-defined body of model-verification theory exists which provides guidance in this critical area of modeling.[17] At least two aspects are important in logistical modeling: (1) surface relevancy and (2) internal consistency.

Surface relevancy relates to the believable nature of model outputs. In essence, does the model output reflect what the manager expects to see about the situation under study? Managerial confidence is critical to the ultimate implementation of a design solution. Therefore, a common procedure is to start the analysis by replicating the existing logistical system. This provides outputs for managerial review that correlate with operating results.

Within the model, a number of relationships must be validated to assure that the model will not lose its validity once it is utilized in design situations. The manner in which flow data are handled must be free of bias, the functional relationships must be consistent, and the feedback mechanisms must be stable. Mathematical and statistical tests are available to assist in the validation of a model's internal consistency.[18]

Regardless of the care taken in testing model validity, an element of error remains a constant possibility. First, it is impossible to calibrate for all possible situations. This danger increases as the model becomes more dynamic. Second, it is never possible to eliminate or identify all compensating errors in a specific validity test. Although such errors may wash out in a validity test, their interrelation may become significant under alternative test situations. Every effort should be made to develop the best possible model, keeping in mind inherent limitations of the modeling process when evaluation results.

The validation process should be initiated by checking system totals such as total logistics costs, total throughput, and overall customer service levels. The process should be continued to check activity, costs, and customer service for each input level within the model. The acceptable variance level depends on the issues being addressed, input accuracy, and modeling assumptions. A preferred accepted variance level is less than ±5 per cent, but ±10 per cent is often adequate if the model is calibrated based on the known error percentage.

Conclusion—Decision Support System Development

The major responsibility of project management in DSS selection is to evaluate the recommendations of the specialist in terms of time and cost. It is to be

---

[17] Peter Gilmour, *Development of a Dynamic Simulation Model for Planning Physical Distribution Systems: Validation* (unpublished Ph. D. dissertation, Michigan State University, 1971), Chap. 2.

[18] Ibid.

expected that the specialist will be more concerned with development of broad-gauged models requiring complex integrative techniques. Management must balance this desire for exacting answers, perfect information, and sophistication with related cost and time requirements. In addition, senior management must understand the capability and limitations of proposed techniques. Although technical evaluation of problem requirements is an area of specialized talent, deciding if the cost/benefits warrant the use of a DSS is a project managerial responsibility. Neglect of this responsibility at an early stage of study development is perhaps the greatest cause for subsequent failure. Once testing and validation have been completed, the DSS can be applied to the specific logistics planning situation. The application is referred to as the system implementation phase.

DECISION SUPPORT SYSTEM IMPLEMENTATION

The third and final phase of logistics planning is system implementation that consists of two modules: (1) project analysis and (2) systems evaluation. The first involves utilization of the DSS and any supportive analyses to select the best logistics redesign alternatives. The second module is a proactive program to continue evaluation and improvement of the system. These two implementation modules are reviewed next.

Project Analysis

The steps of project analysis consist of: (1) basic system use, (2) sensitivity analysis, (3) heuristic procedures, and (4) formulation of recommendations.

Basic System Use

Basic system use consists of establishing and conducting a set of computer runs of the system and analyzing the results. Using the validated DSS, it is necessary to plan a series of DSS computer runs to arrive at the best design solution for the given logistics issues being addressed.

In a technical sense, the formulation of the computer run plan or experimental design is concerned with measuring dependency. For example, given an independent event such as an increase in orders, what will be the impact on the dependent event, logistical cost? To date, there has been relatively limited development of techniques to assist the manager in analysis of experimental data generated by computer models.[19] If only one cause-effect relationship were of concern, a number of basic statistical measurements could assist in evaluation.[20] The problem is that a logistical design analysis is multivariate. Therefore, basic techniques of solution variance measurement do not offer a great deal of practical help.[21]

In the use of a model, the researcher must arrive at several basic decisions aimed at zeroing in on a solution. The structure and sequence of carrying out

---

[19] Geoffrey Gordon, *System Simulation* (Englewood Cliffs, N. J.: Prentice-Hall, Inc., 1969), pp. 18–22; H. Watson, *Computer Simulation in Business* (New York: John Wiley & Sons, 1981).

[20] K. D.Tocher, *The Art of Simulation* (London: English University Press Ltd., 1963), Chap. 2.

[21] Gilmour, op. cit., Chap. 2.

these decisions serve as the experimental design for analysis. In logistical system design problems, four basic determinations are necessary to form an experimental design:[22] (1) state the initial conditions and objectives in the form of parameters and constraints to limit the range of analysis; (2) decide to what degree or over what range of values particular parameters and/or constraints will be permitted to vary in order to establish the necessary measures of system response to arrive at a solution; (3) define the number and sequence of model applications or runs necessary to arrive at a solution; and (4) to the extent practical, measure significant differences in output values (total cost and customer service) as a function of parameter or constraint variance.

The utilization of a logistical DSS involves a great deal of trial-and-error analysis preceded by postulation concerning probable outcomes. Thus, in practical application the number of model runs to include in the experimental design will be a function of the range and variance of output values. This trial-and-error procedure is referred to as sensitivity analysis.

Sensitivity Analysis

In sensitivity analysis, the objective is to see how design solutions vary as a result of systematically changing parameter and constraint values. The process of sensitivity analysis provides a way in which management can pretest alternative distribution policies. In many ways, the real payoff from an integrated logistical system study depends upon the range of sensitivity testing. Given a valid model, the design solution will represent the best possible logistical arrangement in terms of management parameters and constraints. However, this does not mean that the study is over. One of the greatest benefits of a DSS is the ability to ask "what if" questions without taking a chance with the existing business.

In the project planning module, management constraints are introduced concerning output objectives, design parameters, and measurement standards. Each introduces an unknown degree of restraint on the problem solution. By holding all other factors constant, the sensitivity of managerial assumptions can be evaluated in terms of total cost and customer service impact.

To illustrate the importance of such a diagnostic procedure, consider a typical problem confronted by management in logistical system design. Namely, what level of customer service performance should the system provide? The reader will recall that one measure of customer service level is concerned with inventory availability, which, in turn, is a function of safety-stock size.

Figure 12–2 charts the results of using sensitivity analysis to isolate the cost effect of increasing service availability from the existing level of 92 per cent to as close to 100 per cent as possible. To complete the analysis, the constraint dealing with service was relaxed on a systematic basis and total cost for achieving the specified availability was determined. For example, the constraint was first relaxed from 92 to 94 per cent, and the associated design was identified. This procedure was continued until the total-cost curve associated with the service function could be constructed. In the example illustrated in

---

[22] Developed from P. J. Kiviat, *Digital Computer Simulation Modeling Concepts* (Santa Monica, Calif.: Rand Corporation, 1967), p. 18; and M. Asimow, *Introduction to Design* (Englewood Cliffs, N. J.: Prentice-Hall, Inc., 1962).

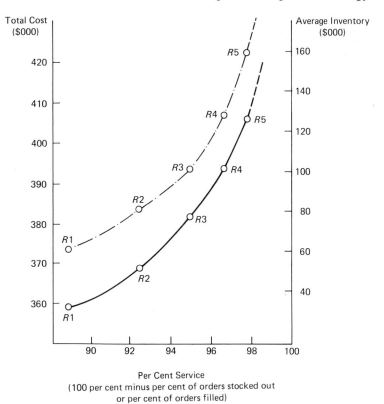

Figure 12–2 Illustration of Using Sensitivity Analysis in Logistical Design

Figure 12–2 five computer runs were required to construct the curve. The chart illustrates both total cost and inventory cost.

An objective in sensitivity analysis is to select critical variables by comprehensive diagnosis. By making value differentials in potentially critical variables and measuring how violently the design solution reacts, it is often possible to limit analysis quickly to those variables that really matter.

In reference to Figure 12–1, a feedback loop is incorporated in the recommended study steps between project procedure and project planning. This linkage reflects the recursive nature of sensitivity analysis. Once the model is fully operational, any or all of the restrictions developed during project planning may be subjected to sensitivity analysis. For example, constraints may be relaxed, measurement standards may be varied, objectives may be altered, and even project scope may be expanded or contracted. The prime requirement to permit comprehensive sensitivity analysis is the availability of data and sufficient model adaptability.

Heuristic Procedure

DSS use, by its very nature, is an interaction process wherein the user attempts to formulate a logistical design utilizing computer capabilities to assist in the development. As noted earlier, when discussing experimental design and sensitivity analysis the utilization of a model involves a great deal of trial-and-error analysis preceded by postulation concerning probable outcomes. To reduce analysis cost, a great deal of attention has focused on the development of a logical procedure to limit the range of solution options to a manageable number. It is becoming increasingly common to refer to the solution approach as a heuristic procedure.[23]

A heuristic approach to problem-solving closely parallels the thought process of the human mind. In essence, it is a steplike procedure that narrows in on the solution by systematic elimination of the alternatives. Such an approach does not necessarily result in selection of an optimal solution. The step procedure requires review at each decision point with related explanation at each step of the procedure. Thus, the solution once derived requires little interpretation on the part of the planner.

In logistical design, modeling constitutes only one aspect of the overall study. Regardless of the technical nature of the model employed, chances are it will be used a number of times under different design constraints to arrive at a solution. The very nature of system design is experimental since management is seeking a more satisfactory level of cost and/or service performance. Thus, whereas the technique employed may be precise in its analytical capabilities, the managerial process of analysis is not.

For example, assume that the desired end result of the analysis is to select the number, size, and location of distribution warehouses. Inventory policy is assumed constant, and a number of warehouses is assumed to start the analysis. The total heuristic process attempts to reduce location alternatives to a minimum consistent with cost-service objectives. Managerial intervention is planned at critical points in the search process in order to guarantee acceptable results.

Under heuristic procedures, a given network of facilities is modeled and measured on the basis of cost and service capability. This information is given to management for evaluation. The assumption is made that management has sufficient appreciation of realistic requirements not to eliminate a vital aspect of the solution. As a result of this evaluation, additional distribution facilities are added to or deleted from the network by managerial discretion.

The modified system state is then evaluated. As new facilities are added or deleted, existing warehouses are reviewed in terms of continued desirability. Once again, results are compiled for managerial review. This process continues until the most acceptable network of warehouses is determined.[24]

To assist management in the solution process, a number of DSS offer preprogrammed heuristic procedures. These procedures, often referred to as model heuristics, consist of analysis rules which automatically test the sensitivity of selected parameters which are typically major focal points in strategic planning. The primary purpose of the preprogrammed analysis routines is to increase the efficiency of the modeling process. It is important to remember that model heuristic procedures are based upon assumptions that will direct the solution process and influence outcome. Naturally, the planner must fully understand the assumptive logic behind the model heuristics to avoid solution bias.

---

[23] Kiviat, ibid., p 18.

[24] The initial model using this procedure in a logistical system design was reported by Harvey N. Shycon and Richard B. Maffei, "Simulation—Tools for Better Distribution," *Harvard Business Review* Vol. 38 (November–December 1960), pp. 65–75.

Formal heuristic procedures serve to highlight the fact that the most comprehensive computer models are at best an aid to management when developing a strategic plan. To a significant degree, modeling is more an art than a science. Soundly developed heuristic analysis procedures serve to increase the trial-and-error efficiency.

Formulation of Recommendations

The most common question asked by senior management is "What can I expect to see as the end result of logistical system redesign?" Unfortunately, unless considerable evaluation is completed and a summary report prepared, the executive will see a voluminous stack of computer printouts. The mental barrier to approaching such a mass of data can greatly reduce the benefit gained from the study as a result of the need to "dig it out." Therefore, the best procedure is to develop a study summary report of significant findings. Such a report will contain the following information: (1) a statement of system customer service capabilities, including an estimate of performance probability, (2) an estimate of total fixed and variable cost expressed as a cost of sales for a specified operating period, (3) a comparison of service and cost projections for the redesigned system in comparison to the current system for identical time periods, (4) estimated results of several alternative service policies and related costs of performance, and (5) a format of required transport facility, communication, and inventory capabilities under the integrated system.

The results of the overall redesign effort will contain infinitely more detail than the information listed above. In the final analysis, recommendations to support implementation must quantify two basic decision elements: (1) cost-benefit evaluations and (2) risk appraisal.

Cost-Benefit Evaluations. As the feasibility of strategic planning, potential benefits were identified as service improvement, cost reduction, and cost prevention. It was noted that these benefits were not mutually exclusive and that a sound strategy might realize all simultaneously. To evaluate the potential of implementing a particular logistical strategy, a comparative analysis must be completed of present cost and service capabilities to conditions projected under a revamped system. The ideal benefit analysis compares the two systems fully implemented for a base period and then projects comparative operations across the planning horizon. Thus, benefits can be projected on the basis of one-time savings which result from system reconfiguration as well as recurring operating economies. The importance of viewing cost-benefit results across the planning horizon is illustrated by the following examples.

Illustration I. The planning situation called for a 10-year evaluation of required warehousing capacity. The existing system consisted of six regional distribution warehouses. A sales growth of 50 per cent was forecast over the 10-year planning horizon. Management specified that customer service be maintained at or above the current level of 80 per cent of all orders being serviced at lowest possible total cost and within a five-day total order cycle.

Heuristic analysis established three design alternatives that management desired to evaluate in detail: (1) expand existing facilities, (2) expand existing facilities plus add two facilities, and (3) expand existing facilities plus add three

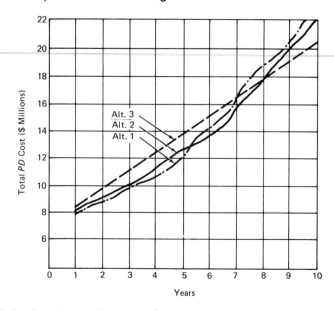

Figure 12–3   Total Cost—Illustration I

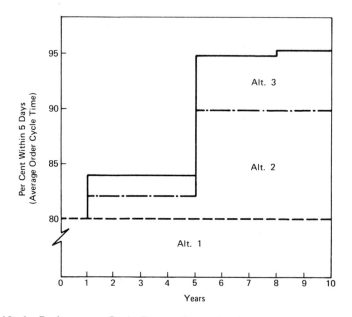

Figure 12–4   Performance Cycle Time—Illustration I

facilities. The cost-service results of the detailed simulation runs are graphically illustrated in Figures 12–3 and 12–4.

A surprising result was that total logistical system cost over the planning horizon was similar for each alternative. Each alternative experienced increasing costs over time. However, trade-offs between the various physical distribution components in each situation were substantially different. Alternative 1 experienced highest transport costs coupled with lowest inventory costs. The situation was reversed in the case of alternative 3.

Despite similar total system costs, a significant differential existed between the customer service capabilities of the three alternatives. Although not expected, all three systems realized the stated managerial service goals. Over the planning horizons, however, alternative 3 realized greater than 90 per cent of all orders being serviced within a five-day performance cycle. Thus, alternative 3 was about 10 per cent more effective than alternative 1 at approximately the same total cost.

The preplanning management expectation was that additional warehouses would be required to maintain desired service standards, and that the total system cost associated with adding facilities would increase substantially. The simulated results provided a flexible plan for expanding service capabilities, if and when desired, as part of the total marketing offering. In the interim, cost-service objectives could be realized by retaining and expanding the existing warehouses.

Illustration II. The planning situation involved inventory planning for a market area consisting of eight states. In this situation the marketing organization desired the addition of a second warehouse to improve service capability and average order cycle by reducing transit time. Expectations were that the total cost of servicing the overall market would increase as a result of adding the second facility. A second alternative for improving customer service was to increase the safety stock at the existing warehouse. Increased safety stock was expected to improve average order cycle time by reducing back-orders. The existing average order cycle time was 4.6 days with 75 per cent of all orders filled within 5 days. Marketing desired a 10 per cent improvement at minimum total cost.

Addition of the warehouse (alternative 1) reduced the average order cycle time to 4.1 days, while increasing the orders filled within 5 days from 75 to 92 per cent. Increasing safety stock at the existing warehouse (alternative 2) reduced the average order cycle by 0.3 day, to 4.3 days. This was equivalent to improving the percentage of orders filled within 5 days from 75 to 87 per cent. Over the 10-year planning horizon, the addition of a second warehouse provided the lowest-total-cost alternative.

The service-cost relationships of the two alternatives are illustrated in Figures 12–5 and 12–6. In this situation the warehouse addition resulted in the lowest cost and provided the highest average customer service. It is interesting to note that the addition of a warehouse was the more costly alternative for approximately the first three years of simulated operations, but the least costly for the aggregated 10 years. Thus, marketing could realize a 12 per cent increase in service capability for the initial three years at the lowest total cost by increasing safety stocks at the existing warehouse. Establishment of a second warehouse to be operational by the fourth year would realize an additional 5 per cent improvement in service and a continuation of the least-cost arrangement. This relationship of cost and service over the planning horizon is one of the many situations simulated to date which illustrates the importance of dynamic planning structure.

Illustration III. A final planning illustration shows total system service relationships on: (1) the number and sequencing of warehouse locations, (2) inventory cost related to performance delays for an eight-location structure, and (3) market area adjustment to postpone timing of warehouse additions.

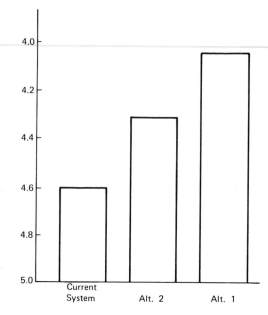

Figure 12–5 Performance Cycle Time—Illustration II

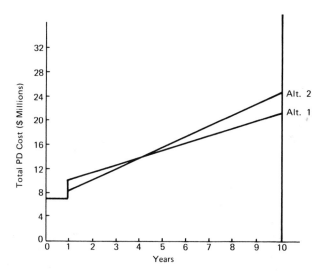

Figure 12–6 Total Cost—Illustration II

The general relationship of service as a function of the number and sequencing of warehouse additions is illustrated in Figure 12–7. A specific marketing situation was evaluated over a 10-year period in an effort to identify the shortest possible average order cycle. A locational model was used to select the sequence and number of warehouse locations constrained only by permissible annual capital investment. Inventory performance was held constant at 85 per cent of all orders being filled within the average order-cycle time. Given the initial six warehouse locations, an expansion plan was selected from a list of 35

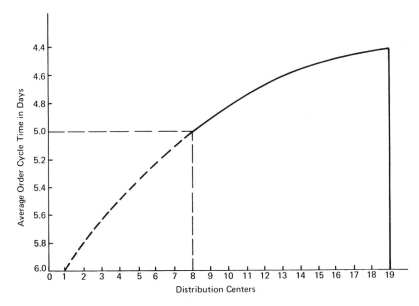

Figure 12–7 Relationship of Distribution Centers to Average Performance Cycle Time—Illustration III

potential warehouse additions. The facility planning model isolated the expansion sequence by selecting additional warehouses on the basis of the incremental relationship between minimum added cost and maximum service.

In total, performance cycle time was reduced from 6.0 to 4.4 days by expanding the locational structure from 1 to 19 warehouses. As anticipated, improvement in simulated average order time increased at a decreasing rate as additional warehouses were added. No improvement was realized beyond 19 warehouses.

Based upon the expansion sequence illustrated in Figure 12–7, management elected to evaluate the addition of two warehouses beyond the existing six. An analysis was conducted to determine the relationship of inventory investment cost to average performance delays for the eight-warehouse configuration. In effect, the original constraint of 85 per cent of all orders being satisfied within 5.0 average order-cycle days was simulated to obtain the service improvement possible from increased safety-stock levels. For the particular number and location of warehouses it was determined that an increase from $7 to $14 million of annual inventory cost would be required to increase service from 85 to 100 per cent of all orders filled within 5.0 average order-cycle days (Figure 12–8).

Next, the alternative of adding two warehouses was subjected to sensitivity analysis, wherein market area assignments to specific warehouses were allowed to shift a maximum of twice during the 10-year planning horizon. The objective was to determine if a trade-off could be realized between investment and operating cost at little or no sacrifice in customer service. The sensitivity testing resulted in a plan to postpone the first facility by one year and the second facility by two years. The situations illustrated demonstrate the results and recommendations expected from cost-benefit evaluations. Each example was selected from an overall strategic planning situation to illustrate the importance of a planning time horizon. The illustrations indicate the depth of cost-benefit

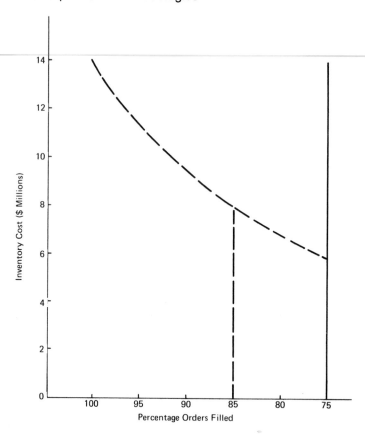

Figure 12–8 Percentage of Orders Filled in 5.0 Average Performance-Cycle Days—Eight-Warehouse Configuration—One Year—Illustration III

justification that should support a recommendation to adopt a specific logistical strategy.

Risk Appraisal. A second type of justification necessary to support planning recommendations is an appraisal of risk involved in the proposed strategic plan. Risk relates to the probability of whether or not assumptions underlying the study will, in fact, materialize, as well as an appraisal of potential hazards related to system switchover.

Risk related to assumptive logic of the plan can be quantified by selected sensitivity runs. For example, assumptions can be varied, and the resultant impact upon the performance under the proposed strategy can be calculated. The end result of this form of appraisal should be a financial evaluation of downside risk involvement if the predictions upon which the plan is predicated do not fully materialize.

Risk related to system switchover can also be quantified. The implementation of a strategic logistical plan, as noted earlier, may take several operating years. The typical procedure is to develop an implementation schedule to guide system switchover. To evaluate the risk associated with unanticipated delay, a series of contingency plans can be tested and reduced to an estimated loss of anticipated benefits.

Formulation of Recommendations

A great deal of planning effort can be wasted if the recommended logistical design is not clearly articulated. No blueprint exists regarding the ideal method for supporting a plan or presenting recommendations. Setting aside the detail, a good test of the strength of the recommendation's supportive logic is to see if the benefits and risks can be summarized clearly into a short statement for executive review. Details can be generated to the extent necessary to support planning conclusions when and if needed.

One positive result of using a DSS when developing a logistical design is that a time-phased implementation program can be specified. Once management has selected a final logistics design, the DSS can be used to develop an implementation program. It would be a rare situation when an across-the-board revision of a logistical system could be implemented. The DSS is a valuable tool for selection of the steps that will provide the greatest payoff if implemented at once. A five-year, or any other time period, implementation program can be developed with a measure of expected results. Priorities and checkpoints are necessary to guide revision of the existing system. The changing nature of business requires that constant checks be performed to test the continued validity of the system model.

From the viewpoint of scheduling and control, the techniques of PERT and CPM offer management a methodology to assist in plan implementation.[25] Since full implementation of a logistics redesign might be expected to span several years, operational planning for specific time periods will specify changes in system structure or operating procedure scheduled for implementation.

System Evaluation

The final module of implementation referred to as systems evaluation includes programs of: (1) ongoing usage and (2) enhancement.

Ongoing Usage Program

From a managerial viewpoint, a final logistics system design never really exists. The redesign implementation plan should constantly be adjusted to take advantage of change. The organization that develops a logistical DSS, formulates a redesign implementation plan, and then disregards the model forfeits a powerful planning tool. The continuous process of planning is illustrated in Figure 12–1 by a feedback linkage between implementation and system definition.

Enhancement Program

The logistics system itself is dynamic and should be continually evaluated to identify the DSS limitations as well as to take advantage of its capabilities to address other logistics situations. Early project success, continued support by top logistics management, and a designated person(s) responsible for the DSS through an information center concept will assure that subsequent projects result in enhancements in the information base and the DSS itself.

---

[25] See Chapter 14, pages 464–68.

A proactive program for utilization is a major factor toward achieving the benefits attributed to DSS. These benefits are significant, including: (1) increased insights regarding cost/service/-productivity trade-offs, (2) specific productivity/ROI improvements, (3) better decision-making over time as the prototype DSS is enhanced by improving the knowledge base and intelligence, (4) improvements to MIS and data base, and (5) flexibility for broad range of "what if" analyses.

Cost reductions possible through more effective decision-making and control range from 5 to 20 per cent of annual materials and logistics costs. Customer service and general productivity improvements can also result from DSS implementation.

COMMENTS ON MANAGEMENT INFORMATION SYSTEM DESIGN

The logistics management information systems include the following scope: (1) purchasing and materials management, (2) operations and manufacturing support, and (3) physical distribution management. The major functions for on-line transaction systems are listed in Table 12–6.

Traditional MIS Design

The basic phases for the traditional or historical approach to information systems development are similar to those presented in Figure 12–1. Phase I would provide the feasibility assessment with a system proposal and project work plan. The second phase of systems development following a traditional life cycle methodology requires two levels of specificity. The first level continues the analysis building upon the system requirements created in the initial phase. The second level of specificity is the detailed system design. The traditional development cycle includes: (1) requirements and specifications, (2) design, (3) programming, (4) testing and integration, (5) deployment, and (6) maintenance.[26]

After the user has approved the input and output of the system, processing flows are designed which incorporate the input, output, and data structure created in the first portion of the design step. A narrative description of each processing step is created as a guide for the development phase.

The next step, programming and testing, may constitute the largest from the standpoint of time investment, but it is second in importance to the previous step of system design. History has shown all too vividly that a shallow emphasis on design leads to an extended programming and testing phase with resulting project delays and budget overruns. The cause of this phenomenon is the lack or absence of integration, understanding, and detail in the design step of the second phase. Significant advantages have been made in application development tools that generate program code faster than traditional methods.

---

[26] For a more detailed discussion of the development cycle, see J. Martin, *An Information Systems Manifesto* (Englewood Cliffs, N. J.: Prentice-Hall, Inc., 1984), Chap. 11, p. 180; and L. E. Long, *Design and Strategy for Corporate Information Services* (Englewood Cliffs, N. J.: Prentice-Hall, Inc., 1982), Part II, Chap. 3–6; R. G. Murdick and J. E. Ross, *Information Systems for Modern Management* (Englewood Cliffs, N. J.: Prentice-Hall, Inc., 1975).

TABLE 12–6   Major Functions in Logistics On-line Transactions Systems

Purchasing and Materials Management

1. Order control/expediting
2. Receiving and inspection control
3. Transportation
4. Debit memo/accounting interface
5. Buyer and management tools
6. Document generation and processing

Operations and Manufacturing Management

1. Forecasting
2. Production planning (input-output control)
3. Master production scheduling (MPS)
4. Capacity requirements planning (CRP)
5. Materials requirements planning (MRP)
6. Shop floor control
7. Standard product costing

Physical Distribution Management

1. Forecasting
2. Order administration/processing
3. Shipment planning
4. Transportation/shipping
5. Inventory management and control
6. Warehouse operations

The third and final phase, implementation, runs approximately concurrently with programming and testing. Implementation begins with the planning necessary to identify the tasks that will ensure a smooth system startup. System and user documentation and training are completed prior to conversion and parallel testing. Users and operations personnel participate in conversion and parallel testing which is dress rehearsal for the final step in this phase, live operations.

This phase also includes evaluations and monitoring of the system utilization. The original plan is reviewed and variances from expectations are quantified. This information is valuable as a point of reference when estimating the next project. Additionally, postinstallation support is provided to the user and operations personnel in the form of spot visits and postinstallation interviews.

Need to Reexamine the Development Cycle

The traditional development cycle described above is typical of the methodologies developed prior to the tools and techniques of the 1980s. These advanced tools, as listed in Table 12–7, require significant changes in the methodologies to receive full benefit in the development of application systems.

An example of new methodologies for more effective system development is prototyping. Prototyping has been applied historically to test complex engineering designs before the final product development. The prototype is built to test the principles, ensure that the system works, and obtain suggestions to incorporate in the final system.

TABLE 12-7 Tools That Identify Significant Change Potential in MIS Methodologies

---

1. Advanced application languages (fourth generation—nonprocedural)
2. Fifth-generation techniques that generate program code automatically
3. Computer-aided design and graphics
4. Data-modeling tools
5. Software engineering techniques
6. Prototyping languages for DSS and MIS
7. Linking of microprocessors and minicomputers to accomplish distributed processing
8. Artificial-intelligence software
9. Information centers to assist users
10. End-user languages

J. Martin states that complex data-processing systems need prototyping because many changes are likely to be made for the final system.[27] Prototyping was not feasible prior to the 1980s because the cost of developing a prototype was approximately the same as programming the working or "fielded" system. The availability of advanced "fourth generation" software allows development of application with much less time and effort, making it practical to develop prototype models. The systems analyst working with the logistics user can create a prototype to demonstrate basic processing, report screens, and data preparation. The user and analyst then through their dialogue and usage of the system are in a position to define the modifications desired for the final system. These new tools are being applied to logistics system design.[28] Therefore, it is clear that the development methodologies need to be redesigned or at least be reexamined to take advantage of the new information technologies.

SUMMARY

In this chapter a three-phase procedure was presented (Figure 12-1) as a recommended managerial guide to logistics system redesign. To illustrate the use of the guide, the first major section presented a general overview of the initial phase—systems definition. This phase is general and can be applied to all logistics design situations. The next sections discussed the second and third phases—systems development and implementation using decision support systems. The final section presented comments on the guide relative to the design of a logistics management information system.

Emphasis throughout the chapter has been placed upon managerial responsibility rather than technical detail. Particular attention was directed to the

---

[27] Martin, op. cit., pp. 46–47.

[28] O. K. Helferich, "Advanced Software Applied to Logistics Management," *Computers in Manufacturing: Distribution Management* (Pennsauken, N. J.: Auerbach Publishers, Inc., 1985), O. K. Helferich and D. G. Seguin, "Fourth Generation Software—An Overview for the Materials and Logistics Manager," *National Council of Physical Distribution Management Proceedings* (Chicago, NCPDM, 1984, pp. 85–99); and O. K. Helferich and Ray C. Rowland, "Expert Systems Software: An Overview for the Materials and Logistics Manager," *National Council of Physical Distribution Management Proceedings* (Chicago, NCPDM, 1984, pp. 249–260).

critical nature of the logistics manager and staff in feasibility assessment, project planning, specification development, testing and validation, project analysis, and system evaluation. The entire chapter stressed managerial involvement in the overall logistics system redesign project. Attention in Chapter 13 is directed to a review of the decision support technique available for logistics system redesign.

QUESTIONS

1. What is the basic objective in a system redesign study? Is it normally a one-time activity?
2. In performing a feasibility assessment, why is the situational analysis extremely important? What is the role of developing a supporting logic?
3. Are the design constraints specified at the early stage of a study capable of being modified at a later point in the system redesign? Why would this be done and to what extent is it practical?
4. Does the nontechnical manager have responsibility in model development?
5. What is meant by validity checking and calibration?
6. Why is geoclassification of data important to logistical studies?
7. What is sensitivity analysis, and what part does it play in experimental design?
8. Compare decision support systems versus an on-line transaction system in terms of the most significant similarities and differences in the redesign process.
9. What role does prototyping have in the developing of (1) decision support systems and (2) on-line transaction systems?
10. Discuss the formulation of an implementation program as a result of a logistical redesign study. What would you consider to be the major ingredients of such a plan?

CHAPTER 13

Design and Analysis Techniques

This chapter presents an overview of logistical system design techniques. Throughout earlier chapters, the systems approach was presented as a method whereby complex logistical arrangements can be analyzed and evaluated. The techniques reviewed in this chapter represent tools capable of applying systems and information technology to logistical strategic, tactical, and operational planning.

The initial section categorizes typical design problems faced in logistical system analysis. The objective is to provide a framework to match analysis technique to problem. The second section discusses important considerations and evaluative criteria to use when selecting an analysis technique. The third section describes symbolic replications, which are the most basic and simple logistics planning models. The fourth section reviews two major classes of analytical models. The fifth section discusses and illustrates the characteristics of simulation models. The final section presents a procedure for identifying and evaluating analytical alternatives.

LOGISTICAL DESIGN PROBLEMS

A logistical strategy consists of a long-range commitment of financial and human resources to the movement and storage operations of an enterprise. The specific objective of the strategic plan is to provide an operating structure capable of attaining performance goals at the lowest total cost. It is the strategic plan that delineates where warehouse facilities will be located, where and which assortments and quantities of materials and finished inventories will be stocked, how transportation will be performed, which techniques of materials handling will be employed, the methods and procedures of order processing and procurement, as well as all other aspects of logistical operations. Perhaps the most important aspect of the strategic plan is that it provides the mechanism by which logistical operations are coordinated into an integrated effort.

The strategic planning process is appropriately viewed as a continuous process. The typical plan should be concerned with a series of modifications to an existing logistical system. Such planned system modifications are implemented over an extended time period. In this sense, the planning situation is more appropriately identified as system redesign, as contrasted to a system design. In every organization, a limit exists regarding the extent of structural change that can be effectively implemented during a given time period. For example, the opening or closing of two distribution warehouses may represent the maximum facility change an organizatiion can handle during a fiscal year while maintaining day-to-day operational and tactical control of logistical performance. Thus, the implementation of a strategic plan may span a substantial time period.

The extended time required to activate a total logistical system strategy means that there is a good chance that the original plan will be modified prior to final implementation. The planning process as well as the analytical techniques require periodic reevaluation of system design alternatives while implementation is underway. Assuming a vigorous and ever-changing competitive situation, the period of implementation may never end.

To assist management in the formulation and review of strategic and tactical plans, a wide range of logistical models have been developed. As noted earlier, a model consists of a body of information, relationships, and restrictions about a unique situation accumulated for purposes of systems analysis.[1] The model represents a substitute for actual testing of potential strategies. When analytic or numerical computation procedures are incorporated in the model, it is typically referred to as an analysis technique. Identification as an analysis technique means that the model incorporates a computational procedure whereby system design alternatives can be evaluated and quantified. In this chapter, primary attention is directed to a managerial description of logistical analysis techniques and considerations. Analysis techniques may or may not require computer analysis, depending upon the size and complexity of the planning process. Analysis techniques are appropriately viewed as one and only one aspect of formulating the logistical plan. To clarify this point in the reader's mind, it is suggested that the *Managerial Guide to Logistical Redesign* illustrated in Figure 12–1 be reviewed.[2] The techniques of logistical system design are aids to assist in the overall process of formulating strategic and tactical plans.

Owing to the relative newness of both logistics and quantitative techniques, one might wonder how extensively such techniques are actually employed in

---

[1] A comprehensive classification of model types is found in Jay W. Forrester, *Industrial Dynamics* (Cambridge, Mass.: The MIT Press, 1961), Chapter 4.

[2] See Chapter 12, pp. 349–87.

logistical planning. An analysis of 75 industrial enterprises revealed that 43 were currently involved in logistical modeling. Among the firms using computerized techniques, 73 different models were reported.[3] The firms that reported being "into" modeling normally were multiple-model users. Such models ranged from small-scale special-purpose applications to large-scale total-system-design techniques. Thus, at least for a substantial number of enterprises, the use of computerized techniques to assist in logistical planning is a "here today" activity.

The first requirement in the process of analyzing a logistical design alternative is the identification of the specific problem. A major criticism of design and evaluation procedures is that there have been too many situations where investigators have attempted to fit the problem to the analysis technique rather than identifying the correct approach for solving the problem. This section identifies and discusses characteristics of typical planning situations confronted by logistical analysts.

Logistical analysis situations can be categorized into three categories. The first consists of strategic issues involved in a major commitment of resources over an extended planning horizon typically longer than one year. Facility location and distribution channel design questions represent strategic planning situations. The second category consists of tactical issues wherein resource commitment is not as significant and the planning horizon is not as long as a strategic situation. An analysis investigating inventory level or position within the logistical system is an example of a tactical issue. The final category considers day-to-day operational issues such as what distribution facility to use for a particular shipment or how to consolidate customer orders.[4]

Logistics planners typically face issues related to each category. The ability to identify the specific issue and select an appropriate analysis technique is the key to effective planning. The following parts discuss the general questions involved in strategic and tactical planning. This chapter is concerned primarily with strategic and tactical planning situations, the application of logistical techniques to operations problems is not discussed. Chapter 14 provides a comprehensive discussion of techniques useful in making such operational evaluations.

Strategic Issues

Strategic logistical issues typically seek to identify the best flow and allocation of inventory over an extended planning horizon. The general managerial questions in this category include: (1) warehouse and plant locations, (2) distribution system changes as a result of changing products and markets, and (3) customer warehouse assignment. In general, strategic questions concern long-term facility location and customer-facility assignment under either stable or changing environmental conditions. The overall objective is to minimize the flow-related costs of moving inventory from manufacturing to markets. Flow-related costs are expenses incurred as a result of the production and movement of goods

---

[3] Robert G. House and George C. Jackson, *Trends in Computer Applications in Transportation and Distribution Management* (Columbus, Ohio: Ohio State University, 1976).

[4] For a discussion of these model categorizations, see Paul S. Bender, William D. Northrup, and Jeremy F. Shapiro, "Practical Modeling for Resource Management," *Harvard Business Review*, Vol. 59 (March–April 1981), pp. 163–73.

such as variable production cost, handling cost, and transportation cost. Since such analysis considers an extended planning horizon and is primarily investigating flow-related costs, most strategic issues can be evaluated using aggregate flow volumes rather than requiring detailed transaction data. Thus, for a strategic level analysis, the individual orders or transactions can be summarized to aggregate flows such as annual demand to a market area. In general, the analysis objective is to identify the network of distribution facilities and sourcing policies that minimize operational expenses for the specified planning conditions. The ability to aggregate orders allows the analysis to effectively apply certain modeling techniques, but it also means that questions that must consider the time relationships between orders cannot be analyzed using strategic planning tools.

Tactical Issues

Tactical issues involve less risky and shorter-range considerations than strategic situations. The major objective is to identify distribution policies that achieved desired objectives most effectively and efficiently. The general questions that can be categorized as tactical planning issues include: (1) shipment policy evaluation, (2) production-distribution coordination, (3) customer service level, (4) inventory cost/service trade-off analysis, and (5) distribution impact of forecast alternatives.

Shipment policy evaluation investigates issues such as the locations and rules for shipment consolidation or load planning. Specific questions that might be investigated include the effects of alternative weight limits and holding times for shipment consolidation. The impacts of changes in production cycles or lead times are examples of issues that involve distribution-production coordination. Such changes directly impact the level of finished-goods inventory required to meet alternative customer service levels. Customer service issues often require the capability to evaluate performance over time to perform an adequate analysis of order cycle time or inventory availability. The specific questions that might be addressed include the customer service impact of changing order cycle times or replenishment order times, the impact of order consolidation policies, or the impact of order prioritization. For analysis of customer service, a common concern is the projection of inventory levels required to maintain a prescribed performance level. The selection of the overall inventory strategy requires the consideration of alternative inventory replenishment logics, safety-stock levels, and order quantities. A final tactical issue concerns the impact of forecast methodology on logistical performance. Forecast considerations that affect logistical performance include the forecast technique, the forecast cycle, the forecast accuracy, and the level of forecast aggregation.

For an accurate evaluation of the above issues tactical analysis requires the incorporation of time as well as locational considerations in logistical planning. The anlaysis must consider the timing of demand on the system across a network of facilities. The analysis must also consider the dynamic impact of stockouts and overstocks on sytem performance. Tactical issues generally involve system dynamics, whereas strategic issues are concerned with the appropriate network of facility locations.

The above discussion identifies the major issues facing a logistics planner. The following section discusses the considerations for strategic and tactical design modeling.

DESIGN MODELING

When it is desirable to use logistical modeling as a tool for strategic or tactical anaylsis, the initial requirement is to identify and evaluate alternative analysis techniques. The first part of this section discusses desirable attributes to consider when evaluating alternative models. The second part discusses application requirements that impact model selection. Each type of consideration is important to fitting the correct analysis technique to a planning situation.

Model Attributes

An ideal planning model for strategic and tactical planning incorporates four primary attributes. These attributes, which should be evaluated when considering the application of a model to a specific analysis situation, provide direction concerning model identification and selection. These attributes are: (1) modular construction, (2) accuracy, (3) simplicity, and (4) adaptability. Each attribute and related implications are defined and discussed below.

Modular Construction

The concept of a modular construction refers to analysis techniques which were developed as a set of standard processes or procedures which can be arranged into a number of different analysis combinations. The process being modeled is ideally subdivided into the smallest activities that represent aspects of the process. For example, the processing of customer orders might be subdivided into the activities of order receipt, order entry, order processing, order picking, loading, and shipment. Each activity should be designed as an individual component which is as independent as possible of the other modules.

Modular construction provides the advantage of increased flexibility since the individual activities can be combined in a number of different ways, thus providing for the evaluation of a larger number of alternatives. In addition, a tool that is modularly constructed is much easier to change since it is only necessary to change the specific module dealing with an activity. For example, if it is desired to incorporate a transportation consolidation logic within an overall logistics planning model, it should only be necessary to develop a representative module and insert it within the picking and shipping activities. The other advantage of the modular approach is that smaller modules are easier to define, develop, and incorporate into an overall analysis technique. It is easier to verify that all individual parts operate correctly within a large system when the analysis technique has modular design.

Accuracy

Accuracy is a second major model attribute. Although it is obvious that an accurate model is better than an inaccurate one, accuracy consideration comes in degrees and at various costs. An accurate analysis, in terms of level of detail and assumptions, leads to realistic and acceptable conclusions. Accuracy may be expressed in terms of a technique's level of detail or fit with the business situation. The level of detail reflects the tool's ability to consider problem detail at a level that is both realistic and tractable. The analysis must be sufficiently detailed so decision-makers can accept that the solution is realistic to their business. The details might include the number of markets and products analyzed or the detailed events and activities that are modeled.

When designing or selecting an analysis technique, a planner must identify the desired degree of accuracy. The accuracy level should be specified in terms of allowable error and analysis scope. Allowable error can be specified in terms of the calibration of technique results to historical performance. The comparisons might include system throughput, logistical costs, or service level. Accuracy specification must also determine the level of time comparison. For example, are accuracy comparisons desired annually, monthly, or weekly? In addition to the temporal and spatial dimensions of accuracy, a planner must also identify the specific variables that will be used to measure accuracy.

The second accuracy consideration concerns the scope of the analysis. Although, from a systems perspective, it might be necessary to include all the activities within the logistical system that interrelate, such a comprehensive analysis is not always possible or practical. It is often necessary to reduce the scope of the analysis to a problem size that can be effectively analyzed. For example, while warehouse operations are initiated by customer orders, it is typically not necessary to include an analysis of order processing when evaluating the impact of an automated warehouse system. Based upon the manager's knowledge of the logistical system interactions, the analysis scope must be selected to consider the interactions that are important and disregard the rest. This accuracy consideration requires that a planner be able to identify and omit elements of an analysis that will minimally impact the outcome.

The third accuracy consideration concerns the nature of the data available for the analysis. The accuracy of the technique should be commensurate with the accuracy of available data. It does not make sense to utilize a very detailed and precise analysis technique when accurate data are not available or when assumptions must be made to establish the values for a significant number of data elements.

Simplicity

A third consideration, which is tied to accuracy, concerns simplicity of the analysis. While the analysis must include enough detail to support realistic and implementable conclusions, the fundamental objective of parsimony must be considered. Instead of attempting to perform a detailed analysis of complex relationships, the analysis should be attempted with a technique that is as simple as possible. If a simple approach does not yield enough accuracy, then a more complex analysis may be justified. However, it does not make sense to begin with a complex, and probably expensive and time-consuming, analysis when a simpler approach will provide adequate results. The general rule is to start as simply as possible and add complexity as justified.

Adaptability

Technique adaptability is the fourth consideration when evaluating either a computer or manual procedure for analysis. The technique should be adaptable and flexible enough to accommodate variations in the analysis such as the inclusion of multiple distribution center locations or multiple stages within manufacturing. An adaptable technique allows a single analysis approach to be used for a wide range of problems without modification. Although the adaptability usually comes at the price of efficiency in analysis, it is usually a better analysis trade-off to have flexibility over speed, given today's low computing cost.

Application Requirements

In addition to the attributes suggested above, three additional application requirements are important when evaluating analysis techniques. However, these considerations relate to the characteristics of the problem rather than the attributes of the technique. These considerations are: (1) the number of stages and echelons, (2) whether or not the analysis is computerized, and (3) the sensitivity capability. Each consideration is discussed below.

Multiple Echelons

The number of stages or echelons refers to the number of levels within the distribution channel.[5] Each channel institution represents one stage. Figure 13–1 illustrates a two- and three-level distribution system. Many distribution analysis techniques, particularly for the inventory management area, make the implicit assumption that the distribution system is single-staged. This assumption facilitates the analysis by ignoring the impact of other channel levels. Although it is often useful to make this assumption, the planner must be careful when eliminating channel institutions from consideration. For example, if master production scheduling significantly impacts the distribution center inventory levels, it would be a mistake not to consider the scheduling when analyzing distribution center inventory policy. The same problem potentially exists when utilizing a technique to evaluate distribution center locations. If the objective is to evaluate potential locations for both regional distribution centers and field warehouses given fixed locations for plants and customers, the analytical technique must be capable of performing a three-stage analysis. Owing to the significant interrelationships between echelons, it would not be wise to use an analysis technique to independently locate the regional facilities and field warehouses. When there are significant interactions between echelons, the planner should select a technique that can adequately consider levels in the distribution channel.

Computerization

The second application consideration is the degree of computerization of the technique. In today's environment of decreasing costs of information technology, it is becoming more cost-effective to perform analysis using computers. While computerization usually provides for a quicker and less tedious analysis, the planner must trade off the analysis in speed with the corresponding decrease in flexibility and the increased time required to identify or develop a technique.

---

[5] Arthur M. Geoffrion, "A Guide to Computer-Assisted Methods for Distribution Planning," *Sloan Management Review*, Vol. 16 (Winter 1975), pp. 17–41.

Two Stage Distribution Channel

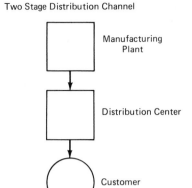

Manufacturing
Plant

Distribution Center

Customer

Three Stage Distribution Channel

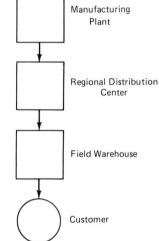

Manufacturing
Plant

Regional Distribution
Center

Field Warehouse

Customer

Figure 13–1 Distribution Echelons

The increasing availability of "canned" or "off the shelf" computerized techniques makes the consideration less important than it was in the past.

Sensitivity Analysis

The last application consideration is the technique's capability to perform sensitivity analysis. Sensitivity analysis is the ability to evaluate the relative impact that changes in input data would have on solution results. To illustrate, in a total logistical system analysis, an example of sensitivity analysis would be the evaluation of the impact of a 10-per-cent increase in transportation rates on the solution. Through sensitivity analysis, the planner should be able to determine whether or not a change would result in a significant impact on system performance.

Sensitivity analysis accomplishes two goals. First, the planner can identify the impact that cost or demand changes would have on system performance. Second, the planner can identify the potential impact of data assumptions. For example, if there is no significant impact identified when the transportation rates increase by 10 per cent, the planner could conclude that the transportation rate accuracy is not particularly important to the results of the analysis. Therefore, it would not be necessary to place significant resources into the development of accurate transportation rates. On the other hand, the planner may find that the solution is very sensitive to transportation rates, therefore, the planning process requires a critical review of transportation rates and assumptions.

SYMBOLIC REPLICATIONS

The first category of tools available to assist in strategic and tactical planning are symbolic replications that include: (1) comparative analysis, (2) break-even analysis, and (3) flowcharting.

Comparative Analysis

One of the most widely used procedures for evaluating the desirability between two courses of action is to calculate the comparative total cost.[6] The procedure is easy to utilize. The primary requirement is identification of cost accounts appropriate to each alternative method of operation.

For purposes of illustration, assume that a decision is required between: (1) continued direct shipment to a market area, or (2) use of a public warehouse facility. The typical circumstance that might lead to such a review is a managerial belief that total cost could be reduced by use of consolidated transportation to a warehouse located in the market with local distribution beyond. Another motivation may be a belief that customer service can be improved, thereby increasing sales penetration as a result of having an inventory locally available. Table 13–1 presents a total cost evaluation of the alternatives, including the managerial assumptions necessary to complete the analysis. If the warehouse facility is established, transportation cost for customer delivery can be reduced by $125,000 for the volume currently sold in the market. However, when all other costs are included in the analysis, establishment of a warehouse facility will raise total cost by $58,540. Thus, if the primary objective is to reduce total cost, the most appropriate alternative is to continue the practice of direct customer physical distribution.

From a marketing viewpoint, the availability of local inventory would increase the service capability in terms of speed and consistency of delivery, owing to the reduced distance of warehouse to customer shipments. Given the assumption that before-tax profit is 15 per cent of sales, additional sales in the amount of $390,267 would be required to offset the added distribution costs. However, to assure the validity of the total-cost estimates, the comparative

---

[6] This form of analysis was the initial application of total costing. See Howard T. Lewis, James W. Culliton, and Jack D. Steel, *The Role of Air Freight in Physical Distribution* (Boston: Division of Research Graduate School of Business Administration, Harvard University, 1956).

TABLE 13–1   Comparative Analysis: Direct Versus Public Warehouse Distribution

Account	Total Cost	
	Direct	Warehouse
Transportation		
Warehouse CL		$200,000
Customer LTL	$450,000	230,000
Customer TL	210,000	105,000
Total transportation	$660,000	$535,000
Other		
Plant processing	$130,000	$100,000
Inventory	87,500	175,000
Warehouse		110,000
Inventory control		7,500
Order processing		1,040
Managerial	17,000	24,500
Total other	$234,500	$418,040
Total cost	$894,500	$953,040
Savings direct	$ 58,540	

Assumptions:
1. Annual sales to market $7 million, standard cost of manufacturing 50% total volume 100,000 cwt.
2. Customer order mix 50% TL and 50% LTL and warehouse CL.
3. Freight rates in ($χcwt):
   Plant to warehouse: CL $2.00
   Plant to customer: LTL $9.00, TL $4.20.
   Warehouse to customer: LTL $4.60; TL $2.10.
4. Total day average inventory:
   Plant direct: 30 days at plant
   Warehouse: 15 days at plant. 10 days rail transit. 35 days at warehouse—total 60 days.
5. Inventory carrying cost 30% of standard cost.
6. Warehouse cost—public facility, no fixed cost.
   Order processing: $20 per order, one order per week.
   Inventory control: 7.5 cents/cwt.
   Warehouse: $1.10/cwt.
7. Managerial and allocated amount of overall supervision required to manage market area physical distribution activities.
8. 15% profit before tax.

evaluation would be again required on the basis of the incremental additional tonnage added as a result of sales increase.

In terms of capability and comprehensive treatment, comparative analysis has many limitations. First, the array of shipment sizes must be averaged. Second, the approach has limited capability to evaluate alternative volume levels. Third, the analysis is static. Fourth, the range of designs tested is limited to those which management feels are acceptable alternatives. Fifth, facility locations must be assumed and held constant under any given design configuration. Thus, the interrelationship of facility location is not treated in the design configuration. Finally, the approach is not able to handle trade-offs between customer service and cost requirements with the same precision as other integrative techniques.

These limitations render comparative analysis deficient for large-scale integrative studies. The approach is useful for evaluation of proposed modification to limited parts of an existing system. For example, as illustrated, it can be employed to check if a given market area has reached a sufficient volume to support replacement of direct shipments with a warehouse. The comparative analysis is quick and inexpensive, and it requires a minimum amount of technical expertise or computation capacity. If used with care and on specific types of problems, it can represent a useful short-range planning tool.

Break-Even Analysis

A more sophisticated approach to evaluating system design alternatives is break-even analysis. The objective in *break-even analysis* is to evaluate the changing nature of total cost as a function of volume. Two or more alternative system designs are identified as potential systems. For example, assume that an enterprise is evaluating the alternatives of direct versus private warehouse physical distribution to a specific market. In addition, an alternative exists between establishment of a mechanized versus an automated facility in the event that utilization of warehousing represents the lowest-total-cost method of physical distribution. The initial step is to isolate the appropriate costs, similar to the procedure followed in comparative analysis. Once costs have been identified, the major difference is that they are then divided for purposes of analysis into fixed and variable groupings for each alternative.[7]

Each alternative will have different cost functions in each category. Some will have higher fixed costs than others. The variable costs of handling more-or-less average shipments will also be substantially different among alternative systems. For any given volume one system will have the lowest combination of fixed and variable costs and therefore will be the lowest-cost logistical alternative under consideration.

---

[7] To review costing procedures and problems related to isolating logistical costs, see Chapter 9, pages 270–73.

TABLE 13-2 Example Costs for Break-Even Analysis

Account	Physical Distribution Alternatives		
	(1)	*(2)*	*(3)*
		Warehouse	*Warehouse*
	Direct	*Mechanized*	*Automated*
Fixed[a]	$10,000	$50,000	$100,000
Variable ($/cwt)			
Inbound transportation	—	$0.25	$0.25
Outbound transportation	$3.00	$1.00	1.00
Material handling	—	0.75	0.25
Total variable	$3.00	$2.00	$1.50

[a] Fixed cost includes cost of average inventory commitment to each system alternative.

Table 13–2 provides an assumed grouping of fixed and variable costs related to transportation, inventory, and materials handling for the alternatives of direct distribution, a mechanized warehouse, and an automated warehouse.

When using break-even analysis, an attempt is made to express variable-cost relationships for each system in a formula. These formulas are linear in relationship and represent the variable cost of an additional average shipment to the market under study. Fixed costs are held constant. By testing alternative volumes of average shipments, it is possible to locate the level at which one system achieves lower cost than the next. The series of formulas represent the models of alternative systems under study.

Using the data presented in Table 13–2 the alternatives are ranked on the basis of relative fixed cost. The analysis starts with the lowest-fixed-cost system. The formulation of this illustration requires that two break-even points be determined: (1) direct versus mechanized warehouse, and (2) mechanized versus automated warehouse. With x representing the two break points, F = fixed cost, and V = variable costs, the analysis is as follows:

$$x_1 = \frac{F_2 - F_1}{V_1 - V_2}$$

$$= \frac{50,000 - 10,000}{3.00 - 2.00}$$

$$= \frac{40,000}{1.00}$$

$$= 40,000 \text{ cwt or } 4,000,000 \text{ pounds}$$

$$x_2 = \frac{F_3 - F_2}{V_2 - V_3}$$

$$= \frac{100,000 - 50,000}{2.00 - 1.50}$$

$$= \frac{50,000}{.50}$$

$$= 100,000 \text{ cwt or } 10,000,000 \text{ pounds}$$

The results are illustrated in graphic form in Figure 13–2.

Given the three alternatives in the illustration, direct distribution from the manufacturing plant would be the lowest-cost alternative if the volume was less than 4 million pounds. Beyond 4 million pounds a mechanized warehouse would be justified; however, automation would not be economically feasible until the volume reached or exceeded 10 million pounds.

Break-even simulation has many of the same limitations as comparative analysis. Location is assumed, range of system alternatives is limited, and service-cost relationships are lacking. Because testing can consider performance at alternative volume levels, break-even analysis eliminates one of the main deficiencies of comparative analysis.

Break-even analysis has limited usefulness as a planning tool. It is frequently utilized to aid operational decision-making. For example, if alternative

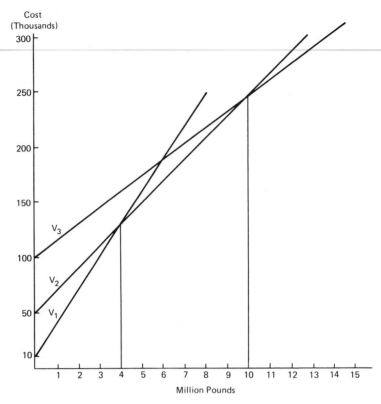

Figure 13–2 Least-Cost Chart: Break-Even Analysis

methods of direct distribution exist to service a given market, break-even simulation can be formulated on the basis of fixed and variable costs of each as a function of shipment size. Given a particular shipment, it is possible to select the direct distribution alternative that should be utilized. Even if a warehouse exists in the service area, the model can provide valuable cost information to help decide if the shipment should be sent directly from the factory. Under certain conditions it may be less expensive to bypass the warehouse and ship direct.

Flowcharting

A final tool in the category of symbolic replications is to use *flowcharts or flow diagrams* to replicate alternative logistical systems. The procedure consists of diagramming the physical product and communication flows as connecting linkages between facility nodes. Once the diagram is completed, cost accounts associated with each node and category of linkage are identified. These costs are then grouped together to formulate a total-cost projection for the system configuration illustrated by the flow diagram at a specified volume level. Given the flowchart, the costing procedure is identical to comparative analysis as illustrated in Table 13–1.

Flow diagrams represent the first step in the development of most computer models. However, the emphasis in modeling is on identification of components, variables, functional relationships, parameters, and constraints for purposes of model formulation and programming. In the case of direct use of flowcharting to aid in strategic planning, a different diagram must be developed for each alternative system.

Figure 13–3 illustrates a two production plant/three distribution warehouse logistical system. This system has the following characteristics: (1) each of the production plants ships to all three distribution centers; (2) distribution warehouses have a communication capacity with each other and with central control; (3) distribution centers can interbranch-transfer when the situation is warranted; (4) when conditions justify, shipments can be made direct from production plants to customers; (5) customer orders are routed direct to distribution warehouses for shipment, if possible; and (6) inventory and production control is maintained at the central inventory control location, which is linked to distribution warehouses by data transmission.

The system detailed in Figure 13–3 represents a major simplification because no detail is developed for major activity centers. In flowcharting the complete structure of a physical distribution system, the normal procedure would be development of diagrams for each subsystem. The procedure would be even more complex if the flowchart attempted to replicate the total logistical system.

In terms of capability to replicate or conduct a comprehensive system design, flowcharts have the same limitations as both comparative analysis and break-even analysis. Although flowcharting can be used to identify alternatives, it must be supplemented by some form of costing to serve as an aid to system planning. Thus, although comparative analysis, break-even analysis, and system flowcharting provide tools to assist in limited research, more powerful and comprehensive techniques are needed for tackling complex distribution system studies. The next two sections review such techniques.

ANALYTIC TECHNIQUES

Two main categories of analytical techniques useful in logistical system design are presented in this section. The *first* category consists of center-of-gravity techniques, which are useful when the major concern is the location of a single facility such as a warehouse or a terminal. The *second* category consists of a variety of linear programming techniques that have been adapted to logistical system design problems.

The unique feature of an analytical technique is the capability to isolate a precise mathematical solution to the problem under analysis. Thus, within the framework of assumptions and constraints of the analysis, the solution will represent a mathematical optimum. The main disadvantage of approaching complex design situations with analytical techniques is the requirement that all relationships be fully identified and quantified. To the extent that the technical requirements for formulating a problem on an analytical basis can be satisfied, they represent an ideal application of models to logistical system strategic planning.

Center of Gravity

This part illustrates the use of an analytical technique to assist in the location of a single distribution warehouse or manufacturing plant. A number of methods,

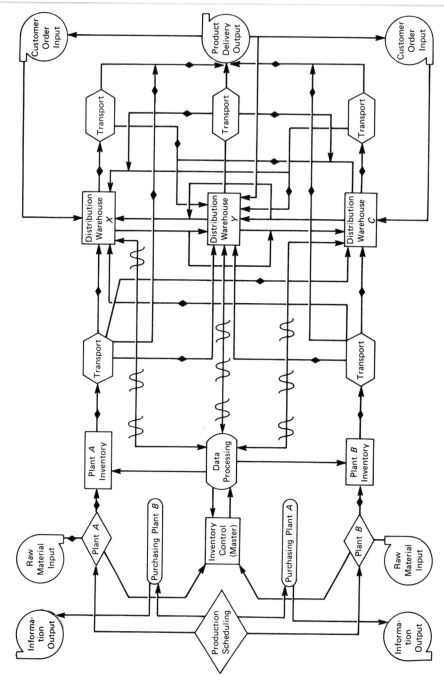

Figure 13-3 Two Production Plant/Three Distribution Warehouse System Flowchart

both mathematical and nonmathematical, can be applied to the problem of a single location. The cost and complexity of the technique should be matched to the difficulty of the problem. Here an analytical technique for solving the location problem is presented. By use of this technique, it is possible to locate a facility at the ton center, mile center, ton-mile center, or time-ton-mile center within a service territory—whichever results in lowest total cost. Where it is necessary to locate multiple distribution warehouses in a total system network, techniques similar to those discussed in following section should be used.

The technique employed evolves from analytic geometry. The model is based upon Cartesian coordinates. In a system of Cartesian coordinates, the horizontal, or east-west, axis is labeled the x axis. The vertical, or north-south, axis is labeled the y axis. Together these two axes differentiate four quadrants, which are customarily numbered as illustrated in Figure 13–4.

Any given point in a quadrant can be identified with reference to the x and y coordinates. The y coordinate of a point is called its *ordinate*. The ordinate is found by measuring its distance from the x axis, parallel to the y axis. The x coordinate of a point is referred to as its *abscissa*. This is the distance from the vertical y axis,, measured parallel to the x axis. Taken together, the abscissa and ordinate form the coordinates of a given point, the abscissa being given first. Figure 13–4 illustrates the abscissa and ordinate point A in the positive or northeast quadrant. In Figure 13–4 the distance Ox_1 equals the abscissa of point A, and the distance Oy_1 equals the ordinate. Assuming the values of 40 miles for x_1 and 30 miles for y_1, the coordinates of point A would be read as $A(40, 30)$. The use of uniform mileage scales along the axes permits all points in the quadrant to be relatively located.

By use of this basic system of orientation, it is possible to replicate the geographic market area in which the warehouse facility is to be located. All delivery points are plotted in the Cartesian plane. Each delivery point is identified by a subscript and placed in the replicated market with reference to its coordinates. In other words, destinations are plotted with reference to their abscissa and ordinate, measured on a uniform mileage scale.

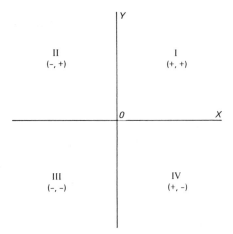

Figure 13–4 Cartesian Coordinates

The algebraic method for solving the location problem identifies the coordinate position of the proposed distribution warehouse. The computation is essentially a weighted average of a given number of independent variables, with the dependent variable being the warehouse location. The algebraic process is solved for the abscissa and ordinate of the warehouse. For simplicity, it is convenient to solve independently for the x- and y-coordinate location of the warehouse.

The algebraic solution may use either the weighted average x and y coordinates or the medium location. The location, which has become accepted as being more efficient by geographers, takes the median location as the coordinate that has half the demand on each side.[8] The formula for this calculation depends upon the independent variables, which are expressed in the location measure employed.

In the algebraic formulation the data utilized as basic measurement input represent independent variables. The resultant warehouse location is the dependent variable. The location problem is structured with identical service standards required from all potential distribution warehouse locations. Given this service standard, the objective is to minimize transportation costs.

Generally, it is accepted that transportation costs are a function of time, weight, and distance. Historically, however, when mathematical techniques were employed, not all of these cost factors were included as independent variables in the measurement device. Four solutions to the location problem are presented: (1) the ton-center solution, (2) the mile-center solution, (3) the ton-mile-center solution, and (4) the time-ton-mile-center solution. As the titles suggest, the first three are limited to variables related to weight and distance. The fourth includes both of these plus time as cost-influencing factors.

Ton-Center Solution

In the ton-center solution, the point located represents the center of gravity or center of movement in the market area. When obtaining a ton-center solution, the assumption is that the center of movements represents the least-cost location. However, accepting cost as a function of time, weight, and distance reveals the basic limitation of the measurement device—only weight is given consideration.

All outlets are plotted in the Cartesian plane and identified by subscripts. To express tonnage requirements to each destination, annual tonnage is reduced to standard trailer units. The standard trailer utilized is a 48-foot semivan with a capacity of 40,000 pounds. Once each destination location is determined and the total trailer loads to each are known, the warehouse location may be determined.

The location solution is found by adding the products of location and delivery frequency to each destination from the x coordinate and dividing by the total number of trailers. The process is repeated from the y coordinate. The result is a location in terms of x and y for the distribution warehouse. The final location solution indicates the point that provides the balance of weight between

[8] For a complete discussion of the location ananlysis alternatives, see Gerard Rushton, *Opltimal Location of Facilities* (Wentworth, N.H.: Compress, Inc., 1979).

destinations over a specific period. This basic algebraic procedure is followed for all mathematically derived location solutions with appropriate modifications necessary to handle the inclusion of different variables. The algebraic formula for the ton-center computation is

$$x = \frac{\sum_{i=1}^{n} x_i F_i}{\sum_{i=1}^{n} F_i} \qquad y = \frac{\sum_{i=1}^{n} y_i F_i}{\sum_{i=1}^{n} F_i}$$

where

x, y = unknown coordinate values of the warehouse
x_n, y_n = delivery locations, designated by appropriate subscript
F_n = annual tonnage to each destination, expressed as standard trailers, identified by appropriate subscript

Mile-Center Solution

The mile-center solution isolates that geographical point which results in the least combined distance to all delivery points. The assumption underlying the solution is that delivery costs are a function of mileage. Therefore, if mileage is minimized, a least-cost location is determined. The basic deficiency in the mile-center solution is the omission of tonnage and time considerations.

Unlike the ton-center solution, the mile-center solution cannot be determined simply by solving for the weighted average along each coordinate. To find the mile center it is necessary to establish the distance of each destination from an original warehouse location, thereby obtaining a mileage value. This value is determined by utilizing the general formula for finding the length of a straight line connecting two points. The exact procedure is developed below.

Because the solution requires an initial x and y value for the distribution center, the final solution is found by a trial-and-error procedure. Starting with initial values for x and y, each time a computation is completed, new values are generated for the warehouse in terms of x and y. The location problem is solved when the new values are equated to zero or within an acceptable tolerance of the previous values. For example, if the initial values of x and y are 30 and 40, respectively, the location solution is obtained by utilizing these values to determine the new warehouse coordinates. Assuming that the new values obtained are $x = 36$ and $y = 43$, the procedure has failed to set the new values equal to the original values. Thus, additional computation is required. For the second computation, the most recent values, $x = 36$ and $y = 43$, are employed. If the second computation results in the values $x = 36$ and $y = 43$, the location solution equates to zero, and the problem is optimized.

In trial-and-error solutions, an acceptable tolerance of ± 1 mile is usually established for the x and y warehouse coordinates. This means that solutions are correct within a 4-square-mile area. If through trial and error, values for x and y within this tolerance are reached, the location is accepted as the center of the 4-square-mile area. This results in a maximum location error of 1 mile.

The algebraic formula for determining the mile-center solution is

$$x = \frac{\sum\limits_{i=1}^{n} \dfrac{x_i}{d_i}}{\sum\limits_{i=1}^{n} \dfrac{1}{d_i}} \qquad y = \frac{\sum\limits_{i=1}^{n} \dfrac{y_i}{d_i}}{\sum\limits_{i=1}^{n} \dfrac{1}{d_i}}$$

where

x, y = unknown coordinate values of the warehouse
x_n, y_n = delivery locations, designated by appropriate subscript
d_n = location until the trial-and-error procedure is completed

The value for d expressing the distance from a warehouse can be determined from direct measurement on the coordinate plane or by utilization of the following straight-line formula:

$$d_n = \sqrt{(x_n - x)^2 + (y_n - y)^2}$$

where

d_n = distance between destination and warehouse, designated by appropriate subscript
x, y = given coordinates of warehouse
x_n, y_n = delivery location, designated by appropriate subscript

Because the value of d for all destinations changes each time a new set of warehouse coordinates is determined, the distance formula is utilized in each step of the trial-and-error procedure.

Ton-Mile-Center Solution

The ton-mile-center solution combines the variables of weight and distance in selecting the warehouse locations. The assumption is that costs are a function of ton-miles. The ton-mile solution is superior to the mile-center solution, because it takes frequency of delivery to each destination into consideration in selecting the warehouse location. It is superior to the simple ton-center solution, since the impact of distance is taken into consideration. The solution once more calls for trial and error, since d is included in the formulation.

The ton-mile formulation is

$$x = \frac{\sum\limits_{i=1}^{n} \dfrac{x_i F_i}{d_i}}{\sum\limits_{i=1}^{n} \dfrac{F_i}{d_i}} \qquad y = \frac{\sum\limits_{i=1}^{n} \dfrac{y_i F_i}{d_i}}{\sum\limits_{i=1}^{n} \dfrac{F_i}{d_i}}$$

where

x, y = unknown coordinate values of the warehouse
x_n, y_n = delivery locations designated by appropriate subscript

F_n = annual tonnage to each location, expressed as standard trailers identified by appropriate subscript

d_n = delivery location differentiated in terms of miles from the initial warehouse location and sequentially from each new location until the trial-and-error procedure is completed

Time-Ton-Mile-Center Solution

The fourth location measurement device includes all cost-influencing variables. Because costs are a function of time, weight, and distance, the warehouse location derived as a product of this device should represent a superior least-cost location. The procedure for selecting the time-ton-mile solution is trial and error, because both the time and distance factors are differentiated from a given warehouse location.

The formulation is as follows:

$$x = \frac{\sum_{i=1}^{n} \frac{x_i F_i}{M_i}}{\sum_{i=1}^{n} \frac{F_i}{M_i}} \qquad y = \frac{\sum_{i=1}^{n} \frac{y_i F_i}{M_i}}{\sum_{i=1}^{n} \frac{F_i}{M_i}}$$

where

x, y = unknown coordinate value of warehouse

x_n, y_n = delivery locations, designated by apropriate subscript

F_n = annual tonnage to each location expressed as standard trailers, identified by appropriate subscript

M_n = delivery location differentiated in terms of miles per minute from the initial warehouse location and sequentially from each new location until the trial-and-error procedure is completed

To arrive at a value of M_n it is necessary to ascertain both the distance and time to all destinations from the given warehouse location. The distance value is determined by use of the basic distance formula. The time in minutes to each destination is found by calculating a time value from the coordinate plane. An estimate of delivery time must include number of miles, type of highway, and traffic. A general rule is that time per mile decreases as the number of miles per stop increases. To account for the basic factors that influence driving time, zones representing attainable movement rates should be established for the market area. These zones consist of two basic types: rural and urban. Such estimates must be developed from engineering time studies for each alternative warehouse location. Given the values of distance and time through rural and urban zones, M_n is calculated in the following manner:

$$M_n = \frac{d_n}{t_n}$$

where

M_n = attainable miles per minute to the appropriate delivery location

$d_n = \sqrt{(x_n - x)^2 + (y_n - y)^2}$

t_n = total time to the location

The location of a single facility is commonly confronted in logistical planning. The very fact that a total system revision is rarely conducted for immediate implementation makes a simple approach to the evaluation of a single-facility location a useful aid to management. In cases where inbound transportation is an important cost, the model can easily be modified to include both inbound and outbound transportation cost. The next section discusses more comprehensive analytical techniques.

Linear Programming

As a category of analytical techniques, linear programming is among the most widely used strategic and tactical planning tools. Linear programming, which is classified as an optimization technique, selects the optimal course of action from a number of available options while considering specific constraints. House and Karrenbauer provide the following definition of optimization with regard to distribution.[9]

> An optimization model considers the aggregate set of requirements from the customers, the aggregate set of production possibilities for the producers, the potential intermediary points, the transportation alternatives, and develops the optimal system. The model determines on a aggregate flow basis where the warehouses should be, where the stocking points should be, how big the warehouses should be, and what kinds of transportation options should be implemented.

In order to solve a problem using linear programming, several qualification conditions must be satisfied. First, choice must exist in that two or more activities or locations must be competing for limited resources. For example, shipments must be capable of being made to a customer from at least two locations. Second, all pertinent relationships in the problem structure must be deterministic and capable of linear approximation.[10] Unless these enabling conditions are satisfied, a solution derived from linear programming, while mathematically optimal, will not be valid for logistical planning.

While linear programming is frequently used for logistical strategic planning, it is more widely applied to problems of an operating nature such as assignment and allocation. Within the broad class of optimization, distribution analysts have applied two different solution methodologies for distribution analysis.

Network Optimization

One of the most widely used forms of linear programming for logistics problems is network optimization. Network optimization treats the distribution

---

[9] Robert G. House and Jeffrey J. Karrenbauer, "Logistics System Modeling," *International Journal of Physical Distribution and Materials Management*, Vol. 8 (May 1978), pp. 189–99.

[10] For expanded treatments of linear programming, see George B. Dantzig, *Linear Programming and Extensions* (Princeton, N.J.: Princeton University Press, 1963); Harold Greenberg, *Integer Programming* (New York: Academic Press, Inc., 1971); G. Hadley, *Linear Programming* (Reading, Mass.: Addison-Wesley Publishing Company, Inc., 1962); Samuel B. Richmond, *Operations Research for Management Decisions* (New York: The Ronald Press Company, 1968); Ronald H. Ballou, "Dynamic Warehouse Location Analysis," *Journal of Marketing Research*, Vol. 5 (August 1968), pp. 271–76; and R. A. Howard, "Dynamic Programming," *Management Science*, Vol. 13 (January 1966), p. 317.

TABLE 13-3   Basic Transportation Method Matrix

Source Locations	Demand Locations			
	a_1	a_2	a_3	a_i
b_1	c_{11}	c_{21}	c_{31}	c_{i1}
b_2	c_{12}	c_{22}	c_{32}	c_{i2}
b_3	c_{13}	c_{23}	c_{33}	c_{i3}
b_j	c_{1j}	c_{2j}	c_{3j}	c_{ij}

channel as a network consisting of nodes and arcs. Costs are incurred to move the goods between nodes. The network model objective is to minimize the variable production, primary and secondary transportation movement, and throughput costs subject to supply, demand, and capacity constraints.[11]

One of the more straightforward approaches to network optimization is the transportation method which derived its name from early applications directed at the minimization of transportation cost. In part, the popularity of the transportation method is that no formulas need be developed or manipulated to arrive at an optimal solution. The general formulation of the transportation method is in terms of a matrix relating demand-and-supply locations.

Table 13-3 illustrates an example matrix formulation of a transportation problem. In the matrix a_1 represents demand, b_j represents the location of supply, and c_{ij} represents the cost of transportation from any supply location b_j to demand location a_i. The matrix represents a network of geographical points connected by links over which the transportation flow can be routed. The matrix illustrated in Table 13-3 represents the classical linear programming problem structure. Given the limited supply at source locations and variable requirements at demand locations, the objective is to satisfy all requirements at the lowest possible transportation cost.

The computation for locating the optimal solution consists of a routinized addition and subtraction procedure. Typical assignment and allocation problems are illustrated in Chapter 14 from inception to attainment of solution optimality. For the solution to satisfy optimality conditions: (1) the cost of an individual shipment is the product of the quantity and the transportation cost, and (2) the total cost of the objective function must be the sum of the individual costs.

The general application of the transportation method in system design studies dealing with location is to individually isolate the optimum for a variety of different locational structures. For example, if the objective is to select from a list of possible warehouse locations the one additional facility that will result in

---

[11] For extended discussions of applications of network modeling to logistical problem-solving, see (1) Fred Glover, John Hultz, and Darwin Klingman, "Improved Computer-Based Planning Techniques. Part I." *Interfaces*, Vol. 8 (August 1978), pp. 16–25; (2) Fred Glover, Gene Jones, David Kerney, Darwin Klingman, and John Mote, "An Integrated Production Distribution, and Inventory Planning System," *Interfaces*, Vol. 9 (November 1979), pp. 25–35; or (3) Fred Glover and Darwin Klingman, "Network Applications in Industry and Government," *AIIE Transactions*, Vol. 9 (November 4, 1977), pp. 363–376.

lowest total system cost, the computation procedure would consist of a series of optimal quantifications. The existing system would be tested with each potential facility "in solution." The final solution would be the combination of existing warehouses plus the additional facility which results in lowest total cost in comparison to all alternatives tested. Because the solution is limited by the preselected locations, optimality is limited to the specific problem formatted.

Beyond the basic considerations for all analytical techniques, network optimization has specific advantages and disadvantages which both enhance and inhibit its application for distribution analysis. On the advantage side, solution times and ease of communication between specialists and nonspecialists are the primary advantages of network models.[12] Network models may also be applied using monthly rather than annual time increments, thus allowing for across-time analysis of macro inventory level changes.[13] However, the use of monthly time increments forces a reduction in scope of the analysis such as the number of markets, distribution facilities, or products. Network formulations may also incorporate fixed costs to replicate facility ownership. The results of a network model identify the optimum set of distribution facilities and material flows for the problem as formulated.

Mixed-Integer Optimization

The other optimization solution technique that has been successfully applied to logistical problems is mixed-integer programming with decomposition. Similar to network optimization, mixed-integer programming identifies the optimum set of facilities and product flows for the model as formulated. The mixed-integer programming formulation offers a great deal of flexibility to incorporate many of the complexities and idiosyncrasies found in logistical applications. The primary advantage of the mixed-integer format is that fixed as well as different levels of variable cost can be included in the determination of the objective solution. For example, the demand can be treated on a noninteger basis and allow demand allocation between multiple warehouses, while warehouse capacity and transportation equipment can be evaluated on an integer basis, thus requiring increments to system capacity in specific step increases. The mixed-integer approach permits a high degree of practicality to accommodate restrictions found in day-to-day logistical operations.

Along with advances in mixed-integer programming, a major development in linear programming from the viewpoint of logistical planning was the application of *decomposition* to the design solution.[14] The benefit of decomposition is that it permits multiple commodities to be incorporated into logistical system design. Most firms have a variety of product which are purchased in varied assortments and quantities by customers. While such products may be shipped

---

[12] Glover, Hultz, et al., op. cit.

[13] Glover, Jones, et al., op. cit.

[14] For a discussion of the application of decomposition to logistical system design, see A. M. Geoffrion and G. W. Graves, "Multicommodity Distribution System Design by Benders Decomposition," *Management Science*, Vol. 20 (January 1974), pp. 822–44; and Arthur M. Geoffrion, "Better Distribution Planning with Computer Models," *Harvard Business Review*, Vol. 54 (July–August 1976), pp. 92–99.

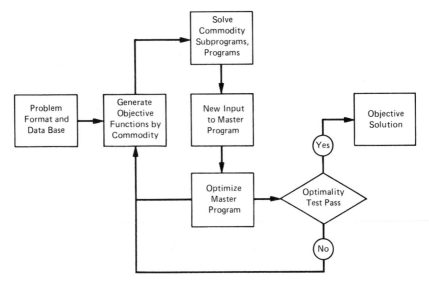

Figure 13–5   Mixed-Integer Solution Flow with Decomposition Feature

and stored together, they are not interchangeable from the viewpoint of servicing customer requirements.

To handle this realistic requirement the decomposition technique provides a procedure for dividing the multicommodity situation into a series of single-commodity problems. The procedure for arriving at commodity assignment follows an iterative process wherein costs associated with each commodity are tested for convergence until a minimum cost or optimal solution is isolated.

This decomposition procedure has been incorporated in a *multicommodity distribution system design program* that includes a mixed-integer algorithm for evaluating the configuration of warehouse location.[15] The procedure for arriving at a system design follows a two-stage iterative process. *First*, given the location structure, individual commodities are optimally assigned to minimize cost. This aspect of the design procedure is similar to the basic transportation solutions. However, it is formatted on a multiproduct basis using the decomposition technique. *Second*, a mixed-integer algorithm is utilized to enumerate the facility structure in terms of individual commodity customer's assignments. The combined solution is tested for optimality and the two-step procedure is repeated until convergence is within accepted tolerance.[16] Figure 13–5 illustrates the combined linear programming procedure.

Conclusion—Optimization Techniques

The network and mixed-integer approaches provide effective tools for analysis of location-related issues such as facility location, optimum product flow, and capacity allocation. Mixed-integer approaches are typically more flexible in terms of capacity to accommodate operational nuances, while network

[15] Ibid.

[16] Ibid.

approaches are more computationally efficient. Both types of linear programming optimization approaches are effective techniques for evaluating situations where there are significant facility capacity limitations.

Notwithstanding the value of optimization, linear programming confronts some major problems when dealing with complex logistical system designs. First, to format a comprehensive system design, it is necessary to develop explicit functional relationships for the full range of design options. Second, the optimality feature of the technique is relative, being only as valid as the design problem definition. Too many simplifying assumptions can render the solution mathematically optimal but useless in terms of business practice. Third, the capability of existing linear programming procedures is typically limited to a system configuration with only three echelons. Thus, problems requiring the analysis of flows from manufacturing plants to warehouses and then to customers can be treated. However, it is difficult to perform a total channel analysis. A fifth weakness is the limitation regarding problem size. While optimization techniques are capable for solving moderately sized problems such as, 2 echelons, 15 plants, 45 distribution centers, 3 commodities, and 50 market areas, optimization techniques become less capable when the situation involves larger problem sizes.[17] It is possible, particularly when the business situation being planned includes multiple divisions or diverse commodity groups, that an accurate analysis may require more than two echelons, more product groups, or more market areas. For example, research by House and Jamie indicates that a relatively large number of market areas (greater than 150) is necessary to accurately evaluate a large list of potential distribution facilities (greater than 20).[18]

Table 13–4 provides a qualitative evaluation of an optimization model's ability to treat the issues identified as important for logistical analysts. The "comments" column provides a brief rationale for the evaluation. The evaluation offers comments that characterize the class of solution techniques in general, although it may not be applicable for a specific model.

SIMULATION TECHNIQUES

This section discusses two forms of computer simulation widely used in logistical strategic and tactical planning. The first category is static simulation and the second is dynamic simulation. The label *simulation* can be applied to almost any attempt to replicate a situation. Shannon defines simulation as:[19] "the process of designing a model of a real system and conducting experiments with this model for the purpose either of understanding the behavior of the system or of evaluating various strategies within the limits imposed by a criterion or set of criteria for the operation of the system."

---

[17] Geoffrion and Graves, op. cit.

[18] Robert G. House and Kenneth D. Jamie, "Measuring the Impact of Alternative Market Classification Systems in Distribution Planning," *Journal of Business Logistics*, Vol. 2, No. 2 (1981), pp. 1–31.

[19] Robert E. Shannon, *Systems Simulation: The Art and Science* (Englewood Cliffs, N.J.: Prentice-Hall, Inc., 1975), p 1.

TABLE 13-4   Applicaton of Optimization for Specific Logistics Problem Types

Problem	Evaluation	Comments
1. Warehouse and plant location analysis	Good	Provides optimal locations and assignments under optimization assumptions
2. Distribution system requirements for changing products and markets	Poor	Does not address tactical inventory considerations
3. Customer warehouse realignment	Good	Good for large-scale problems particularly when capacity is a consideration
4. Shipment policy evaluation	Fair	May assist in evaluation of pool points for shipping
5. Production-distribution coordination	Fair	Provides good tool if capacity or production source is primary issue
6. Customer service improvement (fill rate)	Poor	Does not model order processing or temporal inventory availability
7. Inventory cost/service trade-off analysis	Poor	Inadequate consideration of inventory dynamics
8. Distribution forecasting	Poor	No consideration of temporal dimension

Static Simulation

In a static simulation, an attempt is made to describe an existing or potential logistical system design in the form of a computer model. All components of the total logistical system are replicated and total cost is generated by utilization of a numeric computation procedure. Within a logistical context, static simulation implies that a mathematical model can be constructed that replicates the flow of goods through a specified channel and evaluates the cost and performance characteristics of the defined network structure.

The essential feature of static simulation is that logistical flow is aggregated at a specific point-in-time rather than an across-time analysis. In this sense, the primary difference between static and dynamic simulation is the manner in which time-related events are treated. Whereas dynamic simulation evaluates system performance across time, in static simulation no attempt is made to structure time-period interplay. Static simulation treats each operating period within the overall planning horizon as a finite interval. Final results represent an assumption of operating performance for each period in the planning horizon. For example, in the formulation of a five-year simulated plan, each year is simulated as an independent event. Likewise, the simulated activity for the year would be processed on an aggregated basis, as if total performance took place at one point in time.

Static simulation seeks to estimate the outcome of a specified plan or course of future action. If the potential system design is identified, the primary purpose of the simulation would be to quantify total cost and threshold custome service.[20]

---

[20] The threshold service concept is critical to system design studies. See Chapter 9, pages 292–94 for a complete discussion.

Used in this sense the static simulator provides a tool for rapidly measuring the capabilities and cost related to system design and sensitivity analyses.[21]

An expanded use of static simulation involves a heuristic computation procedure to assist in the selection of warehouses. In this capacity, the static simulator can be programmed to evaluate and quantify various networks of warehouses from a potential list of facility locations provided during problem formatting.

When utilized to help identify the facility structure of the logistical system, the typical heuristic procedure is to include all plausible locations in the initial simulation. Customer destinations are assigned to each potential warehouse on the basis of the lowest-total-cost. One of the main benefits of simulation is that the design problem can be structured on a multiecheloned basis, and delivery points can be assigned to warehouses or directly to manufacturing plants, whichever offers lowest-total-cost delivery. The warehouse evaluation routine can be established to replicate a system design that: (1) represents lowest total cost, (2) provides maximum customer service, and/or (3) provides a specified service level at the lowest associated total cost.

Given the design objective, the simulation deletes warehouse locations one at a time from the maximum to a managerially specified minimum or until only one facility remains in the system. The typical delete procedure eliminates the most costly warehouse from the remaining "in-system" facilities on a marginal cost basis. The demand previously serviced by the casualty warehouse is then reassigned to the next-lowest-cost supply point and the quantification procedure repeated. If a full system delete process is desired, the static simulation will require as many iterations as there are potential warehouse locations under consideration.

The system design solution is obtained by comparison of the total cost and threshold service capabilities among the configurations resulting from the deletion procedure. This analysis is performed by direct comparison of output reports. There is no assurance that the combination of facilities selected as a result of the delete procedure will represent the optimum or even the near-optimum facility configuration. The fact that a warehouse location is no longer available for consideration in subsequent replications once it is deleted is one of the major shortcomings of static simulation procedures.

Figure 13–6 illustrates the solution flow for a typical static simulation model. The system design algorithm illustrates the facility deletion procedure discussed above.

The main advantage of static simulation is that it is simpler, less expensive to operate, and more flexible than other comprehensive design techniques. The replication capabilities of a multiecheloned static simulator create almost unlimited design possibilities. Unlike the mathematical programming approaches, the simulation approach does not guarantee an optimum solution. However, static simulation offers a very flexible tool that may be used to evaluate a wide range of complex channel structures. As a result of the process

---

[21] For examples of static simulators used for logistical planning, see Harvey N. Shycon and Richard B. Maffei, "Simulation—Tool for Better Distribution," *Harvard Business Review*, Vol. 38 (November–December 1960), pp. 65–75; Alfred Kuehn and M. J. Hamburger, "A Heuristic Program for Locating Warehouses," *Management Science*, Vol. 10 (July 1963), pp. 543–666; *WHAMOL* (Benton Harbor, Mich.: Whirlpool Corporation Physical Distribution Department, 1973); and *Net Sim* (East Lansing, Mich.: Dialog Systems Inc., 1985).

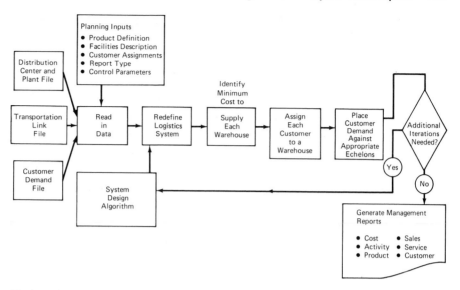

Figure 13-6 Static Simulation Solution Flow

of numerical computation, static simulation does not require explicit functional relationships. If the system or proposed design modification can be described, it can be simulated. The capabilities and operating range of a comprehensive static simulator can incorporate significantly more detail than optimization techniques such as more markets, products, distribution facilities, and shipment sizes.

Table 13–5 provides a summary evaluation of the capabilities of static simulation to investigate the planning issues outlined earlier. The static methodology, with or without heuristic procedures, can be used to investigate issues similar to those addressed by optimization.

Dynamic Simulation

Dynamic or event-oriented simulation offers another technique that has been employed to investigate logistical planning issues. In contrast to location considerations involved in strategic planning, tactical issues require detailed analysis involving time. Dynamic simulation is performed across time so that operating dynamics may impact the planning solution. A dynamic model simulates specific events that occur at points over a time horizon. The types of distribution events that might be simulated include customer or replenishment order processing, customer or replenishment order shipment, or shipment consolidation.

In Figure 13–7 the functional interrelationships of a dynamic simulator are displayed to illustrate the recursive relationship. The initial simulation cycle results in a system state identified as $t + 1$. Operational relationships and feedback influence the system state in two ways. First, for the initial cycle, the study-period deficiencies in system capability are generated in terms of extra demand loads with related operational penalties. Second, given initial system status, deficiencies and/or abundancies lead to modifications in system status, shown as $t + 1 \ldots n$. Such modifications are reflected as new values for

TABLE 13–5   Application of Static Simulation for Specific Logistics Problem Types

Problem	Evaluation	Comments
1. Warehouse and plant location analysis	Good	Does not necessarily provide optimal assignments or locations but does offer more flexibility
2. Distribution system requirements for changing products and markets	Poor	Does not address tactical inventory considerations
3. Customer warehouse realignment	Good	Good for large-scale problems when assignment flexibility is desired
4. Shipment policy evaluation	Fair	May assist in evaluation of pool points for shipping
5. Production-distribution coordination	Poor	May address production source problem but will not consider capacity nor production rules
6. Customer service improvement (fill rate)	Poor	Does not model order processing or temporal inventory availability
7. Inventory cost/service trade-off analysis	Poor	Inadequate consideration of inventory dynamics
8. Distribution forecasting	Poor	No consideration of temporal dimension

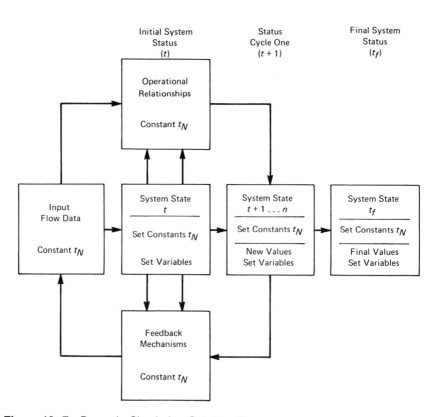

Figure 13–7   Dynamic Simulation Solution Flow

system-state set variables. This process is repeated until no improvement in system state is possible, and the system t_f (final system) has been structured.

The events are simulated at specified time intervals to capture operating dynamics. Thus, the model can be used to trace individual customer transactions, maintain stock status on individual inventory items, and consolidate groups of orders into shipments. Since dynamic simulation follows each transaction at a detailed rather than aggregate level, the model can accurately evaluate the detailed cost and service impacts of changes in inventory policies, consolidation and shipment policies, production policies, or uncertainty in demand or lead times. At such detail levels, there can be thousands or even tens of thousands of variables involved. Current optimization technology and knowledge of logistical system interactions do not permit the identification of optimal solutions. A dynamic simulation model can be used effectively as a testing environment to identify and evaluate logistical policies whose performance depend upon both spatial and temporal factors.

Dynamic simulation has been employed in a number of analyses to investigate logistical system performance. Bowersox describes the LREPS model for use in evaluating the inventory and cost impacts of long-scale distribution systems.[22] On a more functional scale, Whybark has demonstrated the use of dynamic simulation as a tool for the analysis of forecasting technique effectiveness, while Jackson and Masters have demonstrated dynamic simulation as a means for evaluating alternative freight consolidation strategies.[23]

Among the most advanced dynamic simulators is the Simulated Product Sales Forecasting (SPSF) model.[24] The SPSF testing environment consists of four dynamically interrelated modules: the operations module, the demand module, the forecast module, and the analysis module. Each module provides a specific function in the overall operation of the testing environment. Figure 13–8 illustrates the general design of the SPSF testing environment.

The demand module generates simulated product orders. Orders representing different quantities, levels of business, and patterns of occurrence can be developed by the demand module. From a design viewpoint, the demand module uses four different procedures to generate orders. The primary difference between individual procedures is the degree to which marketing and industry factors are included in the generation process. The significant point

[22] For a complete report on the LREPS model, see Donald J. Bowersox et al. *Dynamic Simulation of Physical Distribution Systems* (East Lansing, Mich.: Division of Research, Michigan State University, 1973); Donald J. Bowersox, "Dynamic Simulation of Physical Distribution," *Distribution Worldwide* (December 1972), pp. 24–31; and Donald J Bowersox, Omar Keith Helferich, and Edward J. Marien, "Physical Distribution Planning with Simulation," *International Journal of Physical Distribution* (October 1971), pp. 38–42. Portions of the followings sections and figures are based upon these references by the author.

[23] D. Clay Whybark, "A Comparison of Adaptive Forecasting Techniques," *The Logistics and Transportation Review* (July 1973), pp. 13–26. For a detailed discussion of the freight consolidation research, see George D. Jackson, "Evaluating Order Consolidation Strategies Using Simulation," *Journal of Business Logistics*, Vol. 2, No. 2 (1981), pp. 110–138; or James M. Masters, "The Effects of Freight Consolidation on Customer Service," *Journal of Business Logistics*, Vol. 2, Vol. 2, No. 1 (1980), pp. 55–74.

[24] For more complete discussions of the SPSF approach, see Donald J. Bowersox, David J. Closs, John T. Mentzer, Jr., and Jeffrey R. Sims, *Simulated Product Sales Forecasting* (East Lansing, Mich.: Michigan State University Press, 1979).

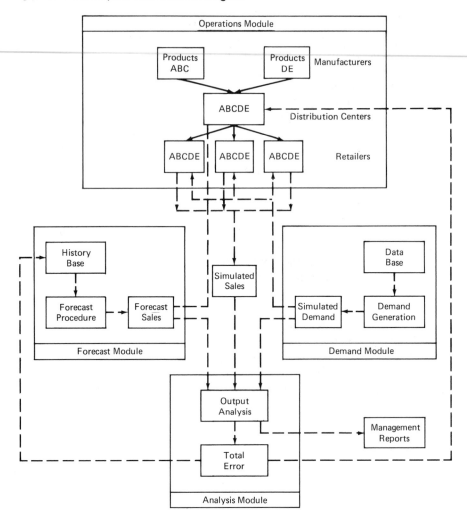

Figure 13–8 SPSF Testing Environment General Design

about the demand module is that it permits the analyst to control the nature of demand confronted by the remainder of the SPSF system. The module output is a daily order flow that simulates the business situation under analysis. These orders are transmitted to both the operations and analysis modules. Thus, a simulated history is established which specifies what could be sold in a specific planning situation.

The forecast module generates an estimate of future sales for use in establishing inventory levels at facilities within the distribution system being simulated. The module provides four different exponential smoothing forecasting procedures, ranging in complexity from simple to triple adaptive. The data base for the forecast module is limited to sales history decomposed into level trend and seasonal components. The partial data base contrasts with the comprehensive data that are available to the demand module. The forecasts generated are input to both the operations and analysis modules and represent the best estimate of what should be sold.

The operations module is a dynamic simulation of the physical distribution system selected for the situation under study. This model has the capability to perform total physical distribution operations in a multiecheloned system structure. The uncertainty inherent in typical operations is replicated in the simulator through the use of stochastic lead times. The typical lead-time components are order-processing and transit times. Thus, utilizing input from both the demand and forecast modules, the operations module simulates performance of the specified distribution system and its associated policies across the forecast period time horizon.

The output of the individual modules is combined in the analysis module. The demand module creates a simulated demand environment. Using less information, the forecast module produces an estimate of individual product demand at each facility. The forecast is used to establish desired inventory levels. The operations module incorporates spatial and temporal uncertainty to simulate the quantity that the system is capable of selling. Using this combination of inputs, the analysis module is in a unique position to report and analyze system performance. First, the module provides management information describing the activity, performance, and costs of logistical operations. This capability provides information to evaluate cost and service characteristics of alternative system designs. Second, the analysis module has access to demand (what could be sold), and the simulated operational results (what was sold). Thus, the module can isolate why sales do not match demand. Failure to realize all available sales can be categorized as resulting from either forecast or operating deficiencies.

The capability to identify factors that cause the planning situation under examination to enjoy less than fully available demand is one of the primary contributions of the dynamic SPSF testing environment. The only planning technique capable of investigaing the day-to-day operating dynamics required for the above activities is through the application of a dynamic simulation technique. This discussion has illustrated the level of detail that can be investigated using the dynamic simulation technology.

The main advantage of dynamic simulation is that it incorporates the realism of day-to-day operations. A system design can be evaluated in terms of specific customer service capabilities on an order-by-order basis. Unlike linear programming and static simulation, dynamic simulation can measure directly the cost benefits of alternative safety-stocking policies. As such, dynamic simulation is the only planning tool that can estimate the full integration of temporal and spatial variables upon system design.

Table 13-6 offers a summary evaluation of the capabilities of the dynamic simulation approach. The reader can see that the level of detail and the incorporation of temporal variables make dynamic simulation a good tool for the evaluation of the tactical issues faced by logistical planners. However, the extreme level of detail and the lack of optimizing algorithms make the dynamic simulation approach inefficient when investigating strategic issues such as location or capacity allocation.

Conclusion—Simulation Techniques

Capability to format the problem in a comprehensive manner is the main attribute of simulation techniques in approaching partial or total system

TABLE 13–6   Application of Dynamic Simulation for Specific Logistics Problem Types

1. Warehouse and plant location analysis	Poor	Too much operational detail so not enough emphasis can be placed on the assignment of location algorithms
2. Distribution system requirements for changing products and markets	Good	Provides total system analysis of distribution system performance under the proposed conditions
3. Customer warehouse realignment	Fair	Too detailed for problems, usually no assignment algorithm
4. Shipment policy evaluation	Good	Provides for analysis of both pool point locations and shipment consolidation policies
5. Production-distribution coordination	Good	Offers capability to alter production policies and rules while providing cost and service implications for the entire system
6. Customer service improvement (fill rate)	Good	Provides accurate measure of inventory availability as matched against orders
7. Inventory cost/service trade-off analysis	Good	Usually good tool but may not provide enough inventory capacity due to detail required for other capabilities
8. Distribution forecasting	Good	Includes the temporal dimension so that the impact of forecast methodology on distribution operations can be investigated

planning. Simulation techniques do not require exact functional relationships. And, in turn, they cannot provide optimum solutions.

Static simulation is a useful tool for evaluating alternative locational arrangements of warehouse facilities and assignment of customer service territories. While relatively easy and inexpensive to use, the heuristic delete-location algorithm used to select location configuration does not offer complete enumeration of all available facility locations. The static simulation approach fails to incorporate time relationships critical to selected logistical planning situations.

Dynamic simulation is the most comprehensive of the available planning techniques. Because of its feedback mechanisms, dynamic simulation is also complex and requires considerable computer time to replicate performance under alternative design configurations. The main advantage of the dynamic approach is that it incorporates the impact of time into performance evaluation. Analysis of system performance across time provides the foundation for planning inventory strategy in relation to order-by-order customer service performance. Thus the full impact of the location configuration upon safety stock can be evaluated directly using dynamic simulation.

The comprehensive nature of dynamic simulation restricts its flexibility to adapt to a wide variety of facility location schemes. Therefore, a practical approach to total system planning is to utilize either linear programming or static simulation initially to reduce the range of possible locations. Next, dynamic simulation can be employed to render the final system design and to plan implementation. With the dual-technique application, the major attributes of both techniques can be enjoyed in system strategic planning.

TECHNIQUE REVIEW

The development of logistical analysis techniques is proceeding at a rapid pace, particularly with the advent of the low-cost computing brought about by the introduction of the personal computer. While rapid technological development has greatly increased the potential and cost-effectiveness of performing significant planning analysis, it has made it more difficult to keep up with the introduction of new analysis techniques. Since there is a wide range of techniques available to investigate logistical issues, a planner must be careful to select the appropriate tool for analysis.

This section discusses the considerations for identifying and evaluating analysis techniques. The first part identifies some timely sources for identifying analysis techniques currently available and under development. The second part discusses considerations in evaluating technique alternatives.

Technique Identification

Since the development of analysis procedures and computer software to support these analyses is dynamic, it is impossible for any textbook to maintain current information. For this reason, the best sources for information describing techniques, models, and applications are through current literature such as journals, trade magazines, and trade shows. The journals typically document new and unique applications, while the trade magazines and trade shows survey and demonstrate the capabilities of the techniques. Table 13–7 lists some of these sources for information regarding the availability and application of distribution planning and analysis techniques.

Technique Evaluation

Once the analyst has identified the alternative techniques that may be used for the analysis, the next task is to evaluate which is best. This selection is one of the most difficult aspects of using a computerized or procedural analysis technique. This segment identifies and discusses the most significant considerations. There are six criteria to use when evaluating the analysis techniques. These considerations are: (1) technique fit, (2) ease of use, (3) hardware requirements, (4) flexibility, (5) data support, and (6) track record. The following segments discuss each of these characteristics.

Fit

The technique fit consideration concerns applicability to the problem being investigated. A major criticism that has been leveled against management science and modeling is that there were many attempts to force the use of a

TABLE 13–7   Distribution Model Sources

Current Journals

1. *Journal of Business Logistics*
   Council of Logistics Management, Oakbrook, Ill.
2. *Interfaces*
   The Institute of Management Sciences, Providence, RI
3. *International Journal of Physical Distribution and Materials Management*
   MBC University Press Limited, West Yorkshire, England

Software Surveys

1. *Survey of Software for Physical Distribution*
   Published annually for the National Council of Physical Distribution Management
   Annual Meeting by Arthur Anderson and Company
2. *Guide to Computer Systems and Software*
   Published annually as an element of Chilton's *Distribution Guide*
3. Survey of Software for Physical Distribution
   Published annually as a segment of *Traffic Management*

Expositions

1. *Distribution Computer Expo*
   Held annually in Chicago during May
2. *Vendor Exhibitions*
   Held in conjunction with the annual meeting of the National Council of Physical
   Distribution Management in the fall.

specific model, even though it may not be the best one for the issue under investigation.

The technique-problem fit should be evaluated in terms of characteristics of the technique, the activities modeled, the accuracy, and the level of detail. The analysts must evaluate characteristics to ensure that the technique can provide a cost-effective solution to the planning solution. From the discussion in the last section, it is apparent that it would not be appropriate to use dynamic simulation technique for location analysis. The fit should also be evaluated in terms of the activities that may significantly impact the results. For example, when customer orders are held for freight consolidation, associated policies must be considered in any analysis of customer service.

The third and fourth fit considerations are the related issues of accuracy and detail. The planner must define the accuracy and detail that are necessary for management to feel comfortable and confident concerning the analysis results. Once management agrees to the desired level of accuracy and detail, the planner must select a technique that provides the desired deliverables.

Ease of Use

The second major consideration is the ease of use or "user friendliness" as it is commonly termed. When evaluating alternative techniques, the planner must consider the ease with which data can be entered and maintained, the analysis performed, and the results can be obtained and interpreted. A technique that uses interactive data entry and editing is invariably easier to use than the older batch-entry analysis tools.

Hardware

The third major consideration is the computer hardware that is required by the analysis technique. While in the past, hardware considerations were significant, they are less significant today due to the advances in information technology and computer compatibility. An increasing number of analysis techniques currently operate on microprocessors. While the compatibility problems have become less important, it is still necessary to evaluate whether the desired technique can be used on available computer hardware.

Flexibility

The fourth major consideration concerns the flexibility of the technique. The ideal technique should be flexible enough to handle various policies and situations such as multiple echelons, different product groups, or various inventory or consolidation policies. The flexibility ensures that the technique will be capable of exploring a wide range of alternatives and will not limit the investigations to variations on the way the logistical system operates today.

Data Support

The fifth major consideration is the data-support services that are provided through the technique. One of the most difficult aspects of working with an analysis tool is the entry, updating, and manipulation of the data elements required for the analysis. The data manipulation part of the process can be both tedious and time consuming. Ideally, the analysis technique should incorporate procedures for changing the characteristics of products, markets, and orders as well as for changing costs. These procedures may be provided directly in the technique or through an interface into an external data-base package.

Track Record

The final consideration is the track record or history of the technique developers. This consideration concerns questions such as: Has the technique been applied before? What were the results of previous applications? Are there potential problems in application or interpretation? It is important that managers obtain as much information as possible regarding the history of model application.

SUMMARY

Chapter 13 described the issues and analysis techniques involved in logistical system design. The first section categorizes the logistical design problems into strategic and tactical issues. Typical strategic issues include warehouse and plant location analysis, changing product and market requirements, and warehouse assignment analysis. Tactical issues include transport policy evaluation, production policy, customer service, inventory cost and service trade-offs, and integrated system analysis. The second section discussed important considerations in the application of models to logistical system design. The section identifies the desirable model attributes of modularity, accuracy, simplicity, and adaptability. The section also discusses application characteristics that impact analysis technique selection such as multiple echelons, computerization, and sensitivity requirements. The third section explained the application of symbolic replication such as comparative and break-even analysis for performing limited analyses. The fourth section described and discussed the application of various types of analytic techniques available for strategic analyses. The fifth section described static and dynamic simulation as alternative approaches to provide detailed and flexible analysis for both strategic and tactical planning. The final section identified the major considerations for evaluating alternative techniques. The considerations include fit, ease of use, hardware compatibility, flexibility, data support, and track record.

In total, the chapter provided a comprehensive review of analysis tools applicable to logistical, strategic, and tactical planning. Attention in Chapter 14 is directed to operational planning techniques.

QUESTIONS

1. Define and discuss the major issues that are faced by logistical strategic, and tactical planners.
2. What are the major differences between the characteristics and capabilities of linear programming and static simulation?
3. What major advantage critical to logistical system design does dynamic simulation have over static simulation and linear programming?
4. Compare and contrast the center of gravity models with the linear programming models.
5. Discuss the considerations that should be addressed when evaluating alternative analysis techniques.
6. Discuss the requirement differences between strategic and tactical logistical planning.
7. What are the major differences between analytic models and simulation models?
8. Describe the process by which a simulation technique is utilized in combination with managerial inputs during a logistical system design study.
9. Why is dynamic representation essential to spatial and temporal unification?
10. Discuss the main advantages and applications of using symbolic replications to aid in logistical system planning.

Operations Techniques

Attention in this chapter is directed to quantitative techniques used in day-to-day logistical management. This orientation contrasts the treatment of design techniques in Chapter 13 in two ways. First, the focal point of technique application within this chapter is to operational decision-making given the logistical system design. Second, most techniques presented seek solutions to specific problems without regard to impact upon total system performance. In terms of fit into the various types of logistical planning, the techniques illustrated in this chapter are classified as operational planning tools.

This chapter follows a unique structure in comparison to other chapters in that no attempt is made to integrate the discussion of individual techniques. Each group is viewed as a tool set that can be utilized by a logistical manager if and when justified by the planning situation. The initial section deals with the basic logic of decision-making under conditions of uncertainty. Next, techniques related to facility operations are presented. The third section is devoted to solving allocation and assignment problems. The fourth section deals with a set of techniques that can assist in the determination of routing requirements. The final section presents scheduling techniques.

Two groups of techniques that have previously been discussed appropriately fall into the operational classification. In Chapter 4 forecasting techniques were discussed. In Chapter 7 statistical and simulation techniques applicable to formulating safety-stock strategy were treated, as well as analytic techniques dealing with economic order quantity. In both situations the judgment was made to include technique discussion in the chapter developing the functional subject because of uniqueness of application. The techniques discussed in this chapter are not as specialized.

DESIGN FOR DECISION

The major variable in logistical operations is the ever-present uncertainty. A logistical manager must always be gauging the probability of disruptions such as unexpected shipment delays, work stoppages, material shortages, and price changes. The essence of contingency planning is to estimate the probability that a disruption will occur and to plan the corrective action consistent with operational goals. To a significant degree, the best approach for coping with the probability of such disruptive events occurring is to maintain familiarity with the prevailing market conditions. Given this knowledge, statistical decision techniques can be utilized to help formulate a logical course of action.

Maximum-Minimum Related Criteria

A number of logic rules have been worked out to help a decision-maker select a course of action that will either maximize payout or minimize risk. These basic criteria are useful in establishing the extremes of a pessimistic or optimistic outlook.

A maximum criterion is based on the assumption that all possible future events will go contrary to the best interest of the enterprise. Therefore, the pessimistic decision attempts to minimize future risks at the sacrifice of potential gains in payoff. The example in Table 14–1 is used to illustrate decision rules applied by a pessimistic decision-maker. The Payoff Table indicates the various payoffs associated with the decision alternatives to be made, in this case whether to build a small, medium, or large warehouse. The payoff is dependent on customer demand which is assumed to be uncertain at this point in time. Using the maximum procedure the decision-maker first selects the minimum payoff possible with each decision alternative and then the maximum payoff is selected from this group. For example the minimum payoffs for decisions 1, 2, and 3, respectively, are $5,000, $4,000, and $1,000. Selecting the largest of these indicates that the decision to build the small warehouse is best.

The maximax procedure affords the decision-maker an optimistic or aggressive approach to deciding. Under the maximum outlook the maximum payoff potential for each decision alternative is considered. From this group the decision which has the potential for the greatest payoff overall is selected. For our example this implies choosing between $10,000, $12,000, or $15,000 for decision alternatives 1, 2, or 3, respectively. The outcome differs since using this aggressive approach as the course of action now is to build a large warehouse.

TABLE 14–1 Payoff Table

Decision Alternatives	Possible Outcomes		
	Low Customer Demand	Medium Customer Demand	High Customer Demand
1. Build small warehouse	$10,000	$ 8,000	$ 5,000
2. Build medium warehouse	4,000	12,000	8,000
3. Build large warehouse	1,000	6,000	15,000

TABLE 14–2 Opportunity Loss Table

Decision Alternatives	Low Customer Demand	Medium Customer Demand	High Customer Demand
1. Build small warehouse	$ 0	−$4,000	−$10,000
2. Build medium warehouse	− 6,000	0	− 7,000
3. Build large warehouse	− 9,000	− 6,000	0

There is a third way of analyzing this problem which involves looking at the opportunity loss associated with the various alternatives. Utilizing the information in Table 14–1, an Opportunity Loss Table, Table 14–2, can be constructed. For a given customer demand the greatest payoff potential should be isolated. For the other decision alternatives the differences in payoffs should be assessed. For example, if customer demand is low, $10,000 is the greatest potential payoff. But if a medium warehouse is constructed, the payoff is only $4,000. This represents an opportunity loss of $6,000. For a large warehouse, $10,000 − $1,000 = $9,000 opportunity loss.

Under the minimax regret procedure the maximum opportunity loss for each alternative is determined. The final selection is then made of the course of action which minimizes the regret the decision-maker will face by choosing the lowest value. From Table 14–2 the values of −$10,000, −$7,000, and −$9,000 are isolated as the maximum regret values associated with the various decision alternatives. Using the minimax regret procedure, the course of action would be to build a medium warehouse.

In this example the decision of which option to use was very influential in determining the outcome. This is to be expected because the emphasis of the decision criteria varies with each method. The maximum procedure uses a pessimistic outlook choosing the best alternative from the worst that can happen with each potential course of action, thereby minimizing the risk. Potential payoff is maximized by the optimistic decision-maker choosing the best payoff of the best potential payoffs for each alternative utilizing the maximax procedure. The minimax regret procedure focuses on minimizing losses from a marginal perspective.

Decision Trees

Another approach to the selection process is the use of decision trees. In most complex situations, a number of options are confronted as a result of any initial decision. Formulation of an overall plan requires evaluation of a total course of action. Initial probabilities and payoffs must be appraised followed by the conditional additional probabilities associated with each subsequent course of action. The decision tree enables the manager to assess a relatively complex situation systematically.

Decision trees consist of three parts: (1) the initial decision point, (2) the paths, and (3) the branches. The whole tree represents the decision problem. The paths, which may consist of several branches, represent the various probabilities and events of a particular outcome. The branches represent various outcomes. Each set of decisions has one outcome and an associated probability.

ALTERNATIVE COURSES OF ACTION	INITIAL PROBABILITY	CONDITIONAL PROBABILITY	NET PROFIT	JOINT PROBABILITY

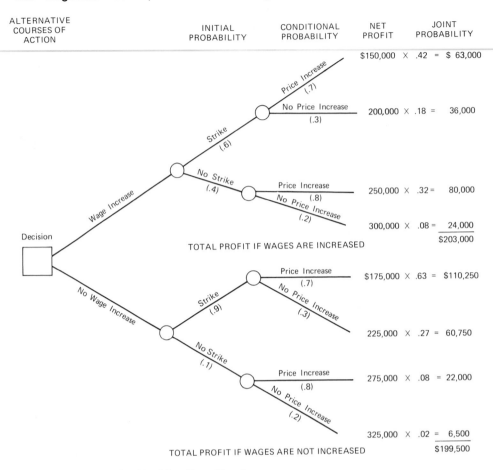

$150,000 × .42 = $ 63,000

200,000 × .18 = 36,000

250,000 × .32 = 80,000

300,000 × .08 = 24,000
$203,000

TOTAL PROFIT IF WAGES ARE INCREASED

$175,000 × .63 = $110,250

225,000 × .27 = 60,750

275,000 × .08 = 22,000

325,000 × .02 = 6,500
$199,500

TOTAL PROFIT IF WAGES ARE NOT INCREASED

Figure 14–1 Decision-Tree Structure

To illustrate, assume that a logistical manager is concerned with the likelihood of a strike and the associated possibility of a price increase. To assist in the formulation of a strategy, it is necessary to estimate the initial probability of a strike occurring under the various courses of action that the upper management can pursue. If wages are increased, management may determine that a strike is less likely. Next, an estimated cost must be determined for the fulfillment of the material plan with and without a wage increase, with or without a strike, as well as with or without a material price increase. If wages are increased, the probability of a strike is estimated to be 0.6. The conditional probability of a price increase is judged to be 0.7 if a strike occurs and 0.8 if it does not. However, a price increase following the strike would be greater than if it is granted without a strike. Under each set of conditional probabilities, the cost of material management operations has to be calculated in terms of net profit impact. In other words, any loss of product sale caused by failure to maintain supply and the greater labor costs if wages are increased have been taken into consideration in arriving at the estimated net profit of each event. The decision structure is presented in Figure 14–1.

Figure 14–1 provides the end products of the various events and the expected profit impact for the decision as to whether wages should be increased or not.

Under the best estimate of probable future events resulting from the initial decision on the part of management, the best decision appears to be to increase wages, thus decreasing the chance of a strike.

The decision-tree structure and problem illustrated are relatively simple in comparison to those that might be confronted in an actual planning situation. Similar to all decision aids, the value of the decision tree is directly related to the correct assignment of probabilities, which is sometimes very difficult. For instance, if it was assumed that the wage increase being considered only had a 30-per-cent probability of averting a strike, then it would be a better decision not to offer it at all.

Capital Budgeting

A number of situations occur in logistical operations where a decision must be made regarding the external purchase or internal performance of a service or manufacture of a component part. Typical service situations requiring do-or-buy analysis are private versus common carrier, public versus private warehousing, and internal study versus use of consultants. However, the most frequent type of make-or-buy situation concerns the manufacturing alternative of internal fabrication or external procurement. The typical manufacturing situation is illustrated. As a general rule, a manufacturing enterprise desires to make as many parts of its finished product line as economically practical. For the most part, raw materials must be purchased from outside sources, since few firms are vertically integrated to the point where they operate extraction of commodity processing facilities.[1]

Ammer has presented a general set of conditions that are helpful in the initial appraisal of the decision to make or buy.[2] These are summarized in Table 14–3. Beyond the general conditions favoring making or buying, the final decision results from the most efficient allocation of available capital. To aid in evaluation, the materials manager can apply expected value analysis to project the probable gain of investing in the necessary fabrication equipment as opposed to alternative uses of capital. In general, any investment is expected to provide a return on investment that meets corporate financial planning criteria.

Although the expected-value criterion is one of the most widely advocated methods of evaluating alternative courses of action, it requires considerable knowledge concerning the decision. In the case of the make-or-buy decision, the technique is extremely useful since the costs of each basic option are normally well defined. Assuming that the costs and other pertinent factors are nearly equal, the final decision is one of evaluating alternative application of financial resources. The basic concept is illustrated by an example application. Assume that the materials manager has a choice of spending $50,000 in any area that will improve overall costs of procurement. Three major options are available. The first is to invest in fabrication equipment that would result in making rather than buying a specific part. The second option is to improve warehouse

[1] Wilbur B. England, *Modern Procurement Management*, 5th ed. (Homewood, Ill.: Richard D. Irwin, Inc., 1970), pp. 72–81, provides an excellent summary of conditions encouraging or discouraging making versus purchasing.

[2] Dean S. Ammer, *Materials Management and Purchasing*, 4th ed. (Homewood, Ill.: Richard D. Irwin, 1980), pp. 349–56.

TABLE 14–3 Factors Favoring Make-or-Buy Decisions

Factors Favoring Fabrication	Factors Favoring Procurement
1. If the part can be more cheaply fabricated than purchased.	1. If the necessary facilities are not available and there are more profitable opportunities for investing company capital.
2. If the cost is nearly equal (because fabrication reduces the number of vendors the firm must rely upon).	
3. If the part is vital and requires extremely close quality control.	2. If existing facilities can be more economically employed to make other parts.
4. If the part can be produced on existing equipment and is of the type in which the firm has considerable manufacturing experience	3. If the existing personnel skills cannot be readily adapted to making the parts.
5. If the fabrication process requires no extensive investment in facilities already available at supplier plants.	4. If patents or other legal barriers prevent the company from making the parts.
6. If the requirements for the part are projected to be both relatively large and stable.	5. If the expected requirements for the part are either temporary or seasonal.

TABLE 14–4 Expected Cost Benefit

Option	Three-Year Cost Reduction
Fabrication equipment	$100,000
Warehouse receiving	95,000
Inventory and method	125,000

receiving facilities to reduce the amount of overtime currently required by dock personnel. The third is to improve the existing methods used to control overall procurement inventories. The problem is to select one of these alternative areas for investing the $50,000.

The first step is to project the potential cost savings of each option over a future time period. Assume that a basic corporate return on investment policy is that all capital investment must be recovered by cost-benefit savings within a three-year period. The best judgment of management is that the payoffs involved in each option are adequate to satisfy the cost-benefit criterion. The estimates of payoff are presented in Table 14–4. Although this payback method is one approach to evaluating cost benefit, it does have the weakness that it does not consider the time value of money or future income streams.

However, each projected cost saving involves a certain degree of risk that the expected results will not materialize. The second step is to assign a relative probability to the expected realization of each potential cost benefit.

Establishment of the probability is a judgment based upon evaluation of relative risk. For example, perhaps a potential vendor of the part in question will develop a new technology that will result in a price reduction if the part is purchased rather than fabricated. Alternatively, the demand for the part may

TABLE 14–5   Expected Value of Capital Expenditures

Option	Cost-Benefit Possibilities	Probability	Expected Value
Fabrication equipment	$100,000	0.6	$60,000
	60,000	0.4	24,000
			$84,000
Warehouse receiving	$ 95,000	0.8	$76,000
	80,000	0.2	16,000
			$92,000
Inventory control	$125,000	0.5	$62,500
	10,000	0.5	5,000
			$67,000

not materialize at the level anticipated, which will result in noneconomical deployment of the new fabrication equipment. Each of the options has similar contingencies that could result in the anticipated savings not materializing. Based on a careful evaluation of all facts, management on a scale of 0.01 to 1.0 estimates the following probabilities of realizing the complete expected cost reduction: (1) fabrication equipment 0.6, (2) warehouse receiving 0.8, and (3) inventory control method 0.5. For each situation the fallback position has been determined, if due to the risks involved, the full cost benefits are not achieved. The expected comparative value among the three options is calculated for each option by multiplying the probability of attainment and the cost benefit for each scenario. The sum of the expected values for the optimistic and pessimistic scenarios is then added to arrive at an expected value for each capital budget alternative. The results are presented in Table 14–5.

Using the expected-value criterion to guide the investment decision, the choice would be to complete the improvement of warehouse receiving facilities. Even though this option has the lowest estimated cost benefit, it has the highest expected value, owing to the high probability that the expected cost benefits will indeed be realized.

In conclusion, no statistical or financial aid to decision-making can serve as a substitute for management judgment. The perception of the manager in estimating the probability of various events is the key to identifying the appropriate course of adjustment action. The main benefit of decision techniques is that they force a logical and consistent interpretation of the facts as perceived by management. Thus, when decision techniques are used, a systematic method for reviewing alternatives is applied. The benefit gained is consistency.

FACILITY OPERATIONS

Statistical techniques can assist in a number of special situations confronted in the operation of warehouse and manufacturing facilities. Three such technique applications are illustrated in this section: (1) receiving, (2) inspection, and (3) facility sizing.

Receiving

Material and finished-goods receiving are typical areas in an enterprise where waiting lines or queues can develop. Queueing analysis is applicable to any situation where (1) some material, person, vehicle, or other element arrives at a facility for servicing; (2) at times, it is necessary to wait in line; (3) the desired service is received; (4) the object in question leaves the system.[3] Thus, queueing analysis could just as readily be applied to a doctor's office, barber shop, a retail store, the overall manufacturing process, or any other similar situation.

As in most areas of applied mathematics, queueing theory uses specialized terminology that should be understood by the reader. The *arrival rate* refers to the average rate at which trucks arrive at the unloading dock. Normally, it is expressed as the number of arrivals per unit of time. The *service rate* refers to the average rate at which trucks can be unloaded. It is expressed as the number of trucks serviced per unit of time. The *distribution pattern* for arrival and unloading has a significant impact upon waiting-line analysis. If no logical or consistent pattern of arrival and unloading exists, then a *random distribution pattern* is experienced. The probabilities of arrival and servicing can usually be expressed in the form of statistical distributions. Arrivals are typically expressed in the form of a *Poisson distribution*, whereas servicing is an *exponential distribution*.[4] Prior to using one of the hypothetical distribution relationships, the observed distribution should be compared with the theoretical relationship using a X^2 test of fit.

The Poisson distribution or the distribution of arrival times is expressed as

$$P(x) = \frac{(\lambda t)^x e^{-\lambda t}}{x!}$$

where

$P(x)$ = probability of arrival
t = unit of time
λ = average number of arrivals per unit of time
x = arrivals
e = base of the natural logarithm = 2.718

The equation yields the probability that there will be x arrivals in time t with the average arrival rate of λ units. Figure 14–2 illustrates the Poisson distribution.

The probability of service time is exponential and is expressed as follows:

$$P(t) = Me^{-Mt}$$

where

$P(t)$ = probability of service time t
t = unit of time
M = average servicing time

[3] For an expanded discussion, see Harvey M. Wagner, *Principles of Operations Research* (Englewood Cliffs, N.J.: Prentice-Hall, Inc., 1975), Chap. 20.

[4] The reader not familiar with basic statistical concepts should skip this section and resume reading at "Inspection," page 437.

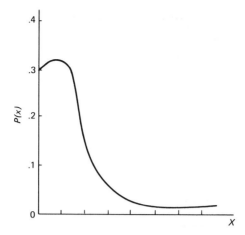

Figure 14–2 Poisson Distribution—Probability Function

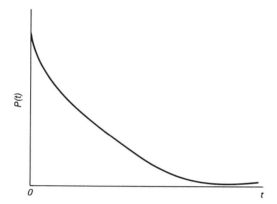

Figure 14–3 Exponential Distribution—Probability Function

The average service time overall is $\bar{t} = 1/M$. Figure 14–3 illustrates the exponential density function.

A final term used in queueing analysis is *channel*. Channel refers to the number of processing devices in the situation under analysis. For example, if one unloading dock is available, then the system is *single-channel*. If more than one channel exists in the problem, then it is *multiple-channel*.

The queueing-analysis problem represents a quantification of the receiving situation to allow management to test different ideas or queue-reduction solutions. To illustrate, assume that an unbiased data bank has been collected about arrival and unloading of trucks at a warehouse dock. The average time between arrivals of trucks at the dock is 30 minutes. Table 14–6 presents the measured unloading times for the trucks and the related frequency distribution.

Based on the data available, the unloading dock can be simulated. The first task is to simulate the arrival of a loaded truck. Based upon the average arrival-time analysis, there is a high probability that at least one truck will arrive every 30 minutes. Using a random-number table, the number of arrivals each 30-minute period can be approximated. In a similar manner, random-number tables can be used to approximate the expected unloading time for each

TABLE 14–6 Queueing Analysis Data

Number of Trucks	Unloading Time (minutes)	Percentage Distribution Unloading Times
10	35	10
30	40	30
40	45	40
20	50	20

TABLE 14–7 Simulated Arrival and Service Data

30-Minute Time Periods	Simulated Arrivals	Simulated Service Time (minutes)
1	0	
2	2	45–50
3	1	40
4	1	40
5	0	
6	0	
7	0	
8	1	50
9	0	
10	2	40–50
11	0	
12	1	45
13	0	
14	1	40
15	1	45
16	2	45–40
17	2	50–35
18	1	45
19	0	
20	0	
21	0	

arrival. A sample of the simulated operational data that can be generated using random numbers and the probabilities of arrival and unloading time is presented in Table 14–7.

Once the arrival and service pattern is determined, the queueing solution is to seek the lowest-cost way to complete the unloading. The cost of unloading consists of warehouse labor plus idle time of truck drivers and equipment while in the queue. Assuming that the necessary number of unloading docks or channels are available, the problem is to decide the size of the labor crew that will most economically service the arriving vehicles. The standard work rule is that trucks are unloaded on a first come–first service basis. For purposes of queue analysis, it is assumed if there is one arrival, it will occur at the start of the 30-minute period, and if two trucks arrive, the second will be ready for servicing at the start of the sixteenth minute of the 30-minute period.

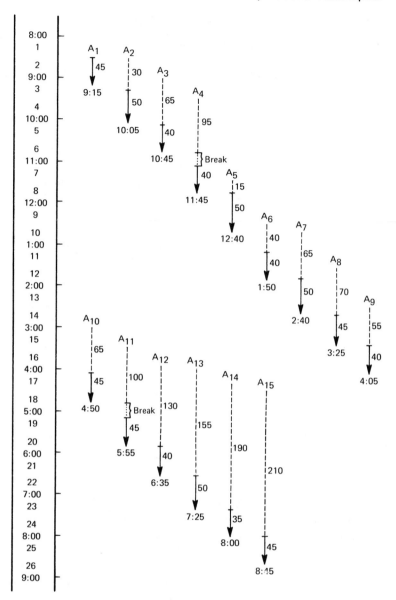

Figure 14-4   Simulated Queue Time Pattern

Figure 14–4 represents the simulated arrival and servicing patterns for the data displayed in Table 14–7. The numbers on the left side of Figure 14–4 represent 30-minute time periods. The dashed line represents waiting time once the truck has arrived. The solid line represents servicing time once the unloading starts. The total time in the queue is the combination of the waiting and servicing time.

Based on Figure 14–4 the total idle time of drivers and equipment is 1,285 minutes, an average time per driver in the queue of 85.69 minutes. Table 14–8 presents the cost of warehouse labor and idle drivers and equipment. The

TABLE 14–8   Queue Cost Factors

Warehouse regular rate/hour	$ 3.50
Warehouse overtime rate/hour	5.25
Driver and equipment rate/hour	20.00

TABLE 14–9   One Warehouse Shift

Warehouse regular rate	$196.00
Warehouse overtime rate	156.19
Driver and equipment rate	409.32
Total cost	$761.51

TABLE 14–10   Two Warehouse Shifts

Warehouse regular rate shift A	$196.00
Warehouse regular rate shift B	196.00
Warehouse overtime rate shift B	15.44
Driver and equipment rate	123.75
Total cost	$531.19

assumption is that idle transport equipment could be utilized if not in the queue.

Based on the data in Figure 14–4, it will be necessary for the warehouse dock crew to work 12.25 hours to complete the servicing of trucks scheduled to arrive on the simulated day. All hours over eight are paid at overtime rates.

The total cost of using a single seven-man unloading crew is presented in Table 14–9.

An alternative unloading procedure would be the addition of more warehouse personnel to unload or service the arriving trucks faster. To illustrate, a second crew of seven men is added under a work schedule that starts at 10 A.M. and ends when the last truck is unloaded. The regular crew is limited to an 8-hour shift.

While the simulated queue pattern is not presented, the result would be a reduction in average waiting time from 85.69 minutes to 25 minutes per truck. Table 14–10 provides the related cost data for the two-crew unloading alternative. A queue pattern for the two-crew unloading alternative similar to that in Figure 14–4 can be developed from the data presented.

In the illustration the queue has been substantially reduced by adding the second crew with a daily saving of $230.32. Based on a 250-day work year, the annualized cost benefit would be $57,580.

This simple illustration points out the type of analysis required by the materials management organization in order to realize smooth operations at the lowest possible total cost. One frequent belief is that when common carriers are used, the in-queue time is not important. Therefore, the proper solution to the queue situation is to use the lowest amount of warehouse labor that will get the trucks unloaded in time for the materials or parts to be ready for manufacturing use. This logic is faulty for two reasons. First, over an extended time, driver and equipment idle time of common carriers will be reflected in the rate per hundredweight charged for their service. Second, most tariffs provide for a specific delay charge unless trucks are serviced within a specified time period.

A number of variations can be applied to a waiting-line simulation to seek better servicing rate or lower costs. For example, when private trucks are used, an attempt can be made to eliminate random arrival by scheduling. Scheduled arrival will reduce the waiting queue. A second potential modification is to relax the first come–first service rule to move trucks with critical materials or higher-than-average delay charges rapidly through the queue.

In essence, the main point of emphasis in receiving is establishment of an unloading procedure that will meet manufacturing requirements at the lowest total cost. As in most areas of logistics, care must be exercised to assure that all relevant costs are considered in the decision process.

Inspection

One of the basic objectives of materials management is quality maintenance. Inferior quality is the single greatest cause for failure of supplies to be delivered on time. The materials management inspection responsibility is aimed at checking a representative sample of materials and parts to assure that they meet specification. Such inspection may be done at the vendor's manufacturing plant or after the material is received. The location of inspection depends upon the critical nature of the item in question and its overall vulnerability to damage while in transit. The more susceptible a given material or part is to quality problems, the greater the need to work with the vendor to ensure consistent quality.

The cost of 100-per-cent inspection is, in most cases, prohibitive.[5] Therefore, some form of inspection or quality control by statistical sampling is required. In most fabrication situations, a degree of random fluctuations in specific parts is expected to occur. The purpose of the inspection sample is to measure the degree of fluctuation or damage to determine if the fabrication or transportation process is out of control.

Sampling consists of selecting a predetermined number of items from a large lot or shipment for careful inspection. The sample size and method of selection are structured in such a way to assure that it is representative of the total group.[6] Based upon a careful inspection of the sample, the inspector follows a predetermined statistical inference procedure with respect to acceptance or rejection of the entire shipment. For each material or part, a predetermined required reliability sets the basic standard for acceptance or rejection.

For example, assume that a shipment of a specific part consists of 400 units. It has been determined that a 10-per-cent, or 40-unit, sample is adequate to project the overall condition of the shipment with a 95-per-cent confidence of correct appraisal.[7] The sampling procedure under this situation could be a

---

[5] Robert E. McGarrah, *Production and Logistics Management* (New York: John Wiley & Sons, Inc., 1963), pp. 7–20.

[6] Ibid.

[7] Ninety-five-per-cent confidence means that the sample size will be adequate to make a valid inspection 95 out of 100 times. It does not mean that deficiencies will exists 5 per cent of the time.

complete inspection of every tenth part. If all 40 parts meet specifications, the entire shipment would be accepted. If one defect was discovered in the sample of 40, then several options might be followed.

First, the total lot could be rejected. However, this could result in unnecessary expense of return shipment and possible shortage of a critical part. Second, the total lot could be inspected, with separation of those parts that do and do not meet specifications. A final choice, if only one or a limited number of defects was discovered in the initial sample, is to take a second random sample to cross-verify results. The degree of tolerance in acceptance or rejection, as well as the amount of additional inspection caused by a defect, will depend upon the tolerance range established for the part.

Facility Sizing

Determination of facility size is a subset of strategic planning which must be implemented as part of the operational planning effort. Once the decision has been made to establish a particular facility at a given location, it is necessary to determine size. Facility sizing involves an analysis of activities to be performed at the facility, coupled with an estimate of inventory space requirements. The focal point of concern in the example is inventory since other requirements for space, such as order processing or light fabrication, are unique to each enterprise's plans. Sizing a warehouse facility was noted initially in Chapter 8. The technique described here can be utilized for all types of facility planning requirements. The example is based on a warehouse situation. The overall sizing analysis requires that four tasks be completed: (1) data identification, (2) determination of gross space requirements, (3) throughput analysis, (4) cost analysis. Each is discussed and illustrated.

Data Identification

Several elements of basic data are required to estimate facility size requirements. First, demand forecasts are critical to sizing since they quantify the throughput requirements of the facility. The inherent errors of forecast techniques require that the final estimate of demand be calculated on the basis of management prediction. Care should be taken to include only warehouse service area demand that will pass through the facility in the prediction. The second type of data required for sizing concerns the characteristics of products and orders to be stored and shipped from the warehouse. The critical product feature is cubic displacement, since it determines the size required to store a specific amount of product. The critical aspects of customer order patterns are the size, frequency, and variation in time between orders. Data collected on existing product and customer configurations must be modified to reflect potential changes. The third type of data required to complete the analysis are estimates of the fixed and variable costs associated with alternative courses of action. Assumptions regarding each type of data are introduced as appropriate.

Determination of Gross Space Requirements

The determination of gross space requires five steps. The basic data required to render facility sizing are presented in Table 14–11. The forecasted annual

TABLE 14-11 Facility Requirements Determination

	(1) Monthly Sales ($000)	(2) Monthly Sales[a] (000s of cubic feet)	(3) Average Inventory[b] (000s of cubic feet)	(4) Area Requirement[c] (square feet)	(5) Adjusted Gross Area Requirement[d] (square feet)
January	11,200	560	1,120	70,000	93,333
February	11,800	590	1,180	73,750	98,333
March	13,200	660	1,320	82,500	110,000
April	12,900	645	1,290	80,625	107,500
May	12,100	605	1,210	75,625	100,833
June	13,500	675	1,350	84,375	112,500
July	14,800	740	1,480	92,500	123,333
August	14,800	740	1,480	92,500	123,333
September	13,600	680	1,360	85,000	113,333
October	11,900	595	1,190	74,375	99,167
November	10,400	520	1,040	65,000	86,667
December	11,800	590	1,180	73,750	98,333
Total	152,000				

[a] An average value of $20/cubic foot is assumed on the average for the overall product line.
[b] On the basis of an average of six turns per year, the average inventory level is twice the monthly sales volume.
[c] Assuming an average usable stacking height of 16 feet, the area requirement for the facility is the cube divided by 16.
[d] The actual area required for storage is estimated to be 75 per cent of gross requirements

demand of $152 million in facility throughput is presented on a monthly basis in column 1 as the first step in the analysis. The sales forecast provides an estimate of demand level and expected seasonal variation. In the second step of the analysis, sales dollars are converted to cubic throughput requirements, as indicated in column 2 of Table 14–11. In the example situation an average price to cubic displacement ratio of $20 per cubic foot is assumed.

Given sales in cubic feet the third step is to estimate average inventory level. An estimate of average inventory can be calculated based on an analysis of past orders or by the use of past inventory turnover experience. For this illustration an annual turn factor of six times is assumed. Using this turn factor, the average inventory for each period in cubic feet is computed to be twice the monthly sales volume. This calculation is presented in column 3, Table 14–11. If the facility is to service a situation where a high degree of seasonality is experienced in either manufacturing or sales accompanied by inventory buildup, the calculation of average inventory based on turns would not provide useful results. In such situations a detailed analysis of the timing of inventory buildup and depletion rate is required.

The fourth step is to estimate square-foot warehouse requirements. The assumed usable vertical storage height for the product line is 16 feet. The actual figure will depend upon product stacking capability and the planned materials-handling system. To determine area requirements, the monthly average inventory is divided by 16. The results are presented in column 4, Table 14–11.

In the fifth step of the analysis an adjustment must be made to convert required storage space to gross warehouse size. The amount of loss space varies by the overall functions to be performed at the facility, the product, and the actual layout. For the illustration it is assumed that the usable product storage represents 75 per cent of gross space. To compute the gross facility size on a monthly basis, the storage area requirement is divided by 0.75. The results are provided in column 5, Table 14–11.

The result of steps 1 through 5 is a monthly gross facility requirement. Next, a throughput analysis is required.

Throughput Analysis

Given the gross space requirement, it is necessary to evaluate month-to-month requirements, in terms of private warehouse or alternative forms of storage, such as public warehouses or transportation equipment. Since the size of a private facility cannot be adjusted on a monthly basis, a form of make-or-buy analysis must be performed to determine the ideal size throughout the year. For illustration, it is assumed that the choice is between private construction and public warehouse overflow storage. In terms of overall problem solution, the facility combination that results in the lowest total annual cost represents the ideal solution.

The throughput analysis is presented in Table 14–12. A range of possible warehouse sizes is taken directly from column 5, Table 14–11, and is ranked in descending order of monthly gross requirements—column 1, Table 14–12. Assuming that each estimate of monthly gross requirements represents a feasible warehouse size, the relative throughput of private and public utilization is calculated in dollar sales. The sales throughput for private utilization is presented in column 2, and for public utilization in column 3, Table 14–12.

Since the first *level of capacity* in Table 14–12 represents the maximum size needed for any month, the entire annual volume can be stored and shipped from the private facility. Thus, the throughput in column 2 represents the total annual sales volume of $152 million. For smaller facility sizes, since these sizes were based on a lower monthly throughput, not all of the volume may be

TABLE 14–12 Throughput Analysis

(1) Possible Warehouse Sizes (square feet)	(2) Sales Throughput Through Private Facility ($000)	(3) Sales Throughput Through Public Facility ($000)
123,333	152,000	0
113,333	149,600	2,400
112,500	149,300	2,700
110,000	148,100	3,900
107,500	146,600	5,400
100,833	141,800	10,200
99,167	140,400	11,600
98,333	139,600	12,400
93,333	133,600	18,400
86,667	124,800	27,200
0	0	152,000

shipped from the private facility. For example, for the second possible warehouse size of 113,333 square feet, the size requirement is based on a monthly volume of $13,600,000. At this capacity level, any monthly volume over that level must be shipped through a public facility. In this case, since the next highest month has a volume of $14.8 million, the volume that must be shifted to the public facility is $2.4 million [(14.8 million − 13.6 million) × 2]. The throughput volume through the private facility in column 2 and the volume through the public facility are then adjusted to reflect this shift. The volume splits for the other possible facility sizes are each illustrated.

If the smallest possible private warehouse is constructed, $27.2 million in sales is serviced using a public warehouse facility. Other options are to use all public warehousing or to build some size of private facility to accommodate from minimum to maximum gross requirements.

Cost Analysis

To arrive at a final solution, a total-cost analysis of the available options is necessary. This requires that the fixed and variable costs through the private facility as well as the cost of utilizing a public warehouse be estimated. The results of this analysis are presented in Table 14–13. To complete the analysis several cost factors are needed. First, throughput must be converted to weight, since variable cost is typically a function of pounds. Based on an assumed sales value of $2 per pound, the throughput ratios are restated in hundred-pound equivalents for each type of warehouse in columns 2 and 5, Table 14–13.

TABLE 14–13   Facility Cost Analysis

(1) Warehouse Size (square feet)	(2) Private Facility Throughput[a] (00's of pounds)	(3) Private Facility Variable Costs[b] ($000)	(4) Private Facility Fixed Costs[c] ($000)	(5) Public Facility Throughput[a] (00's of pounds)	(6) Public Facility Variable Costs[d] ($000)	(7) Total Annual Operating Costs ($000)
123,333	760,000	190.00	92.50	0	0	282.50
113,333	748,000	187.00	85.00	12,000	6.00	278.00
112,500	746,500	186.63	84.38	13,500	6.75	277.76
110,000	740,500	185.13	82.50	19,500	9.75	277.38
107,500	733,000	183.25	80.63	27,000	13.50	277.38
100,833	709,000	177.25	75.62	51,000	25.50	278.37
99,167	702,000	175.50	74.38	58,000	29.00	278.88
98,333	698,000	174.50	73.75	62,000	31.00	279.25
93,333	668,000	167.00	70.00	92,000	46.00	283.00
86,667	624,000	156.00	65.00	136,000	68.00	289.00
0	0	0	0	760,000	380.00	380.00

[a] The product mix is assumed to have an average value of $2/pound.
[b] Based on an arbitrary handling and throughput cost of $0.25/hundredweight of volume moved through the facility.
[c] A $0.75/square foot fixed charge is assessed against the private facility.
[d] Based on an arbitrary handling and throughput cost of $0.50/hundredweight of volume moved through the public facility.

To calculate private warehouse costs, a variable cost of $0.25 per hundred pounds was assumed to reflect such factors as labor, handling equipment, and supplies. For private fixed costs, a figure of $0.75 per square foot is assumed to reflect such items as depreciation, insurance, heat, taxes, light, and administrative overhead. No economy of scale as a function of warehouse size is factored into either cost figure, owing to the narrow range of alternative sizes. The appropriate costs are presented in columns 3 and 4 of Table 14–13.

For the public warehouse facility an assumed rate quotation of $0.50 per hundredweight is used to calculate cost. In the case of public facilities, the cost includes both fixed and variable costs of the warehouse, however, from the user's viewpoint, charges are assessed on the basis of hundredweight throughput. Once again, the analysis does not include the possibility of rate reductions that might be obtained by offering larger volumes to the public warehouse. These costs are illustrated in column 6, Table 14–13.

The total cost of each alternative is illustrated in column 7, Table 14–13. The ideal size of warehouse is between 107,500 and 110,000 square feet of gross space.

As noted at the outset of the sizing analysis, the analysis is only as good as the supporting assumptions regarding demand and cost. For example, what would be the effect if variable cost associated with the public warehouse declined to $0.40 per hundredweight or if demand increased 10 per cent?

The sizing application illustrated has for simplicity been limited to a single-year time frame. In actual situations the analysis is complicated by the need to consider expected life duration of the warehouse as well as changes in demand, cost, and product data across the planning horizon. The ideal solution is the selection of a facility size that results in the least total cost based upon discounted cash flow across the planning horizon. The technique illustrated can be expanded to deal with across-time requirements planning.

ALLOCATION AND ASSIGNMENT

With allocation and assignment problems the decision-maker is certain about the operational planning conditions. Although a number of limitations and restrictions may exist, the objective of allocation is to determine the optimal course of action taking all important factors into consideration. The *allocation* problem exists under conditions of adequate supply as contrasted to the *assignment* problem, wherein a choice situation is confronted as a result of shortage.

The most common technique for solving this type of operational problem is *linear programming*. The capabilities of linear programming were reviewed in Chapter 12. In this chapter one linear programming procedure, the *transportation method*, is illustrated as an appropriate method to solve allocation and assignment problems. The procedure is designed to optimize or maximize a single function referred to as the objective function. Even though it derives its name from its early use in transportation scheduling, the basic method is applicable to other situations.

Allocation: Adequate Supply

The general structure of the allocation problem is that a given number of product source points and product demand points exist in a network and the cost of shipping a volume from each source to each destination is known. The sources and destinations may represent manufacturing plants, warehouses, or customers. The problem is to select those assignments that minimize shipping cost while satisfying the capacity and demand requirements of each source and destination.

To solve the problem using the transportation procedure, the following data are required:

1. The capacities of each source (e.g., manufacturing plant).
2. The requirements of a destination (e.g., warehouse).
3. The transportation cost per unit from each source to each destination.

The only general restriction beyond deterministic and linear relationships is that a one-for-one substitution must be possible when using the transportation method. For example, if it is decided not to ship 100 units of a product from a specific plant to a specific warehouse, it must be possible to substitute a similar number of units from a different plant.

In the example two plants located in New York and Los Angeles each produce the product in question. Shipments are made from the two plants to four warehouses located across the country.

Three types of data are required to operationalize the transportation method. Tables 14–14, 14–15, and 14–16 present the data.

Problem Initialization

The first step is to develop a matrix that arranges supply, demand, and transportation cost data. However, this matrix must maintain a balance between supply and demand; if supply does not equal demand, a dummy source or destination must be added to account for the difference. In the initial matrix, an "other" or dummy destination is added, since the manufacturing capacity

TABLE 14–14   Weekly Availability of Manufacturing at Each Plant

Plant Location	Manufacturing Schedule
New York	4,000
Los Angeles	3,500
Total manufacturing (units per week)	7,500

TABLE 14–15   Weekly Requirements at Individual Warehouses

Warehouse	Unit Requirement
Atlanta	1,500
Chicago	2,000
San Francisco	2,000
Pittsburgh	1,000

TABLE 14–16 Transportation Cost from Each Plant to Each Warehouse (Dollars per Unit)

Warehouses / Plants	Atlanta	Chicago	San Francisco	Pittsburgh
New York	+5	+4	+11	+3
Los Angeles	+10	+7	+2	+9

exceeds demand. The transportation cost to the dummy destination is zero, since no product is actually shipped.

An initial solution is necessary to start the procedure. The initial solution can be determined in a number of ways, among which are: (1) existing assignments, (2) present lowest-cost solution found by inspection, (3) managerially preferred method, and (4) the northwest corner rule (NCR).[8] The NCR is used in this example because it offers a systematic and logical method to arrive at an initial solution. The following procedures are used when implementing the NCR.

1. Begin in the upper left corner of the matrix and compare the demand of the column with the supply in the row. Place the smaller of these two values in that matrix location. If this fills the demand, move to the next location to the right and fill this demand, if possible. Continue this until the supply is exhausted for the row.
2. Moving to the next-lower row, again compare the demand with the supply. Select the smaller of the two quantities and place it in that location. Move to the next column or row and follow the same procedure.
3. After completing the second row, move to the third and fourth row, and so on, following steps 1 and 2.

Matrix I, Table 14–17, is the cost matrix with the dummy column inserted. Since the transportation method is a maximizing procedure, transportation costs are expressed as negatives. If a negative value is used to express cost, a direct readout of the profit impact is possible. Matrix II shows the initial feasible solution of the problem obtained through the NCR method.

Matrix II, Table 14–18, represents a possible allocation, but not necessarily the least-cost alternative. The matrix must now be evaluated for more economical alternatives. Through analysis of each vacant square in the matrix, it can be determined if the least-cost solution has been found. If not, a better solution is possible by varying the shipping assignments within the established constraints.

---

[8] An alternative approach to arriving at an initial solution is the Vogel approximation. See Nyles V. Reinfield and William R. Vogel, *Mathematical Programming* (Englewood Cliffs, N.J.: Prentice-Hall, Inc., 1958).

TABLE 14–17   Matrix I: Cost Matrix with Dummy Column

Plants \ Warehouses	Atlanta	Chicago	San Francisco	Pittsburgh	Other	Total Supply
New York	−5	−4	−11	−3	0	4,000
Los Angeles	−10	−7	−2	−9	0	3,500
Total Supply	1,500	2,000	2,000	1,000	1,000	

TABLE 14–18   Matrix II: Initial Solution—NCR Procedure

Plants \ Warehouses	Atlanta	Chicago	San Francisco	Pittsburgh	Other	Total Supply
New York	1,500 / −5	2,000 / −4	500 / −11	−3	0	4,000
Los Angeles	−10	−7	1,500 / −2	1,000 / −9	1,000 / 0	3,500
Total Supply	1,500	2,000	2,000	1,000	1,000	

Solution Procedure

To evaluate the matrix, the following steps are performed.

1. Place a zero in the margin of the first row. This is a row value. Now, for each nonempty location in that row, determine the column value by using the following equation:

$$\text{transportation cost} = \text{row value} + \text{column value}$$

or

$$\text{column value} = \text{transportation cost} - \text{row value}$$

Place the column value in the margin of the column. The appropriate column should then be used to find the row value for another row, and the process should be repeated until each row and column has a value. Only nonempty locations are used to find these values.

2. Now every vacant location is evaluated by means of the following equation:

vacant value = row value + column value − transportation cost

This is done for all vacant locations and the value is placed, in parentheses, in that location.

3. If all the values in parentheses are nonnegative, the solution is optimal. However, if there are negative values, a better solution exists. A better solution can be obtained by transferring units to the warehouse with the negative value, or the warehouse with the most negative value if there is more than one.

4. If units must be transferred, trace a path starting at the location with the most negative value and put a plus (+) in that location. Continue tracing a path until returning to the original row, alternately placing plus and minus in the nonempty locations. This process, in effect, balances the rows and columns so that units can be shifted to the desired location. Remember, all locations except the first one on this path must be nonempty, and all angles on the path must be right angles.

5. Review the path and find the warehouse with the smallest number of units and a minus in it. This is the number of units to transfer to a new warehouse. Transfer this number of units and balance the remainder of the matrix by adding or subtracting this value from the locations along the path as denoted by the sign. The number of nonvacant locations should equal the number of rows plus the number of columns minus 1 at all times during the solution procedure. If this is not the case, a degenerative situation is said to exist, and special steps must be taken to resolve the situation. The necessary procedure will be discussed later.

6. Return to step 1 and evaluate the new matrix.

Solution Evaluation

Using the rules already given, the solution presented in maxtrix II, Table 14–18, can be evaluated for optimality. First, obtain row and column values using the nonempty locations. If a value of zero is arbitrarily assigned to R_1, then C_1 can be computed as follows:

$$C_1 = -5 - 0 = -5$$

where R_1 is the row value for row 1 and C_1 is the column value for column 1.

Additional column values can be identified through this procedure until column 3 is reached:

$$C_3 = -11 - R_1$$
$$= -11 - 0$$
$$= -11$$

C_3 is now used to find R_2:

$$R_2 = \text{transportation cost} - C_3$$
$$= -2 - (-11)$$
$$= 9$$

The value of R_2 is now placed in the margin, and the process continues as before until all row and column values have been determined. When each row and column has been assigned an appropriate value, each vacant location is evaluated using the following formula:

$$V_{ij} = R_i + C_j - TC_{ij}$$

where

V_{ij} = value to be put in the vacant location at the intersection of the ith row and jth column

R_i = row value for row i

C_j = column value for column j

TC_{ij} = cost (negative) of sending 1 unit from source i to demand point j

To illustrate this procedure, for the matrix location designation Los Angeles (R_2) to Chicago (C_2), the calculation is as follows:

$$\begin{aligned}
V_{2,2} &= R_2 + C_2 - TC_{2,2} \\
&= 9 + (-4) - (-7) \\
&= 12
\end{aligned}$$

The 12 is placed in that matrix location in parentheses. Matrix III, Table 14–19, is the matrix after all row and column values have been found and all vacant locations have been evaluated.

Upon analysis of matrix III it can be determined that units should be transferred into the New York to Pittsburgh route since it is the most negative. Since the matrix on this path location with the least number of units and a minus sign contains an allocation of 500 units (New York–San Francisco), this is the number of units to be transferred. This is the existing allocation from the New York plant to the Pittsburgh warehouse. When the number of units to be shifted has been determined, the quantities of each of the matrix locations on the path must be adjusted and balanced to maintain the correct relationship

TABLE 14–19   Matrix III: Solution 1

	Column Value	−5	−4	−11	−18	−9	
Row Value	Warehouses / Plants	Atlanta	Chicago	San Francisco	Pittsburgh	Other	Total Supply
0	New York	1,500 / −5	2,000 / −4	500 / −11	(−15) / −3	(−9) / 0	4,000
9	Los Angeles	(14) / −10	(12) / −7	1,500 / −2	1,000 / −9	1,000 / 0	3,500
	Total Supply	1,500	2,000	2,000	1,000	1,000	

Total Cost = $33,000

between the supply and demand at each location. To do this, 500 units are placed in the New York–Pittsburgh location by subtracting 500 units each from the New York–San Francisco and Los Angeles–Pittsburgh locations and adding 500 units to the Los Angeles–San Francisco location. This is accomplished in matrix IV, Table 14–20, and matrix V, Table 14–21.

Notice that the totals in supply and demand must remain the same after each transfer iteration. Matrix VI, Table 14–22, now brings together the new routes from matrix V, Table 14–21, and the cost data from matrix III, Table 14–19.

The solution procedure is repeated until a solution is isolated, which yields all nonnegative values for vacant locations. In total, it is necessary to generate three matrices before all negative values are eliminated.

As can be seen in matrix VII, Table 14–23, each of the empty matrix locations has a nonnegative value, so this set of assignments provides the optimum method of allocation.

Matrix VIII, Table 14–24, provides a simplified form of matrix VII showing only the loads to be shipped from each manufacturing plant to each warehouse. The savings between the initial matrix and the final one are $8,000. Although this problem could have been solved just as well using trial-and-error techniques, larger problems require a systematic approach. The transportation

TABLE 14–20 Matrix IV: Path to Balance Supply and Demand After Transfer

Warehouses / Plants	Atlanta	Chicago	San Francisco	Pittsburgh	Other	Total Supply
New York	1,500	2,000	500 (−)	(+)		4,000
Los Angeles			1,500 (+)	1,000 (−)	1,000	3,500
Total Supply	1,500	2,000	2,000	1,000	1,000	

TABLE 14–21 Matrix V: Reallocation

Warehouses / Plants	Atlanta	Chicago	San Francisco	Pittsburgh	Other	Total Supply
New York	1,500	2,000		500		4,000
Los Angeles			2,000	500	1,000	3,500
Total Supply	1,500	2,000	2,000	1,000	1,000	

TABLE 14–22 Matrix VI: Solution 2

Row Value	Warehouses / Plants	Atlanta	Chicago	San Francisco	Pittsburgh	Other	Total Supply
Column Value		−5	−4	4	−3	6	
0	New York	1,500 / −5	2,000 (−) / −4	(15) / −11	500 (+) / −3	(6) / 0	4,000
−6	Los Angeles	(−1) / −10	(−3) (+) / −7	2,000 / −2	500 (−) / −9	1,000 / 0	3,500
	Total Supply	1,500	2,000	2,000	1,000	1,000	

Total Cost = $25,500

TABLE 14–23 Matrix VII: Optimal Solution

Row Value	Warehouses / Plants	Atlanta	Chicago	San Francisco	Pittsburgh	Other	Total Supply
Column Value		−5	−4	1	−3	3	
0	New York	1,500 / −5	1,500 / −4	(12) / −11	1,000 / −3	(3) / 0	4,000
−3	Los Angeles	(2) / −10	500 / −7	2,000 / −2	(3) / −9	1,000 / 0	3,500
	Total Supply	1,500	2,000	2,000	1,000	1,000	

Total Cost = $24,000

TABLE 14–24 Matrix VIII: Optimal Shipping Assignments

Warehouses / Plants	Atlanta	Chicago	San Francisco	Pittsburgh	Other	Total Supply
New York	1,500	1,500		1,000		4,000
Los Angeles		500	2,000		1,000	3,500
Total Supply	1,500	2,000	2,000	1,000	1,000	

TABLE 14–25   Matrix IX: Example of Degenerate Solution

Warehouses / Plants	Atlanta	Chicago	San Francisco	Pittsburgh	Other	Total Supply
New York	1,500	2,000				3,500
Los Angeles			2,000	1,000	1,000	4,000
Total Supply	1,500	2,000	2,000	1,000	1,000	

algorithm provides a technique for manual implementation of linear programming methods. However, for larger problems, the required calculations quickly become tedious. The simplex algorithm or procedure is another method of solving allocation or assignment problems. The simplex procedure has two advantages over the transportation method. First, the simplex method is general and can solve other types of linear programming problems. Second, many computer software packages are available that use the simplex procedure to solve linear programming problems.

Degeneracy

As noted previously, the degenerate situation arises when the number of nonempty matrix locations is more or less than the number of rows plus the number of columns. An example of a degenerate situation is presented in matrix IX, Table 14–25. After the development of each matrix, the analyst must check for the degenerate condition. Steps must be taken to either increase or decrease the number of nonempty matrix locations before the transportation procedure can be continued.

When the initial allocation method produces too many nonempty matrix locations, the possibility of alternative row and column values is introduced. This would make it difficult to compute the resultant vacant square values (V_{ij}) so the matrix could not be evaluated further. When this form of degeneracy occurs, the allocations to some of the nonempty matrix locations must be combined until the correct number of nonempty locations is obtained. After this task is completed, the normal solution procedure can continue.

If there are not enough nonempty matrix locations, as demonstrated in matrix IX, Table 14–25, then an additional square or squares must be filled in. This can be accomplished by allocating 0 units to any of the matrix locations which are presently empty. This provides enough nonempty matrix locations to compute the row and column values. Once this new matrix location has been selected and filled in, the problem can be solved in the normal manner treating the location with 0 units just as any other nonempty location.

Assignment: Short Supply

The short-supply problem occurs when the inventory available to ship falls short of that required at the destinations. The problem is to select a product allocation plan that minimizes the loss associated with the shortage.

The transportation method can be used to solve the short-supply problem by structuring a dummy plant (origin) rather than a dummy warehouse to handle the differential between supply and demand. For example, if the New York plant in the allocation example had a decreased amount of inventory available because of a strike or parts shortage, a shortage would exist. In this instance the total supply is 6,000 units, while the demand remains at 6,500 units. Since the demand of at least one of the warehouses cannot be fully satisfied, it is necessary to determine the location(s) which the shortage will affect least.

The procedure attempts to minimize the total costs of the system, which, in this example, include the normal transportation cost per unit and a per unit penalty cost associated with the loss of sales if the warehouse is not supplied. Table 14–26 provides estimates of the per-unit shortage cost to each warehouse.

These shortages are added to the original transportation costs from Table 14–16 to provide a "pseudo" total cost, which includes transportation and penalty cost. For example, since Atlanta has a penalty cost of $2 per unit and the transportation cost from New York to Atlanta is $5 per unit, the approximation for total cost is $7 per unit. The dummy plant supplies an amount equivalent to the shortage (500 units). The cost associated with the dummy plant includes the out-of-stock cost but not the transportation cost. All costs are shown as negative values. Using the NCR initialization procedure, the first solution is illustrated in Table 14–27. The total cost of the initial solution is $51,000.

TABLE 14–26 Cost of Stockout at Warehouses

LOCATION	COST
Atlanta	2
Chicago	5
San Francisco	4
Pittsburgh	3

TABLE 14–27 Short-Supply Matrix

Warehouse / Plants	Atlanta	Chicago	San Francisco	Pittsburgh	Total Supply
New York	1,500 / −7	1,000 / −9	−15	−6	2,500
Los Angeles	−12	1,000 / −12	2,000 / −6	500 / −12	3,500
Dummy	−2	−5	−4	500 / −3	500
Total Supply	1,500	2,000	2,000	1,000	6,500

Total Cost = $51,000

TABLE 14–28 Final Short-Supply Matrix

Warehouse / Plants	Atlanta	Chicago	San Francisco	Pittsburgh	Total Supply
New York	1,000	500		1,000	2,500
Los Angeles		1,500	2,000		3,500
Dummy	500				500
Total Supply	1,500	2,000	2,000	1,000	6,500

Total Cost = $48,500

The optimal solution for the situation is achieved via the transportation procedure previously described. After four iterations, the final solution, with a total cost of $48,500, is shown in Table 14–28.

ROUTING

One of the most common situations confronted in logistical operations is the need to route transportation vehicles. The problem is to select the delivery sequence of the vehicle so it makes all required stops while minimizing traveling time or distance. Three types of routing situations are illustrated in this section: (1) separate origin-destination points, (2) coincident origin and destination points, and (3) routing with vehicle capacity constraints. While the basic problems are similar, for each situation the technique that handles the specific requirement most efficiently is illustrated.

Separate Origin-Destination Points

The objective in this type of routing is to select the sequence of stops that minimizes the distance while visiting all intermediate locations. The data required are origin, list of all delivery locations, and a measure of either distance or elapsed time between all locations. Figure 14–5 illustrates the network

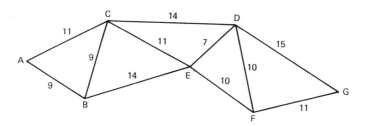

Figure 14–5 Example of Routing Network Separate Origin—Destination

TABLE 14–29 Origin-Destination Pairings and Distance—Separate Origin and Destination

A	B	C	D	E	F	G
AB = 9	BC = 9	CD = 14	DG = 15	ED = 7	FE = 10	GD = 15
AC = 11	BE = 14	CE = 11	DF = 10	EF = 10	FD = 10	GF = 11
	BA = 9	CA = 11	DC = 14	EB = 14	FG = 11	
		CB = 9	DE = 7	EC = 11		

assumed for the application example. The locations are identified as points A through F, and the numerical values represent the distance between any two sets of locations.

The solution procedure illustrated is known as the *listing method*. The initial step is to list all origins along with the destinations that can be serviced from each location and the related distance. This step is illustrated in Table 14–29.

To initiate the solution procedure, a value of zero is assigned to the route origin. For the example, A is assumed as the routing origin location. A new listing is then completed wherein all routes that lead to location A are deleted. This listing and all subsequent iterations necessary to arrive at the final solution are presented in Table 14–30.

The second iteration is to select the lowest distance from the origin, which is $AB = 9$ in the example. B is then assigned the value 9, and all locations that list B as a destination are deleted. The value of B is obtained by adding the value of A to the distance of the AB route.

The third iteration is to select the least distance route with B as the origin which is BC. A new iteration is then developed in which C is assigned the accumulated distance value of $B + BC$, which is 18. Then all remaining locations with C as a destination are deleted.

This iteration procedure is repeated until all the points requiring delivery are sequenced. The final route of A–B–C–E–D–F–G is reached in nine iterations and has an optimum distance of 57.

In a problem of this size it was not difficult to isolate the optimum route. The primary advantage of the listing method is that it provides a systematic means to reduce routes to a manageable size. In this situation 720 possible routes were quickly delineated. If the number of destinations increases, the problem can become unmanageable by manual methods. For example, with only 10 locations there are 3.6×10^5 possible routes. If the number of locations increases to 20, the possible routes expand to 1.2×10^{17}. For larger problems, computer techniques can be used. However, even computerized solution procedures can soon be overpowered by the sheer volume of routing options.[9]

Coincident Origin-Destination Points

A typical routing situation is dispatch of a vehicle for multiple delivery and/or pickups, with eventual return to the originating location. The complicating

[9] O'Neil and Whybark state that the largest problem they could solve in 2,000 seconds on a CDC 6500 involved 10 customers and 3 vehicles. See Brian F. O'Neil and D. Clay Whybark, "The Multiple-Vehicle Routing Problem," *The Logistics and Transportation Review*, Vol. 11 (December 1975), p. 161.

TABLE 14–30 Steps to Select Optimum Route—Separate Origin and Destination

Iteration 1: Deletion of A Destinations

$A = 0$	B	C	D	E	F	G
$AC = 11$	$BC = 9$	$CD = 14$	$DG = 15$	$ED = 7$	$FE = 10$	$GD = 15$
$AB = 9$	$BE = 14$	$CE = 11$	$DF = 10$	$EF = 10$	$FD = 10$	$GF = 11$
		$CB = 9$	$DC = 14$	$EB = 14$	$FG = 11$	
			$DE = 7$	$EC = 11$		

Iteration 2: Deletion of B Destinations

$A = 0$	$B = 9$	C	D	E	F	G
	$BC = 9$	$CD = 14$	$DG = 15$	$ED = 7$	$FE = 10$	$GD = 15$
	$BE = 14$	$CE = 11$	$DF = 10$	$EF = 10$	$FD = 10$	$GF = 11$
			$DC = 14$	$EC = 11$	$FG = 11$	
			$DE = 7$			

Optimum route = $A–B$ = 9

Iteration 3: Deletion of C Destinations

$A = 0$	$B = 9$	$C = 18$	D	E	F	G
	$BE = 14$	$CD = 14$	$DG = 15$	$ED = 7$	$FE = 10$	$GD = 15$
		$CE = 11$	$DF = 10$	$EF = 10$	$FD = 10$	$GF = 11$
			$DE = 7$		$FG = 10$	

Optimum route = $A–B–C$ = 18

Iteration 4: Deletion of E Destinations

$A = 0$	$B = 9$	$C = 18$	D	$E = 29$	F	G
		$CD = 14$	$DG = 15$	$ED = 7$	$FD = 10$	$GD = 15$
			$DF = 10$	$EF = 10$	$FG = 11$	$GF = 11$

Optimum route = $A–B–C–E$ = 29

Iteration 5: Deletion of D Destinations

$A = 0$	$B = 9$	$C = 18$	$D = 36$	$E = 29$	F	G
			$DG = 15$	$EF = 10$	$FG = 11$	$GF = 11$
			$DF = 10$			

'Optimum route = $A–B–C–E–D$ = 36

Iteration 6: Deletion of F Destinations

$A = 0$	$B = 9$	$C = 18$	$D = 36$	$E = 29$	$F = 46$	G
			$DG = 15$		$FG = 11$	

Optimum route = $A–B–C–E–D–F$ = 46

Iteration 7: Final Route

$A = 0$	$B = 9$	$C = 18$	$D = 36$	$E = 29$	$F = 46$	$G = 57$

Optimum route = $A–B–C–E–D–F–G$ = 57

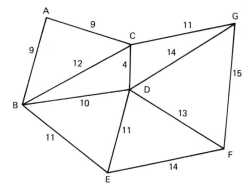

Figure 14–6   Example of Routing Network Coincident Origin and Destination

**TABLE 14–31   Origin-Destination Distances—
Coincident Origin and Destination**

	A	B	C	D	E	F	G
A	0						
B	9	0					
C	9	12	0				
D	13	10	4	0			
E	20	11	15	11	0		
F	26	23	17	13	14	0	
G	20	23	11	14	25	15	0

factor is the need to return to the origin as the final destination. This situation is generally referred to as the "traveling-salesman" problem. A wide variety of analytic and numeric techniques have been applied to this problem.[10] The most feasible solution procedures for large-scale problems are nonoptimizing. One such procedure is illustrated.

The example problem reflects a typical warehouse delivery problem. The vehicle departs warehouse location *A* and makes deliveries to customers at locations *B, C, D, E, F,* and *G.* The possible routes and the respective distances are illustrated in Figure 14–6. The first step is to create a table that contains the distances between any two points in the system. In the example a simplifying assumption is made that to reach a customer not directly connected to the warehouse location, it is necessary to pass through intermediate points. While this assumption simplifies the illustration, it is not necessary to the solution procedure. Table 14–31 presents the distance relationships of the network.

[10] See Frederick S. Hillier and Gerald J. Liebermann, *Introduction to Operations Research* (San Francisco: Holden-Day, Inc., 1967), pp. 218–22; John D. C. Little, Katta G. Murtz, Dura W. Sweeney, and Caroline Karel, "An Algorithm for the Traveling Salesman Problem," *Operations Research*, Vol. 11 (November–December 1963), pp. 972–89; Arthur V. Hill and D. Clay Whybark, *Comparing Exact Solution Procedures for the Multiple-Vehicle Routing Problem* (West Lafayette, Ind.: Krannert Graduate School of Industrial Administration, Purdue University, Paper No. 551, May 1976); Samuel B. Richmond, *Operations Research for Management Decisions* (New York: The Ronald Press Company, 1968), pp. 461–65; Robert L. Karg and Gerald L. Thompson, "A Heuristic Approach to Solving Traveling Salesman Problems," *Management Science*, Vol. 10 (January 1964), pp. 225–48.

TABLE 14–32   Iterations to Select Route—Coincident Origin and Destination

Iteration 1:
$A–B–A = 9 + 9 = 18$

Iteration 2:
$A–C–B–A = 9 + 12 + 9 = 30$
$A–B–C–A = 9 + 12 + 9 = 30$

Iteration 3:
$A–D–B–C–A = 13 + 10 + 12 + 9 = 44$
$A–B–D–C–A = 9 + 10 + 4 + 9 = 32$
$A–B–C–D–A = 9 + 12 + 4 + 13 = 38$

Iteration 4:
$A–E–B–D–C–A = 20 + 11 + 10 + 4 + 9 = 54$
$A–B–E–D–C–A = 9 + 11 + 11 + 4 + 9 = 44$
$A–B–D–E–C–A = 9 + 10 + 11 + 15 + 9 = 54$
$A–B–D–C–E–A = 9 + 10 + 4 + 15 + 20 = 58$

Iteration 5:
$A–F–B–E–D–C–A = 26 + 23 + 11 + 11 + 4 + 9 = 84$
$A–B–F–E–D–C–A = 9 + 23 + 14 + 11 + 4 + 9 = 70$
$A–B–E–F–D–C–A = 9 + 11 + 14 + 13 + 4 + 9 = 60$
$A–B–E–D–F–C–A = 9 + 11 + 11 + 13 + 17 + 9 = 70$
$A–B–E–D–C–F–A = 9 + 11 + 11 + 4 + 17 + 26 = 78$

Iteration 6:
$A–G–B–E–F–D–C–A = 20 + 23 + 11 + 14 + 13 + 4 + 9 = 94$
$A–B–G–E–F–D–C–A = 9 + 23 + 25 + 14 + 13 + 4 + 9 = 97$
$A–B–E–G–F–D–C–A = 9 + 11 + 25 + 15 + 13 + 4 + 9 = 86$
$A–B–E–F–G–D–C–A = 9 + 11 + 14 + 15 + 14 + 4 + 9 = 76$
$A–B–E–F–D–G–C–A = 9 + 11 + 14 + 13 + 14 + 11 + 9 = 81$
$A–B–E–F–D–C–G–A = 9 + 11 + 14 + 13 + 4 + 11 + 20 = 82$

Final Route: $A–B–E–F–G–D–C–A = 76$

The solution procedure is initiated by random selection of a customer destination from the list. In the example, location B is added with a round-trip distance of 18. Since only one possible round-trip route exists, the distance is optimum. This and all additional iterations necessary to select a final route are illustrated in Table 14–32.

In the second iteration a third customer location is inserted into the list. In the example destination C was selected. The result of the second iteration was a distance of 30, regardless of the round-trip route selected. The iteration procedure is continued with the repeated insertion of additional customer locations. The shortest round-trip route is selected each time as the interim solution until all customer destinations are included. The final route of $A–B–E–F–G–D–C–A$ with a distance value of 76 is isolated with six iterations.

The round-trip route identified in the example is the optimum. However, the procedure does not guarantee an optimal solution. Several enhancements have been suggested to improve the procedure for application to large-scale problems.[11]

---

[11] Karg and Thompson, op. cit.

Routing with Vehicle Capacity Constraints

A third type of routing procedure involves the addition of vehicle capacity constraints to the solution procedure. The problem is to schedule a limited number of vehicles from a central facility subject but not limited to the following constraints:[12]

1. The delivery requirements to all destinations must be satisfied.
2. Vehicle capacity may not be violated.
3. The total time or distance traveled by a given vehicle may not exceed a predetermined amount.

An additional conditions or constraint typical of this type of problem is that the number of vehicles in the fleet is limited, and they may have different maximum capacities. The objective of the solution procedure is to select the vehicle assignments and the best possible routing. The technique illustrated is known as the "savings" method, which is a nonoptimizing solution procedure.[13]

The example problem consists of a fleet of vehicles that are dispatched from origin, P_0, and must make deliveries to 10 destinations identified as P_1 through P_{10}. The destinations are located at a distance of $d_{y,0}$ from the origin and $d_{y,z}$ from each other. Table 14–33 presents the distances for all routes included in the assumed network. For example, $d_{1,0} = 9$, $d_{2,0} = 12$, while $d_{2,1} = 5$. In

[12] For a more detailed example, see N. Christofides and S. Eilon, "An Algorithm for the Vehicle Dispatching Problem," *Operational Research Quarterly*, Vol. 20 (September 1969), No. 3, pp. 309–18.

[13] Ibid. For other approaches, see M. Held and R. M. Karp, "A Dynamic Programming Approach to Sequencing Problems," *Journal of the Society of Industrial Applied Mathematics*, Vol. 10 (1962), p. 196; R. L. Hays, "The Delivery Problem," *Report MSR 106* (Pittsburgh, Pa.: Carnegie Institute of Technology, Graduate School of Industrial Administration); G. Clarke and J. W. Wright, "Scheduling of Vehicles from a Central Depot to a Number of Delivery Points," *Operations Research*, Vol. 12 (May–June 1964), pp. 568–81.

TABLE 14–33 Demand Requirements and Route Lengths

Load q_i ⟶ z	P_0	P_1	P_2	P_3	P_4	P_5	P_6	P_7	P_8	P_9	P_{10}
200	9	P_1									
75	12	5	P_2								
100	16	8	7	P_3							
150	19	11	11	5	P_4						
200	21	13	14	12	8	P_5					
300	24	19	12	18	12	7	P_6				
50	28	19	18	21	16	11	6	P_7			
200	31	25	25	25	21	14	12	7	P_8		
300	35	26	28	24	25	19	16	11	6	P_9	
200	40	33	31	26	26	23	19	18	15	12	P_{10}

addition, the requirements of each destination customer are listed in cubic feet in the columns of Table 14–33 labeled "Load q_i". This demand must be satisfied by deployment of the fleet capacity as illustrated in Table 14–34.

The computational procedure is as follows:

1. Initially, assume that there are enough vehicles to allocate one to every customer. Since there are 10 customers, that is the number of vehicles shown in the 300-cubic-foot (ft^3) size in Table 14–34. If a single customer demand exceeds the capacity of the vehicle, split the load and consider only the remainder of the load. For example, if P_1 demanded a 1,000-ft^3 delivery volume, one of the 800-ft^3 trucks would be assigned to it and the remaining 200 ft^3 would be the only volume to be considered in the analysis. Following this procedure, an initial vehicle allocation is determined as illustrated in Table 14–35. One vehicle of the smallest capacity is initially allocated to each customer and provides an initial solution to the problem.

2. The development of a savings matrix is the next step in the algorithm. This savings, denoted $S_{y,z}$, is the time or distance that is saved if the routes $P_0 \rightarrow P_y \rightarrow P_0$ and $P_0 \rightarrow P_z \rightarrow P_0$ are combined to form a single route $P_0 \rightarrow P_y \rightarrow P_z \rightarrow P_0$. The entire savings matrix is shown in Table 14–36. The savings in each of the cells is determined with the following formula:

$$S_{y,z} = d_{0,y} + d_{0,z} - d_{y,z}$$

where $d_{y,z}$ is the route length from Table 14–33. To illustrate this computation:

$$\begin{aligned} S_{1,2} &= d_{0,1} + d_{0,2} - d_{1,2} \\ &= 9 + 12 - 5 \\ &= 16 \end{aligned}$$

This is the value of 16 at the intersection of column P_1 with row P_2. The remaining values are computed similarly.

TABLE 14–34 Available Vehicle Sizes

Size (cubic feet)	Number
300	10
400	3
800	2

TABLE 14–35 Available Vehicle Capacity and Initial Vehicle Allocation to Customers

Trucks	300 ft^3	400 ft^3	800 ft^3
Available	10	3	2
Allocated	10	0	0

TABLE 14–36 "Savings" Matrix

Load q_i

	P_0	P_1	P_2	P_3	P_4	P_5	P_6	P_7	P_8	P_9	P_{10}
200	②	P_1									
75	②	16	P_2								
100	②	17	21	P_3							
150	②	17	20	30	P_4						
200	②	17	19	25	32	P_5					
300	②	14	24	22	31	38	P_6				
50	②	18	22	23	31	38	46	P_7			
200	②	15	18	22	29	38	43	52	P_8		
300	②	18	19	27	29	37	43	52	60	P_9	
200	②	16	21	30	33	38	45	50	56	63	P_{10}

The circled values in some of the cells, $t_{y,z}$, indicate whether the customer combinations P_y and P_z are in a tour. This designator has the following values:

$t_{y,z} = 1$ if two customers are linked on a vehicle route
$t_{y,z} = 0$ if the customers are not linked on a vehicle route
$t_{y,z} = 2$ if the customer is served exclusively by a single vehicle

Zero entries are not shown in Table 14–36. For the initial problem, set all $t_{y,0} = 2$, meaning that one vehicle is used to serve each customer. For ease of computation, the matrix of Table 14–36 is ordered from left to right on the basis of increased savings $S_{y,z}$.

3. At this stage the iterative process is initiated until each savings-assignment matrix is evaluated for further route improvements. The procedure is to search the matrix for the largest savings subject to the following conditions for any cell (y, z):
    a. $t_{y,0}$ and $t_{z,0}$ are > 0.
    b. P_y and P_z are not already allocated on the same vehicle run.
    c. Amending Table 14–36 by removing the trucks allocated to loads q_y and q_z and adding a vehicle to cover the load q_y and q_z does not cause the vehicles allocated to exceed the vehicles available in any column of Table 14–35.

4. Next, a cell is selected where there are two routes that can be combined into a single tour. A value of $t_{y,z} = 1$ is placed in the cell, and all $t_{y,z}$ values are adjusted so that the sum of $t_{y,z}$ across a row, plus $t_{y,z}$ down the column where $y = z$, is always equal to 2. Where $t_{j,0} = 0$, set $q_j = 0$ and make q_j equal the total load on the tour for all other j. This procedure terminates when no further consolidation is possible.

TABLE 14–37 Savings-Assignment Matrix After One Iteration

Load q_i

	P_0										
200	②	P_1									
75	②	16	P_2								
100	②	17	21	P_3							
150	②	17	20	30	P_4						
200	②	17	19	25	32	P_5					
300	②	14	24	22	31	38	P_6				
50	②	18	22	23	31	38	46	P_7			
200	②	15	18	22	29	38	43	52	P_8		
500	①	18	19	27	29	37	43	52	60	P_9	
										①	
500	①	16	21	30	33	38	45	50	56	63	P_{10}

To illustrate this procedure, the delivery problem is traced through its initial iterations. From Table 14–36 the greatest amount of savings can be obtained by combining routes $P_0 \rightarrow P_9 \rightarrow P_0$ and $P_0 \rightarrow P_{10} \rightarrow P_0$, since $S_{9,10} = 63$. The other three conditions expressed in step 3 can also be met; namely, $t_{9,0}$ and $t_{10,0}$ are greater than 0, P_9 and P_{10} are not already on the same route, and $q_9 + q_{10} = 500$, which is below the capacity of an available vehicle. Now that the two routes to be combined have been selected, the mechanics outlined in step 4 of the procedure above must be repeated. The necessary changes in the values of $t_{y,z}$ and q_i are made in the new savings-assignment matrix illustrated in Table 14–37. To follow these through, a $t_{y,z}$ value of 1 is placed at the intersection of column P_9 and row P_{10}. In addition, the values of $t_{y,z}$ must be adjusted to fulfill the conditions specified in step 4. Since the sum of $t_{y,z}$ across row P_9 and down column P_9 must sum to 2, $t_{0,9}$ must be set to 1. The same is true for the sum of the $t_{y,z}$ across row P_{10}, so $t_{0,10}$ is set to 1 also. The q_i's are also adjusted to reflect the total volume of the shipment, Table 14–37. In this case $q_9^* = q_{10}^* = q_9 + q_{10} = 300 + 200 = 500$, where q_i is the volume before and q_i^* is the volume after the routing change. Through this change in routing, one 800-ft^3 vehicle has been substituted for two 300-ft^3 vehicles and a savings of 63 time or distance units has been obtained. The revised vehicle-allocation table is shown in Table 14–38. The adjustments for the iteration have been completed, so the new matrix can be evaluated for further improvements. After an analysis with regard to the criteria expressed in step 3 of the procedure, it appears that a 60-unit savings can be obtained through a combination of routes $P_0 \rightarrow P_8 \rightarrow P_0$ and $P_0 \rightarrow P_9 \rightarrow P_{10} \rightarrow P_0$. The required adjustments are made in the values of $t_{y,z}$ and q_i, and the revised matrix is presented in Table 14–39. The new route is $P_0 \rightarrow P_8 \rightarrow P_9 \rightarrow P_{10} \rightarrow P_0$, and the volume involved is 700 ft^3. Table 14–40 shows the new vehicle allocation.

TABLE 14–38 Vehicle-Allocation Table After One Iteration

Trucks	$300\ ft^3$	$400\ ft^3$	$800\ ft^3$
Available	10	3	2
Allocated	8	0	1

TABLE 14–39 Savings-Assignment Matrix After Two Iterations

Load q_i	P_0	P_1	P_2	P_3	P_4	P_5	P_6	P_7	P_8	P_9	P_{10}
	P_0										
200	②	P_1									
75	②	16	P_2								
100	②	17	21	P_3							
150	②	17	20	30	P_4						
200	②	17	19	25	32	P_5					
300	②	14	24	22	31	38	P_6				
50	②	18	22	23	31	38	46	P_7			
700	①	15	18	22	29	38	43	52	P_8		
									①		
—		18	19	27	29	37	43	52	60	P_9	
										①	
700	①	16	21	30	33	38	45	50	56	63	P_{10}

TABLE 14–40 Vehicle-Allocation Table of Two Iterations

Trucks	$300\ ft^3$	$400\ ft^3$	$800\ ft^3$
Available	10	3	2
Allocated	7	0	1

This iterative procedure is followed until there are no more identifiable route consolidations. In this illustration this requires four more iterations, but the final matrix and allocation table are shown in Tables 14–41 and 14–42, respectively. A graphic presentation of the final route is shown in Table 14–43. A statement of the finalized routes along with the volume assigned to each is illustrated in Table 14–44.

Although this procedure is relatively complex, it does offer a practical procedure for evaluating routing problems with capacity limitations. This solution technique is appropriate for either manual or machine computation.

TABLE 14–41   Savings-Assignment Matrix—Final Iteration

Load q_i	P_0	P_1	P_2	P_3	P_4	P_5	P_6	P_7	P_8	P_9	P_{10}
275	①	P_1									
275	①	①	P_2								
750	①			P_3							
—				①	P_4						
—					①	P_5					
750	①					①	P_6				
750	①							P_7			
—								①	P_8		
—									①	P_9	
750	①									①	P_{10}

TABLE 14–42   Final Vehicle-Allocation Table

Trucks	$300\ ft^3$	$400\ ft^3$	$800\ ft^3$
Available	10	3	2
Allocated	1	0	2

TABLE 14–43   Graphic Presentation of "Best" Routes

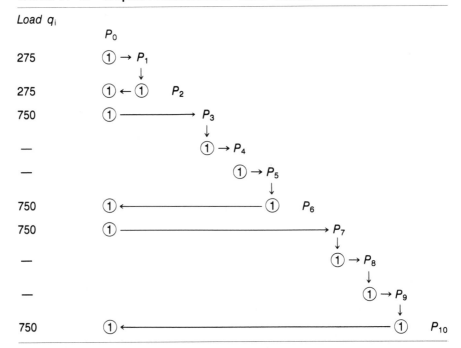

TABLE 14–44 Final Routes and Volume

Volume	Route
275	$P_0 \rightarrow P_1 \rightarrow P_2 \rightarrow P_0$
750	$P_0 \rightarrow P_3 \rightarrow P_4 \rightarrow P_5 \rightarrow P_6 \rightarrow P_0$
750	$P_0 \rightarrow P_7 \rightarrow P_8 \rightarrow P_9 \rightarrow P_{10} \rightarrow P_0$

SCHEDULING

The major management responsibility in logistical design studies is to assure that valid results are realized within time and budget expectations. Fortunately, several scheduling techniques are available that can be easily adopted to the logistical research project.

Scheduling is concerned with planning and the accomplishment of nonrepetitive projects. In addition, scheduling is concerned with the most efficient utilization of resources during the study. During the 1950s sophisticated project planning and progress evaluation techniques were developed. The techniques help managers maintain control over manpower, money, material, and machinery allocated to a project. Two scheduling techniques, the *program evaluation review technique* (PERT) and the *critical path method* (CPM), are reviewed in this section.[14] Both PERT and CPM are variations of more general critical path planning approaches. First, characteristics common to both techniques are reviewed and then the peculiarities of each discussed. For purposes of illustration, the techniques are discussed in terms of a logistical system strategic design study.

Basic Critical Path Concepts

The heart of critical path planning is a graphic portrayal of the project work plan. This graph, or network as it is commonly called, displays the interdependencies between activities leading to project completion.

The critical path concept is designed to satisfy the following five project management requirements:

1. Evaluate progress toward attainment of project completion.
2. Focus attention on potential and actual problems during the project.
3. Provide frequent and accurate status reports at critical check points.
4. Provide a regular and updated prediction of when the project will be completed.
5. Provide at any time during the project determination of the shortest completion time if priorities and resources are shifted.

The Network

The network is a flowchart of project events joined by lines that represent activities. The activities illustrate project interrelationships and interdependencies. Events are usually represented by circles, and activities are illustrated by

[14] For a more detailed discussion, see Wagner, op. cit., pp. 150–51.

arrows that connect events. A project event is a significant occurrence. Events signify the start or completion of at least one activity and represent the achievement of a project goal.

Activities in a project network may be real or dummy. Real activities represent tasks that must be completed to advance from one node to another. Real activities expend project resources. Dummy activities illustrate the dependency of one event to another for project-planning purposes. Dummy activities do not expend project resources. All events are numbered in the network chart. Although the activity arrow lengths have no relationship to the time required to accomplish an event, arrows always connect lower- and higher-numbered events.

PERT Project Illustrations

To illustrate project planning and control, the PERT technique is discussed as applied to design of a logistical system. When this planning project is completed, the best set of warehouse locations is determined along with the customer assignments and inventory policies.

The illustration that follows could be developed using either PERT or CPM. The primary difference is that PERT deals only with timing, whereas CPM considers the trade-offs between the time and cost requirements of a project.

Project Design

The initial step is to divide the overall project into specific tasks. These tasks become activities in the project network. These activities are initiated and terminated by an event. The events and the activities which link them must be sequenced on the network under a logical set of ground rules which allow the determination of important critical and subcritical paths. These ground rules include the fact that no successor event can be considered complete until all predecessor events have been completed, and no "looping" is allowed.

Since activities represent the time necessary to advance from one event to the next, the second step in the scheduling process is to estimate the time necessary to complete each activity. One fundamental difference between PERT and CPM is the nature of the time estimates. CPM uses exact or deterministic times, while PERT uses probabilistic estimates. A PERT schedule requires three time estimates for each activity. These are:

1. *Optimistic time*—the elapsed time if the activity proceeds perfectly, represented by a.
2. *Pessimistic time*—the elapsed time if extreme difficulty is experienced, represented by b.
3. *Most likely completion time*—the expected time, represented by m.

The basic activities and time estimates for the example project are contained in Table 14–45.

The third step is to structure the project in a PERT network, identify the necessary dummy activities as well as the interrelationships between events, and calculate the mean elapsed time (t_e) for each activity. The PERT network is illustrated by Figure 14–7. The following formula is used to develop mean

TABLE 14–45   Project Activities and Variable Time Estimates

Activity	a	m	b
A. Situation audit	1	2	4
B. Problem definition	1	1	2
C. Selection of analytical tool	1	2	3
D. Specification of alternatives	1	2	4
E. Definition of data requirements	1	1	2
F. Collection and preparation of demand data	2	3	5
G. Collection and preparation of cost data	3	5	8
H. Collection and preparation of freight data	4	5	8
I. Validate data and model	2	3	5
J. Initial model runs	1	2	4
K. Preliminary report preparation	2	4	5
L. Model runs for alternative analysis	3	5	7
M. Analysis of model results	1	2	3
N. Final report preparation	2	3	4

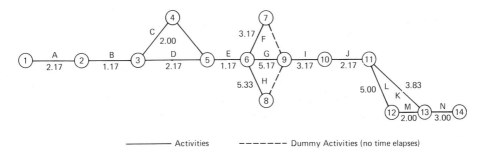

——————— Activities   – – – – – – Dummy Activities (no time elapses)

Figure 14–7   PERT Network for a System Design Project

elapsed times giving a weight of 4 to the most likely time and 1 each to the optimistic and pessimistic times:

$$t_e = \frac{a + 4m + b}{6}$$

This formulation approximates a normal distribution with a relatively low coefficient of variation. The resultant data are presented in Table 14–46.

The fourth and final step is to identify the critical path for the project. The path with the longest mean elapsed time (t_e) represents the critical path. All other paths are called *slack paths* because the final project completion date does not depend upon completing events along the slack path. Table 14–47 presents the determination of the critical path in the example project. Although not all possible paths have been explored in Table 14–47, the total elapsed time for many of the alternatives has been computed and the critical path has been determined.

Once the schedule analysis is completed, management attention is directed to the activities on the critical path. It is important that these activities be completed on schedule, since any delay will delay the overall project completion date.

TABLE 14–46 Activity-Weighted Elapsed Time

Activity	a	m	b	t_e
A	1	2	4	2.17
B	1	1	2	1.17
C	1	2	3	2.00
D	1	2	4	2.17
E	1	1	2	1.17
F	2	3	5	3.17
G	3	5	8	5.17
H	4	5	8	5.33
I	2	3	5	3.17
J	1	2	4	2.17
K	2	4	5	3.83
L	3	5	7	5.00
M	1	2	3	2.00
N	2	3	4	3.00

TABLE 14–47 Path Identification and Average Elapsed Time

Path	Activity Average Elapsed Time	Total Elapsed Time
1–2–3–4–6–7–8–11–12–13–14–16–17	2.17 + 1.17 + 2.00 + 1.17 + 3.17 + 3.17 + 2.17 + 3.83 + 3.00	= 21.85
1–2–3–5–6–7–9–11–12–13–14–16–17	2.17 + 1.17 + 2.17 + 1.17 + 5.17 + 3.17 + 2.17 + 3.83 + 3.00	= 24.02
1–2–3–5–6–7–10–11–12–13–14–16–17	2.17 + 1.17 + 2.17 + 1.17 + 5.33 + 3.17 + 2.17 + 3.83 + 3.00	= 24.18
[a]1–2–3–5–6–7–10–11–12–13–15–16–17	2.17 + 1.17 + 2.17 + 1.17 + 5.33 + 3.17 + 2.17 + 5.00 + 2.00 + 3.00	= 27.35
1–2–3–5–6–7–9–11–12–13–15–16–17	2.17 + 1.17 + 2.17 + 1.17 + 5.17 + 3.17 + 2.17 + 5.00 + 2.00 + 3.00	= 27.19

[a] Critical path.

The final project schedule is based upon the network having the longest total elapsed time. The highest sum of the t_e's for a path on the network is the project critical path.

The procedure for CPM is very similar to that for PERT. The fundamental difference is that CPM uses exact time estimates and incorporates cost or budget figures. Therefore, CPM is particularly applicable to projects of a deterministic nature, where time and cost data can be projected from past experience or estimated with a high degree of certainty. For this reason, the method is used extensively in the construction industry.

The previous example of the system design project will be used to demonstrate CPM, however, a complete analysis is not performed. The subset of activities shown in Figure 14–8 will be discussed in detail.

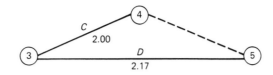

Figure 14–8 Partial PERT Network for a System Design Project

TABLE 14–48   Time and Cost Estimates for Activity C

Resource Allocation	Cost	Time
Normal	$2,000	2.00
110% normal	2,250	1.90
120% normal	2,700	1.80
130% normal	4,000	1.70

TABLE 14–49   Time and Cost Estimates for Activity D

Resource Allocation	Cost	Time
Normal	$2,500	2.17
110% normal	3,000	2.10
120% normal	3,700	2.00
130% normal	4,700	1.90

For each of the activities specified in the network, the project manager must develop the best cost and time estimates possible. These estimates include an approximation of the expected time with the normal amount of resources applied as well as speed-up approximations when additional resources are applied. Time and cost estimates for activities C and D are presented in Tables 14–48 and 14–49, respectively. The resource allocation may represent manpower or computer commitments.

The critical path method analyzes the cost and time trade-offs characteristic of each activity to determine where resources can be applied most beneficially. Since activity D lies on the critical path, CPM would call for the project manager to allocate additional resources to this activity to speed up project completion. By allocating $500 more to this activity, the project length can be decreased by 0.07 period while a $700 allocation to activity C would not shorten the project. An allocation of $1,200 to activity D would enable the entire project to be shortened by 0.17 period. However, any increased allocation of resources to D alone would not result in a shorter project time, since activity C along with D lies on the critical path at this point.

In addition to trade-offs between activities that lie on different paths, there may be trade-offs between activities that lie on the same path. Given that D and H both lie on the critical path, it may be less expensive to cut 0.17 period from the schedule by allocating resources to activity H than by allocating resources to D. However, the time required for the project would be the same in either case.

In addition to providing the information to expedite the project, CPM also provides information concerning resources that may be deallocated without affecting the schedule of the project. In Figure 14–8, for example, the project manager may observe that it is possible to complete activity C with only 90 per cent of the resource allocation if the time is increased to 2.17 periods. Since this is not on the critical path, this would not delay the project completion date. The critical path method also provides the necessary data for estimating time and cost at any point during the project in the event that it becomes desirable to expedite the project.

Since the number of alternative paths and costs considered quickly becomes unmanageable even in small projects, it is usually necessary that the network analysis be performed by computer. Fortunately, many medium and large computer facilties have existing programs that can be used for this purpose.

Many of these programs allow for the incorporation of resource requirements for each activity. The resources can be defined as money, materials, labor, and equipment of various types. The supply of these resources for given time periods is also provided to the program. The program can then deduct the resources required from the resources available to determine schedule feasibility, resource utilization, or cash-flow requirements. If the schedule is determined to be infeasible, decision rules incorporated into these programs will modify the optimum schedule disregarding resource constraints into a feasible plan.

SUMMARY

The intent of this chapter was to introduce and illustrate a variety of quantitative techniques available for use in day-to-day logistical decision-making. In total, the chapter covered five groupings of techniques, related to: (1) basic decision-making, (2) facility operations, (3) allocation and assignment, (4) routing, and (5) scheduling. No attempt was made to integrate the groupings because of the specialized nature of the technique application. Thus, the chapter sections are problem-oriented and stand independently. What the groupings have in common is that they all present techniques applicable to operational and tactical planning situations.

QUESTIONS

1. What is the major shortcoming of using various decision criteria in day-to-day operations? What is the major benefit?
2. Why would an enterprise under certain circumstances elect to purchase a component part even though it could manufacture it more economically?
3. In the utilization of queueing analysis, why are arrivals typically expressed in the form of Poisson distribution, whereas servicing is an exponential distribution?
4. Discuss the impact of single versus multiple receiving channels upon the queueing solution.
5. Why is it beneficial and safe to use sampling in this inspection procedure related to quality control?

6. In general terms, why is linear programming a useful tool for consideration when allocating product from plants to warehouses?

7. Describe the basic purpose of the northwest corner rule.

8. Why is it important to include capacity constraints in selected types of routing problems? Provide an illustration.

9. What can one hope to gain by the use of a project scheduling technique?

10. Discuss the differences between PERT and CPM. What is the role of a dummy activity in the PERT analysis?

FUTURE ENVIRONMENTS

Dimensions of Change—
A Seminar Focus

This concluding chapter offers perspectives on the future direction of logistical management. The chapter commences with a brief look at the anticipated setting for future logistics operations. The remaining sections introduce specific seminar subjects supported by starter issues and questions.

THE SETTING—1990 AND BEYOND

Given the extreme changes that have occurred in logistical management concepts and practices during the past three decades, an appropriate question is: What can we expect to happen during the remainder of the twentieth century? The primary determinant of the shape and form of future logistical systems will be the nature of the demand that must be serviced.

Current projections are that the gross national product of the United States will exceed 4 trillion dollars by 1990 and will continue to grow for the remainder of the century. Significant growth is projected for both goods and services. In comparison to today, a significantly larger share of the total population of United States will participate in the "good life" projected for the 1990s. In terms of logistical demands, operating systems of the future will face complex performance requirements. Even more so than today, logistical systems will be required to support multiple-product distribution to heterogeneous markets through a variety of marketing channels. The return movement of inventory for recycling and/or recall will continue to be an integral part of future logistics. This important area of "reverse logistics" will require two-way logistical system movement flexibility.

Barring a catastrophic event, it is difficult not to expect an increase in total population of the United States exceeding 50 million people during the remainder of the twentieth century. To put this population growth in perspective, at a bare minimum it will be necessary to provide logistical support for one additional person for every four in the United States today.

The outlook for the remainder of the century is the presence of the two main ingredients required for growth—money and people. However, significant differences are expected in lifestyle and related social priorities. Despite some earlier predictions to the contrary, evidence now supports the position that the consuming public will demand more product-contained services and conveniences in items purchased for in-home consumption. For instance, such products as frozen meat might well be precooked and ready for consumption when purchased. To the extent that this service/convenience pattern develops, more value will be added to the typical product before it begins the logistical process. To support the trend, the complexity of the total manufacturing/marketing system will increase.

Ever present in future society will be the continued problems and pressures of energy and ecology. The dependence of the logistical system upon a ready supply of energy is and will continue to be a critical concern. The cost of energy will remain significant for the logistical sector during the foreseeable future. From an ecological viewpoint, continued pressures will exist to reduce the negative impact of logistics on the environment. Such pressures reflect socially worthwhile goals, but ecological compliance will be costly. To some degree, ecological considerations will eliminate selected logistical alternatives currently available such as specific forms of packaging and selected materials handling equipment. Finally, the remainder of the twentieth century is projected to be a period during which selected raw materials will remain in relative short supply.

THE SEMINAR FOCUS CONCEPT

The following sections of Chapter 15 provide eight seminar topics suitable for small group discussion. The topics are not presented in a priority sequence. The topics range from computers to managerial issues to multinational logistics. Each topic is introduced by a brief presentation on the basic seminar subject. The presentation is designed to highlight the potential of the seminar topic to improve logistical productivity, or it presents a problem or concern that managers are expected to confront in the future. The topical sessions are not comprehensive in that no attempt is made to present all sides of the issue or situation. At the conclusion of each seminar topic, six issues and questions are presented to initiate student discussion. It is expected that supplemental reading and research on the subject will result in lively presentation and discussion.

SEMINAR FOCUS ONE: HOW ADEQUATE IS THE UNITED STATES LOGISTICAL SUPPORT POTENTIAL

Assuming full maturity of integrated logistics, is the United States present logistical infrastructure and capability adequate to satisfy future demands? Some experts feel that given the maintenance of a 5-per-cent level of unemployment, the logistical infrastructure and managerial practices today will be hard-pressed if not unable to satisfy future demand. In our society, logistics is second only to personal services as a consumer of labor. Logistics is a labor-intensive process. The situation becomes even more critical when marginal workers must be employed as a result of full employment. Logistical systems are forced to employ more than their rightful share of such marginal workers because of the extensive manual tasks involved. Physical handling of goods does not rank high in employment choice when alternative jobs are available. Thus, marginal entries to the work force are the prime source of manual labor needed to keep the goods moving. The result has been and will continue to be a problem of maintaining adequate labor productivity.

One substitute for labor deficiency is the development and application of new logistical technology. For the past three decades, our logistical system has kept pace with growth by applying new technology to the performance of traditional logistical tasks. For example, load capacity of transportation vehicles has been expanded in water, rail, truck, and air operations. Today, each mode can carry larger payloads faster and cheaper than was considered possible a few years ago. In a similar vein, computing and information transmission have provided a method of receiving and processing customer orders faster and more accurately, while simultaneously capturing critical performance measurement data. During the past decade significant advances have been made in automation of both unit-load and package warehouses.

Across the board, technological developments have been applied to keep pace with increasing tonnage demands placed upon the national logistical system. Considering the track record, even the most severe critic would have to acknowledge outstanding performance. However, after all is said and done, by 1990 the logistical system will continue to utilize massive amounts of physical labor to perform required tasks. Despite the United States logistical system's historical track record of having adequate capability to deliver industrial output, the existing system is now strained, and the situation will become increasingly critical in the decades ahead.

From the viewpoint of technology assessment, the prospects for continued development to satisfy future logistical demands are not encouraging. For example, load capabilities and transportation speeds have reached near maximum for our highway, rail, harbor, and airport infrastructures. Future technology can be expected to pay off at a significantly slower rate. It appears safe to conclude that new technology will not provide the total answer for satisfying tomorrow's logistical demand.

The problems created by the emerging situation are capable of solution. However, performing more of the same activities in logistics in the manner they have been performed during the past three decades is not the solution. The past practice of overpowering the logistical mission by deployment of new technology will no longer be viable. The challenge for the coming decade is to develop *new* ways to satisfy logistical requirements, as contrasted to attempting to perform *old* ways more efficiently. The solution rests with innovative applications of technology available today within a new and permissive framework. Many traditions and practices which characterize today's national logistics structure are both archaic and symbolic of a bygone era.

In summary, regarding demand versus adequacy, the remaining years of the twentieth century are projected to be a period of continued affluence. The sheer numbers of people and their requirements will place unprecedented demands upon logistical performance. Complexity of the logistical process will increase as a result of changing lifestyles, continued high cost of energy, ecological compliance requirements, and the constant potential of recurring material shortages. Unlike the past three decades, the United States cannot look forward to a steady stream of new technology as the solution to satisfying logistical requirements. Almost all recent improvements in logistical operating capability have resulted from technological developments. In a sense, the United States has overpowered problems of logistical growth by technology deployment. Now, for the first time since World War II, the continued development of logistically related technology is not encouraging.

A variety of approaches to help meet future logistical requirements do exist within the philosophy of integrated logistics. Each represents a new or different way of formulating and conducting logistical operations using currently available technology. To be fully implemented, each concept requires a major change in current logistical operating practices. *The significant point is that the application of today's technology to cope with tomorrow's logistical needs depends upon innovative management.* While many legal and/or regulatory barriers exist to hinder innovation, the most serious problem may be management attitude and inflexibility.

Issues and Questions

1. What major changes can be forecasted for the logistical infrastructure?
2. Is the marginal labor claim presented a justified position? How about the position that management attitude and inflexibility represent the greatest barriers to innovative change?
3. The discussion makes the point that future advances cannot depend upon technological developments to solve problems associated with growth.
    a. Does this position present a fair assessment of future technology?
    b. If the position is correct, why so much attention to "high-tech" development?
4. What is a traditional logistical task?

5. Present an example of a new or innovative way to perform an old logistical task.

6. If the United States and the remainder of the world cannot depend upon technological development to assist in satisfying future growth-related logistical requirements, what is the solution? Do you agree with the "doomsday" technology assessment?

SEMINAR FOCUS TWO: ASSESSMENT AND CONTROL TO IMPROVE LOGISTICS PERFORMANCE

Assessment and control systems are the key to ensuring that logistical operations are consistent with management's plans for profitability and performance. By improving operational efficiency and tracking progress toward logistics goals, assessment and control systems help support an organization's efforts to achieve customer service objectives, meet planned output levels, and control assets such as inventory investment.

Logistics assessment and control serves several primary functions. *First*, they measure performance through reports, audits, and observations. *Second*, they make comparison of measured performance against standards or goals. *Third*, they identify areas for corrective action. A diagram of this process is presented in Figure 15–1. The objective of the system is to measure and report information that will assist management in achieving the stated organizational objectives.

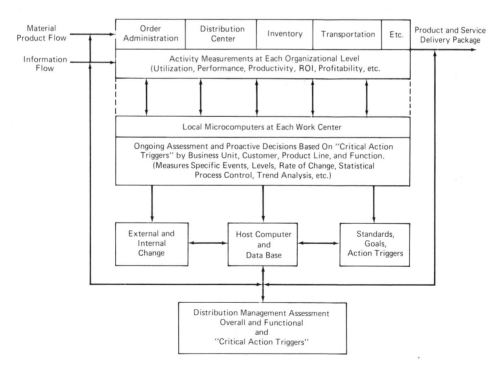

Figure 15–1   Distribution Control System Concept

In general, methods to help measure, compare, and guide (control) logistics performance have not received adequate attention in the development of transaction-processing systems. Increased competition and erratic marketplace growth have forced industry to concentrate on control to help improve productivity. Necessary productivity improvements can only be achieved with formal and comprehensive measurement systems. Successful companies also must have standards of performance for each logistical activity. To be effective, assessment and control systems should be integrated with transaction and planning systems such as order entry and processing, logistics requirements planning, inventory management, master production scheduling, warehousing, and transportation.

Most advanced logistics systems provide detailed data to measure past performance—"a report card." There is far too little emphasis given to measures that permit managers to be "proactive"—take action to prevent problems rather than measuring after-the-fact performance. Action triggers are necessary to be proactive. Action triggers are measures that suggest a level of action to prevent future nonperformance. The trigger could indicate potential problems due to constrained resources, such as lack of equipment, and/or other systems malfunctions. An example of an action trigger is a priority customer order that is not progressing within specified tolerance. This priority order would be isolated for special managerial consideration in an effort to eliminate a critical customer service breakdown. Another example of an action trigger could be identification of greater than planned order processing activity that could signal a potential problem in terms of warehouse capacity to process orders for shipment.

The development of an action-trigger capability requires the construction of a knowledge base. The knowledge base provides a series of dynamic and static measures that assist in assessment and control. Examples of a dynamic measure would be ratios for current periods compared to previous periods. The dynamic measure would compare ratios for all periods to the base and form the knowledge to respond to an action trigger by recommending a corrective action before the operational problem develops.

The implementation of assessment and control has the potential to significantly improve logistical performance. The ROI potential of improved assessment and control may be far greater than most managers realize.

Issues and Questions

1. What are the possible measures of organizational effectiveness for logistics? Is it possible to define the one most important measure for a company?
2. Define three action triggers and three dynamic measures that would be important to a vice president of logistics in (a) a consumer packaged goods company and (b) an industrial products company with equipment and parts.
3. How are utilization, performance, and productivity related?
4. How is logistics assessment and control similar to an automated production control process? What are some of the differences?
5. Does an MRP (or DRP) system eliminate the need for a separate logistics assessment and control system?
6. Should productivity measurement improve managers' diagnostic capabilities and, therefore, their effectiveness?

SEMINAR FOCUS THREE: ORGANIZATIONAL EVALUATION

Chapter 10 was devoted to the subject of logistical organization. The general case was presented that the effectiveness and efficiency of overall logistical operations can typically be improved by grouping authority and responsibility into a single organizational unit.

The development of an integrated logistical organization typicaly takes place over time. The development pattern presented in Chapter 10 identified three types of organization patterns currently observable in business. Type I organization is characterized by the formal recognition of a limited functional group concerned with physical distribution and/or materials management. The focal characteristic of the Type II stage of organizational development is the establishment of an officer-level executive responsible for physical distribution and/or materials management. Included with positioning logistics at the officer level, Type II organization structures typically group more functions within the formal integrated structure.

The most comprehensive form of logistical organization was identified as Type III. In many ways a Type III organization structure represents the maximum integration of logistical functions. In the Type III structure all functions related to physical distribution, manufacturing support, and purchasing are grouped into a single organization. In this most comprehensive concept of logistical organization, all planning and operational activities are coordinated within a single structure.

Research into practices throughout industry supports the conclusion that Type III organization structures are rapidly growing in popularity. In part, the integration of logistics is being supported by rapid advancements in management information system capabilities. The combination of advanced transaction-processing systems, decision-support systems, and assessment and control capabilities provides the information necessary to manage integrated logistics on a national or global basis.

Despite significant evidence to the contrary, not all firms embrace and support evolution toward a Type III organizational structure. Three arguments can be made counter to the evolutionary trend: (1) the case for functional specialization, (2) the case for functional decentralization, and (3) the case for horizontal expansion.

The Case for Functional Specialization

Whereas the Type III organization structure favors integration of the three logistical operation areas of physical distribution, manufacturing support, and procurement, a counter viewpoint is to develop deep specialization in each area in an effort to improve efficiency. The position contrary to the Type III logic is that each area requires sufficient asset deployment and operating expenditures in a large corporation to justify specialization.

Those who favor such specialization present the argument that cross-area trade-offs are really limited to transportation efficiency and that such benefits can be realized without organization integration of all logistical functions given modern MIS capabilities. The position in defense of functional specialization is that economy of scale can be realized while improving control as a result of detailed knowledge regarding physical distribution, manufacturing support, or purchasing. This specialization could be lost or restricted in a Type III structure. As one executive put it, it's the old case of the cavalry versus the infantry.

The Case for Functional Decentralization

The position in favor of functional decentralization is an extension of the concept of functional specialization presented above. Those who favor decentralization argue that the functions of physical distribution, manufacturing support, and purchasing should be integrated but not at the national or headquarters level. The decentralization advocate favors pushing logistical operations down to the industrial business unit and, if possible, to the plant management, distribution warehouse, or sales region level of the organization. The central logic supporting decentralization is that the most relevant organization level to integrate logistics in an effective strategic context is at the day-to-day operational level of the enterprise. Advocates of functional decentralization support a view of the headquarter's activities being restricted to coordination and staff support.

The Case for Horizontal Expansion

The horizontal organization perspective is becoming increasingly popular among large consumer products companies. The horizontal organization is somewhat analogous to the Type III structure in that widespread integration is advocated. However, whereas the Type III integration is vertical from physical distribution to manufacturing support to purchasing, the horizontal organization limits operational concern to a single functional area such as physical distribution across several businesses. This type of organization was identified as Type IV in Chapter 10.

An example of integration in a horizontal structure would be the performance of physical distribution operations for a number of business units by one service organization. Providing that several different business units sell to the same class of trade or to different customers located within a given geographical concentration, the most significant productivity gains could well be realized by concentration of all physical distribution operations into a single organization. A similar grouping in purchasing would be a concentrated maintenance, repair, and operating organization (MRO).

The question of how big is too big to control economy of scale is the critical issue. In theory, a single logistical organization could have the depth and breadth to operate both as a Type III vertical extension and a Type IV horizontal structure.

Issues and Questions

1. Support or reject the assumptions made in Chapter 10 that Type III organizations are gaining in popularity.
2. What is the meant by the statement, "It's the old case of the cavalry versus the infantry."
3. Is the position that functional specialization will increase productivity justified?

4. Why would an organization be more effective if control was decentralized? Does this run contrary to the concept of integration that is at the very heart of logistical management?
5. Is horizontal expansion, Type IV, really different than vertical expansion, Type III?
6. Does a concept of "super organization" exist that can satisfy all concerns?

SEMINAR FOCUS FOUR: ARTIFICIAL INTELLIGENCE FOR MATERIALS AND LOGISTICS MANAGEMENT[1]

The commercialization of artificial intelligence (AI) is seen as the most significant advance in computer science since the invention of the computer. Is this "Second Computer Age," as it is sometimes referred to, significant for the materials and logistics professional? Although it is too early to fully assess, the evidence suggests an affirmative response. What was, until recently, an esoteric niche within the sprawling discipline of AI has moved within reach, and industry has begun to accept the technology. The objective of this seminar focus is to provide an introduction to artificial intelligence with comments regarding its applicability in logistical management.

Artificial Intelligence Defined

AI is the portion of computer science concerned with designing smart computer systems where the systems exhibit the characteristics typically associated with intelligence in human behavior. These characteristics include: (1) understanding language, (2) learning, (3) reasoning, and (4) solving problems. Applications stemming from AI research and spurring it on include expert systems (knowledge engineering), computer-aided instruction, voice synthesis and recognition, vision systems, natural language translators, game-playing systems, and robotics.

AI applications are beginning to emerge from computer science laboratories. Able to mimic—if not duplicate—human thought processes, such as reasoning, perception, and even learning, these applications are expected to open vast new opportunities for automation in the office, factory, and home. In the process, many observers believe, they will profoundly alter the way people work, live, and think about themselves.

Natural language systems will help revolutionize computer-assisted instruction. Programs under development enable students to ask questions of the computer and receive insightful advice, an educational experience comparable to one-on-one instruction with a human expert.

Natural language programs that allow computer users to ask questions in ordinary English represent a core product for AI. Programs for accessing large data bases are a prime application for natural language systems and are already entering the market. Systems that immediately understand everyday English are making computers accessible to anyone who can write. Thus, there will be

---

[1] Adapted from O. K. Helferich, "Computers that Mimic Human Thought—Artificial Intelligence for Materials and Logistics Management," *Journal of Business Logistics* (Oakbrook, Ill.: National Council of Physical Distribution Management, Vol. 5, No. 2, pp. 123–27, 1984).

less need for people to learn how to structure questions or commands in computer syntax. Managers at a number of companies routinely use AI program(s) to call up data just by tapping out memolike requests.

AI research also focuses on improving optical character recognition to enable robots to make decisions based on visual input. Using AI technology, a computer can rapidly sort through signals coming from cameras and other sensors to identify images and sounds—reacting instantly without the agonizing delays that conventional systems require to decipher the meaning of a spoken sentence or recognize a visual image. Artificial sight and hearing is useful in guiding robot arms.

Voice-recognition products have been available since the early 1970s. Use in these areas will increase as electronics continue to drop in price and AI techniques develop more comprehensive "feature recognition."

An Overview of Expert Systems

Expert systems and computer-aided instruction appear to have significant application in logistics. These systems embody the accumulated knowledge of authority. With so-called "expert programs," computers can act as intelligent assistants, providing advice and making assessments in specialized areas of expertise.

Expert systems consist of very large data bases of information integrated with a collection of the best rules-of-thumb that can be applied to identify problem solutions. Based on human knowledge, expert systems seek to solve problems beyond the capabilities of conventionally programmed computers. Expert systems are a way of capturing, codifying, and making available to others specialized human expertise.

The success of expert systems has demonstrated the commercial viability of the concept. Programs, for example, exist to help in the following situations: (1) medical diagnosis, (2) mineral exploration, (3) configuration of computer systems to meet specific customer needs at the lowest possible cost, and (4) engineering structural design.

How an Expert System Works

Expert systems use a problem-solving capability that is superior to conventionally programmed machines. They make use of knowledge about a problem to find short-cut solutions—a technique known as heuristic problem-solving.

The knowledge of the expert consists largely of rules-of-thumb that have come to be called heuristics. Heuristics has been successfully utilized in simulation modeling for many years. It enables a human expert to apply experience and knowledge based on educated guesses and rules that have worked in the past. This approach allows the expert to deal with ill-structured problems where incomplete data also complicate the solution methodology(ies).

A typical expert system consists of a knowledge base, an inference engine, and a workspace. The relationship is illustrated in Figure 15–2.

The inference engine is usually a small, fixed program that solves problems by using inference rules and by interpreting knowledge and facts contained in

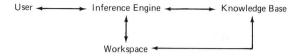

Figure 15–2 Typical Expert System Structure

the knowledge base. This program should not have to change when a new piece of knowledge is added to the system, as is often the case in traditional programs. The workspace is an area of memory set aside for storing a description of the problem constructed by the system from the facts supplied by the user, or inferred from the knowledge base.

The Methods of Expert Systems

Three methods are employed to represent knowledge in expert systems: (1) production rules, (2) semantic networks, and (3) first-order logic.

Production rules are two-part rules, expressed in an "if-then" format. The rule contains in its left-hand side information about when the rule should be used. The right-hand side specifies an action to be taken when the rule is used. A typical rule might be: "*If* customer service is at 85 per cent *and* inventory levels are at a two-week supply *and* the order cycle is three months, *then* consider increasing safety stocks or shortening the order-cycle time."

A *semantic network* is a scheme for representing abstract relations among objects in the system's knowledge domain, such as membership in a class. Examples include ROBIN IS-A BIRD, SPARROW IS-A BIRD, BIRD IS-A ANIMAL. These kinds of representations can be represented graphically by a network of nodes and links where nodes represent objects and links represent the relations among the objects. In the above example, the nodes would represent the objects ROBIN, SPARROW, BIRD, and ANIMAL. The links would represent the relation IS-A, and the network as a whole forms a taxonomy.

First-order logic is a formal way of representing logical propositions and relations between propositions. It is issued mainly in theorem-proving applications.

Each of these methods has advantages. For example, production rules are especially useful for representing procedural knowledge—methods for accomplishing goals. Semantic networks are good for representing relations among objects, and frame-based semantic networks can store an immense amount of knowledge about object properties and relations. First-order logic offers a way for explicitly expressing nearly any type of knowledge.

Which is used most frequently? The trend has been to combine representations, with each scheme being used, for the knowledge it represents best. A system might use production rules to define procedures for discovering attributes of objects, semantic networks to define the relationships among the objects referenced in the rules, and frames to describe the objects typical attributes.

TABLE 15–1 Potential Application of Expert Systems in Logistics

Management assessment or audit	Distribution audit programs
Inventory planning and control	Policy determination, diagnosing problems, controlling operations
Information systems strategy	Hardware configurations, software selection
Freight rate negotiation	Strategy determination
Production planning and control	Planning determination, diagnosing problems, controlling operations
Transportation routing and selection	Policy selection, monitoring operations, diagnosing problems, controlling operations
Purchasing analysis	Negotiation strategies, vendor selection

Expert Systems in Logistics Management

An extrapolation from the current applications in industry to the field of logistics indicates that there are many areas waiting to be harvested. Table 15–1 identifies some potential applications of expert systems within logistics management.

The state of the art in programming these systems is progressing rapidly. Telecommunications add the possibility of putting the knowledge system on-line for general access. The basic assumption more or less shared by many AI researchers has been that all important human experience and intelligence will ultimately be analyzed as a set of rules and principles. Given enough time, research, computation power, and programming sophistication, computers have the potential to replicate humans and then improve on their shelfs. By contrast, some software executives believe artificial intelligence is still an academic discipline and represents at best a theoretical goal. One thing appears certain: during future years you will be hearing a great deal more about artificial intelligence and expert system applications to a wide variety of complex management decisions. Logistical management will be no exception.

Issues and Questions

1. What are the basic steps in building an expert system?
2. How are decision-support systems of the early 1980s different from the expert systems possible with artificial intelligence techniques?
3. Define an approach to evaluate an expert system utilized in a logistics analysis situation.
4. Why are some professionals in the field of computer science skeptical of the application's potential for expert systems to business situations?
5. Select and develop an AI approach for one of the materials and logistics areas mentioned in the text.
6. How does the use of expert systems offer opportunities for training of the logistics workforce—both professional and paraprofessional?

SEMINAR FOCUS FIVE: MEGA DISTRIBUTION SERVICES

Changes to the distribution environment have given rise to another institutional change represented by the formation of third party mega distribution service companies (MDSC). These companies are formed or developed to provide a broad range of distribution services to their customers at a profit. As a result, their customers turn over a great deal of responsibility for distribution operations to the MDSC. The functions performed by the MDSC may include warehousing, transportation, information processing, order processing, and freight consolidation. This seminar focus reviews the environmental changes that have resulted in the development of MDSCS and then specifically discusses the service offering typically provided.

Environmental Changes

There are three environmental changes that have brought about the recent rise in the provision of mega distribution services. These changes are deregulation, emphasis on return on assets, and specialization potential. Each is briefly discussed.

As discussed in Chapter 5, the deregulation of the transportation industry has dramatically increased the potential and occurrence of negotiation for transportation rates and services. Such negotiations result in lower transportation costs and more specialized services when they are beneficial to both the carrier and shipper. For example, the existence of consistent high-volume transportation demand for a specific market area provides significant potential for lower transportation charges in contrast to a situation where demand is low and inconsistent. As a result of this potential, a market opportunity has emerged for businesses to perform consolidation activities in an effort to achieve maximum transportation economies. The consolidation potential is greater when a large number of organizations combine shipments.

The second environmental change that has given rise to the MDSC is the widespread emphasis on the return on assets. This emphasis has resulted in a desire, on the part of many corporations, to use their distribution assets, such as transportation and distribution warehouses, to generate revenue. In order to generate revenue, the enterprise develops a program that offers distribution capabilities for hire. The result is a service that benefits the new MDSC and its customer. For the MDSC, a profit-generating business is formed. For the customer, assets are freed when operations are turned over to a MDSC. Distribution expense for the customer becomes a variable rather than fixed cost, and the assets for the distribution services customer are reduced, resulting in elimination of ROI pressures. This form of MDSC has only been possible since relaxation of entry conditions in transportation and the authorization to operate in several different types of for-hire services that have resulted since deregulation.

The third change that has brought about the development of MDSCs is the increased benefits of specialization. These benefits include the cost reductions that result from use of automated or more specialized equipment and higher volume processes. For example, if a distribution service firm can increase overall transaction volume, it may be able to justify the acquisition of more sophisticated handling, storage, or transportation equipment.

Service Offering

The MDSCs provide some combination of five distribution services. These services are: (1) warehousing, (2) transportation, (3) information processing, (4) order processing, and (5) freight consolidation. The warehouse services include the handling and storage of product as well as the management of inventories. The transportation services include both inbound and outbound movement through the use of the transportation capacity of the MDSC. The information-processing services include the maintenance and tracking of sales and cost information in order to support the performance analysis for their distribution services customers. Since the distribution service company is providing information to an extensive number of customers, more comprehensive performance analysis reporting can be justified than a single firm might be able to afford. Order-processing services provide significant economies by joint processing of the requirements of MDSC customers. Freight consolidation offers the opportunity to enjoy economies of scale. This might mean that the shipments of competitors are being consolidated together. However, the benefits of consolidation would accrue to both. Where a small company may not be able to afford expertise in a wide range of distribution services such as analysis negotiation, operations, and personnel, the MDSC can provide this expertise.

Issues and Questions

1. What are the potential antitrust problems brought about by MDSC organizations? Are the potential rewards worth the risk?
2. What are the potential conflicts that may develop as a vital distribution service is contracted to an outside vendor? What precautions should be taken?
3. Should special laws or government action be taken to control the MDSC?
4. What criteria should an enterprise use to determine whether it should develop the structure to offer itself as a MDSC?
5. What criteria should be used to evaluate the use of an outside distribution service vendor?
6. What should be the responsibility of the MDSC in terms of marketing and sales?

SEMINAR FOCUS SIX: INFORMATION TECHNOLOGY

Historians are describing the current stage of civilization as the information age. Today's developments in terms of both computer and communications hardware along with the required software have advanced much faster than the ability to apply such technology. At the same time, these technology advances are being seen as one method to increase logistical effectiveness by moving information rather than moving goods and services. This seminar focus reviews some of these advances and discussed implications for logistical management.

New Languages

One of the most dramatic technology advances involves new computer programming languages. In the era when information resources were expensive and human resources were less costly, programming languages required much structure on the part of the human resource in order to minimize the machine resource requirements. Table 15–2 briefly defines the characteristics of first-, second-, and third-generation programming languages. In the case of all these languages, programmers were required to instruct computers on what to do and specifically in how to do it. This required that the programmer provide the instructions describing where to find data and exactly how to process the information. Fourth- and fifth-generation languages ease the process of communicating with the computer by permitting the program to be developed in a more "English-like" language. In addition, the new languages only require the programmer to instruct the computer on what needs to be done and not on how to do it. For example, instead of requiring the programmer to provide instructions on how to process a file to generate a summary of sales by month, fourth-generation languages only require the programmer to tell the computer to summarize the product sales by month. The computer then generates the specific instructions and performs the operations to provide the summary. The new languages can generate report formats, develop summary statistics, and provide report headings.

The development of such advanced languages implies that less technical background is required to effectively program computers. Where it used to require a significant amount of education and training to enable an individual to develop computer programs, advanced programming languages have reduced, although not eliminated, that requirement. This advance has allowed

TABLE 15–2   Programming Language Characteristics

Generation	Example	Descriptions
First	Machine code	Requires that the programmer enter machine instructions and specific variable addresses. Requires that the programmer communicate with the computer in the computer's internal language.
Second	Assembly language	Instead of instruction codes and specific addresses, assembly languages allow the programmer to use neumonic instruction codes and labels for variables. This allows programs to be more intelligible to programmers but required the computer to perform some translation and therefore made it a little less efficient.
Third	Compiled languages such as FORTRAN or COBOL	The third-generation languages use English instructions which instruct the computer to perform a number of internal operations. While third-generation languages are more understandable, they require a significant amount of structure and specificity. These languages require that the computer perform a significant translation, resulting in less efficient computer operation.

people with minimal background in computers and possibly with a strong background in systems and functional areas to be able to address some of their own information-processing needs.

End-User Computing

Due in part to the development of these user-friendly languages and also to the severe shortage of programmers, there has been a trend to decentralize computer utilization to the end or functional user. Instead of making requests for information processing and reporting to the MIS department and having the request placed in a backlog queue, end-user computing seeks to provide functional users with the tools that enable them to develop their own reports and applications. The birth of software products such as spreadsheets, database packages, report generators, and decision-support systems has made it feasible for a moderately trained individual to develop extensive applications and perform functional analysis. These applications range from spreadsheet analysis of specific alternatives to the development of a freight-recording system to aid in the negotiation of transportation rates. Not only does end-user computing decrease the time required for application development, it also brings the development effort closer to the decision level. As a result, user-developed applications generally reflect more closely the desires and exact needs of the functional manager. For example, if a functional manager designs screens, reports, and processes, there is little potential for communication problems between MIS and the user. The major potential problem is that end-users may not make the most efficient use of the hardware or the application development resource. The current argument is that it is more cost-effective to allow the hardware to be used inefficiently than to reduce the effectiveness of a highly trained functional managers.

Issues and Questions

1. The development of end-user computing and fourth-generation languages implies the shifting of some information-processing roles. What changes are seen in the logistical management organization to accommodate for these changes? Discuss whether these changes will have positive or negative impacts on logistical productivity.
2. What changes will advances in information technology bring about in the training requirements for entry-level logistical positions?
3. Given that there will be trained information technology people in the logistical organization, should these individuals receive primary training in logistics or in information technology? What are the arguments for each position?
4. Do fourth- and fifth-generation languages really provide productivity improvements that they have promised, or is this merely a marketing promise? In what types of logistical applications have the benefits been found?
5. The development of these new languages and end-user computing significantly increases the potential for duplication of effort as specific logistical operations begin developing their own applications. What procedures should be put in place to minimize duplication, and what controls should be established to maintain information and decision-making integrity?

6. Should there be changes in the education and training process for logistical managers in order for them to support end-user computing? What should these changes be?

SEMINAR FOCUS SEVEN: COMPUTER-INTEGRATED MANUFACTURING

Computer-integrated manufacturing (CIM), in its broadest context, is a managerial approach to problem-solving as contrasted to a specific computer application. The focus of CIM is on the automated flow of information among the various groups involved in manufacturing. This usually includes manufacturing, engineering, production, planning, and other support groups. CIM consists of a cluster of powerful technologies used to coordinate the use of computers throughout manufacturing operations.

An Overview of CIM

CIM comprises three types of integration: (1) information, (2) hardware, and (3) human behavior.

Integration of information involves the linking together of computer-aided design, computer-aided manufacturing, planning, and control systems. The linkage and interface require compatible software and a common data base.

The physical flow of the product is structured to resemble continuous flow processing through the application of CIM methodologies. The product flows through the phases of the production cycle, through production steps of a manufacturing cell, and between manufacturing cells more quickly utilizing CIM.

The phases of the production cycle are more closely linked utilizing CIM. Therefore, the different functional departments must develop a high degree of coordination and agree on priority. The effective use of CIM thus only is achieved if the various groups operate as one team with well-defined goals.

CIM Information Flow

A full CIM approach would allow the coordination of information flow for a product (or part) from engineering design, through planning, production, and related manufacturing support operations. The level of activity and resulting required information vary as the product moves through the system. The information needed at the business unit and plant level usually includes: (1) issues and opportunities, (2) overall systems, and (3) management. At the production department level, the information is similar to that for the plant, but involves local issues and resources. The information needs at the production workstation and machine level become machine- and task-specific.

The Role of Management in CIM

CIM concepts have already begun to change the appearance and operative practices of many manufacturing operations. However, not all of the CIM applications have been cost-beneficial. CIM installation failures frequently have resulted from lack of understanding of CIM. Education is therefore a necessity, but not sufficient precondition to achieving a successful CIM implementation.

CIM potentially covers a wide variety of computer applications in the production process. The implications of CIM may differ significantly from the experience of the management and technical staff. These managers, therefore, might find the CIM integration requirements difficult to accept. There is a need for developing the proper educational environment to achieve the maximum benefit from a CIM implementation.

CIM System Design

Successful CIM programs require: (1) defining strategy and (2) development of plans. Each is briefly reviewed.

The first requirement is for business unit/corporate level strategies. These strategies determine the objectives of the CIM in terms of the expected results. The specific CIM strategies can then be developed. The CIM strategies consider the amount and timing of investment, level of integration, phases of production to receive emphasis, and computer technologies to be utilized. The business unit, manufacturing, and CIM strategies must be matched, with differences resolved, before proceeding to the CIM system development.

Just as any new complex methodology requires a plan, successful CIM implementation also needs adequate planning. The planning procedure is similar to the three-phased system design procedures presented in Chapter 12.

Issues and Questions

1. What are the important manufacturing issues that impact on the CIM strategy?
2. List and discuss the roles of the computer technologies usually associated with a full CIM implementation.
3. What is the role of education in achieving a successful CIM implementation?
4. Using the design chart (Figure 12–1) in Chapter 12, prepare an outline of a procedure to develop a CIM system.
5. Select three specific CIM objectives (e.g., shorter production cycles). Define how CIM might be used to achieve the objectives and the computer applications (tools) necessary to achieve the desired ends.
6. Discuss how an audit (assessment) should be conducted of current manufacturing operations to determine the need for a CIM system.
7. How should logistics management information systems and CIM interface?

SEMINAR FOCUS EIGHT: MULTINATIONAL LOGISTICS[2]

Prior to the last few decades, international business for many enterprises was more or less an afterthought—the opportunity to enjoy some incremental volume. The outlook is that the dominant form of future business will involve

---

[2] Adapted from Donald J. Bowersox and Jay U. Sterling, "Multinational Logistics," *Journal of Business Logistics* (Oakbrook, Ill.: National Council of Physical Distribution Management, Vol. 3, No. 2, pp. 15–23, 1982).

global competitiveness of vast and complex multinational institutions. In today's environment the only relevant focus for logistical planning and operations is a global perspective.

Progressive enterprises recognize they must produce and distribute products worldwide to achieve substantial long-term success in growth markets. To gain and maintain competitive superiority and achieve maximum manufacturing economies of scale, it is necessary to capitalize on the inherent advantages of all nations within which a firm operates.

Such a global perspective has created a need for the development of a logic to guide worldwide logistical management. This logistical logic must be capable of controlling the complex process of asset deployment within and between a large number of countries which have different laws, cultures, levels of economic development, and national aspirations. There are only a few instances where multinational companies have implemented the logistics concept on a truly international scale. The general consensus is that planning practices of many multinational businesses leave a great deal to be desired. Typically, such planning effort is operationally, as opposed to strategically, oriented.

Development of a coordinated international logistics logic is timely for two reasons. First, the potential of a global movement/storage system provides an opportunity for a higher order of trade-off and synergistics benefits than is attainable from logistical planning on a nation-by-nation basis. Second, the limited concepts of physical distribution and materials management create the danger of a dysfunctional interface when applied individually to multinational situations. The acceptance of either philosophy as the dominant logic in a multinational setting creates the potential danger of suboptimization. Only a unified logistics system has the potential to guide the orderly, efficient flow of assets from global material sourcing, into a multinational manufacturing and assembly complex, through a variety of domestic distribution systems to customers located throughout the world. Multinational logistics offers the potential for such an integrated logic. The problem is that such an integrated logic does not currently exist.

What exists is a series of individual national physical distribution and material procurement systems, each with its own legal and operating infrastructure and management style. From within this vast range of national characteristics, each multinational concern must develop a unique and coordinated logistical capability.

The Prerequisites for Global Success

What logistical prerequisites or qualifications must an enterprise possess to compete on a multinational basis? Beyond the fundamental economic and technological resource base, several managerial attributes appear desirable.

First, it is mandatory that the participating enterprises have an integrated logic of logistics that is commonly accepted by its managers. Specifically, the overall organizational structure must have the capability to transfer knowledge and skills required to succeed on a global basis to all national operations. It must also be organized to provide both visibility and accountability to strategic movement and storage. Global operations require a substantial degree of central control if they are to be effective.

Second, multinational logistics requires a unique set of performance measurement standards. Primary concerns are the substantial fluctuations in national currencies, the varying inflation rates among both industrialized and developing countries, and the necessity to manufacture or assemble locally which less-developed countries frequently impose on foreign ownership. It is clear that an enterprise planning multinational activities needs to develop measurement standards that reflect realistic estimates of the value added in the logistical process. For example, it is necessary to develop procedures and methods to trade and barter products and commodities to realize a unit of payment that has universal worth.

Third, enterprises engaged in multinational manufacturing and distribution need to plan for greater inventory holdings than are typically required to support domestic operations. The average United States manufacturing firm has between 25 and 30 per cent of its assets committed to inventory. Retailing counterparts characteristically approach or exceed 50 per cent. By the simple fact of geography, lead times are longer in international logistics, and variations from average transit times increase significantly. As a result, multinational pipeline inventories will be larger than typically required for domestic operations. Likewise, the range of potential uncertainties inherent in multinational arrangements requires increased safety stocks to avoid supply discontinuities and demand variations.

Fourth, beyond inventory, it appears reasonable to estimate that overall costs of logistics, as a percentage of revenue, will be greater for multinationals than for their domestic counterparts. This increase in logistical cost per unit results in part from the geographic realities of international logistics, as well as from the substitution of logistical services for other activities. Specifically, longer transit times between continents and sometimes across continents may require more storage. However, international sourcing provides an opportunity to postpone final assembly by performing this function at selected forward locations within the logistical system. Thus, the key to efficient multinational operations is to make sourcing decisions based on the least cost of both procurement and conversion.

Fifth, the methods by which logistical costs are accounted for may also be unique to multinational arrangements. The typical practice in domestic logistics is to combine the burden of capital and direct expenditure to arrive at the lowest possible total cost of operation. In multinational situations the desirability of investing capital in distribution-related assets (beyond inventory) may be substantially reduced by economic and political uncertainties. In fact, the typical multinational enterprise may not seek an overall capital allocation process that supports profitable operations independent of national borderlines. The risk of host countries seeking to control the enterprise's local operations in such a way as to serve their own national interests is always present. The logistical conclusion is that the multinational may place a much greater emphasis on expensing rather than capitalizing costs of logistical operations.

A sixth, and final, requirement for involvement in international logistics is the need to master a complex set of business relationships. This managerial concern is not unique to logistical operations, but it is pertinent. Without a doubt, the details involved in international movement are among the most extensive of any operational area. To the extent that an enterprise shifts from a primarily domestic to a multinational base, managerial control must be directed to a mass of documentation and detail that expands geometrically with the number of involved nations.

Issues and Questions

1. Some logistics managers are of the opinion that multinational logistics is only the collection of a group of national logistics requirements. Therefore, in reality international logistics as a separate discipline does not exist. Do you support or reject this position and why?

2. Is it logical that larger inventories will be required to support international logistics?

3. Why would a multinational enterprise seek to "expense" logistical operations? Discuss the full ramifications of this concept.

4. What dangers exist in trading or bartering as a form of payment?

5. Discuss and illustrate the notion of higher level synergism that is possible when business is conducted on a multinational basis.

6. How could physical distribution and materials management cause a dysfunctional interface when applied individually to multinational situations?

APPENDICES

Marketing Channel Structure

Unlike those concerned with logistics, marketing managers have traditionally acknowledged that distribution channels consist of a fantastically complex network of organizations grouped in a variety of combinations.[1] Each organization linked in a distribution channel exists for a reason and performs services in anticipation of a return on investment and effort. The marketing task is never considered complete until the final owner has been satisfied with respect to pretransaction anticipations. In fact, a considerable degree of marketing effort centers around measurement of pretransaction anticipation and posttransaction satisfaction. Thus, marketing horizons are not limited by the operating boundaries of the enterprise. The basic acknowledgment of a wider spectrum of planning and the realistic approach to interorganizational relationships render a channel approach superior to that of a single firm. The marketing approach eliminates the limitations of dealing only with vertically controlled systems.[2]

Four general approaches are used by marketing writers to study and describe channels: (1) descriptive institutional, (2) graphic, (3) commodity groupings, and (4) functional.

DESCRIPTIVE INSTITUTIONAL APPROACH

The institutional approach to channel analysis focuses on the identification, description, and classification of middlemen institutions. Such institutions are grouped with respect to the marketing services they perform. Figure I–1 typifies

---

[1] The purpose of this appendix is to provide a brief overview of the conventional marketing approach to channel description. A great deal of the terminology is based upon *Note on Marketing Channels* (Boston: Harvard Business School, 1965), ICH 10M65, EA-M-480.

[2] See Chapter 3, page 83.

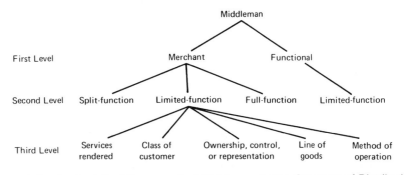

Figure I–1 An Analytical Framework of Middlemen in the Structure of Distribution

the analytical framework. At the first level, the distinction is made between merchant and functional middlemen. Merchant middlemen take title to the goods with all the ownership risks. Functional middlemen escape the risks of ownership but provide some necessary service to both client and customer.

At the second level, the distinction between range and type of wholesale services is made. Full-function middlemen typically buy in large quantities, break-bulk, assemble, assort, sell, and deliver. In performing these activities, the full-function middleman maintains a warehouse, employs a sales force that calls on the trade regularly, provides for physical distribution, extends trade credit, manages the collection of accounts, and serves in an advisory capacity or as an informational link to both suppliers and customers. The limited-function wholesaler is so designated because the range of services offered falls short of that provided by a full-function middleman. On the other hand, the split-function middleman usually operates as both a retailer and wholesaler.

The third level of Figure I–1 represents descriptive criteria commonly applied to the various categories of wholesalers specified by the first two levels. Every student of business administration should have a working understanding of marketing institutions, because they serve as the basis for all other methods of studying channel structures.

Merchant Middlemen

Included in this section are those wholesalers who buy and sell of their own initiative, thereby dealing with the risks of ownership.

Regular Wholesalers

The service, or regular, wholesaler operates a full-function enterprise. Usually the firm is independently owned and handles consumer goods. The regular wholesale firm purchases in large volume from producers and manufacturers, accepts delivery at one or more of its warehouses, breaks down and stores its purchases, sends out its sales force to canvass the trade, assembles orders in relatively small quantities, delivers orders to its customers, extends credit, assumes the risks of inventory and receivables, offers advisory service to its customers, and supplies marketing information to both customers and suppliers. The regular wholesale firm predominates as a retail source of supply in many mass-distributed consumer-goods lines.

Industrial Distributor

The industrial distributor is also classified as a regular or full-function wholesaler. As such, these distributors provide essentially the same services enumerated previously. The industrial distributor is differentiated from other full-function wholesalers by customers serviced and by the nature of inventory sold. Customers purchase goods for consumption, use within their enterprise, or as an unfinished item subject to further processing. Although retailers are not technically excluded as a class of customer, in practice they are a minimal source for the distributor. Most of the distributor's trade comes from manufacturing firms, public utilities, railroads, mines, and service establishments (e.g., doctors, barbers, beauticians, hotels and restaurants). The industrial distributor often specializes in servicing one industry segment, such as automotive or mining.

Drop Shippers

Drop shippers are limited-function wholesalers in that they seldom take physical possession of the goods. Commodities such as coal, lumber, construction materials, agricultural products, and heavy machinery are bulky and require the economies of shipment by carload lots. The drop shipper purchases the carload from the supplier in anticipation of a future order. Once a buyer is found, the drop shipper assumes the responsibility and ownership of shipment until it is accepted by the customer. Because no warehouse facilities are maintained, the drop shipper's risk of title bearing varies with the time lag between purchase and sale of the carload. Apart from this risk, the drop shipper also incurs the risks and costs of credit extension and receivables collection. A distinction between the practice of drop shipping and the drop shipper is important. Drop shipping is the practice of shipping an order direct from the supplier to the customer, although a middleman might be involved in the transactions. For example, central purchasing might purchase a large quantity of bulk merchandise. Instead of direct shipment to the firm's distribution warehouse; the company might allocate portions of the shipment directly to its retail store. This practice is termed *drop shipping*. The drop shipper, on the other hand, is a distinct middleman who arranges for shipment, takes title, assumes responsibility for shipment, and functions as a merchant middleman in the overall distribution channel.

Cash-and-Carry Wholesalers

Cash-and-carry wholesalers are limited-function middlemen who operate on a cash basis with no merchandise delivery. Chiefly found in the grocery trade, they were established to serve the small retailer whose order size was not large enough to justify delivery. By stocking staple merchandise, employing no salespersons, and eliminating delivery services and credit, such middlemen can economically serve the small retailer. To take advantage of such services, the retailer must travel to the warehouse, find and assemble an order, carry it to a central checkout location, pay cash, load it on a truck, and transport the order to the retail location.

Wagon Distributors (Jobbers)

Utilized mainly by the grocery trade, the wagon distributor is a limited-function wholesaler who specializes in high-margin specialty items or quick-turnover perishables. This intermediary purchases from producers, may or may not maintain a warehouse, and employs one or more drivers to call on the trade regularly. Sales and delivery are performed simultaneously. The customer selects merchandise from the truck's limited assortment and closes the transaction with a cash payment.

Rack Jobbers

Rack jobbers or service merchandisers are classified as full-function intermediaries in that they perform all the regular wholesaling functions plus some retailing functions. Dealing in extensive lines of nonfood merchandise, driver-salesmen regularly service grocer accounts. Typically, a sales representative on call performs a stock control function to ensure that display racks are adequately stocked, properly price-marked, and arranged in an attractive manner. Generally, a rack jobber will be responsible for stock rotation. The retailer is usually billed on a consignment basis, paying only for merchandise sold since the jobber's last visit.

Assembling Wholesalers

Primarily dealing in agricultural products, the assembling wholesaler reverses the common procedure in terms of order size. This category of wholesaler buys the output of many small farmers, assembles and grades the product, ships in economical quantities to central markets, and sells in large quantities than those purchased.

Semijobbers

Semijobbers are designated split-function middlemen, because they operate at both the wholesale and retail level of the channel of distribution. Usually semijobbers are limited- or full-function wholesalers who indulge in some retail sales, conversely, they are retailers who find it advantageous to be classified as wholesalers for at least a small portion of their operation. An illustration of the former is automative suppliers. The second case is not typical of any particular retailing segment but is illustrative of a strategy aimed at gaining lower prices or developing business in two separate market segments.

Functional Middlemen

Wholesalers in the functional category do not take title; nevertheless, they perform many wholesale functions. All middlemen included in this classification are, by definition, limited-function wholesalers, because they do not assume the risks of inventory ownership.

Selling Agents

Selling agents serve their clients in lieu of a sales organization. They are contracted to sell output of one or more manufacturers as long as the lines handled are supplementary and do not compete directly. Because their principals are generally small firms, as illustrated by the textile industry, they are often called upon for financial assistance in terms of loans, carrying credit for the client, or collecting receivables. Furthermore, agents serve as collectors, analysts, and dispensers of marketing data. For these services, selling agents are remunerated on a commission basis.

Manufacturers' Agents

Manufacturers' agents are similar to selling agents in that they act as substitutes for a direct sales organization, are hired on a continuing contractual basis, represent relatively small enterprises, provide market intelligence, and are reimbursed by commissions. They differ from selling agents inasmuch as they do not sell the entire output of their clients, are limited to a specific geographic territory, and have little control over prices, discounts, and credit terms. A manufacturer's agent or representative usually represents a number of manufacturers who produce noncompetitive but related lines.

Commission Merchants

Unlike agents, commission merchants rarely are used on a regular contractual basis. Instead, they are engaged for a single transaction, or, more commonly, to facilitate the disposal of a particular lot of goods. Once contracted, the commission merchant takes possession but not title of the goods, provides warehousing facilities, and displays either a sample or the entire lot to prospective purchasers. Once negotiations begin, the commission merchant is usually empowered to accept the best offer, as long as it exceeds a previously stipulted minimum price. To facilitate good offerings and speed the closing of transactions, the commission merchant may choose to extend credit at risk. In practice, commission merchants commonly extend credit, bill the customer, collect the account, provide a final accounting, and remit the proceeds less commission to the principal. Such a wholesaling operation is of vital importance to the marketing of livestock, grain, and other agricultural products.

Brokers

Brokers serve as catalytic agents to classes of buyers and sellers that would normally have considerable difficulty in meeting for purposes of negotiation. A broker's entire function is to stimulate and arrange contacts between the two groups. It is understood that brokers do not permanently represent either buyer or seller. Furthermore, they do not handle the goods, rarely take physical possession, nor do they provide financial assistance to clients. The brokerage fee is paid by the principal, whether it is the buyer or the seller. In no case can a broker legally receive a fee from both parties to a transaction. Brokers are widely used in foreign trade by small manufacturers of convenience goods and by wholesale grocers.

Auction Companies

Auction companies are widely used in marketing fruit, tobacco, and livestock. They provide a physical setting conducive to marketing specific lots of commodities. Facilities are usually available to all those offering commodities and to all those bidding for them. The auction company is paid by the seller at a flat fee per transaction or a percentage of the sale.

Petroleum Bulk Stations

Stations provide the storage and wholesale distribution for the petroleum industry. Such establishments may be owned by refining companies and operated on a basis similar to that of manufacturers' sales branches. Alternatively, they may be owned and operated independently.

GRAPHIC APPROACH

Flow graphs are a useful technique to identify the flow of ownership title of raw materials and finished products. These graphs illustrate the range of alternatives in institutional selection at all levels of the markeing process.

The graphic approach to describing a structure of distribution is shown in Figures I–2 and I–3. In Figure I–2 the most common variations in consumer-goods channels are illustrated. Of the four channels shown, the most typical for the consumer is the wholesale-retail-consumer channel. Most mass-produced

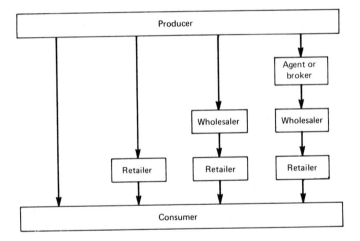

Figure I–2 Typical Channel Structure Alternatives in Consumer-Goods Distribution

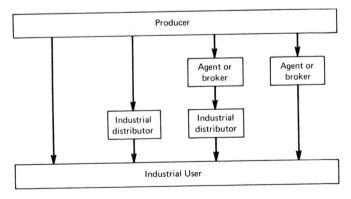

Figure I–3 Typical Channel Structure Alternatives in Industrial-Goods Distribution

consumer goods reach the market through a wholesaler and retailer. The channel selected by the manufacturer depends upon the characteristics of the product, the buying habits of the consumer, and the overall marketing strategy of the firm. For example, a large personal sales force is required for successful marketing of a product nationwide directly to the consumer. Such companies as Avon Products and Fuller have selected this method of distribution. On the other hand, a manufacturer with limited capital resources and a limited product line might elect to hire a broker or an agent to sell products in consumer channels.

In Figure I–3 a description of alternative channels for industrial-goods distribution is presented. Most high-volume items in industrial markets move directly from producer to consumer. Industrial distributors often handle supplies, replacement parts, and small orders of bulk items. In this sense the industrial middleman performs much the same function as the wholesaler in consumer channels. One major difference between consumer and industrial channels is that incidence of functional middlemen such as selling agents, brokers, and manufacturers' agents is much greater in industrial than in commercial channels.

The structures described in Figures I–2 and I–3 should be regarded as general patterns. There are a great number of possible variations in channel structure in addition to those shown in these charts depending on the product, the customer, and the entrepreneurial vision of the channel members. The neat graphs of distribution channels have been confused by the expanded tendency toward *scrambled merchandising*.[3] An organization once considered only a wholesaler may now function within the channel as a retailer as well as a wholesaler. Retailers and manufacturers in turn have assumed many traditional duties of wholesalers. This extension of activities has been referred to as *integrated wholesaling*.[4] Under integrated wholesaling, the retail operation performs the functions traditionally assumed by the wholesale intermediary.

The main advantage of a graphic approach is that it illustrates the many links in modern marketing. By the use of graphs the multiplicity of institutions is focused in a logical sequence. However, the simplicity of flow diagrams tends to understate some complexities of designing the proper channel structure for an individual firm.

COMMODITY GROUPING

In an effort to limit the range of considerations in channel planning, several studies have been completed with the objective of defining channel structure in detail for specific commodities.[5] Generally empirical in nature, commodities

---

[3] *Scrambled merchandising* refers to the identical product being offered for sale in several different types of retail outlets, for example, garden rakes sold at gasoline service stations as well as in hardware, garden, discount, and department stores. Also referred to as *channel jumping* and *conglomerate marketing*. See Chapter 3, page 80.

[4] Theodore N. Beckman and William R. Davidson, *Marketing*, 7th ed. (New York: The Ronald Press Company, 1962), pp. 348–64.

[5] For a historical review of the development of marketing channel logic and selected industry examples, see Richard M. Clewett, *Marketing Channels* (Homewood, Ill.: Richard D. Irwin, Inc., 1954).

studies combine a description of institutions with a graphic illustration of primary ownership flows. Although they are very useful in specific situations, such commodity-channel treatments are too specific for general planning.

FUNCTIONAL TREATMENTS

The functional approach to channel structure developed as a result of attempts to provide a logical explanation of the overall marketing process. Figure I–4 illustrates the most commonly agreed-upon listing of functions. A function, in a marketing sense, represents a major economic activity that must be performed to some degree in the marketing of all products. In the marketing of many products, a given function may be performed by a number of institutions and intermediaries between the point of original sale and final sale. For example, storage may be performed by a producer, wholesaler, retailer, and even by a user. On the other hand, market financing might be performed by only one institution in the total process of marketing a product. Marketing has been defined as a process—one in which no person or institution is self-sufficient. It involves many participants and consists of various functional components. One must consider each of these functions and their interrelationships to understand the totality of the process. Beckman and Davidson have segmented the functional relationships into exchange functions, physical distribution functions, and facilitating functions.[6] The exchange functions include the buying and selling activities. The physical distribution functions include the transportation and storage activities. The facilitating functions include standardization, market financing, risk bearing, and market information and research activities.

The functional approach to marketing provides a framework for evaluation of alternative channel structures with respect to total channel capability. Initial listing of marketing functions has been greatly expanded by subsequent developments of functional analysis. Functional analysis concentrates upon the interrelation of various functions in the total marketing process. Particularly noteworthy are the developments of Alderson with respect to the role of middlemen in the marketing process.[8] In the Alderson treatment, the essential

[6] Beckman and Davidson, op. cit.

[7] Ibid., p. 390.

[8] Wroe Alderson, *Marketing Behavior and Executive Action* (Homewood, Ill.: Richard D. Irwin, Inc., 1957).

Figure I–4 Marketing Functions[7]

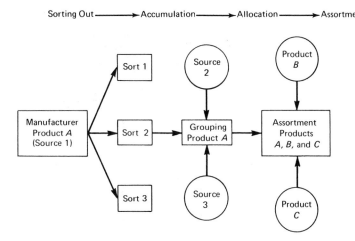

Figure I–5 Alderson's Process of Sorting

role of marketing intermediary is one of reconciling a narrow conglomeration of products from single sources into a wide inventory assortment at the point of final sales. This involves several steps, which can be best accomplished by a specialized middleman.

The entire process of changing conglomerations to assortments was labeled *sorting* in the Alderson treatment.[9] The marketing channel serves to perform the sorting activity, which consists of four steps. The initial step involves the *sorting out* of large conglomerations and results in one large supply being reclassified into small lots of various types of goods according to the requirements of the sorter. Next, a larger supply, perhaps from different locations, is *accumulated* over a period of time to provide a larger grouping of specialized but homogeneous goods. The third step in the sorting process consists of *allocation*. In allocation the total supply is apportioned either within corporate facilities or among market outlets. Finally, *assortment* takes place, which constitutes the building of individual supplies into a combination of different products or an assortment in accordance with an anticipated pattern of demand. Alderson's process of sorting is illustrated in Figure I–5. In Figure I–5 the four aspects of sorting are illustrated in the sequence most commonly found in the marketing process.

Staudt, Taylor, and Bowersox built upon Alderson's concept of sorting and have generalized four principles that justify the existence of marketing intermediaries: (1) the principle of minimum total transactions, (2) the principle of massed reserves, (3) the principle of proximity, and (4) the principle of postponement.[10]

The *principle of minimum total transactions* acknowledges that the total process of sorting is reduced by having a limited number of middlemen. This principle has wide application in finished-goods and agricultural-commodity distribution. In essence, the principle advocates specialization in the marketing process. Figure I–6 illustrates the principle of minimum total transactions.

[9] Ibid.

[10] Thomas A. Staudt, Donald A. Taylor, and Donald J. Bowersox, *A Managerial Introduction to Marketing*, 3rd ed. (Englewood Cliffs, N.J.: Prentice-Hall, Inc., 1976), pp. 278–82.

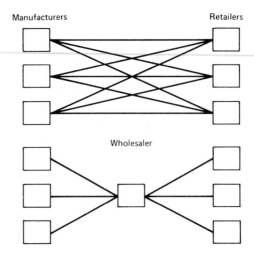

Figure I–6   Principle of Minimum Total Transactions

The *principle of massed reserves* is concerned with the storage of goods in the distribution channel. Goods in the form of inventories exist at each stop in the process of concentration and dispersal. Such stops are defined at the producer level, accumulation level, assortment level, and the household. The amount of goods in inventory when intermediaries are used is less than would otherwise he required.[11] This principle assumes exacting inventory control and consistent product delivery.

The *principle of proximity* states that the specialized intermediary should be located close to the marketplace. Close proximity provides better positioning to render final assortments in a manner most satisfactory and timely to market demand.

The principle of postponement was introduced in Chapter 2 as a strategic consideration in logistical system design.[12] With postponement, physical changes in product form and identity should be delayed as long as practical in the manufacturing and distribution process. Inventories should be retained in homogeneous lots to reduce the risk associated with the sorting process detailed by Alderson.

In total, the four principles lend credence to the logic of including specialized middlemen in a channel of distribution. To a significant degree, the objective of each principle is more effectively realized by cooperation within a middleman structure.

[11] See page 84.

[12] See pages 57–58.

Mechanized Warehouse Establishment

Establishing a mechanized warehouse involves a series of decisions, which, in total, mold the structure within which material handling and inventory storage will be performed. The following discussion is oriented to managers who have not previously established a warehouse. This review provides a working background to help avoid typical mistakes and indicates the type of information required to establish a warehouse. Decisions made in one area will influence decisions in other areas. Such interrelationships must be recognized to develop an integrated warehouse system.

PLANNING THE DISTRIBUTION WAREHOUSE

The initial decisions are those related to planning the warehouse. The modern notion that warehouses provide an enclosure for material handling requires detailed analysis before the size, type, and shape of the facility can be determined. Too, the buildings are designed and under construction before the material-handling system is finalized. A master plan of related areas such as material handling, layout, space requirement, and design should be developed, and a specific site for the warehouse selected. Construction decisions are the most rigid in implementation. They establish the character of the warehouse, which, in turn, determines the degree of attainable handling efficiency.

Site Selection

Location analysis techniques are available to assist in selecting a general area for warehouse location. These were discussed in Chapter 13. Once locational analysis is completed, a specific building site must be selected. Three areas in a community may be considered for location: (1) commercial zone, (2) outlying areas served by motor carrier only, and (3) central or downtown area.

The primary factors in site selection are the availability of services and cost. The cost of procurement is the most important governing factor. A warehouse need not be located in a major industrial area. In city after city, one can observe warehouses among industrial plants and in areas zoned for light or heavy industry. This is not necessary because most warehouses can operate legally under the restrictions placed upon commmercial property.

Beyond procurement costs, such setup and operating expenses as rail sidings, utility hookups, taxes, insurance rates, and highway access require evaluation. These expenses vary among sites. For example, a food-distribution firm recently rejected what otherwise appeared to be a totally satisfactory site because of insurance rates. The site was located near the end of the water main. During most of the day, adequate water supplies were available to handle operational and emergency requirements. The only possible water problem would occur during two short periods each day. From 6:30 A.M. to 8:30 A.M. and from 5:00 P.M. to 7:00 P.M., the demand for water along the line was so great that a sufficient supply was not available to handle emergencies. Because of this deficiency, abnormally high insurance rates were required, and the site was rejected.

Several other requirements must be satisfied before the site is purchased. The site must offer adequate room for expansion. Necessary utilities must be available. The site's soil must be capable of supporting the structure and must be sufficiently high to afford proper drainage. Additional requirements may be situationally necessary, depending upon the structure to be constructed. In summary, the final selection of the site must be preceded by extensive analysis.

Product-Mix Considerations

A second and independent area of quantitative analysis is a precise study of the products to be distributed through the proposed warehouse. The design and operation of a proposed warehouse are related directly to the character of the product mix. Each product should be analyzed in terms of annual sales, stability of demand, weight, bulk, and packaging. It is also desirable to determine the total size, bulk, and weight of the average order processed through the warehouse. These data provide necessary information for determining requirements in warehouse space, design and layout, material-handling equipment, operating procedures, and controls.

Expansion

Future expansion is often neglected when an enterprise is considering an immediate extension of its warehouse facilities. Inclusion of a warehouse component into the logistical structure should be based partially upon estimated requirements for future operations. Well-managed organizations often establish 5- to 10-year expansion plans. Such expansion considerations may require purchase or option of a site three to five times the size of the initial structure.

Special construction is often considered to ease expansion without seriously affecting normal operations. Some walls may be constructed of semipermanent materials to allow easy removal. Floor areas, designed to support heavy movements, are extended to these walls in a manner that facilitates expansion.

Selection of Material-Handling System

A material-handling system is one of the initial considerations. Movement is the main function within a warehouse. Consequently, the warehouse is viewed as a structure designed to facilitate maximum product flow. In Chapter 8, material-handling alternatives ranging from mechanized to automated were discussed. It is important to stress that the material-handling system must be selected early in the warehouse design stage.

Warehouse Layout

Layout consists of developing a floor plan that will facilitate product flow, and the layout of a warehouse depends on the proposed system of material handling. The layout and the material-handling system must be planned together.

It is difficult to generalize because of the variety of layouts available to fit specific needs. If pallets are utilized, the first step is to determine the size of the pallets. A pallet of nonstandard size may be desirable for specialized products, but, whenever possible, standardized pallets should be used because of their lower cost. The most common sizes are 40 by 48 inches and 32 by 40 inches. In general, the larger the pallet load, the lower the cost of movement per pound or package over a given distance. One fork-lift-truck operator can move a large load in the same time and with the same effort required to move a smaller load. The packages to be placed on the pallet and the related patterns will determine, to a certain extent, the size of pallet best suited to the operation. Regardless of the size finally selected, management should adopt one size for the total operation.

The second step in planning a layout involves the positioning of pallets. There are two basic methods in a mechanized warehouse: (1) 90 degree, or square, and (2) angle. Ninety-degree, or square, placement is most common throughout industry. Square placement means that the pallet is positioned perpendicular to the aisle. Angular placement means that the pallet is placed at an angle. The angles employed range from 10 degrees to 45 degrees, with 26 1/2 degrees most common. Figure II–1 shows the two methods of positioning. The square method is widely used because of layout ease. The angle method, however, offers the potential for improved operating efficiency. Aisle width can be reduced because the fork-lift truck can position a pallet in the angle placement system without making a full 90-degree turn. Operating efficiency is

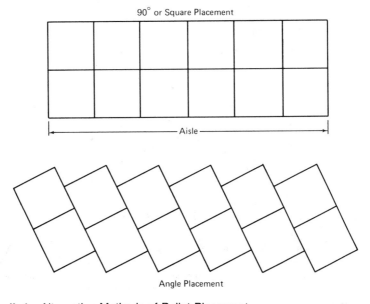

Figure II–1 Alternative Methods of Pallet Placement

increased because of the ease of placement resulting from the shorter turn. Under certain conditions, reduced aisles offset space losses due to angling. The method of pallet placement in a particular layout will depend upon the specific problems experienced. Often the two methods can be combined to arrive at the most efficient overall layout.

Once all details have been isolated, the handling equipment selected must be integrated into a final layout. The path of product flow will depend upon the material-handling system. To indicate the relationship between material handling and layout, two systems and their respective layouts are reviewed. The following illustrations represent only two of many possible layouts.

Layout A, illustrated in Figure II–2, represents a material-handling system with related layout utilizing fork-lift trucks for inbound and transfer movements and tractor-trailers for order selection. The products are assumed adaptable to a palletized operation. This layout is greatly simplified because offices, special area, and details are omitted.

The floor plan in layout A is approximately square. The advocates of this type of system feel that a square structure provides the best plan for operating efficiency. As indicated in Chapter 8, products are typically clustered in a specific area of the warehouse for order selection. Such is the case in layout A.

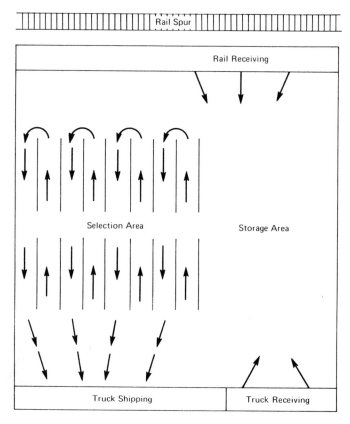

Figure II–2 Layout A

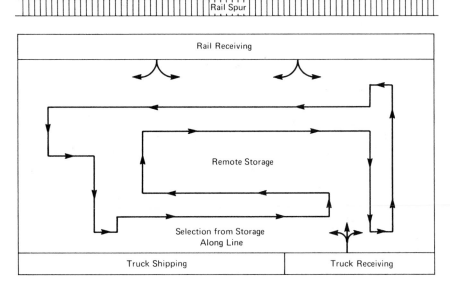

Figure II–3   Layout *B*

This area is labeled the selection area, and its primary purpose is to minimize the distance order pickers must cover when selecting an order.

The selection area is supported by a storage area. When products are received by rail or truck, they are palletized and placed in the storage area. The selection area is then replenished from storage as required. When a compact selection area is utilized, products are placed in this area according to weight, bulk, and velocity characteristics, in an attempt to minimize outbound-movement problems. Special orders are then accumulated by the order selector moving a tractor and trailer through the selection are. The arrows in layout *A* indicate the flow of product movements.

Layout *B*, as illustrated in Figure II–3, represents a material-handling system utilizing fork-lift trucks for inbound and transfer movements and a continuous-movement towline for order selection. As in layout *A*, products are assumed adaptable to pallets, and the illustration is greatly simplified. The floor plan is rectangular. In a system with a continuous-movement towline, the special selection area is omitted with selection directly from storage. Products are moved from rail and truck receiving areas into storage areas adjacent to the towline. The orders are then selected directly from storage and loaded onto four-wheel trucks, which are propelled by the towline. Merchandise is placed in the storage area to minimize inbound movement. Because the towline moves all products with equal efficiency, the weight, bulk, and velocity considerations are not important for outbound movement. The arrows in layout *B* indicate major product movements. The line in the center of the layout illustrates the path of the towline.

As indicated, both layouts *A* and *B* are greatly simplified; their purpose is to indicate the relationship of material-handling systems and warehouse layouts.

Both represent mechanized warehouses and are not applicable to automated or information-directed handling.

Precise Determination of Warehouse Space

Several methods are used to estimate the final size of the required warehouse. Each starts with a sales forecast or some projection of the total tonnage expected during a given period. This tonnage is then used to develop base and safety stocks. Some techniques consider firm and peak utilization rates. Neglecting utilization rates can result in overbuilding, with corresponding cost increases. It is important to note, however, that one of the major complaints of warehouse managers is the underestimate of warehouse size requirements by management. A good practice is to allow 10 per cent additional space to account for increased volume, new products, and so on. Size determination techniques were discussed in Chapter 14.

Warehouse Design

Warehouse design is a special area of planning usually contracted to an architect. Design and construction characteristics must not hinder product flow. Consequently, management must communicate to the architect the need for unrestricted movement. In order to design a warehouse properly, the architect will require specifications for the size of the structure, layout, and predetermined path of material-handling equipment. The material-handling specialist must work closely with the design specialist to develop an integrated system.

Careful attention should be paid to placement of overhead obstructions such as lights, steampipes, sprinkler systems, and heating ducts. These items must be kept above the tiering height to provide material-handling clearance. The placement of supporting columns is also an important design consideration. Generally, some latitude exists in positioning, depending upon which ways the columns run in relation to the supporting walls of the structure. Column placement is important to ensure a minimum of restricted storage bays. The floor areas, which must be specially treated for sufficient hardness, depend upon the predetermined path of the material-handling equipment.

These items illustrate just a few reasons why the warehouse must be designed to facilitate product flow. The modern warehouse is founded on the efficient use of every cubic foot of space and available material-handling equipment, and the structure should be designed to stimulate this efficiency.

The Integrated Plan

Once management has selected a site and planned the size, layout, material-handling equipment, and design, construction may begin. A small-scale physical model of the proposed structure, using a model and templates, provides a clear three-dimensional image of the proposed structure. A scale 1/4 inch equal to 1 foot is a standard size. Such a model will help pinpoint minor shortcomings of the proposed structure so that modifications can be made prior to construction.

INITIATING WAREHOUSE OPERATIONS

To initiate operation, management must stock merchandise, hire personnel, develop work procedures, establish a method of billing and inventory control, and initiate a system of local delivery.

Stocking the Warehouse

The ideal procedure to follow when stocking a warehouse is to obtain the complete inventory prior to initiating operations. The individual products to be distributed through the warehouse and the quantities of each in the basic inventory were determined when the warehouse was planned. The problem in stocking is to schedule the arrival of this merchandise to achieve an orderly inbound flow. The time required to initially stock a warehouse depends upon the number and quantity of products; it may take over 30 days to complete initial stocking.

In the storage area, products are assigned in full pallet loads to a predetermined pallet position. Two common methods of slot assignment are variable and fixed. The variable-slot placement system allows the product position to be changed each time a new shipment arrives in order to utilize warehouse space efficiently. With the fixed-slot placement system, a permanent position is assigned to each product placed in the selection area. The product retains this position as long as volume of movement maintains the same level. If volume increases or decreases, the product is reassigned. Fixed placement has an advantage over variable-slot placement because it provides a method of immediately locating a product. However, with computer-controlled warehouse locator systems this is not a problem. Regardless of which slot system is employed, each inbound product should be assigned an initial location.

Personnel Training

Hiring and training personnel qualified to operate a warehouse present serious problems. Regardless of how efficient the proposed system is in theory, in practice it will be only as good as the operating personnel. Proper training of personnel is necessary to ensure results from the system.

Training is not a difficult task if executed properly. The full workforce should begin work prior to the arrival of merchandise. People hired for specific assignments should be fully indoctrinated in their jobs and the role they play in the total system. Examination of the scale model and tours of the actual structure will familiarize the personnel with the system.

After indoctrination, each group of employees should be given specific training. Personnel hired to operate a warehouse may be grouped in the following categories: administrators, supervisors, selectors, equipment operators, laborers, and miscellaneous workers (maintenance, salvage, and so forth).

Prior to actual operations, it is desirable to simulate the various activities that each group of workers will perform. This type of training provides hands-on experience under near-typical working conditions. When initial stocking begins, the workforce receives experience in merchandise handling under typical conditions. Normally, the manufacturer supplying the basic material-handling equipment sends an instructor to help train equipment operators under both simulation and initial stocking. Once the basic inventory is in stock, it is a good practice to spend some time running sample orders through the warehouse. Simulated orders can be selected and loaded into delivery trucks, and the merchandise may then be treated as a new arrival and transferred back into stock.

Developing Work Procedures

The development of work procedures goes hand in hand with the training of warehouse personnel. Design of a material-handling systtem generally includes work procedures. It is management's responsibility to see that all personnel understand and use these procedures.

In the mechanized warehouse, approximately 65 per cent of the floor personnel are employed in some phase of order selection. Modifications of two basic methods of order picking are employed in distribution warehouses: (1) individual selection, and (2) area selection. Under the individual system, one selector completes a total order. This system is not used widely. Its primary application is when a large number of small orders are selected for repack or consolidated shipment on the same truck. Under the more commonly used area selection system, each selector is assigned a certain portion of the warehouse, and many selectors handle portions of the same order. Because each has a thorough knowledge of the selection area, no time is lost in locating items.

Specific procedures must also be established for receiving and shipping. Merchandise received must be checked to ensure its inclusion into the inventory accounting system. If pallets are used, the merchandise must be stacked in patterns to ensure maximum load stability. Personnel working in shipping must have a knowledge of loading procedures. In specific types of operations, particularly when merchandise changes ownership, items must be checked during loading.

Work procedures are not restricted to floor personnel. A definite procedure must be established for proper handling of inventory control records. Most firms employ some type of computer system. The purchasing or reordering of merchandise for the warehouse can cause a serious operational problem if proper procedures are lacking. Normally, there is little cooperation between buyers and the warehouse personnel if the facility is operating below capacity. The buyer tends to purchase in the quantity that will afford the best price, and little attention is given to the problem of space utilization. Under such conditions, the danger of overstocking the warehouse always exists. The problem can be avoided if the proper procedures are employed.

Buyers should be required to check with the warehouse manager before any abnormally large orders or new products are purchased. Some feel so strongly about this point that buyers are required to obtain a space allotment for all merchandise ordered. An equally serious problem is the quantity of cases ordered at a given time. The buyer should be required to order in pallet-multiple quantities. For example, if a product is placed upon pallets in a pattern containing 50 cases, the buyer should order in multiples of 50. If an order is placed for 110 cases, upon arrival the cases will fill two pallets plus ten on a third pallet. The extra 10 cases will require the same space as 50 and will require the same amount of movement effort. These illustrations indicate a few of the operational bottlenecks that can result from poor work procedures.

Security Systems

In a broad sense, security in a warehouse involves protection against merchandise pilferage and deterioration. Each form of security is worth management attention.

Pilferage Protection

Protection against theft of merchandise has become a major factor in warehouse operations. Such protection is required with respect to employees and as a result of the increased vulnerability of firms to riots and civil disturbances. All normal precautions employed throughout the enterprise should be strictly enforced at each warehouse. Security begins at the fence. As standard procedure, only authorized personnel should be permitted into the facility and surrounding grounds, and entry to the warehouse yard should be controlled through a single gate. Without exception, no private automobile—regardless of management rank or customer status—should be allowed to penetrate the yard adjacent to the warehouse.

To illustrate the importance of the guidelines stated, the following actual experience may be helpful. The particular firm enforced the rule that no private vehicles should be permitted in the warehouse yard. Exceptions were made for two handicapped office employees. One night after work, one of these employees accidentally discovered a bundle taped under a fender of the car. Subsequent checking revealed that the car was literally a delivery truck. The matter was promptly reported to security, who informed the employee not to alter any packages taped to the car and to continue parking inside the yard. Over the next several days, the situation was fully uncovered, with the ultimate arrest and conviction of seven warehouse employees who confessed to stealing over $100,000 of company merchandise. The firm would have been better off if it had originally purchased the small transport vehicle that was procured after the incident to provide rides from the regular parking lots to the office for the handicapped employees.

Shortages are always a major consideration in warehouse operations. Many are honest mistakes in order selection and shipment, but the purpose of security is to restrict theft from all angles. The majority of thefts occur during normal working hours.

Computerized inventory-control and order-processing systems help in the protection of merchandise being carried out the doors. No merchandise should be released from the warehouse unless accompanied by a computer-release document. If samples are authorized for the use of salespersons, this merchandise should be separate from other inventory. Not all pilferage is on a one-by-one basis. Numerous cases have been discovered where organized efforts between warehouse personnel and truckers resulted in deliberate overpicking, or high-for-low-value product substitution in order to move unauthorized merchandise out of the warehouse "in system." Employee rotation, total counts, and occasional complete line-item checks can reduce vulnerability to such collaboration.

A final comment is in order concerning the increased incidence of hijacking over-the-road trailer loads from yards or while in transit. Hijacking has become a major concern during the past decade. Over-the-road hijack prevention is primarily a law-enforcement matter, but in-yard total unit theft can be eliminated by tight security provisions.

Product Deterioration

With the warehouse, a number of factors can reduce a product or material to a nonusable or nonmarketable state. The most obvious form of product deterioration is damage from careless transfer or storage. Another major form of deterioration is noncompatibility of products stored in the same facility.

Of concern at this point is the deterioration that results from improper warehouse work procedures. For example, when pallets of merchandise are stacked in high cubes, a marked change in humidity or temperature can cause packages supporting the stack to fall. The warehouse represents an environment that must be carefully controlled or measured to provide proper product protection.

A constant concern is the carelessness of warehouse employees. In this respect, the fork-lift truck may well be management's worst enemy. Regardless of how often fork-lift truck operators are warned against carrying overloads, some still attempt such shortcuts when not properly supervised. In one situation, a stack of four pallets was dropped off the fork truck at the receiving dock of a food warehouse. Standard procedure was to move merchandise two pallets per load. The value of the damaged merchandise exceeded the average daily profit of two supermarkets. Product deterioration from careless handling within the warehouse is a form of loss that cannot be insured against. Such losses constitute 100-per-cent cost with no compensating revenue.

Billing and Inventory Control

Most firms handling a large number of products with varied turnover characteristics find it economical to employ computers for billing and inventory control. Inputs are prepared for each case of merchandise received at the warehouse. When an order is received, products are listed in order of warehouse placement. For example, if an area method of selection is employed, the order will be grouped by areas and listed in either numerical or slot order for the selector. It is possible to print at inventory of merchandise on hand at any given time. The computer inventory must be checked at times against a physical inventory in order to ensure accuracy in receiving and shipping records.

Initiating and Programming Local Delivery

Most shipments from distribution warehouses are made to customers by truck. When private trucking is utilized, a problem is encountered in scheduling movements to ensure maximum utilization at minimum cost. Routing techniques discussed in Chapter 14 have been developed to assist management in solving this problem. In programming local deliveries, the objective is to minimize the cost of distribution, which may be expressed as a function of vehicle mileage, for example.

Safety and Maintenance

Accident prevention is a paramount concern within the warehouse. A well-balanced safety program should include constant examination of work procedures and equipment to locate and correct unsafe conditions before they result in accidents. Accidents occur when workers become careless or are exposed to mechanical and/or physical hazards. The floors of a warehouse may cause accidents if not properly cleaned. During normal operation, rubber and glass deposits collect along aisles and, from time to time, broken cases will cause product seepage onto the floor. Proper cleaning procedures can reduce the risk of accidents from these hazards. Work environment safety has become a major concern of government under such programs as OSHA and cannot be neglected by management.

A preventive maintenance program is necessary for material-handling equipment. Unlike production machines, movement equipment is not stationary, and it is easy to neglect proper maintenance. A preventive maintenance program requiring a periodic check of all handling equipment should be installed.

PRODUCTIVITY MEASUREMENT

A final consideration in warehouse operations is the measurement of system productivity. Two general approaches are to measure productivity on a physical or dollar basis. Each type of measure is discussed with a concluding discussion on measurement standards.

Physical Systems of Productivity Measurement

Physical systems of measurement consist of unit and weight evaluations. For example, a unit measure may be cases moved per work-hour or pallets per work-hour. Generally, a tabulation is made of units handled in each functional area of the warehouse. The physical unit system of measurement is also a convenient method for evaluating individual employees.

Weight systems employ a popular measure referred to as tons per work-hour (usually written TPWH). TPWH may be computed for the total warehouse or for individual functional areas. Normally the TPWH figure for the total werehouse is obtained by adding together the tons of merchandise received (TR) and shipped (TS) and then dividing the sum by the number of total direct handling hours. The formula is:

$$TPWH = \frac{TR + TS}{\text{hours}}$$

Dollar System of Productivity Measurement

The most widely used dollar measure is one expressing warehouse expense as a percentage of the cost of merchandise delivered to the warehouse during a given period. Relating the dollar figures to a percentage figure partially omits the problems of changing dollar values between time periods. The problem of different rates of change in prices and wages still exists. The dollar system is inadequate for measuring efficiency between two warehouse systems because of regional cost differences.

Measurement Standards

The selection of standards presents a delicate management problem. The standard is the primary reason for measuring various activities. The various measures result in figures that may be compared to standards, thereby determining whether specific functions or employees deviate substantially from the expected level of activity.

A performance standard can be set only after one has a thorough knowledge of all particulars relating to the job. Extreme care should be taken in making warehouse comparisons on the basis of physical measures and related standards. Management should realize that there is no such thing as an absolute standard for measuring warehouse efficiency. Figures vary substantially between warehouses, depending upon methods of calculation and the various details of operation. Each warehouse should be considered as a special operation, and specific standards should be established on the basis of the potential of that operation. Physical standards offer a convenient means of making internal employee comparisons. For example, order selectors may be evaluated to point out which workers are exceptionally fast or slow The results of such an evaluation may be compared with accuracy figures to determine which selectors require additional training and supervision.

Regardless of which system of standards is employed, if applied to evaluate various workers, it should represent a reasonable goal rather than an optimum effort. Setting standards is a difficult problem which deserves management attention. Only if measuring techniques are consistently applied and performance standards realistically developed will management have a true picture of warehouse efficiency.

APPENDIX **III**

Manufacturing Location Analysis

Current economic literature contains many contributions aimed at developing a general theory of industrial location. Several such contributions were reviewed throughout the text. These theoretical studies address the problem of explaining geographic distribution of plant capacity. The main criterion permeating the majority of published works is the rational allocation of scarce resources. Thus, most location literature has been devoted to explaining socially acceptable goals generated from classical competitive economics.

However, the principle of free economic action and profit maximization may lead to personal goals inconsistent with social goals. Given imperfections in social and economic organization, individual entrepreneurs may find profit opportunities derived from astute location decisions. It may appear that economic theory and applied business practice are, therefore, incompatible. This view is quite incorrect. The function of location theory is to abstract from practice so that all elemental forces affecting location may be identified. Once these forces are appropriately defined, they implicitly form the foundation of public policy, which is aimed at achieving maximum economic welfare. One result of location theory is, therefore, the formation of adequate public policy to guide the nation's economic welfare. Given this orientation, the complete acceptance of general location forces for the purpose of solving an individual location problem may be inappropriate. However, theory aids in identification of fundamental forces affecting location and thus assists in the organization of an applied method for locating a specific plant. Applied methodology can be developed within the guideposts so conveniently developed by economic theorists.[1]

This appendix presents plant location initially in terms of the influencing factors. A general procedure and checklist to determine plant location then follow.

PLANT LOCATION FACTORS

Location theorists point out that all location factors can be grouped and summarized under two broad categories: (1) least-cost factors (profit-maximizing factors) and (2) intangible factors. To select a proper plant

---

[1] For a comprehensive review of location theories, see M. J. Webber, *Impact of Uncertainty on Location* (Cambridge, Mass.: The MIT Press, 1972), Chaps. 2 and 3; and Melvin L. Greenhut and H. Ohta, *Theory of Spatial Pricing and Market Areas* (Durham, N. C.: Duke University Press, 1975), and C. M. Warnenburg (trans.) and Peter Hall (ed.), *Von Thunen's Isolated State* (Oxford: Pergamon Press, 1966).

519

location, a complete evaluation of the influence of each category of factors on a particular location problem is necessary. Thus, it is important that all location factors be clearly understood.

Location Cost Factors

Location cost factors may be divided between transfer costs and production costs.[2] Transfer costs are defined as the costs that result from the movement of raw materials to the proposed plant site and those that are incurred by shipping finished products to market.[3] Production costs include all other costs related to plant operation. To achieve the least-cost location, the sum of all transfer costs and production costs must be minimized.[4] External economies due to clustering of plants can also be significant. Intangibles may be defined as those elements affecting costs that may not be classified in transfer or production accounts.

Transfer Costs

Transfer costs as a factor in plant location traditionally have been considered by assuming that all other location influences are negligible.[5] Such an assumption tends to minimize important location forces and, therefore, should be employed with considerable caution. On the other hand, this approach allows a detailed and unrestricted treatment of this very important factor. Transfer costs frequently are a dominant element in plant location. Because they are readily quantifiable, transfer cost analysis provides a convenient starting point for solving locational problems. In Chapter 13 analytical techniques were presented which may be employed to arrive at the geographical point of least transfer costs. However, it is essential to keep in mind that transfer costs are only one of many location influences. The point of least transfer cost normally will have to be amended to accommodate other location elements in selecting the profit-maximizing plant site. Five principal methods of movement are available to transport raw materials and finished products: rail, truck, air, water, and pipeline. The particular method capable of solving a given movement problem depends upon the commodity to be moved, distance, weight, size of shipment, speed required, cost, and so on.[6] Given the alternative methods capable of moving a particular commodity, the specific method or combination of methods employed is selected on the basis of cost and type of service required. Cost in all cases should be held to a minimum under the

[2] Hoover presented as the core of his thesis two influential cost categories—transfer and process. Although not utilized in a similar manner, these cost categories have been adopted for the present treatment. See Edgar M. Hoover, *The Location of Economic Activity* (New York: McGraw-Hill Book Company, 1948).

[3] Transfer costs are defined to include all cost components as developed in the total cost discussion. For a complete discussion of transportation, see Chapter 6.

[4] Only costs that vary between alternative locations are influential in plant location. For example, the cost of raw materials, per se, is not important unless this basic cost is geographically variable.

[5] For example, see D. Philip Locklin, *Economics of Transportation*, rev. ed. (Homewood, Ill.: Richard D. Irwin, Inc., 1972), p. 67.

[6] The capabilities and limitations of various modes of transport are discussed in greater detail in Chapter 5.

standards of service necessary to satisfy market requirements. Thus, when service requirements are satisfied, the combination of methods that results in the lowest total transfer cost may be determined by utilizing the total cost techniques introduced in Chapter 9. The combination of transfer methods and resultant costs can be materially altered by the geographical point at which the production plant is located. Consequently, in selecting a plant location, it is necessary to isolate the one best geographical point from which service requirements may be satisfied at the lowest total transfer cost.

Intercity transfer costs may be divided into two components: the costs associated with accumulation of raw materials and those related to product distribution. Accumulation costs result from the movement of raw materials or semifinished products to the point of manufacture. Distribution costs are derived from shipment of finished products to the final market through all intermediary steps. A particular plant location may be pulled toward the market or toward the source of raw materials, depending on which location minimizes the sum of accumulation and distribution costs. In some cases, as will be shown, a location between the market and the source of raw materials may yield the lowest total transfer costs.

Materials-Oriented Industries. The plants in a particular industry may be located near the source of raw materials because of the unique location of the raw material or because of a great weight loss in the process of production. Extractive industries as characterized by agriculture, mining, and lumbering must be located at the point where raw materials are available in economic quantities. In agriculture, the supply and quantity of land suited to particular crops play the dominant roles. In mining, it is the location of deposits; in lumber, it is the location of forests.

Industries in which, because of the nature of the product, great weight loss is experienced in production tend to locate plants near the source of raw materials.[7] Sugar beet refining and cotton ginning are excellent examples.[8] The net result of such locations is to reduce total transfer costs, because the weight shipped to market is significantly less than the weight of raw materials. A third element causing plants to be located near raw materials is the perishability of the materials. Many agricultural canning and freezing processes are examples. The great canning and freezing complex in central New Jersey, with its vast fresh fruit and vegetable acreages and large processing centers, illustrates this condition. To some unmeasurable extent, this location factor is offset by technological improvement in transportation equipment, for example, refrigerated cars and trucks.

In summary, several major forces influence transfer costs for particular industries, thereby making the point of least transfer cost one in close proximity to the source of raw materials. These forces are: (1) great loss of weight in raw materials during processing or production, (2) availability of raw materials for extractive industries, and (3) perishability of the raw material.

---

[7] Webber, op. cit., pp. 11–13.

[8] For example, about one sixth of the weight of sugar beets is retained in the extracted sugar. This is also important in cane sugar production; the mature cane is about 10 per cent fiber, 18 per cent sugar, and 72 per cent water. Stanley Vance, *American Industries* (Englewood Cliffs, N. J.: Prentice-Hall, Inc., 1955), p. 557.

Market-Oriented Industries. Industries that add weight during the production of finished products, experience large differentials in rates between raw materials and finished products, or produce a highly perishable finished product tend to locate plants near the market.[9]

A typical weight-gaining process is found in the beverage industry. Water, a major ingredient in the final product, causes substantial weight gains during production. Because adequate water supplies are found in most potential locations, it is economically desirable to ship concentrates rather than finished products. The weight added to the final product by the addition of water causes transfer costs to be lowest when it is added near the market.[10]

It is interesting to note that in the total marketing effort of the firm, advertising may somewhat modify the impact of transfer cost factors. If advertising can develop a product image that commands a higher price, this increased revenue may absorb the added transfer expense associated with a location at a point distant from the market. This is of particular importance to firms selling to a national market in which the production process does not allow the use of concentrated syrups. In the beer industry, for example, the accepted meaning of a "premium beer" is that it sells at a price above that of locally brewed products. Although there may indeed be quality difference, it is not the only foundation for classifying a beer as premium for marketing purposes. However, the basic market orientation rule is not greatly influenced by this special case. If concentrates can be employed, the location impact of advertising may be channeled toward more productive sources while lower transfer rates are enjoyed. Primary examples of such physical distribution decisions are the policies followed by the major soft drink producers.

Even when weight differentials between raw materials and finished products are negligible, the plant may be attracted to a market location. A general characteristic of rates is that lower rates are placed upon cruder materials, with the rate increasing as the product reaches final stages of fabrication.[11] Therefore, transfer rates tend to increase with the stage of manufacture. Historically, this condition reflects the value of the service principle in rate making. That is, in some loose way it was assumed that the higher the value a commodity could command, the more easily it could absorb a higher freight rate. The monopoly position enjoyed by the railroads up to the 1930s allowed such discrimination. Newer modes of transportation in competition with the railroads have impaired the railroad's ability to continue such practices. Value of service in modern rate-making theory refers to the rate that may be charged by a competing form of transport equivalent service. Under this new concept, the spread between raw-materials rates and finished-product rates is likely to diminish in the future.

---

[9] There is considerable confusion in current literature regarding whether perishability, service, and so on are location forces requiring a market orientation as a result of transfer expense, or location forces requiring a market orientation owing to consumer preferences. Unquestionably, both forces are important. A clear separation could be obtained only by studying specific industrial location problems.

[10] In some cases where other than "any quantity" rates prevail, for example, if rates in carload lots are lower than rates on less-than-carload lots, it may be possible to increase weight without increasing total costs. Furthermore, within a limited range, increased weights may decrease cost. See Locklin, op. cit., pp. 73 and 78.

[11] Ibid.

To the extent that this differential diminishes, such discrimination will become of lesser consequence in plant location.

If the final product is characterized by extreme perishability, there may be additional reasons why a market-oriented location should be selected. Special handling and the requirement for extreme speed may tend to increase the cost of transferring commodities such as baked goods, ice cream, and delicatessen foods. Under such conditions, production close to markets minimizes such transfer expense.

In summary, transfer forces pulling plant locations to a market proximity are: (1) weight gains during production, (2) differential freight rates between raw materials and finished products, and (3) perishability of the finished product.

Location at Other Points. A third group of industries traditionally has been labeled "foot-loose." This is because the transfer costs related to their particular manufacturing process allow selection of a plant location either at markets, at raw materials, or at an intermediate point. If a particular industry is truly-foot-loose, transfer costs may play a small role in determining plant location. For example, research and development firms are quite independent of the transfer forces under consideration.

But this is not the situation for all the firms that select plant sites at points separated from raw materials or markets. In some special cases, a plant located at an intermediate point represents the least-cost transfer location. The earlier discussion illustrating why plants are attracted to materials or markets was based upon the assumption that freight expense for a through movement was less than the expense incurred from movements to and from an intermediate point. Although this is normally true, there are some notable exceptions.

Probably the best-known exception to the general rule is the granting of in-transit privileges by the transport companies. The most widely utilized in-transit privileges are milling and fabrication. In both cases, the raw material may be shipped to a production point, then to final destination, at a combined cost slightly higher than the through rate. Utilization of this artificial removal of the "diseconomy" of short hauls is particularly influential when the pull of the materials and the pull of the market are otherwise almost equal. Examples of in-transit privileges can be found in the grain and steel industries. In-transit privileges allow management considerably more freedom in the selection of plant sites. The net effect of in-transit privileges is to promote the dispersion of industry.[12]

Intermediate location may also stem from the use of transshipment points. Location at transshipment points can be highly beneficial to industries processing raw materials which have low transport costs into final products normally associated with high transport costs. In such cases location at junction points may greatly reduce aggregate transport costs. Water facilities are among the cheapest methods of movement for the transport of bulky raw materials. Processing may then take place during the rehandling operation. This has the

---

[12] For more detailed discussions, see Martin Beckman, *Location Theory* (New York: Random House, 1968); James T. Kreafsey, *Transportation Economic Analysis* (Lexington, Mass.: Lexington Books, 1975); P. Dicken and P. E. Lloyd, *Location in Space: A Theoretical Approach to Economic Geography* (New York: Harper & Row, Publishers, 1972); and Edward J. Taaffe and Howard L. Gauthier, Jr., *Geography of Transportation* (Englewood Cliffs, N. J.: Prentice-Hall, Inc., 1973).

net effect of reducing unnecessary rehandling cost. Location at such junction points means that raw materials may move via water transportation, and finished products may be shipped via the cheapest satisfactory means of reaching the market. The importance of Pittsburgh and Youngstown as steel centers may be attributed in part to the availability of water transportation facilities.

Additional factors that pull plants to intermediate locations result from the need to utilize several raw materials or serve several different markets. A firm that utilizes a number of raw materials in processing can usually realize lowest transfer costs by locating at collection points. A collection point is a location that has minimum aggregate accumulation costs for various raw materials. On the other hand, a distribution point is a location that has minimum distribution costs to various markets. When one material or one market cannot be identified as the primary determinant of lowest transport costs, an acceptable compromise location at intermediate least-cost points may be the alternative.

In summary, if an industry can be categorized as truly foot-loose, plants may be located at any point, and transfer costs may not be a dominant location element. Particular industries tend to locate plants at intermediate points, depending upon certain economic forces. In these special cases, transfer costs will be minimized at an intermediate location.

Distorting Influences. The transfer factors thus far indicated combine to point out the one best location that results in lowest total transfer costs for each plant. Several factors may act to displace the least-cost location, based only on minimum transfer costs. Processing costs, competition, and intangible elements that displace this location will be considered shortly.

At this point, some additional transfer factors of an institutional nature must be considered. One such element is simply the availability of transportation facilities. Extensive industrial development of the northeastern United States may be attributed in part to this condition. At one time, no geographical point within this region was farther than 10 miles from a railroad.[13] The influence of topography and its effect upon transportation facilities cannot be overemphasized. Waterways are restricted to rivers, valleys, lakes, bays, and relatively level areas where canals can be constructed. Other natural barriers influence the character of various modes of transportation. The transportation network is a powerful element that limits the availability of locations to points along the current configuration of transfer routes.

Rate discrimination among commodities and geographic areas will also modify location decisions. Utilization of base-point pricing or uniform blanket rates may completely distort the influences of transportation costs. In addition, rate policies of the various carriers can influence the location of industries. Although rates are subject to regulation, the point must be kept in mind that effective rates are set by the carrier. Close proximity to facilities does not necessarily mean lowest rates. Another important point is that published rates do not necessarily reflect the rate at which freight actually moves. It is necessary to make a detailed study of rates under which relevant commodities actually move rather than to accept published rates.

In conclusion, transfer costs as location factors can attract plants to the point of raw materials, or of markets, or to some intermediate point. Which prevails

[13] Locklin, op. cit., p. 49.

will depend upon the service necessary to meet individual market requirements and the cost of achieving this service at alternative locations. Because of the general importance of transfer costs in plant location, techniques that minimize this factor offer convenient starting points for the solution of location problems.

Production Costs

Production costs consist of all expenses necessary to convert raw materials into finished products. The production costs related to any given manufacturing process are geographically variable. Such geographical differences may be directly traced to forces of immobility. To the extent that any factor necessary for production of a product is mobile, it will tend to move to the geographical area of greatest reward.[14] From the viewpoint of production costs, the most economical location is one that combines the cheapest critical immobile factors with the necessary array of inexpensive mobile factors. Major production costs may be grouped into three categories, each of which is, in varying degrees, an important location factor. These are: (1) rent, (2) labor, and (3) power. Each of these is discussed next.

Rent. In broad perspective, rent includes the following production costs: land, taxes, and capital.

Land Cost. Land prices may reflect wide regional differences. These cost differences result from the immobile characteristics of land and the wide variation in the natural endowment of individual sites. Variations in costs among specific sites stem primarily from scarcity. The general rule is that the more intensive the demand for land in a given area, the greater will be the cost. Normally, land cost diminishes as distance increases from the city center. Although the cost of land within the central city may be high, it usually offers certain economies that offset this high purchase price. Among these advantages are more adequate transport supply and a more flexible labor market. The price of a parcel of land must, therefore, be considered in light of other location advantages it may provide.

For any manufacturer, there are two classes of plant sites. First, sites with existing structures may be purchased or rented. Although vacant plants are found in abundance, the adaptability to specific location requirements may be limited. Because the average life of a real estate improvement is often in excess of 20 years, this durability results in a standing stock of plant facilities that have limited adaptability to individual tenants. The second alternative is to purchase vacant land. Construction normally requires a substantial capital outlay that tends to bind the firm to a permanent location, thus decreasing mobility. Whether to rent or buy is primarily a financial question to be considered in light of company policy.

Tax Cost. The influence of tax cost on location decisions is elusive, to say the least. Common knowledge dictates that a firm will attempt to locate at the point of least aggregate tax cost. It also follows that the 50 bodies of state tax laws, not

---

[14] Hoover adequately summarizes the influence of mobility on location in the following quote: "The price of a freely mobile factor would be the same everywhere and would not affect the location of production or other factors at all." See Hoover, op. cit., p. 69.

to mention uncounted community ordinances, will render distinctly different tax assessments in various geographical areas. Yet empirical studies point out that tax costs are, at best, relatively unimportant, secondary influences in location. Greenhut reviews four studies, which all agree that the incentives offered by lower taxes were not the determining factors in locating industries.[15] The location influence attributed to taxes was concluded to be of primary concern only in selecting between various sites within a particular area. Taxes may play a minor role in the decision to relocate, but the combined role of these and other costs casts the influence. Tax costs are especially influential when political boundaries, such as state lines, separate the communities under consideration. In addition, taxes are primary cost factors for firms with a high proportion of assets which are taxable under state and local ordinances. For example, if a firm requires a large acreage of land to undertake production, property taxes may become important location elements. In such cases, the firm tends to move toward areas offering comparatively lower property tax levies.

Capital Cost. The cost of capital is an important factor in plant location, but this does not mean that the manufacturer must be geographically near the source of funds. Capital is the most mobile of the elements influencing location. The major significance of capital rests upon availability and cost. For a business to grow, it must have ready access to capital at reasonable cost. Neither of these requirements is directly related to location. Availability is more nearly connected to the financial status of the firm requesting loans and the character of executives employed by the firm than it is to location. The cost of capital is a direct result of the money market, although this, too, may depend upon the intrinsic character of the firm. Historically, capital has been considered an influential factor in location. Today, financial requirements are rarely, if ever, critical determinants. The decline of the influence of capital upon location is generally attributed to the rise in mobility of capital funds.

Labor. The location influence of labor affects manufacturing firms in different ways. These variations tend to pull the location of particular industries toward the geographical point that will best satisfy labor requirements. Although the cumulative influence of labor upon location is difficult to measure, for some companies it is the greatest single influence motivating plant relocation.

Since there are great variations in labor requirements among industries, a number of firms are attracted by low labor rates. Traditionally, wage levels in the United States have been lowest in the southern states. Accordingly, many firms that are labor intensive and operate on low margins locate in the South to take advantage of large numbers of low-wage, unskilled workers. Wages paid are important determinants of location but only one aspect of the labor-cost factor. From the viewpoint of the employer, productivity, skill requirements, stability, and labor legislation also must be considered.

Location advantages of an area that offers low wage rates may be offset by low productivity rates. Hoover points out that high wage rates do not necessarily attract job seekers or repel employers.[16] Low production costs

[15] Melvin L. Greenhut, *Plant Location in Theory and Practice* (Chapel Hill, N. C.: University of North Carolina Press, 1956), p. 126. For a technical analysis, see also Melvin L. Greenhut, *A Theory of the Firm in Economic Space* (Austin, Tex.: Lone Star Publishers, Inc., 1971).

[16] Hoover, op. cit., p. 103.

may be found in areas with relatively high wage rates. The essential concern for the manufacturer is the productivity of labor and labor's response to maintaining low overhead costs. Hot climates are normally considered areas of low productivity. Although this statement has not been substantiated, to the extent that it is true, the low-wage advantage of the South may be offset by decreased productivity.

Firms that require highly skilled labor normally locate in close proximity to the areas that offer such skill. When other critical factors force manufacturers to move from areas of skilled labor, this loss may be offset by bringing skilled operators to train the local unskilled labor force. It is possible to offset the lack of skilled workers, but this is a costly and time-consuming process.

Regardless of the planning and analysis taken prior to locating in a particular area, low labor costs will not be realized if the local labor force proves unstable. High labor turnover is expensive. Retraining and loss of productivity are cost factors that cannot be recovered easily.

Labor laws can also cause cost differences between geographical areas. Virtually all industries are subject to state labor laws. Workmen's Compensation insurance rates normally are applied against payrolls at rates varying substantially among the states. Although not a limiting factor to some firms, compensation charges may represent a substantial cost to the manufacturer when a large work force is employed.

The size of the necessary labor force can also limit location possibilities. Those manufacturers who require large work forces normally are restricted to densely populated areas. In any community, the available supply of labor is basically represented by the workers unemployed. Response of labor to geographical wage differences is often restricted because of movement expense. Although the mobility of labor may be somewhat "sticky," migration can materially affect the local labor supply in times of increased demand.

Power. Historically, the location of power resources has been an outstanding factor in the selection of plant sites. But power, like capital and labor, has gained mobility throughout the years. For some early industries, the most attractive sites were located at the fall lines of navigable streams. At this point, water could be harnessed to turn power wheels at minimum cost.

Technological developments have altered the location influence of both power and fuel. Although some plants are still attracted by the availability of cheap and abundant power, in most industries the cost of power as a percentage of total cost is small. Aluminum reduction plants are examples of firms attracted to water-power sites. Natural gas, in the production of glass, and accessibility to coal and coke in steel production are other examples of power-oriented industries. Because of more or less uniform availability, the location of the average plant will not be chosen solely because of power or fuel cost differentials.

In summary, the location factors of rent, labor, and power can influence the cost structure of a plant located at different geographical points. To the degree that production factors are immobile, costs will vary geographically. Thus, to find the point of least production cost for a given plant, it becomes necessary to evaluate alternative cost structures resulting from different potential locations. To a large extent, these geographical cost differences result from forces of external economies of location. Therefore, prior to concluding the discussion of location cost factors, attention is directed to external economies of location.

External Economies of Location

External economies of location refer to cost reductions that result from the geographical clustering of plants.[17] The forces of concentration explain why the least-cost locations for many plants tend to congregate within a few industrial areas. For particular plants such cost reductions may be direct or indirect. Direct cost reductions evolve from the increased demand for interchangeable factors of production and transportation resulting when a large number of plants locate within a single industrial complex. Indirect cost reductions stem from other benefits realized from location in close proximity to an industrial population.

Examples of direct cost reductions are: (1) lower total transfer costs resulting from better transport facilities, (2) reduced production costs due to a ready supply of technically trained labor, and (3) specialization of supplies allowing lower unit costs for materials, supplies, and services. These direct cost reductions explain to a large extent the forces underlying least-cost analysis.

Indirect cost reductions are not as easily qualified. Greenhut refers to this category of influences as a group of generally neglected location forces.[18] He points out that indirect cost-reducing factors may be separated from basic cost factors, because they emphasize the relationship between physical distance and costs in terms other than those of transfer and labor costs. Insurance is an example of a cost factor reduced by locating in an industrial community. A particular type of insurance may be available because of better protective facilities or familiarity of an insurance company with local hazards. Although the cost of insurance is a direct expense, the reduction in cost resulting from excellent protection represents the influence of indirect economies of concentration. Advertising costs can also be reduced by location in highly populated areas. Lower expense may be incurred to achieve equal population coverage.

The combined influence of external economies of location is to attract plants to industrial complexes. Individual firms attempt to locate plants in close proximity to other plants in order to enjoy mutual benefits of spatial concentration. To a large extent these same forces may influence a particular firm to centralize individual plants in order to realize maximum benefits from external economies.[19]

Intangible Location Factors

A final group of location forces influencing site selection is often classified as intangible factors. Intangible factors may be divided into two categories for discussion purposes. The first category contains cost-revenue influencing

---

[17] External economies of location, as the phrase is used here, are similar to the forces referred to by Weber as agglomerative. He defined an agglomerative force as "An aggregate cost-reducing influence resulting from spatial interdependence." In external economies of location, economies of spatial interdependence are considered from the viewpoint of direct and indirect reductions. The original discussion of agglomerative forces did not develop this distinction in great detail. See Carl J. Friedrich (trans.), *Alfred Weber's Theory of Location of Industries* (Chicago: University of Chicago Press, 1928), p. 134.

[18] Greenhut, *Plant Location in Theory and Practice*, op. cit., p. 168.

[19] Hoover expands this consideration to include individual benefits realized by centralizing all plants owned by an individual firm. See Hoover, op. cit., p. 80.

factors that result from personal contacts of company executives. The second group is personal preferences that influence site selection.

Cost-Revenue Influencing Factors

Plant locations may be altered to capitalize on the personal contacts and influences of management. Such factors may directly influence the availability of materials, capital, and sales. The availability of capital may be related to personal friendships and confidences that exist between management and creditors. Special requests for rush materials or spare parts in order to eliminate production bottlenecks may be given urgent consideration if friendly relations exist. Last of all, additional sales may be realized by community contacts developed by executives.

All of these intangible factors influence the cost-revenue structure of a particular firm. Without this aspect of personal consideration, location forces are impersonal results of cost and competitive factors. With consideration of personal influence, locations may be altered to increase profitability. Obviously, this influence is paramount to small manufacturing firms, which in some cases may find their only economic justification based upon such personal relationships.

Personal Preferences

Personal preferences influence plant location as a result of adjustments made to accommodate human needs and desires. A particular community may be selected because it offers desirable types of recreation, housing, or educational facilities. A particular region may be selected because it offers an enjoyable climate. Although such factors cannot be conveniently analyzed within the framework of economic analysis, the fact remains that purely personal considerations can be important determinants of plant location. Intangible considerations alter the ideal economic location. The freedom available in selecting sites to fit intangible specifications is somewhat narrow if profit-maximization principles are strictly employed. For any particular firm, these factors may be influential only in selecting between communities located within close proximity to each other.

GENERAL PROCEDURE

Plant location procedure consists of an organized development of location factors within a working framework. Selection of a plant site is a compromise among various location forces. Because location is conceivably possible at an infinite number of geographical points, the final decision requires an orderly elimination of undesirable locations until the one best plant site is selected. Fortunately, the natural and logical process of plant location provides a satisfactory location procedure, which consists of plant analysis and field analysis. Table III–1 presents a detailed checklist. This section discusses general procedure to plant location.

The location decision is a complex process that is difficult to standardize because of the numerous factors both quantitative and qualitative. The trade-offs vary by industry and also by management groups.

TABLE III–I   Plant Location Checklist

I. Plant analysis
   A. Logistical analysis
      1. Logistical systems analysis
         a. Current production points
         b. Current warehouse locations
      2. Long-term expansion plans and policies
      3. Primary transfer requirements
      4. Modes of transportation capable of satisfying transfer demands
         a. Raw-material movement
         b. Finished-products movement
   B. Production analysis
      1. Raw-material requirements
         a. Present point of purchase
         b. Quantity purchased
         c. Alternative purchase points
      2. Characterisitics of production process
         a. General factors
         b. Special factors dependent upon location
      3. Labor requirements
         a. Number of skilled and unskilled workers
         b. Degree of labor organization acceptable
         c. Number of people to be transferred
      4. Power and utility requirements
   C. Market analysis
      1. Geographical location of major market segments
      2. Competition analysis
         a. Production locations
         b. Major markets serviced and relative strength in each
   D. Managerial location preferences
   E. Location specifications for new plant
      1. Logistical requirements
      2. Production requirements
      3. Market requirements
      4. Managerial preferences
   F. Cost Analysis at present manufacturing location
      1. Transportation
      2. Production
II. Field analysis
   A. Regional analysis
      1. Least-cost transfer location
         a. Arrival at alternative points using different raw-material purchase points
      2. Selection of region(s) to be given detailed analysis
      3. Analysis of location factors variable between states
         a. Legal structure
         b. Political environment
         c. Corporate laws and tax structures
         d. Labor laws and labor conditions
         e. State financial status
         f. Industries currently located in state
         g. Cost-of-living index
      4. Selection of state(s) to be evaluated in detail based upon regional analysis and location specifications

TABLE III–1 *(Continued)*

B. Community analysis
    1. General description of community(ties)
    2. Income trends
    3. Consumer characteristics
    4. Retail sales trends
    5. Population and growth patterns
    6. Industrial climate
        a. Existing industry
        b. Local laws
        c. Labor situation
        d. Community attitude toward industry
        e. Amount of cooperation available
    7. Municipal services
        a. Water systems
        b. Waste systems
        c. Solid waste disposal systems
    8. Ecological factors
        a. State regulations
        b. Local regulations
        c. Impact statement requirements
        d. Conditions of sites for the planned operations
    9. Community utilities
        a. Gas
        b. Oil
        c. Power
        d. Other
    10. Quality of life factors
        a. Appearance of community
        b. Cost of living
        c. Housing conditions
        d. Educational facilities
        e. Recreational facilities
        f. Character and quality of local government
        g. Health and welfare
        h. Police and fire protection
        i. Cultural opportunities
        j. Religious
        k. Climate
    11. Selection of community(ties) on the basis of location specification to be
        evaluated for a plant site
C. Work force environment
    1. Availability of required labor
    2. Wages and hours
    3. Benefits package in area
    4. Union/management relationships
    5. Productivity
    6. Human resource policies
    7. Training opportunities
    8. Commuting patterns
    9. Legislative environment
    10. Relocation assistance available
    11. Sources to assist in finding labor

TABLE III–1 (*Continued*)

    D. Transportation services
        1. Rail service
          a. General
          b. At the potential sites
        2. Truck service
          a. Highway system
          b. Trucking service
          c. Other highway services
        3. Air service
          a. Airport services
          b. Air carriers
        4. Other services
          a. Water transportation
          b. Pipelines
    E. Materials and services
        1. Material availability
        2. General supplier services
        3. Technical services
    F. Site analysis
        1. Geo considerations
          a. Size
          b. Soil content
          c. Drainage
        2. Utility Availability
        3. Availability of required transportation facilities
        4. Costs
          a. Procurement
          b. Landscaping, etc.
        5. Selection of a site(s) based upon location specifications
    G. Specific site analysis
        1. Type of site
        2. Topographic considerations
        3. Geographic factors
        4. Geologic considerations
        5. Availability of utilities
        6. Transportation services
        7. Costs
          a. Procurement
          b. Landscaping
          c. Improvements
        8. Zoning
        9. Deed covenants
          a. Land use
          b. Impact statement
          c. Space standards
      10. Buildings
          a. Buildings available
          b. Leasing
III. Final location selection
    A. Proposed Costs at alternative sites
        1. Continuing production and distribution costs
        2. Initial establishment costs
    B. Comparative analysis of proposed costs with costs experienced at current location
    C. Final selection of new location based upon least-cost comparison

The location decisions are made by a management team. The team usually includes representatives from operations, engineering, real estate development, logistics, and human resources.

PLANT ANALYSIS

The first step in applying location theory to practice is an appropriate evaluation of the three categories of location factors as they apply to the individual plant location problem. This stage of evaluation is referred to as plant analysis. For plants currently operating, one purpose of plant analysis is to determine if relocation is desirable. With the assumption that a new location is desirable, careful analysis of all location elements will determine what specifications the new location must meet. Similarly for new plants, analysis must be completed to isolate relevant location specifications.

It is during plant analysis that location theory can be applied to the specifics of an individual problem. The critical cost factors for the new plant should be identified, and a detailed cost study of current operations should be completed. This will allow comparative cost analysis between the current location and potential new sites. In most cases identification of cost factors requires extensive data collection. The net result is ideally a number of specifications that can be transposed into dollar costs. For example, the amount of labor required, the point of raw-material procurement, the power requirements, and the many other factors noted earlier should be quantified in order to guide field research. A detailed study of market areas and competitive forces should be completed in order to determine what general geographic areas appear to contain a profit-maximizing location. Finally, the impact of intangible elements should be given complete analysis.

The final result of extensive plant analysis is a set of location specifications designed to guide the process of site selection. If one or two location factors evolve as critical, they should be identified during plant analysis. Only after the location problem has been analyzed in the magnitude here indicated is field analysis ready to be undertaken.

FIELD ANALYSIS

Field analysis consists of three steps necessary to reduce the geographic area of concern to a few potential locations. Evaluation of location alternatives should be completed at the regional, community, and site levels of consideration. Field analysis procedure is not viewed as a limiting process. Selection of the one best community need not be made prior to conducting a search for satisfactory factory sites. Several search areas can be considered simultaneously, including their alternative communities and respective factory locations.

Individual states are not considered focal points of attention. Without doubt, some states offer advantages for location, while others have distinct disadvantages. But the potential geographic territory included in a search area is indifferent to political boundaries. Consequently, several different states may be considered simultaneously as location prospects.

Regional Evaluation

The first step in selecting a specific site from a potential geographic area is regional evaluation. The task at this stage of selection is to determine which areas qualify for detailed field examination. The total area under consideration will vary according to the specifications of individual firms. In cases where inexpensive labor is the primary location influence, examination may be limited to only a few regions. If proximity to markets is a primary requirement, regional possibilities will be in the general locale of major market areas. Competitive or intangible influences may limit the regional areas to just a few. Whatever the specifications, the first step is to identify the geographic areas that meet the broad location requirements.

The second step is to determine which of the alternative regions will be most economical for achieving location objectives. Consideration begins with the assumption that all costs are regionally variable. Each potential region is evaluated by examining the expense of satisfying location requirements. The differential in cost between alternative regions will vary with particular industries. For any particular firm, regional evaluation will identify geographic areas that will satisfy location requirements at least cost. The regions that present possibilities for most economic operation become the search areas for particular communities.

Community Evaluation

Up to this point, the firm considering plant location has, by the process of elimination, selected a few general areas within which communities capable of satisfying location requirements must be identified. Community evaluation should include the availability of necessary facilities. Such factors as availability of utilities, adequate labor force, and transportation must be examined. If a particular community appears to have the necessary characteristics in this respect, a more detailed investigation is undertaken.

Detailed investigation consists of measuring all facilities in terms of potential costs of manufacturing. If all facilities are available at a reasonable cost, investigation is extended to include intangible characteristics of the community. The character of local politics and the community's attitude toward industrial development must be considered. Of primary concern is the question of compatibility between the firm and the community: Will the proposed building and manufacturing operations meet with the approval of the community? Not understanding all implications of such intangible factors can result in a serious and expensive mistake on the part of the firm. The firm must also consider if the community fulfills the environmental desires of the personnel to be transferred. Living conditions must be examined in terms of such factors as recreational facilities, cost of living, and adequate housing. If the community offers incentives, complete details should be examined. Analysis of these and all other factors of importance will point out which communities are the best potential locations for conducting manufacturing operations. Evaluation of potential sites still remains.

Site Evaluation

Evaluation of available sites represents the last step in plant location. Only if the community meets all other requirements will the search be necessary.

Selection of a site to construct a new plant can normally be completed in all industrially minded communities. In location problems where an already constructed plant is sought, evaluation of sites may be necessary prior to community delineation.

In selecting a site, attention must once again be directed to cost analysis and consideration of intangibles. In addition, physical requirements and topographic features must be considered. Naturally, the direct cost of procurement is one governing factor. Other costs, such as obtaining rail sidings, utility hook-ups, and highway access, also require evaluation. From the intangible aspect, the firm must determine if the neighborhood is consistent with the desired image of the firm. For some firms, close proximity with "linked" industries may be desirable.

Only after satisfactory plant sites have been determined is the location process near completion. At this point, the firm's executives are armed with the necessary facts to make an intelligent location decision. Sufficient information should now be available to determine the area, community, and site that offer the best plant location.

Because all location factors have been under consideration throughout plant and field analysis, the forces of cost, market competition, and intangible location factors have guided the selection procedure. To aid in selecting between alternative sites, comparative cost analysis is helpful. The total costs of operation at each potential site should be compared to total costs experienced at the old location. Such cost analysis will clearly point out the benefits gained from relocation.

Software Evaluation Guide

The significant advances in information technology along with the increasing demand require that distribution management become more aware and involved in decisions regarding software selection.

The objective of this appendix is to aid this evaluation by providing guidelines concerning software features and capabilities. The ideal software evaluation process consists of a five-step procedure. These steps are: (1) functional definition, (2) importance measures, (3) alternative identification, (4) rating, and (5) selection and negotiation. The following discussion briefly describes each.

Functional Definition

The first step is to define functions and features to be included in the software system. The functions include the logistical activities that the system must perform along with the features it should incorporate when performing the activities. The feature list should be developed using the knowledge of those who must work with the system and descriptions of requirements currently available. Table IV–1 provides an extensive, although not necessarily exhaustive, list of modules and features that should be included in a contemporary logistical information system. The features are segmented into modules of: (1) order entry, (2) order processing, (3) inventory accounting, (4) accounts payable, (5) accounts receivable, (6) purchasing, (7) forecasting, (8) transportation, (9) warehouse management, and (10) other general features. When defining the features, input should be obtained from the functional managers, the functional operations personnel, and the information systems people.

Importance Measurement

The second step requires the importance ranking for each function and feature. The importance of each feature should be established by a joint task force of logistical and information systems managers. Each feature should be rated on an importance scale from 1 to 3. A rating of 3 implies that the function or feature is absolutely necessary, while a rating of 1 implies that the feature is nice but not necessary. The features' importance rating should be entered in the appropriate column in Table IV–1.

Alternative Identification

The third step is to identify the alternative software that should be considered. Alternatives can be identified through vendor information as well as through other software resources such as those identified in Table 13–8. The vendors should be requested to provide information that is detailed enough to support a critical review of the features and capabilities of each package.

TABLE IV–1 Logistical Information System Functional Features List

Feature	Importance Rating	Package Rating	Score
I. Order management			
1. On-line entry			
2. On-line inquiry			
3. Order edit and verification			
4. Order modification			
5. Order acknowledgment			
6. Order status inquiry and modification			
7. Inventory availability check			
8. Multiple ship to locations			
9. Order pricing			
10. Credit checking			
11. Price and discount extensions			
12. Returned-order processing			
13. Multiple-order types			
14. Multiple-order release/ship dates			
15. Hold for future order processing			
16. Assign order source			
17. Allow for multiple-order sources			
II. Order processing			
1. Inventory reservation			
2. Update inventory status			
3. Create back-order			
4. Process back-order			
5. Generate pick labels and documentation			
6. Shipment verification			
7. Generate invoice			
III. Warehouse operations			
1. Assign storage locations			
2. Handle bin and bulk storage			
3. Storage location management			
4. Initiate stock retrieval			
5. Assist warehouse scheduling			
6. Generate warehouse performance measures			
IV. Transportation			
1. Shipment consolidation			
2. Shipment routing			
3. Dispatching			
4. Vehicle loading			
5. Shipment tracing and expediting			
6. Shipment rating			
7. Freight payment			
V. Forecasting			
1. Forecast technique alternatives			
2. Forecast data maintenance			

TABLE IV–1 (*Continued*)

Feature	Importance Rating	Package Rating	Score
3. Forecast data filtering			
4. Forecast parameter selection			
5. Weekly forecast time brackets			
6. Promotional forecast considerations			
7. Bottom-up forecast generation			
8. Top-down forecast generation			
9. Product group analysis			
VI. Inventory management			
1. Provide alternative inventory management logics			
2. Compute inventory parameters			
3. Provide summary analysis by warehouse and product			
4. Initiate replenishment orders			
5. Track replenishment orders			
6. Project inventory requirements by location			
VII. Inventory accounting			
1. Maintain inventory balance for			
a. Customer orders			
b. Warehouse transfers			
c. Receipts			
d. Returns			
e. Shrinkage			
2. Inventory aging			
3. Stock rotation			
4. Inventory costing			
5. Lot control			
6. Cycle counting			
VIII. General features			
1. Multiple currencies			
2. Multiple warehouse and echelons			
3. Audit trail			

Rating

The fourth step is a rating of the individual software based on extenated ability to meet each of the prescribed features. For each feature, the review should rate each alternative on a scale from 0 to 2. A value of 0 implies that the software does not support a specific feature, while a 2 implies it performs exactly as specified in the feature.

The overall rating for each alternative is determined by multiplying the importance rating for a specific feature by the specific supplier rating to obtain the score. For example, if the enterprise required an on-line entry and inquiry system, the importance rating for this feature would be 3. If a particular alternative provided on-line inquiry but did not support on-line entry, the rating might be 1. The vendor's resulting score for this feature is 3 (3 × 1). The software overall score is the sum of the scores for individual features. The alternative with the highest overall score is the one that best meets the needs of the firm.

Selection and Negotiation

While the above analysis provides a quantitative evaluation of alternative software, the final task requires a qualitative evaluation of the software and its supplier. This task requires that management consider the system features and characteristics that do not allow for a quantitative evaluation and incorporate these aspects into the analysis. Elements that might be included include the language the software is written in, the track record, familiarity with the software and/or hardware, and software flexibility. Once these qualitative elements have been included in the analysis, management must select the best alternative and negotiate with the supplier.

This appendix provides a brief overview of a software evaluation process. There are texts and seminars that provide a more in-depth review of the process. Table IV-1 offers an extensive list of desirable functionality and features.

Simchip—A Manual Logistical Game

Simchip is a logistical management decision simulation based on four firms supplying five market areas with potato chips. Each firm produces potato chips in 1-pound bags and distributes to the five areas in the week following production. The overall objective of the simulation is to make maximum gross distribution profits for a time period specified by the umpire. Product sales result in revenue generation. Warehouse and inventory costs, production costs, transportation costs, and distribution costs result in expense generation.

The purpose of Simchip is to demonstrate the basic interrelationship between several important elements of logistics. The game has not been designed to present all possible alternatives in a dynamic setting, but to focus on the key elements of the task to provide important background perspective for the student.

In order to focus on the logistics task, some simplifying assumptions have been made. These assumptions include a simplified market structure, a limited product line, and the elimination of promotional and advertising decisions.

The explanation of Simchip is divided into three general parts. The first part, entitled "Information on Key Variables," presents detailed data on all the variables used in the simulation. The second part, entitled "Explanation of Forms and Procedures Used by the Player," explains the forms and procedures used in actually playing the game. The third section illustrates the forms utilized by the players in recording decisions.

The game may be played for as many periods as specified by the umpire. The reader should carefully review all materials in the appendix and thoroughly understand the simulation procedure before completing any decision forms.

INFORMATION ON KEY VARIABLES

Market Data

Consumer demand for the product is the key determinant in the firm's sales. Each firm starts the simulation with an equal share of the total market. Consumer demand based on past sales history fluctuates ±15 per cent. As the simulation develops, each firm's market share will vary depending on the efficiency of production and physical distribution.

Raw Material

	Cost	Package	Pounds/ Cubic Foot
Potatoes	$ 8.42/cwt	100-lb bags	6.66
Salt	3.470/cwt	100-lb bags	12.50
Oil	32.42/drum	50-gal drum, 400 lb	44.44
1-lb bags	44.00/M	1,000 bags, 260 lb	9.64

Warehouse and Inventory

Each firm has two types of warehouse facilities available for raw materials storage.

Private

12,500 square feet, 20 feet clear.
80% usable cube = 200,000 cubic feet.
Warehouse overhead charge = $2,866/week.
Warehouse operation = throughput = total receipts + total production (from status report) ÷ 2 × $0.32/cwt.

Public

A public warehouse will be used after 200,000 cubic feet have been placed in a private warehouse.

Cubic Feet	Cost/Cubic Foot
0–100,000	$0.030
100,000–500,000	0.020
500,000 and above	0.010

(*Note*: Cost includes delivery from warehouse to factory.)

Raw-Material and Finished-Inventory Carrying Cost

Ending raw-material inventory (at cost) × 20% ÷ 52.
Finished-goods inventory carrying cost = waste × unit wholesale price
× 30% ÷ 52.

Production Capacity

Capacity

Each firm operates a cooking plant at its home market location (see Figure V–1). This plant has a cooking capacity of 20,000 pounds/day normal, 5,000 pounds/day overtime, and an additional 20,000 pounds by scheduling Saturday

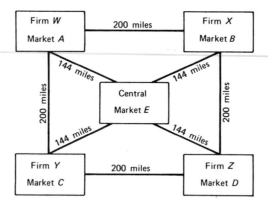

Figure V–1   Simchip 1—Market Structure

production. Production must be completed in the week prior to the following week's anticipated sales.

Production Overhead

Fixed overhead charge regardless of production—$7,500/week. A portion of this overhead is for the reusable cartons utilized in delivery.

Cooking Costs

The production of finished potato chips requires raw potatoes, oil, salt, and bags. Costs are incurred as raw materials are converted to chips.

Cooking Conversion—1,000 Pounds of Finished Chips

Potatoes (lb)	4,370	$367.940
Salt (lb)	50	1.736
Oil (lb)	400	32.420
Bags (lb)	1,000	44.000
		$446.096
	Total cost	Cost/lb
	$446.10	$0.446

Cooking Costs—Regular

Basic (lb)	lb/day	Saturday/lb
10,000	$0.440	$0.638
11,000	0.430	0.638
12,000	0.420	0.638
13,000	0.410	0.638
14,000	0.400	0.638
15,000	0.390	0.566
16,000	0.380	0.566
17,000	0.370	0.566
18,000	0.360	0.566
19,000	0.350	0.566
20,000	0.340	0.566

Cooking Costs—Overtime

Basic (lb)	Per lb
0–2,500	$0.568
2,501–5,000	0.492

Transportation Costs (Inbound Raw Materials)

Transportation of raw materials is accomplished by rail, common-carrier motor truck, and private truck. All raw materials are received from Central City.

Company Truck (No Lead Time)

	Capacity (lb)	
	Truck A	Truck B
Potatoes	60,000	24,000
Salt	50,000	20,000
Oil	96,000	38,000
Bags	10,000	4,000

	Cost	
	Truck A	Truck B
Basic	$200/week	$130/week
Per mile	$0.30	$0.20
Average mile/hour	40	45
Loading-unloading time	4 hours	4 hours
Driver's wages	$15/hour	$15 hour

Central City—Rail (2 Weeks Lead Time) (No Maximum)

0–480,000 lb	$0.30/cwt
480,000–960,000 lb	0.26/cwt
960,000–1,440,000 lb	0.25/cwt
1,440,000–any Q lb	0.24/cwt

Central City—Truck (1 Week Lead Time)

	LTL	TL
Potatoes	0–30,000 lb	30,000–50,000 lb[a]
	$1.00/cwt	$0.70/cwt
Salt	0–25,000 lb	25,000–60,000 lb[a]
	$1.10/cwt	$0.70/cwt
Oil	0–48,000 lb	48,000–96,000 lb[a]
	$0.60/cwt	$0.40/cwt
Bags	0–5,000 lb	5,000–10,000 lb[a]
	$1.70/cwt	$1.30/cwt

[a] Maximum weight/shipment.

Distribution Costs (Finished Products)

Company Truck

	Truck A	Truck B
Per mile	$0.45	$0.30
Average mile/hour	40	45
Unloading time	1 hour	1 hour
Driver's wages	$12/hour	$12/hour
Capacity		
Cartons	1,620	600
Pounds	9,720	3,600

Common Carrier

	LTL: 0–9,000 lb	TL: Over 9,000 lb
Central (144 miles)	$7.00/cwt	$6.00/cwt
Adjacent (145–200 miles)	$7.80/cwt	$6.80/cwt
Distant (over 200 miles)	$8.40/cwt	$7.60/cwt

Distribution in Market Area—Basic Cost/Market $500,000[a]

	Cost/cwt
Under 2,000	$0.54
2,001–5,000	0.52
5,001–10,000	0.50
10,001–15,000	0.48
15,001–20,000	0.46
20,000–25,000	0.44
25,001–30,000	0.42
Over 30,000	0.40

[a] The cost is added once each decision period for each market in which distribution is made. This cost represents storage in transit and distribution in the various market areas.

EXPLANATION OF FORMS AND PROCEDURES USED BY THE PLAYER

Status Report

The status report provides the basis for planning each period's actions and aids in preparing the operating statement. It is filled out by the umpire. The form contains your company's share of each market and the amount of waste you had last period. You are to assume that you will sell the amount proposed if you produce and distribute that amount to each market. The percentage share may be compared to past percentages to get an idea of your distribution in each market as compared to that of the other companies. Waste is the amount produced and distributed to each market that was not sold.

Remember, this is a simulation and your score will be determined by how well by control your logistical system. Coordination among team members is of prime importance!

Decision-Recording Form

Production Schedule

This schedule will be completed, showing production for each day and the total for the week.

Raw-Material Inventory Status

Beginning inventory and purchase orders due will be provided by the umpire at the start of the simulation. After this, you will be responsible for completing this form in duplicate and returning one copy to the umpire each period. The starting inventory will be the same figure as last period's ending inventory. Usage (obtained from the production worksheet) and receipts (obtained from the warehouse worksheet) are applied to beginning inventory to obtain ending inventory.

All new orders placed and those placed in previous periods and not received during the period are deleted.

Distribution Schedule

This schedule is provided in three parts:

Total Distribution. This form is to be filled out completely showing the market and the day of distribution. Total q will show the daily distribution; total p will show the total distribution to each market. These two totals must be equal.

Company Truck Distribution. This schedule will show your truck schedule for each day of the week and the total pounds distributed. If the truck is used to pick up raw material, the route will be entered in the market column and miles recorded. [*Example*: Your firm is located in market B. You make a raw material pickup in Central (E). Market column would show B-E-B-; miles, 288; pounds and distribution stops, blank. If you loaded your truck with 9,000 pounds of chips and delivered 4,500 to market D and 4,500 pounds to E, and then picked up the raw material, the form would be Market, B-D-E-B, miles, 488; pounds, 9,000; distribution stops, 2.]

Common-Carrier Distribution. This schedule will show the daily distribution by market and pounds when using a common carrier.

Note: The combined totals of parts 2 and 3 must equal the total distribution in part 1.

Operating Statement

The worksheets provided are cross-referenced to assist you in preparing your operating statement.

General

The decision-recording form and the operating statement will be completed and turned in to the umpire on the day announced by your instructor. Fill out these forms completely and accurately, for they are subject to audit at any time during the simulation. File each period's worksheets so that you will be able to support your figures.

STATUS REPORT

Company _____   End of Period _____

Market	Proposed demand in pounds	Per cent share last period	Waste last period in #
A			
B			
C			
D			
E			

Total   _____ _____ _____

Sales Computations:

    Total distribution in $ = distribution last period × $1.690
    Total waste in $ = waste last period × $1.690

Total Distribution Less Total Waste = Total Net Sales

    $ _____ − $ _____ = $ _____

DECISION-RECORDING FORM

Company _____   End of Period _____

Production schedule:

M	T	W	TH	F	S	S
#	#	#	#	#	#	#

Raw materials inventory status:

	Potatoes #	Oil #	Salt #	Bags #
Starting inventory				
Usage (−)				
Receipts (+)				
Ending inventory				
Over due				

#	period				
_____	_____				
_____	_____				
_____	_____				
_____	_____				
_____	_____				
_____	_____				
Total Committed					

DISTRIBUTION SCHEDULE

1. Total distribution:

	M	T	W	TH	F	S	Total(p)
Local							
Mkt							
Mkt							
Mkt							
Mkt							
Total(q)							

2. Company truck distribution:

	Truck A				Truck B				
	Routing	Miles	Pounds	Stops	Routing	Miles	Pounds	Stops	Total #
M									
T									
W									
TH									
F									
S									

Total   ___ ___ ___   ___ ___ ___

3. Common carrier distribution:

	Market	Pounds	Market	Pounds	Market	Pounds	Total #
M							
T							
W							
TH							
F							
S							

OPERATING STATEMENT

A. Sales (in Dollars) $ _____

B. Warehouse and Inventory Costs

     B-1. Warehouse overhead $ _____2866_____

     B-2. Warehouse operations $ _____

     B-3. Extra warehousing (public) $ _____

     B-4. Raw material inventory carrying cost $ _____

     B-5. Finished good inventory carrying cost $ _____

     Subtotal $ _____

C. Production Costs

     C-1. Overhead $ _____

     C-2. Cooking conversion $ _____

     C-3. Cooking costs–regular $ _____

     C-4. Cooking costs–overtime

     Subtotal $ _____

D. Transportation Costs–Inbound Raw Materials

     D-1. Company truck

         Fixed charge $ _____330.00_____

         Variable charge $ _____

     D-2. Common carrier–rail $ _____

     D-3. Common carrier–truck $ _____

     Subtotal $ _____

E. Distribution Cost–Outbound (Finished Product)

     E-1. Company truck variable $ _____

     E-2. Common carrier truck $ _____

     E-3. Distribution in market $ _____

     Subtotal $ _____

     Total Cost $ _____

     Profit for Period $ _____

WORKSHEET–WAREHOUSE AND INVENTORY COST

B-1. Warehouse Overhead (Private) $ _____

B-2. Warehouse Operations (Raw Material Handling)

    Raw Material Receipts During Period

	#	Order No.
Potatoes	_____	_____
Salt	_____	_____
Oil	_____	_____
1 # Bags	_____	_____
Total Receipts (a) _____

    Raw materials used during period (#)
    (Production worksheet) (b) _____

    Total (a) & (b) _____ ÷ 2 × .32/cwt = _____

B-3. Extra Warehousing (Public)

    Cubic ft. used during period   _____
    × Appropriate rate   _____
    Extra warehousing cost for period $ _____

B-4. Raw Material Inventory Carrying Cost

    Beginning Raw Materials Inventory

Potatoes	_____ × 8.42/cwt	= _____
Oil	_____ × 32.42/drum	= _____
Salt	_____ × 3.470/cwt	= _____
Bags	_____ × 44.00/M	= _____

    Total (a) $ _____

    Ending Raw Materials Inventory

Potatoes	_____ × 8.42/cwt	= _____
Oil	_____ × 32.42/drum	= _____
Salt	_____ × 3.470/cwt	= _____
Bags	_____ × 44.00/M	= _____

    Total (b) $ _____

    Total (a) and (b) $ _____ ÷ 2 = (c) $ _____

    (c) _____ × 20% ÷ 52 =

    Period raw material inventory carrying cost $ _____

B-5. Finished Goods Inventory Carrying Cost

    Period waste (status report) _____
    × Unit wholesale price _____ $1.690.
    $ _____ × 30% ÷ 52 =
    Period finished goods inventory carrying cost $ _____

C. Production Costs:

C-1. Overhead $ _____7500_____

C-2. Cooking Conversion

Quantity cooked this period _____ (finished)

Potatoes   _____ × \$.0842/lb = _____

Salt   _____ × \$.0347/lb = _____

Oil   _____ × \$.081/lb   = _____

Bags   _____ × \$.044/bag = _____

Total Conversion Cost _____

C-3. Cooking Costs–Regular

Quantity cooked   ×   rate/lb   = total cooking cost

M _____ × _____ = _____

T _____ × _____ = _____

W _____ × _____ = _____

TH _____ × _____ = _____

F _____ × _____ = _____

S _____ × _____ = _____

Total   _____

C-4. Cooking Cost–Overtime

Daily output in excess of 20,000 lb × rate

_____ × _____ =

_____ × _____ =

_____ × _____ =

Total   _____

D. Transportation Costs:

Inbound Raw Materials:

D-1. Company Truck   Fixed Charge \$ _____

*Total mileage per period × rate

Track A _____ × _____\$.45_____ = _____

Track B _____ × _____\$.30_____ = _____

(Driving time + loading time) × driver's wages

(_____ + _____) × \$12 = _____

Total _____

*Separate truck mileage between raw materials hauling and finished goods delivery.

D-2. Common Carrier—Rail

Total lbs	×	Rate

_____ × _____ ×

_____ × _____ ×

_____ × _____ × _____

Total _____

D-3. Common Carrier—Truck

Total Lbs/Shipment × Rate (LTL OR TL)

Potatoes _____ × _____ = _____

Salt   _____ × _____ = _____

Oil   _____ × _____ = _____

Bags   _____ × _____ = _____

Total _____

E. Distribution Cost:

Outbound Finished Product

E-1. Company Truck

*Total mileage per period × rate

Truck A _____ × _____ $.45 _____ = _____

Truck B _____ × _____ $.30 _____ = _____

Driving time + unloading time ×   drivers' wages   = _____

(_____ + _____) × $12.00   = _____

Total _____

*Separate truck mileage between raw materials hauling and finished goods delivery.

E-2. Common Carrier—Truck

Market	Pounds	×	Rate (LTL or TL)

_____ _____ × _____ = _____

_____ _____ × _____ = _____

_____ _____ × _____ = _____

_____ _____ × _____ = _____

_____ _____ × _____ = _____

_____ _____ × _____ = _____

Total _____

E-3. Distribution In Market

No. of markets in which distribution is made × fixed distribution charge =

_____ × _____ = _____

Pounds delivered in Market:

A _____ × _____ $250. _____ = _____

B _____ × _____ = _____

C _____ × _____ = _____

D _____ × _____ = _____

E _____ × _____ = _____

Total _____

LOGA—A Computerized Logistics Simulator

LOGA (LOgistics GAme) is a simulated four-firm industry in which individual company success is measured in an interactive competitive environment. The simulator replicates a business operation in which company representatives manage all aspects of logistical operations. The management of each participating firm must make and implement decisions in an effort "to procure materials, schedule production, and deliver the right quantity of the right goods to the right place at the right time at the *least total cost*." The game is competitive in that all firms compete for industry profits and market share.

One must remember that a simulator cannot duplicate all complexities of a competitive business world. However, you will find yourself deeply involved and highly motivated. Versions of LOGA have been operational for over ten years, during which it has been regularly utilized in executive seminars and university classes.

A tangible benefit realized from LOGA is the opportunity to manage the total logistical system. Regardless of success or failure, understanding of overall logistical management will be strengthened. LOGA requires simultaneous coordination of finished goods and raw materials, inventory management, transportation procurement, production scheduling, warehousing, sales promotion, advertising, and marketing research, while keeping in mind time lags and competitive interactions from other firms. The game places primary emphasis on decision-making and implementation of the total systems approach. However, it is not just a work exercise. A considerable amount of enjoyment results from your effort to "outsmart" competition.

FIRM AND INDUSTRY COMPETITIVE STRUCTURE

Each firm is located in a local market which is an equal distance from the central market. No firm is located in the central market. Each firm is therefore equidistant from two of the three other local markets. The remaining local market is twice as far away as the central market. The market configuration illustrated in Figure VI–1 illustrates distance relationships.

All firms have the same manufacturing and potential warehouse facility configuration. In the home market, each firm has a manufacturing plant, a raw-material private warehouse, and a finished-goods private warehouse. In other markets, each firm has a private finished-goods distribution center, public warehousing, and the potential to change both. No public warehousing is available for raw materials. Table VI–1 illustrates the market area number and firm number for each industry.

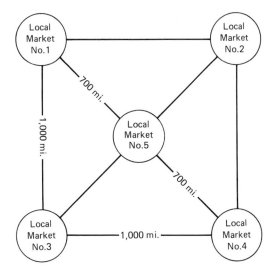

Figure VI–1 Geographical Market Structure

TABLE VI–1 Firm Location and Home Market Area

Market Number	Industry and Team		
	East	Central	West
1	Giants	Vikings	Rams
2	Redskins	Lions	49ers
3	Eagles	Packers	Falcons
4	Colts	Bears	Cowboys
5	Super Bowl	Super Bowl	Super Bowl

All the firms produce and market a hypothetical product known as a Spartan. Spartans are manufactured from three basic raw materials: aluminum, plastic, and steel. These materials are used in fixed proportions: 4 units of aluminum, 8 units of plastic, and 12 units of steel per finished Spartan. Raw materials have varying procurement times to reach the manufacturing plant. Plastic and steel are available locally; aluminum must be purchased from a distant source.

Basic Spartan demand is approximately 9,600 units per week for all markets combined. The Central market demand is about 3,200 units per week. Each of the local markets demand approximately 1,600 units per week. When initiating the simulation, each firm has 25 per cent of the Central market, 49 per cent of its home local market, and 17 per cent of all other local markets. As the competitive strategies and tactics of each firm interact, these percentages will change.

Sales analysis and forecasting have determined an expected seasonal pattern of demand for all five markets. However, past experience has proven such estimates are accurate only to within plus or minus 5 per cent. Sales forecasts

TABLE VI–2 Forecasted Spartan Demand Pattern

Variation of Week #	Demand Index Value
1	1.00
2	.95
3	.90
4	.85
5	.90
6	1.00
7	1.05
8	1.10
9	1.15
10	1.10
11	1.00
12	1.00

are also subject to unpredictable fluctuations which randomly occur in individual markets. Table VI–2 reports the expected seasonal sales.

DECISION-MAKING

The logistical management task is to provide a specified level of product availability at the associated lowest total cost. This is achieved by having a specified amount of Spartans available for sale in each market.

To assist in decision-planning, the logistical department's tasks are discussed by functional areas. The overall decision-making responsibilities of the logistical department include the following tasks:

1. Raw-material purchasing.
2. Scheduling the number of Spartans to produce, when to produce them, and how fast to produce them, in light of probable demand and inventories on hand.
3. Determination of warehouse space needed for raw materials at the plant and for Spartans in each of the five markets.
4. Selection of type of finished-goods warehousing to use—public and/or private.
5. Selection of transportation mode—truck and/or rail.
6. Product allocation to specific markets.
7. Selection of the number, type, and sequence of sales promotions.

8. Planning advertising for each market.

9. Requesting promotion, advertising, and/or demand marketing research.

For efficient operations, it is recommended that teams organize along functional areas and designate a member responsible for each decision area. Coordination of the integrated logistical system is the responsibility of the overall team.

Transportation

A significant aspect of logistical success depends upon transportation decisions. One primary transportation decision is modal selection. For fast delivery, to reduce the threat of stockouts or a production shutdown, truck transportation is available. On the other hand, lower-cost-per-unit rail transportation may be adequate. In specific situations, less-than-volume load (LVL) shipments may be desired. Charges and transit times for each mode and size of shipments are illustrated in Table VI–3.

TABLE VI–3 Transportation

Inbound Transportation of Raw Materials—Unit Rates and Transit Times

Material		Rail Transportation		Truck Transportation	
		VL[a] (14,000 units)	LVL (less than 14,000 units)	VL[1a] (6,500 units)	LVL (less than 6,500 units)
Plastic	Rate:	$ .15	$ .20	$ .23	$ .30
	Transit Time:	1 week	2 weeks	Overnight	Overnight
Steel	Rate:	$ .21	$ .29	$ .31	$ .40
	Transit Time:	2 weeks	3 weeks	Overnight	Overnight
Aluminum	Rate:	Any quantity	$ .28	$1.00	$1.50
	Transit Time:		8 weeks	1 week	1 week

Outbound Transportation of Finished Goods—Unit Rates and Transit Times

Distance		Rail Transportation		Truck Transportation	
		VL[a] (280 units)	LVL (less than 280 units)	VL[a] (130 units)	LVL (less than 130 units)
700 miles[b]	Rate:	$5.50	$7.50	$9.70	$11.70
	Transit Time:	1 week	1 week	Overnight	Overnight
1,000 miles[c]	Rate:	$7.00	$9.00	$13.00	$15.00
	Transit Time:	1 week	2 weeks	Overnight	Overnight
1,400 miles[d]	Rate:	$9.00	$11.00	$17.40	$19.40
	Transit Time:	1 week	2 week	Overnight	Overnight

[a] VL has no overflow penalty charges.
[b] Distance from Market 5 to any other.
[c] Distance from Market 1 to 2, 3 to 4, etc.
[d] Distance from Market 1 to 4, 2 to 3, etc.

An order placement charge of $75 is assessed for the documentation of each order placed with suppliers. A shipment documentation charge of $75 is assessed for documenting each shipment.

For the most part, transportation transit times are dependable. However, during heavy demand periods, equipment shortages and inconsistency in transit times may be experienced.

Production Scheduling

Within the constraint of plant capacity, the logistics department is responsible for scheduling production. To support the production schedule, materials must be procured. In this regard, the sales forecast indices presented in Table VI–2 are helpful to guide planning. Raw-material transportation charges are assessed when the order is placed.

The per-unit manufacturing cost structure is influenced by utilization of plant capacity. Over- or underutilization results in higher per-unit costs of production. The logistical department is charged for any excess costs resulting from over-or underutilization of capacity. The standard per-unit cost of production is charged to manufacturing. A schedule of these excess charges is contained in Table VI–4.

Normal practice is to schedule production two weeks in advance. Occasions will develop wherein you may desire to increase or decrease scheduled production quantities. "Expedited" orders are adjustments with one week's delay. "At once" modifications take place during the current week. If a production schedule must be curtailed because of raw-material shortage or production schedules exceeding maximum capacity, a forced reduction penalty

TABLE VI–4 Plant Capacity and Production Charges

Rated plant capacity	2,700 units per week
Optimum level of weekly production	2,430 units per week (90% of rate capacity)
Maximum level of weekly production	3,375 units per week (125% of rate capacity)
Cost per unit of *change* for *expedited* changes	$2.00
Cost per unit of *change* for *at once* changes	$3.50
Cost per unit of *change* for forced reduction in production schedule	$3.50

Examples of production charges for production above or below optimum production cost point	% of Capacity Used	Units Produced	Production Charge
	0%	0	$219,000
	50	1,350	43,300
	75	2,025	5,400
	90	2,430	0
	100	2,700	2,700
	115	3,110	16,200
	125	3,375	32,400

is charged. To initiate the game, 2,400 units have been scheduled for production.

Spartans produced during a given week are transferred to the factory adjacent to the finished-goods warehouse. These Spartans are *only* available for sale in the home market during the week they are produced. Shipments cannot be made to other markets until the next week.

Inventory Planning

Inventory planning is responsible for having an adequate supply of raw materials and a strategic supply of Spartans in selected markets. Failure to plan properly may result in production shutdown or a stockout. A production shutdown may or may not be critical, depending on inventory levels. In contrast, if Spartan stockouts occur, a company is normally penalized through lost sales and may lose market share. If you stockout in a market in which a competitor has adequate Spartans available, you will lose a portion of market share. In selected instances, the inventories of all firms might be zero in a specific market. In such situations, the industry will experience a reduction in future demand in that market.

Inventory carrying charges are assessed against both raw materials and finished goods. A 15 per cent per year carrying charge is assessed against the average total weekly dollar value of all raw materials on hand. (Each unit of plastic is worth $3, steel, $4; and aluminum, $7.) Spartans are assessed at 24 per cent per year on an estimated value of $250. All goods in process, in storage, and in transit at the end of a week are assessed this charge.

For purposes of inventory planning, the following order of actions should always be kept in mind:

1. Warehouse capacity is adjusted.
2. Raw materials are received.
3. Outbound shipments from warehouses are made.[1]
4. Spartans are produced and received in the home market warehouses.[2]
5. Shipments are received at all warehouses.[2]
6. Sales in the markets are made and deducted from inventory.

Warehousing

The logistical department is responsible for the storage of raw materials and finished goods. To facilitate this task, the company operates a raw-material and finished-goods warehouse at the factory. Finished-goods public warehouse space can also be contracted for within the home market. In the other four markets, the firm has the option of utilizing private or public warehousing.

At the start of the game, the firm has the following warehouse space (Table VI–5).

In some instances, the present warehousing capacity may be inadequate. Additional private space can be obtained within three weeks for both raw

---

[1] The shipment is accumulated from inventory according to the following order: (1) demurrage and detention, (2) public warehouse, (3) company warehouse.

[2] Receipts are placed in inventory according to the following order: (1) company warehouse, (2) public warehouse, (3) demurrage and detention.

TABLE VI–5 Warehouse Capacity

Raw-material warehouse	60,000 units
Finished-goods warehouse—private	
a. Home market	1,700 units
b. Small nonhome market	200 units
c. Central market	600 units
Finished-goods warehouse—public	
a. Home market	300 units
b. Small nonhome market	100 units
c. Central market	500 units

materials and finished goods. Public warehouse space can be added immediately. If additional space is not added, the firm will automatically be charged demurrage and detention for storage in transport vehicles. Demurrage and detention charges are assessed only when private and public warehouse space is filled.

In markets where warehouse capacity is judged excessive, a reduction can be scheduled. For private warehouse operations, two weeks are required before becoming effective. Public warehouse capacity may be reduced instantaneously. If warehouse capacity is less than inventory at any point during the week, the overflow inventory is subject to demurrage and detention charges. Each time warehouse capacity is changed, a fixed charge of $300 is incurred.

The costs to operate private warehouses are basically of two types: space utilization and per-unit handling. Space costs are fixed and based on total available warehouse space. The per-unit handling cost is variable and based on utilization of the warehouse. The charge is assessed on warehouse receipts. The most efficient utilization rate is around 70 per cent of peak capacity. As the utilization increases, the handling costs are constant until 70 per cent of peak is reached. Storage in excess of 70 per cent of peak results in increased per-unit rates. The rate of increase is not specified to participants since labor productivity is a major problem. Participants will have to "test" the sensitivity of this cost factor. Public warehouse handling is fixed per unit and is charged upon receipt of Spartans. Table VI–6 provides warehouse cost schedules.

Advertising and Promotion

Advertising and promotional campaigns will be initiated when announced by the administrator. Due to the seasonal demand for finished goods, advertising and promotional expenditures normally do not start until mid-year. Once advertising and promotions are introduced, market shares are subject to alternation. Expenditures for these programs are necessary to maintain market share. The effects of advertising and promotion are somewhat different. However, each takes effect *immediately*.

Advertising causes *total demand* to increase in each market. As additional dollars are spent, demand increases at a diminishing rate. In instances where stockout has occurred and the firm has lost a portion of its demand, additional advertising will help to stimulate market-share recovery. Advertising expendi-

TABLE VI-6   Warehouse Cost

Cost of Private Warehouse Operation

	Finished Goods	Raw Material
Fixed cost per unit of capacity per week	$ .40	$.02
Material handling cost per unit received[a]	$2.40	$.06

Cost of Public Warehouse Operation

	Public Warehouse	Finished Goods D&D	Raw Material D&D
Storage cost per unit in inventory at week's end	$1.00	$6.40	$ .16
Material handling cost per unit received	$3.75	—	—

[a] At the 70 per cent warehouse utilization.

TABLE VI-7   Sales Promotion Plans

Promotion Period	Promotion 1 Allocated Cost	Promotion 2 Allocated Cost	Promotion 3 Allocated Cost
1	$ 19,000	$24,000	$ 60,000
2	36,000	14,400	120,000
3	23,000	9,000	20,000
4	12,000	6,000	—
5	7,000	3,600	—
6	3,000	1,800	—
7	—	1,200	—
	$100,000	$60,000	$200,000

tures are distributed to each market area as specified. For instance, you may allocate $100 for Market 1, $0 for Market 2, $1,000 for Market 3, $50 for Market 4, and $3,000 for Market 5.

Promotions help a firm maintain market share. The promotional department can initiate any one of the available three plans that it so desires. However, only one plan may be started each week, and a given plan may not be reinitiated until it has expired. If a plan was initiated and has expired, it may be repeated. If more than one plan are used, their effect is combined. The plans available are listed in Table VI–7.

The allocation of promotional effort to specific markets is according to per-market percentage of firm total sales. For instance, if the sales in the Central market are 50 per cent of the firm's total sales, 50 per cent of promotion charges are allocated to that market.

To accommodate competitive dynamics, customer loyalty is introduced. By having customer loyalty, a certain portion of each firm's previous week's market share is considered "safe" from competitive inroads. That is, customers will

TABLE VI–8   Customer Loyalty

Market	"Safe" % of Previous Market Share
Home	60
Central	55
Nonhome	40

postpone purchases until succeeding weeks if a stockout occurs. The "safe" percentages are listed in Table VI–8.

The portions of the markets not reserved as "safe" are placed in a "pool." From the pool, demand is reallocated on the basis of relative expenditures for both advertising and promotion in the market. Thus, a firm's individual market demand can be calculated as its "safe" share of total demand plus share of the pooled demand.

When advertisting and sales promotions are in effect, one fifth of the total expenditure is charged to the logistical department. This is justified since logistics received one fifth of the revenue from sales for performance measurement. Thus, only one fifth of expenditure placed on decision sheets is allocated to logistical management.

COMPETITIVE OBJECTIVES—PERFORMANCE CRITERIA

LOGA has two closely related competitive objectives. First, each company should attempt to earn the highest total gross profit during the competition. Second, each company should attempt to maximize its total company market share. Total gross profit is an indication of overall past performance, while market share is a long-run barometer indicative of future potential.

The winners are those teams achieving the highest performance index. This performance index is determined by multiplying "total to date" gross profit by "average to date" market share. If, for example, your team achieved a total to-date gross profit of $200,000 and a 25 per cent average total market share, your index of performance would be 50,000 (200,000 × .25).

Before reaching a final decision on who wins, game administrators will check "in transit pipelines," Spartan inventories, warehouse capacity, and raw materials on order to determine a firm's competitive posture. If a firm has attempted a "game end" strategy, its performance index will be discounted by the game administrator.

MARKETING RESEARCH INFORMATION

Confidential reports are available to each firm regarding selected competitive activities. These reports become available when advertising and promotion are initiated. The cost of such information varies according to the desired number and selection of reports. Such information can assist a firm in competing more effectively by knowing, at least in part, what is occurring in the market. The

TABLE VI–9 MRI Reports

MRI #	Identification	Ref. No.	Cost
Promotion			
1	Total allocated promotion expenditures and no. of promotions for each company	None	$800
2	Itemization of promotion types for requested competitors	Competitors #1–#4	$500 per competitor
3	Total allocated promotion expenditures for each market	None	$2,000
4	Itemization by company of promotion expenditures in requested markets	Markets #1–#5	$900 per market
5	Itemization by market of promotion expenditures for requested competitors	Competitors #1–#4	$1,000 per competitor
Advertising			
6	Total advertising of each company	None	$1,800
7	Total advertising in each market	None	$3,500
8	Itemization by company of advertising in requested markets	Markets #1–#5	$900 per market
9	Itemization by market of advertising of requested companies	Competitors #1–#4	$900 per competitor
Demand			
10	Itemization by company of demand in requested markets	Markets #1–#5	$800 per market
11	Itemization by market of demand of requested companies	Competitors #1–#4	$1,000 per competitor
12	Total demand in all companies	None	$1,200
13	Total demand in all markets	None	$1,500

data provided are accurate most of the time to within plus or minus 10 per cent. Marketing research in this simulation will in no way provide "perfect information" for decision-making. Totals may not agree as they are estimated independently of market and company estimates.

Three types of marketing research are available: promotion marketing research, advertising marketing research, and demand marketing research. These market research information (MRI) reports are listed in Table VI–9. To obtain them, determine the MRI numbers and competitive and marketing numbers, if required, and insert them on the marketing research decision sheet number 5.

MANAGEMENT REPORTS

Two reports other than market research reports are presented to the firm after each round. The first report is the financial statement. It summarizes all cost data for the current rounds and the year to date. The second report is the operations reports. It enumerates current and in-transit raw material and Spartan inventories. It also shows the current and contracted warehouse space in each market.

The operations report should be used for comparative purposes. A comparison of current inventory with currently available warehouse capacity tells a firm whether detention and demurrage charges will be incurred. Comparison of current and projected production schedules indicates whether sufficient raw materials will be available to meet production requirements. If any of the comparisons indicate trouble, the manager of the firm will have to decide on what corrective action to take in its next decision.

RECORDING DECISIONS

For each week, each firm is required to complete a decision sheet set on the forms accompanying this report. These forms must be handed in promptly at the end of each decision round. They are entered as submitted without alteration. All five sheets of the set must be completed through item 5 and turned in for each round, even if advertising, promotion, and marketing research are not in effect. Firms are encouraged to maintain a duplicate copy of each decision sheet.

LOGA DECISION SHEET: I

Team Name_____ Number_____

Decision for Week Number_____

Sheet Number_____

Industry Name_____ Number_____

	(1)
	(2-3)
1	(4)
	(5)
	(6)

(Blank)

RAW MATERIAL ORDERS

  Plastic:

    Rail Transportation   (7-12)

    Truck Transportation   (13-18)

  Steel:

    Rail Transportation   (19-24)

    Truck Transportation   (25-30)

  Aluminum:

    Rail transportation   (31-36)

    Truck Transportation   (37-42)

PRODUCTION SCHEDULING

  Rush   (43-48)

  Expedite   (49-54)

  Regular   (55-60)

Note: Write justify data using no decimals or commas, i.e., | 1 | 0 | 0 |

LOGA DECISION SHEET: II

Team Name _____ Number _____	(1)
Decision for Week Number _____	(2-3)
Sheet Number _____	(4)
Industry Name _____ Number _____	(5)
WAREHOUSE CAPACITY CHANGES	(6)
Raw Material Warehouse	(7-12)
Market No. 1 Finished Goods: Private	(13-18)
Public	(19-24)
Market No. 2 Finished Goods: Private	(25-30)
Public	(31-36)
Market No. 3 Finished Goods: Private	(37-42)
Public	(43-48)
Market No. 4 Finished Goods: Private	(49-54)
Public	(55-60)
Market No. 5 Finished Goods: Private	(61-66)
Public	(67-72)

Note: Indicate a decrease in capacity by using a minus sign, i.e., $\boxed{} \boxed{-} \boxed{1} \boxed{0} \boxed{0}$

LOGA DECISION SHEET: III

Team Name_____ Number_____

Decision for Week Number_____

Sheet Number_____

Industry Name _____ Number_____

	(1)
	(2-3)
3	(4)
	(5)
	(6)

SPARTAN FINISHED GOODS SHIPMENT SCHEDULING

Origin Market No.	Via Mode No.	Destination Market No.	Quantity						
									(7-15)
									(16-24)
									(25-33)
									(34-42)
									(43-51)
									(52-60)
									(61-69)
									(70-78)

MARKET:	No.	East	Central	West	MODES:	No.	Type
	1	Giants	Vikings	Rams		1	Rail
	2	Redskins	Lions	49ers		2	Truck
	3	Eagles	Packers	Falcons			
	4	Colts	Bears	Cowboys			
	5	Super Bowl	Super Bowl	Super Bowl			

Note: VL/LVL shipment sizes automatically determined based on quantity shipped; VL has no overflow penalty charge.

LOGA DECISION SHEET: IV

Team Name _____ Number _____   (1)

Decision for Week Number_____   (2-3)

Sheet Number_____   4   (4)

Industry Name_____ Number _____   (5)

ADVERTISING AND SALES PROMOTION: (6-7)

   Sales Promotion Plan Number (1, 2, or 3)   (8)

   Allocation of Advertising Funds: (9)

      Market No. 1   (10-17)

      Market No. 2   (18-25)

      Market No. 3   (26-33)

      Market No. 4   (34-41)

      Market No. 5   (42-49)

                                                                         (50-59)

Is Market Research desired? (Enter "1" for *Yes* and "0" for *No*)   (60)

Note: Amounts not to exceed % $99,999 per market.

LOGA DECISION SHEET: V

Team Name_____ Number_____

Decision for Week Number_____

Sheet Number _____

Industry Name _____ Number_____

(1)
(2-3)
5 (4)
(5)
(6-7)

Requested Report	MRI No.		Enter competitor or market number on which you desire information					
First								(8-15)
Second								(16-23)
Third								(24-31)
Fourth								(32-39)
Fifth								(40-47)
Sixth								(48-55)
Seventh								(56-63)
Eighth								(64-71)
Ninth								(72-79)

Firms can request up to nine reports. Thirteen MRI reports are available as listed in the participant manual. The columns below indicate the numbers corresponding with either markets or competitors.

No.	East	Central	West
1	Giants	Vikings	Rams
2	Redskins	Lions	49ers
3	Eagles	Packers	Falcons
4	Colts	Bears	Cowboys
5	Super Bowl	Super Bowl	Super Bowl

AUTHOR INDEX

SUBJECT INDEX